World
Organ
Organ

Protocol on th
Kingdom of S

Protocole d'A
Royaume d'A

Protocolo de A
de Arabia Sau

Geneva 11 December 2005

CAMBRIDGE
UNIVERSITY PRESS

CAMBRIDGE UNIVERSITY PRESS
Cambridge, New York, Melbourne, Madrid, Cape Town, Singapore, São Paulo

Cambridge University Press
The Edinburgh Building, Cambridge CB2 8RU, UK

Published in the United States of America by Cambridge University Press, New York

www.cambridge.org
Information on this title: www.cambridge.org/9780521707633

First published 2007

Printed in the United Kingdom at the University Press, Cambridge

A catalogue record for this publication is available from the British Library

Library of Congress Cataloguing in Publication data

ISBN 978-0-521-70763-3 paperback

The Protocol of Accession for each new Member of the WTO contains the terms it has negotiated to become a Member, and which have been accepted by all other Members of the WTO in the General Council or at a Ministerial Conference. The Protocol includes annexes for the commitments made by the new member for trade in goods and in services.

Please note: This brief introduction is provided for information purposes only and therefore does not form part of the official Protocol of Accession. The Protocol of Accession reproduced in this publication does not have the legal standing of the original Protocol which is entrusted to and kept at the WTO Secretariat in Geneva.

Le Protocole d'accession de chaque nouveau Membre de l'OMC énonce les modalités que celui-ci a négociées pour devenir Membre et qui ont été acceptées par tous les autres Membres de l'OMC au Conseil général ou á la Conférence ministérielle. Il contient des annexes renfermant les engagements souscrits par le nouveau Membre dans les domaines du commerce des marchandises et du commerce des services.

Prière de noter: Cette brève introduction est fournie uniquement pour information et ne fait dono pas partie du Protocole d'accession officiel. Le Protocole d'accession reproduit dans cette publication n'a pas le statut juridique du Protocole original, lequel a été confié au Secrétariat de l'OMC qui en assure la garde.

El Protocolo de Adhesión correspondiente a cada nuevo Miembro de la OMC contiene las condiciones que éste ha negociado para adquirir su condición de Miembro, y que han sido aceptadas por todos los demás Miembros de la OMC en el Consejo General o en una Conferencia Ministerial. El Protocolo comprende anexos donde figuran los compromisos contraídos por el nuevo Miembro en lo que respecta al comercio de mercancías y de servicios.

Sírvanse notar: Esta breve introducción se proporciona únicamente a efectos informativos y, por consiguiente, no forma parte del Protocolo oficial de Adhesión. El Protocolo de Adhesión reproducido en la presente publicación no tiene la condición jurídica del Protocolo original, confiado a la Secretaría de la OMC en Ginebra y depositado en ésta.

PROTOCOL

ON THE ACCESSION OF THE KINGDOM OF SAUDI ARABIA

Preamble

The World Trade Organization (hereinafter referred to as the "WTO"), pursuant to the approval of the General Council of the WTO accorded under Article XII of the Marrakesh Agreement Establishing the World Trade Organization (hereinafter referred to as the "WTO Agreement"), and the Kingdom of Saudi Arabia,

Taking note of the Report of the Working Party on the Accession of the Kingdom of Saudi Arabia to the WTO Agreement reproduced in document WT/ACC/SAU/61, dated 1 November 2005 (hereinafter referred to as the "Working Party Report"),

Having regard to the results of the negotiations on the accession of the Kingdom of Saudi Arabia to the WTO Agreement,

Agree as follows:

PART I - GENERAL

1. Upon entry into force of this Protocol pursuant to paragraph 8, the Kingdom of Saudi Arabia accedes to the WTO Agreement pursuant to Article XII of that Agreement and thereby becomes a Member of the WTO.

2. The WTO Agreement to which the Kingdom of Saudi Arabia accedes shall be the WTO Agreement, including the Explanatory Notes to that Agreement, as rectified, amended or otherwise modified by such legal instruments as may have entered into force before the date of entry into force of this Protocol. This Protocol, which shall include the commitments referred to in paragraph 315 of the Working Party Report, shall be an integral part of the WTO Agreement.

3. Except as otherwise provided for in paragraph 315 of the Working Party Report, those obligations in the Multilateral Trade Agreements annexed to the WTO Agreement that are to be implemented over a period of time starting with the entry into force of that Agreement shall be implemented by the Kingdom of Saudi Arabia as if it had accepted that Agreement on the date of its entry into force.

4. The Kingdom of Saudi Arabia may maintain a measure inconsistent with paragraph 1 of Article II of the GATS provided that such a measure was recorded in the list of Article II Exemptions annexed to this Protocol and meets the conditions of the Annex to the GATS on Article II Exemptions.

PART II - SCHEDULES

5. The Schedules reproduced in Annex I to this Protocol shall become the Schedule of Concessions and Commitments annexed to the General Agreement on Tariffs and Trade 1994 (hereinafter referred to as the "GATT 1994") and the Schedule of Specific Commitments annexed to the General Agreement on Trade in Services (hereinafter referred to as "GATS") relating to the Kingdom of Saudi Arabia. The staging of the concessions and commitments listed in the Schedules shall be implemented as specified in the relevant parts of the respective Schedules.

6. For the purpose of the reference in paragraph 6(a) of Article II of the GATT 1994 to the date of that Agreement, the applicable date in respect of the Schedules of Concessions and Commitments annexed to this Protocol shall be the date of entry into force of this Protocol.

PART III - FINAL PROVISIONS

7. This Protocol shall be open for acceptance, by signature or otherwise, by the Kingdom of Saudi Arabia until 31 December 2005.

8. This Protocol shall enter into force on the thirtieth day following the day upon which it shall have been accepted by the Kingdom of Saudi Arabia.

9. This Protocol shall be deposited with the Director-General of the WTO. The Director-General of the WTO shall promptly furnish a certified copy of this Protocol and a notification of acceptance by the Kingdom of Saudi Arabia thereto pursuant to paragraph 9 to each Member of the WTO and to the Kingdom of Saudi Arabia.

This Protocol shall be registered in accordance with the provisions of Article 102 of the Charter of the United Nations.

Done at Geneva this eleventh day of November, two thousand and five, in a single copy in the English, French and Spanish languages, each text being authentic, except that a Schedule annexed hereto may specify that it is authentic in only one of these languages.

PROTOCOLE D'ACCESSION DU ROYAUME D'ARABIE SAOUDITE

Préambule

L'Organisation mondiale du commerce (ci-après dénommée "l'OMC"), eu égard à l'approbation du Conseil général de l'OMC donnée en vertu de l'article XII de l'Accord de Marrakech instituant l'Organisation mondiale du commerce (ci-après dénommé "l'Accord sur l'OMC") et le Royaume d'Arabie saoudite (ci-après dénommé "l'Arabie saoudite"),

Prenant note du rapport du Groupe de travail de l'accession de l'Arabie saoudite à l'OMC qui figure dans le document WT/ACC/SAU/61 daté du 1er novembre 2005 (ci-après dénommé "le rapport du Groupe de travail"),

Eu égard aux résultats des négociations sur l'accession de l'Arabie saoudite à l'OMC,

Conviennent de ce qui suit:

PARTIE I – DISPOSITIONS GÉNÉRALES

1. À compter de la date à laquelle le présent protocole entrera en vigueur, l'Arabie saoudite accédera à l'Accord sur l'OMC conformément à l'article XII dudit accord et deviendra ainsi Membre de l'OMC.

2. L'Accord sur l'OMC auquel l'Arabie saoudite accédera sera l'Accord sur l'OMC, y compris les Notes explicatives de cet accord, tel qu'il aura été rectifié, amendé ou autrement modifié par des instruments juridiques qui seront entrés en vigueur avant la date d'entrée en vigueur du présent protocole. Le présent protocole, qui comprendra les engagements mentionnés au paragraphe 315 du rapport du Groupe de travail, fera partie intégrante de l'Accord sur l'OMC.

3. Sauf dispositions contraires du paragraphe 315 du rapport du Groupe de travail, les obligations découlant des accords commerciaux multilatéraux annexés à l'Accord sur l'OMC qui doivent être mises en œuvre au cours d'une période commençant au moment de l'entrée en vigueur dudit accord seront mises en œuvre par l'Arabie saoudite comme si elle avait accepté cet accord à la date de son entrée en vigueur.

4. L'Arabie saoudite peut maintenir une mesure incompatible avec le paragraphe 1 de l'article II de l'AGCS pour autant que cette mesure soit inscrite sur la liste d'exemptions des obligations énoncées à l'article II, qui est annexée au présent protocole, et qu'elle satisfasse aux conditions qui sont indiquées dans l'Annexe de l'AGCS sur les exemptions des obligations énoncées à l'article II.

PARTIE II – LISTES

5. Les Listes annexées au présent protocole deviendront la Liste de concessions et d'engagements annexée à l'Accord général sur les tarifs douaniers et le commerce de 1994 (ci-après dénommé "le GATT de 1994") et la Liste d'engagements spécifiques annexée à l'Accord général sur le commerce des services (ci-après dénommé "l'AGCS") de l'Arabie saoudite. Les concessions et les engagements inscrits sur les Listes seront mis en œuvre par étapes ainsi qu'il est spécifié dans les parties pertinentes des Listes.

6. Dans le cas de la référence à la date du GATT de 1994 que contient le paragraphe 6 a) de l'article II dudit accord, la date applicable en ce qui concerne les Listes de concessions et d'engagements annexées au présent protocole sera la date d'entrée en vigueur du présent protocole.

PARTIE III – DISPOSITIONS FINALES

7. Le présent protocole sera ouvert à l'acceptation de l'Arabie saoudite, par voie de signature ou autrement, jusqu'au 31 décembre 2005.

8. Le présent protocole entrera en vigueur le trentième jour qui suivra celui où il aura été accepté.

9. Le présent protocole sera déposé auprès du Directeur général de l'OMC. Le Directeur général de l'OMC remettra dans les moindres délais à chaque Membre de l'OMC et à l'Arabie saoudite une copie certifiée conforme du présent protocole et une notification d'acceptation dudit protocole par l'Arabie saoudite conformément au paragraphe 9.

Le présent protocole sera enregistré conformément aux dispositions de l'article 102 de la Charte des Nations Unies.

Fait à Genève, le onze novembre deux mille cinq, en un seul exemplaire, en langues française, anglaise et espagnole, les trois textes faisant foi, si ce n'est qu'une liste ci-annexée peut préciser ne faire foi que dans une seule de ces langues.

PROTOCOLO DE ADHESIÓN DEL REINO DE ARABIA SAUDITA

Preámbulo

La Organización Mundial del Comercio (denominada en adelante la "OMC"), de conformidad con la aprobación del Consejo General otorgada en aplicación del artículo XII del Acuerdo de Marrakech por el que se establece la Organización Mundial del Comercio (denominado en adelante "Acuerdo sobre la OMC"), y el Reino de Arabia Saudita,

Tomando nota del informe del Grupo de Trabajo sobre la Adhesión del Reino de Arabia Saudita al Acuerdo sobre la OMC que figura en el documento WT/ACC/SAU/61, de fecha 1 de noviembre de 2005 (denominado en adelante el "informe del Grupo de Trabajo"),

Habida cuenta de los resultados de las negociaciones celebradas para la adhesión del Reino de Arabia Saudita al Acuerdo sobre la OMC,

Acuerda lo siguiente:

PARTE I - DISPOSICIONES GENERALES

1. A partir de la entrada en vigor del presente Protocolo conforme al párrafo 8, el Reino de Arabia Saudita se adhiere al Acuerdo sobre la OMC de conformidad con el artículo XII de ese Acuerdo y, por tanto, se convierte en Miembro de la OMC.

2. El Acuerdo sobre la OMC al que se adhiere el Reino de Arabia Saudita será el Acuerdo sobre la OMC, incluidas las Notas Explicativas de dicho Acuerdo, rectificado, enmendado o modificado de cualquier otro modo por los instrumentos jurídicos que hayan entrado en vigor antes de la fecha de entrada en vigor del presente Protocolo. Este Protocolo, que incluirá los compromisos mencionados en el párrafo 315 del informe del Grupo de Trabajo, formará parte integrante del Acuerdo sobre la OMC.

3. Salvo que se establezca lo contrario en el párrafo 315 del informe del Grupo de Trabajo, las obligaciones de los Acuerdos Comerciales Multilaterales anexos al Acuerdo sobre la OMC que deben aplicarse durante un período de tiempo que se inicia con la entrada en vigor de ese Acuerdo serán aplicados por el Reino de Arabia Saudita como si hubiera aceptado ese Acuerdo en la fecha de su entrada en vigor.

4. El Reino de Arabia Saudita podrá mantener una medida incompatible con el párrafo 1 del artículo II del AGCS siempre que esa medida se registre en la lista de exenciones de las obligaciones del artículo II anexa al presente Protocolo y cumpla las condiciones del Anexo del AGCS sobre Exenciones de las Obligaciones del Artículo II.

PARTE II - LISTAS

5. Las Listas reproducidas en el anexo I del presente Protocolo pasarán a ser la Lista de concesiones y compromisos anexa al Acuerdo General sobre Aranceles Aduaneros y Comercio de 1994 (denominado en adelante el "GATT de 1994") y la Lista de compromisos específicos anexa al Acuerdo General sobre el Comercio de Servicios (denominado en adelante "AGCS") relativas al Reino de Arabia Saudita. El escalonamiento de concesiones y compromisos enumerados en las Listas se aplicará del modo especificado en las partes pertinentes de las respectivas Listas.

6. A los efectos de la referencia que se hace en el apartado a) del párrafo 6 del artículo II del GATT de 1994 a la fecha de dicho Acuerdo, la fecha aplicable en lo que concierne a las Listas de

concesiones y compromisos anexas al presente Protocolo será la fecha de entrada en vigor de este Protocolo.

PARTE III - DISPOSICIONES FINALES

7. El presente Protocolo estará abierto a la aceptación, mediante firma o de otro modo, del Reino de Arabia Saudita hasta el 31 de diciembre de 2005.

8. El presente Protocolo entrará en vigor treinta días después de su aceptación por el Reino de Arabia Saudita.

9. El presente Protocolo se depositará en poder del Director General de la OMC. El Director General de la OMC remitirá sin dilación una copia autenticada del presente Protocolo, así como la notificación de su aceptación por el Reino de Arabia Saudita, de conformidad con el párrafo 9, a cada uno de los Miembros de la OMC y al Reino de Arabia Saudita.

El presente Protocolo será registrado de conformidad con las disposiciones del Artículo 102 de la Carta de las Naciones Unidas.

Hecho en Ginebra el once de noviembre de dos mil cinco, en un solo ejemplar y en los idiomas español, francés e inglés, siendo cada uno de los textos igualmente auténtico, excepto que una Lista anexa determine que su texto es auténtico solamente en uno de esos idiomas.

ANNEX I /ANNEXE I/ANEXO I

KINGDOM OF SAUDI ARABIA

ROYAUME D'ARABIE SAOUDITE

REINO DE ARABIA SAUDITA

Schedule CLVIII - Kingdom of Saudi Arabia

This Schedule is authentic only in the English language

Schedule CLVIII - Kingdom of Saudi Arabia

This Schedule is authentic only in the English language

PART I - MOST-FAVOURED-NATION TARIFF
SECTION I - Agricultural Products
SECTION I - A Tariffs

Notes:
1. The "final bound rate" of duty, if differing from the "bound rate at date of accession", will be implemented in the year specified in the "implementation" column and on the day/month the Kingdom of Saudi Arabia accedes to the WTO. Tariff reductions will be implemented according to the dates specified in the "implementation" column (no other staged reductions are implied) unless there is an asterisk (*) in the "implementation" column. In these cases, rates will be reduced in equal annual increments from the rate indicated in the "bound rate at date of accession" column to the rate indicated in the "final bound rate" column. The designation "P" indicates that the products are prohibited for importation.
2. a) Applied tariffs on raw cane sugar of subheading 170111 shall be no higher than applied tariffs on beet sugar of subheading 170112.
b) Applied tariffs on lupines falling to subheading 121490 shall be no higher than applied tariffs on soya-bean oil-cake of subheading 230400.

3. a) Access conditions (i.e., applied and bound rates of duty) on rapeseed/colza/canola and their products (i.e., 120500, 120890, 151410, 151490 and 230640) shall be no less favourable than those applied on comparable soya products. The tariff lines for the comparable soya products are: soya beans (120100); flours of soya beans (120810); soyabean oil (150710 and 150790); and soya bean oil-cake (230400) respectively.
b) Access conditions (i.e., applied and bound rates of duty) in the case of barley (i.e., 100300) shall be no less favourable than those applied on corn (i.e., 100590).
c) Access conditions (i.e., applied and bound rates of duty) on dried leguminous vegetables (feed peas/Pisum sativum) (i.e., 071310) shall be no less favourable than those applied on oil-cake and other solid residues - of rape or colza seeds (i.e., 230640) and oil-cake and other solid residues (soya-bean oil), (i.e., 230400) respectively.

4. All products within the specific Headings of : 0406 (Cheese and curd); 0713 (Dried leguminous vegetables); and 2004 (Other Vegetables prepared or preserved otherwise than by vinegar or acetic acid, frozen, other than products of heading No. 2006) would have identical tariff treatment (both applied and bound).

HS	Description	Bound rate at date of accession	Final Bound rate	Implementation	Present concession established	INR	Concession first incorporated in a GATT Schedule	Earlier INRs	ODCs
0101	Live horses, asses, mules and hinnies.								
010110	-Pure-bred breeding animals								
01011010	--Of Arab breed	5				CE25,US			0
01011020	--Other	5				US			0
010190	-Other								
01019010	--Horses for sport	5							0
01019020	--Ponies	5							0
01019030	--Asses	15							0
01019040	--Mules	15							0
01019050	--Hinnies	15							0

HS	Description	Bound rate at date of accession	Final Bound rate	Implementation	Present concession established	INR	Concession first incorporated in a GATT Schedule	Earlier INRs	ODCs
01019090	--Other	5							0
0102	Live bovine animals.								
01021000	-Pure-bred breeding animals	5							0
01029000	-Other	7				UY			0
0103	Live swine.								
01031000	-Pure-bred breeding animals	P							0
01039	-Other:								
01039100	--Weighing less than 50 kg	P							0
01039200	--Weighing 50 kg or more	P							0
0104	Live sheep and goats.								
010410	-Sheep								
01041010	--Breeding sheep	7							0
01041090	--Other sheep	7				UY			0
010420	-Goats								
01042010	--Pure-bred breeding goats	7							0
01042090	--Other goats	7							0
0105	Live poultry, that is to say, fowls of the species Gallus domesticus, ducks, geese, turkeys and guinea fowls.								
01051	-Weighing not more than 185 g:								
01051100	--Fowls of the species Gallus domesticus	5				US			0
01051200	--Turkeys	15							0
01051900	--Other	15							0
01059	-Other:								
010592	--Fowls of the species Gallus domesticus, weighing not more than 2,000 g								
01059210	---Other fowl, of the species Gallus domesticus, weighing not more than 2,000 g, layers	15							0
01059220	---Other fowl, of the species Gallus domesticus, weighing not more than 2,000 g, broilers	15							0
01059230	---Other fowl, of the species Gallus domesticus, weighing not more than 2,000 g, breeding fowls	15							0
01059290	---Other fowl, of the species Gallus domesticus, weighing not more than 2,000 g	15							0
010593	--Fowls of the species Gallus domesticus, weighing more than 2,000 g								
01059310	---Other fowl, of the species Gallus domesticus, weighing more than 2,000 g, layers	15							0

HS	Description	Bound rate at date of accession	Final Bound rate	Implementation	Present concession established	INR	Concession first incorporated in a GATT Schedule	Earlier INRs	ODCs
01059320	---Other fowl, of the species Gallus domesticus, weighing more than 2,000 g, broilers	15							0
01059330	---Other fowl, of the species Gallus domesticus, weighing more than 2,000 g, breeding fowls	15							0
01059390	---Other fowl, of the species Gallus domesticus, weighing more than 2,000 g	15							0
010599	--Other								
01059910	---Tame ducks and geese	15							0
01059920	---Turkeys	15							0
01059990	---Other fowl, not chicken	15							0
0106	Other live animals.								
01061	-Mammals:								
01061100	--Primates	15							0
01061200	--Whales, dolphins and porpoises (mammals of the order Cetacea); manatees and dugongs (mammals of the order Sirenia)	15							0
010619	--Other								
01061910	---Camels	7							0
01061920	---Tame and wild rabbits	15							0
01061930	---Gazelles and deer	15							0
01061940	---Dogs	15							0
01061950	---Foxes, minks and other fur animals	15							0
01061960	---Animals for zoos, scientific and research labs	15							0
01061990	---Other	15							0
01062000	-Reptiles (including snakes and turtles)	15							0
01063	-Birds:								
01063100	--Birds of prey	15							0
01063200	--Psittaciformes (including parrots, parakeets, macaws and cockatoos)	15							0
010639	--Other								
01063910	---Tame and wild pigeons, partridges, pheasants, quail, snipe, sand grouse, wild ducks and similar animals	15							0
01063920	---Ornamental birds	15							0
01063990	---Other	15							0
010690	-Other								
01069010	--Bees and other insects	15							0
01069090	--Other	15							0

HS	Description	Bound rate at date of accession	Final Bound rate	Implementation	Present concession established	INR	Concession first incorporated in a GATT Schedule	Earlier INRs	ODCs
0201	Meat of bovine animals, fresh or chilled.								
02011000	-Carcasses and half-carcasses	7				CN,UY			0
02012000	-Other cuts with bone in	7				DO,HN,UY			0
02013000	-Boneless	5				CA,CE25,DO,HN,MX,US,UY			0
0202	Meat of bovine animals, frozen.								
02021000	-Carcasses and half-carcasses	7				UY			0
02022000	-Other cuts with bone in	6				CA,KG,US,UY			0
020230	-Boneless								
02023010	--Bovine minced meat, frozen	6				AU,CA,CE25,KG,US,UY			0
02023090	--Other, of bovine meat, frozen	6				AU,CA,CE25,KG,US,UY			0
0203	Meat of swine, fresh, chilled or frozen.								
02031	-Fresh or chilled:								
02031100	--Carcasses and half-carcasses	P							0
02031200	--Hams, shoulders and cuts thereof, with bone in	P							0
02031900	--Other	P							0
02032	-Frozen:								
02032100	--Carcasses and half-carcasses	P							0
02032200	--Hams, shoulders and cuts thereof, with bone in	P							0
02032900	--Other	P							0
0204	Meat of sheep or goats, fresh, chilled or frozen.								
02041000	-Carcasses and half-carcasses of lamb, fresh or chilled	7				AU,KG,NZ,UY			0
02042	-Other meat of sheep, fresh or chilled:								
02042100	--Carcasses and half-carcasses	6				AU,KG,NZ,UY			0
02042200	--Other cuts with bone in	6				AU,KG,NZ,UY			0
02042300	--Boneless	6				AU,KG,NZ,UY			0
02043000	-Carcasses and half-carcasses of lamb, frozen	7				AU,KG,NZ,UY			0
02044	-Other meat of sheep, frozen:								
02044100	--Carcasses and half-carcasses	7				AU,KG,NZ,UY			0
02044200	--Other cuts with bone in	7				AU,KG,NZ,UY			0
020443	--Boneless								
02044310	---Sheep minced meat, frozen	7				AU,KG,NZ,UY			0
02044390	---Other, of sheep meat, frozen	7				AU,KG,NZ,UY			0
020450	-Meat of goats								
0204501	--Carcasses and half-carcasses:								
02045011	---Fresh or chilled goat carcasses	7				KG,NZ			0
02045012	---Frozen goat carcasses	7				KG,NZ			0

HS	Description	Bound rate at date of accession	Final Bound rate	Implementation	Present concession established	INR	Concession first incorporated in a GATT Schedule	Earlier INRs	ODCs
0204502	--Other cuts with bone in:								
02045021	---Fresh or chilled cuts with bone in of goats	7				KG,NZ			0
02045022	---Frozen cuts with bone in of goats	7				KG,NZ			0
0204503	--Boneless:								
02045031	---Fresh or chilled boneless goat meat	7				KG,NZ			0
02045032	---Frozen boneless goat meat	7				KG,NZ			0
0205	Meat of horses, asses, mules or hinnies, fresh, chilled or frozen.								
02050010	-Horse meat	15							0
02050090	-Other meat of asses, mules or hinnies	P							0
0206	Edible offal of bovine animals, swine, sheep, goats, horses, asses, mules or hinnies, fresh, chilled or frozen.								
02061000	-Of bovine animals, fresh or chilled	6				KG,NZ,US,UY			0
02062	-Of bovine animals, frozen:								
02062100	--Tongues	6				KG,NZ,PY,US,UY			0
02062200	--Livers	6				KG,NZ,US,UY			0
02062900	--Other	6				KG,NZ,US,UY			0
02063000	-Of swine, fresh or chilled	P							0
02064	-Of swine, frozen:								
02064100	--Livers	P							0
02064900	--Other	P							0
020680	-Other, fresh or chilled								
02068010	---Sheep and goat offal, fresh	7				NZ,UY			0
02068090	---Other animal offal, fresh	10				NZ,UY			0
020690	-Other, frozen								
0206901	---Of sheep and goats:								
02069011	----Sheep and goat tongues, frozen	6				AU,KG,NZ,UY			0
02069012	----Sheep and goat livers, frozen	6				AU,KG,NZ,UY			0
02069019	----Other sheep and goat offal, frozen	6				AU,KG,NZ,UY			0
02069090	---Other animal offal, frozen	6				UY			0
0207	Meat and edible offal, of the poultry of heading 01.05, fresh, chilled or frozen.								
02071	-Of fowls of the species Gallus domesticus:								
02071100	--Not cut in pieces, fresh or chilled	20 or SR 1/net kg				CN,KG,PY,US			0
02071200	--Not cut in pieces, frozen	20 or SR 1/net kg				CE25,CN,KG,PY,US			0
020713	--Cuts and offal, fresh or chilled								
02071310	---Poultry minced meat, chilled	20 or SR 1/net kg				KG			0

HS	Description	Bound rate at date of accession	Final Bound rate	Implementation	Present concession established	INR	Concession first incorporated in a GATT Schedule	Earlier INRs	ODCs
02071390	---Other, of poultry meat, chilled	20 or SR 1/net kg				KG			0
020714	--Cuts and offal, frozen								
02071410	---Poultry minced meat, frozen	20 or SR 1/net kg				CN,KG,MX,US			0
02071490	---Other, of poultry meat, frozen	20 or SR 1/net kg				CN,KG,US			0
02072	-Of turkeys:								
02072400	--Not cut in pieces, fresh or chilled	15				KG			0
02072500	--Not cut in pieces, frozen	15				KG,US			0
02072600	--Cuts and offal, fresh or chilled	15				KG			0
02072700	--Cuts and offal, frozen	20 or SR 1/net kg				KG,US			0
02073	-Of ducks, geese or guinea fowls:								
02073200	--Not cut in pieces, fresh or chilled	25	20	2010		KG			0
02073300	--Not cut in pieces, frozen	25	20	2010		KG			0
02073400	--Fatty livers, fresh or chilled	25	20	2010		KG			0
02073500	--Other, fresh or chilled	25	20	2010		KG			0
02073600	--Other, frozen	20				KG			0
0208	Other meat and edible meat offal, fresh, chilled or frozen.								
020810	-Of rabbits or hares								
02081010	---Rabbit meat, fresh	25	20	2010					0
02081020	---Rabbit meat, frozen	25	20	2010					0
02082000	-Frogs' legs	P							0
02083000	-Of primates	15							0
02084000	-Of whales, dolphins and porpoises (mammals of the order Cetacea); of manatees and dugongs (mammals of the order Sirenia)	15							0
02085000	-Of reptiles (including snakes and turtles)	15							0
020890	-Other								
0208901	---Camel:								
02089011	----Camel meat, fresh or chilled	0							0
02089012	----Camel meat, frozen	0							0
0208902	---Gazelles and deer:								
02089021	----Gazelle or deer meat, fresh or chilled	25							0
02089022	----Gazelle or deer meat, frozen	25							0
0208903	---Wild pigeons, partridges, pheasants, quail, snipe, sand grouse and wild ducks								
02089031	----Pigeon or similar meat, fresh or chilled	25							0
02089032	----Pigeon or similar meat, frozen	25							0

HS	Description	Bound rate at date of accession	Final Bound rate	Implementation	Present concession established	INR	Concession first incorporated in a GATT Schedule	Earlier INRs	ODCs
02089090	---Other meat, not elsewhere classified	15							0
0209	Pig fat, free of lean meat, and poultry fat, not rendered or otherwise extracted, fresh, chilled, frozen, salted, in brine, dried or smoked.								
02090010	---Pig fat	P							0
02090090	---Other	15				DO,HN			0
0210	Meat and edible meat offal, salted, in brine, dried or smoked; edible flours and meals of meat or meat offal.								
02101	-Meat of swine:								
02101100	--Hams, shoulders and cuts thereof, with bone in	P							0
02101200	--Bellies (streaky) and cuts thereof	P							0
02101900	--Other	P							0
02102000	-Meat of bovine animals	15							0
02109	-Other, including edible flours and meals of meat and meat offal:								
02109100	--Of primates	15							0
02109200	--Of whales, dolphins and porpoises (mammals of the order Cetacea); of manatees and dugongs (mammals of the order Sirenia)	15							0
02109300	--Of reptiles (including snakes and turtles)	15							0
021099	--Other								
02109910	---Of poultry livers	15							0
02109920	---In flour or meal form (mince or burger)	15							0
02109990	---Other	15							0
0401	Milk and cream, not concentrated nor containing added sugar or other sweetening matter.								
040110	-Of a fat content, by weight, not exceeding 1 %								
04011030	---Long life liquid milk in packages exceeding one litre	40	25	2010		AU			0
04011090	---Other	15							0
040120	-Of a fat content, by weight, exceeding 1 % but not exceeding 6 %								
04012030	---Long life liquid milk in packages exceeding one litre	40	25	2010		AU			0
04012090	---Other	15							0
040130	-Of a fat content, by weight, exceeding 6 %								

HS	Description	Bound rate at date of accession	Final Bound rate	Implementation	Present concession established	INR	Concession first incorporated in a GATT Schedule	Earlier INRs	ODCs
04013030	---Long life liquid milk in packages exceeding one litre	40	25	2010		AU,CE25			0
04013090	---Other	10							0
0402	Milk and cream, concentrated or containing added sugar or other sweetening matter.								
04021	-In powder, granules or other solid forms, of a fat content, by weight, not exceeding 1.5 %:								
04021010	---Milk powder for industrial purposes	10				AU,CE25,NZ,US,UY			0
04021090	---Other low fat solid milk	10				CE25,NZ,US,UY			0
04022	-In powder, granules or other solid forms, of a fat content, by weight, exceeding 1.5 %:								
040221	--Not containing added sugar or other sweetening matter								
04022110	---Milk powder for industrial purposes	15				AU,CE25,NZ,UY			0
04022190	---Other solid unsweetened milk,	10				CE25,NZ,UY			0
040229	--Other								
04022910	---Milk powder for industrial purposes	15				AU,NZ,UY			0
04022990	---Other solid sweetened milk, over 1.5% fat	15				NZ,UY			0
04029	-Other:								
040291	--Not containing added sugar or other sweetening matter								
04029110	---Other milk, unsweetened	10				NZ,UY			0
04029120	---Other cream, unsweetened	10				CE25,NZ,UY			0
040299	--Other								
04029910	---Other Milk, sweetened	10				CE25,NZ,UY			0
04029920	---Other cream, sweetened	10				NZ,UY			0
0403	Buttermilk, curdled milk and cream, yogurt, kephir and other fermented or acidified milk and cream, whether or not concentrated or containing added sugar or other sweetening matter or flavoured or containing added fruit, nuts or cocoa.								
04031000	-Yoghurt	10				DO,HN,US			0
040390	-Other								
04039010	---Labnah	15							0
04039020	---Laban	15							0
04039030	---Cottage cheese	10				US			0
04039090	---Other milk and cream	10				DO,HN,US			0

HS	Description	Bound rate at date of accession	Final Bound rate	Implementation	Present concession established	INR	Concession first incorporated in a GATT Schedule	Earlier INRs	ODCs
0404	Whey, whether or not concentrated or containing added sugar or other sweetening matter; products consisting of natural milk constituents, whether or not containing added sugar or other sweetening matter, not elsewhere specified or included.								
04041000	-Whey and modified whey, whether or not concentrated or containing added sugar or other sweetening matter	10				US			0
04049000	-Other	10				US			0
0405	Butter and other fats and oils derived from milk; dairy spreads.								
04051000	-Butter	6				AU,CE25,DO,HN,NZ,UY			0
04052000	-Dairy spreads	15				DO,HN,NZ,UY			0
04059000	-Other	10				AU,CE25,DO,HN,NZ,UY			0
0406	Cheese and curd.								
04061000	-Fresh (unripened or uncured) cheese, including whey cheese, and curd	6				AU,CE25,DO,HN,NZ,UY			0
04062000	-Grated or powdered cheese, of all kinds	6				AU,DO,HN,NZ,US,UY			0
04063000	-Processed cheese, not grated or powdered	6				AU,CE25,DO,HN,NZ,US,UY			0
04064000	-Blue-veined cheese	6				NZ,UY			0
040690	-Other cheese								
04069010	---Fresh fermented cream cheese	6				CA,DO,HN,NZ,US,UY			0
04069020	---Solid or semi-solid cheese	6				AU,CA,CE25,DO,HN,NZ,US,UY			0
04069090	---Other cheese	6				AU,CA,CE25,DO,HN,NZ,US,UY			0
0407	Birds' eggs, in shell, fresh, preserved or cooked.								
0407001	---Fresh:								
04070011	----Fresh birds' eggs for hatching	10							0
04070019	----Other fresh birds' eggs	25 or SR 0.08/each				CE25,CN			0
04070090	---Other eggs in shells	25 or SR 0.08/each				CN			0
0408	Birds' eggs, not in shell, and egg yolks, fresh, dried, cooked by steaming or by boiling in water, moulded, frozen or otherwise preserved, whether or not containing added sugar or other sweetening matter.								
04081	-Egg yolks:								
04081100	--Dried	25 or SR 0.08/each	20	2010					0

HS	Description	Bound rate at date of accession	Final Bound rate	Implementation	Present concession established	INR	Concession first incorporated in a GATT Schedule	Earlier INRs	ODCs
04081900	--Other	25 or SR 0.08/each	20	2010					0
04089	-Other:								
04089100	--Dried	25 or SR 0.08/each	20	2010					0
04089900	--Other	25 or SR 0.08/each	20	2010					0
04090000	Natural honey.	6				AU,DO,HN,KG,MX,PY,US,UY			0
0410	Edible products of animal origin, not elsewhere specified or included.								
04100010	---Tortoise eggs	15							0
04100020	---Bird's nests	15							0
04100090	---Other edible products of animal Origin	15							0
05010000	Human hair, unworked, whether or not washed or scoured; waste of human hair.	15							0
0502	Pigs', hogs' or boars' bristles and hair; badger hair and other brush making hair; waste of such bristles or hair.								
05021000	-Pigs', hogs' or boars' bristles and hair and waste thereof	P							0
05029000	-Other	15							0
05030000	Horsehair and horsehair waste, whether or not put up as a layer with or without supporting material.	15							0
0504	Guts, bladders and stomachs of animals (other than fish), whole and pieces thereof, fresh, chilled, frozen, salted, in brine, dried or smoked.								
05040010	---Animal guts	15				UY			0
05040020	---Animal stomachs	15				UY			0
05040090	---Other animal parts	15				UY			0
0505	Skins and other parts of birds, with their feathers or down, feathers and parts of feathers (whether or not with trimmed edges) and down, not further worked than cleaned, disinfected or treated for preservation; powder and waste of feathers or parts of feathers.								
05051000	-Feathers of a kind used for stuffing; down	15							0
05059000	-Other	15							0
0506	Bones and horn-cores, unworked, defatted, simply prepared (but not cut to shape), treated with acid or degelatinised; powder and waste of these products.								

HS	Description	Bound rate at date of accession	Final Bound rate	Implementation	Present concession established	INR	Concession first incorporated in a GATT Schedule	Earlier INRs	ODCs
05061000	-Ossein and bones treated with acid	15							0
05069000	-Other	15							0
0507	Ivory, tortoise-shell, whalebone and whalebone hair, horns, antlers, hooves, nails, claws and beaks, unworked or simply prepared but not cut to shape; powder and waste of these products.								
05071000	-Ivory; ivory powder and waste	15							0
050790	-Other								
05079010	---Tortoise-shell, Whalebone and whale-bone hair	15							0
05079020	---Horns, antlers, hooves, nails, claws	15							0
0508	Coral and similar materials, unworked or simply prepared but not otherwise worked; shells of molluscs, crustaceans or echinoderms and cuttle-bone, unworked or simply prepared but not cut to shape, powder and waste thereof.								
05080010	---Coral	15							0
05080020	---Black coral	15							0
05080030	---Shells of molluscs, crustaceans or echinoderms	15							0
05080090	---Cuttlebone and similar material	15							0
0509	Natural sponges of animal origin.								
05090010	---Crude sponges	15							0
05090020	---Prepared sponges	15							0
0510	Ambergris, castoreum, civet and musk; cantharides; bile, whether or not dried; glands and other animal products used in the preparation of pharmaceutical products, fresh, chilled, frozen or otherwise provisionally preserved.								
05100010	---Ambergris, castoreum, civet, musk	15							0
05100090	---Other animal products	15							0
0511	Animal products not elsewhere specified or included; dead animals of Chapter 1 or 3, unfit for human consumption.								
05111000	-Bovine semen	6				CA,US			0
05119	-Other:								
051191	--Products of fish or crustaceans, molluscs or other aquatic invertebrates; dead animals of Chapter 3								
05119110	---Inedible fish eggs	15							0
05119120	---Dead animals of marine life	15							0

HS	Description	Bound rate at date of accession	Final Bound rate	Implementation	Present concession established	INR	Concession first incorporated in a GATT Schedule	Earlier INRs	ODCs
05119190	---Other products of fish, crustaceans, etc.	15							0
051199	--Other								
05119910	---Kermes and similar insects	15							0
05119920	---Silkworm eggs	15							0
05119930	---Ant eggs	15							0
05119940	---Animal blood, other dead animals and inedible meat	15							0
05119950	---Sinews and tendons, and similar waste of raw hides	15							0
05119990	---Other animal products, not elsewhere specified	15							0
0601	Bulbs, tubers, tuberous roots, corms, crowns and rhizomes, dormant, in growth or in flower; chicory plants and roots other than roots of heading 12.12.								
06011000	-Bulbs, tubers, tuberous roots, corms, crowns and rhizomes, dormant	15				DO,HN			0
06012000	-Bulbs, tubers, tuberous roots, corms, crowns and rhizomes, in growth or in flower; chicory plants and roots	15							0
0602	Other live plants (including their roots), cuttings and slips; mushroom spawn.								
060210	-Unrooted cuttings and slips								
06021010	---Grapevines (grapeslips)	15				DO,HN			0
06021090	---Other unrooted cuttings and slips	15				DO,HN			0
060220	-Trees, shrubs and bushes, grafted or not, of kinds which bear edible fruit or nuts								
06022010	---Palm tree seedlings	15				DO,HN			0
06022090	---Other edible fruit trees or bushes	15				DO,HN			0
060230	-Rhododendrons and azaleas, grafted or not								
06023010	---Ornamental shrubs	15							0
06023090	---Other rhododendrons or azaleas	15							0
06024000	-Roses, grafted or not	15							0
06029000	-Other	6				DO,HN			0
0603	Cut flowers and flower buds of a kind suitable for bouquets or for ornamental purposes, fresh, dried, dyed, bleached, impregnated or otherwise prepared.								
06031000	-Fresh	5				EC,MX			0
06039000	-Other	5				EC,MX			0

HS	Description	Bound rate at date of accession	Final Bound rate	Implementation	Present concession established	INR	Concession first incorporated in a GATT Schedule	Earlier INRs	ODCs
0604	Foliage, branches and other parts of plants, without flowers or flower buds, and grasses, mosses and lichens, being goods of a kind suitable for bouquets or for ornamental purposes, fresh, dried, dyed, bleached, impregnated or otherwise prepared.								
06041000	-Mosses and lichens	15				DO,HN			0
06049	-Other:								
06049100	--Fresh	15							0
06049900	--Other	5				EC			0
0701	Potatoes, fresh or chilled.								
07011000	-Seed	10				CE25			0
07019000	-Other:								
ex07019000	- From 1 January to 31 May	25	15	2010		DO,HN			0
ex07019000	- From 1 June to 31 December	15				DO,HN			0
0702	Tomatoes, fresh (or chilled)								
ex07020000	- From 1 September to 30 April	15				DO,HN			0
ex07020000	- From 1 May to 31 August	25	15	2010		DO,HN			0
0703	Onions, shallots, garlic, leeks and other alliaceous vegetables, fresh or chilled.								
070310	-Onions and shallots								
0703101	--Onions:								
07031011	---Onions for food								
ex07031011	- From 1 November to 31 May	12				DO,HN			0
ex07031011	- From 1 June to 31 October	25	15	2010		DO,HN,KG			0
07031012	---Onions (for sowing)	5				DO,HN,KG			0
07031020	--Shallots	5				DO,HN,KG			0
07032000	-Garlic	15				CN,MX,UY			0
07039000	-Leeks and other alliaceous vegetables	15							0
0704	Cabbages, cauliflowers, kohlrabi, kale and similar edible brassicas, fresh or chilled.								
07041000	-Cauliflowers and headed broccoli	15				AU,DO,HN			0
07042000	-Brussels sprouts	15							0
07049000	-Other	15							0
0705	Lettuce (Lactuca sativa) and chicory (Cichorium spp.), fresh or chilled.								
07051	-Lettuce:								
07051100	--Cabbage lettuce (head lettuce)	15							0
07051900	--Other	15							0
07052	-Chicory:								
07052100	--Witloof chicory (Cichorium intybus var. foliosum)	15							0

HS	Description	Bound rate at date of accession	Final Bound rate	Implementation	Present concession established	INR	Concession first incorporated in a GATT Schedule	Earlier INRs	ODCs
07052900	--Other	6							0
0706	Carrots, turnips, salad beetroot, salsify, celeriac, radishes and similar edible roots, fresh or chilled.								
07061000	-Carrots and turnips								
ex07061000	- From 1 Februray to 31 May	25	15	2010		DO,HN			0
ex07061000	- From 1 June to 31 January	15				DO,HN			0
07069000	-Other	15							0
0707	Cucumbers and gherkins, fresh or chilled.								
ex07070000	- From 1 May to 31 August	25	15	2010		DO,HN			0
ex07070000	- From 1 September to 30 April	15				DO,HN			0
0708	Leguminous vegetables, shelled or unshelled, fresh or chilled.								
07081000	-Peas (Pisum sativum)	15				DO,HN			0
07082000	-Beans (Vigna spp., Phaseolus spp.)	15				DO,HN			0
070890	-Other leguminous vegetables								
07089010	--Kidney beans	15				DO,HN			0
07089090	--Other leguminous vegetables	15							0
0709	Other vegetables, fresh or chilled.								
07091000	-Globe artichokes	8							0
07092000	-Asparagus	8				DO,HN			0
07093000	-Aubergines (egg-plants)	10				DO,HN			0
07094000	-Celery other than celeriac	15							0
07095	-Mushrooms and truffles:								
07095100	--Mushrooms of the genus Agaricus	15				DO,HN			0
07095200	--Truffles	15							0
07095900	--Other	15							0
07096000	-Fruits of the genus Capsicum or of the genus Pimenta	15				DO,HN			0
07097000	-Spinach, New Zealand spinach and orache spinach (garden spinach)	15							0
070990	-Other								
07099010	--Pumpkins	15							0
07099020	--Marrow								
ex07099020	- From 1 August to 31 May	15							0
ex07099020	- From 1 June to 31 July	25	15	2010					0
07099030	--Olives	15							0
07099040	--Okra:								
ex07099040	- From 1 June to 31 August	25	15	2010					0
ex07099040	- From 1 September to 31 May	15							0
07099050	--Parsley	15							0

HS	Description	Bound rate at date of accession	Final Bound rate	Implementation	Present concession established	INR	Concession first incorporated in a GATT Schedule	Earlier INRs	ODCs
07099060	--Coriander	15							0
07099090	--Other vegetables	12				LK			0
0710	Vegetables (uncooked or cooked by steaming or boiling in water), frozen.								
07101000	-Potatoes	12							0
07102	-Leguminous vegetables, shelled or unshelled:								
07102100	--Peas (Pisum sativum)	15	12	2010*					0
07102200	--Beans (Vigna spp., Phaseolus spp.)	15	12	2010*					0
07102900	--Other	15							0
07103000	-Spinach, New Zealand spinach and orache spinach (garden spinach)	15							0
07104000	-Sweet corn	6				US			0
07108000	-Other vegetables	10							0
07109000	-Mixtures of vegetables	10				US			0
0711	Vegetables provisionally preserved (for example, by sulphur dioxide gas, in brine, in sulphur water or in other preservative solutions), but unsuitable in that state for immediate consumption.								
07112000	-Olives	15							0
07113000	-Capers	15							0
07114000	-Cucumbers and gherkins	15				DO,HN			0
07115	-Mushrooms and truffles:								
07115100	--Mushrooms of the genus Agaricus	6							0
07115900	--Other	6							0
07119000	-Other vegetables; mixtures of vegetables	6				US			0
0712	Dried vegetables, whole, cut, sliced, broken or in powder, but not further prepared.								
07122000	-Onions	10							0
07123	-Mushrooms, wood ears (Auricularia spp.), jelly fungi (Tremella spp.) and truffles:								
07123100	--Mushrooms of the genus Agaricus	15							0
07123200	--Wood ears (Auricularia spp.)	15							0
07123300	--Jelly fungi (Tremella spp.)	15							0
07123900	--Other	15							0
07129000	-Other vegetables; mixtures of vegetables	15							0
0713	Dried leguminous vegetables, shelled, whether or not skinned or split.								
07131000	-Peas (Pisum sativum)	6				AU,CA,US			0
07132000	-Chickpeas (garbanzos)	6				AU,MX,US			0
07133	-Beans (Vigna spp., Phaseolus spp.):								

HS	Description	Bound rate at date of accession	Final Bound rate	Implementation	Present concession established	INR	Concession first incorporated in a GATT Schedule	Earlier INRs	ODCs
071331	--Beans of the species Vigna mungo (L.) Hepper or Vigna radiata (L.) Wilczek								
07133110	---Beans, for sowing, dried	6				KG			0
07133120	---Beans, for food, dried	6				KG			0
071332	--Small red (Adzuki) beans (Phaseolus or Vigna angularis)								
07133210	---Red beans for sowing, dried	6				DO,HN			0
07133220	---Red beans for food, dried	6				DO,HN			0
071333	--Kidney beans, including white pea beans (Phaseolus vulgaris)								
07133310	---Kidney beans for sowing, dried	6				DO,HN,KG			0
07133320	---Kidney beans for food, dried	6				DO,HN,KG			0
07133900	--Other	6				DO,HN,KG,US			0
07134000	-Lentils	6				DO,HN			0
07135000	-Broad beans (Vicia faba var. major) and horse beans (Vicia faba var. equina, Vicia faba var. minor)	6				AU,DO,HN			0
071390	-Other								
07139010	---Mung beans, dried	6				DO,HN			0
07139090	---Other dried leguminous vegetables	6							0
0714	Manioc, arrowroot, salep, Jerusalem artichokes, sweet potatoes and similar roots and tubers with high starch or inulin content, fresh, chilled, frozen or dried, whether or not sliced or in the form of pellets; sago pith.								
07141000	-Manioc (cassava)	15				DO,HN			0
07142000	-Sweet potatoes	15				DO,HN			0
071490	-Other								
07149010	---Salep	15							0
07149020	---Jerusalem artichokes	15							0
07149090	---Other roots and tubers	15				DO,HN			0
0801	Coconuts, Brazil nuts and cashew nuts, fresh or dried, whether or not shelled or peeled.								
08011	-Coconuts:								
08011100	--Desiccated	6				DO,HN,LK,PH			0
08011900	--Other	6				DO,HN,LK,PH			0
08012	-Brazil nuts:								
08012100	--In shell	15							0
08012200	--Shelled	15							0
08013	-Cashew nuts:								

HS	Description	Bound rate at date of accession	Final Bound rate	Implementation	Present concession established	INR	Concession first incorporated in a GATT Schedule	Earlier INRs	ODCs
08013100	--In shell	10				DO,HN,IN			0
08013200	--Shelled	10				DO,HN,IN,SV			0
0802	Other nuts, fresh or dried, whether or not shelled or peeled.								
08021	-Almonds:								
08021100	--In shell	6				KG,US			0
08021200	--Shelled	6				US			0
08022	-Hazelnuts or filberts (Corylus spp.):								
08022100	--In shell	15							0
08022200	--Shelled	15							0
08023	-Walnuts:								
08023100	--In shell	15							0
08023200	--Shelled	15							0
08024000	-Chestnuts (Castanea spp.)	15							0
080250	-Pistachios								
08025010	---Pistachios, in shells	15							0
08025020	---Pistachios, shelled	15							0
080290	-Other								
0802901	---Pine nuts:								
08029011	----Pine nuts, in shells	15							0
08029012	----Pine nuts, shelled	15							0
08029020	---Green seed (Bank)	15							0
0802909	---Other:								
08029091	----Other nuts, in shells	12							0
08029092	----Other nuts, shelled	12							0
08030000	Bananas, including plantains, fresh or dried.	5				DO,EC,HN,MX,PH			0
0804	Dates, figs, pineapples, avocados, guavas, mangoes and mangosteens, fresh or dried.								
080410	-Dates								
08041010	---Fresh dates	40							0
08041020	---Dried dates	40							0
08041030	---Dried and Pressed Dates	40							0
08041090	---Other dates	40							0
080420	-Figs								
08042010	---Fresh figs	15							0
08042020	---Dried figs	15							0
08043000	-Pineapples	10				DO,EC,HN			0
08044000	-Avocados	10				DO,HN,MX			0
080450	-Guavas, mangoes and mangosteens								
08045010	---Guavas	8				DO,EC,HN,MX			0
08045020	---Mangoes (See Endnote 1)	6				AU,DO,EC,HN,MX,PH,PK			0

HS	Description	Bound rate at date of accession	Final Bound rate	Implementation	Present concession established	INR	Concession first incorporated in a GATT Schedule	Earlier INRs	ODCs
08045030	---Mangosteens	8				DO,EC,HN			0
0805	Citrus fruit, fresh or dried.								
08051000	-Oranges	10				DO,HN,UY			0
08052000	-Mandarins (including tangerines and satsumas); clementines, wilkings and similar citrus hybrids	13				DO,HN,UY			0
08054000	-Grapefruit	10				DO,HN			0
080550	-Lemons (Citrus limon, Citrus limonum) and limes (Citrus aurantifolia, Citrus latifolia)								
08055010	---Fresh lemons	10				DO,HN,MX,UY			0
08055020	---Dried lemons	15				DO,HN,UY			0
08059000	-Other	15	12	2008		DO,HN,MX			0
0806	Grapes, fresh or dried.								
08061000	-Fresh	5				US			0
08062000	-Dried	5				KG,US			0
0807	Melons (including watermelons) and papaws (papayas), fresh.								
08071	-Melons (including watermelons):								
08071100	--Watermelon:								
ex08071100	- From 1 May to 31 August	25	15	2010		DO,HN,KG			0
ex08071100	- From 1 September to 30 April	15				DO,HN			0
08071910	--Melon (muskmelon):								
ex08071910	- From 1 May to 31 August	25	15	2010		DO,HN			0
ex08071910	- From 1 September to 30 April	12				DO,HN			0
ex08071990	- From 1 September to 30 April	15				DO,HN			0
08071990	--Other								
ex08071990	- From 1 May to 31 August	25	15	2010		DO,HN			0
08072000	-Papaws (papayas)	15				DO,HN			0
0808	Apples, pears and quinces, fresh.								
08081000	-Apples	5				CE25,NZ,US			0
080820	-Pears and quinces								
08082010	--Pears, fresh	5				NZ,US			0
08082020	--Quince, fresh	7							0
0809	Apricots, cherries, peaches (including nectarines), plums and sloes, fresh.								
08091000	-Apricots	15							0
08092000	-Cherries	15							0
08093000	-Peaches, including nectarines	15							0
08094000	-Plums and sloes	10							0
0810	Other fruit, fresh.								
08101000	-Strawberries	12				US			0

HS	Description	Bound rate at date of accession	Final Bound rate	Implementation	Present concession established	INR	Concession first incorporated in a GATT Schedule	Earlier INRs	ODCs
08102000	-Raspberries, blackberries, mulberries and loganberries	15							0
08103000	-Black, white or red currants and gooseberries	15							0
08104000	-Cranberries, bilberries and other fruits of the genus Vaccinium	15							0
08105000	-Kiwifruit	10				NZ			0
08106000	-Durians	15							0
081090	-Other								
08109010	---Pomegranates, fresh	10				DO,HN			0
08109020	---Medlar, fresh	15				DO,HN			0
08109030	---Prickly pear, fresh	15							0
08109090	---Other fruit, fresh	15				DO,HN			0
0811	Fruit and nuts, uncooked or cooked by steaming or boiling in water, frozen, whether or not containing added sugar or other sweetening matter.								
08111000	-Strawberries	15	12	2008		MX			0
08112000	-Raspberries, blackberries, mulberries, loganberries, black, white or red currants and gooseberries	15							0
08119000	-Other	10							0
0812	Fruit and nuts, provisionally preserved (for example, by sulphur dioxide gas, in brine, in sulphur water or in other preservative solutions), but unsuitable in that state for immediate consumption.								
08121000	-Cherries	15							0
08129000	-Other	10				IN			0
0813	Fruit, dried, other than that of headings Nos. 08.01 to 08.06; mixtures of nuts or dried fruits of this Chapter.								
08131000	-Apricots	15				KG			0
08132000	-Prunes	6				US			0
08133000	-Apples	15							0
081340	-Other fruit								
08134010	---Cherries, dried	15				KG			0
08134020	---Tamarind, dried	10				KG			0
08134030	---Pears, dried	15				KG			0
08134090	---Other dried fruit	15				KG			0
08135000	-Mixtures of nuts or dried fruits of this Chapter	15				KG			0

HS	Description	Bound rate at date of accession	Final Bound rate	Implementation	Present concession established	INR	Concession first incorporated in a GATT Schedule	Earlier INRs	ODCs
08140000	Peel of citrus fruit or melons (including watermelons), fresh, frozen, dried or provisionally preserved in brine, in sulphur water or in other preservative solutions.	15				DO,HN			0
0901	Coffee, whether or not roasted or decaffeinated; coffee husks and skins; coffee substitutes containing coffee in any proportion.								
09011	-Coffee, not roasted:								
09011100	--Not decaffeinated	5				DO,EC,HN,SV			0
09011200	--Decaffeinated	5				DO,EC,HN,SV			0
09012	-Coffee roasted:								
09012100	--Not decaffeinated	5				DO,EC,HN,MX,US			0
09012200	--Decaffeinated	5				DO,EC,HN,MX			0
09019000	-Other	15	12	2008		DO,HN,MX			0
0902	Tea, whether or not flavoured.								
09021000	-Green tea (not fermented) in immediate packings of a content not exceeding 3 kg (See Endnote 2)	7				LK			0
09022000	-Other green tea (not fermented)	7							0
090230	-Black tea (fermented) and partly fermented tea, in immediate packings of a content not exceeding 3 kg								
09023010	---Tea, in small packings of a content not exceeding 3 g (See Endnote 3)	6				IN,LK			0
09023090	---Other (See Endnote 4)	6				IN,LK			0
09024000	-Other black tea (fermented) and other partly fermented tea (See Endnote 5)	6				IN,LK			0
09030000	Maté.	15							0
0904	Pepper of the genus Piper; dried or crushed or ground fruits of the genus Capsicum or of the genus Pimenta.								
09041	-Pepper:								
09041100	--Neither crushed nor ground	10				DO,HN,LK			0
09041200	--Crushed or ground	15				DO,HN			0
09042000	-Fruits of the genus Capsicum or of the genus Pimenta, dried or crushed or ground	10				DO,HN			0
09050000	Vanilla.	15							0
0906	Cinnamon and cinnamon-tree flowers.								
09061000	-Neither crushed nor ground	15							0
09062000	-Crushed or ground	15							0
09070000	Cloves (whole fruit, cloves and stems).	12				DO,HN,LK			0
0908	Nutmeg, mace and cardamoms.								

HS	Description	Bound rate at date of accession	Final Bound rate	Implementation	Present concession established	INR	Concession first incorporated in a GATT Schedule	Earlier INRs	ODCs
09081000	-Nutmeg	15							0
09082000	-Mace	P							0
09083000	-Cardamoms	7				DO,HN,IN			0
0909	Seeds of anise, badian, fennel, coriander, cumin or caraway; juniper berries.								
09091000	-Seeds of anise or badian	15							0
09092000	-Seeds of coriander	10							0
09093000	-Seeds of cumin	15							0
09094000	-Seeds of caraway	15							0
09095000	-Seeds of fennel; juniper berries	10							0
0910	Ginger, saffron, turmeric (curcuma), thyme, bay leaves, curry and other spices.								
09101000	-Ginger	10				DO,HN,IN			0
09102000	-Saffron	15				DO,HN			0
09103000	-Turmeric (curcuma)	10				IN			0
09104000	-Thyme; bay leaves	15							0
09105000	-Curry	15							0
09109	-Other spices:								
09109100	--Mixtures referred to in Note 1 (b) to this Chapter	10				IN			0
091099	--Other								
09109910	---Fenugreek	10				DO,HN,IN,US			0
09109990	---Other spices	10				DO,HN,IN,US			0
1001	Wheat and meslin.								
10011000	-Durum wheat	25				US			0
100190	-Other								
10019010	---Wheat, normal	25				AU,US			0
10019020	---Wheat, thin	25				US			0
10019030	---Wheat and rye, mixed	25				US			0
10020000	Rye.	15							0
10030000	Barley.	5				AU,CA,CE25,US			0
1004	Oats.								
10040010	---Grey oats (or black)	10				US			0
10040020	---White oats (or yellow)	10				US			0
1005	Maize (corn).								
10051000	-Seed	5							0
100590	-Other								
10059010	---Golden corn	5				US			0
10059020	---White corn	7				US			0
10059030	---Brown corn	7				US			0
10059090	---Other corn	5				US			0

HS	Description	Bound rate at date of accession	Final Bound rate	Implementation	Present concession established	INR	Concession first incorporated in a GATT Schedule	Earlier INRs	ODCs
1006	Rice.								
10061000	-Rice in the husk (paddy or rough)	5				IN,US,UY			0
10062000	-Husked (brown) rice	7				AU,US,UY			0
10063000	-Semi-milled or wholly milled rice, whether or not polished or glazed	5				AU,IN,PK,US,UY			0
10064000	-Broken rice	7				US,UY			0
10070000	Grain sorghum.	10				US			0
1008	Buckwheat, millet and canary seed; other cereals.								
10081000	-Buckwheat	25							0
10082000	-Millet	8				IN			0
10083000	-Canary seed	15							0
10089000	-Other cereals	5				US			0
1101	Wheat or meslin flour.								
11010010	---Wheat Flour	25				AU,US			0
11010020	---Flour of mixed wheat and rye	25				AU,US			0
1102	Cereal flours other than of wheat or meslin.								
11021000	-Rye flour	15							0
11022000	-Maize (corn) flour	10							0
11023000	-Rice flour	10							0
ex11023000	Non-glutinous rice flour	5							0
110290	-Other								
11029010	---Barley flour	15							0
11029020	---Oat flour	15							0
11029030	---Grain sorghum flour	15							0
11029040	---Buckwheat flour	25							0
11029050	---Millet flour	15							0
11029090	---Other flour	15							0
1103	Cereal groats, meal and pellets.								
11031	-Groats and meal:								
110311	--Of wheat								
11031110	---Wheat groats	20				CE25			0
11031120	---Wheat meal	20				CE25			0
110313	--Of maize (corn)								
11031310	---Maize groats	15							0
11031320	---Maize meal	15							0
110319	--Of other cereals								
11031910	---Crushed grains of barley	15							0
11031920	---Crushed grains of sorghum	15							0
11031930	---Crushed grains of darnel	15							0
11031940	---Crushed grains of dark wheat	20							0

HS	Description	Bound rate at date of accession	Final Bound rate	Implementation	Present concession established	INR	Concession first incorporated in a GATT Schedule	Earlier INRs	ODCs
11031950	---Crushed grains of millet	15							0
11031990	---Other crushed grains	15							0
11032000	-Pellets	15							0
1104	Cereal grains otherwise worked (for example, hulled, rolled, flaked, pearled, sliced or kibbled), except rice of heading 10.06; germ of cereals, whole, rolled, flaked or ground.								
11041	-Rolled or flaked grains:								
11041200	--Of oats	15							0
110419	--Of other cereals								
11041910	---Rolled or flaked wheat grains	15							0
11041920	---Rolled or flaked rye grains	15							0
11041930	---Rolled or flaked buckwheat grains	15							0
11041940	---Rolled or flaked millet grains	15							0
11041950	---Rolled or flaked sorghum grains	15							0
11041960	---Rolled or flaked maize grains	15							0
11041990	---Rolled or flaked grains of other cereals	15							0
11042	-Other worked grains (for example, hulled, pearled, sliced or kibbled):								
11042200	--Of oats	15							0
11042300	--Of maize (corn)	15							0
110429	--Of other cereals								
11042910	---Other worked wheat grains	15							0
11042920	---Other worked rye grains	15							0
11042930	---Other worked buckwheat grains	15							0
11042940	---Other worked millet grains	15							0
11042950	---Other worked sorghum grains	15							0
11042990	---Other worked Grains of other cereals	15							0
11043000	-Germ of cereals, whole, rolled, flaked or ground	15							0
1105	Flour, meal, powder, flakes, granules and pellets of potatoes.								
110510	-Flour, meal and powder								
11051010	---Potato flour	15							0
11051020	---Potato meal	15							0
11051030	---Potato powder	15							0
11052000	-Flakes, granules and pellets	15							0
1106	Flour, meal and powder of the dried leguminous vegetables of heading 07.13, of sago or of roots or tubers of heading 07.14 or of the products of Chapter 8.								

HS	Description	Bound rate at date of accession	Final Bound rate	Implementation	Present concession established	INR	Concession first incorporated in a GATT Schedule	Earlier INRs	ODCs
110610	-Of the dried leguminous vegetables of heading 07.13								
1106101	---Flour:								
11061011	----Pea flour	15							0
11061012	----Chick pea flour	15							0
11061013	----String bean flour	15							0
11061014	----Haricot bean flour	15							0
11061015	----Lentil flour	15							0
11061016	----Kidney bean flour	15							0
11061019	----Flour of other dried legumes	15							0
1106102	---Meal:								
11061021	----Pea meal	15							0
11061022	----Chick pea meal	15							0
11061023	----String bean meal	15							0
11061024	----Haricot bean meal	15							0
11061025	----Lentil bean meal	15							0
11061026	----Kidney bean meal	15							0
11061029	----Meal of other dried legumes	15							0
110620	-Of sago or of roots or tubers of heading 07.14								
11062010	---Sago flour	15							0
11062020	---Sago meal	15							0
1106203	---Flour and meal of roots and tubers:								
11062031	----Manioc flour	15							0
11062032	----Arrowroot flour	15							0
11062033	----Salep flour	15							0
11062034	----Jerusalem artichoke flour	15							0
11062035	----Sweet potato flour	15							0
11062039	----Flour of other roots and tubers	15							0
110630	-Of the products of Chapter 8								
11063010	---Chestnut flour, meal and powder	15							0
11063020	---Almond flour, meal and powder	15							0
11063030	---Date flour, meal and powder	15							0
11063040	---Banana Flour, meal and powder	15							0
11063050	---Coconut flour, meal and powder	12				LK			0
11063060	---Tamarind flour, meal and powder	15							0
11063070	---Flour, meal and powder of fruit peelings	15							0
11063080	---Flour of lemon	15							0
11063090	---Other flour, meal and powder	15							0
1107	Malt, whether or not roasted.								
11071000	-Not roasted	15							0

HS	Description	Bound rate at date of accession	Final Bound rate	Implementation	Present concession established	INR	Concession first incorporated in a GATT Schedule	Earlier INRs	ODCs
11072000	-Roasted	15							0
1108	Starches; inulin.								
11081	-Starches:								
11081100	--Wheat starch	10				US			0
11081200	--Maize (corn) starch	15							0
11081300	--Potato starch	15							0
11081400	--Manioc (cassava) starch	15							0
110819	--Other starches								
11081910	---Rice starch	10							0
11081920	---Arrowroot starch	10							0
11081930	---Sago starch	10							0
11081990	---Other starches	10							0
11082000	-Inulin	15							0
11090000	Wheat gluten, whether or not dried.	15							0
1201	Soya beans, whether or not broken.								
12010010	---Whole soy beans	6				US			0
12010020	---Broken soy beans	6				US			0
1202	Ground-nuts, not roasted or otherwise cooked, whether or not shelled or broken.								
12021000	-In shell	15				US			0
12022000	-Shelled, whether or not broken	10				KG,US			0
12030000	Copra.	15							0
12040000	Linseed, whether or not broken.	15							0
1205	Rape or colza seeds, whether or not broken.								
12051000	-Low erucic acid rape or colza seeds	6				AU,US			0
12059000	-Other	6				AU,US			0
12060000	Sunflower seeds, whether or not broken.	10				US			0
1207	Other oil seeds and oleaginous fruits, whether or not broken.								
12071000	-Palm nuts and kernels	15							0
12072000	-Cotton seeds	10				CE25			0
12073000	-Castor oil seeds	15							0
12074000	-Sesamum seeds	12				MX			0
12075000	-Mustard seeds	15							0
12076000	-Safflower seeds	15							0
12079	-Other:								
12079100	--Poppy seeds	P							0
120799	--Other								
12079910	---Poppy	P							0
12079920	---Hemp seeds	P							0
12079990	---Other seeds	15							0

HS	Description	Bound rate at date of accession	Final Bound rate	Implementation	Present concession established	INR	Concession first incorporated in a GATT Schedule	Earlier INRs	ODCs
1208	Flours and meals of oil seeds or oleaginous fruits, other than those of mustard.								
12081000	-Of soya beans	6				US			0
12089000	-Other	6				US			0
1209	Seeds, fruit and spores, of a kind used for sowing.								
12091000	-Sugar beet seed	15				KG			0
12092	-Seeds of forage plants:								
12092100	--Lucerne (alfalfa) seed	5				AU,KG,US			0
12092200	--Clover (Trifolium spp.) seed	10							0
12092300	--Fescue seed	15							0
12092400	--Kentucky blue grass (Poa pratensis L.) seed	15							0
12092500	--Rye grass (Lolium multiflorum Lam., Lolium perenne L.) seed	5				US			0
12092600	--Timothy grass seed	10				US			0
120929	--Other								
12092910	---Lupine seed	5				US			0
12092990	---Other seeds of forage plants	5				KG,US			0
12093000	-Seeds of herbaceous plants cultivated principally for their flowers	10							0
12099	-Other:								
120991	--Vegetable seeds								
12099110	---Tomato seeds	5				KG,US			0
12099120	---Leek seeds	5				KG,US			0
12099130	---Radish seeds	5				KG,US			0
12099140	---Carrot seeds	5				KG,US			0
12099150	---Cucumber seeds	5				KG,US			0
12099160	---Marrow seeds	5				KG,US			0
12099170	---Pumpkin seeds	5				KG,US			0
12099180	---Eggplant seeds	5				KG,US			0
1209919	---Other:								
12099191	----Lettuce seeds	5				CE25,KG,US			0
12099192	----Cress seeds	5				KG,US			0
12099193	----Capsicum seeds	5				KG,US			0
12099199	----Other vegetable seeds	5				KG,US			0
12099900	--Other	5				US			0
1210	Hop cones, fresh or dried, whether or not ground, powdered or in the form of pellets; lupulin.								
12101000	-Hop cones, neither ground nor powdered nor in the form of pellets	15							0

HS	Description	Bound rate at date of accession	Final Bound rate	Implementation	Present concession established	INR	Concession first incorporated in a GATT Schedule	Earlier INRs	ODCs
12102000	-Hop cones, ground, powdered or in the form of pellets; lupulin	15							0
1211	Plants and parts of plants (including seeds and fruits), of a kind used primarily in perfumery, in pharmacy or for insecticidal, fungicidal or similar purposes, fresh or dried, whether or not cut, crushed or powdered.								
12111000	-Liquorice roots	15							0
12112000	-Ginseng roots	15							0
12113000	-Coca leaf	P				KG			0
12114000	-Poppy straw	P				KG			0
121190	-Other								
12119010	---Black Caraway plants	6				KG,US			0
12119020	---Black poppy plants	P							0
12119030	---Chips and pieces of aloeswood, and other aromatic woods	6				DO,HN,KG,US			0
12119040	---Mint	6				KG			0
12119050	---Desert flower	6				KG			0
12119060	---Indian hemp	P				KG			0
12119070	---Cleaning sticks for teeth	6				KG			0
12119090	---Other plants used in perfumes or pharmacy	6				DO,EC,HN,KG,US			0
1212	Locust beans, seaweeds and other algae, sugar beet and sugar cane, fresh, chilled, frozen or dried, whether or not ground; fruit stones and kernels and other vegetable products (including unroasted chicory roots of the variety Cichorium intybus sativum) of a kind used primarily for human consumption, not elsewhere specified or included.								
121210	-Locust beans, including locust bean seeds								
12121010	---Locust beans	15							0
12121020	---Locust bean seeds	15							0
12122000	-Seaweeds and other algae	8				PH			0
12123000	-Apricot, peach (including nectarine) or plum stones and kernels	15							0
12129	-Other:								
12129100	--Sugar beet	15							0
121299	--Other								
12129910	---Melon seeds, unroasted	15							0
12129930	---Sugar cane	15							0

HS	Description	Bound rate at date of accession	Final Bound rate	Implementation	Present concession established	INR	Concession first incorporated in a GATT Schedule	Earlier INRs	ODCs
12129940	---Pumpkin, squash and marrow seeds, unroasted	15							0
12129990	---Other unroasted stones and kernels	15							0
1213	Cereal straw and husks, unprepared, whether or not chopped, ground, pressed or in the form of pellets.								
12130010	---Straw	15							0
12130090	---Other	15							0
1214	Swedes, mangolds, fodder roots, hay, lucerne (alfalfa), clover, sainfoin, forage kale, lupines, vetches and similar forage products, whether or not in the form of pellets.								
12141000	-Lucerne (alfalfa) meal and pellets	15							0
121490	-Other								
12149010	---Lupine	15				AU			0
12149020	---Vetch, vetchling and chickling vetch	15							0
12149090	---Other forage products	15							0
1301	Lac; natural gums, resins, gum-resins and oleoresins (for example, balsams).								
13011000	-Lac	6				KG			0
13012000	-Gum Arabic	15							0
130190	-Other								
13019010	---Tragacanth	15				KG			0
13019020	---Mastic	15				KG			0
13019030	---Benzoin	15				KG			0
13019040	---Asafoetida	15				KG			0
13019050	---Myrrh	15				KG			0
13019060	---Olibanum	15				KG			0
13019070	---Frankincense	15				KG			0
13019080	---Storax	15				KG			0
1301909	---Other:								
13019091	----Gum resins	15				KG			0
13019092	----Oleoresins	15				KG			0
13019093	----Natural resins	15				KG			0
13019099	----Other resins	15				KG			0
1302	Vegetable saps and extracts; pectic substances, pectinates and pectates; agar-agar and other mucilages and thickeners, whether or not modified, derived from vegetable products.								
13021	-Vegetable saps and extracts:								

HS	Description	Bound rate at date of accession	Final Bound rate	Implementation	Present concession established	INR	Concession first incorporated in a GATT Schedule	Earlier INRs	ODCs
13021100	--Opium	P							0
13021200	--Of liquorice	15							0
13021300	--Of hops	15							0
13021400	--Of pyrethrum or of the roots of plants containing rotenone	15							0
130219	--Other								
13021910	---Hashish	P							0
13021920	---Ginseng extract	15							0
13021930	---Tahinah (sesame juice)	20							0
13021940	---Aloes	15				DO,HN			0
13021950	---Myrrh	15							0
13021960	---Mannite	15							0
13021970	---Other medical extracts	15				DO,HN			0
13021990	---Other extracts	15				DO,HN			0
13022000	-Pectic substances, pectinates and pectates	15							0
13023	-Mucilages and thickeners, whether or not modified, derived from vegetable products:								
13023100	--Agar-agar	8				PH			0
13023200	--Mucilages and thickeners, whether or not modified, derived from locust beans, locust bean seeds or guar seeds	15							0
13023900	--Other (See Endnote 6)	8				PH			0
1401	Vegetable materials of a kind used primarily for plaiting (for example, bamboos, rattans, reeds, rushes, osier, raffia, cleaned, bleached or dyed cereal straw, and lime bark).								
14011000	-Bamboos	8				EC			0
14012000	-Rattans	15							0
140190	-Other								
14019010	---Osier	15							0
14019020	---Reeds	15							0
14019090	---Other plaiting materials	8				EC			0
14020000	Vegetable materials of a kind used primarily as stuffing or as padding (for example, kapok, vegetable hair and eel-grass), whether or not put up as a layer with or without supporting material.	15							0
14030000	Vegetable materials of a kind used primarily in brooms or in brushes (for example, broomcorn, piassava, couch-grass and istle), whether or not in hanks or bundles.	15							0

HS	Description	Bound rate at date of accession	Final Bound rate	Implementation	Present concession established	INR	Concession first incorporated in a GATT Schedule	Earlier INRs	ODCs
1404	Vegetable products not elsewhere specified or included.								
140410	-Raw vegetable materials of a kind used primarily in dyeing or tanning								
14041010	---Wood for dyeing or tanning	15				DO,HN			0
14041020	---Bark for dyeing or tanning	15				DO,HN			0
14041030	---Gall for dyeing or tanning	15							0
14041040	---Henna for dyeing or tanning	15							0
14041090	---Other materials for dyeing Or tanning	15				DO,HN			0
14042000	-Cotton linters	15							0
140490	-Other								
14049010	---Hard seeds, pips, hulls and nuts for craving	15							0
14049090	---Other vegetable products not elsewhere specified	10							0
1501	Pig fat (including lard) and poultry fat, other than that of heading 02.09 or 15.03.								
15010010	---Poultry fat	15							0
15010020	---Fat from poultry bones and fat from poultry waste	15							0
15010030	---Lard and other pig fats	P							0
1502	Fats of bovine animals, sheep or goats, other than those of heading 15.03.								
15020010	---Bovine animal fat	6				US			0
15020020	---Sheep and goat fat	6							0
1503	Lard stearin, lard oil, oleostearin, oleo-oil and tallow oil, not emulsified or mixed or otherwise prepared.								
1503001	---Oleostearin:								
15030011	----Styrene of Pig	P							0
15030019	----Other Styrene	10							0
1503002	---Oleo-margarine:								
15030021	----Margarine of Pig	P							0
15030029	----Other Margarine	10							0
1503009	---Other:								
15030091	----Fat of Pig	P							0
15030099	----Other fats	10							0
1504	Fats and oils and their fractions, of fish or marine mammals, whether or not refined, but not chemically modified.								
15043000	-Fats and oils and their fractions, of marine mammals	15							0

HS	Description	Bound rate at date of accession	Final Bound rate	Implementation	Present concession established	INR	Concession first incorporated in a GATT Schedule	Earlier INRs	ODCs
15050000	Wool grease and fatty substances derived therefrom (including lanolin).	15							0
15060000	Other animal fats and oils and their fractions, whether or not refined, but not chemically modified.	15							0
1507	Soya-bean oil and its fractions, whether or not refined, but not chemically modified.								
15071000	-Crude oil, whether or not degummed	15							0
15079000	-Other	12							0
1508	Ground-nut oil and its fractions, whether or not refined, but not chemically modified.								
15081000	-Crude oil	15							0
15089000	-Other	15							0
1509	Olive oil and its fractions, whether or not refined, but not chemically modified.								
15091000	-Virgin	12				CE25			0
15099000	-Other	12				CE25			0
15100000	Other oils and their fractions, obtained solely from olives, whether or not refined, but not chemically modified, including blends of these oils or fractions with oils or fractions of heading 15.09.	12				CE25			0
1511	Palm oil and its fractions, whether or not refined, but not chemically modified.								
15111000	-Crude oil	15				DO,HN			0
15119000	-Other	12				DO,HN			0
1512	Sunflower-seed, safflower or cotton-seed oil and fractions thereof, whether or not refined, but not chemically modified.								
15121	-Sunflower-seed or safflower oil and fractions thereof:								
15121100	--Crude oil	6				AU			0
15121900	--Other	8				AU,US			0
15122	-Cotton-seed oil and its fractions:								
15122100	--Crude oil, whether or not gossypol has been removed	10				AU,US			0
15122900	--Other	10				AU,US			0
1513	Coconut (copra), palm kernel or babassu oil and fractions thereof, whether or not refined, but not chemically modified.								
15131	-Coconut (copra) oil and its fractions:								
15131100	--Crude oil	6				PH			0
15131900	--Other	6				IN,PH			0

HS	Description	Bound rate at date of accession	Final Bound rate	Implementation	Present concession established	INR	Concession first incorporated in a GATT Schedule	Earlier INRs	ODCs
15132	-Palm kernel or babassu oil and fractions thereof:								
15132100	--Crude oil	15							0
15132900	--Other	15	12	2008					0
1514	Rape, colza or mustard oil and fractions thereof, whether or not refined, but not chemically modified.								
15141	-Low erucic acid rape or colza oil and its fractions:								
15141100	--Crude oil	15				AU			0
15141900	--Other	12				AU			0
15149	-Other:								
15149100	--Crude oil	15				AU			0
15149900	--Other	12				AU			0
1515	Other fixed vegetable fats and oils (including jojoba oil) and their fractions, whether or not refined, but not chemically modified.								
15151	-Linseed oil and its fractions:								
15151100	--Crude oil	15							0
15151900	--Other	15							0
15152	-Maize (corn) oil and its fractions:								
15152100	--Crude oil	6				US			0
15152900	--Other	8				US			0
15153000	-Castor oil and its fractions	10				IN			0
15154000	-Tung oil and its fractions	15							0
15155000	-Sesame oil and its fractions	15							0
15159000	-Other	15							0
1516	Animal or vegetable fats and oils and their fractions, partly or wholly hydrogenated, inter-esterified, re-esterified or elaidinised, whether or not refined, but not further prepared.								
15161000	-Animal fats and oils and their fractions	15							0
15162000	-Vegetable fats and oils and their fractions	10				DO,HN,US			0
1517	Margarine; edible mixtures or preparations of animal or vegetable fats or oils or of fractions of different fats or oils of this Chapter, other than edible fats or oils or their fractions of heading 15.16.								
151710	-Margarine, excluding liquid margarine								
15171010	---Margarine of animal origin	10				DO,HN			0
15171020	---Margarine of vegetable origin	10				DO,HN			0

HS	Description	Bound rate at date of accession	Final Bound rate	Implementation	Present concession established	INR	Concession first incorporated in a GATT Schedule	Earlier INRs	ODCs
15171090	---Other margarine	10				DO,HN			0
151790	-Other								
15179010	---Liquid margarine	6				US			0
15179090	---Other mixtures of animal or vegetable fats or oils	6				US			0
15180000	Animal or vegetable fats and oils and their fractions, boiled, oxidised, dehydrated, sulphurised, blown, polymerised by heat in vacuum or in inert gas or otherwise chemically modified, excluding those of heading 15.16; inedible mixtures or preparations of animal or vegetable fats or oils or of fractions of different fats or oils of this Chapter, not elsewhere specified or included.	10							0
1520	Glycerol, crude; glycerol waters and glycerol lyes.								
15200010	---Glycerol, crude	15	12	2008					0
15200020	---Glycerol waters and glycerol lyes	15	12	2008					0
1521	Vegetable waxes (other than triglycerides), beeswax, other insect waxes and spermaceti, whether or not refined or coloured.								
15211000	-Vegetable waxes	15							0
152190	-Other								
15219010	---Spermaceti, crude, pressed or refined	15							0
15219020	---Beeswax, whether or not colored	15							0
15219040	---Insect waxes, whether or not colored	15							0
1522	Degras; residues resulting from the treatment of fatty substances or animal or vegetable waxes.								
15220010	---Degras (fish oil treated with nitric acid)	15				DO,HN			0
15220020	---Residues from the treatment Of fatty substances	15				DO,HN			0
1601	Sausages and similar products, of meat, meat offal or blood; food preparations based on these products.								
16010011	----Sausage of Pig or animal blood	P				CE25			0
16010019	----Others of other animals	10				CE25,US			0
1601002	---Packed in tight containers (canned or the like):								
16010021	----Canned sausage of Pig or animal blood	P							0
16010029	----Others of other animals	6				US			0
1601003	---Frozen								

HS	Description	Bound rate at date of accession	Final Bound rate	Implementation	Present concession established	INR	Concession first incorporated in a GATT Schedule	Earlier INRs	ODCs
16010031	----Frozen sausage of Pig	P							0
16010039	----Others of other animals	10				US			0
1602	Other prepared or preserved meat, meat offal or blood.								
160210	-Homogenised preparations								
16021010	---Baby food from meat, homogenized	15							0
16021090	---Other homogenized meat preparations	15							0
16022000	-Of liver of any animal	10				US			0
16023	-Of poultry of heading 01.05:								
16023100	--Of turkeys	10				US			0
16023200	--Of fowls of the species Gallus domesticus	6				US			0
16023900	--Other	6				US			0
16024	-Of swine:								
16024100	--Hams and cuts thereof	P							0
16024200	--Shoulders and cuts thereof	P							0
16024900	--Other, including mixtures	P							0
160250	-Of bovine animals								
16025010	---Pastrami	8				US			0
16025090	---Other bovine canned meats (See Endnote 7)	8				AU,PH,US			0
160290	-Other, including preparations of blood of any animal								
16029010	---Foodstuff preparations more than 20% meat	15							0
1602902	---Offal of any animal:								
16029021	----Tongues	15							0
16029029	----Other offal (except liver)	15							0
16029030	---Preparations of animal blood	P							0
16029090	---Other prepared or preserved meat	15							0
1603	Extracts and juices of meat, fish or crustaceans, molluscs or other aquatic invertebrates.								
16030010	---Meat extracts and meat juices	15							0
1701	Cane or beet sugar and chemically pure sucrose, in solid form.								
17011	-Raw sugar not containing added flavouring or colouring matter:								
170111	--Cane sugar								
17011110	---Raw cane sugar for industrial use	11				AU,DO,HN,MX,SV			0
17011190	---Other cane sugar	11				DO,HN,MX,SV			0
170112	--Beet sugar								

HS	Description	Bound rate at date of accession	Final Bound rate	Implementation	Present concession established	INR	Concession first incorporated in a GATT Schedule	Earlier INRs	ODCs
17011210	---Beet sugar for industrial refining and filtering	15	12	2008		DO,HN			0
17011290	---Other beet sugar	15	12	2008		DO,HN			0
17019	-Other:								
17019100	--Containing added flavouring or colouring matter	10				DO,HN			0
170199	--Other								
1701991	---Refined:								
17019911	----Refined sugar crystals	15				CE25,DO,HN,KG			0
17019912	----Refined sugar moulds	15				CN,DO,HN,KG			0
17019913	----Castor sugar	20				CN,DO,HN,KG			0
17019920	---Sugar candy, neither flavored or colored	10				DO,HN,KG			0
17019930	---Chemically pure sucrose	10				DO,HN,KG			0
17019990	---Other sucrose	10				DO,HN,KG			0
1702	Other sugars, including chemically pure lactose, maltose, glucose and fructose, in solid form; sugar syrups not containing added flavouring or colouring matter; artificial honey, whether or not mixed with natural honey; caramel.								
17021	-Lactose and lactose syrup:								
17021100	--Containing by weight 99 % or more lactose, expressed as anhydrous lactose, calculated on the dry matter	15				DO,HN			0
17021900	--Other	15				DO,HN			0
17022000	-Maple sugar and maple syrup	15							0
17023000	-Glucose and glucose syrup, not containing fructose or containing in the dry state less than 20 % by weight of fructose	15							0
17024000	-Glucose and glucose syrup, containing in the dry state at least 20 % but less than 50 % by weight of fructose, excluding invert sugar	15							0
17025000	-Chemically pure fructose	15							0
17026000	-Other fructose and fructose syrup, containing in the dry state more than 50 % by weight of fructose, excluding invert sugar	6							0
170290	-Other, including invert sugar and other sugar and sugar syrup blends containing in the dry state 50 % by weight of fructose								
17029010	---Maltose, whether or nor chemically pure	15	12	2008					0
17029020	---Sucrose, chemically impure	15	12	2008					0

HS	Description	Bound rate at date of accession	Final Bound rate	Implementation	Present concession established	INR	Concession first incorporated in a GATT Schedule	Earlier INRs	ODCs
17029030	---Invert sugar, whether or not chemically pure	15	12	2008					0
17029040	---Fructose, chemically impure	15	12	2008					0
17029050	---Sugar liquids	15	12	2008					0
17029060	---Caramel	15	12	2008					0
17029070	---Artificial honey	15	12	2008					0
17029090	---Other sugar	15	12	2008					0
1703	Molasses resulting from the extraction or refining of sugar.								
17031000	-Cane molasses	10				DO,HN			0
17039000	-Other	15				DO,HN			0
1704	Sugar confectionery (including white chocolate), not containing cocoa.								
17041000	-Chewing gum, whether or not sugar-coated	10				DO,HN,US			0
170490	-Other								
17049010	---Sugar confectionary, candy drops, with wrapping	8				DO,EC,HN,US			0
17049020	---Toffee (caramels), Turkish delights, nougat	8				DO,EC,HN,US			0
17049030	---Almond candy, pistachio candy and similar	8				DO,EC,HN,US			0
17049040	---Fruit jellies, fruit pastes, licorice	8				DO,EC,HN,US			0
17049050	---Cough drops	6				DO,EC,HN,US			0
17049060	---Halawa tahiniah	15							0
17049070	---Sugar powder containing fruit flavor	8				CE25,DO,HN,US			0
17049080	---White Chocolate with Alcohol	P				US			0
17049090	---Other sugar confectionery	8				DO,EC,HN,SV			0
18010000	Cocoa beans, whole or broken, raw or roasted.	8				DO,EC,HN			0
18020000	Cocoa shells, husks, skins and other cocoa waste.	15	13	2008		DO,HN			0
1803	Cocoa paste, whether or not defatted.								
18031000	-Not defatted	8				DO,EC,HN			0
18032000	-Wholly or partly defatted	15	13	2008		DO,HN			0
18040000	Cocoa butter, fat and oil.	15	13	2008		DO,HN			0
18050000	Cocoa powder, not containing added sugar or other sweetening matter.	8				DO,HN			0
1806	Chocolate and other food preparations containing cocoa.								
180610	-Cocoa powder, containing added sugar or other sweetening matter								
18061010	---Cocoa powder with peptone or milk	10				DO,HN,US			0

HS	Description	Bound rate at date of accession	Final Bound rate	Implementation	Present concession established	INR	Concession first incorporated in a GATT Schedule	Earlier INRs	ODCs
18061090	---Other sweetened cocoa powder	10				DO,HN,US			0
180620	-Other preparations in blocks, slabs or bars weighing more than 2 kg or in liquid, paste, powder, granular or other bulk form in containers or immediate packings, of a content exceeding 2 kg								
18062010	---Powder for making ice-cream, containing cocoa, bulk	6				DO,HN			0
18062020	---Sugar confectionary, containing cocoa, bulk	15				DO,HN,US			0
18062030	---Confectionery products with cocoa, bulk	15				DO,HN,US			0
18062090	---Other bulk cocoa products	15				DO,HN,US			0
18063	-Other, in blocks, slabs or bars:								
180631	--Filled								
18063110	---Chocolate with Alcohol	P				AU,CE25,DO,EC,HN			0
18063190	---Other stuffed Chocolate	15				AU,CE25,DO,EC,HN,US			0
180632	--Not filled								
18063210	---Non - stuffed Chocolate with Alcohol	P				DO,HN			0
18063290	---Other non-stuffed Chocolate	15				DO,HN,US			0
180690	-Other								
18069010	---Powder for making ice-cream, with cocoa, non-bulk	8				AU,DO,EC,HN,US			0
18069020	---Other sugar confectionary, with cocoa, bulk	8				AU,DO,EC,HN,US			0
18069030	---Confectionery products with cocoa, non-bulk	8				AU,DO,EC,HN,US			0
18069090	---Other non-bulk cocoa products	8				AU,DO,EC,HN,US			0
1901	Malt extract; food preparations of flour, groats, meal, starch or malt extract, not containing cocoa or containing less than 40 % by weight of cocoa calculated on a totally defatted basis, not elsewhere specified or included; food preparations of goods of headings 04.01 to 04.04, not containing cocoa or containing less than 5 % by weight of cocoa calculated on a totally defatted basis, not elsewhere specified or included.								
190110	-Preparations for infant use, put up for retail sale								
19011010	---Baby food with milk base, no cocoa	5				CE25,US			0
19011020	---Baby food with milk base, under 5% cocoa	15				US			0
19011090	---Other baby food	5				US			0

HS	Description	Bound rate at date of accession	Final Bound rate	Implementation	Present concession established	INR	Concession first incorporated in a GATT Schedule	Earlier INRs	ODCs
190120	-Mixes and doughs for the preparation of bakers' wares of heading 19.05								
19012010	---Cereal and flour mixes with fruit flour, cocoa powder	10				AU,CE25,US			0
19012020	---Ready-mixed doughs of cereal flour	6				AU,DO,HN,US			0
19012090	---Other cereal and flour mixes	10				AU,DO,HN,US			0
190190	-Other								
19019010	---Ragi	6				US			0
19019020	---Malted milk	6				US			0
19019030	---Powder for making ice cream	6				US			0
19019090	---Other starch or malt extracts	6				CE25,US			0
1902	Pasta, whether or not cooked or stuffed (with meat or other substances) or otherwise prepared, such as spaghetti, macaroni, noodles, lasagne, gnocchi, ravioli, cannelloni; couscous, whether or not prepared.								
19021	-Uncooked pasta, not stuffed or otherwise prepared:								
190211	--Containing eggs								
19021110	---Macaroni, vermicelli and similar items with eggs	20							0
19021120	---Edible pastas, frozen with eggs	8							0
19021130	---Potato flour chips, macaroni-shaped with eggs	15							0
19021190	---Other uncooked pasta with eggs (See Endnote 8)	8							0
190219	--Other								
19021910	---Macaroni, vermicelli and similar items without eggs	12				CE25,US			0
19021920	---Edible pastas, frozen without eggs	10				US			0
19021930	---Potato flour chips, macaroni-shaped without eggs	10				US			0
19021990	---Other uncooked pasta Without eggs (See Endnote 9)	8				US			0
190220	-Stuffed pasta, whether or not cooked or otherwise prepared								
19022010	---Pasta stuffed with meat	15							0
19022020	---Pasta stuffed with fish, crustaceans and molluscs	15							0
19022090	---Other stuffed pasta	15							0
19023000	-Other pasta	10				PH			0
19024000	-Couscous	15							0

HS	Description	Bound rate at date of accession	Final Bound rate	Implementation	Present concession established	INR	Concession first incorporated in a GATT Schedule	Earlier INRs	ODCs
19030000	Tapioca and substitutes therefor prepared from starch, in the form of flakes, grains, pearls, siftings or in similar forms.	15							0
1904	Prepared foods obtained by the swelling or roasting of cereals or cereal products (for example, corn flakes); cereals (other than maize (corn)) in grain form or in the form of flakes or other worked grains (except flour, groats and meal), pre-cooked, or otherwise prepared, not elsewhere specified or included.								
190410	-Prepared foods obtained by the swelling or roasting of cereals or cereal products								
19041010	---Roasted or swelled cereals containing cocoa	15				CE25,US			0
1904109	---Other:								
19041091	----Corn flakes and similar, roasted	12				US			0
19041099	----Other roasted or swelled cereals	10				CE25,US			0
190420	-Prepared foods obtained from unroasted cereal flakes or from mixtures of unroasted cereal flakes and roasted cereal flakes or swelled cereals								
1904201	---Products obtained from unroasted cereal flakes or from mixtures of unroasted cereal flakes:								
19042011	----Prepared foods obtained from unroasted cereal flakes or from mixtures of unroasted cereal flakes and roasted cereal flakes or swelled cereals	15							0
19042019	----Other	15							0
1904202	---Roasted cereal flakes or swelled cereals:								
19042021	----Containing cocoa	20							0
19042029	----Other	15							0
190430	-Bulgur wheat								
19043010	---Containing cocoa	20							0
19043090	---Other	15							0
190490	-Other								
19049010	---Other cereals containing cocoa	20							0
19049090	---Other cereals	15							0

HS	Description	Bound rate at date of accession	Final Bound rate	Implementation	Present concession established	INR	Concession first incorporated in a GATT Schedule	Earlier INRs	ODCs
1905	Bread, pastry, cakes, biscuits and other bakers' wares, whether or not containing cocoa; communion wafers, empty cachets of a kind suitable for pharmaceutical use, sealing wafers, rice paper and similar products.								
19051000	-Crispbread	15							0
19052000	-Gingerbread and the like	15							0
19053	-Sweet biscuits; waffles and wafers:								
19053100	--Sweet biscuits	10				CE25,DO,HN,US			0
19053200	--Waffles and wafers	6				CE25,US			0
190540	-Rusks, toasted bread and similar toasted products								
19054010	---Rusks	12				US			0
19054090	---Other toasted products	6				US			0
190590	-Other								
19059010	---Ordinary bread	6				DO,HN,US			0
19059020	---Gluten bread prepared for diabetics	6				DO,HN,US			0
19059030	---Pastry (except waffles and wafers) including pizzas	10				DO,HN,US			0
19059040	---Eastern sweetmeats (kunafah, baklawah, etc)	6							0
19059050	---Cake, gateau and similar	10				DO,HN,US			0
19059060	---Empty cachets for pharmaceutical use	6				US			0
19059070	---Sealing wafers	6				US			0
19059080	---Crisps (such as pop corn, chips and the like)	10				DO,HN,US			0
1905909	---Other:								
19059091	----Unleavened bread	6				US			0
19059092	----Pretzels	6				US			0
19059093	----Ordinary biscuits, whether or not salted (See Endnote 10)	8				DO,HN,US			0
19059099	----Other bakers' wares	10				DO,HN,US			0
2001	Vegetables, fruit, nuts and other edible parts of plants, prepared or preserved by vinegar or acetic acid.								
20011000	-Cucumbers and gherkins	15				DO,HN			0
200190	-Other								
2001901	---Vegetables and edible plants:								
20019011	----Mushrooms and truffles preserved with vinegar	8				PY			0
20019012	----Olives and capers preserved with vinegar	10							0

HS	Description	Bound rate at date of accession	Final Bound rate	Implementation	Present concession established	INR	Concession first incorporated in a GATT Schedule	Earlier INRs	ODCs
20019013	----Green peppers preserved with vinegar	10							0
20019014	----Pickles (assorted) preserved With vinegar	10				DO,HN			0
20019015	----Tomatoes preserved with vinegar	10							0
20019019	----Other preserved vegetables	10				DO,HN			0
20019020	---Fruits preserved with vinegar	10				DO,HN			0
2002	Tomatoes prepared or preserved otherwise than by vinegar or acetic acid.								
20021000	-Tomatoes, whole or in pieces	10				CE25,US			0
200290	-Other								
20029010	---Tomato paste	10				DO,HN,US			0
20029090	---Other tomatoes, not vinegar-preserved	10				US			0
2003	Mushrooms and truffles, prepared or preserved otherwise than by vinegar or acetic acid.								
20031000	-Mushrooms of the genus Agaricus	15							0
20032000	-Truffles	15							0
20039000	-Other	15							0
2004	Other vegetables prepared or preserved otherwise than by vinegar or acetic acid, frozen, other than products of heading 20.06.								
20041000	-Potatoes	6				CA,CE25,US			0
200490	-Other vegetables and mixtures of vegetables								
20049010	---Carrots, frozen	6				US			0
20049020	---Peas, frozen	6				US			0
20049030	---Haricot beans, frozen	6				US			0
20049040	---Kidney beans, frozen	6				US			0
20049050	---Asparagus, frozen	6				US			0
20049060	---Spinach, frozen	6				US			0
20049070	---Okra, frozen	6				US			0
20049080	---Mixed vegetables, frozen	6				US			0
20049090	---Other frozen vegetables	6				US			0
2005	Other vegetables prepared or preserved otherwise than by vinegar or acetic acid, not frozen, other than products of heading 20.06.								
200510	-Homogenised vegetables								
20051010	---Baby food Vegetables, prepared	15							0
20051020	---Diet vegetables, prepared	15							0
20051090	---Other homogenized vegetables	15							0

HS	Description	Bound rate at date of accession	Final Bound rate	Implementation	Present concession established	INR	Concession first incorporated in a GATT Schedule	Earlier INRs	ODCs
20052000	-Potatoes	15				US			0
20054000	-Peas (Pisum sativum)	15							0
20055	-Beans (Vigna spp., Phaseolus spp.):								
20055100	--Beans, shelled	10							0
20055900	--Other	15							0
20056000	-Asparagus	10				US			0
20057000	-Olives	10				CE25			0
20058000	-Sweet corn (Zea mays var. saccharata)	6				US			0
200590	-Other vegetables and mixtures of vegetables								
2005901	---Prepared by other products and intended for direct consumption:								
20059011	----Cooked beans	12				US			0
20059012	----Cooked chick peas with sesame oil	10				US			0
20059013	----Vegetables and legumes with sauce	10				US			0
20059019	----Other cooked vegetables	6				US			0
2005909	---Other:								
20059091	----Okra, not frozen	6							0
20059092	----Horse beans, not frozen	6							0
20059093	----Spinach, not frozen	6							0
20059094	----Artichokes, not frozen	6				US			0
20059095	----Mixed vegetables, not frozen	6				US			0
20059096	----Sauekraut	6							0
20059097	----Grape leaves	6							0
20059099	----Other vegetables and plants, not frozen	6				US			0
20060000	Vegetables, fruit, nuts, fruit-peel and other parts of plants, preserved by sugar (drained, glacé or crystallised).	15				DO,HN			0
2007	Jams, fruit jellies, marmalades, fruit or nut purée and fruit or nut pastes, obtained by cooking, whether or not containing added sugar or other sweetening matter.								
200710	-Homogenised preparations								
20071010	---Baby food of fruit	15				DO,HN			0
20071020	---Diet fruit, prepared	15				DO,HN			0
20071090	---Other homogenized fruit preparations	15				DO,HN			0
20079	-Other:								
200791	--Citrus fruit								
20079110	---Marmalades	10				DO,HN			0
20079190	---Other citrus fruit preparations	10				DO,HN			0
200799	--Other								
2007991	---Jams and fruit jellies:								

HS	Description	Bound rate at date of accession	Final Bound rate	Implementation	Present concession established	INR	Concession first incorporated in a GATT Schedule	Earlier INRs	ODCs
20079911	----Peach jams and jellies	6				US			0
20079912	----Apricot jams and jellies	6				US			0
20079913	----Apple jams and jellies	6				US			0
20079914	----Water melon jams and jellies	6							0
20079915	----Cherry Jams and jellies	6				US			0
20079916	----Strawberry jams and jellies	6				US			0
20079917	----Raspberry jams and jellies	6				US			0
20079919	----Other jams and jellies	6							0
20079920	---Apricot sheets	6				US			0
20079930	---Turkish delights	6							0
20079990	---Other fruit and nut pastes	6				US			0
2008	Fruit, nuts and other edible parts of plants, otherwise prepared or preserved, whether or not containing added sugar or other sweetening matter or spirit, not elsewhere specified or included.								
20081	-Nuts, ground-nuts and other seeds, whether or not mixed together:								
200811	--Ground-nuts								
20081110	---Roasted ground nuts, whether or not salted	6				US			0
20081120	---Peanut butter	8				US			0
200819	--Other, including mixtures								
2008191	---Roasted nuts, whether or not salted:								
20081911	----Almonds	6				US			0
20081912	----Pistachios	10				US			0
20081913	----Hazel nuts	10				US			0
20081919	----Other roasted nuts	10				US			0
20081920	---Mixed nuts	10				US			0
20082000	-Pineapples	8				PH,TH			0
20083000	-Citrus fruit	15							0
20084000	-Pears	15							0
20085000	-Apricots	15							0
20086000	-Cherries	15							0
20087000	-Peaches, including nectarines	10				US			0
20088000	-Strawberries	15							0
20089	-Other, including mixtures other than those of subheading 2008.19:								
20089100	--Palm hearts	10				EC			0
20089200	--Mixtures	6				US			0
20089900	--Other	6				US			0

HS	Description	Bound rate at date of accession	Final Bound rate	Implementation	Present concession established	INR	Concession first incorporated in a GATT Schedule	Earlier INRs	ODCs
2009	Fruit juices (including grape must) and vegetable juices, unfermented and not containing added spirit, whether or not containing added sugar or other sweetening matter.								
20091	-Orange juice:								
20091100	--Frozen	6				DO,HN,MX,US			0
20091200	--Not frozen, of a Brix value not exceeding 20	10				DO,HN,US			0
20091900	--Other	10				DO,HN,US			0
20092	-Grapefruit juice:								
20092100	--Of a Brix value not exceeding 20	10				DO,HN,US			0
20092900	--Other	10				DO,HN,US			0
20093	-Juice of any other single citrus fruit:								
200931	--Of a Brix value not exceeding 20								
20093110	---Lemon juice	15				DO,HN			0
20093190	---Other	15				DO,HN			0
20093900	--Other	15				DO,HN			0
20094	-Pineapple juice:								
20094100	--Of a Brix value not exceeding 20	10				DO,HN			0
20094900	--Other	8				DO,HN			0
20095000	-Tomato juice	15				DO,HN			0
20096	-Grape juice (including grape must):								
20096100	--Of a Brix value not exceeding 30	15							0
20096900	--Other	15							0
20097	-Apple juice:								
20097100	--Of a Brix value not exceeding 20	10				DO,HN,US			0
20097900	--Other	10				DO,HN,US			0
200980	-Juice of any other single fruit or vegetable								
20098010	---Date molasses	12							0
2009802	---Mango juice:								
20098021	----Unconcentrated mango juice	10				DO,EC,HN			0
20098029	----Other mango juice	10				DO,HN			0
2009803	---Guava juice:								
20098031	----Concentrated guava juice	10				DO,EC,HN			0
20098039	----Other guava juice	10				DO,EC,HN			0
2009804	---Carrot juice:								
20098041	----Carrot juice, not concentrated	10							0
20098049	----Other carrot juice	10							0
20098090	---Other single fruit juice	10				DO,EC,HN			0
200990	-Mixtures of juices								

HS	Description	Bound rate at date of accession	Final Bound rate	Implementation	Present concession established	INR	Concession first incorporated in a GATT Schedule	Earlier INRs	ODCs
20099010	---Mixtures of juices, not concentrated	8				DO,HN,PY			0
20099090	---Other mixtures of juices	8				DO,HN,PY			0
2101	Extracts, essences and concentrates, of coffee, tea or maté and preparations with a basis of these products or with a basis of coffee, tea or maté; roasted chicory and other roasted coffee substitutes, and extracts, essences and concentrates thereof.								
21011	-Extracts, essences and concentrates, of coffee, and preparations with a basis of these extracts, essences or concentrates or with a basis of coffee:								
21011100	--Extracts, essences and concentrates	6				EC,US			0
210112	--Preparations with a basis of extracts, essences or concentrates or with a basis of coffee								
21011210	---Nescafe, yuban, maxwell, etc.	15							0
21011220	---Coffee paste	15							0
21011290	---Other of Coffee extraction	15							0
210120	-Extracts, essences and concentrates, of tea or maté, and preparations with a basis of these extracts, essences or concentrates or with a basis of tea or maté								
21012010	---Prepared tea preparations	7				LK			0
21012090	---Other prepared tea or mate	7				LK			0
210130	-Roasted chicory and other roasted coffee substitutes, and extracts, essences and concentrates thereof								
21013010	---Roasted chicory and other roasted coffee substitutes	15	12	2008					0
21013020	---Chicory extracts, concentrates and essences	15	12	2008					0
2102	Yeasts (active or inactive); other single-cell micro-organisms, dead (but not including vaccines of heading 30.02); prepared baking powders.								
21021000	-Active yeasts	10							0
210220	-Inactive yeasts; other single-cell micro-organisms, dead								
21022010	---Inactive yeasts for human consumption	15							0
21022020	---Inactive yeasts, etc., For animals	15							0
21022090	---Other micro-organisms	15							0
210230	-Prepared baking powders								

HS	Description	Bound rate at date of accession	Final Bound rate	Implementation	Present concession established	INR	Concession first incorporated in a GATT Schedule	Earlier INRs	ODCs
21023010	---Baking powder	12							0
21023020	---Anras yeast	15							0
21023090	---Other prepared baking powders	12							0
2103	Sauces and preparations therefor; mixed condiments and mixed seasonings; mustard flour and meal and prepared mustard.								
21031000	-Soya sauce	8				PH			0
21032000	-Tomato ketchup and other tomato sauces	15				DO,HN,US			0
210330	-Mustard flour and meal and prepared mustard								
21033010	---Mustard flour	6							0
21033020	---Prepared mustard	6				DO,HN			0
210390	-Other								
21039010	---Mayonnaise	15				DO,HN,US			0
21039020	---Chili sauce	6				DO,HN,US			0
21039030	---Celery salt	6				US			0
21039090	---Other sauces	6				DO,HN,US			0
2104	Soups and broths and preparations therefor; homogenised composite food preparations.								
21041000	-Soups and broths and preparations therefor	8				CH,US			0
21042000	-Homogenised composite food preparations	15							0
21050000	Ice cream and other edible ice, whether or not containing cocoa.	15				DO,HN,PH,US			0
2106	Food preparations not elsewhere specified or included.								
21061000	-Protein concentrates and textured protein substances	6				US			0
210690	-Other								
21069010	---Powders for making table cream	6				AU,CH,US			0
21069020	---Powders for making table jelly	6				AU,CH,US			0
21069030	---Powders for Making ice cream	6				AU,CH,US			0
21069050	---Preparations with a basis of milk for baking	6				AU,CH,US			0
21069060	---Doughs with a basis of sugar for fillings	6				AU,CH,US			0
21069070	---All types of sweetmeats and the like for diabetics	6				AU,CH,US			0
21069080	---Commercial saccharine	6				AU,CH,US			0
2106909	---Other:								
21069091	----Edible tablets such as vanillin	6				AU,CH,US			0

HS	Description	Bound rate at date of accession	Final Bound rate	Implementation	Present concession established	INR	Concession first incorporated in a GATT Schedule	Earlier INRs	ODCs
21069092	----Preparations for making lemonade or other soft drinks	6				AU,CE25,CH,US			0
21069093	----Preparations, often referred to as food additives	6				AU,CH,US			0
21069094	----Natural honey rich in Royal jelly	6				AU,CH,US			0
21069095	----Proteins dissolved in water, used in food preparations	6				AU,CH,US			0
21069096	----Muscle growing preparations	6				AU,CE25,CH,US			0
21069099	----Other food preparations	6				AU,CE25,CH,US			0
2201	Waters, including natural or artificial mineral waters and aerated waters, not containing added sugar or other sweetening matter nor flavoured; ice and snow.								
220110	-Mineral waters and aerated waters								
22011010	---Natural mineral water	15				DO,HN,KG,US			0
22011020	---Artificial mineral water	8				DO,HN,KG,US			0
22011030	---Aerated water	8				DO,HN,KG,US			0
220190	-Other								
22019010	---Ordinary natural water	15				KG			0
22019090	---Other unflavored natural water	8				KG			0
2202	Waters, including mineral waters and aerated waters, containing added sugar or other sweetening matter or flavoured, and other non-alcoholic beverages, not including fruit or vegetable juices of heading 20.09.								
220210	-Waters, including mineral waters and aerated waters, containing added sugar or other sweetening matter or flavoured								
22021010	---Flavored or sweetened mineral water	8				CH,DO,HN,KG			0
2202102	---Aerated water, flavoured or sweetened:								
22021021	----Lemonade	6				CH,DO,HN,KG			0
22021022	----Orange drink (e.g. Miranda)	6				CH,DO,HN,KG			0
22021023	----Cola	6				CH,DO,HN,KG			0
22021029	----Other carbonized drinks	6				CH,DO,HN,KG			0
22021090	---Other flavored water	8				CH,DO,HN,KG			0
220290	-Other								
22029010	---Non-alcoholic beverages, based on Milk	6				CE25,CH,DO,HN,US			0
22029020	---Beverages, based upon cocoa	6				CH,DO,HN,US			0
22029060	---Still beverages	6				CH,DO,HN,US			0
22029070	---Non-alcoholic beer	6				CH,DO,HN,US			0
22029090	---Other flavored non-alcoholic drinks	6				CH,DO,HN,US			0

HS	Description	Bound rate at date of accession	Final Bound rate	Implementation	Present concession established	INR	Concession first incorporated in a GATT Schedule	Earlier INRs	ODCs
22030000	Beer made from malt.	P							0
2204	Wine of fresh grapes, including fortified wines; grape must other than that of heading 20.09.								
22041000	-Sparkling wine	P							0
22042	-Other wine; grape must with fermentation prevented or arrested by the addition of alcohol:								
22042100	--In containers holding 2 litres or less	P							0
22042900	--Other	P							0
22043000	-Other grape must	P							0
2205	Vermouth and other wine of fresh grapes flavoured with plants or aromatic substances.								
22051000	-In containers holding 2 litres or less	P							0
22059000	-Other	P							0
22060000	Other fermented beverages (for example, cider, perry, mead); mixtures of fermented beverages and mixtures of fermented beverages and non-alcoholic beverages, not elsewhere specified or included.	P							0
2207	Undenatured ethyl alcohol of an alcoholic strength by volume of 80 % vol or higher; ethyl alcohol and other spirits, denatured, of any strength.								
220710	-Undenatured ethyl alcohol of an alcoholic strength by volume of 80 % vol or higher								
22071010	---Undenatured ethyl alcohol for medical use	7				DO,HN,SV			0
22071090	---Other undenatured ethyl alcohol	15				DO,HN,SV			0
220720	-Ethyl alcohol and other spirits, denatured, of any strength								
2207201	---Denatured ethyl alchohol:								
22072011	----Inactive ethyl alcohol for medical use	0							0
22072019	----Other inactive ethyl alcohol	15							0
22072090	---Other ethyl alcohol of any strength, denatured	P							0
2208	Undenatured ethyl alcohol of an alcoholic strength by volume of less than 80 % vol; spirits, liqueurs and other spirituous beverages.								
22082000	-Spirits obtained by distilling grape wine or grape marc	P							0
22083000	-Whiskies	P							0
22084000	-Rum and tafia	P							0

HS	Description	Bound rate at date of accession	Final Bound rate	Implementation	Present concession established	INR	Concession first incorporated in a GATT Schedule	Earlier INRs	ODCs
22085000	-Gin and Geneva	P							0
22086000	-Vodka	P							0
22087000	-Liqueurs and cordials	P							0
220890	-Other								
2208901	---Undenatured ethyl alchohol of an alchoholic strength by volume of less than 80% vol:								
22089011	----Active ethyl alcohol for medical uses	7				DO,HN			0
22089019	----Other active ethyl alcohol, non-medical	15				DO,HN			0
22089090	---Other denatured ethyl alcohol under 80%	P							0
2209	Vinegar and substitutes for vinegar obtained from acetic acid.								
22090010	---Vinegar (See Endnote 11)	6				DO,HN,PH,US			0
22090020	---Vinegar substitutes	6				DO,HN,US			0
2301	Flours, meals and pellets, of meat or meat offal, of fish or of crustaceans, molluscs or other aquatic invertebrates, unfit for human consumption; greaves.								
23011000	-Flours, meals and pellets, of meat or meat offal; greaves	15							0
2302	Bran, sharps and other residues, whether or not in the form of pellets, derived from the sifting, milling or other working of cereals or of leguminous plants.								
23021000	-Of maize (corn)	15							0
23022000	-Of rice	15							0
23023000	-Of wheat	12							0
23024000	-Of other cereals	15							0
23025000	-Of leguminous plants	15							0
2303	Residues of starch manufacture and similar residues, beet-pulp, bagasse and other waste of sugar manufacture, brewing or distilling dregs and waste, whether or not in the form of pellets.								
23031000	-Residues of starch manufacture and similar residues	15							0
23032000	-Beet-pulp, bagasse and other waste of sugar manufacture	15							0
23033000	-Brewing or distilling dregs and waste	15							0
23040000	Oil-cake and other solid residues, whether or not ground or in the form of pellets, resulting from the extraction of soyabean oil.	6				US			0

HS	Description	Bound rate at date of accession	Final Bound rate	Implementation	Present concession established	INR	Concession first incorporated in a GATT Schedule	Earlier INRs	ODCs
23050000	Oil-cake and other solid residues, whether or not ground or in the form of pellets, resulting from the extraction of ground-nut oil.	15							0
2306	Oil-cake and other solid residues, whether or not ground or in the form of pellets, resulting from the extraction of vegetable fats or oils, other than those of heading 23.04 or 23.05.								
23061000	-Of cotton seeds	15							0
23062000	-Of linseed	15							0
23063000	-Of sunflower seeds	15							0
23064	-Of rape or colza seeds:								
23064100	--Of low erucic acid rape or colza seeds	6				AU			0
23064900	--Other	6				AU			0
23065000	-Of coconut or copra	15							0
23066000	-Of palm nuts or kernels	15							0
23067000	-Of maize (corn) germ	15							0
23069000	-Other	6							0
2307	Wine lees; argol.								
23070010	---Wine lees	P							0
23070020	---Argol	15							0
23080000	Vegetable materials and vegetable waste, vegetable residues and by-products, whether or not in the form of pellets, of a kind used in animal feeding, not elsewhere specified or included.	15							0
2309	Preparations of a kind used in animal feeding.								
23091000	-Dog or cat food, put up for retail sale	6				US			0
230990	-Other								
23099010	---Fish and ornamental bird food	6				US			0
23099020	---Poultry food	6				US			0
2309903	---Animal feed:								
23099031	----Salt stones, containing animal feed	6				US			0
23099039	----Other salt stones for animal feed	6				US			0
23099040	---Milk substitutes for feeding small animals	6				US			0
23099050	---Concentrated preparations for the forage industry	6				US			0
23099090	---Other animal feeds	6				CE25,US,UY			0
2401	Unmanufactured tobacco; tobacco refuse.								

58

HS	Description	Bound rate at date of accession	Final Bound rate	Implementation	Present concession established	INR	Concession first incorporated in a GATT Schedule	Earlier INRs	ODCs
24011000	-Tobacco, not stemmed/stripped	200 or SR 36/gross kg				DO,HN,IN			SR 0.03/each packet
24012000	-Tobacco, partly or wholly stemmed/stripped	200 or SR 36/gross kg				DO,HN,IN			SR 0.03/each packet
240130	-Tobacco refuse								
24013010	---Tobacco waste suitable for use as tobacco	200 or SR 36/gross kg				DO,HN			SR 0.03/each packet
24013090	---Other tobacco waste	200 or SR 36/gross kg				DO,HN			SR 0.03/each packet
2402	Cigars, cheroots, cigarillos and cigarettes, of tobacco or of tobacco substitutes.								
24021000	-Cigars, cheroots and cigarillos, containing tobacco	200 or SR 300/kg				DO,HN,MX			SR 0.03/each packet
24022000	-Cigarettes containing tobacco	200 or SR 200/each 1000 cigarette				AU,CE25,CH,DO,HN,MX,PH			SR 0.03/each packet
240290	-Other								
24029010	---Cigars as tobacco substitutes	200 or SR 300/kg				DO,HN			SR 0.03/each packet
24029020	---Cigarettes as tobacco substitutes	200 or SR 200/each 1000 cigarette				DO,HN			SR 0.03/each packet
2403	Other manufactured tobacco and manufactured tobacco substitutes; "homogenised" or "reconstituted" tobacco; tobacco extracts and essences.								
240310	-Smoking tobacco, whether or not containing tobacco substitutes in any proportion								
24031010	---Chopped or pressed tobacco for smoking	200 or SR 80/net kg				DO,HN,MX			SR 0.03/each packet
24031020	---Chopped or pressed tobacco for pipes	200 or SR 80/net kg				DO,HN,MX			SR 0.03/each packet
24031030	---Chopped or Pressed tunbak for retail sale	200 or SR 80/net kg				DO,HN,IN			SR 0.03/each packet

HS	Description	Bound rate at date of accession	Final Bound rate	Implementation	Present concession established	INR	Concession first incorporated in a GATT Schedule	Earlier INRs	ODCs
24031090	---Other smoking tobacco	200 or SR 80/net kg				DO,HN,IN,PH			SR 0.03/each packet
24039	-Other:								
24039100	--"Homogenised" or "reconstituted" tobacco	200 or SR 80/net kg				DO,HN			SR 0.03/each packet
240399	--Other								
24039910	---Pressed or liquored tobacco for making snuff	200 or SR 80/net kg				DO,HN			SR 0.03/each packet
24039920	---Chopped or pressed tobacco for chewing	200 or SR 80/net kg				DO,HN			SR 0.03/each packet
24039930	---Snuff	200 or SR 80/net kg				DO,HN			SR 0.03/each packet
24039940	---Jirak	200 or SR 12/gross kg				IN			SR 0.03/each packet
24039950	---Tobacco extracts and essences	200				DO,HN			SR 0.03/each packet
24039960	---Meassil (tobacco mixed with glycerin and flavoring substances	200 or SR 12/gross kg							SR 0.03/each packet
24039990	---Other tobacco substitutes	200 or SR 80/net kg							SR 0.03/each packet
29054300	--Mannitol	15							0
29054400	--D-glucitol (sorbitol)	15							0
29054500	--Glycerol	5.5							0
3301	Essential oils (terpeneless or not), including concretes and absolutes; resinoids; extracted oleoresins; concentrates of essential oils in fats, in fixed oils, in waxes or the like, obtained by enfleurage or maceration; terpenic by-products of the deterpenation of essential oils; aqueous distillates and aqueous solutions of essential oils.								
33011	-Essential oils of citrus fruit:								
33011100	--Of bergamot	10							0
33011200	--Of orange	8				PY			0
33011300	--Of lemon	15							0

HS	Description	Bound rate at date of accession	Final Bound rate	Implementation	Present concession established	INR	Concession first incorporated in a GATT Schedule	Earlier INRs	ODCs
33011400	--Of lime	15							0
33011900	--Other	10				CE25			0
33012	-Essential oils other than those of citrus fruit:								
33012100	--Of geranium	15							0
33012200	--Of jasmin	15							0
33012300	--Of lavender or of lavandin	15							0
33012400	--Of peppermint (Mentha piperita)	15							0
33012500	--Of other mints	15							0
33012600	--Of vetiver	15							0
33012900	--Other	8				PY			0
330130	-Resinoids								
33013010	---Aloes essence	6				US			0
33013090	---Other Perfuming resins	6				US			0
330190	-Other								
3301901	---Aqueous distillates and aqueous solutions of essential oils:								
33019011	----Solutions of essential Oils	10							0
33019012	----Cade water (kady)	10							0
33019013	----Rosewater	10							0
33019014	----Orange flower water	10							0
33019015	----Aqueous solutions of	10							0
33019019	----Other aqueous distilallates of	10							0
33019090	---Other essential oils	10							0
3501	Casein, caseinates and other casein derivatives; casein glues.								
35011000	-Casein	12				NZ			0
350190	-Other								
35019010	---Casein glues	12				NZ			0
35019090	---Other casein derivatives	12				NZ			0
3502	Albumins (including concentrates of two or more whey proteins, containing by weight more than 80 % whey proteins, calculated on the dry matter), albuminates and other albumin derivatives.								
35021	-Egg albumin:								
35021100	--Dried	15							0
35021900	--Other	15							0
35022000	-Milk albumin, including concentrates of two or more whey proteins	15							0
35029000	-Other	15							0

HS	Description	Bound rate at date of accession	Final Bound rate	Implementation	Present concession established	INR	Concession first incorporated in a GATT Schedule	Earlier INRs	ODCs
3503	Gelatin (including gelatin in rectangular (including square) sheets, whether or not surface-worked or coloured) and gelatin derivatives; isinglass; other glues of animal origin, excluding casein glues of heading 35.01.								
35030010	---Gelatin and gelatin derivatives	6				US			0
35030090	---Other	6				US			0
3504	Peptones and their derivatives; other protein substances and their derivatives, not elsewhere specified or included; hide powder, whether or not chromed.								
35040010	---Peptones and their derivatives	6							0
35040090	---Other	15							0
3505	Dextrins and other modified starches (for example, pregelatinised or esterified starches); glues based on starches, or on dextrins or other modified starches.								
350510	-Dextrins and other modified starches								
35051010	---Dextrins	10							0
35051020	---Pregerlatinized starches or	15							0
35051030	---Esterified starches	15							0
35051040	---Soluble starches	15							0
35051090	---Other modified starches	15							0
350520	-Glues								
35052010	---Dextrin glue	15							0
35052020	---Starch glue	15							0
35052030	---Glue composed of untreated	15							0
35052090	---Others	15							0
380910	-With a basis of amylaceous substances								
38091010	---Cloth iron fixers	15							0
38091090	---Other finishing agents of	15							0
3823	Industrial monocarboxylic fatty acids; acid oils from refining; industrial fatty alcohols.								
38231	-Industrial monocarboxylic fatty acids; acid oils from refining:								
38231100	--Stearic acid	6.5							0
38231200	--Oleic acid	6.5							0
38231300	--Tall oil fatty acids	6.5							0
38231900	--Other	6.5							0
38237000	-Industrial fatty alcohols	6.5							0
38246000	-Sorbitol other than that of subheading 2905.44	15							0

HS	Description	Bound rate at date of accession	Final Bound rate	Implementation	Present concession established	INR	Concession first incorporated in a GATT Schedule	Earlier INRs	ODCs
4101	Raw hides and skins of bovine (including buffalo) or equine animals (fresh, or salted, dried, limed, pickled or otherwise preserved, but not tanned, parchment-dressed or further prepared), whether or not dehaired or split.								
41012000	-Whole hides and skins, of a weight per skin not exceeding 8 kg when simply dried, 10 kg when dry-salted, or 16 kg when fresh, wet-salted or otherwise preserved	10				DO,HN,IN,KG,PY,US			0
41015000	-Whole hides and skins, of a weight exceeding 16 kg	10				DO,HN,IN,KG			0
41019000	-Other, including butts, bends and bellies	10				DO,HN,IN,KG			0
4102	Raw skins of sheep or lambs (fresh, or salted, dried, limed, pickled or otherwise preserved, but not tanned, parchment-dressed or further prepared), whether or not with wool on or split, other than those excluded by Note 1 (c) to this Chapter.								
41021000	-With wool on	15				KG			0
41022	-Without wool on:								
41022100	--Pickled	15							0
41022900	--Other	15				KG			0
4103	Other raw hides and skins (fresh, or salted, dried, limed, pickled or otherwise preserved, but not tanned, parchment-dressed or further prepared), whether or not dehaired or split, other than those excluded by Note 1 (b) or 1 (c) to this Chapter.								
41031000	-Of goats or kids	15							0
41032000	-Of reptiles	15				DO,HN			0
41033000	-Of swine	P							0
41039000	-Other	15							0
4301	Raw furskins (including heads, tails, paws and other pieces or cuttings, suitable for furriers' use), other than raw hides and skins of heading 41.01, 41.02 or 41.03.								
43011000	-Of mink, whole, with or without head, tail or paws	15							0
43013000	-Of lamb, the following: Astrakhan, Broadtail, Caracul, Persian and similar lamb, Indian, Chinese, Mongolian or Tibetan lamb, whole, with or without head, tail or paws	15							0

HS	Description	Bound rate at date of accession	Final Bound rate	Implementation	Present concession established	INR	Concession first incorporated in a GATT Schedule	Earlier INRs	ODCs
43016000	-Of fox, whole, with or without head, tail or paws	15							0
43017000	-Of seal, whole, with or without head, tail or paws	15							0
43018000	-Other furskins, whole, with or without head, tail or paws	15							0
43019000	-Heads, tails, paws and other pieces or cuttings, suitable for furriers' use	15							0
50010000	Silk-worm cocoons suitable for reeling.	15							0
50020000	Raw silk (not thrown).	15							0
5003	Silk waste (including cocoons unsuitable for reeling, yarn waste and garnetted stock).								
50031000	-Not carded or combed	15							0
50039000	-Other	15							0
5101	Wool, not carded or combed.								
51011	-Greasy, including fleece-washed wool:								
51011100	--Shorn wool	15				KG			0
51011900	--Other	15				KG			0
51012	-Degreased, not carbonised:								
51012100	--Shorn wool	15							0
51012900	--Other	15							0
51013000	-Carbonised	15				KG			0
5102	Fine or coarse animal hair, not carded or combed.								
51021	-Fine animal hair:								
51021100	--Of Kashmir (cashmere) goats	15				KG			0
51021900	--Other	15				KG			0
51022000	-Coarse animal hair	15							0
5103	Waste of wool or of fine or coarse animal hair, including yarn waste but excluding garnetted stock.								
51031000	-Noils of wool or of fine animal hair	15				KG			0
51032000	-Other waste of wool or of fine animal hair	15							0
51033000	-Waste of coarse animal hair	15							0
52010000	Cotton, not carded or combed.	6				AU,KG,US			0
5202	Cotton waste (including yarn waste and garnetted stock).								
52021000	-Yarn waste (including thread waste)	15							0
52029	-Other:								
52029100	--Garnetted stock	15				KG			0
52029900	--Other	15				KG			0
52030000	Cotton, carded or combed.	15				KG			0

HS	Description	Bound rate at date of accession	Final Bound rate	Implementation	Present concession established	INR	Concession first incorporated in a GATT Schedule	Earlier INRs	ODCs
5301	Flax, raw or processed but not spun; flax tow and waste (including yarn waste and garnetted stock).								
53011000	-Flax, raw or retted	15							0
53012	-Flax, broken, scutched, hackled or otherwise processed, but not spun:								
53012100	--Broken or scutched	15							0
53012900	--Other	15							0
53013000	-Flax tow and waste	15							0
5302	True hemp (Cannabis sativa L.), raw or processed but not spun; tow and waste of true hemp (including yarn waste and garnetted stock).								
53021000	-True hemp, raw or retted	15							0
53029000	-Other	15							0
	Endnote 1--Mango pulp is included in HS 08045020.								
	Endnote 2--Green tea in packs with weight not exceeding 3 kgs and tea in bags of filter paper weight not exceeding 4 gms are included in HS 09021000.								
	Endnote 3--Black tea in bags of filter paper or filter cloth not exceeding 4 gms is included in HS 09023010.								
	Endnote 4--Black tea in packs with weight not exceeding 3 kgs and flavoured tea in packs weight not exceeding 3 kgs are included in HS 09023090.								
	Endnote 5--Black tea in bulk is included in HS 09024000.								
	Endnote 6--Carrageenan is included in HS 13023900.								
	Endnote 7--Corned beef is included in HS 16025090.								
	Endnote 8--"Canton" is included in HS 19021190.								
	Endnote 9--"Bihon" is included in HS 19021990.								
	Endnote 10--Plain biscuits are included in HS 19059093.								
	Endnote 11--Palm vinegar is included in HS 22090010.								

Schedule CLVIII - Kingdom of Saudi Arabia

PART I - MOST-FAVOURED-NATION TARIFF

SECTION I - B Tariff Quotas

Description of products	Tariff item number	Initial quota quantity and in-quota tariff rate	Final quota quantity and inquota tariff rate	Implementation period	Initial negotiating right	Other terms and conditions

Schedule CLVIII - Kingdom of Saudi Arabia

This Schedule is authentic only in the English language

PART I - MOST-FAVOURED-NATION TARIFF
SECTION II - Other Products

Notes:
1. The "final bound rate" of duty, if differing from the "bound rate at date of accession", will be implemented in the year specified in the "implementation" column and on the day/month the Kingdom of Saudi Arabia accedes to the WTO. The "interim" column indicates the bound rate and the year in parentheses, when the rate will be implemented (also on the day/month of accession). Tariff reductions will be implemented according to the dates specified in the "interim" or "implementation" columns (no other staged reductions are implied) unless there is an asterisk (*) in the "implementation" column. In these cases, rates will be reduced in equal annual increments from the rate indicated in the "bound rate at date of accession" column to the rate indicated in the "final bound rate" column, and adjusted for certain years, if necessary, by the rate(s) indicated in the "interim" column. The designation "P" indicates that the products are prohibited for importation.
2. Access conditions (i.e., applied and bound rates of duty) on 870324 (Motor vehicles; engine over 3 litres) shall be no less favourable than those applied on comparable Motor vehicle products as classified under sub-headings 870321, 870322, and 870323.

HS	Description	Bound rate at date of accession	Interim	Final Bound	Implementation	Present concession established	INR	Concession first incorporated in a GATT Schedule	Earlier INRs	ODCs
0301	Live fish.									
03011000	-Ornamental fish	12								0
03019	-Other live fish:									
030191	--Trout (Salmo trutta, Oncorhynchus mykiss, Oncorhynchus clarki, Oncorhynchus aguabonita, Oncorhynchus gilae, Oncorhynchus apache and Oncorhynchus chrysogaster)									
03019110	---For breeding	12								0
03019190	---Other	12								0
030192	--Eels (Anguilla spp.)									
03019210	---Eel for breeding	12								0
03019290	---Other live eel	12								0
030193	--Carp									
03019310	---Carp for breeding	12								0
03019390	---Other live carp	12								0
030199	--Other									
03019910	---Other live fish for breeding	12								0

HS	Description	Bound rate at date of accession	Interim	Final Bound	Implementation	Present concession established	INR	Concession first incorporated in a GATT Schedule	Earlier INRs	ODCs
03019920	---Tilapia (Tilapia Nilotica), (Sarotherodon spp.)	12								0
03019990	---Other live fish	12								0
0302	Fish, fresh or chilled, excluding fish fillets and other fish meat of heading 03.04.									
03021	-Salmonidae, excluding livers and roes:									
03021100	--Trout (Salmo trutta, Oncorhynchus mykiss, Oncorhynchus clarki, Oncorhynchus aguabonita, Oncorhynchus gilae, Oncorhynchus apache and Oncorhynchus chrysogaster)	12								0
03021200	--Pacific salmon (Oncorhynchus nerka, Oncorhynchus gorbuscha, Oncorhynchus keta, Oncorhynchus tschawytscha, Oncorhynchus kisutch, Oncorhynchus masou and Oncorhynchus rhodurus), Atlantic salmon (Salmo salar) and Danube salmon (Hucho hucho)	8					NO			0
03021900	--Other	12								0
03022	-Flat fish (Pleuronectidae, Bothidae, Cynoglossidae, Soleidae, Scophthalmidae and Citharidae), excluding livers and roes:									
03022100	--Halibut (Reinhardtius hippoglossoides, Hippoglossus hippoglossus, Hippoglossus stenolepis)	12								0
03022200	--Plaice (Pleuronectes platessa)	12								0
03022300	--Sole (Solea spp.)	12								0
03022900	--Other	12								0
03023	-Tunas (of the genus Thunnus), skipjack or stripe-bellied bonito (Euthynnus (Katsuwonus) pelamis), excluding livers and roes:									
03023100	--Albacore or longfinned tunas (Thunnus alalunga)	8					EC			0
03023200	--Yellowfin tunas (Thunnus albacares)	12								0
03023300	--Skipjack or stripe-bellied bonito	12								0
03023400	--Bigeye tunas (Thunnus obesus)	12								0
03023500	--Bluefin tunas (Thunnus thynnus)	12								0
03023600	--Southern bluefin tunas (Thunnus maccoyii)	12								0

HS	Description	Bound rate at date of accession	Interim	Final Bound	Implementation	Present concession established	INR	Concession first incorporated in a GATT Schedule	Earlier INRs	ODCs
03023900	--Other	12								0
03024000	-Herrings (Clupea harengus, Clupea pallasii), excluding livers and roes	12								0
03025000	-Cod (Gadus morhua, Gadus ogac, Gadus macrocephalus), excluding livers and roes	12								0
03026	-Other fish, excluding livers and roes:									
03026100	--Sardines (Sardina pilchardus, Sardinops spp.), sardinella (Sardinella spp.), brisling or sprats (Sprattus sprattus)	12								0
03026200	--Haddock (Melanogrammus aeglefinus)	12								0
03026300	--Coalfish (Pollachius virens)	12								0
030264	--Mackerel (Scomber scombrus, Scomber australasicus, Scomber japonicus)									
03026410	---Kingfish (Scomberomorus commerson)	12								0
03026420	---Indian mackerel (Rastrelliger Kanagurta)	12								0
03026490	---Other	12								0
03026500	--Dogfish and other sharks	12								0
03026600	--Eels (Anguilla spp.)	12								0
030269	--Other									
03026910	---Groupers (All genus following the family: serranidae)	8					DO,EC,HN			0
03026920	---Emperors (Lethrinus spp.), (Monotaxis spp.)	8					DO,EC,HN			0
03026930	---Snappers / Jobfishes (All genus following the family: Lutjanidae)	8					DO,EC,HN			0
03026940	---Jacks, Trevallies and Scads (All genus following the family: Carangidae)	8					DO,EC,HN			0
03026950	---pomferts (Pampus argenteus, parastromateus niger)	8					DO,EC,HN			0
03026960	---Sibaiti, Shamm, Nahhash, fresh	8					DO,EC,HN			0
03026970	---Nigroor fish	8					DO,EC,HN			0
03026980	---Striped mullet (Mugil cephalus)	8					DO,EC,HN			0
03026991	----Safi fish	8					DO,EC,HN			0
03026999	----Other fish, fresh	8					DO,EC,HN			0
03027000	-Livers and roes	12								0
0303	Fish, frozen, excluding fish fillets and other fish meat of heading 03.04.									

HS	Description	Bound rate at date of accession	Interim	Final Bound	Implementation	Present concession established	INR	Concession first incorporated in a GATT Schedule	Earlier INRs	ODCs
03031	-Pacific salmon (Oncorhynchus nerka, Oncorhynchus gorbuscha, Oncorhynchus keta, Oncorhynchus tschawytscha, Oncorhynchus kisutch, Oncorhynchus masou and Oncorhynchus rhodurus), Atlantic salmon excluding livers and roes:									
03031100	--Sockeye salmon (red salmon) (Oncorhynchus nerka)	12								0
03031900	--Other	12								0
03032	-Other salmonidae, excluding livers and roes:									
03032100	--Trout (Salmo trutta, Oncorhynchus mykiss, Oncorhynchus clarki, Oncorhynchus aguabonita, Oncorhynchus gilae, Oncorhynchus apache and Oncorhynchus chrysogaster)	8					NO			0
03032200	--Atlantic salmon (Salmo salar) and Danube salmon (Hucho hucho)	5					NO			0
03032900	--Other	12					PK			0
03033	-Flat fish (Pleuronectidae, Bothidae, Cynoglossidae, Soleidae, Scophthalmidae and Citharidae), excluding livers and roes:									
03033100	--Halibut (Reinhardtius hippoglossoides, Hippoglossus hippoglossus, Hippoglossus stenolepis)	12								0
03033200	--Plaice (Pleuronectes platessa)	12								0
03033300	--Sole (Solea spp.)	12								0
03033900	--Other	12								0
03034	-Tunas (of the genus Thunnus), skipjack or stripe-bellied bonito (Euthynnus (Katsuwonus) pelamis), excluding livers and roes:									
03034100	--Albacore or longfinned tunas (Thunnus alalunga)	12								0
03034200	--Yellowfin tunas (Thunnus albacares)	12								0
03034300	--Skipjack or stripe-bellied bonito	12								0
03034400	--Bigeye tunas (Thunnus obesus)	12								0
03034500	--Bluefin tunas (Thunnus thynnus)	12								0
03034600	--Southern bluefin tunas (Thunnus maccoyii)	12								0
03034900	--Other	12								0

HS	Description	Bound rate at date of accession	Interim	Final Bound	Implementation	Present concession established	INR	Concession first incorporated in a GATT Schedule	Earlier INRs	ODCs
03035000	-Herrings (Clupea harengus, Clupea pallasii), excluding livers and roes	12								0
03036000	-Cod (Gadus morhua, Gadus ogac, Gadus macrocephalus), excluding livers and roes	12								0
03037	-Other fish, excluding livers and roes:									
03037100	--Sardines (Sardina pilchardus, Sardinops spp.), sardinella (Sardinella spp.), brisling or sprats (Sprattus sprattus)	12								0
03037200	--Haddock (Melanogrammus aeglefinus)	12								0
03037300	--Coalfish (Pollachius virens)	12								0
030374	--Mackerel (Scomber scombrus, Scomber australasicus, Scomber japonicus)									
03037410	---Kingfish (Scomberomorus commerson)	12								0
03037420	---Indian mackerel (Rastrelliger Kanagurta)	12								0
03037500	--Dogfish and other sharks	12								0
03037600	--Eels (Anguilla spp.)	12								0
03037700	--Sea bass (Dicentrarchus labrax, Dicentrarchus punctatus)	12								0
03037800	--Hake (Merluccius spp., Urophycis spp.)	12					UY			0
030379	--Other (See Endnote 1)									
03037910	---Groupers (All genus following the family: serranidae)	6					DO,EC,HN,UY			0
03037920	---Tilapia (Tilapia Nilotica), (Sarotherodon spp.)	6					DO,EC,HN,UY			0
03037930	---Snappers / Jobfishes (All genus following the family: Lutjanidae)	6					DO,EC,HN,UY			0
03037940	---Jacks, Trevallies and Scads (All genus following the family: Carangidae)	6					DO,EC,HN,UY			0
03037950	---Emperors (Lethrinus spp.), (Monotaxis spp.)	6					DO,EC,HN,UY			0
03037960	---Milkfish (Chanus chanus)	6					DO,EC,HN,UY			0
0303799	---Other									
03037991	----Zabidi fish	6					DO,EC,HN,UY			0
03037992	----Sibaiti, Shamm, Nahhash, frozen	6					DO,EC,HN,UY			0
03037993	----Nigroor fish	6					DO,EC,HN,UY			0
03037994	----Striped mullet (Mugil cephalus)	6					DO,EC,HN,UY			0
03037995	----Safi fish	6					DO,EC,HN,UY			0

HS	Description	Bound rate at date of accession	Interim	Final Bound	Implementation	Present concession established	INR	Concession first incorporated in a GATT Schedule	Earlier INRs	ODCs
03037999	----Other fish, fresh	6					DO,EC,HN,UY			0
03038000	-Livers and roes	12								0
0304	Fish fillets and other fish meat (whether or not minced), fresh, chilled or frozen.									
030410	-Fresh or chilled									
03041010	---Groupers (All genus following the family: serranidae)	8					DO,EC,HN,NO			0
03041020	---Of Emperors (Lethrinus spp.), (Monotaxis spp.)	8					DO,EC,HN,NO			0
03041090	---Other	8					DO,EC,HN,NO			0
030420	-Frozen fillets									
03042010	---Of Groupers (All genus following the family: serranidae)	5					DO,EC,HN,NO,UY			0
03042020	---Of Emperors (Lethrinus spp.), (Monoatxis spp.)	5					DO,EC,HN,NO,UY			0
03042090	---Other	5					DO,EC,HN,NO,UY			0
03049000	-Other	12								0
0305	Fish, dried, salted or in brine; smoked fish, whether or not cooked before or during the smoking process; flours, meals and pellets of fish, fit for human consumption.									
03051000	-Flours, meals and pellets of fish, fit for human consumption	8					EC			0
03052000	-Livers and roes of fish, dried, smoked, salted or in brine	12								0
03053000	-Fish fillets, dried, salted or in brine, but not smoked	8					NO			0
03054	-Smoked fish, including fillets:									
03054100	--Pacific salmon (Oncorhynchus nerka, Oncorhynchus gorbuscha, Oncorhynchus keta, Oncorhynchus tschawytscha, Oncorhynchus kisutch, Oncorhynchus masou and Oncorhynchus rhodurus), Atlantic salmon (Salmo salar) and Danube salmon (Hucho hucho)	5					NO			0
03054200	--Herrings (Clupea harengus, Clupea pallasii)	8					NO			0
03054900	--Other	8					NO			0
03055	-Dried fish, whether or not salted but not smoked:									
03055100	--Cod (Gadus morhua, Gadus ogac, Gadus macrocephalus)	12								0

HS	Description	Bound rate at date of accession	Interim	Final Bound	Implementation	Present concession established	INR	Concession first incorporated in a GATT Schedule	Earlier INRs	ODCs
030559	--Other									
03055910	---Kingfish (Scomberomorus commerson)	8					NO			0
03055920	---Striped mullet (mugil cephalus)	8					NO			0
03056	-Fish, salted but not dried or smoked and fish in brine:									
03056100	--Herrings (Clupea harengus, Clupea pallasii)	12								0
03056200	--Cod (Gadus morhua, Gadus ogac, Gadus macrocephalus)	12								0
03056300	--Anchovies (Engraulis spp.)	12								0
03056900	--Other	12								0
0306	Crustaceans, whether in shell or not, live, fresh, chilled, frozen, dried, salted or in brine; crustaceans, in shell, cooked by steaming or by boiling in water, whether or not chilled, frozen, dried, salted or in brine; flours, meals and pellets of crustaceans, fit for human consumption.									
03061	-Frozen:									
03061100	--Rock lobster and other sea crawfish (Palinurus spp., Panulirus spp., Jasus spp.)	12					DO,HN			0
03061200	--Lobsters (Homarus spp.)	12								0
03061300	--Shrimps and prawns	6					DO,EC,HN,NO			0
03061400	--Crabs	12								0
03061900	--Other, including flours, meals and pellets of crustaceans, fit for human consumption	12								0
03062	-Not frozen:									
03062100	--Rock lobster and other sea crawfish (Palinurus spp., Panulirus spp., Jasus spp.)	12					DO,HN,MX			0
03062200	--Lobsters (Homarus spp.)	12					MX			0
03062300	--Shrimps and prawns	12					DO,HN,MX			0
03062400	--Crabs	12								0
03062900	--Other, including flours, meals and pellets of crustaceans, fit for human consumption	12								0

HS	Description	Bound rate at date of accession	Interim	Final Bound	Implementation	Present concession established	INR	Concession first incorporated in a GATT Schedule	Earlier INRs	ODCs
0307	Molluscs, whether in shell or not, live, fresh, chilled, frozen, dried, salted or in brine; aquatic invertebrates other than crustaceans and molluscs, live, fresh, chilled, frozen, dried, salted or in brine; flours, meals and pellets of aquatic invertebrates other than crustaceans, fit for human consumption.									
03071000	-Oysters	12								0
03072	-Scallops, including queen scallops, of the genera Pecten, Chlamys or Placopecten:									
03072100	--Live, fresh or chilled	12								0
03072900	--Other	12								0
03073	-Mussels (Mytilus spp., Perna spp.):									
03073100	--Live, fresh or chilled	12								0
03073900	--Other	12								0
03074	-Cuttle fish (Sepia officinalis, Rossia macrosoma, Sepiola spp.) and squid (Ommastrephes spp., Loligo spp., Nototodarus spp., Sepioteuthis spp.):									
03074100	--Live, fresh or chilled	6								0
03074900	--Other	6					DO,HN,UY			0
03075	-Octopus (Octopus spp.):									
03075100	--Live, fresh or chilled	6					DO,HN,MX			0
03075900	--Other	6					DO,HN			0
03076000	-Snails, other than sea snails	12								0
03079	-Other, including flours, meals and pellets of aquatic invertebrates other than crustaceans, fit for human consumption:									
03079100	--Live, fresh or chilled	12								0
03079900	--Other	12								0
15041000	-Fish-liver oils and their fractions	15								0
15042000	-Fats and oils and their fractions, of fish, other than liver oils	15								0
16030020	---Extract and juices of fish, crustaceans	15								0
1604	Prepared or preserved fish; caviar and caviar substitutes prepared from fish eggs.									
16041	-Fish, whole or in pieces, but not minced:									
16041100	--Salmon	5								0

HS	Description	Bound rate at date of accession	Interim	Final Bound	Implementation	Present concession established	INR	Concession first incorporated in a GATT Schedule	Earlier INRs	ODCs
16041200	--Herrings	8								0
16041300	--Sardines, sardinella and brisling or sprats	5					EC			0
16041400	--Tunas, skipjack and bonito (Sarda spp.)	5					EC,MX			0
16041500	--Mackerel	8								0
16041600	--Anchovies	8								0
16041900	--Other	12								0
16042000	-Other prepared or preserved fish	8								0
16043000	-Caviar and caviar substitutes	8								0
1605	Crustaceans, molluscs and other aquatic invertebrates, prepared or preserved.									
16051000	-Crab	8								0
16052000	-Shrimps and prawns	8								0
16053000	-Lobster	12								0
16054000	-Other crustaceans	12								0
16059000	-Other	8					EC			0
23012000	-Flours, meals and pellets, of fish or of crustaceans, molluscs or other aquatic invertebrates	15								0
2501	Salt (including table salt and denatured salt) and pure sodium chloride, whether or not in aqueous solution or containing added anti-caking or free-flowing agents; sea water.									
25010010	---Common salt (table salt)	15								0
25010020	---Denatured salt unfit for human consumption	15								0
25010030	---Pure sodium chloride	15								0
25010040	---Salt solutions	15								0
25010090	---Other salts or sea water	15								0
25020000	Unroasted iron pyrites.	15								0
25030000	Sulphur of all kinds, other than sublimed sulphur, precipitated sulphur and colloidal sulphur.	15								0
2504	Natural graphite.									
25041000	-In powder or in flakes	15								0
25049000	-Other	15								0
2505	Natural sands of all kinds, whether or not coloured, other than metal-bearing sands of Chapter 26.									
25051000	-Silica sands and quartz sands	15								0

HS	Description	Bound rate at date of accession	Interim	Final Bound	Implementation	Present concession established	INR	Concession first incorporated in a GATT Schedule	Earlier INRs	ODCs
25059000	-Other	15					AU			0
2506	Quartz (other than natural sands); quartzite, whether or not roughly trimmed or merely cut, by sawing or otherwise, into blocks or slabs of a rectangular (including square) shape.									
250610	-Quartz									
25061010	---Raw quartz, in the form of unsawn agglomerates	15								0
25061090	---Other quartz	15								0
25062	-Quartzite:									
250621	--Crude or roughly trimmed									
25062110	---Raw quartzite	15								0
25062120	---Split or squared quartzite	15								0
25062900	--Other	15								0
2507	Kaolin and other kaolinic clays, whether or not calcined.									
25070010	---Kaolin	15								0
25070090	---Other kaolin clays	15								0
2508	Other clays (not including expanded clays of heading 68.06), andalusite, kyanite and sillimanite, whether or not calcined; mullite; chamotte or dinas earths.									
25081000	-Bentonite	10								0
25082000	-Decolourising earths and fuller's earth	15								0
25083000	-Fire-clay	15								0
25084000	-Other clays	15								0
25085000	-Andalusite, kyanite and sillimanite	15								0
25086000	-Mullite	15								0
25087000	-Chamotte or dinas earths	15								0
2509	Chalk.									
25090010	---Ground chalk for construction	15								0
25090090	---Other chalk	15								0
2510	Natural calcium phosphates, natural aluminium calcium phosphates and phosphatic chalk.									
25101000	-Unground	15								0
25102000	-Ground	15								0
2511	Natural barium sulphate (barytes); natural barium carbonate (witherite), whether or not calcined, other than barium oxide of heading 28.16.									

HS	Description	Bound rate at date of accession	Interim	Final Bound	Implementation	Present concession established	INR	Concession first incorporated in a GATT Schedule	Earlier INRs	ODCs
25111000	-Natural barium sulphate (barytes)	10								0
25112000	-Natural barium carbonate (witherite)	15								0
25120000	Siliceous fossil meals (for example, kieselguhr, tripolite and diatomite) and similar siliceous earths, whether or not calcined, of an apparent specific gravity of 1 or less.	15								0
2513	Pumice stone; emery; natural corundum, natural garnet and other natural abrasives, whether or not heat-treated.									
25131	-Pumice stone:									
25131100	--Crude or in irregular pieces, including crushed pumice ("bimskies")	8								0
25131900	--Other	8								0
251320	-Emery, natural corundum, natural garnet and other natural abrasives									
25132010	---Emery	15					AU			0
25132020	---Natural corundum	15					AU			0
25132030	---Natural carnelian	15					AU			0
25132040	---Tripoli earth	15					AU			0
25132090	---Other natural abrasives, crude or irregular	15					AU			0
2514	Slate, whether or not roughly trimmed or merely cut, by sawing or otherwise, into blocks or slabs of a rectangular (including square) shape.									
25140010	---Raw slate, in the form of unsawn agglomerates	15								0
25140090	---Other slate	15								0
2515	Marble, travertine, ecaussine and other calcareous monumental or building stone of an apparent specific gravity of 2.5 or more, and alabaster, whether or not roughly trimmed or merely cut, by sawing or otherwise, into blocks or slabs of a rectangular (including square) shape.									
25151	-Marble and travertine:									
25151100	--Crude or roughly trimmed	15								0
25151200	--Merely cut, by sawing or otherwise, into blocks or slabs of a rectangular (including square) shape	15								0

HS	Description	Bound rate at date of accession	Interim	Final Bound	Implementation	Present concession established	INR	Concession first incorporated in a GATT Schedule	Earlier INRs	ODCs
251520	-Ecaussine and other calcareous monumental or building stone; alabaster									
25152010	---Building stone, crude or roughly trimmed	15								0
25152020	---Building stone, cut into blocks	15								0
2516	Granite, porphyry, basalt, sandstone and other monumental or building stone, whether or not roughly trimmed or merely cut, by sawing or otherwise, into blocks or slabs of a rectangular (including square) shape.									
25161	-Granite:									
25161100	--Crude or roughly trimmed	15								0
25161200	--Merely cut, by sawing or otherwise, into blocks or slabs of a rectangular (including square) shape	15								0
25162	-Sandstone:									
25162100	--Crude or roughly trimmed	15								0
25162200	--Merely cut, by sawing or otherwise, into blocks or slabs of a rectangular (including square) shape	15								0
251690	-Other monumental or building stone									
25169010	---Other building stone, crude or roughly trimmed	15								0
25169020	---Other building stone, cut into blocks	15								0
2517	Pebbles, gravel, broken or crushed stone, of a kind commonly used for concrete aggregates, for road metalling or for railway or other ballast, shingle and flint, whether or not heat-treated; macadam of slag, dross or similar industrial waste, whether or not incorporating the materials cited in the first part of the heading; tarred macadam; granules, chippings and powder, of stones of heading 25.15 or 25.16, whether or not heat-treated.									
25171000	-Pebbles, gravel, broken or crushed stone, of a kind commonly used for concrete aggregates, for road metalling or for railway or other ballast, shingle and flint, whether or not heat-treated	15								0

HS	Description	Bound rate at date of accession	Interim	Final Bound	Implementation	Present concession established	INR	Concession first incorporated in a GATT Schedule	Earlier INRs	ODCs
25172000	-Macadam of slag, dross or similar industrial waste, whether or not incorporating the materials cited in subheading 2517.10	15								0
25173000	-Tarred macadam	15								0
25174	-Granules, chippings and powder, of stones of heading 25.15 or 25.16, whether or not heat-treated:									
25174100	--Of marble	15								0
25174900	--Other	10								0
2518	Dolomite, whether or not calcined or sintered, including dolomite roughly trimmed or merely cut, by sawing or otherwise, into blocks or slabs of a rectangular (including square) shape; dolomite ramming mix.									
251810	-Dolomite, not calcined or sintered									
25181010	---Crude dolomite, not calcined	15								0
25181020	---Dolomite cut into blocks, not calcined	15								0
251820	-Calcined or sintered dolomite									
25182010	---Crude calcined dolomite	15								0
25182020	---Calcined dolomite cut into blocks	15								0
25183000	-Dolomite ramming mix	15								0
2519	Natural magnesium carbonate (magnesite); fused magnesia; dead-burned (sintered) magnesia, whether or not containing small quantities of other oxides added before sintering; other magnesium oxide, whether or not pure.									
25191000	-Natural magnesium carbonate (magnesite)	15								0
25199000	-Other	15								0
2520	Gypsum; anhydrite; plasters (consisting of calcined gypsum or calcium sulphate) whether or not coloured, with or without small quantities of accelerators or retarders.									
252010	-Gypsum; anhydrite									
25201010	---Gypsum	15								0
25201020	---Anhydrite	15								0
252020	-Plasters									
25202010	---Plaster used in dentistry	15								0
25202090	---Other plaster	15								0

HS	Description	Bound rate at date of accession	Interim	Final Bound	Implementation	Present concession established	INR	Concession first incorporated in a GATT Schedule	Earlier INRs	ODCs
25210000	Limestone flux; limestone and other calcareous stone, of a kind used for the manufacture of lime or cement.	15								0
2522	Quicklime, slaked lime and hydraulic lime, other than calcium oxide and hydroxide of heading 28.25.									
25221000	-Quicklime	15								0
25222000	-Slaked lime	15								0
25223000	-Hydraulic lime	15								0
2523	Portland cement, aluminous cement, slag cement, supersulphate cement and similar hydraulic cements, whether or not coloured or in the form of clinkers.									
25231000	-Cement clinkers	15								0
25232	-Portland cement:									
25232100	--White cement, whether or not artificially coloured	15		12	2008		MX			0
252329	--Other									
25232910	---Other Portland cement	15					MX			0
25232920	---Sulphate resistant cement	15					MX			0
25232990	---Other cement	15								0
25233000	-Aluminous cement	15								0
25239000	-Other hydraulic cements	15								0
25240000	Asbestos.	15								0
2525	Mica, including splittings; mica waste.									
25251000	-Crude mica and mica rifted into sheets or splittings	15								0
25252000	-Mica powder	10								0
25253000	-Mica waste	15								0
2526	Natural steatite, whether or not roughly trimmed or merely cut, by sawing or otherwise, into blocks or slabs of a rectangular (including square) shape; talc.									
252610	-Not crushed, not powdered									
25261010	---Steatite, uncrushed	15								0
25261020	---Talc, uncrushed	15								0
252620	-Crushed or powdered									
25262010	---Steatite, crushed	15								0
25262020	---Talc, crushed	15		13	2008					0

HS	Description	Bound rate at date of accession	Interim	Final Bound	Implementation	Present concession established	INR	Concession first incorporated in a GATT Schedule	Earlier INRs	ODCs
2528	Natural borates and concentrates thereof (whether or not calcined), but not including borates separated from natural brine; natural boric acid containing not more than 85 % of H3BO3 calculated on the dry weight.									
25281000	-Natural sodium borates and concentrates thereof (whether or not calcined)	15								0
25289000	-Other	15								0
2529	Felspar; leucite, nepheline and nepheline syenite; fluorspar.									
25291000	-Felspar	15								0
25292	-Fluorspar:									
25292100	--Containing by weight 97 % or less of calcium fluoride	15								0
25292200	--Containing by weight more than 97 % of calcium fluoride	15								0
25293000	-Leucite; nepheline and nepheline syenite	15								0
2530	Mineral substances not elsewhere specified or included.									
25301000	-Vermiculite, perlite and chlorites, unexpanded	15								0
25302000	-Kieserite, epsomite (natural magnesium sulphates)	15								0
253090	-Other									
2530901	---Natural arsenic sulphates:									
25309011	----Yellow arsenic sulphide (rat poison)	15								0
25309019	----Other arsenic sulphides	15								0
25309020	---Meerschaum and amber	15								0
25309030	---Broken pottery	15								0
25309040	---Earth colours	15								0
25309090	---Other mineral substances	15								0
2601	Iron ores and concentrates, including roasted iron pyrites.									
26011	-Iron ores and concentrates, other than roasted iron pyrites:									
26011100	--Non-agglomerated	15		13	2008					0
26011200	--Agglomerated	15		13	2008					0
26012000	-Roasted iron pyrites	15								0

HS	Description	Bound rate at date of accession	Interim	Final Bound	Implementation	Present concession established	INR	Concession first incorporated in a GATT Schedule	Earlier INRs	ODCs
26020000	Manganese ores and concentrates, including ferruginous manganese ores and concentrates with a manganese content of 20 % or more, calculated on the dry weight.	15								0
26030000	Copper ores and concentrates.	15								0
26040000	Nickel ores and concentrates.	15								0
26050000	Cobalt ores and concentrates.	15								0
26060000	Aluminium ores and concentrates.	10								0
26070000	Lead ores and concentrates.	15								0
26080000	Zinc ores and concentrates.	15								0
26090000	Tin ores and concentrates.	15								0
26100000	Chromium ores and concentrates.	15								0
26110000	Tungsten ores and concentrates.	15								0
2612	Uranium or thorium ores and concentrates.									
26121000	-Uranium ores and concentrates	15								0
26122000	-Thorium ores and concentrates	15								0
2613	Molybdenum ores and concentrates.									
26131000	-Roasted	15								0
26139000	-Other	15								0
26140000	Titanium ores and concentrates.	15								0
2615	Niobium, tantalum, vanadium or zirconium ores and concentrates.									
26151000	-Zirconium ores and concentrates	15								0
26159000	-Other	15								0
2616	Precious metal ores and concentrates.									
26161000	-Silver ores and concentrates	15								0
26169000	-Other	15								0
2617	Other ores and concentrates.									
26171000	-Antimony ores and concentrates	15								0
26179000	-Other	15								0
26180000	Granulated slag (slag sand) from the manufacture of iron or steel.	15								0
26190000	Slag, dross (other than granulated slag), scalings and other waste from the manufacture of iron or steel.	15								0
2620	Ash and residues (other than from the manufacture of iron or steel), containing arsenic, metals or their compounds.									
26201	-Containing mainly zinc:									
26201100	--Hard zinc spelter	15								0

HS	Description	Bound rate at date of accession	Interim	Final Bound	Implementation	Present concession established	INR	Concession first incorporated in a GATT Schedule	Earlier INRs	ODCs
26201900	--Other	15								0
26202	-Containing mainly lead:									
26202100	--Leaded gasoline sludges and leaded anti-knock compound sludges	15								0
26202900	--Other	15								0
26203000	-Containing mainly copper	15								0
26204000	-Containing mainly aluminium	15								0
26206000	-Containing arsenic, mercury, thallium or their mixtures, of a kind used for the extraction of arsenic or those metals or for the manufacture of their chemical compounds	15								0
26209	-Other:									
26209100	--Containing antimony, beryllium, cadmium, chromium or their mixtures	15								0
26209900	--Other	15								0
2621	Other slag and ash, including seaweed ash (kelp); ash and residues from the incineration of municipal waste.									
26211000	-Ash and residues from the incineration of municipal waste	15								0
26219000	-Other	15								0
2701	Coal; briquettes, ovoids and similar solid fuels manufactured from coal.									
27011	-Coal, whether or not pulverised, but not agglomerated:									
27011100	--Anthracite	15								0
27011200	--Bituminous coal	15								0
27011900	--Other coal	15								0
27012000	-Briquettes, ovoids and similar solid fuels manufactured from coal	15								0
2702	Lignite, whether or not agglomerated, excluding jet.									
27021000	-Lignite, whether or not pulverised, but not agglomerated	15								0
27022000	-Agglomerated lignite	15								0
2703	Peat (including peat litter), whether or not agglomerated.									
27030010	---Peat for use as agricultural dust	15								0
27030090	---Other Peat	15								0
2704	Coke and semi-coke of coal, of lignite or of peat, whether or not agglomerated; retort carbon.									

HS	Description	Bound rate at date of accession	Interim	Final Bound	Implementation	Present concession established	INR	Concession first incorporated in a GATT Schedule	Earlier INRs	ODCs
27040010	---Coke and semi-coke of coal, of lignite or peat	15								0
27040020	---Retort coke	10								0
27050000	Coal gas, water gas, producer gas and similar gases, other than petroleum gases and other gaseous hydrocarbons.	15								0
27060000	Tar distilled from coal, from lignite or from peat, and other mineral tars, whether or not dehydrated or partially distilled, including reconstituted tars.	15								0
2707	Oils and other products of the distillation of high temperature coal tar; similar products in which the weight of the aromatic constituents exceeds that of the non-aromatic constituents.									
27071000	-Benzol (benzene)	15								0
27072000	-Toluol (toluene)	15								0
27073000	-Xylol (xylenes)	15								0
27074000	-Naphthalene	15								0
27075000	-Other aromatic hydrocarbon mixtures of which 65 % or more by volume (including losses) distils at 250 °C by the ASTM D 86 method	15								0
27076000	-Phenols	15								0
27079	-Other:									
27079100	--Creosote oils	15								0
27079900	--Other	15								0
2708	Pitch and pitch coke, obtained from coal tar or from other mineral tars.									
27081000	-Pitch	15								0
27082000	-Pitch coke	15								0
27090000	Petroleum oils and oils obtained from bituminous minerals, crude.	8								0
2710	Petroleum oils and oils obtained from bituminous minerals, other than crude; preparations not elsewhere specified or included, containing by weight 70 % or more of petroleum oils or of oils obtained from bituminous minerals, these oils being the basic constituents of the preparations; waste oils.									

HS	Description	Bound rate at date of accession	Interim	Final Bound	Implementation	Present concession established	INR	Concession first incorporated in a GATT Schedule	Earlier INRs	ODCs
27101	-Petroleum oils and oils obtained from bituminous minerals (other than crude) and preparations not elsewhere specified or included, containing by weight 70 % or more of petroleum oils or of oils obtained from bituminous minerals, these oils being the basic constituents of the preparations, other than waste oils :									
271011	--Light oils and preparations									
2710111	---Naphtha:									
27101111	----Light straight run naphtha	5					IN			0
27101112	----Whole naphtha	5					IN			0
27101113	----Reformate	5					IN			0
27101114	----Natural gasoline	5					IN			0
27101119	----Other	5					IN			0
2710112	---Fuel:									
27101121	----Motor gasoline	5					IN			0
27101122	----Jet-fuel (JP-4)	5					IN			0
27101123	----Jet-fuel (JP5, JP-8)	5					IN			0
27101129	----Multi-purpose kerosene	5					IN			0
2710113	---Diesel:									
27101131	----Engine diesel	5					IN			0
27101132	----Generator diesel including marine diesel	5					IN			0
27101133	----Heating diesel	5					IN			0
27101139	----For other purposes	5					IN			0
2710114	---Fuel oils:									
27101141	----Bunker oil	5					IN			0
27101142	----Topped crude	5					IN			0
27101149	----Other	5					IN			0
271019	--Other									
2710191	---Lubricating oils:									
27101911	----Base oils	5					IN			0
27101912	----Gasoline engine lubricating oil	10					IN			0
27101913	----Diesel engine lubricating oil	10					IN			0
27101914	----Gear lubricating oil	10					IN			0
27101915	----Automatic transmission fluid	10					IN			0
27101919	----Other	10					IN			0
2710199	---Oils for other purposes:									
27101991	----Cutting oils	5					IN			0
27101992	----Cleansing oils	5					IN			0

HS	Description	Bound rate at date of accession	Interim	Final Bound	Implementation	Present concession established	INR	Concession first incorporated in a GATT Schedule	Earlier INRs	ODCs
27101993	----Mould release oils	5					IN			0
27101994	----Liquids for hydraulic brakes	10					IN			0
27101995	----Hydraulic and turbo system oils	5					IN			0
27101996	----Transformer and circuit breaker oils	5					IN			0
27101997	----White oils (paraffin oil, Vaseline oil)	5					IN			0
27101998	----Greases	10					IN			0
27101999	----Other	5					IN			0
27109	-Waste oils:									
27109100	--Containing polychlorinated biphenyls (PCBs), polychlorinated terphenyls (PCTs) or polybrominated biphenyls (PBBs)	5					IN			0
27109900	--Other	5					IN			0
2711	Petroleum gases and other gaseous hydrocarbons.									
27111	-Liquefied:									
27111100	--Natural gas	15								0
27111200	--Propane	15								0
27111300	--Butanes	15								0
27111400	--Ethylene, propylene, butylene and butadiene	15								0
27111900	--Other	15								0
27112	-In gaseous state:									
27112100	--Natural gas	15								0
27112900	--Other	15								0
2712	Petroleum jelly; paraffin wax, micro-crystalline petroleum wax, slack wax, ozokerite, lignite wax, peat wax, other mineral waxes, and similar products obtained by synthesis or by other processes, whether or not coloured.									
27121000	-Petroleum jelly	15								0
271220	-Paraffin wax containing by weight less than 0.75 % of oil									
27122010	---Paraffin wax for candle industry	15								0
27122020	---Paraffin wax for impregnating matches	15								0
27122090	---Other paraffin wax under 0.75% oil	15								0
27129000	-Other	15								0
2713	Petroleum coke, petroleum bitumen and other residues of petroleum oils or of oils obtained from bituminous minerals.									

HS	Description	Bound rate at date of accession	Interim	Final Bound	Implementation	Present concession established	INR	Concession first incorporated in a GATT Schedule	Earlier INRs	ODCs
27131	-Petroleum coke:									
27131100	--Not calcined	15								0
27131200	--Calcined	5								0
27132000	-Petroleum bitumen	15								0
27139000	-Other residues of petroleum oils or of oils obtained from bituminous minerals	15								0
2714	Bitumen and asphalt, natural; bituminous or oil shale and tar sands; asphaltites and asphaltic rocks.									
27141000	-Bituminous or oil shale and tar sands	15								0
271490	-Other									
27149010	---Bitumen and asphalt, natural	15								0
27149090	---Other bitumen and asphaltic rock	15								0
27150000	Bituminous mixtures based on natural asphalt, on natural bitumen, on petroleum bitumen, on mineral tar or on mineral tar pitch (for example, bituminous mastics, cut-backs).	15								0
27160000	Electrical energy	15								0
2801	Fluorine, chlorine, bromine and iodine.									
28011000	-Chlorine	5.5					US			0
28012000	-Iodine	5.5					US			0
280130	-Fluorine; bromine									
28013010	---Fluoride	5.5					US			0
28013020	---Bromine	5.5					US			0
2802	Sulphur, sublimed or precipitated; colloidal sulphur.									
28020010	---Sulphur, sublimed or precipitated	5.5					US			0
28020020	---Colloidal sulphur	5.5					US			0
28030000	Carbon (carbon blacks and other forms of carbon not elsewhere specified or included).	5.5					US			0
2804	Hydrogen, rare gases and other non-metals.									
28041000	-Hydrogen	5.5					US			0
28042	-Rare gases:									
28042100	--Argon	12	8 (2008)	5.5	2010*					0
280429	--Other									
28042910	---Helium	5.5					US			0
28042920	---Neon	5.5					US			0
28042990	---Other rare gases	5.5					US			0
28043000	-Nitrogen	12	8 (2008)	5.5	2010*					0

HS	Description	Bound rate at date of accession	Interim	Final Bound	Implementation	Present concession established	INR	Concession first incorporated in a GATT Schedule	Earlier INRs	ODCs
28044000	-Oxygen	20	11.3 (2008)	5.5	2010*					0
28045000	-Boron; tellurium	5.5					US			0
28046	-Silicon:									
28046100	--Containing by weight not less than 99.99 % of silicon	5.5					US			0
28046900	--Other	5.5					AU,US			0
28047000	-Phosphorus	5.5					US			0
28048000	-Arsenic	5.5					US			0
28049000	-Selenium	5.5					US			0
2805	Alkali or alkaline-earth metals; rare-earth metals, scandium and yttrium, whether or not intermixed or interalloyed; mercury.									
28051	-Alkali or alkaline-earth metals:									
28051100	--Sodium	5.5					US			0
28051200	--Calcium	5.5					US			0
280519	--Other									
28051910	---Lithium	5.5					US			0
28051920	---Potassium	5.5					US			0
28051990	---Other alkali metals	5.5					US			0
28053000	-Rare-earth metals, scandium and yttrium, whether or not intermixed or interalloyed	5.5					US			0
28054000	-Mercury	5.5					US			0
2806	Hydrogen chloride (hydrochloric acid); chlorosulphuric acid.									
28061000	-Hydrogen chloride (hydrochloric acid)	5.5					US			0
28062000	-Chlorosulphuric acid	5.5					US			0
2807	Sulphuric acid; oleum.									
28070010	---Sulphuric acid	20	11.3 (2008)	5.5	2010*					0
28070020	---Oleum (oily sulphuric acid)	20	11.3 (2008)	5.5	2010*					0
2808	Nitric acid; sulphonitric acids.									
28080010	---Nitric acid	5.5					US			0
28080020	---Sulphonitric acid	5.5					US			0
2809	Diphosphorus pentaoxide; phosphoric acid; polyphosphoric acids, whether or not chemically defined.									
28091000	-Diphosphorus pentaoxide	5.5					US			0
280920	-Phosphoric acid and polyphosphoric acids									
28092010	---Phosphoric acid	5.5					US			0
28092020	---Polyphosphoric acid	5.5					US			0

HS	Description	Bound rate at date of accession	Interim	Final Bound	Implementation	Present concession established	INR	Concession first incorporated in a GATT Schedule	Earlier INRs	ODCs
2810	Oxides of boron; boric acids.									
28100010	---Oxides of boron	5.5					US			0
28100020	---Boric acid	5.5					US			0
2811	Other inorganic acids and other inorganic oxygen compounds of non-metals.									
28111	-Other inorganic acids:									
28111100	--Hydrogen fluoride (hydrofluoric acid)	5.5					US			0
281119	--Other									
28111910	---Hydrogen cyanide	5.5					US			0
28111990	---Other	5.5					US			0
28112	-Other inorganic oxygen compounds of non-metals:									
28112100	--Carbon dioxide	12	8 (2008)	5.5	2010*					0
28112200	--Silicon dioxide	5.5					US			0
28112300	--Sulphur dioxide	5.5					US			0
281129	--Other									
28112910	---Arsenic trioxide, arsenic pentoxide, arsenic acid	5.5					US			0
28112990	---Other inorganic oxygen compounds of nonmetals	5.5					US			0
2812	Halides and halide oxides of non-metals.									
281210	-Chlorides and chloride oxides									
28121010	---Arsenic trichloride	5.5								0
28121020	---Carbonyl dichloride (phosgene)	5.5					US			0
28121030	---Phosphorous oxychloride	5.5					US			0
28121040	---Phosphorous trichloride	5.5					US			0
28121050	---Phosphorous pentachloride	5.5					US			0
28121060	---Sulphur monochloride	5.5					US			0
28121070	---Sulphur dinochloride	5.5					US			0
28121080	---Thionyl chloride	5.5					US			0
28121090	---Other	5.5					US			0
28129000	-Other	5.5					US			0
2813	Sulphides of non-metals; commercial phosphorus trisulphide.									
28131000	-Carbon disulphide	5.5					US			0
28139000	-Other	5.5					US			0
2814	Ammonia, anhydrous or in aqueous solution.									
28141000	-Anhydrous ammonia	5.5					US			0
28142000	-Ammonia in aqueous solution	5.5					US			0

HS	Description	Bound rate at date of accession	Interim	Final Bound	Implementation	Present concession established	INR	Concession first incorporated in a GATT Schedule	Earlier INRs	ODCs
2815	Sodium hydroxide (caustic soda); potassium hydroxide (caustic potash); peroxides of sodium or potassium.									
28151	-Sodium hydroxide (caustic soda):									
28151100	--Solid	12	8 (2008)	5.5	2010*					0
28151200	--In aqueous solution (soda lye or liquid soda)	12	8 (2008)	5.5	2010*					0
28152000	-Potassium hydroxide (caustic potash)	5.5					US			0
28153000	-Peroxides of sodium or potassium	5.5					US			0
2816	Hydroxide and peroxide of magnesium; oxides, hydroxides and peroxides, of strontium or barium.									
28161000	-Hydroxide and peroxide of magnesium	5.5					US			0
28164000	-Oxides, hydroxides and peroxides, of strontium or barium	5.5					US			0
2817	Zinc oxide; zinc peroxide.									
28170010	---Zinc oxide	5.5					US			0
28170020	---Zinc peroxide	5.5					US			0
2818	Artificial corundum, whether or not chemically defined; aluminium oxide; aluminium hydroxide.									
28181000	-Artificial corundum, whether or not chemically defined	5.5					US			0
28182000	-Aluminium oxide, other than artificial corundum	5.5					AU,US			0
28183000	-Aluminium hydroxide	5.5					US			0
2819	Chromium oxides and hydroxides.									
28191000	-Chromium trioxide	5.5					US			0
28199000	-Other	5.5					US			0
2820	Manganese oxides.									
28201000	-Manganese dioxide	5.5					US			0
28209000	-Other	5.5					US			0
2821	Iron oxides and hydroxides; earth colours containing 70 % or more by weight of combined iron evaluated as Fe2O3.									
28211000	-Iron oxides and hydroxides	5.5					US			0
28212000	-Earth colours	5.5					US			0
28220000	Cobalt oxides and hydroxides; commercial cobalt oxides.	5.5					US			0
28230000	Titanium oxides.	5.5					US			0
2824	Lead oxides; red lead and orange lead.									
28241000	-Lead monoxide (litharge, massicot)	5.5					US			0

HS	Description	Bound rate at date of accession	Interim	Final Bound	Implementation	Present concession established	INR	Concession first incorporated in a GATT Schedule	Earlier INRs	ODCs
28242000	-Red lead and orange lead	5.5					US			0
28249000	-Other	5.5					US			0
2825	Hydrazine and hydroxylamine and their inorganic salts; other inorganic bases; other metal oxides, hydroxides and peroxides.									
28251000	-Hydrazine and hydroxylamine and their inorganic salts	5.5					US			0
28252000	-Lithium oxide and hydroxide	5.5					US			0
28253000	-Vanadium oxides and hydroxides	5.5					US			0
28254000	-Nickel oxides and hydroxides	5.5					US			0
28255000	-Copper oxides and hydroxides	5.5					US			0
28256000	-Germanium oxides and zirconium dioxide	5.5					US			0
28257000	-Molybdenum oxides and hydroxides	5.5					US			0
28258000	-Antimony oxides	5.5					KG,US			0
282590	-Other									
28259010	---Tin oxide	5.5					US			0
28259090	---Other oxide and inorganic salt	5.5					US			0
2826	Fluorides; fluorosilicates, fluoroaluminates and other complex fluorine salts.									
28261	-Fluorides:									
28261100	--Of ammonium or of sodium	5.5					US			0
28261200	--Of aluminium	5.5					US			0
28261900	--Other	5.5					US			0
28262000	-Fluorosilicates of sodium or of potassium	5.5					US			0
28263000	-Sodium hexafluoroaluminate (synthetic cryolite)	5.5					US			0
28269000	-Other	5.5					US			0
2827	Chlorides, chloride oxides and chloride hydroxides; bromides and bromide oxides; iodides and iodide oxides.									
28271000	-Ammonium chloride	5.5					US			0
28272000	-Calcium chloride	5.5					US			0
28273	-Other chlorides:									
28273100	--Of magnesium	5.5					US			0
28273200	--Of aluminium	5.5					US			0
28273300	--Of iron	5.5					US			0
28273400	--Of cobalt	5.5					US			0
28273500	--Of nickel	5.5					US			0

HS	Description	Bound rate at date of accession	Interim	Final Bound	Implementation	Present concession established	INR	Concession first incorporated in a GATT Schedule	Earlier INRs	ODCs
28273600	--Of zinc	5.5					US			0
28273900	--Other	5.5					US			0
28274	-Chloride oxides and chloride hydroxides:									
28274100	--Of copper	5.5					US			0
28274900	--Other	5.5					US			0
28275	-Bromides and bromide oxides:									
28275100	--Bromides of sodium or of potassium	5.5					US			0
28275900	--Other	5.5					US			0
28276000	-Iodides and iodide oxides	5.5					US			0
2828	Hypochlorites; commercial calcium hypochlorite; chlorites; hypobromites.									
28281000	-Commercial calcium hypochlorite and other calcium hypochlorites	5.5					US			0
282890	-Other									
28289010	---Sodium hypochlorite	5.5					US			0
28289020	---Potassium hypochlorite	5.5					US			0
28289030	---Chlorites	5.5					US			0
28289040	---Hypobromites	5.5					US			0
28289090	---Other hypochlorites	5.5					US			0
2829	Chlorates and perchlorates; bromates and perbromates; iodates and periodates.									
28291	-Chlorates:									
28291100	--Of sodium	5.5					US			0
28291900	--Other	5.5					US			0
282990	-Other									
28299010	---Perchlorates	5.5					US			0
28299020	---Bromates and perbromates	5.5					US			0
28299030	---Iodates and periodates	5.5					US			0
2830	Sulphides; polysulphides, whether or not chemically defined.									
28301000	-Sodium sulphides	5.5					US			0
28302000	-Zinc sulphide	5.5					US			0
28303000	-Cadmium sulphide	5.5					US			0
28309000	-Other	5.5					US			0
2831	Dithionites and sulphoxylates.									
28311000	-Of sodium	5.5					US			0
28319000	-Other	5.5					US			0
2832	Sulphites; thiosulphates.									
28321000	-Sodium sulphites	5.5					US			0

HS	Description	Bound rate at date of accession	Interim	Final Bound	Implementation	Present concession established	INR	Concession first incorporated in a GATT Schedule	Earlier INRs	ODCs
28322000	-Other sulphites	5.5					US			0
283230	-Thiosulphates									
28323010	---Sodium thiosulphates	5.5					US			0
28323020	---Calcium thiosulphates	5.5					US			0
28323090	---Other thiosulphates	5.5					US			0
2833	Sulphates; alums; peroxosulphates (persulphates).									
28331	-Sodium sulphates:									
28331100	--Disodium sulphate	5.5					US			0
28331900	--Other	5.5					US			0
28332	-Other sulphates:									
28332100	--Of magnesium	5.5					US			0
28332200	--Of aluminium	5.5					US			0
28332300	--Of chromium	5.5					US			0
28332400	--Of nickel	5.5					US			0
28332500	--Of copper	5.5					US			0
28332600	--Of zinc	5.5					US			0
28332700	--Of barium	5.5					US			0
28332900	--Other	5.5					AU,US			0
28333000	-Alums	5.5					US			0
28334000	-Peroxosulphates (persulphates)	5.5					US			0
2834	Nitrites; nitrates.									
28341000	-Nitrites	5.5					US			0
28342	-Nitrates:									
28342100	--Of potassium	5.5					US			0
28342900	--Other	5.5					US			0
2835	Phosphinates (hypophosphites), phosphonates (phosphites) and phosphates; polyphosphates, whether or not chemically defined.									
28351000	-Phosphinates (hypophosphites) and phosphonates (phosphites)	5.5					US			0
28352	-Phosphates:									
28352200	--Of mono- or disodium	5.5					US			0
28352300	--Of trisodium	5.5					US			0
28352400	--Of potassium	5.5					US			0
28352500	--Calcium hydrogenorthophosphate ("dicalcium phosphate")	5.5					US			0
28352600	--Other phosphates of calcium	5.5					US			0
28352900	--Other	5.5					US			0
28353	-Polyphosphates:									

HS	Description	Bound rate at date of accession	Interim	Final Bound	Implementation	Present concession established	INR	Concession first incorporated in a GATT Schedule	Earlier INRs	ODCs
28353100	--Sodium triphosphate (sodium tripolyphosphate)	5.5					US			0
28353900	--Other	5.5					US			0
2836	Carbonates; peroxocarbonates (percarbonates); commercial ammonium carbonate containing ammonium carbamate.									
28361000	-Commercial ammonium carbonate and other ammonium carbonates	5.5					US			0
28362000	-Disodium carbonate	5.5					US			0
28363000	-Sodium hydrogencarbonate (sodium bicarbonate)	5.5					US			0
28364000	-Potassium carbonates	5.5					US			0
28365000	-Calcium carbonate	12	8 (2008)	5.5	2010*					0
28366000	-Barium carbonate	5.5					US			0
28367000	-Lead carbonates	5.5					US			0
28369	-Other:									
28369100	--Lithium carbonates	5.5					US			0
28369200	--Strontium carbonate	5.5					US			0
28369900	--Other	5.5					US			0
2837	Cyanides, cyanide oxides and complex cyanides.									
28371	-Cyanides and cyanide oxides:									
28371100	--Of sodium	5.5					US			0
28371900	--Other	5.5					US			0
28372000	-Complex cyanides	5.5					US			0
2838	Fulminates, cyanates and thiocyanates.									
28380010	---Fulminates	5.5					US			0
28380020	---Cyanates	5.5					US			0
28380030	---Thiocyanates	5.5					US			0
2839	Silicates; commercial alkali metal silicates.									
28391	-Of sodium:									
28391100	--Sodium metasilicates	5.5					US			0
28391900	--Other	5.5					US			0
28392000	-Of potassium	5.5					US			0
28399000	-Other	5.5					US			0
2840	Borates; peroxoborates (perborates).									
28401	-Disodium tetraborate (refined borax):									
28401100	--Anhydrous	5.5					US			0
28401900	--Other	5.5					US			0
28402000	-Other borates	5.5					US			0

HS	Description	Bound rate at date of accession	Interim	Final Bound	Implementation	Present concession established	INR	Concession first incorporated in a GATT Schedule	Earlier INRs	ODCs
28403000	-Peroxoborates (perborates)	5.5					US			0
2841	Salts of oxometallic or peroxometallic acids.									
28411000	-Aluminates	5.5					US			0
28412000	-Chromates of zinc or of lead	5.5					US			0
28413000	-Sodium dichromate	5.5					US			0
28415000	-Other chromates and dichromates; peroxochromates	5.5					US			0
28416	-Manganites, manganates and permanganates:									
28416100	--Potassium permanganate	5.5					US			0
28416900	--Other	5.5					US			0
28417000	-Molybdates	5.5					US			0
28418000	-Tungstates (wolframates)	5.5					US			0
28419000	-Other	5.5					US			0
2842	Other salts of inorganic acids or peroxoacids (including aluminosilicates whether or not chemically defined), other than azides.									
28421000	-Double or complex silicates, including aluminosilicates whether or not chemically defined	5.5					US			0
28429000	-Other	5.5					US			0
2843	Colloidal precious metals; inorganic or organic compounds of precious metals, whether or not chemically defined; amalgams of precious metals.									
28431000	-Colloidal precious metals	5.5					US			0
28432	-Silver compounds:									
28432100	--Silver nitrate	5.5					US			0
28432900	--Other	5.5					US			0
28433000	-Gold compounds	5.5					US			0
28439000	-Other compounds; amalgams	5.5					US			0
2844	Radioactive chemical elements and radioactive isotopes (including the fissile or fertile chemical elements and isotopes) and their compounds; mixtures and residues containing these products.									
284410	-Natural uranium and its compounds; alloys, dispersions (including cermets), ceramic products and mixtures containing natural uranium or natural uranium compounds									

HS	Description	Bound rate at date of accession	Interim	Final Bound	Implementation	Present concession established	INR	Concession first incorporated in a GATT Schedule	Earlier INRs	ODCs
28441010	---Natural uranium prepared for medical purposes	5.5					US			0
28441090	---Other natural uranium	5.5					US			0
284420	-Uranium enriched in U 235 and its compounds; plutonium and its compounds; alloys, dispersions (including cermets), ceramic products and mixtures containing uranium enriched in U 235, plutonium or compounds of these products									
28442010	---Enriched uranium prepared for medical purposes	5.5					US			0
28442090	---Other enriched uranium	5.5					US			0
284430	-Uranium depleted in U 235 and its compounds; thorium and its compounds; alloys, dispersions (including cermets), ceramic products and mixtures containing uranium depleted in U 235, thorium or compounds of these products									
28443010	---Depleted uranium prepared for medical purposes	5.5					US			0
28443090	---Other depleted uranium	5.5								0
284440	-Radioactive elements and isotopes and compounds other than those of subheading 2844.10, 2844.20 or 2844.30; alloys, dispersions (including cermets), ceramic products and mixtures containing these elements, isotopes or compounds; radioactive residues									
28444010	---Radioactive elements prepared for medical purposes	5					US			0
28444090	---Other radioactive elements	5					US			0
28445000	-Spent (irradiated) fuel elements (cartridges) of nuclear reactors	5.5					US			0
2845	Isotopes other than those of heading 28.44; compounds, inorganic or organic, of such isotopes, whether or not chemically defined.									
28451000	-Heavy water (deuterium oxide)	5.5					US			0
28459000	-Other	5.5					US			0
2846	Compounds, inorganic or organic, of rare-earth metals, of yttrium or of scandium or of mixtures of these metals.									

HS	Description	Bound rate at date of accession	Interim	Final Bound	Implementation	Present concession established	INR	Concession first incorporated in a GATT Schedule	Earlier INRs	ODCs
28461000	-Cerium compounds	5.5					US			0
28469000	-Other	5.5					US			0
28470000	Hydrogen peroxide, whether or not solidified with urea.	5.5					US			0
28480000	Phosphides, whether or not chemically defined, excluding ferrophosphorus.	5.5					US			0
2849	Carbides, whether or not chemically defined.									
28491000	-Of calcium	5.5					US			0
28492000	-Of silicon	5.5					US			0
28499000	-Other	5.5					US			0
2850	Hydrides, nitrides, azides, silicides and borides, whether or not chemically defined, other than compounds which are also carbides of heading 28.49.									
28500010	---Hydrides	5.5					US			0
28500020	---Nitrides	12	8 (2008)	5.5	2010*					0
28500030	---Azides	5.5					US			0
28500040	---Silicides	5.5					US			0
28500050	---Borides	5.5					US			0
2851	Other inorganic compounds (including distilled or conductivity water and water of similar purity); liquid air (whether or not rare gases have been removed); compressed air; amalgams, other than amalgams of precious metals.									
28510010	---Distilled water, conductivity water and similar water	12	8 (2008)	5.5	2010*					0
28510020	---Liquid air and compressed air	5.5					US			0
28510030	---Amalgams	5.5					US			0
28510040	---Cyanogen chloride	5.5					US			0
28510090	---Other inorganic compounds	5.5					US			0
2901	Acyclic hydrocarbons.									
290110	-Saturated									
29011010	---Ethane	5	2.5 (2008), 2.4 (2009)	0	2010		US			0
29011020	---Butanes	5		0	2008		US			0
29011030	---Pentanes	5	2.5 (2008), 2.4 (2009)	0	2010		US			0
29011040	---Hexanes	5	2.5 (2008), 2.4 (2009)	0	2010		US			0
29011050	---Heptanes	5	2.5 (2008), 2.4 (2009)	0	2010		US			0

HS	Description	Bound rate at date of accession	Interim	Final Bound	Implementation	Present concession established	INR	Concession first incorporated in a GATT Schedule	Earlier INRs	ODCs
29011060	---Octanes	5	2.5 (2008), 2.4 (2009)	0	2010		US			0
29011090	---Other saturated acyclic hydrocarbons	5	2.5 (2008), 2.4 (2009)	0	2010		US			0
29012	-Unsaturated:									
29012100	--Ethylene	12	4.8 (2008)	0	2010*		US			0
29012200	--Propene (propylene)	12	4.8 (2008)	0	2010*		US			0
29012300	--Butene (butylene) and isomers thereof	5	2.5 (2008), 2.4 (2009)	0	2010		US			0
29012400	--Buta-1,3-diene and isoprene	5	2.5 (2008), 2.4 (2009)	0	2010		US			0
290129	--Other									
29012910	---Propadiene	5	2.5 (2008), 2.4 (2009)	0	2010		US			0
29012920	---Buta- 1,3 diene	12	4.8 (2008)	0	2010*		US			0
29012930	---Acetylene	20	8 (2008)	0	2010*		US			0
29012940	---Acetylene phenyl	5	2.5 (2008), 2.4 (2009)	0	2010		US			0
29012950	---Methyl acetylene phenyl	5	2.5 (2008), 2.4 (2009)	0	2010		US			0
29012960	---Butene	12	4.8 (2008)	0	2010*		US			0
29012990	---Other unsaturated acyclic hydrocarbons	5	2.5 (2008), 2.4 (2009)	0	2010		US			0
2902	Cyclic hydrocarbons.									
29021	-Cyclanes, cyclenes and cycloterpenes:									
29021100	--Cyclohexane	5	2.5 (2008), 2.4 (2009)	0	2010		US			0
29021900	--Other	5	2.5 (2008), 2.4 (2009)	0	2010		US			0
29022000	-Benzene	12	4.8 (2008)	0	2010*		US			0
29023000	-Toluene	5	2.5 (2008), 2.4 (2009)	0	2010		US			0
29024	-Xylenes:									
29024100	--o-Xylene	12	4.8 (2008)	0	2010*		US			0
29024200	--m-Xylene	5	2.5 (2008), 2.4 (2009)	0	2010		US			0
29024300	--p-Xylene	12	4.8 (2008)	0	2010*		US			0
29024400	--Mixed xylene isomers	5	2.5 (2008), 2.4 (2009)	0	2010		US			0
29025000	-Styrene	12	4.8 (2008)	0	2010*		US			0
29026000	-Ethylbenzene	5	2.5 (2008), 2.4 (2009)	0	2010		US			0

HS	Description	Bound rate at date of accession	Interim	Final Bound	Implementation	Present concession established	INR	Concession first incorporated in a GATT Schedule	Earlier INRs	ODCs
29027000	-Cumene	5	2.5 (2008), 2.4 (2009)	0	2010		US			0
290290	-Other									
29029010	---Tetralyne	5	2.5 (2008), 2.4 (2009)	0	2010		US			0
29029020	---Naphthalene	5	2.5 (2008), 2.4 (2009)	0	2010		US			0
29029090	---Other cyclic hydrocarbons	5	2.5 (2008), 2.4 (2009)	0	2010		US			0
2903	Halogenated derivatives of hydrocarbons.									
29031	-Saturated chlorinated derivatives of acyclic hydrocarbons:									
29031100	--Chloromethane (methyl chloride) and chloroethane (ethyl chloride)	5.5					US			0
29031200	--Dichloromethane (methylene chloride)	5.5					US			0
29031300	--Chloroform (trichloromethane)	5.5					US			0
29031400	--Carbon tetrachloride	5.5					US			0
29031500	--1,2-Dichloroethane (ethylene dichloride)	12	8 (2008)	5.5	2010*					0
290319	--Other									
29031910	---1,1,1-Trichloroethane (methylchloforme)	5.5					US			0
29031990	---Other	5.5					US			0
29032	-Unsaturated chlorinated derivatives of acyclic hydrocarbons:									
29032100	--Vinyl chloride (chloroethylene)	5.5					US			0
29032200	--Trichloroethylene	5.5					US			0
29032300	--Tetrachloroethylene (perchloroethylene)	5.5					US			0
29032900	--Other	5.5					US			0
290330	-Fluorinated, brominated or iodinated derivatives of acyclic hydrocarbons									
29033010	---3,3,3,1,1-Pentafluoro-2-(trifluoromethyl)-prop-1-ene	5.5								0
29033020	---Bromomethane (methyl bromide)	5.5					US			0
29033090	---Other	5.5					US			0
29034	-Halogenated derivatives of acyclic hydrocarbons containing two or more different halogens:									
29034100	--Trichlorofluoromethane	5.5					US			0
29034200	--Dichlorodifluoromethane	5.5					US			0
29034300	--Trichlorotrifluoroethanes	5.5					US			0

HS	Description	Bound rate at date of accession	Interim	Final Bound	Implementation	Present concession established	INR	Concession first incorporated in a GATT Schedule	Earlier INRs	ODCs
29034400	--Dichlorotetrafluoroethanes and chloropentafluoroethane	5.5					US			0
290345	--Other derivatives perhalogenated only with fluorine and chlorine									
29034510	---Chlorotrifluoromethane	5.5					US			0
29034520	---Pentachlorofluoromethane	5.5					US			0
29034530	---Tetrachlorodifluoromethanes	5.5					US			0
29034540	---Heptachlorofluoropropanes	5.5					US			0
29034550	---Hexachlorodifluoropropanes	5.5					US			0
29034560	---Pentachlorotrifluoropropanes	5.5					US			0
29034570	---Tetrachlorotetrafluoropropanes	5.5					US			0
29034580	---Trichloropentafluoropropanes	5.5					US			0
29034590	---Dichlorohexafluoropropanes and chloroheeptafluoropropanes	5.5					US			0
29034600	--Bromochlorodifluoromethane, bromotrifluoromethane and dibromotetrafluoroethanes	5.5					US			0
29034700	--Other perhalogenated derivatives	5.5					US			0
290349	--Other									
29034910	---Derivatives of methane, ethane or propane, halogenated only with flourine and chlorine	5.5					US			0
29034920	---Derivatives of methane, ethane or propane, halogenated only with flourine and bromine	5.5					US			0
29034930	---Chlorodifluoromethane	5.5					US			0
29034940	---Dichlorotrifluoroethanes	5.5					US			0
29034950	---Chlorotetrafluoroethanes	5.5					US			0
29034960	---Dichlorodifluoroethanes	5.5					US			0
29034970	---Chlorodifluoroethanes	5.5					US			0
29034980	---Dichloropentafluoropropanes	5.5					US			0
29034990	---Other	5.5					US			0
29035	-Halogenated derivatives of cyclanic, cyclenic or cycloterpenic hydrocarbons:									
29035100	--1,2,3,4,5,6-Hexachlorocyclohexane	5.5					US			0
29035900	--Other	5.5					US			0
29036	-Halogenated derivatives of aromatic hydrocarbons:									
29036100	--Chlorobenzene, o-dichlorobenzene and p-dichlorobenzene	5.5					US			0
29036200	--Hexachlorobenzene and DDT (1,1,1-trichloro-2,2-bis(p-chlorophenyl)ethane)	5.5					US			0
29036900	--Other	5.5					US			0

HS	Description	Bound rate at date of accession	Interim	Final Bound	Implementation	Present concession established	INR	Concession first incorporated in a GATT Schedule	Earlier INRs	ODCs
2904	Sulphonated, nitrated or nitrosated derivatives of hydrocarbons, whether or not halogenated.									
29041000	-Derivatives containing only sulpho groups, their salts and ethyl esters	5.5					US			0
29042000	-Derivatives containing only nitro or only nitroso groups	5.5					US			0
290490	-Other									
29049010	---Trichloronitromethane (pinacolyl alchohol)	5.5					US			0
29049090	---Other	5.5					US			0
2905	Acyclic alcohols and their halogenated, sulphonated, nitrated or nitrosated derivatives.									
29051	-Saturated monohydric alcohols:									
29051100	--Methanol (methyl alcohol)	12	8 (2008)	5.5	2010*					0
29051200	--Propan-1-ol (propyl alcohol) and propan-2-ol (isopropyl alcohol)	5.5					US			0
29051300	--Butan-1-ol (n-butyl alcohol)	5.5					US			0
29051400	--Other butanols	5.5					US			0
29051500	--Pentanol (amyl alcohol) and isomers thereof	5.5					US			0
29051600	--Octanol (octyl alcohol) and isomers thereof	5.5					US			0
29051700	--Dodecan-1-ol (lauryl alcohol), hexadecan-1-ol (cetyl alcohol) and octadecan-1-ol (stearyl alcohol)	5.5					US			0
290519	--Other									
29051910	---Diethylhexanols	5.5								0
29051990	---Other	5.5					US			0
29052	-Unsaturated monohydric alcohols:									
29052200	--Acyclic terpene alcohols	5.5					US			0
29052900	--Other	5.5					US			0
29053	-Diols:									
29053100	--Ethylene glycol (ethanediol)	12	8 (2008)	5.5	2010*					0
29053200	--Propylene glycol (propane-1,2-diol)	5.5					US			0
29053900	--Other	5.5					US			0
29054	-Other polyhydric alcohols:									
29054100	--2-Ethyl-2-(hydroxymethyl)propane-1,3-diol (trimethylolpropane)	5.5					US			0
29054200	--Pentaerythritol	5.5					US			0
29054900	--Other	5.5					US			0

HS	Description	Bound rate at date of accession	Interim	Final Bound	Implementation	Present concession established	INR	Concession first incorporated in a GATT Schedule	Earlier INRs	ODCs
29055	-Halogenated, sulphonated, nitrated or nitrosated derivatives of acyclic alcohols:									
29055100	--Ethchlorvynol (INN)	5.5								0
29055900	--Other	5.5					US			0
2906	Cyclic alcohols and their halogenated, sulphonated, nitrated or nitrosated derivatives.									
29061	-Cyclanic, cyclenic or cycloterpenic:									
29061100	--Menthol	5.5					US			0
29061200	--Cyclohexanol, methylcyclohexanols and dimethylcyclo-hexanols	5.5					US			0
29061300	--Sterols and inositols	5.5					US			0
29061400	--Terpineols	5.5					US			0
29061900	--Other	5.5					US			0
29062	-Aromatic:									
29062100	--Benzyl alcohol	5.5					US			0
29062900	--Other	5.5					US			0
2907	Phenols; phenol-alcohols.									
29071	-Monophenols:									
29071100	--Phenol (hydroxybenzene) and its salts	5.5					US			0
29071200	--Cresols and their salts	5.5					US			0
29071300	--Octylphenol, nonylphenol and their isomers; salts thereof	5.5					US			0
29071400	--Xylenols and their salts	5.5					US			0
29071500	--Naphthols and their salts	5.5					US			0
29071900	--Other	5.5					US			0
29072	-Polyphenols; phenol-alcohols:									
29072100	--Resorcinol and its salts	5.5					US			0
29072200	--Hydroquinone (quinol) and its salts	5.5					US			0
29072300	--4,4'-Isopropylidenediphenol (bisphenol A, diphenylolpropane) and its salts	5.5					US			0
29072900	--Other	5.5					US			0
2908	Halogenated, sulphonated, nitrated or nitrosated derivatives of phenols or phenol-alcohols.									
29081000	-Derivatives containing only halogen substituents and their salts	5.5					US			0
29082000	-Derivatives containing only sulpho groups, their salts and esters	5.5					US			0
29089000	-Other	5.5					US			0

HS	Description	Bound rate at date of accession	Interim	Final Bound	Implementation	Present concession established	INR	Concession first incorporated in a GATT Schedule	Earlier INRs	ODCs
2909	Ethers, ether-alcohols, ether-phenols, ether-alcohol- phenols, alcohol peroxides, ether peroxides, ketone peroxides (whether or not chemically defined), and their halogenated, sulphonated, nitrated or nitrosated derivatives.									
29091	-Acyclic ethers and their halogenated, sulphonated, nitrated or nitrosated derivatives:									
29091100	--Diethyl ether	5.5					US			0
290919	--Other									
29091910	---Tert-butyl methyl ethers	12	8 (2008)	5.5	2010*					0
29091990	---Other acyclic ethers	5.5					US			0
29092000	-Cyclanic, cyclenic or cycloterpenic ethers and their halogenated, sulphonated, nitrated or nitrosated derivatives	5.5					US			0
29093000	-Aromatic ethers and their halogenated, sulphonated, nitrated or nitrosated derivatives	5.5					US			0
29094	-Ether-alcohols and their halogenated, sulphonated, nitrated or nitrosated derivatives:									
29094100	--2,2'-Oxydiethanol (diethylene glycol, digol)	5.5					US			0
29094200	--Monomethyl ethers of ethylene glycol or of diethylene glycol	5.5					US			0
29094300	--Monobutyl ethers of ethylene glycol or of diethylene glycol	5.5					US			0
29094400	--Other monoalkylethers of ethylene glycol or of diethylene glycol	5.5					US			0
29094900	--Other	5.5					US			0
29095000	-Ether-phenols, ether-alcohol-phenols and their halogenated, sulphonated, nitrated or nitrosated derivatives	5.5					US			0
29096000	-Alcohol peroxides, ether peroxides, ketone peroxides and their halogenated, sulphonated, nitrated or nitrosated derivatives	5.5					US			0
2910	Epoxides, epoxyalcohols, epoxyphenols and epoxyethers, with a three-membered ring, and their halogenated, sulphonated, nitrated or nitrosated derivatives.									

HS	Description	Bound rate at date of accession	Interim	Final Bound	Implementation	Present concession established	INR	Concession first incorporated in a GATT Schedule	Earlier INRs	ODCs
29101000	-Oxirane (ethylene oxide)	5.5					US			0
29102000	-Methyloxirane (propylene oxide)	5.5					US			0
29103000	-1-Chloro-2,3-epoxypropane (epichlorohydrin)	5.5					US			0
29109000	-Other	5.5					US			0
29110000	Acetals and hemiacetals, whether or not with other oxygen function, and their halogenated, sulphonated, nitrated or nitrosated derivatives.	5.5					US			0
2912	Aldehydes, whether or not with other oxygen function; cyclic polymers of aldehydes; paraformaldehyde.									
29121	-Acyclic aldehydes without other oxygen function:									
29121100	--Methanal (formaldehyde)	5.5					US			0
29121200	--Ethanal (acetaldehyde)	5.5					US			0
29121300	--Butanal (butyraldehyde, normal isomer)	5.5					US			0
29121900	--Other	5.5					US			0
29122	-Cyclic aldehydes without other oxygen function:									
29122100	--Benzaldehyde	5.5					US			0
29122900	--Other	5.5					US			0
29123000	-Aldehyde-alcohols	5.5					US			0
29124	-Aldehyde-ethers, aldehyde-phenols and aldehydes with other oxygen function:									
29124100	--Vanillin (4-hydroxy-3-methoxybenzaldehyde)	5.5					US			0
29124200	--Ethylvanillin (3-ethoxy-4-hydroxybenzaldehyde)	5.5					US			0
29124900	--Other	5.5					US			0
29125000	-Cyclic polymers of aldehydes	5.5					US			0
29126000	-Paraformaldehyde	5.5					US			0
29130000	Halogenated, sulphonated, nitrated or nitrosated derivatives of products of heading 29.12.	5.5					US			0
2914	Ketones and quinones, whether or not with other oxygen function, and their halogenated, sulphonated, nitrated or nitrosated derivatives.									
29141	-Acyclic ketones without other oxygen function:									

HS	Description	Bound rate at date of accession	Interim	Final Bound	Implementation	Present concession established	INR	Concession first incorporated in a GATT Schedule	Earlier INRs	ODCs
29141100	--Acetone	5.5					US			0
29141200	--Butanone (methyl ethyl ketone)	5.5					US			0
29141300	--4-Methylpentan-2-one (methyl isobutyl ketone)	5.5					US			0
29141900	--Other	5.5					US			0
29142	-Cyclanic, cyclenic or cycloterpenic ketones without other oxygen function:									
29142100	--Camphor	5.5					US			0
29142200	--Cyclohexanone and methylcyclohexanones	5.5					US			0
29142300	--Ionones and methylionones	5.5					US			0
29142900	--Other	5.5					US			0
29143	-Aromatic ketones without other oxygen function:									
29143100	--Phenylacetone (phenylpropan-2-one)	5.5					US			0
29143900	--Other	5.5					US			0
29144000	-Ketone-alcohols and ketone-aldehydes	5.5					US			0
29145000	-Ketone-phenols and ketones with other oxygen function	5.5					US			0
29146	-Quinones:									
29146100	--Anthraquinone	5.5					US			0
29146900	--Other	5.5					US			0
29147000	-Halogenated, sulphonated, nitrated or nitrosated derivatives	5.5					US			0
2915	Saturated acyclic monocarboxylic acids and their anhydrides, halides, peroxides and peroxyacids; their halogenated, sulphonated, nitrated or nitrosated derivatives.									
29151	-Formic acid, its salts and esters:									
29151100	--Formic acid	5.5					US			0
29151200	--Salts of formic acid	5.5					US			0
29151300	--Esters of formic acid	5.5					US			0
29152	-Acetic acid and its salts; acetic anhydride:									
291521	--Acetic acid									
29152110	---Acetic acid denatured and unusable as vinegar	5.5					US			0
29152120	---Acetic acid useable as vinegar	5.5					US			0
29152200	--Sodium acetate	5.5					US			0
29152300	--Cobalt acetates	5.5					US			0
29152400	--Acetic anhydride	5.5					US			0

HS	Description	Bound rate at date of accession	Interim	Final Bound	Implementation	Present concession established	INR	Concession first incorporated in a GATT Schedule	Earlier INRs	ODCs
29152900	--Other	5.5					US			0
29153	-Esters of acetic acid:									
29153100	--Ethyl acetate	5.5					US			0
29153200	--Vinyl acetate	5.5					US			0
29153300	--n-Butyl acetate	5.5					US			0
29153400	--Isobutyl acetate	5.5					US			0
29153500	--2-Ethoxyethyl acetate	5.5					US			0
29153900	--Other	5.5					US			0
29154000	-Mono-, di- or trichloroacetic acids, their salts and esters	5.5					US			0
29155000	-Propionic acid, its salts and esters	5.5					US			0
29156000	-Butanoic acids, pentanoic acids, their salts and esters	5.5					US			0
29157000	-Palmitic acid, stearic acid, their salts and esters	5.5					US			0
29159000	-Other	5.5					US			0
2916	Unsaturated acyclic monocarboxylic acids, cyclic monocarboxylic acids, their anhydrides, halides, peroxides and peroxyacids; their halogenated, sulphonated, nitrated or nitrosated derivatives.									
29161	-Unsaturated acyclic monocarboxylic acids, their anhydrides, halides, peroxides, peroxyacids and their derivatives:									
29161100	--Acrylic acid and its salts	6.5					US			0
29161200	--Esters of acrylic acid	6.5					US			0
29161300	--Methacrylic acid and its salts	6.5					US			0
29161400	--Esters of methacrylic acid	6.5					US			0
29161500	--Oleic, linoleic or linolenic acids, their salts and esters	6.5					US			0
29161900	--Other	6.5					US			0
29162000	-Cyclanic, cyclenic or cycloterpenic monocarboxylic acids, their anhydrides, halides, peroxides, peroxyacids and their derivatives	6.5					US			0
29163	-Aromatic monocarboxylic acids, their anhydrides, halides, peroxides, peroxyacids and their derivatives:									
29163100	--Benzoic acid, its salts and esters	6.5					US			0
29163200	--Benzoyl peroxide and benzoyl chloride	6.5					US			0
29163400	--Phenylacetic acid and its salts	6.5					US			0

HS	Description	Bound rate at date of accession	Interim	Final Bound	Implementation	Present concession established	INR	Concession first incorporated in a GATT Schedule	Earlier INRs	ODCs
29163500	--Esters of phenylacetic acid	6.5					US			0
29163900	--Other	6.5					US			0
2917	Polycarboxylic acids, their anhydrides, halides, peroxides and peroxyacids; their halogenated, sulphonated, nitrated or nitrosated derivatives.									
29171	-Acyclic polycarboxylic acids, their anhydrides, halides, peroxides, peroxyacids and their derivatives:									
29171100	--Oxalic acid, its salts and esters	6.5					US			0
29171200	--Adipic acid, its salts and esters	6.5					US			0
29171300	--Azelaic acid, sebacic acid, their salts and esters	6.5					US			0
29171400	--Maleic anhydride	6.5					US			0
29171900	--Other	6.5					US			0
29172000	-Cyclanic, cyclenic or cycloterpenic polycarboxylic acids, their anhydrides, halides, peroxides, peroxyacids and their derivatives	6.5					US			0
29173	-Aromatic polycarboxylic acids, their anhydrides, halides, peroxides, peroxyacids and their derivatives:									
29173100	--Dibutyl orthophthalates	6.5					US			0
29173200	--Dioctyl orthophthalates	6.5					US			0
29173300	--Dinonyl or didecyl orthophthalates	6.5					US			0
29173400	--Other esters of orthophthalic acid	6.5					US			0
29173500	--Phthalic anhydride	6.5					US			0
29173600	--Terephthalic acid and its salts	12	8 (2008)	6.5	2010					0
29173700	--Dimethyl terephthalate	6.5					US			0
29173900	--Other	6.5					US			0
2918	Carboxylic acids with additional oxygen function and their anhydrides, halides, peroxides and peroxyacids; their halogenated, sulphonated, nitrated or nitrosated derivatives.									
29181	-Carboxylic acids with alcohol function but without other oxygen function, their anhydrides, halides, peroxides, peroxyacids and their derivatives:									
29181100	--Lactic acid, its salts and esters	6.5					US			0
29181200	--Tartaric acid	6.5					US			0
29181300	--Salts and esters of tartaric acid	6.5					US			0
29181400	--Citric acid	6.5					US			0

HS	Description	Bound rate at date of accession	Interim	Final Bound	Implementation	Present concession established	INR	Concession first incorporated in a GATT Schedule	Earlier INRs	ODCs
29181500	--Salts and esters of citric acid	6.5					US			0
29181600	--Gluconic acid, its salts and esters	6.5					US			0
291819	--Other									
29181910	---2,2-Diphynyl-2-hydroxyacetic acid (benzilic acid)	6.5								0
29181990	---Other	6.5								0
29182	-Carboxylic acids with phenol function but without other oxygen function, their anhydrides, halides, peroxides, peroxyacids and their derivatives:									
29182100	--Salicylic acid and its salts	6.5					US			0
29182200	--O-Acetylsalicylic acid, its salts and esters	6.5					US			0
29182300	--Other esters of salicylic acid and their salts	6.5					US			0
29182900	--Other	6.5					CH,US			0
29183000	-Carboxylic acids with aldehyde or ketone function but without other oxygen function, their anhydrides, halides, peroxides, peroxyacids and their derivatives	6.5					US			0
29189000	-Other	6.5					US			0
29190000	Phosphoric esters and their salts, including lactophosphates; their halogenated, sulphonated, nitrated or nitrosated derivatives.	6.5					US			0
2920	Esters of other inorganic acids of non-metals (excluding esters of hydrogen halides) and their salts; their halogenated, sulphonated, nitrated or nitrosated derivatives.									
29201000	-Thiophosphoric esters (phosphorothioates) and their salts; their halogenated, sulphonated, nitrated or nitrosated derivatives	6.5					US			0
292090	-Other									
29209010	---Trimethyl phosphite	6.5					US			0
29209020	---Triethyl phosphite	6.5					US			0
29209030	---Dimethyl phosphite	6.5					US			0
29209040	---Diethyl phosphite	6.5					US			0
29209090	---Other	6.5					US			0
2921	Amine-function compounds.									
29211	-Acyclic monoamines and their derivatives; salts thereof:									

HS	Description	Bound rate at date of accession	Interim	Final Bound	Implementation	Present concession established	INR	Concession first incorporated in a GATT Schedule	Earlier INRs	ODCs
29211100	--Methylamine, di- or trimethylamine and their salts	6.5					US			0
29211200	--Diethylamine and its salts	6.5					US			0
292119	--Other									
29211910	---Bis(2-chloroethyl)ethylamine	6.5					US			0
29211920	---Chloromethine (INN) (bis(2-chloroethyl)methylamine)	6.5					US			0
29211930	---Trichloromethine (INN) (tris(2-chloroethyl)methylamine)	6.5					US			0
29211940	---N,N-dialkyl(methyl, ethyl, n-propyl or isopropyl) 2-chloroethylamines and their protonated salts	6.5					US			0
29211990	---Other	6.5					US			0
29212	-Acyclic polyamines and their derivatives; salts thereof:									
29212100	--Ethylenediamine and its salts	6.5					US			0
29212200	--Hexamethylenediamine and its salts	6.5					US			0
29212900	--Other	6.5					US			0
29213000	-Cyclanic, cyclenic or cycloterpenic mono- or polyamines, and their derivatives; salts thereof	6.5					US			0
29214	-Aromatic monoamines and their derivatives; salts thereof:									
29214100	--Aniline and its salts	6.5					US			0
29214200	--Aniline derivatives and their salts	6.5					US			0
29214300	--Toluidines and their derivatives; salts thereof	6.5					US			0
29214400	--Diphenylamine and its derivatives; salts thereof	6.5					US			0
29214500	--1-Naphthylamine (alpha-naphthylamine), 2-naphthylamine (beta-naphthylamine) and their derivatives; salts thereof	6.5					US			0
29214600	--Amfetamine (INN), benzfetamine (INN), dexamfetamine (INN), etilamfetamine (INN), fencamfefamin (INN), lefetamine (INN), levamfetamine (INN), mefenorex (INN) and phentermine (INN); salts thereof	6.5					US			0
29214900	--Other	6.5					US			0
29215	-Aromatic polyamines and their derivatives; salts thereof:									

HS	Description	Bound rate at date of accession	Interim	Final Bound	Implementation	Present concession established	INR	Concession first incorporated in a GATT Schedule	Earlier INRs	ODCs
29215100	--o-, m-, p-Phenylenediamine, diaminotoluenes, and their derivatives; salts thereof	6.5					US			0
29215900	--Other	6.5					US			0
2922	Oxygen-function amino-compounds.									
29221	-Amino-alcohols, other than those containing more than one kind of oxygen function, their ethers and esters; salts thereof:									
29221100	--Monoethanolamine and its salts	6.5					US			0
29221200	--Diethanolamine and its salts	6.5					US			0
292213	--Triethanolamine and its salts									
29221310	---Triethanolamine	6.5								0
29221390	---Other	6.5					US			0
29221400	--Dextropropoxyphene (INN) and its salts	6.5					US			0
292219	--Other									
29221911	----N,N-Dimethyl-2-aminoethanols and their protonated salts	6.5					US			0
29221912	----N,N-Diethyl-2-aminoethanols and their protonated salts	6.5					US			0
29221919	----Other	6.5					US			0
29221920	---Ethyldiethanolamine	6.5					US			0
29221930	---Methyldiethanolamine	6.5					US			0
29221990	---Other	6.5					US			0
29222	-Amino-naphthols and other amino-phenols, other than those containing more than one kind of oxygen function, their ethers and esters; salts thereof:									
29222100	--Aminohydroxynaphthalenesulphonic acids and their salts	6.5					US			0
29222200	--Anisidines, dianisidines, phenetidines, and their salts	6.5					US			0
29222900	--Other	6.5					US			0
29223	-Amino-aldehydes, amino-ketones and amino-quinones, other than those containing more than one kind of oxygen function; salts thereof:									
29223100	--Amfepramone (INN), methadone (INN) and normethadone (INN); salts thereof	6.5								0
29223900	--Other	6.5					US			0

HS	Description	Bound rate at date of accession	Interim	Final Bound	Implementation	Present concession established	INR	Concession first incorporated in a GATT Schedule	Earlier INRs	ODCs
29224	-Amino-acids, other than those containing more than one kind of oxygen function, and their esters; salts thereof:									
29224100	--Lysine and its esters; salts thereof	6.5					US			0
29224200	--Glutamic acid and its salts	6.5					US			0
29224300	--Anthranilic acid and its salts	6.5					US			0
29224400	--Tilidine (INN) and its salts	6.5					US			0
29224900	--Other	6.5					US			0
29225000	-Amino-alcohol-phenols, amino-acid-phenols and other amino-compounds with oxygen function	6.5					US			0
2923	Quaternary ammonium salts and hydroxides; lecithins and other phosphoaminolipids, whether or not chemically defined.									
29231000	-Choline and its salts	6.5					US			0
29232000	-Lecithins and other phosphoaminolipids	6.5					US			0
29239000	-Other	6.5					US			0
2924	Carboxyamide-function compounds; amide-function compounds of carbonic acid.									
29241	-Acyclic amides (including acyclic carbamates) and their derivatives; salts thereof:									
29241100	--Meprobamate (INN)	6.5								0
29241900	--Other	6.5					US			0
29242	-Cyclic amides (including cyclic carbamates) and their derivatives; salts thereof:									
29242100	--Ureines and their derivatives; salts thereof	6.5					US			0
29242300	--2-Acetamidobenzoic acid (N-acetylanthranilic acid) and its salts	6.5					US			0
29242400	--Ethinamate (INN)	6.5					US			0
29242900	--Other	6.5					US			0
2925	Carboxyimide-function compounds (including saccharin and its salts) and imine-function compounds.									
29251	-Imides and their derivatives; salts thereof:									
29251100	--Saccharin and its salts	6.5					US			0
29251200	--Glutethimide (INN)	6.5					US			0

HS	Description	Bound rate at date of accession	Interim	Final Bound	Implementation	Present concession established	INR	Concession first incorporated in a GATT Schedule	Earlier INRs	ODCs
29251900	--Other	6.5					US			0
29252000	-Imines and their derivatives; salts thereof	6.5					US			0
2926	Nitrile-function compounds.									
29261000	-Acrylonitrile	6.5					US			0
29262000	-1-Cyanoguanidine (dicyandiamide)	6.5					US			0
29263000	-Fenproporex (INN) and its salts; methadone (INN) intermediate (4-cyano-2-dimethylamino-4,4-diphenylbutane)	6.5					US			0
29269000	-Other	6.5					US			0
29270000	Diazo-, azo- or azoxy-compounds.	6.5					US			0
29280000	Organic derivatives of hydrazine or of hydroxylamine.	6.5					US			0
2929	Compounds with other nitrogen function.									
29291000	-Isocyanates	6.5					US			0
292990	-Other									
29299010	---N,N-Dialkyl (methyl, ethyl, n-propyl or isopropyl) phosphoramidic dihalides	6.5					US			0
29299020	---Dialkyl (methyl, ethyl, n-propyl or isopropyl) phosphoramidic dihalides N,N-dialkyl (methyl, ethyl, n-propyl or isopropyl) phosphoramidates	6.5					US			0
29299090	---Other	6.5					US			0
2930	Organo-sulphur compounds.									
29301000	-Dithiocarbonates (xanthates)	6.5					US			0
29302000	-Thiocarbamates and dithiocarbamates	6.5					US			0
29303000	-Thiuram mono-, di- or tetrasulphides	6.5					US			0
29304000	-Methionine	6.5					US			0
293090	-Other									
29309010	---[S-2 dialkyl (methyl, ethyl, n-propyl or isopropyl) amino)ethyl] hydrogen alkyl (methyl, ethyl, n-propyl or isopropyl) phosphonothioates and their O-alkyl (£ C10, including cycloalkyl) esters; alkylated and protonated salts thereof	6.5					US			0
29309020	---2-Chloroethylchloromethylsulphide	6.5					US			0
29309030	---Bis(2-chloroethyl)sulphide	6.5					US			0
29309040	---Bis(2-chloroethylthio)methane	6.5					US			0
29309050	---1,2-Bis(2-chloroethylthio)ethane	6.5					US			0
29309060	---1,3-Bis(2-chloroethylthio)-n-propane	6.5					US			0
29309070	---1,4-Bis(2-chloroethylthio)-n-butane	6.5					US			0
29309080	---1,5-Bis(2-chloroethylthio)-n-pentane	6.5					US			0
2930909	---Other:									

HS	Description	Bound rate at date of accession	Interim	Final Bound	Implementation	Present concession established	INR	Concession first incorporated in a GATT Schedule	Earlier INRs	ODCs
29309091	----Bis(2-chloroethylthiomethyl)ether	6.5					US			0
29309092	----Bis(2-chloroethylthioethyl)ether	6.5					US			0
29309093	----O,O-Diethyl S-[2 diethyl amino) ethyl] phosphorothioates and its alkylated protonated salts	6.5					US			0
29309094	----N,N-Dialkyl (methyl, ethyl, n-propyl or isopropyl)aminoethane-2-thiols and their protonated salts	6.5					US			0
29309095	----Thiodiglycol (INN) (bis(2-hydoxyethyl)sulphide)	6.5					US			0
29309096	----O-Ethyl S-phethyl ethylphosphonothiolothionates (fonofos)	6.5					US			0
29309097	----Containing a phosphorus atom to which is bonded one methyl, ethyl, n-propyl or isopropyl group but not further carbon atoms	6.5					US			0
29309099	----Other	6.5					US			0
2931	Other organo-inorganic compounds.									
29310010	---O-alkyl (£ C10, including cycloalkyl) alkyl (methyl, ethyl, n-propyl or isopropyl) phosphonofluoridates	6.5					US			0
29310020	---O-alkyl (£ C10, including cycloalkyl) N,N-dialkyl (methyl, ethyl, n-propyl or isopropyl) phosphoraamidocyanidates	6.5					US			0
29310030	---2-Chlorovinyldichloroarsine	6.5					US			0
29310040	---Bis(2-Chlorovinyl)dichloroarsine	6.5					US			0
29310050	---Tris(2-Chlorovinyl)arsine	6.5					US			0
29310060	---Alkyl (methyl, ethyl, n-propyl or isopropyl) phosphonyldifluorides	6.5					US			0
29310070	---[S-2-(dialkyl (methyl, ethyl, n-propyl or isopropyl) amino)ethyl] hydrogen alkyl (methyl, ethyl, n-propyl or isopropyl) phosphonites and their O-alkyl (£ C10, including cycloalkyl) esters; alkylated and protonated salts thereof	6.5					US			0
29310080	---O-Isopropyl methylphosphonochloridate	6.5					US			0
2931009	---Other:									
29310091	----Containing a phosphorus atom to which is bonded one methyl, ethyl, n-propyl or isopropyl group but not further carbon atoms	6.5					US			0
29310099	----Other	6.5					US			0

HS	Description	Bound rate at date of accession	Interim	Final Bound	Implementation	Present concession established	INR	Concession first incorporated in a GATT Schedule	Earlier INRs	ODCs
2932	Heterocyclic compounds with oxygen hetero-atom(s) only.									
29321	-Compounds containing an unfused furan ring (whether or not hydrogenated) in the structure:									
29321100	--Tetrahydrofuran	6.5					US			0
29321200	--2-Furaldehyde (furfuraldehyde)	6.5					US			0
29321300	--Furfuryl alcohol and tetrahydrofurfuryl alcohol	6.5					US			0
29321900	--Other	6.5					US			0
29322	-Lactones:									
29322100	--Coumarin, methylcoumarins and ethylcoumarins	6.5					US			0
29322900	--Other lactones	6.5					US			0
29329	-Other:									
29329100	--Isosafrole	6.5					US			0
29329200	--1-(1,3-Benzodioxol-5-yl)propan-2-one	6.5					US			0
29329300	--Piperonal	6.5					US			0
29329400	--Safrole	6.5					US			0
29329500	--Tetrahydrocannabinols (all isomers)	6.5					US			0
29329900	--Other	6.5					US			0
2933	Heterocyclic compounds with nitrogen hetero-atom(s) only.									
29331	-Compounds containing an unfused pyrazole ring (whether or not hydrogenated) in the structure:									
29331100	--Phenazone (antipyrin) and its derivatives	6.5					US			0
29331900	--Other	6.5					US			0
29332	-Compounds containing an unfused imidazole ring (whether or not hydrogenated) in the structure:									
29332100	--Hydantoin and its derivatives	6.5					US			0
29332900	--Other	6.5					US			0
29333	-Compounds containing an unfused pyridine ring (whether or not hydrogenated) in the structure:									
29333100	--Pyridine and its salts	6.5					US			0
29333200	--Piperidine and its salts	6.5					US			0

HS	Description	Bound rate at date of accession	Interim	Final Bound	Implementation	Present concession established	INR	Concession first incorporated in a GATT Schedule	Earlier INRs	ODCs
29333300	--Alfentanil (INN), anileridine (INN), bezitramide (INN), bromazepam (INN), difenoxin (INN), diphenoxylate (INN), dipipanone (INN), fentanyl (INN), ketobemidone (INN), methylphenidate (INN), pentazocine (INN), pethidine (INN), pethidine (INN) intermediate A, phencyclidine (INN) (PCP), phenoperidine (INN), pipradrol (INN), piritramide (INN), propiram (INN) and trimeperidine (INN); salts thereof	6.5					US			0
293339	--Other									
29333910	---3-Quinuclidinyl benzilate	6.5					CH,US			0
29333920	---Quinuclidine-3-ol	6.5					CH,US			0
29333990	---Other	6.5					CH,US			0
29334	-Compounds containing in the structure a quinoline or isoquinoline ring-system (whether or not hydrogenated), not further fused:									
29334100	--Levorphanol (INN) and its salts	6.5					CH			0
29334900	--Other	6.5					CH,US			0
29335	-Compounds containing a pyrimidine ring (whether or not hydrogenated) or piperazine ring in the structure:									
29335200	--Malonylurea (barbituric acid) and its salts	6.5								0
29335300	--Allobarbital (INN), amobarbital (INN), barbital (INN), butalbital (INN), butobarbital, cyclobarbital (INN), methylphenobarbital (INN), pentobarbital (INN), phenobarbital (INN), secbutabarbital (INN), secobarbital (INN) and vinylbital (INN); salts thereof	6.5					US			0
29335400	--Other derivatives of malonylurea (barbituric acid); salts thereof	6.5					US			0
29335500	--Loprazolam (INN), mecloqualone (INN), methaqualone (INN) and zipeprol (INN); salts thereof	6.5					US			0
29335900	--Other	6.5					CH,US			0
29336	-Compounds containing an unfused triazine ring (whether or not hydrogenated) in the structure:									
29336100	--Melamine	12	8 (2008)	6.5	2010		US			0
29336900	--Other	6.5					CH,US			0

HS	Description	Bound rate at date of accession	Interim	Final Bound	Implementation	Present concession established	INR	Concession first incorporated in a GATT Schedule	Earlier INRs	ODCs
29337	-Lactams:									
29337100	--6-Hexanelactam (epsilon-caprolactam)	6.5					US			0
29337200	--Clobazam (INN) and methyprylon (INN)	6.5					US			0
29337900	--Other lactams	6.5					CH,US			0
29339	-Other:									
29339100	--Alprazolam (INN), camazepam (INN), chlordiazepoxide (INN), clonazepam (INN), clorazepate, delorazepam (INN), diazepam (INN), estazolam (INN), ethyl loflazepate (INN), fludiazepam (INN), flunitrazepam (INN), flurazepam (INN), halazepam (INN), lorazepam (INN), lormetazepam (INN), mazindol (INN), medazepam (INN), midazolam (INN), nimetazepam (INN), nitrazepam (INN), nordazepam (INN), oxazepam (INN), pinazepam (INN), prazepam (INN), pyrovalerone (INN), temazepam (INN), tetrazepam (INN) and triazolam (INN); salts thereof	6.5					CH,US			0
29339900	--Other	6.5					CH,US			0
2934	Nucleic acids and their salts, whether or not chemically defined; other heterocyclic compounds.									
29341000	-Compounds containing an unfused thiazole ring (whether or not hydrogenated) in the structure	6.5					US			0
29342000	-Compounds containing in the structure a benzothiazole ring-system (whether or not hydrogenated), not further fused	6.5					US			0
29343000	-Compounds containing in the structure a phenothiazine ring-system (whether or not hydrogenated), not further fused	6.5					US			0
29349	-Other:									
29349100	--Aminorex (INN), brotizolam (INN), clotiazepam (INN), cloxazolam (INN), dextromoramide (INN), haloxazolam (INN), ketazolam (INN), mesocarb (INN), oxazolam (INN), pemoline (INN), phendimetrazine (INN), phenmetrazine (INN) and sufentanil (INN); salts thereof	6.5					US			0
29349900	--Other	6.5					US			0
29350000	Sulphonamides.	6.5					CH,US			0

HS	Description	Bound rate at date of accession	Interim	Final Bound	Implementation	Present concession established	INR	Concession first incorporated in a GATT Schedule	Earlier INRs	ODCs
2936	Provitamins and vitamins, natural or reproduced by synthesis (including natural concentrates), derivatives thereof used primarily as vitamins, and intermixtures of the foregoing, whether or not in any solvent.									
29361000	-Provitamins, unmixed	0					US			0
29362	-Vitamins and their derivatives, unmixed:									
29362100	--Vitamins A and their derivatives	0					US			0
29362200	--Vitamin B1 and its derivatives	0								0
29362300	--Vitamin B2 and its derivatives	0								0
29362400	--D- or DL-Pantothenic acid (Vitamin B3 or Vitamin B5) and its derivatives	0								0
29362500	--Vitamin B6 and its derivatives	0								0
29362600	--Vitamin B12 and its derivatives	0								0
29362700	--Vitamin C and its derivatives	0					US			0
29362800	--Vitamin E and its derivatives	0								0
29362900	--Other vitamins and their derivatives	0					US			0
29369000	-Other, including natural concentrates	0					US			0
2937	Hormones, prostaglandins, thromboxanes and leukotrienes, natural or reproduced by synthesis; derivatives and structural analogues thereof, including chain modified polypeptides, used primarily as hormones.									
29371	-Polypeptide hormones, protein hormones and glycoprotein hormones, their derivatives and structural analogues:									
29371100	--Somatotropin, its derivatives and structural analogues	0					US			0
29371200	--Insulin and its salts	0					US			0
29371900	--Other	0					US			0
29372	-Steroidal hormones, their derivatives and structural analogues:									
29372100	--Cortisone, hydrocortisone, prednisone (dehydrocortisone) and prednisolone (dehydrohydrocortisone)	0					US			0
29372200	--Halogenated derivatives of adrenal corticosteroidal hormones	0					US			0
29372300	--Oestrogens and progestogens	0					US			0
29372900	--Other	0					US			0

HS	Description	Bound rate at date of accession	Interim	Final Bound	Implementation	Present concession established	INR	Concession first incorporated in a GATT Schedule	Earlier INRs	ODCs
29373	-Catecholamine hormones, their derivatives and structural analogues:									
29373100	--Epinephrine	0					US			0
29373900	--Other	0					US			0
29374000	-Amino-acid derivatives	0					US			0
29375000	-Prostaglandins, thromboxanes and leukotrienes, their derivatives and structural analogues	0					US			0
29379000	-Other	0					US			0
2938	Glycosides, natural or reproduced by synthesis, and their salts, ethers, esters and other derivatives.									
29381000	-Rutoside (rutin) and its derivatives	6.5					US			0
29389000	-Other	6.5					US			0
2939	Vegetable alkaloids, natural or reproduced by synthesis, and their salts, ethers, esters and other derivatives.									
29391	-Alkaloids of opium and their derivatives; salts thereof:									
29391100	--Concentrates of poppy straw; buprenorphine (INN), codeine, dihydrocodeine (INN), ethylmorphine, etorphine (INN), heroin, hydrocodone (INN), hydromorphone (INN), morphine, nicomorphine (INN), oxycodone (INN), oxymorphone (INN), pholcodine (INN), thebacon (INN) and thebaine; salts thereof	0					US			0
29391900	--Other	0					US			0
29392	-Alkaloids of cinchona and their derivatives; salts thereof:									
29392100	--Quinine and its salts	0								0
29392900	--Other	0								0
29393000	-Caffeine and its salts	0					US			0
29394	-Ephedrines and their salts:									
29394100	--Ephedrine and its salts	0								0
29394200	--Pseudoephedrine (INN) and its salts	0					US			0
29394300	--Cathine (INN) and its salts	0					US			0
29394900	--Other	0								0
29395	-Theophylline and aminophylline (theophylline-ethylenedia-mine) and their derivatives; salts thereof:									
29395100	--Fenetylline (INN) and its salts	0					US			0

HS	Description	Bound rate at date of accession	Interim	Final Bound	Implementation	Present concession established	INR	Concession first incorporated in a GATT Schedule	Earlier INRs	ODCs
29395900	--Other	0					US			0
29396	-Alkaloids of rye ergot and their derivatives; salts thereof:									
29396100	--Ergometrine (INN) and its salts	0					US			0
29396200	--Ergotamine (INN) and its salts	0					US			0
29396300	--Lysergic acid and its salts	0								0
29396900	--Other	0								0
29399	-Other:									
293991	--Cocaine, ecgonine, levometamfetamine, metamfetamine (INN), metamfetamine racemate; salts, esters and other derivatives thereof									
29399110	---Cocaine	P								0
29399190	---Other	0					US			0
29399900	--Other	0					US			0
29400000	Sugars, chemically pure, other than sucrose, lactose, maltose, glucose and fructose; sugar ethers, sugar acetals and sugar esters, and their salts, other than products of heading 29.37, 29.38 or 29.39.	6.5					US			0
2941	Antibiotics.									
29411000	-Penicillins and their derivatives with a penicillanic acid structure; salts thereof	0					IN			0
29412000	-Streptomycins and their derivatives; salts thereof	0								0
29413000	-Tetracyclines and their derivatives; salts thereof	0								0
29414000	-Chloramphenicol and its derivatives; salts thereof	0								0
29415000	-Erythromycin and its derivatives; salts thereof	0					AU			0
29419000	-Other	0					IN,US			0
29420000	Other organic compounds.	6.5					IN,US			0
3001	Glands and other organs for organo-therapeutic uses, dried, whether or not powdered; extracts of glands or other organs or of their secretions for organo-therapeutic uses; heparin and its salts; other human or animal substances prepared for therapeutic or prophylactic uses, not elsewhere specified or included.									

HS	Description	Bound rate at date of accession	Interim	Final Bound	Implementation	Present concession established	INR	Concession first incorporated in a GATT Schedule	Earlier INRs	ODCs
30011000	-Glands and other organs, dried, whether or not powdered	0								0
30012000	-Extracts of glands or other organs or of their secretions	0					US			0
30019000	-Other	0					US			0
3002	Human blood; animal blood prepared for therapeutic, prophylactic or diagnostic uses; antisera and other blood fractions and modified immunological products, whether or not obtained by means of biotechnological processes; vaccines, toxins, cultures of micro-organisms (excluding yeasts) and similar products.									
30021000	-Antisera and other blood fractions and modified immunological products, whether or not obtained by means of biotechnological processes	0					US			0
30022000	-Vaccines for human medicine	0					US			0
30023000	-Vaccines for veterinary medicine	0					US			0
300290	-Other									
30029010	---Saxitoxin	0					US			0
30029020	---Ricin	0					US			0
30029090	---Other	0					US			0
3003	Medicaments (excluding goods of heading 30.02, 30.05 or 30.06) consisting of two or more constituents which have been mixed together for therapeutic or prophylactic uses, not put up in measured doses or in forms or packings for retail sale.									
30031000	-Containing penicillins or derivatives thereof, with a penicillanic acid structure, or streptomycins or their derivatives	0					US			0
30032000	-Containing other antibiotics	0					DO,HN,US			0
30033	-Containing hormones or other products of heading 29.37 but not containing antibiotics:									
30033100	--Containing insulin	0					US			0
30033900	--Other	0					US			0
30034000	-Containing alkaloids or derivatives thereof but not containing hormones or other products of heading 29.37 or antibiotics	0								0

HS	Description	Bound rate at date of accession	Interim	Final Bound	Implementation	Present concession established	INR	Concession first incorporated in a GATT Schedule	Earlier INRs	ODCs
30039000	-Other	0					US			0
3004	Medicaments (excluding goods of heading 30.02, 30.05 or 30.06) consisting of mixed or unmixed products for therapeutic or prophylactic uses, put up in measured doses (including those in the form of transdermal administration systems) or in forms or packings for retail sale.									
30041000	-Containing penicillins or derivatives thereof, with a penicillanic acid structure, or streptomycins or their derivatives	0					DO,HN,US			0
30042000	-Containing other antibiotics	0					CH,DO,HN,US			0
30043	-Containing hormones or other products of heading 29.37 but not containing antibiotics:									
30043100	--Containing insulin	0					US			0
30043200	--Containing corticosteroid hormones, their derivatives and structural analogues	0					CH,US			0
30043900	--Other	0					CH,US			0
30044000	-Containing alkaloids or derivatives thereof but not containing hormones, other products of heading 29.37 or antibiotics	0					CH,US			0
30045000	-Other medicaments containing vitamins or other products of heading 29.36	0					CA,CH,DO,HN,IN,US			0
300490	-Other									
30049010	---Medical solutions put up in measured doses or in forms or packing for retail sale	0					CA,CH,DO,HN,IN,US			0
30049090	---Other medicaments	0					CA,CH,DO,HN,IN,US			0
3005	Wadding, gauze, bandages and similar articles (for example, dressings, adhesive plasters, poultices), impregnated or coated with pharmaceutical substances or put up in forms or packings for retail sale for medical, surgical, dental or veterinary purposes.									
30051000	-Adhesive dressings and other articles having an adhesive layer	0					CH,DO,HN,US			0
300590	-Other									

HS	Description	Bound rate at date of accession	Interim	Final Bound	Implementation	Present concession established	INR	Concession first incorporated in a GATT Schedule	Earlier INRs	ODCs
30059010	---Cotton wool	0					US			0
3005902	---Gauze, bandages and similar article:									
30059021	----Wadding covered or saturated with pharmaceuticals	0					US			0
30059022	----Wadding not covered or saturated with pharmaceuticals	0					US			0
30059090	---Other adhesive	0					US			0
3006	Pharmaceutical goods specified in Note 4 to this Chapter.									
300610	-Sterile surgical catgut, similar sterile suture materials and sterile tissue adhesives for surgical wound closure; sterile laminaria and sterile laminaria tents; sterile absorbable surgical or dental haemostatics									
30061010	---Sterile surgical catgut for surgical closures	0					US			0
30061020	---Sterile laminaria	0					US			0
30061030	---Sterile absorbable surgical or dental haemostatics	0					US			0
30061040	---Sterilized surgical plasters	0					US			0
30062000	-Blood-grouping reagents	0					US			0
30063000	-Opacifying preparations for X-ray examinations; diagnostic reagents designed to be administered to the patient	0					US			0
30064000	-Dental cements and other dental fillings; bone reconstruction cements	0					US			0
30065000	-First-aid boxes and kits	0					US			0
30066000	-Chemical contraceptive preparations based on hormones, on other products of heading 29.37 or on spermicides	0								0
30067000	-Gel preparations designed to be used in human or veterinary medicine as a lubricant for parts of the body for surgical operations or physical examinations or as a coupling agent between the body and medical instruments	6.5	4.8 (2008), 2.4 (2009)	0	2010		US			0
30068000	-Waste pharmaceuticals	0					DO,HN,IN			0
31010000	Animal or vegetable fertilisers, whether or not mixed together or chemically treated; fertilisers produced by the mixing or chemical treatment of animal or vegetable products.	12	8 (2008)	6.5	2010*		US			0

HS	Description	Bound rate at date of accession	Interim	Final Bound	Implementation	Present concession established	INR	Concession first incorporated in a GATT Schedule	Earlier INRs	ODCs
3102	Mineral or chemical fertilisers, nitrogenous.									
31021000	-Urea, whether or not in aqueous solution	12	8 (2008)	6.5	2010*		US			0
31022	-Ammonium sulphate; double salts and mixtures of ammonium sulphate and ammonium nitrate:									
31022100	--Ammonium sulphate	12	8 (2008)	6.5	2010*		US			0
31022900	--Other	12	8 (2008)	6.5	2010*		US			0
31023000	-Ammonium nitrate, whether or not in aqueous solution	12	8 (2008)	6.5	2010*		US			0
31024000	-Mixtures of ammonium nitrate with calcium carbonate or other inorganic non-fertilising substances	12	8 (2008)	6.5	2010*		US			0
31025000	-Sodium nitrate	12	8 (2008)	6.5	2010*		US			0
31026000	-Double salts and mixtures of calcium nitrate and ammonium nitrate	12	8 (2008)	6.5	2010*		US			0
31027000	-Calcium cyanamide	12	8 (2008)	6.5	2010*		US			0
31028000	-Mixtures of urea and ammonium nitrate in aqueous or ammoniacal solution	12	8 (2008)	6.5	2010*		US			0
31029000	-Other, including mixtures not specified in the foregoing subheadings	12	8 (2008)	6.5	2010*		US			0
3103	Mineral or chemical fertilisers, phosphatic.									
31031000	-Superphosphates	12	8 (2008)	6.5	2010*		US			0
31032000	-Basic slag	12	8 (2008)	6.5	2010*		US			0
310390	-Other									
31039010	---Bicalcium phosphate	12	8 (2008)	6.5	2010*		US			0
31039020	---Decomposed bicalcium phosphate	12	8 (2008)	6.5	2010*		US			0
31039030	---Natural, heat treated, calcarious aluminium phosphate	12	8 (2008)	6.5	2010*		US			0
31039040	---Mixtures of phosphatic fertilizers	12	8 (2008)	6.5	2010*		US			0
31039090	---Other	12	8 (2008)	6.5	2010*		US			0
3104	Mineral or chemical fertilisers, potassic.									
31041000	-Carnallite, sylvite and other crude natural potassium salts	12	8 (2008)	6.5	2010*		US			0
31042000	-Potassium chloride	12	8 (2008)	6.5	2010*		US			0
31043000	-Potassium sulphate	12	8 (2008)	6.5	2010*		US			0
310490	-Other									
31049010	---Magnesium and potassium bi-sulphate	12	8 (2008)	6.5	2010*		US			0
31049020	---Mixtures of potassic fertilizers	12	8 (2008)	6.5	2010*		US			0

HS	Description	Bound rate at date of accession	Interim	Final Bound	Implementation	Present concession established	INR	Concession first incorporated in a GATT Schedule	Earlier INRs	ODCs
3105	Mineral or chemical fertilisers containing two or three of the fertilising elements nitrogen, phosphorus and potassium; other fertilisers; goods of this Chapter in tablets or similar forms or in packages of a gross weight not exceeding 10 kg.									
31051000	-Goods of this Chapter in tablets or similar forms or in packages of a gross weight not exceeding 10 kg	12	8 (2008)	6.5	2010*		US			0
31052000	-Mineral or chemical fertilisers containing the three fertilising elements nitrogen, phosphorus and potassium	12	8 (2008)	6.5	2010*		US			0
31053000	-Diammonium hydrogenorthophosphate (diammonium phosphate)	12	8 (2008)	6.5	2010*		US			0
31054000	-Ammonium dihydrogenorthophosphate (monoammonium phosphate) and mixtures thereof with diammonium hydrogenorthophosphate (diammonium phosphate)	12	8 (2008)	6.5	2010*		US			0
31055	-Other mineral or chemical fertilisers containing the two fertilising elements nitrogen and phosphorus:									
31055100	--Containing nitrates and phosphates	12	8 (2008)	6.5	2010*		US			0
31055900	--Other	12	8 (2008)	6.5	2010*		US			0
31056000	-Mineral or chemical fertilisers containing the two fertilising elements phosphorus and potassium	12	8 (2008)	6.5	2010*		US			0
31059000	-Other	12	8 (2008)	6.5	2010*		US			0
3201	Tanning extracts of vegetable origin; tannins and their salts, ethers, esters and other derivatives.									
32011000	-Quebracho extract	6.5								0
32012000	-Wattle extract	6.5								0
32019000	-Other	6.5								0
3202	Synthetic organic tanning substances; inorganic tanning substances; tanning preparations, whether or not containing natural tanning substances; enzymatic preparations for pre-tanning.									
32021000	-Synthetic organic tanning substances	6.5								0
32029000	-Other	6.5								0

HS	Description	Bound rate at date of accession	Interim	Final Bound	Implementation	Present concession established	INR	Concession first incorporated in a GATT Schedule	Earlier INRs	ODCs
3203	Colouring matter of vegetable or animal origin (including dyeing extracts but excluding animal black), whether or not chemically defined; preparations as specified in Note 3 to this Chapter based on colouring matter of vegetable or animal origin.									
3203001	---Of plant origin:									
32030011	----Natural indigo	6.5								0
32030019	----Other plant coloring matter	6.5								0
32030020	---Coloring matter of animal origin	6.5								0
3204	Synthetic organic colouring matter, whether or not chemically defined; preparations as specified in Note 3 to this Chapter based on synthetic organic colouring matter; synthetic organic products of a kind used as fluorescent brightening agents or as luminophores, whether or not chemically defined.									
32041	-Synthetic organic colouring matter and preparations based thereon as specified in Note 3 to this Chapter:									
32041100	--Disperse dyes and preparations based thereon	6.5								0
32041200	--Acid dyes, whether or not premetallised, and preparations based thereon; mordant dyes and preparations based thereon	6.5					CH			0
32041300	--Basic dyes and preparations based thereon	6.5								0
32041400	--Direct dyes and preparations based thereon	6.5								0
32041500	--Vat dyes (including those usable in that state as pigments) and preparations based thereon	6.5								0
32041600	--Reactive dyes and preparations based thereon	6.5								0
32041700	--Pigments and preparations based thereon	6.5								0
32041900	--Other, including mixtures of colouring matter of two or more of the subheadings 3204.11 to 3204.19	6.5								0
32042000	-Synthetic organic products of a kind used as fluorescent brightening agents	6.5								0
320490	-Other									

HS	Description	Bound rate at date of accession	Interim	Final Bound	Implementation	Present concession established	INR	Concession first incorporated in a GATT Schedule	Earlier INRs	ODCs
32049010	---Synthetic indigo	6.5								0
32049090	---Other synthetic organic coloring products	6.5								0
32050000	Colour lakes; preparations as specified in Note 3 to this Chapter based on colour lakes.	6.5								0
3206	Other colouring matter; preparations as specified in Note 3 to this Chapter, other than those of heading 32.03, 32.04 or 32.05; inorganic products of a kind used as luminophores, whether or not chemically defined.									
32061	-Pigments and preparations based on titanium dioxide:									
32061100	--Containing 80 % or more by weight of titanium dioxide calculated on the dry matter	12	8 (2008)	6.5	2010*		AU			0
32061900	--Other	6.5								0
32062000	-Pigments and preparations based on chromium compounds	6.5								0
32063000	-Pigments and preparations based on cadmium compounds	6.5								0
32064	-Other colouring matter and other preparations:									
32064100	--Ultramarine and preparations based thereon	6.5								0
32064200	--Lithopone and other pigments and preparations based on zinc sulphide	6.5								0
32064300	--Pigments and preparations based on hexacyanoferrates (ferrocyanides and ferricyanides)	6.5								0
32064900	--Other	6.5								0
32065000	-Inorganic products of a kind used as luminophores	6.5								0
3207	Prepared pigments, prepared opacifiers and prepared colours, vitrifiable enamels and glazes, engobes (slips), liquid lustres and similar preparations, of a kind used in the ceramic, enamelling or glass industry; glass frit and other glass, in the form of powder, granules or flakes.									
32071000	-Prepared pigments, prepared opacifiers, prepared colours and similar preparations	20		6.5	2010*					0

HS	Description	Bound rate at date of accession	Interim	Final Bound	Implementation	Present concession established	INR	Concession first incorporated in a GATT Schedule	Earlier INRs	ODCs
32072000	-Vitrifiable enamels and glazes, engobes (slips) and similar preparations	20		6.5	2010*					0
32073000	-Liquid lustres and similar preparations	20		6.5	2010*					0
32074000	-Glass frit and other glass, in the form of powder, granules or flakes	20		6.5	2010*					0
3208	Paints and varnishes (including enamels and lacquers) based on synthetic polymers or chemically modified natural polymers, dispersed or dissolved in a non-aqueous medium; solutions as defined in Note 4 to this Chapter.									
320810	-Based on polyesters									
32081010	---Varnish from polyesters	20		6.5	2010*					0
32081090	---Other paint based on polyesters	20		6.5	2010*					0
320820	-Based on acrylic or vinyl polymers									
32082010	---Varnish from acrylic or vinyl, non-water base	20		6.5	2010*					0
32082090	---Other paints from acrylic or vinyl polymers, non-water base	20		6.5	2010*					0
320890	-Other									
32089010	---Varnish from other polymers, non-water base	20		6.5	2010*					0
32089090	---Other paints from other polymers, non-water base	20		6.5	2010*					0
3209	Paints and varnishes (including enamels and lacquers) based on synthetic polymers or chemically modified natural polymers, dispersed or dissolved in an aqueous medium.									
320910	-Based on acrylic or vinyl polymers									
32091010	---Varnish from acrylic or vinyl polymers, water-base	20		6.5	2010*					0
32091090	---Other paint from acrylic or vinyl polymers, water-base	20		6.5	2010*					0
320990	-Other									
32099010	---Varnish from other polymers, water based	20		6.5	2010*					0
32099090	---Other paints from other polymers, water-based	20		6.5	2010*					0
3210	Other paints and varnishes (including enamels, lacquers and distempers); prepared water pigments of a kind used for finishing leather.									

HS	Description	Bound rate at date of accession	Interim	Final Bound	Implementation	Present concession established	INR	Concession first incorporated in a GATT Schedule	Earlier INRs	ODCs
32100010	---Other varnish	20		6.5	2010*					0
32100020	---Prepared water pigments for finishing leather	20		6.5	2010*					0
32100090	---Other paints	20		6.5	2010*					0
32110000	Prepared driers.	6.5								0
3212	Pigments (including metallic powders and flakes) dispersed in non-aqueous media, in liquid or paste form, of a kind used in the manufacture of paints (including enamels); stamping foils; dyes and other colouring matter put up in forms or packings for retail sale.									
32121000	-Stamping foils	20		6.5	2010*					0
321290	-Other									
32129010	---Dyes and other coloring matter, for retail	20		6.5	2010*					0
32129090	---Other pigments for paint manufacture	20		6.5	2010*					0
3213	Artists', students' or signboard painters' colours, modifying tints, amusement colours and the like, in tablets, tubes, jars, bottles, pans or in similar forms or packings.									
321310	-Colours in sets									
32131010	---Colors in sets with modifying tints	6.5								0
32131090	---All other types of colors in sets	6.5								0
32139000	-Other	6.5								0
3214	Glaziers' putty, grafting putty, resin cements, caulking compounds and other mastics; painters' fillings; non-refractory surfacing preparations for façades, indoor walls, floors, ceilings or the like.									
321410	-Glaziers' putty, grafting putty, resin cements, caulking compounds and other mastics; painters' fillings									
32141010	---Oil based glaziers' putty	6.5								0
32141020	---Grafting and sealing paints for painting casks, etc.	6.5								0
32141030	---Resin mastics for technical usages	6.5								0
32141040	---Soluble glass based mastics for bonding the engines	6.5								0
32141050	---Zinc oxichloride based mastics for pasting of wood, etc	6.5								0

HS	Description	Bound rate at date of accession	Interim	Final Bound	Implementation	Present concession established	INR	Concession first incorporated in a GATT Schedule	Earlier INRs	ODCs
32141060	---Magnesium oxichloride based mastics for filling wood	6.5								0
32141070	---Sulphur based mastics used as hard filling	6.5								0
32141080	---Plastic based mastics used for preventing leakage	6.5								0
3214109	---Other:									
32141091	----Zinc oxide and glycerol based mastics for metal or pipe	6.5								0
32141092	----Rubber based mastics used for pipes	6.5								0
32141093	----Compound stamping wax used for filling, proofing	6.5								0
32141094	----Fillings to prepare surfaces for painting	6.5								0
32141099	----Other mastics and painters' fillings	6.5								0
32149000	-Other	6.5								0
3215	Printing ink, writing or drawing ink and other inks, whether or not concentrated or solid.									
32151	-Printing ink:									
32151100	--Black	12	8 (2008)	6.5	2010*					0
32151900	--Other	12	8 (2008)	6.5	2010*		AU			0
321590	-Other									
32159010	---Writing and drawing ink	6.5								0
32159020	---Copying ink	6.5								0
32159030	---Ink for ballpoint pens	6.5								0
32159040	---Ink for typing machines	6.5								0
32159050	---Stamping ink	6.5								0
32159060	---Ink for typing machines' ribbons	6.5								0
32159070	---Ink for numbering	6.5								0
32159080	---Invisible ink	6.5								0
32159090	---Other ink	6.5								0
3302	Mixtures of odoriferous substances and mixtures (including alcoholic solutions) with a basis of one or more of these substances, of a kind used as raw materials in industry; other preparations based on odoriferous substances, of a kind used for the manufacture of beverages.									
33021000	-Of a kind used in the food or drink industries	6.5					CE25,CH			0
33029000	-Other	6.5					CH			0

HS	Description	Bound rate at date of accession	Interim	Final Bound	Implementation	Present concession established	INR	Concession first incorporated in a GATT Schedule	Earlier INRs	ODCs
3303	Perfumes and toilet waters.									
33030010	---Perfumes, liquid or solid	10	9.8 (2007), 8 (2008), 7.6 (2009)	6.5	2010		CH,DO,HN			0
33030020	---Eaux de cologne	10	9.8 (2007), 8 (2008), 7.6 (2009)	6.5	2010		CH,DO,HN			0
33030090	---Other perfumes and toilet water	10	9.8 (2007), 8 (2008), 7.6 (2009)	6.5	2010		CH,DO,HN			0
3304	Beauty or make-up preparations and preparations for the care of the skin (other than medicaments), including sunscreen or sun tan preparations; manicure or pedicure preparations.									
33041000	-Lip make-up preparations	6.5					CH,DO,HN			0
33042000	-Eye make-up preparations	6.5					CH,DO,HN			0
330430	-Manicure or pedicure preparations									
33043010	---Nail polish and paint	6.5					CH,DO,HN			0
33043020	---Nail polish remover	6.5					CH,DO,HN			0
33043090	---Other manicure and pedicure products	6.5					CH,DO,HN			0
33049	-Other:									
330491	--Powders, whether or not compressed									
33049110	---Cosmetic powder for babies	6.5					CH,DO,HN			0
33049190	---Other cosmetic powder (See Endnote 2)	6.5					CH,DO,HN			0
330499	--Other									
33049910	---Toilet vinegar (See Endnote 3)	6.5					CH,DO,HN			0
33049920	---Sun-tan products (See Endnote 3)	6.5					CH,DO,HN			0
33049930	---Skin softening products (See Endnote 3)	6.5					CH,DO,HN			0
33049940	---Preparation for face make-up and paint make-up (See Endnote 3)	6.5					CH,DO,HN			0
33049990	---Other beauty products (See Endnote 3)	6.5					CH,DO,HN			0
3305	Preparations for use on the hair.									
33051000	-Shampoos	12	8 (2008)	6.5	2010*		DO,HN			0
33052000	-Preparations for permanent waving or straightening	6.5					DO,HN			0
33053000	-Hair lacquers	6.5								0
330590	-Other									
33059010	---Hair oil	6.5					AU			0

HS	Description	Bound rate at date of accession	Interim	Final Bound	Implementation	Present concession established	INR	Concession first incorporated in a GATT Schedule	Earlier INRs	ODCs
33059020	---Hair cream	6.5					AU			0
33059030	---Hair dyeing products	6.5					AU			0
33059090	---Other hair products	6.5					AU			0
3306	Preparations for oral or dental hygiene, including denture fixative pastes and powders; yarn used to clean between the teeth (dental floss), in individual retail packages.									
330610	-Dentifrices									
33061010	---Tooth paste	12	8 (2008)	6.5	2010*					0
33061020	---Denture cleaning products	6.5								0
33061090	---Other dentifrices	6.5								0
33062000	-Yarn used to clean between the teeth (dental floss)	6.5								0
330690	-Other									
33069010	---Mouth wash	6.5								0
33069020	---Denture fixing products	6.5								0
33069090	---Other dental products	6.5								0
3307	Pre-shave, shaving or after-shave preparations, personal deodorants, bath preparations, depilatories and other perfumery, cosmetic or toilet preparations, not elsewhere specified or included; prepared room deodorisers, whether or not perfumed or having disinfectant properties.									
330710	-Pre-shave, shaving or after-shave preparations									
33071010	---Shaving cream and foam	12	8 (2008)	6.5	2010*					0
33071090	---Other pre-shave or after-shave products	6.5								0
33072000	-Personal deodorants and antiperspirants	6.5					DO,HN			0
33073000	-Perfumed bath salts and other bath preparations	6.5								0
33074	-Preparations for perfuming or deodorizing rooms, including odoriferous preparations used during religious rites:									
330741	--Agarbatti and other odoriferous preparations which operate by burning									
33074110	---Liquid odoriferous burning products	6.5								0
33074120	---Powdered odoriferous burning products	6.5								0

HS	Description	Bound rate at date of accession	Interim	Final Bound	Implementation	Present concession established	INR	Concession first incorporated in a GATT Schedule	Earlier INRs	ODCs
33074130	---Incense (sticks)	6.5								0
33074190	---Other odoriferous burning products	6.5								0
330749	--Other									
33074910	---Cosmetic products in an aerosol can	6.5								0
33074920	---Activated carbon used for deodorizing refrigerators	6.5								0
33074990	---Other deodorizing products	6.5								0
330790	-Other									
33079010	---Hair removers	12	8 (2008)	6.5	2010*					0
33079020	---Perfumed or cosmetic coated tissue	6.5								0
33079040	---Solutions for contact lens	6.5								0
33079050	---Cosmetic and toilet products for animals	6.5								0
33079090	---Other cosmetic products	6.5								0
3401	Soap; organic surface-active products and preparations for use as soap, in the form of bars, cakes, moulded pieces or shapes, whether or not containing soap; organic surface-active products and preparations for washing the skin, in the form of liquid or cream and put up for retail sale, whether or not containing soap; paper, wadding, felt and nonwovens, impregnated, coated or covered with soap or detergent.									
34011	-Soap and organic surface-active products and preparations, in the form of bars, cakes, moulded pieces or shapes, and paper, wadding, felt and nonwovens, impregnated, coated or covered with soap or detergent:									
340111	--For toilet use (including medicated products)									
34011130	---Shaving soap	20		6.5	2010*		DO,HN			0
34011140	---Medicated soap	20		6.5	2010*		DO,HN			0
34011150	---Disinfectant soap	20		6.5	2010*		DO,HN			0
34011170	---Paper, wadding, felt and nonwovens, with toilet soap	6.5								0
34011180	---toilet soap	20		6.5	2010*		DO,HN			0
34011190	---other soap	20		6.5	2010*		DO,HN			0
340119	--Other									
34011920	---Tall oil soap	20		6.5	2010*					0
34011930	---Artificial soap prepared for special use	20		6.5	2010*					0

HS	Description	Bound rate at date of accession	Interim	Final Bound	Implementation	Present concession established	INR	Concession first incorporated in a GATT Schedule	Earlier INRs	ODCs
34011940	---Paper, wadding, felt and nonwovens, with other soap	6.5								0
34011990	---Other soap in bars and cakes	20		6.5	2010*		DO,HN			0
340120	-Soap in other forms									
34012010	---Soap in the form of powder	20		6.5	2010*		DO,HN			0
34012020	---Soap in the form of paste	20		6.5	2010*		DO,HN			0
34012030	---Soap in the form of aqueous solutions (liquids)	20		6.5	2010*		DO,HN			0
34012090	---Other soap	20		6.5	2010*		DO,HN			0
34013000	-Organic surface-active products and preparations for washing the skin, in the form of liquid or cream and put up for retail sale, whether or not containing soap	20		6.5	2010*					0
3402	Organic surface-active agents (other than soap); surface-active preparations, washing preparations (including auxiliary washing preparations) and cleaning preparations, whether or not containing soap, other than those of heading 34.01.									
34021	-Organic surface-active agents, whether or not put up for retail sale:									
34021100	--Anionic	20		6.5	2010*		DO,HN			0
34021200	--Cationic	20		6.5	2010*					0
34021300	--Non-ionic	20		6.5	2010*					0
34021900	--Other	20		6.5	2010*					0
340220	-Preparations put up for retail sale									
34022010	---Organic surface-active agents, like clorox, for retail	20		6.5	2010*					0
3402202	---Washing preparations:									
34022021	----Dry-powdered organic surface-active agents, for retail	20		6.5	2010*					0
34022022	----Fluid organic surface-active agents, for retail	20		6.5	2010*					0
34022029	----Other organic surface-active agents, for retail	20		6.5	2010*					0
34029000	-Other	20		6.5	2010*		DO,HN			0

HS	Description	Bound rate at date of accession	Interim	Final Bound	Implementation	Present concession established	INR	Concession first incorporated in a GATT Schedule	Earlier INRs	ODCs
3403	Lubricating preparations (including cutting-oil preparations, bolt or nut release preparations, anti-rust or anti-corrosion preparations and mould release preparations, based on lubricants) and preparations of a kind used for the oil or grease treatment of textile materials, leather, furskins or other materials, but excluding preparations containing, as basic constituents, 70 % or more by weight of petroleum oils or of oils obtained from bituminous minerals.									
34031	-Containing petroleum oils or oils obtained from bituminous minerals:									
34031100	--Preparations for the treatment of textile materials, leather, furskins or other materials	6.5								0
340319	--Other									
34031910	---Lubricating products for decreasing friction	6.5								0
34031920	---Pulling oils and lubricants	6.5								0
34031930	---Oils for cutting tools	6.5								0
34031940	---Bolt or nut release products	6.5								0
34031950	---Anti-rust and anti-corrosion products	6.5								0
34031990	---Other petroleum-based lubricating products	6.5								0
34039	-Other:									
34039100	--Preparations for the treatment of textile materials, leather, furskins or other materials	6.5								0
34039900	--Other	6.5								0
3404	Artificial waxes and prepared waxes.									
34041000	-Of chemically modified lignite	6.5								0
34042000	-Of poly(oxyethylene) (polyethylene glycol)	6.5								0
340490	-Other									
34049010	---Stamping wax	6.5								0
34049090	---Other prepared waxes	6.5								0

HS	Description	Bound rate at date of accession	Interim	Final Bound	Implementation	Present concession established	INR	Concession first incorporated in a GATT Schedule	Earlier INRs	ODCs
3405	Polishes and creams, for footwear, furniture, floors, coachwork, glass or metal, scouring pastes and powders and similar preparations (whether or not in the form of paper, wadding, felt, nonwovens, cellular plastics or cellular rubber, impregnated, coated or covered with such preparations), excluding waxes of heading 34.04.									
34051000	-Polishes, creams and similar preparations for footwear or leather	6.5					DO,HN			0
34052000	-Polishes, creams and similar preparations for the maintenance of wooden furniture, floors or other woodwork	6.5					DO,HN			0
34053000	-Polishes and similar preparations for coachwork, other than metal polishes	6.5					DO,HN			0
34054000	-Scouring pastes and powders and other scouring preparations	6.5								0
340590	-Other									
34059010	---Polishes for glass and mirrors	6.5		5.5	2015		DO,HN			0
34059020	---Polishes for metals	6.5		5.5	2015					0
34059090	---Other polishes	6.5		5.5	2015		DO,HN			0
34060000	Candles, tapers and the like.	6.5					DO,HN			0
3407	Modelling pastes, including those put up for children's amusement; preparations known as "dental wax" or as "dental impression compounds", put up in sets, in packings for retail sale or in plates, horseshoe shapes, sticks or similar forms; other preparations for use in dentistry, with a basis of plaster (of calcined gypsum or calcium sulphate).									
34070010	---Dental wax	6.5								0
34070020	---Dentistry paste	6.5								0
34070030	---Modelling pastes for children's amusement	6.5								0
34070090	---Other pastes	6.5		5.5	2015					0
3506	Prepared glues and other prepared adhesives, not elsewhere specified or included; products suitable for use as glues or adhesives, put up for retail sale as glues or adhesives, not exceeding a net weight of 1 kg.									

HS	Description	Bound rate at date of accession	Interim	Final Bound	Implementation	Present concession established	INR	Concession first incorporated in a GATT Schedule	Earlier INRs	ODCs
35061000	-Products suitable for use as glues or adhesives, put up for retail sale as glues or adhesives, not exceeding a net weight of 1 kg	12	8 (2008)	6.5	2010*					0
35069	-Other:									
35069100	--Adhesives based on polymers of headings 39.01 to 39.13 or on rubber	12	8 (2008)	6.5	2010*					0
35069900	--Other	12	8 (2008)	6.5	2010*					0
3507	Enzymes; prepared enzymes not elsewhere specified or included.									
350710	-Rennet and concentrates thereof									
35071010	---Calves' rennet	6.5								0
35071090	---Other rennets	6.5								0
350790	-Other									
35079010	---Enzyme preparations for tenderizing meats	6.5								0
35079020	---Enzyme preparations for purifying fruit juices	6.5								0
35079030	---Enzyme preparations for removing starch from clothes	6.5								0
35079040	---Pancreatic enzymes	6.5								0
35079050	---Pepsin enzymes	6.5								0
35079060	---Malt enzymes	6.5								0
35079090	---Other enzymes	6.5								0
36010000	Propellent powders.	6.5								0
36020000	Prepared explosives, other than propellent powders.	6.5								0
3603	Safety fuses; detonating fuses; percussion or detonating caps; igniters; electric detonators.									
36030010	---Percussion and detonating caps, igniters	6.5								0
36030090	---Safety fuses, blasting fuses	6.5								0
3604	Fireworks, signalling flares, rain rockets, fog signals and other pyrotechnic articles.									
36041000	-Fireworks	6.5								0
36049000	-Other	6.5								0
36050000	Matches, other than pyrotechnic articles of heading 36.04.	20		6.5	2010*		DO,HN			0

HS	Description	Bound rate at date of accession	Interim	Final Bound	Implementation	Present concession established	INR	Concession first incorporated in a GATT Schedule	Earlier INRs	ODCs
3606	Ferro-cerium and other pyrophoric alloys in all forms; articles of combustible materials as specified in Note 2 to this Chapter.									
36061000	-Liquid or liquefied-gas fuels in containers of a kind used for filling or refilling cigarette or similar lighters and of a capacity not exceeding 300 cm3	6.5								0
360690	-Other									
36069010	---Lighter flints	6.5								0
36069090	---Other combustile materials, for retail	6.5								0
3701	Photographic plates and film in the flat, sensitised, unexposed, of any material other than paper, paperboard or textiles; instant print film in the flat, sensitised, unexposed, whether or not in packs.									
37011000	-For X-ray	6.5								0
37012000	-Instant print film	6.5								0
37013000	-Other plates and film, with any side exceeding 255 mm	6.5								0
37019	-Other:									
37019100	--For colour photography (polychrome)	6.5								0
37019900	--Other	6.5								0
3702	Photographic film in rolls, sensitised, unexposed, of any material other than paper, paperboard or textiles; instant print film in rolls, sensitised, unexposed.									
37021000	-For X-ray	12	8 (2008)	6.5	2010*					0
37022000	-Instant print film	6.5								0
37023	-Other film, without perforations, of a width not exceeding 105 mm:									
37023100	--For colour photography (polychrome)	6.5								0
37023200	--Other, with silver halide emulsion	6.5								0
37023900	--Other	6.5								0
37024	-Other film, without perforations, of a width exceeding 105 mm:									
37024100	--Of a width exceeding 610 mm and of a length exceeding 200 m, for colour photography (polychrome)	6.5								0
37024200	--Of a width exceeding 610 mm and of a length exceeding 200 m, other than for colour photography	6.5								0

HS	Description	Bound rate at date of accession	Interim	Final Bound	Implementation	Present concession established	INR	Concession first incorporated in a GATT Schedule	Earlier INRs	ODCs
37024300	--Of a width exceeding 610 mm and of a length not exceeding 200 m	6.5								0
37024400	--Of a width exceeding 105 mm but not exceeding 610 mm	6.5								0
37025	-Other film, for colour photography (polychrome):									
37025100	--Of a width not exceeding 16 mm and of a length not exceeding 14 m	6.5								0
37025200	--Of a width not exceeding 16 mm and of a length exceeding 14 m	6.5								0
37025300	--Of a width exceeding 16 mm but not exceeding 35 mm and of a length not exceeding 30 m, for slides	6.5								0
37025400	--Of a width exceeding 16 mm but not exceeding 35 mm and of a length not exceeding 30 m, other than for slides	6.5								0
37025500	--Of a width exceeding 16 mm but not exceeding 35 mm and of a length exceeding 30 m	6.5								0
37025600	--Of a width exceeding 35 mm	6.5								0
37029	-Other:									
37029100	--Of a width not exceeding 16 mm	6.5								0
37029300	--Of a width exceeding 16 mm but not exceeding 35 mm and of a length not exceeding 30 m	6.5								0
37029400	--Of a width exceeding 16 mm but not exceeding 35 mm and of a length exceeding 30 m	6.5								0
37029500	--Of a width exceeding 35 mm	6.5								0
3703	Photographic paper, paperboard and textiles, sensitised, unexposed.									
37031000	-In rolls of a width exceeding 610 mm	6.5								0
37032000	-Other, for colour photography (polychrome)	6.5								0
37039000	-Other	6.5								0
37040000	Photographic plates, film, paper, paperboard and textiles, exposed but not developed.	6.5								0
3705	Photographic plates and film, exposed and developed, other than cinematographic film.									
37051000	-For offset reproduction	6.5								0
37052000	-Microfilms	6.5								0
37059000	-Other	6.5								0

HS	Description	Bound rate at date of accession	Interim	Final Bound	Implementation	Present concession established	INR	Concession first incorporated in a GATT Schedule	Earlier INRs	ODCs
3706	Cinematographic film, exposed and developed, whether or not incorporating sound track or consisting only of sound track.									
370610	-Of a width of 35 mm or more									
37061010	---Cinema film, over 34 mm wide for education and similar	6.5								0
37061090	---Other cinema film over 34 mm wide	6.5								0
370690	-Other									
37069010	---Cinema film, under 35 mm wide for education and similar	6.5								0
37069090	---Other cinema film under 35 mm wide	6.5								0
3707	Chemical preparations for photographic uses (other than varnishes, glues, adhesives and similar preparations); unmixed products for photographic uses, put up in measured portions or put up for retail sale in a form ready for use.									
37071000	-Sensitising emulsions	6.5								0
370790	-Other									
37079010	---Developers for photography	6.5								0
37079020	---Fixers for photography	6.5								0
37079030	---Intensifying solutions and diluting solutions	6.5								0
37079040	---Processing solutions for photography	6.5								0
37079050	---Cleaning (washing) solutions for photography	6.5								0
37079090	---Other chemical preparations for photography	6.5								0
3801	Artificial graphite; colloidal or semi-colloidal graphite; preparations based on graphite or other carbon in the form of pastes, blocks, plates or other semi-manufactures.									
38011000	-Artificial graphite	6.5								0
38012000	-Colloidal or semi-colloidal graphite	6.5								0
38013000	-Carbonaceous pastes for electrodes and similar pastes for furnace linings	6.5								0
380190	-Other									
38019010	---Mixtures of graphite with mineral oils	6.5								0
38019090	---Other graphite preparations	6.5								0

HS	Description	Bound rate at date of accession	Interim	Final Bound	Implementation	Present concession established	INR	Concession first incorporated in a GATT Schedule	Earlier INRs	ODCs
3802	Activated carbon; activated natural mineral products; animal black, including spent animal black.									
38021000	-Activated carbon	6.5					LK			0
38029000	-Other	6.5								0
38030000	Tall oil, whether or not refined.	6.5								0
38040000	Residual lyes from the manufacture of wood pulp, whether or not concentrated, desugared or chemically treated, including lignin sulphonates, but excluding tall oil of heading 38.03.	6.5								0
3805	Gum, wood or sulphate turpentine and other terpenic oils produced by the distillation or other treatment of coniferous woods; crude dipentene; sulphite turpentine and other crude para-cymene; pine oil containing alpha-terpineol as the main constituent.									
38051000	-Gum, wood or sulphate turpentine oils	6.5					DO,HN			0
38052000	-Pine oil	6.5					DO,HN			0
38059000	-Other	6.5								0
3806	Rosin and resin acids, and derivatives thereof; rosin spirit and rosin oils; run gums.									
38061000	-Rosin and resin acids	6.5					DO,HN			0
38062000	-Salts of rosin, of resin acids or of derivatives of rosin or resin acids, other than salts of rosin adducts	6.5								0
38063000	-Ester gums	6.5								0
38069000	-Other	6.5								0
38070000	Wood tar; wood tar oils; wood creosote; wood naphtha; vegetable pitch; brewers' pitch and similar preparations based on rosin, resin acids or on vegetable pitch.	6.5								0
3808	Insecticides, rodenticides, fungicides, herbicides, anti-sprouting products and plant-growth regulators, disinfectants and similar products, put up in forms or packings for retail sale or as preparations or articles (for example, sulphur-treated bands, wicks and candles, and fly-papers).									
380810	-Insecticides									

HS	Description	Bound rate at date of accession	Interim	Final Bound	Implementation	Present concession established	INR	Concession first incorporated in a GATT Schedule	Earlier INRs	ODCs
38081010	---Liquid insecticides	10	9.8 (2007), 8 (2008), 7.6 (2009)	6.5	2010		CH,IN,US			0
38081020	---Powder insecticides	10	9.8 (2007), 8 (2008), 7.6 (2009)	6.5	2010		CH,IN,US			0
38081030	---Insecticides in aerosol cans	10	9.8 (2007), 8 (2008), 7.6 (2009)	6.5	2010		CH,IN,US			0
38081090	---Other insecticides	10	9.8 (2007), 8 (2008), 7.6 (2009)	6.5	2010		CH,IN,US			0
38082000	-Fungicides	6.5					CH,US			0
38083000	-Herbicides, anti-sprouting products and plant-growth regulators	6.5					CH,US			0
38084000	-Disinfectants	12	8 (2008)	6.5	2010*		US			0
38089000	-Other	6.5					CH,US			0
3809	Finishing agents, dye carriers to accelerate the dyeing or fixing of dyestuffs and other products and preparations (for example, dressings and mordants), of a kind used in the textile, paper, leather or like industries, not elsewhere specified or included.									
38099	-Other:									
380991	--Of a kind used in the textile or like industries									
38099110	---Cloth and towel smoothers	6.5								0
38099190	---Other finishing agents used in the textile industry	6.5								0
38099200	--Of a kind used in the paper or like industries	6.5								0
38099300	--Of a kind used in the leather or like industries	6.5								0
3810	Pickling preparations for metal surfaces; fluxes and other auxiliary preparations for soldering, brazing or welding; soldering, brazing or welding powders and pastes consisting of metal and other materials; preparations of a kind used as cores or coatings for welding electrodes or rods.									

HS	Description	Bound rate at date of accession	Interim	Final Bound	Implementation	Present concession established	INR	Concession first incorporated in a GATT Schedule	Earlier INRs	ODCs
38101000	-Pickling preparations for metal surfaces; soldering, brazing or welding powders and pastes consisting of metal and other materials	6.5								0
38109000	-Other	6.5								0
3811	Anti-knock preparations, oxidation inhibitors, gum inhibitors, viscosity improvers, anti-corrosive preparations and other prepared additives, for mineral oils (including gasoline) or for other liquids used for the same purposes as mineral oils.									
38111	-Anti-knock preparations:									
38111100	--Based on lead compounds	6.5								0
38111900	--Other	6.5								0
38112	-Additives for lubricating oils:									
38112100	--Containing petroleum oils or oils obtained from bituminous minerals	12	8 (2008)	6.5	2010*					0
38112900	--Other	12	8 (2008)	6.5	2010*					0
38119000	-Other	6.5								0
3812	Prepared rubber accelerators; compound plasticisers for rubber or plastics, not elsewhere specified or included; anti-oxidising preparations and other compound stabilisers for rubber or plastics.									
38121000	-Prepared rubber accelerators	6.5								0
38122000	-Compound plasticisers for rubber or plastics	6.5								0
38123000	-Anti-oxidising preparations and other compound stabilisers for rubber or plastics	10	9.8 (2007), 8 (2008), 7.6 (2009)	6.5	2010		CH			0
38130000	Preparations and charges for fire-extinguishers; charged fire-extinguishing grenades.	6.5								0
38140000	Organic composite solvents and thinners, not elsewhere specified or included; prepared paint or varnish removers.	12	8 (2008)	6.5	2010*		DO,HN			0
3815	Reaction initiators, reaction accelerators and catalytic preparations, not elsewhere specified or included.									
38151	-Supported catalysts:									
38151100	--With nickel or nickel compounds as the active substance	6.5								0

HS	Description	Bound rate at date of accession	Interim	Final Bound	Implementation	Present concession established	INR	Concession first incorporated in a GATT Schedule	Earlier INRs	ODCs
38151200	--With precious metal or precious metal compounds as the active substance	6.5								0
38151900	--Other	6.5								0
38159000	-Other	6.5								0
38160000	Refractory cements, mortars, concretes and similar compositions, other than products of heading 38.01.	6.5								0
38170000	Mixed alkylbenzenes and mixed alkylnaphthalenes, other than those of heading 27.07 or 29.02.	6.5								0
38180000	Chemical elements doped for use in electronics, in the form of discs, wafers or similar forms; chemical compounds doped for use in electronics.	5		0	2008		US			0
38190000	Hydraulic brake fluids and other prepared liquids for hydraulic transmission, not containing or containing less than 70 % by weight of petroleum oils or oils obtained from bituminous minerals.	6.5								0
38200000	Anti-freezing preparations and prepared de-icing fluids.	6.5								0
38210000	Prepared culture media for development of micro-organisms.	6.5								0
38220000	Diagnostic or laboratory reagents on a backing, prepared diagnostic or laboratory reagents whether or not on a backing, other than those of heading 30.02 or 30.06; certified reference materials.	5								0
3824	Prepared binders for foundry moulds or cores; chemical products and preparations of the chemical or allied industries (including those consisting of mixtures of natural products), not elsewhere specified or included.									
38241000	-Prepared binders for foundry moulds or cores	6.5								0
38242000	-Naphthenic acids, their water-insoluble salts and their esters	6.5								0
38243000	-Non-agglomerated metal carbides mixed together or with metallic binders	6.5								0
38244000	-Prepared additives for cements, mortars or concretes	6.5								0
38245000	-Non-refractory mortars and concretes	6.5								0

HS	Description	Bound rate at date of accession	Interim	Final Bound	Implementation	Present concession established	INR	Concession first incorporated in a GATT Schedule	Earlier INRs	ODCs
38247	-Mixtures containing perhalogenated derivatives of acyclic hydrocarbons containing two or more different halogens:									
38247100	--Containing acyclic hydrocarbons perhalogenated only with fluorine and chlorine	6.5								0
38247900	--Other	6.5								0
382490	-Other									
38249010	---Ink removers, in containers for retail sale	6.5								0
38249020	---Compounds for correction of writings on stencil	6.5								0
38249030	---Ammoniacal gas liquors and spent oxide	6.5								0
38249040	---Oxillite	6.5								0
38249050	---Additives for hardening the varnish or glue	6.5								0
38249060	---Absorbing compounds for creating vacuum in tubes	6.5								0
38249070	---Sodium calcine prepared by impregnating pure calcine	6.5								0
38249080	---Anti-rust preparations	6.5								0
3824909	---Other:									
38249091	----Anti-slip preparations for transmission belts	6.5								0
38249092	----Liquids for starting operation of petroleum engines	6.5								0
38249093	----Gelatin-based pastes for printing	6.5								0
38249094	----Radiator coolant containing glycolethyl	12	8 (2008)	6.5	2010*					0
38249099	----Other chemical preparations	6.5								0
3825	Residual products of the chemical or allied industries, not elsewhere specified or included; municipal waste; sewage sludge; other wastes specified in Note 6 to this Chapter.									
38251000	-Municipal waste	6.5								0
38252000	-Sewage sludge	6.5								0
38253000	-Clinical waste	0								0
38254	-Waste organic solvents:									
38254100	--Halogenated	6.5								0
38254900	--Other	6.5								0

HS	Description	Bound rate at date of accession	Interim	Final Bound	Implementation	Present concession established	INR	Concession first incorporated in a GATT Schedule	Earlier INRs	ODCs
38255000	-Wastes of metal pickling liquors, hydraulic fluids, brake fluids and anti-freeze fluids	6.5								0
38256	-Other wastes from chemical or allied industries:									
38256100	--Mainly containing organic constituents	6.5								0
38256900	--Other	6.5								0
38259000	-Other	6.5								0
3901	Polymers of ethylene, in primary forms.									
39011000	-Polyethylene having a specific gravity of less than 0.94	12	8 (2008)	6.5	2010*		US			0
39012000	-Polyethylene having a specific gravity of 0.94 or more	12	8 (2008)	6.5	2010*		US			0
39013000	-Ethylene-vinyl acetate copolymers	6.5					US			0
39019000	-Other	6.5					US			0
3902	Polymers of propylene or of other olefins, in primary forms.									
39021000	-Polypropylene	12	8 (2008)	6.5	2010*		US			0
39022000	-Polyisobutylene	6.5					US			0
39023000	-Propylene copolymers	6.5					US			0
39029000	-Other	6.5					US			0
3903	Polymers of styrene, in primary forms.									
39031	-Polystyrene:									
39031100	--Expansible	12	8 (2008)	6.5	2010*		US			0
39031900	--Other	12	8 (2008)	6.5	2010*		US			0
39032000	-Styrene-acrylonitrile (SAN) copolymers	6.5					US			0
39033000	-Acrylonitrile-butadiene-styrene (ABS) copolymers	6.5					US			0
39039000	-Other	6.5					US			0
3904	Polymers of vinyl chloride or of other halogenated olefins, in primary forms.									
39041000	-Poly(vinyl chloride), not mixed with any other substances	6.5					US			0
39042	-Other poly(vinyl chloride):									
39042100	--Non-plasticised	6.5					US			0
39042200	--Plasticised	6.5					US			0
39043000	-Vinyl chloride-vinyl acetate copolymers	6.5					US			0
39044000	-Other vinyl chloride copolymers	6.5					US			0
39045000	-Vinylidene chloride polymers	6.5					US			0
39046	-Fluoro-polymers:									
39046100	--Polytetrafluoroethylene	6.5					US			0
39046900	--Other	6.5					US			0

HS	Description	Bound rate at date of accession	Interim	Final Bound	Implementation	Present concession established	INR	Concession first incorporated in a GATT Schedule	Earlier INRs	ODCs
39049000	-Other	6.5					US			0
3905	Polymers of vinyl acetate or of other vinyl esters, in primary forms; other vinyl polymers in primary forms.									
39051	-Poly(vinyl acetate):									
39051200	--In aqueous dispersion	12	8 (2008)	6.5	2010*		US			0
39051900	--Other	12	8 (2008)	6.5	2010*		US			0
39052	-Vinyl acetate copolymers:									
39052100	--In aqueous dispersion	6.5					US			0
39052900	--Other	6.5					US			0
39053000	-Poly(vinyl alcohol), whether or not containing unhydrolysed acetate groups	6.5					US			0
39059	-Other:									
39059100	--Copolymers	6.5					US			0
39059900	--Other	6.5					US			0
3906	Acrylic polymers in primary forms.									
39061000	-Poly(methyl methacrylate)	6.5					US			0
39069000	-Other	6.5					US			0
3907	Polyacetals, other polyethers and epoxide resins, in primary forms; polycarbonates, alkyd resins, polyallyl esters and other polyesters, in primary forms.									
39071000	-Polyacetals	6.5					US			0
39072000	-Other polyethers	6.5					US			0
39073000	-Epoxide resins	10	9.8 (2007), 8 (2008), 7.6 (2009)	6.5	2010		CH,US			0
39074000	-Polycarbonates	6.5					US			0
39075000	-Alkyd resins	12	8 (2008)	6.5	2010*		US			0
39076000	-Poly(ethylene terephthalate)	6.5					US			0
39079	-Other polyesters:									
39079100	--Unsaturated	12	8 (2008)	6.5	2010*		US			0
39079900	--Other	12	8 (2008)	6.5	2010*		US			0
3908	Polyamides in primary forms.									
39081000	-Polyamide-6, -11, -12, -6,6, -6,9, -6,10 or -6,12	6.5					US			0
39089000	-Other	6.5					US			0
3909	Amino-resins, phenolic resins and polyurethanes, in primary forms.									
39091000	-Urea resins; thiourea resins	12	8 (2008)	6.5	2010*		US			0
39092000	-Melamine resins	12	8 (2008)	6.5	2010*		US			0

HS	Description	Bound rate at date of accession	Interim	Final Bound	Implementation	Present concession established	INR	Concession first incorporated in a GATT Schedule	Earlier INRs	ODCs
39093000	-Other amino-resins	6.5					US			0
39094000	-Phenolic resins	12	8 (2008)	6.5	2010*		US			0
39095000	-Polyurethanes	6.5					US			0
39100000	Silicones in primary forms.	6.5					US			0
3911	Petroleum resins, coumarone-indene resins, polyterpenes, polysulphides, polysulphones and other products specified in Note 3 to this Chapter, not elsewhere specified or included, in primary forms.									
39111000	-Petroleum resins, coumarone, indene or coumarone-indene resins and polyterpenes	6.5					US			0
39119000	-Other	6.5					US			0
3912	Cellulose and its chemical derivatives, not elsewhere specified or included, in primary forms.									
39121	-Cellulose acetates:									
39121100	--Non-plasticised	6.5					US			0
39121200	--Plasticised	6.5					US			0
39122000	-Cellulose nitrates (including collodions)	6.5					US			0
39123	-Cellulose ethers:									
39123100	--Carboxymethylcellulose and its salts	6.5					LK,US			0
39123900	--Other	6.5					US			0
39129000	-Other	6.5					US			0
3913	Natural polymers (for example, alginic acid) and modified natural polymers (for example, hardened proteins, chemical derivatives of natural rubber), not elsewhere specified or included, in primary forms.									
39131000	-Alginic acid, its salts and esters	6.5					US			0
39139000	-Other	6.5					US			0
39140000	Ion-exchangers based on polymers of headings 39.01 to 39.13, in primary forms.	6.5					US			0
3915	Waste, parings and scrap, of plastics.									
39151000	-Of polymers of ethylene	6.5								0
39152000	-Of polymers of styrene	6.5								0
39153000	-Of polymers of vinyl chloride	6.5								0
39159000	-Of other plastics	6.5								0

HS	Description	Bound rate at date of accession	Interim	Final Bound	Implementation	Present concession established	INR	Concession first incorporated in a GATT Schedule	Earlier INRs	ODCs
3916	Monofilament of which any cross-sectional dimension exceeds 1 mm, rods, sticks and profile shapes, whether or not surface-worked but not otherwise worked, of plastics.									
391610	-Of polymers of ethylene									
39161010	---Monofilament of ethylene polymers over 1 mm wide	6.5								0
39161020	---Rods, sticks and profile shapes of ethylene polymers	6.5								0
391620	-Of polymers of vinyl chloride									
39162010	---Monafilament of vinyl chloride over 1 mm wide	6.5								0
39162020	---Rods, sticks and profile shapes of vinyl chloride	6.5								0
391690	-Of other plastics									
39169010	---Monafilament of other plastics over 1 mm wide	6.5								0
39169020	---Rods, sticks and profile shapes of other plastics	6.5								0
3917	Tubes, pipes and hoses, and fittings therefor (for example, joints, elbows, flanges), of plastics.									
39171000	-Artificial guts (sausage casings) of hardened protein or of cellulosic materials	6.5								0
39172	-Tubes, pipes and hoses, rigid:									
39172100	--Of polymers of ethylene	12	8 (2008)	6.5	2010*					0
ex39172100	---For use in civil aircraft	0								0
39172200	--Of polymers of propylene	6.5								0
ex39172200	---For use in civil aircraft	0								0
39172300	--Of polymers of vinyl chloride	15	14.6 (2007), 11.9 (2008), 9.2 (2009)	6.5	2010		DO,HN			0
ex39172300	---For use in civil aircraft	0					DO,HN			0
39172900	--Of other plastics	6.5								0
ex39172900	---For use in civil aircraft	0								0
39173	-Other tubes, pipes and hoses:									
39173100	--Flexible tubes, pipes and hoses, having a minimum burst pressure of 27.6 MPa	6.5								0
ex39173100	---For use in civil aircraft	0								0

HS	Description	Bound rate at date of accession	Interim	Final Bound	Implementation	Present concession established	INR	Concession first incorporated in a GATT Schedule	Earlier INRs	ODCs
391732	--Other, not reinforced or otherwise combined with other materials, without fittings									
39173210	---Sipping tubes (straws)	6.5					DO,HN			0
39173290	---Other	6.5					DO,HN			0
39173300	--Other, not reinforced or otherwise combined with other materials, with fittings	6.5					DO,HN			0
ex39173300	---For use in civil aircraft	0					DO,HN			0
39173900	--Other	6.5								0
ex39173900	---For use in civil aircraft	0								0
39174000	-Fittings	6.5								0
ex39174000	--For use in civil aircraft	0								0
3918	Floor coverings of plastics, whether or not self-adhesive, in rolls or in the form of tiles; wall or ceiling coverings of plastics, as defined in Note 9 to this Chapter.									
39181000	-Of polymers of vinyl chloride	12	8 (2008)	6.5	2010*					0
39189000	-Of other plastics	12	8 (2008)	6.5	2010*					0
3919	Self-adhesive plates, sheets, film, foil, tape, strip and other flat shapes, of plastics, whether or not in rolls.									
39191000	-In rolls of a width not exceeding 20 cm	6.5								0
39199000	-Other	6.5								0
3920	Other plates, sheets, film, foil and strip, of plastics, non-cellular and not reinforced, laminated, supported or similarly combined with other materials.									
39201000	-Of polymers of ethylene	12	8 (2008)	6.5	2010*		AU			0
39202000	-Of polymers of propylene	12	8 (2008)	6.5	2010*					0
39203000	-Of polymers of styrene	12	8 (2008)	6.5	2010*					0
39204	-Of polymers of vinyl chloride:									
39204300	--Containing by weight not less than 6 % of plasticisers	6.5								0
392049	--Other									
39204910	---Table cover (wats)	12	8 (2008)	6.5	2010*					0
39204990	---Other	12	8 (2008)	6.5	2010*					0
39205	-Of acrylic polymers:									
39205100	--Of poly(methyl methacrylate)	12	8 (2008)	6.5	2010*					0
39205900	--Other	12	8 (2008)	6.5	2010*					0
39206	-Of polycarbonates, alkyd resins, polyallyl esters or other polyesters:									

HS	Description	Bound rate at date of accession	Interim	Final Bound	Implementation	Present concession established	INR	Concession first incorporated in a GATT Schedule	Earlier INRs	ODCs
39206100	--Of polycarbonates	12	8 (2008)	6.5	2010*					0
39206200	--Of poly(ethylene terephthalate)	6.5								0
39206300	--Of unsaturated polyesters	6.5								0
39206900	--Of other polyesters	6.5					IN			0
39207	-Of cellulose or its chemical derivatives:									
39207100	--Of regenerated cellulose	6.5								0
39207200	--Of vulcanised fibre	6.5								0
39207300	--Of cellulose acetate	6.5								0
39207900	--Of other cellulose derivatives	6.5								0
39209	-Of other plastics:									
39209100	--Of poly(vinyl butyral)	6.5								0
39209200	--Of polyamides	6.5								0
39209300	--Of amino-resins	6.5								0
39209400	--Of phenolic resins	6.5								0
39209900	--Of other plastics	6.5								0
3921	Other plates, sheets, film, foil and strip, of plastics.									
39211	-Cellular:									
39211100	--Of polymers of styrene	15		6.5	2010*					0
39211200	--Of polymers of vinyl chloride	15	14.6 (2007), 11.9 (2008), 9.2 (2009)	6.5	2010					0
39211300	--Of polyurethanes	15	14.6 (2007), 11.9 (2008), 9.2 (2009)	6.5	2010					0
39211400	--Of regenerated cellulose	15	14.6 (2007), 11.9 (2008), 9.2 (2009)	6.5	2010					0
39211900	--Of other plastics	15	14.6 (2007), 11.9 (2008), 9.2 (2009)	6.5	2010					0
39219000	-Other	6.5								0
3922	Baths, shower-baths, sinks, wash-basins, bidets, lavatory pans, seats and covers, flushing cisterns and similar sanitary ware, of plastics.									
39221000	-Baths, shower-baths, sinks and wash-basins	6.5					DO,HN			0
39222000	-Lavatory seats and covers	6.5								0
39229000	-Other	6.5								0
3923	Articles for the conveyance or packing of goods, of plastics; stoppers, lids, caps and other closures, of plastics.									

HS	Description	Bound rate at date of accession	Interim	Final Bound	Implementation	Present concession established	INR	Concession first incorporated in a GATT Schedule	Earlier INRs	ODCs
392310	-Boxes, cases, crates and similar articles									
39231010	---Plastic boxes, cases, and crates used for carrying poultry	15	14.6 (2007), 11.9 (2008), 9.2 (2009)	6.5	2010		DO,HN			0
39231020	---Plastic boxes, cases, and crates used for carrying dairy products	15	14.6 (2007), 11.9 (2008), 9.2 (2009)	6.5	2010		DO,HN			0
39231090	---Plastic boxes, cases, and crates used to carry all other products	15	14.6 (2007), 11.9 (2008), 9.2 (2009)	6.5	2010		DO,HN			0
39232	-Sacks and bags (including cones):									
39232100	--Of polymers of ethylene	20		6.5	2010*		DO,HN,KG			0
39232900	--Of other plastics	20		6.5	2010*					0
39233000	-Carboys, bottles, flasks and similar articles	20		6.5	2010*					0
39234000	-Spools, cops, bobbins and similar supports	6.5								0
39235000	-Stoppers, lids, caps and other closures	20		6.5	2010*		DO,HN			0
39239000	-Other	20		6.5	2010*					0
3924	Tableware, kitchenware, other household articles and toilet articles, of plastics.									
392410	-Tableware and kitchenware									
39241010	---Containers for keeping the ice and foods, plastic	15	14.6 (2007), 11.9 (2008), 9.2 (2009)	6.5	2010		DO,HN			0
39241020	---Plastic forks, spoons, and knives	20		6.5	2010*					0
39241030	---Plastic plates and cups	20		6.5	2010*					0
39241040	---Babies' feeding bottles	15	14.6 (2007), 11.9 (2008), 9.2 (2009)	6.5	2010		IN			0
39241090	---Other plastic kitchenware	15	14.6 (2007), 11.9 (2008), 9.2 (2009)	6.5	2010		DO,HN			0
392490	-Other									
39249010	---Plasticware holders for the bathroom	15	14.6 (2007), 11.9 (2008), 9.2 (2009)	6.5	2010					0
39249030	---Ash trays	15	14.6 (2007), 11.9 (2008), 9.2 (2009)	6.5	2010		DO,HN			0

HS	Description	Bound rate at date of accession	Interim	Final Bound	Implementation	Present concession established	INR	Concession first incorporated in a GATT Schedule	Earlier INRs	ODCs
39249040	---Plastic nursing bottles	15	14.6 (2007), 11.9 (2008), 9.2 (2009)	6.5	2010		DO,HN			0
39249090	---Other houseware plasticware holders not for the kitchen or bathroom	15	14.6 (2007), 11.9 (2008), 9.2 (2009)	6.5	2010					0
3925	Builders' ware of plastics, not elsewhere specified or included.									
39251000	-Reservoirs, tanks, vats and similar containers, of a capacity exceeding 300 litres	6.5					DO,HN			0
39252000	-Doors, windows and their frames and thresholds for doors	12	8 (2008)	6.5	2010*		DO,HN			0
39253000	-Shutters, blinds (including Venetian blinds) and similar articles and parts thereof	6.5					DO,HN			0
39259000	-Other	6.5					DO,HN			0
3926	Other articles of plastics and articles of other materials of headings 39.01 to 39.14.									
39261000	-Office or school supplies	6.5					DO,HN			0
392620	-Articles of apparel and clothing accessories (including gloves, mittens and mitts)									
39262010	---Medical gloves of plastic	12	8 (2008)	6.5	2010*		DO,HN			0
39262090	---Other garments	6.5					DO,HN			0
39263000	-Fittings for furniture, coachwork or the like	6.5					DO,HN			0
39264000	-Statuettes and other ornamental articles	6.5					DO,HN			0
392690	-Other									
3926903	---Medical and pharmaceutical articles:									
39269031	----Containers for samples	12	8 (2008)	6.5	2010*		DO,HN			0
ex39269031	-----For use in civil aircraft	0					DO,HN,US			0
39269032	----Medical plates for culture	12	8 (2008)	6.5	2010*		DO,HN			0
ex39269032	-----For use in civil aircraft	0					DO,HN,US			0
39269039	----Other	12	8 (2008)	6.5	2010*		DO,HN			0
ex39269039	-----For use in civil aircraft	0					DO,HN,US			0
ex39269040	----For use in civil aircraft	0					DO,HN,US			0
39269040	---Plastic screws, bolts, rings and similar parts	6.5					DO,HN			0
39269050	---Plastic locks of handbags, suitcase angles, arches, etc	6.5					DO,HN			0

HS	Description	Bound rate at date of accession	Interim	Final Bound	Implementation	Present concession established	INR	Concession first incorporated in a GATT Schedule	Earlier INRs	ODCs
ex39269050	----For use in civil aircraft	0					DO,HN,US			0
3926906	---Furniture coverings, goods' coverings, carriage coverings and similar protective articles:									
39269061	----Plastic coverings for furniture, vehicles and similar, for goods	6.5					DO,HN			0
ex39269061	-----For use in civil aircraft	0					DO,HN,US			0
39269069	----Other	6.5					DO,HN			0
ex39269069	-----For use in civil aircraft	0					DO,HN,US			0
39269070	---Plastic transmission and conveyor belts	6.5								0
ex39269070	----For use in civil aircraft	0					US			0
ex39269080	----For use in civil aircraft	0					DO,HN,US			0
39269080	---Plastic technical items for industrial and agricultural	6.5					DO,HN			0
3926909	---Other:									
ex39269091	-----For use in civil aircraft	0					DO,HN,US			0
39269091	----Rosaries	20		6.5	2010*		DO,HN			0
ex39269092	-----For use in civil aircraft	0					DO,HN,US			0
39269092	----Plastic imitation glass for watches	6.5					DO,HN			0
ex39269093	-----For use in civil aircraft	0					DO,HN,US			0
39269093	----Plastic fans	6.5					DO,HN			0
4001	Natural rubber, balata, gutta-percha, guayule, chicle and similar natural gums, in primary forms or in plates, sheets or strip.									
39269099	----Other miscellaneous plastic items	6.5					DO,HN			0
ex39269099	-----For use in civil aircraft	0					DO,HN,US			0
40011000	-Natural rubber latex, whether or not pre-vulcanised	15								0
40012	-Natural rubber in other forms:									
40012100	--Smoked sheets	15								0
40012200	--Technically specified natural rubber (TSNR)	15								0
40012900	--Other	15								0
40013000	-Balata, gutta-percha, guayule, chicle and similar natural gums	15								0
4002	Synthetic rubber and factice derived from oils, in primary forms or in plates, sheets or strip; mixtures of any product of heading 40.01 with any product of this heading, in primary forms or in plates, sheets or strip.									

HS	Description	Bound rate at date of accession	Interim	Final Bound	Implementation	Present concession established	INR	Concession first incorporated in a GATT Schedule	Earlier INRs	ODCs
40021	-Styrene-butadiene rubber (SBR); carboxylated styrene-butadiene rubber (XSBR):									
40021100	--Latex	15								0
40021900	--Other	15		13	2008					0
40022000	-Butadiene rubber (BR)	8								0
40023	-Isobutene-isoprene (butyl) rubber (IIR); halo-isobutene-isoprene rubber (CIIR or BIIR):									
40023100	--Isobutene-isoprene (butyl) rubber (IIR)	8								0
40023900	--Other	8								0
40024	-Chloroprene (chlorobutadiene) rubber (CR):									
40024100	--Latex	8								0
40024900	--Other	8								0
40025	-Acrylonitrile-butadiene rubber (NBR):									
40025100	--Latex	8								0
40025900	--Other	8								0
40026000	-Isoprene rubber (IR)	8								0
40027000	-Ethylene-propylene-non-conjugated diene rubber (EPDM)	8								0
40028000	-Mixtures of any product of heading 40.01 with any product of this heading	8								0
40029	-Other:									
40029100	--Latex	8								0
40029900	--Other	8								0
40030000	Reclaimed rubber in primary forms or in plates, sheets or strip.	15								0
40040000	Waste, parings and scrap of rubber (other than hard rubber) and powders and granules obtained therefrom.	15								0
4005	Compounded rubber, unvulcanised, in primary forms or in plates, sheets or strip.									
40051000	-Compounded with carbon black or silica	7								0
40052000	-Solutions; dispersions other than those of subheading 4005.10	15								0
40059	-Other:									
40059100	--Plates, sheets and strip	15								0
40059900	--Other	15								0

HS	Description	Bound rate at date of accession	Interim	Final Bound	Implementation	Present concession established	INR	Concession first incorporated in a GATT Schedule	Earlier INRs	ODCs
4006	Other forms (for example, rods, tubes and profile shapes) and articles (for example, discs and rings), of unvulcanised rubber.									
40061000	-Camel-back strips for retreading rubber tyres	15								0
400690	-Other									
40069010	---Tubes of unvulcanized rubber	15								0
40069020	---Discs, rings and joints of unvulcanized rubber	15								0
40069030	---Threads of unvulcanized rubber	15								0
40069040	---Plates, sheets and strips of unvulcanized rubber	15								0
40069090	---Other unvulcanized rubber	15		13	2010					0
40070000	Vulcanised rubber thread and cord.	15		13	2010					0
4008	Plates, sheets, strip, rods and profile shapes, of vulcanised rubber other than hard rubber.									
40081	-Of cellular rubber:									
40081100	--Plates, sheets and strip	15								0
40081900	--Other	15								0
40082	-Of non-cellular rubber:									
40082100	--Plates, sheets and strip	15		13	2010					0
40082900	--Other	15								0
ex40082900	---For use in civil aircraft	0					US			0
4009	Tubes, pipes and hoses, of vulcanised rubber other than hard rubber, with or without their fittings (for example, joints, elbows, flanges).									
40091	-Not reinforced or otherwise combined with other materials:									
400911	--Without fittings									
40091110	---For transportation	15								0
40091190	---Other	15								0
400912	--With fittings									
40091210	---For transportation	15								0
ex40091210	----For use in civil aircraft	0					US			0
ex40091290	----For use in civil aircraft	0					US			0
40091290	---Other	15								0
40092	-Reinforced or otherwise combined only with metal:									
400921	--Without fittings									
40092110	---For transportation	15								0

HS	Description	Bound rate at date of accession	Interim	Final Bound	Implementation	Present concession established	INR	Concession first incorporated in a GATT Schedule	Earlier INRs	ODCs
40092190	---Other	15								0
400922	--With fittings									
40092210	---For transportation	15								0
ex40092210	----For use in civil aircraft	0					US			0
ex40092290	----For use in civil aircraft	0					US			0
40092290	---Other	15								0
40093	-Reinforced or otherwise combined only with textile materials:									
400931	--Without fittings									
40093110	---For transportation	15								0
40093190	---Other	15								0
400932	--With fittings									
40093210	---For transportation	15								0
ex40093210	----For use in civil aircraft	0					US			0
ex40093290	----For use in civil aircraft	0					US			0
40093290	---Other	15								0
40094	-Reinforced or otherwise combined with other materials:									
400941	--Without fittings									
40094110	---For transportation	15								0
40094190	---Other	15								0
400942	--With fittings									
40094210	---For transportation	15								0
ex40094210	----For use in civil aircraft	0					US			0
40094290	---Other	15								0
ex40094290	----For use in civil aircraft	0					US			0
4010	Conveyor or transmission belts or belting, of vulcanised rubber.									
40101	-Conveyor belts or belting:									
40101100	--Reinforced only with metal	15								0
40101200	--Reinforced only with textile materials	15								0
40101300	--Reinforced only with plastics	15								0
40101900	--Other	15								0
40103	-Transmission belts or belting:									
40103100	--Endless transmission belts of trapezoidal cross-section (V-belts), V-ribbed, of an outside circumference exceeding 60 cm but not exceeding 180 cm	15								0

HS	Description	Bound rate at date of accession	Interim	Final Bound	Implementation	Present concession established	INR	Concession first incorporated in a GATT Schedule	Earlier INRs	ODCs
40103200	--Endless transmission belts of trapezoidal cross-section (V-belts), other than V-ribbed, of an outside circumference exceeding 60 cm but not exceeding 180 cm	15								0
40103300	--Endless transmission belts of trapezoidal cross-section (V-belts), V-ribbed, of an outside circumference exceeding 180 cm but not exceeding 240 cm	15								0
40103400	--Endless transmission belts of trapezoidal cross-section (V-belts), other than V-ribbed, of an outside circumference exceeding 180 cm but not exceeding 240 cm	15								0
40103500	--Endless synchronous belts, of an outside circumference exceeding 60 cm but not exceeding 150 cm	15								0
40103600	--Endless synchronous belts, of an outside circumference exceeding 150 cm but not exceeding 198 cm	15								0
40103900	--Other	15								0
4011	New pneumatic tyres, of rubber.									
40111000	-Of a kind used on motor cars (including station wagons and racing cars)	7								0
40112000	-Of a kind used on buses or lorries	7					CN,IN			0
40113000	-Of a kind used on aircraft	15								0
ex40113000	--For use in civil aircraft	0					US			0
40114000	-Of a kind used on motorcycles	15								0
40115000	-Of a kind used on bicycles	10					IN			0
40116	-Other, having a "herring-bone" or similar tread:									
40116100	--Of a kind used on agricultural or forestry vehicles and machines	15		13	2008					0
40116200	--Of a kind used on construction or industrial handling vehicles and machines and having a rim size not exceeding 61 cm	15		13	2008					0
40116300	--Of a kind used on construction or industrial handling vehicles and machines and having a rim size exceeding 61 cm	15		13	2008					0
40116900	--Other	15		13	2008					0
40119	-Other:									

HS	Description	Bound rate at date of accession	Interim	Final Bound	Implementation	Present concession established	INR	Concession first incorporated in a GATT Schedule	Earlier INRs	ODCs
40119200	--Of a kind used on agricultural or forestry vehicles and machines	15								0
40119300	--Of a kind used on construction or industrial handling vehicles and machines and having a rim size not exceeding 61 cm	15								0
40119400	--Of a kind used on construction or industrial handling vehicles and machines and having a rim size exceeding 61 cm	15								0
40119900	--Other	10								0
4012	Retreaded or used pneumatic tyres of rubber; solid or cushion tyres, tyre treads and tyre flaps, of rubber.									
40121	-Retreaded tyres:									
40121100	--Of a kind used on motor cars (including station wagons and racing cars)	15								0
ex40121100	---For use in civil aircraft	0					US			0
40121200	--Of a kind used on buses or lorries	15								0
ex40121200	---For use in civil aircraft	0					US			0
40121300	--Of a kind used on aircraft	15								0
ex40121300	---For use in civil aircraft	0					US			0
40121900	--Other	15								0
ex40121900	---For use in civil aircraft	0					US			0
40122000	-Used pneumatic tyres	15								0
ex40122000	--For use in civil aircraft	0					US			0
40129000	-Other	10					IN			0
4013	Inner tubes, of rubber.									
40131000	-Of a kind used on motor cars (including station wagons and racing cars), buses or lorries	15								0
40132000	-Of a kind used on bicycles	10								0
40139000	-Other	15								0
4014	Hygienic or pharmaceutical articles (including teats), of vulcanised rubber other than hard rubber, with or without fittings of hard rubber.									
40141000	-Sheath contraceptives	15		13	2010					0
401490	-Other									
40149010	---Water skins, ice sacks, enemas, and the like	15								0
40149020	---Teats	15								0

HS	Description	Bound rate at date of accession	Interim	Final Bound	Implementation	Present concession established	INR	Concession first incorporated in a GATT Schedule	Earlier INRs	ODCs
40149090	---Other hygienic rubber articles	12								0
4015	Articles of apparel and clothing accessories (including gloves, mittens and mitts), for all purposes, of vulcanised rubber other than hard rubber.									
40151	-Gloves, mittens and mitts:									
40151100	--Surgical	15		13	2010		LK			0
401519	--Other									
40151910	---Gloves for fire extinguishing	8								0
40151990	---Gloves for other uses	10								0
401590	-Other									
40159010	---For divers and firemen	12								0
40159020	---Apparel for surgeons and x-ray operators	12								0
40159030	---Belts	12								0
40159040	---Coats, overcoats, baby clothes and the like	12								0
40159090	---Other	12								0
4016	Other articles of vulcanised rubber other than hard rubber.									
40161000	-Of cellular rubber	15								0
ex40161000	--For use in civil aircraft	0					US			0
40169	-Other:									
40169100	--Floor coverings and mats	15								0
40169200	--Erasers	15								0
40169300	--Gaskets, washers and other seals	15								0
ex40169300	---For use in civil aircraft	0					US			0
40169400	--Boat or dock fenders, whether or not inflatable	15								0
401695	--Other inflatable articles									
40169510	---Pneumatic mattresses, pillows and backrests	15								0
40169590	---Other inflatable articles of vulcanized rubber	15								0
401699	--Other									
ex40169910	----For use in civil aircraft	0					US			0
40169910	---Adhesive plasters for repairing tires and tubes	15		13	2010					0
ex40169920	----For use in civil aircraft	0					US			0
40169920	---Letters, figures and similar articles for stamps	15								0

HS	Description	Bound rate at date of accession	Interim	Final Bound	Implementation	Present concession established	INR	Concession first incorporated in a GATT Schedule	Earlier INRs	ODCs
40169930	---Vulcanized rubber parts of railway and tramway locomotives	15								0
ex40169930	----For use in civil aircraft	0					US			0
40169940	---Vulcanized rubber parts of tractors and motor vehicles	15								0
ex40169940	----For use in civil aircraft	0					US			0
40169950	---Vulcanized rubber parts of military tanks	15								0
ex40169950	----For use in civil aircraft	0					US			0
40169990	---Other articles of vulcanized rubber	15		13	2010					0
ex40169990	----For use in civil aircraft	0					US			0
4017	Hard rubber (for example, ebonite) in all forms, including waste and scrap; articles of hard rubber.									
ex40170010	----For use in civil aircraft	0					US			0
40170010	---Powder, waste and scraps of hard rubber	15								0
40170020	---Valves, taps and sprayers for medical enemas	15								0
ex40170020	----For use in civil aircraft	0					US			0
ex40170030	----For use in civil aircraft	0					US			0
40170030	---Hygienic bathroom appliances and the like	15								0
40170040	---Jugs and basins	15								0
ex40170040	----For use in civil aircraft	0					US			0
40170050	---Stoppers	15								0
ex40170050	----For use in civil aircraft	0					US			0
40170060	---Washers and gaskets of hard non-cellular rubber	15								0
ex40170090	----For use in civil aircraft	0					US			0
40170090	---Other hard rubber	15								0
4104	Tanned or crust hides and skins of bovine (including buffalo) or equine animals, without hair on, whether or not split, but not further prepared.									
41041	-In the wet state (including wet-blue):									
41041100	--Full grains, unsplit; grain splits	10					DO,HN,IN,KG,PY			0
41041900	--Other	10					DO,HN,IN,KG,PY			0
41044	-In the dry state (crust):									
41044100	--Full grains, unsplit; grain splits	10					DO,HN,IN,KG,PY			0
41044900	--Other	10					DO,HN,IN,KG,PY			0

HS	Description	Bound rate at date of accession	Interim	Final Bound	Implementation	Present concession established	INR	Concession first incorporated in a GATT Schedule	Earlier INRs	ODCs
4105	Tanned or crust skins of sheep or lambs, without wool on, whether or not split, but not further prepared.									
41051000	-In the wet state (including wet-blue)	15								0
41053000	-In the dry state (crust)	15								0
4106	Tanned or crust hides and skins of other animals, without wool or hair on, whether or not split, but not further prepared.									
41062	-Of goats or kids:									
41062100	--In the wet state (including wet-blue)	15								0
41062200	--In the dry state (crust)	15								0
41063	-Of swine:									
41063100	--In the wet state (including wet-blue)	P								0
41063200	--In the dry state (crust)	P								0
41064000	-Of reptiles	15								0
41069	-Other:									
41069100	--In the wet state (including wet-blue)	15					KG			0
41069200	--In the dry state (crust)	15					KG			0
4107	Leather further prepared after tanning or crusting, including parchment-dressed leather, of bovine (including buffalo) or equine animals, without hair on, whether or not split, other than leather of heading 41.14.									
41071	-Whole hides and skins:									
41071100	--Full grains, unsplit	10					DO,HN,IN,KG,PY			0
41071200	--Grain splits	10					DO,HN,IN,KG,PY			0
41071900	--Other	10					DO,HN,IN,KG,PY			0
41079	-Other, including sides:									
41079100	--Full grains, unsplit	12					DO,HN			0
41079200	--Grain splits	12					DO,HN			0
41079900	--Other	10					DO,HN,IN			0
41120000	Leather further prepared after tanning or crusting, including parchment-dressed leather, of sheep or lamb, without wool on, whether or not split, other than leather of heading 41.14.	15								0

HS	Description	Bound rate at date of accession	Interim	Final Bound	Implementation	Present concession established	INR	Concession first incorporated in a GATT Schedule	Earlier INRs	ODCs
4113	Leather further prepared after tanning or crusting, including parchment-dressed leather, of other animals, without wool or hair on, whether or not split, other than leather of heading 41.14.									
41131000	-Of goats or kids	15								0
41132000	-Of swine	P								0
41133000	-Of reptiles	15								0
41139000	-Other	15					KG			0
4114	Chamois (including combination chamois) leather; patent leather and patent laminated leather; metallised leather.									
41141000	-Chamois (including combination chamois) leather	15								0
41142000	-Patent leather and patent laminated leather; metallised leather	15								0
4115	Composition leather with a basis of leather or leather fibre, in slabs, sheets or strip, whether or not in rolls; parings and other waste of leather or of composition leather, not suitable for the manufacture of leather articles; leather dust, powder and flour.									
41151000	-Composition leather with a basis of leather or leather fibre, in slabs, sheets or strip, whether or not in rolls	10					KG,PY			0
41152000	-Parings and other waste of leather or of composition leather, not suitable for the manufacture of leather articles; leather dust, powder and flour	10					PY			0
42010000	Saddlery and harness for any animal (including traces, leads, knee pads, muzzles, saddle cloths, saddle bags, dog coats and the like), of any material.	15					DO,HN			0

162

HS	Description	Bound rate at date of accession	Interim	Final Bound	Implementation	Present concession established	INR	Concession first incorporated in a GATT Schedule	Earlier INRs	ODCs
4202	Trunks, suit-cases, vanity-cases, executive-cases, brief-cases, school satchels, spectacle cases, binocular cases, camera cases, musical instrument cases, gun cases, holsters and similar containers; travelling-bags, insulated food or beverages bags, toilet bags, rucksacks, handbags, shopping-bags, wallets, purses, map-cases, cigarette-cases, tobacco-pouches, tool bags, sports bags, bottle-cases, jewellery boxes, powder-boxes, cutlery cases and similar containers, of leather or of composition leather, of sheeting of plastics, of textile materials, of vulcanised fibre or of paperboard, or wholly or mainly covered with such materials or with paper.									
42021	-Trunks, suit-cases, vanity-cases, executive-cases, brief-cases, school satchels and similar containers:									
420211	--With outer surface of leather, of composition leather or of patent leather									
42021110	---Leather trunks and suitcases	15					DO,HN			0
42021120	---Leather briefcases	15					DO,HN			0
42021130	---Leather school satchels	15					DO,HN			0
42021190	---Other leather cases and trunks	15					DO,HN			0
420212	--With outer surface of plastics or of textile materials									
42021210	---Textile or plastic trunks and suitcases	10					CN			0
42021220	---Textile or plastic briefcases	10					CN			0
42021230	---Textile or plastic school satchels	10					CN			0
42021290	---Other textile or plastic cases or trunks	10					CN			0
420219	--Other									
42021910	---Cases and trunks with outer surface of wood	15								0
42021920	---Cases and trunks with outer surface of iron	15								0
42021990	---Other cases and trunks	15								0
42022	-Handbags, whether or not with shoulder strap, including those without handle:									
42022100	--With outer surface of leather, of composition leather or of patent leather	15					DO,HN			0

HS	Description	Bound rate at date of accession	Interim	Final Bound	Implementation	Present concession established	INR	Concession first incorporated in a GATT Schedule	Earlier INRs	ODCs
42022200	--With outer surface of plastic sheeting or of textile materials	10								0
42022900	--Other	15								0
42023	-Articles of a kind normally carried in the pocket or in the handbag:									
42023100	--With outer surface of leather, of composition leather or of patent leather	10					DO,HN,IN			0
42023200	--With outer surface of plastic sheeting or of textile materials	10								0
42023900	--Other	15								0
42029	-Other:									
42029100	--With outer surface of leather, of composition leather or of patent leather	15								0
42029200	--With outer surface of plastic sheeting or of textile materials	15								0
42029900	--Other	15								0
4203	Articles of apparel and clothing accessories, of leather or of composition leather.									
42031000	-Articles of apparel	8					DO,EC,HN			0
42032	-Gloves, mittens and mitts:									
42032100	--Specially designed for use in sports	15								0
42032900	--Other	10					DO,HN			0
42033000	-Belts and bandoliers	15								0
42034000	-Other clothing accessories	8								0
4204	Articles of leather or of composition leather, of a kind used in machinery or mechanical appliances or for other technical uses.									
4204001	---Conveyor belts and transmission belts:									
42040011	----Conveyor and transmission belts of leather, for industrial use	15								0
42040019	----Other	15								0
42040030	---Tubes and pipes of leather	15								0
42040040	---Plastic clothes racks	15								0
42040090	---Other conveyor and transmission belts of leather, for industrial use	15								0
4205	Other articles of leather or of composition leather.									
42050010	---Chamois leather made especially for wiping cars	15								0
42050020	---Covers of puff seats, unstuffed	10								0

HS	Description	Bound rate at date of accession	Interim	Final Bound	Implementation	Present concession established	INR	Concession first incorporated in a GATT Schedule	Earlier INRs	ODCs
42050030	---Shoe strings, of leather	15								0
42050040	---Desk pads of leather or covered with leather	15								0
42050050	---Waterskins and other ornamented articles	15								0
42050060	---Parts of straps, buckles, locks and frames, leather	15								0
42050090	---Other leather articles	15								0
4206	Articles of gut (other than silk-worm gut), of goldbeater's skin, of bladders or of tendons.									
420610	-Catgut									
42061010	---Catguts, unsterilized, used in tennis rackets, etc.	15								0
42061020	---Thick guts, dressed and cut into shapes	15								0
420690	-Other									
42069010	---Articles made of bladders, such as tobacco pouches	15								0
42069020	---Articles made of tendons, such as machine belts	15								0
42069090	---Other articles of guts or bladders	15								0
4302	Tanned or dressed furskins (including heads, tails, paws and other pieces or cuttings), unassembled, or assembled (without the addition of other materials) other than those of heading 43.03.									
43021	-Whole skins, with or without head, tail or paws, not assembled:									
43021100	--Of mink	15								0
43021300	--Of lamb, the following: Astrakhan, Broadtail, Caracul, Persian and similar lamb, Indian, Chinese, Mongolian or Tibetan lamb	15								0
43021900	--Other	15								0
43022000	-Heads, tails, paws and other pieces or cuttings, not assembled	15								0
43023000	-Whole skins and pieces or cuttings thereof, assembled	15								0
4303	Articles of apparel, clothing accessories and other articles of furskin.									
430310	-Articles of apparel and clothing accessories									
43031010	---Men's outergarments of furskins	15								0

HS	Description	Bound rate at date of accession	Interim	Final Bound	Implementation	Present concession established	INR	Concession first incorporated in a GATT Schedule	Earlier INRs	ODCs
43031090	---Other fur apparel	15								0
43039000	-Other	15								0
4304	Artificial fur and articles thereof.									
43040010	---Artificial fur in the form of pieces	15								0
43040020	---Men's outergarments of artificial fur	15								0
43040090	---Other articles of artificial fur	15								0
4401	Fuel wood, in logs, in billets, in twigs, in faggots or in similar forms; wood in chips or particles; sawdust and wood waste and scrap, whether or not agglomerated in logs, briquettes, pellets or similar forms.									
44011000	-Fuel wood, in logs, in billets, in twigs, in faggots or in similar forms	5								0
44012	-Wood in chips or particles:									
44012100	--Coniferous	5								0
44012200	--Non-coniferous	5								0
44013000	-Sawdust and wood waste and scrap, whether or not agglomerated in logs, briquettes, pellets or similar forms	5								0
44020000	Wood charcoal (including shell or nut charcoal), whether or not agglomerated.	5								0
4403	Wood in the rough, whether or not stripped of bark or sapwood, or roughly squared.									
440310	-Treated with paint, stains, creosote or other preservatives									
44031010	---Telephone poles treated with preservatives	5								0
44031090	---Other wood treated with preservatives	5								0
440320	-Other, coniferous									
44032020	---Telephone poles of coniferous wood	5								0
44032090	---Other coniferous wood	5								0
44034	-Other, of tropical wood specified in Subheading Note 1 to this Chapter:									
440341	--Dark Red Meranti, Light Red Meranti and Meranti Bakau									
44034120	---Telephone poles of coniferous wood	5								0
44034190	---Other	5								0
440349	--Other									
44034920	---Telephone, telegraph or electric power poles.	5								0
44034990	---Other	5								0

HS	Description	Bound rate at date of accession	Interim	Final Bound	Implementation	Present concession established	INR	Concession first incorporated in a GATT Schedule	Earlier INRs	ODCs
44039	-Other:									
440391	--Of oak (Quercus spp.)									
44039120	---Telephone, telegraph or electric power poles.	5								0
44039190	---Other	5								0
440392	--Of beech (Fagus spp.)									
44039220	---Telephone, telegraph or electric power poles.	5								0
44039290	---Other	5								0
440399	--Other									
44039910	---For manufacture of match sticks	5								0
44039920	---Telephone, telegraph or electric power poles.	5								0
44039990	---Other	5								0
4404	Hoopwood; split poles; piles, pickets and stakes of wood, pointed but not sawn lengthwise; wooden sticks, roughly trimmed but not turned, bent or otherwise worked, suitable for the manufacture of walking-sticks, umbrellas, tool handles or the like; chipwood and the like.									
440410	-Coniferous									
44041010	---Hoopwood for barrel starves and paritions, coniferous	5								0
44041020	---Split poles used as partitions, etc., coniferous	5								0
44041030	---Wooden sticks trimmed but not turned, coniferous	5								0
44041040	---Pointed stakes of wood, coniferous	5								0
44041050	---Chipwood, coniferous	5								0
44041090	---Other coniferous poles and stakes	5								0
440420	-Non-coniferous									
44042010	---Hoopwood for barrel starves, partitions, non-coniferous	5								0
44042020	---Split poles used as partitions, etc., non-coniferous	5								0
44042030	---Wooden sticks, non-coniferous	5								0
44042040	---Pointed stakes of wood, non-coniferous	5								0
44042050	---Chipwood, non-coniferous	5								0
44042090	---Other non-coniferous poles and stakes	5								0

HS	Description	Bound rate at date of accession	Interim	Final Bound	Implementation	Present concession established	INR	Concession first incorporated in a GATT Schedule	Earlier INRs	ODCs
4405	Wood wool; wood flour.									
44050010	---Wood wool	5								0
44050020	---Wood flour	5								0
4406	Railway or tramway sleepers (cross-ties) of wood.									
44061000	-Not impregnated	5								0
44069000	-Other	5								0
4407	Wood sawn or chipped lengthwise, sliced or peeled, whether or not planed, sanded or end-jointed, of a thickness exceeding 6 mm.									
440710	-Coniferous									
44071010	---Planed coniferous wood over 6 mm thick	5					CA			0
44071020	---Finger-jointed coniferous wood over 6 mm thick	5					CA			0
44071090	---Other sawn coniferous wood over 6 mm thick	5					CA			0
44072	-Of tropical wood specified in Subheading Note 1 to this Chapter:									
440724	--Virola, Mahogany (Swietenia spp.), Imbuia and Balsa									
44072410	---Planed	5					EC			0
44072420	---Finger-jointed	5					EC			0
44072490	---Other	5					EC			0
440725	--Dark Red Meranti, Light Red Meranti and Meranti Bakau									
44072510	---Planed	5								0
44072520	---Finger-jointed	5								0
44072590	---Other	5								0
440726	--White Lauan, White Meranti, White Seraya, Yellow Meranti and Alan									
44072610	---Planed	5								0
44072620	---Finger-jointed	5								0
44072690	---Other	5								0
44072900	--Other	5								0
44079	-Other:									
440791	--Of oak (Quercus spp.)									
44079110	---Planed oak	5								0
44079120	---Finger-jointed oak	5								0
44079190	---Other sawn oak	5								0
440792	--Of beech (Fagus spp.)									

HS	Description	Bound rate at date of accession	Interim	Final Bound	Implementation	Present concession established	INR	Concession first incorporated in a GATT Schedule	Earlier INRs	ODCs
44079210	---Planed beech	5								0
44079220	---Finger-jointed beech	5								0
44079290	---Other sawn beech	5								0
440799	--Other									
44079910	---Planed other wood	5								0
44079920	---Finger-jointed other wood	5								0
44079990	---Other sawn wood	5								0
4408	Sheets for veneering (including those obtained by slicing laminated wood), for plywood or for other similar laminated wood and other wood, sawn lengthwise, sliced or peeled, whether or not planed, sanded, spliced or end-jointed, of a thickness not exceeding 6 mm.									
440810	-Coniferous									
44081010	---Planed coniferous plywood, not over 6 mm thick	5					DO,HN,ID			0
44081020	---Finger-jointed coniferous plywood, not over 6 mm thick	5					DO,HN,ID			0
44081090	---Other coniferous plywood, not over 6 mm thick	5					DO,HN,ID			0
44083	-Of tropical wood specified in Subheading Note 1 to this Chapter:									
440831	--Dark Red Meranti, Light Red Meranti and Meranti Bakau									
44083110	---Planed	5								0
44083120	---Finger-jointed	5								0
44083190	---Other	5								0
440839	--Other									
44083910	---Planed	5								0
44083920	---Finger-jointed	5								0
44083990	---Other	5								0
440890	-Other									
44089010	---Planed	5								0
44089020	---Finger-jointed	5								0
44089090	---Other	5								0

HS	Description	Bound rate at date of accession	Interim	Final Bound	Implementation	Present concession established	INR	Concession first incorporated in a GATT Schedule	Earlier INRs	ODCs
4409	Wood (including strips and friezes for parquet flooring, not assembled) continuously shaped (tongued, grooved, rebated, chamfered, V-jointed, beaded, moulded, rounded or the like) along any of its edges, ends or faces, whether or not planed, sanded or end-jointed.									
440910	-Coniferous									
44091010	---Tongued wood, coniferous	5								0
44091020	---Chamfered wood, coniferous	5								0
44091030	---Planed panels with rounded edges, coniferous	5								0
44091040	---V-jointed wood, coniferous	5								0
44091050	---Tongued or grooved wood for ceilings, coniferous	5								0
44091060	---Wooden beadings and mouldings, coniferous	20								0
44091070	---Rounded wood, coniferous	5								0
44091090	---Other coniferous wood, continuously shaped	5								0
440920	-Non-coniferous									
44092010	---Tongued wood, non-coniferous	5					EC			0
44092020	---Chamfered wood, non-coniferous	5					EC			0
44092030	---Planed panels with rounded edges, non-coniferous	5					EC			0
44092040	---V-jointed wood, non-coniferous	5					EC			0
44092050	---Tongued or grooved wood for ceilings, non-coniferous	5					EC			0
44092060	---Wooden beadings, mouldings for pictures, non-coniferous	20					EC			0
44092070	---Rounded wood, non-coniferous	5					EC			0
44092090	---Other non-coniferous wood, continuously shaped	5					EC			0
4410	Particle board and similar board (for example, oriented strand board and waferboard) of wood or other ligneous materials, whether or not agglomerated with resins or other organic binding substances.									
44102	-Oriented strand board and waferboard, of wood:									
44102100	--Unworked or not further worked than sanded	5								0

HS	Description	Bound rate at date of accession	Interim	Final Bound	Implementation	Present concession established	INR	Concession first incorporated in a GATT Schedule	Earlier INRs	ODCs
44102900	--Other	5								0
44103	-Other, of wood:									
44103100	--Unworked or not further worked than sanded	5								0
44103200	--Surface-covered with melamine-impregnated paper	5								0
44103300	--Surface-covered with decorative laminates of plastics	5								0
44103900	--Other	5								0
44109000	-Other	5					EC,ID			0
4411	Fibreboard of wood or other ligneous materials, whether or not bonded with resins or other organic substances.									
44111	-Fibreboard of a density exceeding 0.8 g/cm3:									
44111100	--Not mechanically worked or surface covered	5					ID			0
44111900	--Other	5					EC,ID			0
44112	-Fibreboard of a density exceeding 0.5 g/cm3 but not exceeding 0.8 g/cm3:									
44112100	--Not mechanically worked or surface covered	5					CA,ID			0
44112900	--Other	5								0
44113	-Fibreboard of a density exceeding 0.35 g/cm3 but not exceeding 0.5 g/cm3:									
44113100	--Not mechanically worked or surface covered	5								0
44113900	--Other	5								0
44119	-Other:									
44119100	--Not mechanically worked or surface covered	5								0
44119900	--Other	5								0
4412	Plywood, veneered panels and similar laminated wood.									
44121	-Plywood consisting solely of sheets of wood, each ply not exceeding 6 mm thickness:									
44121300	--With at least one outer ply of tropical wood specified in Subheading Note 1 to this Chapter	5					EC			0
44121400	--Other, with at least one outer ply of non-coniferous wood	5					DO,HN			0
44121900	--Other	5					ID			0

HS	Description	Bound rate at date of accession	Interim	Final Bound	Implementation	Present concession established	INR	Concession first incorporated in a GATT Schedule	Earlier INRs	ODCs
44122	-Other, with at least one outer ply of non-coniferous wood:									
44122200	--With at least one ply of tropical wood specified in Subheading Note 1 to this Chapter	5								0
44122300	--Other, containing at least one layer of particle board	5								0
44122900	--Other	5					ID			0
44129	-Other:									
44129200	--With at least one ply of tropical wood specified in Subheading Note 1 to this Chapter	5								0
44129300	--Other, containing at least one layer of particle board	5								0
44129900	--Other	5					ID			0
44130000	Densified wood, in blocks, plates, strips or profile shapes.	5					ID			0
44140000	Wooden frames for paintings, photographs, mirrors or similar objects.	20								0
4415	Packing cases, boxes, crates, drums and similar packings, of wood; cable-drums of wood; pallets, box pallets and other load boards, of wood; pallet collars of wood.									
441510	-Cases, boxes, crates, drums and similar packings; cable-drums									
44151010	---Ordinary boxes and small boxes for packing, wood	20								0
44151020	---Empty match boxes, wood	20								0
44151040	---Cable drums, wood	20								0
44151090	---Other boxes and crates, wood	20								0
44152000	-Pallets, box pallets and other load boards; pallet collars	20								0
44160000	Casks, barrels, vats, tubs and other coopers' products and parts thereof, of wood, including staves.	20								0
4417	Tools, tool bodies, tool handles, broom or brush bodies and handles, of wood; boot or shoe lasts and trees, of wood.									
44170010	---Tools whose active part is of wood	5					ID			0
44170020	---Tool bodies	5					ID			0
44170030	---Tool handles	5					ID			0
44170040	---Broom and brush bodies	5					ID			0
44170050	---Broom and brush handles	5					ID			0

HS	Description	Bound rate at date of accession	Interim	Final Bound	Implementation	Present concession established	INR	Concession first incorporated in a GATT Schedule	Earlier INRs	ODCs
44170060	---Shoe lasts, whether or not with metal base	5					ID			0
44170090	---Other	5					ID			0
4418	Builders' joinery and carpentry of wood, including cellular wood panels, assembled parquet panels, shingles and shakes.									
44181000	-Windows, French-windows and their frames	12					DO,HN			0
44182000	-Doors and their frames and thresholds	12					DO,HN			0
44183000	-Parquet panels	5								0
44184000	-Shuttering for concrete constructional work	5								0
44185000	-Shingles and shakes	5								0
441890	-Other									
44189010	---Handrails for staircases	12								0
44189020	---Cellular wood panels	5								0
44189090	---Other builders' joinery	5								0
44190000	Tableware and kitchenware, of wood.	20					DO,HN			0
4420	Wood marquetry and inlaid wood; caskets and cases for jewellery or cutlery, and similar articles, of wood; statuettes and other ornaments, of wood; wooden articles of furniture not falling in Chapter 94.									
44201000	-Statuettes and other ornaments, of wood	5								0
442090	-Other									
44209010	---Caskets, small boxes and receptacles, etc.	5								0
44209020	---Articles of wood furniture not classified as miscellaneous manufactured products (Chapter 94)	5								0
44209030	---Wood beads	20								0
44209040	---Wood censers	5								0
44209090	---Other wood cases, etc.	5								0
4421	Other articles of wood.									
44211000	-Clothes hangers	20								0
442190	-Other									
44219010	---Wood spools, cops, bobbins, and similar	5								0
44219020	---Wooden farm equipment and cages	5								0
44219030	---Stage decors	5								0

HS	Description	Bound rate at date of accession	Interim	Final Bound	Implementation	Present concession established	INR	Concession first incorporated in a GATT Schedule	Earlier INRs	ODCs
44219040	---Portable ladders, wood	5								0
44219050	---Stepped platforms, wood	5								0
44219060	---Advertisement boards, signboards, road signs, wood	20								0
44219070	---Toothpicks, wood	20								0
44219080	---Screens of different types and their axles, wood	5								0
4421909	---Other:									
44219091	----Washing boards and ironing boards, wood	20								0
44219092	----Clothes pegs (pins), wood	20								0
44219093	----Paving sets, wood	5								0
44219094	----Processed splints for matches	5								0
44219095	----Wooden pegs or pins for shoes	5								0
44219096	----Measures and scales for capacity, wood	20								0
44219099	----Other miscellaneous wood articles	20								0
4501	Natural cork, raw or simply prepared; waste cork; crushed, granulated or ground cork.									
45011000	-Natural cork, raw or simply prepared	15								0
45019000	-Other	15								0
4502	Natural cork, debacked or roughly squared, or in rectangular (including square) blocks, plates, sheets or strip (including sharp-edged blanks for corks or stoppers).									
45020010	---Cubes and blocks for cork manufacturing	15								0
45020020	---Cork plates, cubes and sheets for refrigeration	15								0
45020090	---Other natural cork, shaped	15								0
4503	Articles of natural cork.									
45031000	-Corks and stoppers	15								0
450390	-Other									
45039010	---Floats for fishing nets, natural cork	15								0
45039020	---Spare parts for machinery, natural cork	15								0
45039030	---Discs and rings for lining stoppers, natural cork	15								0
45039040	---Articles for refrigeration industry, natural cork	15								0
45039090	---Other natural cork articles	15								0

HS	Description	Bound rate at date of accession	Interim	Final Bound	Implementation	Present concession established	INR	Concession first incorporated in a GATT Schedule	Earlier INRs	ODCs
4504	Agglomerated cork (with or without a binding substance) and articles of agglomerated cork.									
450410	-Blocks, plates, sheets and strip; tiles of any shape; solid cylinders, including discs									
45041010	---Agglomerated cork for refrigeration or preservation	15								0
45041090	---Other agglomerated cork blocks, sheets, tiles, etc.	15								0
450490	-Other									
45049010	---Floats for fishing nets, agglomerated cork	15								0
ex45049010	----For use in civil aircraft	0					US			0
ex45049020	----For use in civil aircraft	0					US			0
45049020	---Spare parts for machinery, agglomerated cork	15								0
ex45049030	----For use in civil aircraft	0					US			0
45049030	---Stoppers, agglomerated cork	15								0
45049040	---Discs for lining stoppers, agglomerated cork	15								0
ex45049040	----For use in civil aircraft	0					US			0
45049090	---Other articles of agglomerated cork	15								0
ex45049090	----For use in civil aircraft	0					US			0
4601	Plaits and similar products of plaiting materials, whether or not assembled into strips; plaiting materials, plaits and similar products of plaiting materials, bound together in parallel strands or woven, in sheet form, whether or not being finished articles (for example, mats, matting, screens).									
46012000	-Mats, matting and screens of vegetable materials	15								0
46019	-Other:									
46019100	--Of vegetable materials	15								0
46019900	--Other	15								0
4602	Basketwork, wickerwork and other articles, made directly to shape from plaiting materials or made up from goods of heading 46.01; articles of loofah.									
460210	-Of vegetable materials									

HS	Description	Bound rate at date of accession	Interim	Final Bound	Implementation	Present concession established	INR	Concession first incorporated in a GATT Schedule	Earlier INRs	ODCs
46021010	---Baskets of vegetable materials (See Endnote 4)	8					PH			0
46021020	---Handbags and the like of vegetable materials (See Endnote 5)	8					PH			0
46021030	---Travel suitcases and boxes of vegetable materials	10								0
46021040	---Bird cages and similar articles of vegetable materials	10								0
46021050	---Fish traps of vegetable materials	10								0
46021060	---Housekeeping articles of vegetable materials	10								0
46021070	---Envelopes for bottles of vegetable materials	10								0
46021080	---Articles of loofah of vegetable materials	10								0
46021090	---Other articles of vegetable materials	10								0
460290	-Other									
4602901	---Of plastics:									
46029011	----Baskets of plastics	15								0
46029012	----Handbags and the like of plastics	15								0
46029013	----Travel suitcases and boxes of plastics	15								0
46029014	----Bird cages and similar articles of plastics	15								0
46029015	----Fish traps of plastics	15								0
46029016	----Housekeeping articles of plastics	15								0
46029017	----Envelopes for bottles of plastics	15								0
46029018	----Articles of loofah of plastics	15								0
46029019	----Other plastic basketware and the like	15								0
46029090	---Other plastic articles	15								0
47010000	Mechanical wood pulp.	10								0
47020000	Chemical wood pulp, dissolving grades.	10								0
4703	Chemical wood pulp, soda or sulphate, other than dissolving grades.									
47031	-Unbleached:									
47031100	--Coniferous	10								0
47031900	--Non-coniferous	10								0
47032	-Semi-bleached or bleached:									
47032100	--Coniferous	10					CA,US			0
47032900	--Non-coniferous	10					CA			0
4704	Chemical wood pulp, sulphite, other than dissolving grades.									

HS	Description	Bound rate at date of accession	Interim	Final Bound	Implementation	Present concession established	INR	Concession first incorporated in a GATT Schedule	Earlier INRs	ODCs
47041	-Unbleached:									
47041100	--Coniferous	10								0
47041900	--Non-coniferous	10								0
47042	-Semi-bleached or bleached:									
47042100	--Coniferous	10								0
47042900	--Non-coniferous	10								0
47050000	Wood pulp obtained by a combination of mechanical and chemical pulping processes.	10								0
4706	Pulps of fibres derived from recovered (waste and scrap) paper or paperboard or of other fibrous cellulosic material.									
47061000	-Cotton linters pulp	10								0
47062000	-Pulps of fibres derived from recovered (waste and scrap) paper or paperboard	10								0
47069	-Other:									
47069100	--Mechanical	10								0
47069200	--Chemical	10								0
47069300	--Semi-chemical	10								0
4707	Recovered (waste and scrap) paper or paperboard.									
47071000	-Unbleached kraft paper or paperboard or corrugated paper or paperboard	10								0
47072000	-Other paper or paperboard made mainly of bleached chemical pulp, not coloured in the mass	10								0
47073000	-Paper or paperboard made mainly of mechanical pulp (for example, newspapers, journals and similar printed matter)	10								0
470790	-Other, including unsorted waste and scrap									
47079010	---Old newspapers	10								0
47079090	---Other waste and scrap of paper and paperboard	10								0
48010000	Newsprint, in rolls or sheets.	8					US			0
4802	Uncoated paper and paperboard, of a kind used for writing, printing or other graphic purposes, and non perforated punch-cards and punch tape paper, in rolls or rectangular (including square) sheets, of any size, other than paper of heading 48.01 or 48.03; hand-made paper and paperboard.									

HS	Description	Bound rate at date of accession	Interim	Final Bound	Implementation	Present concession established	INR	Concession first incorporated in a GATT Schedule	Earlier INRs	ODCs
48021000	-Hand-made paper and paperboard	10								0
48022000	-Paper and paperboard of a kind used as a base for photo-sensitive, heat-sensitive or electro-sensitive paper or paperboard	10								0
48023000	-Carbonising base paper	10								0
48024000	-Wallpaper base	10								0
48025	-Other paper and paperboard, not containing fibres obtained by a mechanical or chemi-mechanical process or of which not more than 10 % by weight of the total fibre content consists of such fibres:									
48025400	--Weighing less than 40 g/m²	5					CA,ID,US			0
48025500	--Weighing 40 g/m² or more but not more than 150 g/m², in rolls	5					CA,US			0
48025600	--Weighing 40 g/m² or more but not more than 150 g/m², in sheets with one side not exceeding 435 mm and the other side not exceeding 297 mm in the unfolded state	5					CA,US			0
48025700	--Other, weighing 40 g/m² or more but not more than 150 g/m²	5					CA,US			0
48025800	--Weighing more than 150 g/m²	5					CA,US			0
48026	-Other paper and paperboard, of which more than 10 % by weight of the total fibre content consists of fibres obtained by a mechanical or chemi-mechanical process:									
48026100	--In rolls	5					CA,ID,US			0
48026200	--In sheets with one side not exceeding 435 mm and the other side not exceeding 297 mm in the unfolded state	5					CA,ID,US			0
48026900	--Other	5					CA,ID,US			0
4803	Toilet or facial tissue stock, towel or napkin stock and similar paper of a kind used for household or sanitary purposes, cellulose wadding and webs of cellulose fibres, whether or not creped, crinkled, embossed, perforated, surface-coloured, surface-decorated or printed, in rolls or sheets.									
48030010	---Toilet or facial tissue stock, towels for household	15								0
48030090	---Other household or sanitary paper	15								0

HS	Description	Bound rate at date of accession	Interim	Final Bound	Implementation	Present concession established	INR	Concession first incorporated in a GATT Schedule	Earlier INRs	ODCs
4804	Uncoated kraft paper and paperboard, in rolls or sheets, other than that of heading 48.02 or 48.03.									
48041	-Kraftliner:									
48041100	--Unbleached	8					US			0
48041900	--Other	8					US			0
48042	-Sack kraft paper:									
48042100	--Unbleached	10					CA,US			0
48042900	--Other	8					US			0
48043	-Other kraft paper and paperboard weighing 150 g/m² or less:									
48043100	--Unbleached	10					US			0
48043900	--Other	8					US			0
48044	-Other kraft paper and paperboard weighing more than 150 g/m² but less than 225 g/m²:									
48044100	--Unbleached	10					US			0
48044200	--Bleached uniformly throughout the mass and of which more than 95 % by weight of the total fibre content consists of wood fibres obtained by a chemical process	10					US			0
48044900	--Other	10								0
480450	-Other kraft paper and paperboard weighing 225 g/m² or									
48045100	--Unbleached	10					US			0
48045200	--Bleached uniformly throughout the mass and of which more than 95 % by weight of the total fibre content consists of wood fibres obtained by a chemical process	10					US			0
48045900	--Other	10								0
4805	Other uncoated paper and paperboard, in rolls or sheets, not further worked or processed than as specified in Note 3 to this Chapter.									
48051	-Fluting paper:									
48051100	--Semi-chemical fluting paper	8					CA,US			0
48051200	--Straw fluting paper	5					US			0
48051900	--Other	5					US			0
48052	-Testliner (recycled liner board):									
48052400	--Weighing 150 g/m² or less	5					CA,US			0
48052500	--Weighing more than 150 g/m²	5					CA,US			0

HS	Description	Bound rate at date of accession	Interim	Final Bound	Implementation	Present concession established	INR	Concession first incorporated in a GATT Schedule	Earlier INRs	ODCs
48053000	-Sulphite wrapping paper	10								0
48054000	-Filter paper and paperboard	10								0
48055000	-Felt paper and paperboard	10								0
48059	-Other:									
48059100	--Weighing 150 g/m² or less	5					CA,US			0
48059200	--Weighing more than 150 g/m² but less than 225 g/m²	5					CA,US			0
48059300	--Weighing 225 g/m² or more	5					CA,US			0
4806	Vegetable parchment, greaseproof papers, tracing papers and glassine and other glazed transparent or translucent papers, in rolls or sheets.									
48061000	-Vegetable parchment	10								0
48062000	-Greaseproof papers	10								0
48063000	-Tracing papers	10								0
48064000	-Glassine and other glazed transparent or translucent papers	10								0
48070000	Composite paper and paperboard (made by sticking flat layers of paper or paperboard together with an adhesive), not surface-coated or impregnated, whether or not internally reinforced, in rolls or sheets.	5					US			0
4808	Paper and paperboard, corrugated (with or without glued flat surface sheets), creped, crinkled, embossed or perforated, in rolls or sheets, other than paper of the kind described in heading 48.03.									
48081000	-Corrugated paper and paperboard, whether or not perforated	10					PY			0
48082000	-Sack kraft paper, creped or crinkled, whether or not embossed or perforated	10								0
48083000	-Other kraft paper, creped or crinkled, whether or not embossed or perforated	10								0
48089000	-Other	10								0
4809	Carbon paper, self-copy paper and other copying or transfer papers (including coated or impregnated paper for duplicator stencils or offset plates), whether or not printed, in rolls or sheets.									
48091000	-Carbon or similar copying papers	10					ID			0
48092000	-Self-copy paper	10								0
48099000	-Other	10					ID			0

HS	Description	Bound rate at date of accession	Interim	Final Bound	Implementation	Present concession established	INR	Concession first incorporated in a GATT Schedule	Earlier INRs	ODCs
4810	Paper and paperboard, coated on one or both sides with kaolin (China clay) or other inorganic substances, with or without a binder, and with no other coating, whether or not surface-coloured, surface-decorated or printed, in rolls or rectangular (including square) sheets, of any size.									
48101	-Paper and paperboard of a kind used for writing, printing or other graphic purposes, not containing fibres obtained by a mechanical or chemi-mechanical process or of which not more than 10 % by weight of the total fibre content consists of such fibres:									
48101300	--In rolls	5					DO,HN,ID,US			0
48101400	--In sheets with one side not exceeding 435 mm and the other side not exceeding 297 mm in the unfolded state	5					DO,HN,ID,US			0
48101900	--Other	5					DO,HN,ID,US			0
48102	-Paper and paperboard of a kind used for writing, printing or other graphic purposes, of which more than 10 % by weight of the total fibre content consists of fibres obtained by a mechanical or chemi-mechanical process:									
48102200	--Light-weight coated paper	5					DO,HN,US			0
48102900	--Other	10								0
48103	-Kraft paper and paperboard, other than that of a kind used for writing, printing or other graphic purposes:									
48103100	--Bleached uniformly throughout the mass and of which more than 95 % by weight of the total fibre content consists of wood fibres obtained by a chemical process, and weighing 150 g/m² or less	10								0
48103200	--Bleached uniformly throughout the mass and of which more than 95 % by weight of the total fibre content consists of wood fibres obtained by a chemical process, and weighing more than 150 g/m²	10								0
48103900	--Other	10								0
48109	-Other paper and paperboard:									
48109200	--Multi-ply	5					DO,HN,ID			0

HS	Description	Bound rate at date of accession	Interim	Final Bound	Implementation	Present concession established	INR	Concession first incorporated in a GATT Schedule	Earlier INRs	ODCs
48109900	--Other	10					ID			0
4811	Paper, paperboard, cellulose wadding and webs of cellulose fibres, coated, impregnated, covered, surface-coloured, surface-decorated or printed, in rolls or rectangular (including square) sheets, of any size, other than goods of the kind described in heading 48.03, 48.09 or 48.10.									
48111000	-Tarred, bituminised or asphalted paper and paperboard	10					DO,HN			0
48114	-Gummed or adhesive paper and paperboard:									
48114100	--Self-adhesive	5					DO,HN			0
48114900	--Other	5					DO,HN			0
48115	-Paper and paperboard coated, impregnated or covered with plastics (excluding adhesives):									
48115100	--Bleached, weighing more than 150 g/m²	5					DO,HN			0
48115900	--Other	5					DO,HN			0
48116000	-Paper and paperboard, coated, impregnated or covered with wax, paraffin wax, stearin, oil or glycerol	5					DO,HN			0
48119000	-Other paper, paperboard, cellulose wadding and webs of cellulose fibres	8					DO,HN			0
48120000	Filter blocks, slabs and plates, of paper pulp.	10								0
4813	Cigarette paper, whether or not cut to size or in the form of booklets or tubes.									
48131000	-In the form of booklets or tubes	10								0
48132000	-In rolls of a width not exceeding 5 cm	10								0
48139000	-Other	10								0
4814	Wallpaper and similar wall coverings; window transparencies of paper.									
48141000	-Ingrain paper	10								0
48142000	-Wallpaper and similar wall coverings, consisting of paper coated or covered, on the face side, with a grained, embossed, coloured, design-printed or otherwise decorated layer of plastics	10								0

HS	Description	Bound rate at date of accession	Interim	Final Bound	Implementation	Present concession established	INR	Concession first incorporated in a GATT Schedule	Earlier INRs	ODCs
48143000	-Wallpaper and similar wall coverings, consisting of paper covered, on the face side, with plaiting material, whether or not bound together in parallel strands or woven	10								0
48149000	-Other	10								0
48150000	Floor coverings on a base of paper or of paperboard, whether or not cut to size.	10								0
4816	Carbon paper, self-copy paper and other copying or transfer papers (other than those of heading 48.09), duplicator stencils and offset plates, of paper, whether or not put up in boxes.									
48161000	-Carbon or similar copying papers	10								0
48162000	-Self-copy paper	10					ID			0
48163000	-Duplicator stencils	10								0
48169000	-Other	10					ID			0
4817	Envelopes, letter cards, plain postcards and correspondence cards, of paper or paperboard; boxes, pouches, wallets and writing compendiums, of paper or paperboard, containing an assortment of paper stationery.									
48171000	-Envelopes	10								0
48172000	-Letter cards, plain postcards and correspondence cards	10								0
48173000	-Boxes, pouches, wallets and writing compendiums, of paper or paperboard, containing an assortment of paper stationery	10					PY			0
4818	Toilet paper and similar paper, cellulose wadding or webs of cellulose fibres, of a kind used for household or sanitary purposes, in rolls of a width not exceeding 36 cm, or cut to size or shape; handkerchiefs, cleansing tissues, towels, tablecloths, serviettes, napkins for babies, tampons, bed sheets and similar household, sanitary or hospital articles, articles of apparel and clothing accessories, of paper pulp, paper, cellulose wadding or webs of cellulose fibres.									
48181000	-Toilet paper	15								0

HS	Description	Bound rate at date of accession	Interim	Final Bound	Implementation	Present concession established	INR	Concession first incorporated in a GATT Schedule	Earlier INRs	ODCs
48182000	-Handkerchiefs, cleansing or facial tissues and towels	15								0
481830	-Tablecloths and serviettes									
48183010	---Towels	15								0
48183090	---Other	15								0
481840	-Sanitary towels and tampons, napkins and napkin liners for babies and similar sanitary articles									
48184010	---Diapers for children	15								0
48184020	---Sanitary towels for women	15								0
48184030	---Napkins for patients and cripples	10								0
48184040	---Thin pads of paper for absorption of secretions	10								0
48184090	---Other sanitary paper articles	10								0
48185000	-Articles of apparel and clothing accessories	10								0
48189000	-Other	10								0
4819	Cartons, boxes, cases, bags and other packing containers, of paper, paperboard, cellulose wadding or webs of cellulose fibres; box files, letter trays, and similar articles, of paper or paperboard of a kind used in offices, shops or the like.									
481910	-Cartons, boxes and cases, of corrugated paper or paperboard									
48191010	---Cases for perfumes, jewellery and gifts	15					EC,SV			0
48191090	---Other cases	15					EC,SV			0
481920	-Folding cartons, boxes and cases, of non-corrugated paper or paperboard									
48192010	---Non- corrugated paper boxes for perfumes and gifts	15								0
48192090	---Other boxes of non-corrugated paper	15								0
48193000	-Sacks and bags, having a base of a width of 40 cm or more	15								0
48194000	-Other sacks and bags, including cones	15								0
48195000	-Other packing containers, including record sleeves	15					ID			0
48196000	-Box files, letter trays, storage boxes and similar articles, of a kind used in offices, shops or the like	10								0

HS	Description	Bound rate at date of accession	Interim	Final Bound	Implementation	Present concession established	INR	Concession first incorporated in a GATT Schedule	Earlier INRs	ODCs
4820	Registers, account books, note books, order books, receipt books, letter pads, memorandum pads, diaries and similar articles, exercise books, blotting-pads, binders (loose-leaf or other), folders, file covers, manifold business forms, interleaved carbon sets and other articles of stationery, of paper or paperboard; albums for samples or for collections and book covers, of paper or paperboard.									
48201000	-Registers, account books, note books, order books, receipt books, letter pads, memorandum pads, diaries and similar articles	10					ID			0
48202000	-Exercise books	10					ID			0
482030	-Binders (other than book covers), folders and file covers									
48203010	---Binders, etc., with metal fittings	15								0
48203090	---Other	15								0
48204000	-Manifold business forms and interleaved carbon sets	10								0
48205000	-Albums for samples or for collections	10								0
48209000	-Other	10								0
4821	Paper or paperboard labels of all kinds, whether or not printed.									
48211000	-Printed	10					DO,HN			0
48219000	-Other	10					DO,HN			0
4822	Bobbins, spools, cops and similar supports of paper pulp, paper or paperboard (whether or not perforated or hardened).									
48221000	-Of a kind used for winding textile yarn	10								0
48229000	-Other	10								0
4823	Other paper, paperboard, cellulose wadding and webs of cellulose fibres, cut to size or shape; other articles of paper pulp, paper, paperboard, cellulose wadding or webs of cellulose fibres.									
48231	-Gummed or adhesive paper, in strips or rolls:									
48231200	--Self-adhesive	8					DO,HN,US			0
48231900	--Other	10					DO,HN			0

HS	Description	Bound rate at date of accession	Interim	Final Bound	Implementation	Present concession established	INR	Concession first incorporated in a GATT Schedule	Earlier INRs	ODCs
48232000	-Filter paper and paperboard	10					DO,HN			0
48234000	-Rolls, sheets and dials, printed for self-recording apparatus	10					DO,HN			0
48236000	-Trays, dishes, plates, cups and the like, of paper or paperboard	8					DO,HN,US			0
482370	-Moulded or pressed articles of paper pulp									
48237010	---Moulded plates used for carrying eggs	10					DO,HN			0
48237090	---Other moulded articles of paper pulp	10					DO,HN			0
482390	-Other									
ex48239010	----For use in civil aircraft	0					DO,HN,US			0
48239010	---Packing containers for sweets and fruits	10					DO,HN			0
ex48239020	----For use in civil aircraft	0					DO,HN,US			0
48239020	---Cogged or embroidered paper and the like	10					DO,HN			0
48239030	---Spacers and rings of paper	10					DO,HN			0
ex48239030	----For use in civil aircraft	0					DO,HN,US			0
ex48239040	----For use in civil aircraft	0					DO,HN,US			0
48239040	---Angles and joints for stamps and photographs	10					DO,HN			0
48239050	---Tailoring patterns	10					DO,HN			0
ex48239050	----For use in civil aircraft	0					DO,HN,US			0
48239060	---Perforated cards for jacquard spools and similar	10					DO,HN			0
ex48239060	----For use in civil aircraft	0					DO,HN,US			0
48239070	---Cartons used in textile plants, etc.	10					DO,HN			0
ex48239070	----For use in civil aircraft	0					DO,HN,US			0
48239080	---Artificial guts of waterproofing paper for sausages	10					DO,HN			0
ex48239080	----For use in civil aircraft	0					DO,HN,US			0
4823909	---Other:									
ex48239091	-----For use in civil aircraft	0					DO,HN,US			0
48239091	----Manual fans	10					DO,HN			0
ex48239092	-----For use in civil aircraft	0					US			0
48239092	----Paper wool for wrapping	10								0
48239093	----Paper strips for plaiting	10					DO,HN			0
ex48239093	-----For use in civil aircraft	0					DO,HN,US			0
48239094	----Computer form paper	10		0	2008					0
48239099	----Other paper, etc., articles, not elsewhere classified	10					DO,HN			0
ex48239099	-----For use in civil aircraft	0					DO,HN,US			0

HS	Description	Bound rate at date of accession	Interim	Final Bound	Implementation	Present concession established	INR	Concession first incorporated in a GATT Schedule	Earlier INRs	ODCs
4901	Printed books, brochures, leaflets and similar printed matter, whether or not in single sheets.									
490110	-In single sheets, whether or not folded									
49011010	---Printed cards for educational purposes	7								0
49011090	---Other books and leaflets	7								0
49019	-Other:									
49019100	--Dictionaries and encyclopaedias, and serial instalments thereof	7					EC			0
490199	--Other									
49019910	---Books, booklets and pamphlets, printed	7								0
49019920	---Books, booklets and pamphlets in Braille	7					EC			0
49019930	---School and collegiate books	7								0
49019940	---Museums and public libraries indexes, etc.	7								0
49019950	---Children's books	7								0
49019960	---Newspapers, journals and periodicals, bound	7								0
49019990	---Other printed matter	7								0
4902	Newspapers, journals and periodicals, whether or not illustrated or containing advertising material.									
490210	-Appearing at least four times a week									
49021010	---Newspapers printed at least 4 times a week	7								0
49021020	---Magazines printed at least 4 times a week	7								0
49021090	---Other periodicals printed at least 4 times a week	10								0
490290	-Other									
49029010	---Newspapers, other	7								0
49029020	---Magazines, other	7								0
49029030	---Periodicals, other	7								0
49029090	---Other journals, etc.	10								0
4903	Children's picture, drawing or colouring books.									
49030010	---Drawing and painting books for children	10								0
49030020	---Picture albums for children	10								0
49030090	---Other children's books	10								0

HS	Description	Bound rate at date of accession	Interim	Final Bound	Implementation	Present concession established	INR	Concession first incorporated in a GATT Schedule	Earlier INRs	ODCs
49040000	Music, printed or in manuscript, whether or not bound or illustrated.	10								0
4905	Maps and hydrographic or similar charts of all kinds, including atlases, wall maps, topographical plans and globes, printed.									
49051000	-Globes	10								0
49059	-Other:									
49059100	--In book form	10								0
49059900	--Other	10								0
49060000	Plans and drawings for architectural, engineering, industrial, commercial, topographical or similar purposes, being originals drawn by hand; hand-written texts; photographic reproductions on sensitised paper and carbon copies of the foregoing.	10								0
4907	Unused postage, revenue or similar stamps of current or new issue in the country in which they have, or will have, a recognised face value; stamp-impressed paper; banknotes; cheque forms; stock, share or bond certificates and similar documents of title.									
4907001	---Unused stamps of current issue in the country in which they have a recognised face value:									
49070011	----Postage stamps	10								0
49070012	----Fiscal stamps	10								0
49070019	----Other stamps	10								0
49070020	---Papers, cards or envelopes impressed with stamps	10								0
4907003	---Banknotes:									
49070031	----Banknotes in circulation	7								0
49070032	----Banknotes not yet in circulation	7								0
49070040	---Travellers' checks	7								0
49070050	---Negotiable ratified checks	7								0
49070060	---Stocks, shares, and similar, numbered and signed	7								0
49070070	---Stocks, shares, and the like intended for use	10								0
49070080	---Cheque books	10								0
49070090	---Other documents of title	10								0
4908	Transfers (decalcomanias).									

HS	Description	Bound rate at date of accession	Interim	Final Bound	Implementation	Present concession established	INR	Concession first incorporated in a GATT Schedule	Earlier INRs	ODCs
49081000	-Transfers (decalcomanias), vitrifiable	10								0
49089000	-Other	10								0
4909	Printed or illustrated postcards; printed cards bearing personal greetings, messages or announcements, whether or not illustrated, with or without envelopes or trimmings.									
49090010	---Postcards	10								0
49090020	---Greeting and similar cards	10								0
49100000	Calendars of any kind, printed, including calendar blocks.	10								0
4911	Other printed matter, including printed pictures and photographs.									
491110	-Trade advertising material, commercial catalogues and the like									
49111010	---Printed matter for publicity and advertisement	10					DO,HN			0
49111090	---Other	10					DO,HN			0
49119	-Other:									
491191	--Pictures, designs and photographs									
49119110	---Photographs of tourist scenes, etc.	10					DO,HN			0
49119190	---Other pictures and photographs	10					DO,HN			0
491199	--Other									
49119910	---Calendar stands, printed	10					DO,HN			0
49119920	---Educational charts for anatomy, botany and zoology	10					DO,HN			0
49119930	---Tickets for performances, etc.	10					DO,HN			0
49119990	---Other printed matter	10					DO,HN			0
50040000	Silk yarn (other than yarn spun from silk waste) not put up for retail sale.	15								0
50050000	Yarn spun from silk waste, not put up for retail sale.	15								0
50060000	Silk yarn and yarn spun from silk waste, put up for retail sale; silk-worm gut.	15								0
5007	Woven fabrics of silk or of silk waste.									
50071000	-Fabrics of noil silk	10					IN			0
50072000	-Other fabrics, containing 85 % or more by weight of silk or of silk waste other than noil silk	10					IN			0
50079000	-Other fabrics	10					IN			0
51040000	Garnetted stock of wool or of fine or coarse animal hair.	15								0

HS	Description	Bound rate at date of accession	Interim	Final Bound	Implementation	Present concession established	INR	Concession first incorporated in a GATT Schedule	Earlier INRs	ODCs
5105	Wool and fine or coarse animal hair, carded or combed (including combed wool in fragments).									
51051000	-Carded wool	15								0
51052	-Wool tops and other combed wool:									
51052100	--Combed wool in fragments	15								0
51052900	--Other	15								0
51053	-Fine animal hair, carded or combed:									
51053100	--Of Kashmir (cashmere) goats	15								0
51053900	--Other	15								0
51054000	-Coarse animal hair, carded or combed	15								0
5106	Yarn of carded wool, not put up for retail sale.									
51061000	-Containing 85 % or more by weight of wool	15								0
51062000	-Containing less than 85 % by weight of wool	15								0
5107	Yarn of combed wool, not put up for retail sale.									
51071000	-Containing 85 % or more by weight of wool	15								0
51072000	-Containing less than 85 % by weight of wool	15								0
5108	Yarn of fine animal hair (carded or combed), not put up for retail sale.									
51081000	-Carded	15								0
51082000	-Combed	15								0
5109	Yarn of wool or of fine animal hair, put up for retail sale.									
51091000	-Containing 85 % or more by weight of wool or of fine animal hair	15								0
51099000	-Other	15								0
51100000	Yarn of coarse animal hair or of horsehair (including gimped horsehair yarn), whether or not put up for retail sale.	15								0
5111	Woven fabrics of carded wool or of carded fine animal hair.									
51111	-Containing 85 % or more by weight of wool or of fine animal hair:									
511111	--Of a weight not exceeding 300 g/m²									
51111110	---Abayas 85% or more wool, animal hair, under 301 g/m2	12								0

HS	Description	Bound rate at date of accession	Interim	Final Bound	Implementation	Present concession established	INR	Concession first incorporated in a GATT Schedule	Earlier INRs	ODCs
51111190	---Other items 85% or more wool, animal hair under 301g/m2	15								0
511119	--Other									
51111910	---Abayas 85% or more wool, animal hair, over 300 g/m2	12								0
51111990	---Other items 85% or more wool, animal hair, over 300 g/m2	15								0
511120	-Other, mixed mainly or solely with man-made filaments									
51112010	---Abayas of carded wool and manmade filaments	15								0
51112090	---Other articles of carded wool and manmade filaments	15								0
511130	-Other, mixed mainly or solely with man-made staple fibres									
51113010	---Abayas of carded wool and manmade staple fibres	15								0
51113090	---Other articles of carded wool and manmade staple fibres	15								0
511190	-Other									
51119010	---Abayas of carded wool and other materials	15								0
51119090	---Other articles of carded wool and other materials	15								0
5112	Woven fabrics of combed wool or of combed fine animal hair.									
51121	-Containing 85 % or more by weight of wool or of fine animal hair:									
511211	--Of a weight not exceeding 200 g/m²									
51121110	---Abayas of 85% or more combed wool, under 201 g/m2	15								0
51121190	---Other articles 85% or more combed wool, under 201 g/m2	15								0
511219	--Other									
51121910	---Abayas 85% or more combed wool over 200 g/m2	15								0
51121990	---Other articles 85% or more combed wool over 200 g/m2	15								0
511220	-Other, mixed mainly or solely with man-made filaments									
51122010	---Abayas of combed wool and manmade filaments	15								0
51122090	---Other articles of combed wool and manmade filaments	15								0

HS	Description	Bound rate at date of accession	Interim	Final Bound	Implementation	Present concession established	INR	Concession first incorporated in a GATT Schedule	Earlier INRs	ODCs
511230	-Other, mixed mainly or solely with man-made staple fibres									
51123010	---Abayas of combed wool and manmade staple fibres	15								0
51123090	---Other articles of combed wool and manmade staple fibres	15								0
511290	-Other									
51129010	---Abayas of combed wool and other materials	15								0
51129090	---Other articles of combed wool and other materials	15								0
5113	Woven fabrics of coarse animal hair or of horsehair.									
5113001	---Woven fabrics of coarse animal hair:									
51130011	----Abayas of coarse animal hair	15								0
51130019	----Other articles of coarse animal hair	15								0
51130020	---Woven fabrics of horsehair	15								0
5204	Cotton sewing thread, whether or not put up for retail sale.									
52041	-Not put up for retail sale:									
52041100	--Containing 85 % or more by weight of cotton	15								0
52041900	--Other	15								0
52042000	-Put up for retail sale	15								0
5205	Cotton yarn (other than sewing thread), containing 85 % or more by weight of cotton, not put up for retail sale.									
52051	-Single yarn, of uncombed fibres:									
52051100	--Measuring 714.29 decitex or more (not exceeding 14 metric number)	10								0
52051200	--Measuring less than 714.29 decitex but not less than 232.56 decitex (exceeding 14 metric number but not exceeding 43 metric number)	15								0
52051300	--Measuring less than 232.56 decitex but not less than 192.31 decitex (exceeding 43 metric number but not exceeding 52 metric number)	15								0
52051400	--Measuring less than 192.31 decitex but not less than 125 decitex (exceeding 52 metric number but not exceeding 80 metric number)	15								0
52051500	--Measuring less than 125 decitex (exceeding 80 metric number)	15								0

HS	Description	Bound rate at date of accession	Interim	Final Bound	Implementation	Present concession established	INR	Concession first incorporated in a GATT Schedule	Earlier INRs	ODCs
52052	-Single yarn, of combed fibres:									
52052100	--Measuring 714.29 decitex or more (not exceeding 14 metric number)	15								0
52052200	--Measuring less than 714.29 decitex but not less than 232.56 decitex (exceeding 14 metric number but not exceeding 43 metric number)	15								0
52052300	--Measuring less than 232.56 decitex but not less than 192.31 decitex (exceeding 43 metric number but not exceeding 52 metric number)	15								0
52052400	--Measuring less than 192.31 decitex but not less than 125 decitex (exceeding 52 metric number but not exceeding 80 metric number)	15								0
52052600	--Measuring less than 125 decitex but not less than 106.38 decitex (exceeding 80 metric number but not exceeding 94 metric number)	15								0
52052700	--Measuring less than 106.38 decitex but not less than 83.33 decitex (exceeding 94 metric number but not exceeding 120 metric number)	15								0
52052800	--Measuring less than 83.33 decitex (exceeding 120 metric number)	15								0
52053	-Multiple (folded) or cabled yarn, of uncombed fibres:									
52053100	--Measuring per single yarn 714.29 decitex or more (not exceeding 14 metric number per single yarn)	15								0
52053200	--Measuring per single yarn less than 714.29 decitex but not less than 232.56 decitex (exceeding 14 metric number but not exceeding 43 metric number per single yarn)	15								0
52053300	--Measuring per single yarn less than 232.56 decitex but not less than 192.31 decitex (exceeding 43 metric number but not exceeding 52 metric number per single yarn)	15								0
52053400	--Measuring per single yarn less than 192.31 decitex but not less than 125 decitex (exceeding 52 metric number but not exceeding 80 metric number per single yarn)	15								0

HS	Description	Bound rate at date of accession	Interim	Final Bound	Implementation	Present concession established	INR	Concession first incorporated in a GATT Schedule	Earlier INRs	ODCs
52053500	--Measuring per single yarn less than 125 decitex (exceeding 80 metric number per single yarn)	15								0
52054	-Multiple (folded) or cabled yarn, of combed fibres:									
52054100	--Measuring per single yarn 714.29 decitex or more (not exceeding 14 metric number per single yarn)	15								0
52054200	--Measuring per single yarn less than 714.29 decitex but not less than 232.56 decitex (exceeding 14 metric number but not exceeding 43 metric number per single yarn)	15								0
52054300	--Measuring per single yarn less than 232.56 decitex but not less than 192.31 decitex (exceeding 43 metric number but not exceeding 52 metric number per single yarn)	15								0
52054400	--Measuring per single yarn less than 192.31 decitex but not less than 125 decitex (exceeding 52 metric number but not exceeding 80 metric number per single yarn)	15								0
52054600	--Measuring per single yarn less than 125 decitex but not less than 106.38 decitex (exceeding 80 metric number but not exceeding 94 metric number per single yarn)	15								0
52054700	--Measuring per single yarn less than 106.38 decitex but not less than 83.33 decitex (exceeding 94 metric number but not exceeding 120 metric number per single yarn)	15								0
52054800	--Measuring per single yarn less than 83.33 decitex (exceeding 120 metric number per single yarn)	15								0
5206	Cotton yarn (other than sewing thread), containing less than 85 % by weight of cotton, not put up for retail sale.									
52061	-Single yarn, of uncombed fibres:									
52061100	--Measuring 714.29 decitex or more (not exceeding 14 metric number)	15								0
52061200	--Measuring less than 714.29 decitex but not less than 232.56 decitex (exceeding 14 metric number but not exceeding 43 metric number)	15								0

HS	Description	Bound rate at date of accession	Interim	Final Bound	Implementation	Present concession established	INR	Concession first incorporated in a GATT Schedule	Earlier INRs	ODCs
52061300	--Measuring less than 232.56 decitex but not less than 192.31 decitex (exceeding 43 metric number but not exceeding 52 metric number)	15								0
52061400	--Measuring less than 192.31 decitex but not less than 125 decitex (exceeding 52 metric number but not exceeding 80 metric number)	15								0
52061500	--Measuring less than 125 decitex (exceeding 80 metric number)	15								0
52062	-Single yarn, of combed fibres:									
52062100	--Measuring 714.29 decitex or more (not exceeding 14 metric number)	15								0
52062200	--Measuring less than 714.29 decitex but not less than 232.56 decitex (exceeding 14 metric number but not exceeding 43 metric number)	15								0
52062300	--Measuring less than 232.56 decitex but not less than 192.31 decitex (exceeding 43 metric number but not exceeding 52 metric number)	15								0
52062400	--Measuring less than 192.31 decitex but not less than 125 decitex (exceeding 52 metric number but not exceeding 80 metric number)	15								0
52062500	--Measuring less than 125 decitex (exceeding 80 metric number)	15								0
52063	-Multiple (folded) or cabled yarn, of uncombed fibres:									
52063100	--Measuring per single yarn 714.29 decitex or more (not exceeding 14 metric number per single yarn)	15								0
52063200	--Measuring per single yarn less than 714.29 decitex but not less than 232.56 decitex (exceeding 14 metric number but not exceeding 43 metric number per single yarn)	15								0
52063300	--Measuring per single yarn less than 232.56 decitex but not less than 192.31 decitex (exceeding 43 metric number but not exceeding 52 metric number per single yarn)	15								0

HS	Description	Bound rate at date of accession	Interim	Final Bound	Implementation	Present concession established	INR	Concession first incorporated in a GATT Schedule	Earlier INRs	ODCs
52063400	--Measuring per single yarn less than 192.31 decitex but not less than 125 decitex (exceeding 52 metric number but not exceeding 80 metric number per single yarn)	15								0
52063500	--Measuring per single yarn less than 125 decitex (exceeding 80 metric number per single yarn)	15								0
52064	-Multiple (folded) or cabled yarn, of combed fibres:									
52064100	--Measuring per single yarn 714.29 decitex or more (not exceeding 14 metric number per single yarn)	15								0
52064200	--Measuring per single yarn less than 714.29 decitex but not less than 232.56 decitex (exceeding 14 metric number but not exceeding 43 metric number per single yarn)	15								0
52064300	--Measuring per single yarn less than 232.56 decitex but not less than 192.31 decitex (exceeding 43 metric number but not exceeding 52 metric number per single yarn)	15								0
52064400	--Measuring per single yarn less than 192.31 decitex but not less than 125 decitex (exceeding 52 metric number but not exceeding 80 metric number per single yarn)	15								0
52064500	--Measuring per single yarn less than 125 decitex (exceeding 80 metric number per single yarn)	15								0
5207	Cotton yarn (other than sewing thread) put up for retail sale.									
52071000	-Containing 85 % or more by weight of cotton	10								0
52079000	-Other	15								0
5208	Woven fabrics of cotton, containing 85 % or more by weight of cotton, weighing not more than 200 g/m2.									
52081	-Unbleached:									
52081100	--Plain weave, weighing not more than 100 g/m2	10					IN			0
52081200	--Plain weave, weighing more than 100 g/m2	15					KG			0

HS	Description	Bound rate at date of accession	Interim	Final Bound	Implementation	Present concession established	INR	Concession first incorporated in a GATT Schedule	Earlier INRs	ODCs
52081300	--3-thread or 4-thread twill, including cross twill	15								0
52081900	--Other fabrics	10					IN			0
52082	-Bleached:									
52082100	--Plain weave, weighing not more than 100 g/m2	12					CH			0
52082200	--Plain weave, weighing more than 100 g/m2	15					CH,PK			0
52082300	--3-thread or 4-thread twill, including cross twill	15					CH			0
52082900	--Other fabrics	10					CH,KG			0
52083	-Dyed:									
52083100	--Plain weave, weighing not more than 100 g/m2	12					CH			0
52083200	--Plain weave, weighing more than 100 g/m2	15					CH			0
52083300	--3-thread or 4-thread twill, including cross twill	15					CH			0
52083900	--Other fabrics	15					CH			0
52084	-Of yarns of different colours:									
52084100	--Plain weave, weighing not more than 100 g/m2	15					CH			0
52084200	--Plain weave, weighing more than 100 g/m2	15					CH			0
52084300	--3-thread or 4-thread twill, including cross twill	15					CH			0
52084900	--Other fabrics	15					CH			0
52085	-Printed:									
52085100	--Plain weave, weighing not more than 100 g/m2	10					CH,IN			0
52085200	--Plain weave, weighing more than 100 g/m2	10					CH,IN			0
52085300	--3-thread or 4-thread twill, including cross twill	15					CH			0
52085900	--Other fabrics	12					CH			0
5209	Woven fabrics of cotton, containing 85 % or more by weight of cotton, weighing more than 200 g/m2.									
52091	-Unbleached:									
52091100	--Plain weave	15								0
52091200	--3-thread or 4-thread twill, including cross twill	15								0
52091900	--Other fabrics	15								0

HS	Description	Bound rate at date of accession	Interim	Final Bound	Implementation	Present concession established	INR	Concession first incorporated in a GATT Schedule	Earlier INRs	ODCs
52092	-Bleached:									
52092100	--Plain weave	15								0
52092200	--3-thread or 4-thread twill, including cross twill	15								0
52092900	--Other fabrics	10								0
52093	-Dyed:									
52093100	--Plain weave	15								0
52093200	--3-thread or 4-thread twill, including cross twill	15								0
52093900	--Other fabrics	15					KG			0
52094	-Of yarns of different colours:									
52094100	--Plain weave	15								0
52094200	--Denim	15								0
52094300	--Other fabrics of 3-thread or 4-thread twill, including cross twill	15								0
52094900	--Other fabrics	10								0
52095	-Printed:									
52095100	--Plain weave	15								0
52095200	--3-thread or 4-thread twill, including cross twill	15								0
52095900	--Other fabrics	15								0
5210	Woven fabrics of cotton, containing less than 85 % by weight of cotton, mixed mainly or solely with man-made fibres, weighing not more than 200 g/m2.									
52101	-Unbleached:									
52101100	--Plain weave	15								0
52101200	--3-thread or 4-thread twill, including cross twill	10								0
52101900	--Other fabrics	15								0
52102	-Bleached:									
52102100	--Plain weave	10								0
52102200	--3-thread or 4-thread twill, including cross twill	15								0
52102900	--Other fabrics	15								0
52103	-Dyed:									
52103100	--Plain weave	15								0
52103200	--3-thread or 4-thread twill, including cross twill	15								0
52103900	--Other fabrics	5								0
52104	-Of yarns of different colours:									

HS	Description	Bound rate at date of accession	Interim	Final Bound	Implementation	Present concession established	INR	Concession first incorporated in a GATT Schedule	Earlier INRs	ODCs
52104100	--Plain weave	15								0
52104200	--3-thread or 4-thread twill, including cross twill	15								0
52104900	--Other fabrics	15								0
52105	-Printed:									
52105100	--Plain weave	15								0
52105200	--3-thread or 4-thread twill, including cross twill	15								0
52105900	--Other fabrics	15								0
5211	Woven fabrics of cotton, containing less than 85 % by weight of cotton, mixed mainly or solely with man-made fibres, weighing more than 200 g/m2.									
52111	-Unbleached:									
52111100	--Plain weave	15					PK			0
52111200	--3-thread or 4-thread twill, including cross twill	15								0
52111900	--Other fabrics	15					KG			0
52112	-Bleached:									
52112100	--Plain weave	15								0
52112200	--3-thread or 4-thread twill, including cross twill	15								0
52112900	--Other fabrics	15								0
52113	-Dyed:									
52113100	--Plain weave	15								0
52113200	--3-thread or 4-thread twill, including cross twill	15								0
52113900	--Other fabrics	15								0
52114	-Of yarns of different colours:									
52114100	--Plain weave	15								0
52114200	--Denim	15								0
52114300	--Other fabrics of 3-thread or 4-thread twill, including cross twill	15								0
52114900	--Other fabrics	15								0
52115	-Printed:									
52115100	--Plain weave	15								0
52115200	--3-thread or 4-thread twill, including cross twill	15								0
52115900	--Other fabrics	5								0
5212	Other woven fabrics of cotton.									
52121	-Weighing not more than 200 g/m2:									
52121100	--Unbleached	15								0

HS	Description	Bound rate at date of accession	Interim	Final Bound	Implementation	Present concession established	INR	Concession first incorporated in a GATT Schedule	Earlier INRs	ODCs
52121200	--Bleached	15								0
52121300	--Dyed	15								0
52121400	--Of yarns of different colours	15								0
52121500	--Printed	15								0
52122	-Weighing more than 200 g/m2:									
52122100	--Unbleached	15								0
52122200	--Bleached	15								0
52122300	--Dyed	15								0
52122400	--Of yarns of different colours	15								0
52122500	--Printed	10					IN			0
5303	Jute and other textile bast fibres (excluding flax, true hemp and ramie), raw or processed but not spun; tow and waste of these fibres (including yarn waste and garnetted stock).									
53031000	-Jute and other textile bast fibres, raw or retted	10								0
53039000	-Other	15								0
5304	Sisal and other textile fibres of the genus Agave, raw or processed but not spun; tow and waste of these fibres (including yarn waste and garnetted stock).									
53041000	-Sisal and other textile fibres of the genus Agave, raw	15								0
53049000	-Other	15								0
5305	Coconut, abaca (Manila hemp or Musa textilis Nee), ramie and other vegetable textile fibres, not elsewhere specified or included, raw or processed but not spun; tow, noils and waste of these fibres (including yarn waste and garnetted stock).									
53051	-Of coconut (coir):									
53051100	--Raw	15								0
53051900	--Other	12								0
53052	-Of abaca:									
53052100	--Raw	8								0
53052900	--Other	8								0
53059000	-Other	15								0
5306	Flax yarn.									
53061000	-Single	15								0
53062000	-Multiple (folded) or cabled	15								0

HS	Description	Bound rate at date of accession	Interim	Final Bound	Implementation	Present concession established	INR	Concession first incorporated in a GATT Schedule	Earlier INRs	ODCs
5307	Yarn of jute or of other textile bast fibres of heading 53.03.									
53071000	-Single	10					IN			0
53072000	-Multiple (folded) or cabled	10					IN			0
5308	Yarn of other vegetable textile fibres; paper yarn.									
53081000	-Coir yarn	15								0
53082000	-True hemp yarn	15								0
53089000	-Other	15								0
5309	Woven fabrics of flax.									
53091	-Containing 85 % or more by weight of flax:									
53091100	--Unbleached or bleached	15								0
53091900	--Other	15								0
53092	-Containing less than 85 % by weight of flax:									
53092100	--Unbleached or bleached	15								0
53092900	--Other	15								0
5310	Woven fabrics of jute or of other textile bast fibres of heading 53.03.									
53101000	-Unbleached	10					IN			0
53109000	-Other	15								0
53110000	Woven fabrics of other vegetable textile fibres; woven fabrics of paper yarn.	15								0
5401	Sewing thread of man-made filaments, whether or not put up for retail sale.									
540110	-Of synthetic filaments									
54011010	---Synthetic sewing thread, for retail	15								0
54011090	---Synthetic sewing thread, not for retail	15								0
540120	-Of artificial filaments									
54012010	---Artificial filament sewing thread, for retail	15								0
54012090	---Artificial filament sewing thread, not for retail	15								0
5402	Synthetic filament yarn (other than sewing thread), not put up for retail sale, including synthetic monofilament of less than 67 decitex.									
54021000	-High tenacity yarn of nylon or other polyamides	15								0
54022000	-High tenacity yarn of polyesters	15								0
54023	-Textured yarn:									

HS	Description	Bound rate at date of accession	Interim	Final Bound	Implementation	Present concession established	INR	Concession first incorporated in a GATT Schedule	Earlier INRs	ODCs
54023100	--Of nylon or other polyamides, measuring per single yarn not more than 50 tex	15								0
54023200	--Of nylon or other polyamides, measuring per single yarn more than 50 tex	15								0
54023300	--Of polyesters	12								0
54023900	--Other	15								0
54024	-Other yarn, single, untwisted or with a twist not exceeding 50 turns per metre:									
54024100	--Of nylon or other polyamides	15								0
54024200	--Of polyesters, partially oriented	15								0
54024300	--Of polyesters, other	15								0
54024900	--Other	15								0
54025	-Other yarn, single, with a twist exceeding 50 turns per metre:									
54025100	--Of nylon or other polyamides	15								0
54025200	--Of polyesters	15								0
54025900	--Other	15								0
54026	-Other yarn, multiple (folded) or cabled:									
54026100	--Of nylon or other polyamides	15								0
54026200	--Of polyesters	12								0
54026900	--Other	15								0
5403	Artificial filament yarn (other than sewing thread), not put up for retail sale, including artificial monofilament of less than 67 decitex.									
54031000	-High tenacity yarn of viscose rayon	15								0
54032000	-Textured yarn	15								0
54033	-Other yarn, single:									
54033100	--Of viscose rayon, untwisted or with a twist not exceeding 120 turns per metre	15								0
54033200	--Of viscose rayon, with a twist exceeding 120 turns per metre	15								0
54033300	--Of cellulose acetate	15								0
54033900	--Other	15								0
54034	-Other yarn, multiple (folded) or cabled:									
54034100	--Of viscose rayon	15								0
54034200	--Of cellulose acetate	15								0
54034900	--Other	15								0

HS	Description	Bound rate at date of accession	Interim	Final Bound	Implementation	Present concession established	INR	Concession first incorporated in a GATT Schedule	Earlier INRs	ODCs
5404	Synthetic monofilament of 67 decitex or more and of which no cross-sectional dimension exceeds 1 mm; strip and the like (for example, artificial straw) of synthetic textile materials of an apparent width not exceeding 5 mm.									
54041000	-Monofilament	15								0
54049000	-Other	15								0
5405	Artificial monofilament of 67 decitex or more and of which no cross-sectional dimension exceeds 1 mm; strip and the like (for example, artificial straw) of artificial textile materials of an apparent width not exceeding 5 mm.									
54050010	---Artificial monofilament	15								0
54050090	---Other artificial filament yarn and strip	15								0
5406	Man-made filament yarn (other than sewing thread), put up for retail sale.									
54061000	-Synthetic filament yarn	12					IN			0
54062000	-Artificial filament yarn	15								0
5407	Woven fabrics of synthetic filament yarn, including woven fabrics obtained from materials of heading 54.04.									
54071000	-Woven fabrics obtained from high tenacity yarn of nylon or other polyamides or of polyesters	15					IN			0
54072000	-Woven fabrics obtained from strip or the like	15								0
54073000	-Fabrics specified in Note 9 to Section XI	15								0
54074	-Other woven fabrics, containing 85 % or more by weight of filaments of nylon or other polyamides:									
54074100	--Unbleached or bleached	15		12	2008					0
54074200	--Dyed	15								0
54074300	--Of yarns of different colours	15								0
54074400	--Printed	15								0
54075	-Other woven fabrics, containing 85 % or more by weight of textured polyester filaments:									
54075100	--Unbleached or bleached	15					JP			0
54075200	--Dyed (See Endnote 6)	10					IN,JP,PK			0
54075300	--Of yarns of different colours	15					JP			0
54075400	--Printed	10					IN,JP,PK			0

HS	Description	Bound rate at date of accession	Interim	Final Bound	Implementation	Present concession established	INR	Concession first incorporated in a GATT Schedule	Earlier INRs	ODCs
54076	-Other woven fabrics, containing 85 % or more by weight of polyester filaments:									
54076100	--Containing 85 % or more by weight of non-textured polyester filaments	15					JP			0
54076900	--Other	15					JP			0
54077	-Other woven fabrics, containing 85 % or more by weight of synthetic filaments:									
54077100	--Unbleached or bleached	15					JP			0
54077200	--Dyed	15					JP			0
54077300	--Of yarns of different colours	5								0
54077400	--Printed	15								0
54078	-Other woven fabrics, containing less than 85 % by weight of synthetic filaments, mixed mainly or solely with cotton:									
54078100	--Unbleached or bleached	15								0
54078200	--Dyed	15								0
54078300	--Of yarns of different colours	15								0
54078400	--Printed	15								0
54079	-Other woven fabrics:									
54079100	--Unbleached or bleached	15								0
54079200	--Dyed	15								0
54079300	--Of yarns of different colours	10								0
54079400	--Printed	15								0
5408	Woven fabrics of artificial filament yarn, including woven fabrics obtained from materials of heading 54.05.									
54081000	-Woven fabrics obtained from high tenacity yarn of viscose rayon	15								0
54082	-Other woven fabrics, containing 85 % or more by weight of artificial filament or strip or the like:									
54082100	--Unbleached or bleached	15								0
54082200	--Dyed	15								0
54082300	--Of yarns of different colours	15								0
54082400	--Printed	15								0
54083	-Other woven fabrics:									
54083100	--Unbleached or bleached	15								0
54083200	--Dyed	15					JP			0
54083300	--Of yarns of different colours	15					PK			0
54083400	--Printed	15								0
5501	Synthetic filament tow.									

HS	Description	Bound rate at date of accession	Interim	Final Bound	Implementation	Present concession established	INR	Concession first incorporated in a GATT Schedule	Earlier INRs	ODCs
55011000	-Of nylon or other polyamides	15								0
55012000	-Of polyesters	15					PK			0
55013000	-Acrylic or modacrylic	15								0
55019000	-Other	15								0
55020000	Artificial filament tow.	15								0
5503	Synthetic staple fibres, not carded, combed or otherwise processed for spinning.									
55031000	-Of nylon or other polyamides	15								0
55032000	-Of polyesters	15								0
55033000	-Acrylic or modacrylic	15								0
55034000	-Of polypropylene	15								0
55039000	-Other	15								0
5504	Artificial staple fibres, not carded, combed or otherwise processed for spinning.									
55041000	-Of viscose rayon	15								0
55049000	-Other	15								0
5505	Waste (including noils, yarn waste and garnetted stock) of man-made fibres.									
55051000	-Of synthetic fibres	10								0
55052000	-Of artificial fibres	15								0
5506	Synthetic staple fibres, carded, combed or otherwise processed for spinning.									
55061000	-Of nylon or other polyamides	15								0
55062000	-Of polyesters	15								0
55063000	-Acrylic or modacrylic	15								0
55069000	-Other	15								0
55070000	Artificial staple fibres, carded, combed or otherwise processed for spinning.	15								0
5508	Sewing thread of man-made staple fibres, whether or not put up for retail sale.									
550810	-Of synthetic staple fibres									
55081010	---Sewing thread of synthetic staples, retail	10								0
55081090	---Sewing thread of synthetic staples, non-retail	10								0
550820	-Of artificial staple fibres									
55082010	---Sewing thread of artificial staples, for retail	15								0
55082090	---Sewing thread of artificial staples, not for retail	15								0

HS	Description	Bound rate at date of accession	Interim	Final Bound	Implementation	Present concession established	INR	Concession first incorporated in a GATT Schedule	Earlier INRs	ODCs
5509	Yarn (other than sewing thread) of synthetic staple fibres, not put up for retail sale.									
55091	-Containing 85 % or more by weight of staple fibres of nylon or other polyamides:									
55091100	--Single yarn	15								0
55091200	--Multiple (folded) or cabled yarn	15								0
55092	-Containing 85 % or more by weight of polyester staple fibres:									
55092100	--Single yarn	15								0
55092200	--Multiple (folded) or cabled yarn	10					IN			0
55093	-Containing 85 % or more by weight of acrylic or modacrylic staple fibres:									
55093100	--Single yarn	15								0
55093200	--Multiple (folded) or cabled yarn	10					IN			0
55094	-Other yarn, containing 85 % or more by weight of synthetic staple fibres:									
55094100	--Single yarn	15								0
55094200	--Multiple (folded) or cabled yarn	15								0
55095	-Other yarn, of polyester staple fibres:									
55095100	--Mixed mainly or solely with artificial staple fibres	10					IN			0
55095200	--Mixed mainly or solely with wool or fine animal hair	15								0
55095300	--Mixed mainly or solely with cotton	10					IN			0
55095900	--Other	5								0
55096	-Other yarn, of acrylic or modacrylic staple fibres:									
55096100	--Mixed mainly or solely with wool or fine animal hair	15								0
55096200	--Mixed mainly or solely with cotton	10								0
55096900	--Other	15								0
55099	-Other yarn:									
55099100	--Mixed mainly or solely with wool or fine animal hair	15								0
55099200	--Mixed mainly or solely with cotton	15								0
55099900	--Other	10					IN			0
5510	Yarn (other than sewing thread) of artificial staple fibres, not put up for retail sale.									
55101	-Containing 85 % or more by weight of artificial staple fibres:									

HS	Description	Bound rate at date of accession	Interim	Final Bound	Implementation	Present concession established	INR	Concession first incorporated in a GATT Schedule	Earlier INRs	ODCs
55101100	--Single yarn	15								0
55101200	--Multiple (folded) or cabled yarn	15								0
55102000	-Other yarn, mixed mainly or solely with wool or fine animal hair	10					IN			0
55103000	-Other yarn, mixed mainly or solely with cotton	15								0
55109000	-Other yarn	15								0
5511	Yarn (other than sewing thread) of man-made staple fibres, put up for retail sale.									
55111000	-Of synthetic staple fibres, containing 85 % or more by weight of such fibres	15								0
55112000	-Of synthetic staple fibres, containing less than 85 % by weight of such fibres	15								0
55113000	-Of artificial staple fibres	15								0
5512	Woven fabrics of synthetic staple fibres, containing 85 % or more by weight of synthetic staple fibres.									
55121	-Containing 85 % or more by weight of polyester staple fibres:									
55121100	--Unbleached or bleached	15					JP			0
55121900	--Other	10					IN,JP,PK			0
55122	-Containing 85 % or more by weight of acrylic or modacrylic staple fibres:									
55122100	--Unbleached or bleached	15								0
55122900	--Other	10								0
55129	-Other:									
55129100	--Unbleached or bleached	15								0
55129900	--Other	15								0
5513	Woven fabrics of synthetic staple fibres, containing less than 85 % by weight of such fibres, mixed mainly or solely with cotton, of a weight not exceeding 170 g/m².									
55131	-Unbleached or bleached:									
55131100	--Of polyester staple fibres, plain weave	10					JP			0
55131200	--3-thread or 4-thread twill, including cross twill, of polyester staple fibres	15								0
55131300	--Other woven fabrics of polyester staple fibres	15								0
55131900	--Other woven fabrics	15								0
55132	-Dyed:									
55132100	--Of polyester staple fibres, plain weave	15								0

HS	Description	Bound rate at date of accession	Interim	Final Bound	Implementation	Present concession established	INR	Concession first incorporated in a GATT Schedule	Earlier INRs	ODCs
55132200	--3-thread or 4-thread twill, including cross twill, of polyester staple fibres	15								0
55132300	--Other woven fabrics of polyester staple fibres	15								0
55132900	--Other woven fabrics	15								0
55133	-Of yarns of different colours:									
55133100	--Of polyester staple fibres, plain weave	15								0
55133200	--3-thread or 4-thread twill, including cross twill, of polyester staple fibres	10					IN			0
55133300	--Other woven fabrics of polyester staple fibres	15								0
55133900	--Other woven fabrics	15								0
55134	-Printed:									
55134100	--Of polyester staple fibres, plain weave	13								0
55134200	--3-thread or 4-thread twill, including cross twill, of polyester staple fibres	15								0
55134300	--Other woven fabrics of polyester staple fibres	15								0
55134900	--Other woven fabrics	15								0
5514	Woven fabrics of synthetic staple fibres, containing less than 85 % by weight of such fibres, mixed mainly or solely with cotton, of a weight exceeding 170 g/m².									
55141	-Unbleached or bleached:									
55141100	--Of polyester staple fibres, plain weave	15								0
55141200	--3-thread or 4-thread twill, including cross twill, of polyester staple fibres	15								0
55141300	--Other woven fabrics of polyester staple fibres	15								0
55141900	--Other woven fabrics	15								0
55142	-Dyed:									
55142100	--Of polyester staple fibres, plain weave	15								0
55142200	--3-thread or 4-thread twill, including cross twill, of polyester staple fibres	15								0
55142300	--Other woven fabrics of polyester staple fibres	15								0
55142900	--Other woven fabrics	15								0
55143	-Of yarns of different colours:									
55143100	--Of polyester staple fibres, plain weave	15								0
55143200	--3-thread or 4-thread twill, including cross twill, of polyester staple fibres	15								0

HS	Description	Bound rate at date of accession	Interim	Final Bound	Implementation	Present concession established	INR	Concession first incorporated in a GATT Schedule	Earlier INRs	ODCs
55143300	--Other woven fabrics of polyester staple fibres	10								0
55143900	--Other woven fabrics	15								0
55144	-Printed:									
55144100	--Of polyester staple fibres, plain weave	15								0
55144200	--3-thread or 4-thread twill, including cross twill, of polyester staple fibres	15								0
55144300	--Other woven fabrics of polyester staple fibres	15								0
55144900	--Other woven fabrics	15								0
5515	Other woven fabrics of synthetic staple fibres.									
55151	-Of polyester staple fibres:									
55151100	--Mixed mainly or solely with viscose rayon staple fibres	10					IN			0
55151200	--Mixed mainly or solely with man-made filaments	10					IN,JP			0
55151300	--Mixed mainly or solely with wool or fine animal hair	10					IN			0
55151900	--Other	10					IN			0
55152	-Of acrylic or modacrylic staple fibres:									
55152100	--Mixed mainly or solely with man-made filaments	15								0
55152200	--Mixed mainly or solely with wool or fine animal hair	15								0
55152900	--Other	15								0
55159	-Other woven fabrics:									
55159100	--Mixed mainly or solely with man-made filaments	15								0
55159200	--Mixed mainly or solely with wool or fine animal hair	10								0
55159900	--Other	15								0
5516	Woven fabrics of artificial staple fibres.									
55161	-Containing 85 % or more by weight of artificial staple fibres:									
55161100	--Unbleached or bleached	15								0
55161200	--Dyed	15								0
55161300	--Of yarns of different colours	15								0
55161400	--Printed	10								0
55162	-Containing less than 85 % by weight of artificial staple fibres, mixed mainly or solely with man-made filaments:									
55162100	--Unbleached or bleached	15								0

HS	Description	Bound rate at date of accession	Interim	Final Bound	Implementation	Present concession established	INR	Concession first incorporated in a GATT Schedule	Earlier INRs	ODCs
55162200	--Dyed	10								0
55162300	--Of yarns of different colours	10								0
55162400	--Printed	15								0
55163	-Containing less than 85 % by weight of artificial staple fibres, mixed mainly or solely with wool or fine animal hair:									
55163100	--Unbleached or bleached	15								0
55163200	--Dyed	15								0
55163300	--Of yarns of different colours	10								0
55163400	--Printed	15								0
55164	-Containing less than 85 % by weight of artificial staple fibres, mixed mainly or solely with cotton:									
55164100	--Unbleached or bleached	15								0
55164200	--Dyed	15								0
55164300	--Of yarns of different colours	15								0
55164400	--Printed	15								0
55169	-Other:									
55169100	--Unbleached or bleached	15								0
55169200	--Dyed	15								0
55169300	--Of yarns of different colours	15								0
55169400	--Printed	15								0
5601	Wadding of textile materials and articles thereof; textile fibres, not exceeding 5 mm in length (flock), textile dust and mill neps.									
56011000	-Sanitary towels and tampons, napkins and napkin liners for babies and similar sanitary articles, of wadding	15								0
56012	-Wadding; other articles of wadding:									
56012100	--Of cotton	15								0
56012200	--Of man-made fibres	15								0
56012900	--Other	15								0
56013000	-Textile flock and dust and mill neps	15								0
5602	Felt, whether or not impregnated, coated, covered or laminated.									
56021000	-Needleloom felt and stitch-bonded fibre fabrics	15								0
56022	-Other felt, not impregnated, coated, covered or laminated:									
56022100	--Of wool or fine animal hair	15								0
56022900	--Of other textile materials	15								0

HS	Description	Bound rate at date of accession	Interim	Final Bound	Implementation	Present concession established	INR	Concession first incorporated in a GATT Schedule	Earlier INRs	ODCs
56029000	-Other	15								0
5603	Nonwovens, whether or not impregnated, coated, covered or laminated.									
56031	-Of man-made filaments:									
56031100	--Weighing not more than 25 g/m²	15								0
56031200	--Weighing more than 25 g/m² but not more than 70 g/m²	15								0
56031300	--Weighing more than 70 g/m² but not more than 150 g/m²	15								0
56031400	--Weighing more than 150 g/m²	15								0
56039	-Other:									
56039100	--Weighing not more than 25 g/m²	15								0
56039200	--Weighing more than 25 g/m² but not more than 70 g/m²	15								0
56039300	--Weighing more than 70 g/m² but not more than 150 g/m²	15								0
56039400	--Weighing more than 150 g/m²	15								0
5604	Rubber thread and cord, textile covered; textile yarn, and strip and the like of heading 54.04 or 54.05, impregnated, coated, covered or sheathed with rubber or plastics.									
56041000	-Rubber thread and cord, textile covered	15								0
56042000	-High tenacity yarn of polyesters, of nylon or other polyamides or of viscose rayon, impregnated or coated	15								0
56049000	-Other	15								0
56050000	Metallised yarn, whether or not gimped, being textile yarn, or strip or the like of heading 54.04 or 54.05, combined with metal in the form of thread, strip or powder or covered with metal.	15								0
5606	Gimped yarn, and strip and the like of heading 54.04 or 54.05, gimped (other than those of heading 56.05 and gimped horsehair yarn); chenille yarn (including flock chenille yarn); loop wale-yarn.									
56060010	---Gimped yarn and strip and the like	15								0
56060020	---Chenille yarn	15								0
56060030	---Loop wale-yarn	15								0

HS	Description	Bound rate at date of accession	Interim	Final Bound	Implementation	Present concession established	INR	Concession first incorporated in a GATT Schedule	Earlier INRs	ODCs
5607	Twine, cordage, ropes and cables, whether or not plaited or braided and whether or not impregnated, coated, covered or sheathed with rubber or plastics.									
560710	-Of jute or other textile bast fibres of heading 53.03									
56071010	---Jute twine and cord, not plaited	10					IN			0
56071020	---Jute twine and cord, plaited	12					IN			0
56072	-Of sisal or other textile fibres of the genus Agave:									
560721	--Binder or baler twine									
56072110	---Sisal binder twine, not plaited	15								0
56072120	---Sisal binder twine, plaited	15					KG			0
560729	--Other									
56072910	---Sisal other twine, not plaited	15								0
56072920	---Sisal other twine, plaited	15								0
56074	-Of polyethylene or polypropylene:									
560741	--Binder or baler twine									
56074110	---Polyethylene binder twine, not plaited	15					KG			0
56074120	---Polyethylene binder twine, plaited	15								0
560749	--Other									
56074910	---Polyethylene other twine, not plaited	10					IN			0
56074920	---Polyethylene other twine, plaited	10					IN			0
560750	-Of other synthetic fibres									
56075010	---Twine and cord of other synthetics, not plaited	15								0
56075020	---Twine and cord of other synthetics, plaited	15								0
560790	-Other									
56079010	---Other twine and cord, not plaited (See Endnote 7)	8					PH			0
56079020	---Other twine and cord, plaited (See Endnote 7)	8					IN,PH			0
5608	Knotted netting of twine, cordage or rope; made up fishing nets and other made up nets, of textile materials.									
56081	-Of man-made textile materials:									
56081100	--Made up fishing nets	15								0
56081900	--Other	15								0
56089000	-Other	15								0

HS	Description	Bound rate at date of accession	Interim	Final Bound	Implementation	Present concession established	INR	Concession first incorporated in a GATT Schedule	Earlier INRs	ODCs
5609	Articles of yarn, strip or the like of heading 54.04 or 54.05, twine, cordage, rope or cables, not elsewhere specified or included.									
56090010	---Shoelaces	15								0
56090020	---Ropes for hanging laundry	15								0
56090030	---Ropes for dragging or lifting weights	15								0
56090090	---Other articles of twine, cord and the like	15								0
5701	Carpets and other textile floor coverings, knotted, whether or not made up.									
57011000	-Of wool or fine animal hair	15								0
570190	-Of other textile materials									
57019010	---Carpets of silk	10								0
57019020	---Carpets of coarse animal hair	10								0
57019030	---Carpets of cotton	10								0
57019090	---Other	10								0
5702	Carpets and other textile floor coverings, woven, not tufted or flocked, whether or not made up, including "Kelem", "Schumacks", "Karamanie" and similar hand-woven rugs.									
57021000	-"Kelem", "Schumacks", "Karamanie" and similar hand-woven rugs	15		13	2010					0
57022000	-Floor coverings of coconut fibres (coir)	10					IN			0
57023	-Other, of pile construction, not made up:									
570231	--Of wool or fine animal hair									
57023110	---Machine-made carpets of wool, pile, not made up	15								0
57023120	---Rugs and the like of wool, pile, not made up	15								0
57023190	---Other carpets of wool, pile, not made up	15								0
570232	--Of man-made textile materials									
57023210	---Moquette carpets and rugs, pile, not made up	15								0
57023220	---Carpets and rugs of chenille yarn, pile, not made up	15								0
57023290	---Other manmade carpets, pile, not made up	15								0
57023900	--Of other textile materials	15								0

HS	Description	Bound rate at date of accession	Interim	Final Bound	Implementation	Present concession established	INR	Concession first incorporated in a GATT Schedule	Earlier INRs	ODCs
57024	-Other, of pile construction, made up:									
570241	--Of wool or fine animal hair									
57024110	---Machine-made carpets, wool, pile, made up	15								0
57024120	---Rugs and the like, wool, pile, made up	15								0
57024190	---Other carpets, wool, pile, made up	15								0
570242	--Of man-made textile materials									
57024210	---Moquette, carpets and rugs, pile, made up	15								0
5702422	---Carpets and floor coverings of velvet yarn:									
57024221	----Bed covers and table covers of chenile	15								0
57024229	----Other carpets of chenile, pile, made up	15								0
57024230	---Prayer rugs of manmade textiles, pile, made up	15								0
57024290	---Other carpets of manmade textiles, pile, made up	15								0
570249	--Of other textile materials									
5702491	---Of cotton:									
57024911	----Prayer rugs of cotton, pile, made up	15								0
57024919	----Other cotton rugs, pile, made up	15								0
57024990	---Other rugs, pile, made up	15								0
57025	-Other, non pile construction, not made up:									
570251	--Of wool or fine animal hair									
57025110	---Machine-made carpets of wool, not pile or made up	15								0
57025120	---Rugs and the like of wool, not pile or made up	15								0
57025190	---Other carpets, of wool, not pile or made up	15								0
570252	--Of man-made textile materials									
57025210	---Moquette carpets and rugs, not pile or made up	15								0
57025290	---Other manmade textile carpets, not pile or made up	15								0
57025900	--Of other textile materials	15								0
57029	-Other, not of pile construction, made up:									
570291	--Of wool or fine animal hair									

HS	Description	Bound rate at date of accession	Interim	Final Bound	Implementation	Present concession established	INR	Concession first incorporated in a GATT Schedule	Earlier INRs	ODCs
57029110	---Machine-made carpets of wool, not pile, made up	15								0
57029120	---Rugs and the like of wool, not pile, made up	15								0
57029190	---Other wool carpets, not pile, made up	15								0
570292	--Of man-made textile materials									
57029210	---Moquette carpets and rugs, not pile, made up	15								0
57029220	---Prayer rugs of manmade textiles, not pile, made up	15								0
57029290	---Other carpets of manmade textiles, not pile, made up	15								0
570299	--Of other textile materials									
5702991	---Of cotton:									
57029911	----Prayer rugs of cotton, not pile, made up	15								0
57029919	----Other cotton rugs, not pile, made up	15								0
57029990	---Other rugs, not pile, made up	15								0
5703	Carpets and other textile floor coverings, tufted, whether or not made up.									
57031000	-Of wool or fine animal hair	8					PH			0
57032000	-Of nylon or other polyamides	15		12	2008					0
570330	-Of other man-made textile materials									
57033010	---Moquette carpets and rugs, tufted	15		12	2008					0
57033020	---Carpets and rugs of chenille yarn, tufted	15		12	2008					0
57033030	---Prayer rugs of tufted manmade textiles	15		12	2008					0
57033090	---Other tufted manmade textile carpets	15		12	2008					0
570390	-Of other textile materials									
5703901	---Of cotton:									
57039011	----Prayer rugs, cotton, tufted	15								0
57039019	----Other cotton carpets, tufted	15								0
57039090	---Other textile carpets, tufted	15								0
5704	Carpets and other textile floor coverings, of felt, not tufted or flocked, whether or not made up.									
57041000	-Tiles, having a maximum surface area of 0.3 m^2	15								0
57049000	-Other	15								0
5705	Other carpets and other textile floor coverings, whether or not made up.									

HS	Description	Bound rate at date of accession	Interim	Final Bound	Implementation	Present concession established	INR	Concession first incorporated in a GATT Schedule	Earlier INRs	ODCs
5705001	---Bonded pile carpet:									
57050011	----Carpets and rugs of chenille yarn, gummed pile	15								0
57050012	----Prayer rugs, gummed pile	15								0
57050019	----Other gummed pile carpets	15								0
57050020	---Bonded carpets of fibres, carded, assembled by rubber	15								0
57050030	---Knitted or crocheted carpets looking like fur	15								0
57050090	---Other carpets not elsewhere specified	15								0
5801	Woven pile fabrics and chenille fabrics, other than fabrics of heading 58.02 or 58.06.									
580110	-Of wool or fine animal hair									
58011010	---Abayas of wool or fine animal hair	15								0
58011090	---Other woven pile fabrics of wool or fine animal hair	15								0
58012	-Of cotton:									
58012100	--Uncut weft pile fabrics	15								0
58012200	--Cut corduroy	15								0
58012300	--Other weft pile fabrics	15								0
58012400	--Warp pile fabrics, épinglé (uncut)	15								0
58012500	--Warp pile fabrics, cut	15								0
58012600	--Chenille fabrics	15								0
58013	-Of man-made fibres:									
58013100	--Uncut weft pile fabrics	15								0
58013200	--Cut corduroy	15								0
58013300	--Other weft pile fabrics	10								0
58013400	--Warp pile fabrics, épinglé (uncut)	15								0
58013500	--Warp pile fabrics, cut	10								0
58013600	--Chenille fabrics	10								0
580190	-Of other textile materials									
5801901	---Woven fabrics of coarse hair:									
58019011	----Abayas of rough wool	15								0
58019019	----Other articles of rough wool	15								0
58019090	---Other articles of other textiles	15								0
5802	Terry towelling and similar woven terry fabrics, other than narrow fabrics of heading 58.06; tufted textile fabrics, other than products of heading 57.03.									
58021	-Terry towelling and similar woven terry fabrics, of cotton:									

HS	Description	Bound rate at date of accession	Interim	Final Bound	Implementation	Present concession established	INR	Concession first incorporated in a GATT Schedule	Earlier INRs	ODCs
58021100	--Unbleached	15								0
58021900	--Other	15								0
58022000	-Terry towelling and similar woven terry fabrics, of other textile materials	15								0
58023000	-Tufted textile fabrics	15								0
5803	Gauze, other than narrow fabrics of heading 58.06.									
58031000	-Of cotton	15								0
58039000	-Of other textile materials	15								0
5804	Tulles and other net fabrics, not including woven, knitted or crocheted fabrics; lace in the piece, in strips or in motifs, other than fabrics of headings 60.02 to 60.06.									
58041000	-Tulles and other net fabrics	15								0
58042	-Mechanically made lace:									
58042100	--Of man-made fibres	10								0
58042900	--Of other textile materials	15								0
58043000	-Hand-made lace	15								0
58050000	Hand-woven tapestries of the type Gobelins, Flanders, Aubusson, Beauvais and the like, and needle-worked tapestries (for example, petit point, cross stitch), whether or not made up.	15								0
5806	Narrow woven fabrics, other than goods of heading 58.07; narrow fabrics consisting of warp without weft assembled by means of an adhesive (bolducs).									
58061000	-Woven pile fabrics (including terry towelling and similar terry fabrics) and chenille fabrics	15								0
58062000	-Other woven fabrics, containing by weight 5 % or more of elastomeric yarn or rubber thread	15								0
58063	-Other woven fabrics:									
58063100	--Of cotton	15								0
58063200	--Of man-made fibres	15								0
58063900	--Of other textile materials	15								0
58064000	-Fabrics consisting of warp without weft assembled by means of an adhesive (bolducs)	15								0

HS	Description	Bound rate at date of accession	Interim	Final Bound	Implementation	Present concession established	INR	Concession first incorporated in a GATT Schedule	Earlier INRs	ODCs
5807	Labels, badges and similar articles of textile materials, in the piece, in strips or cut to shape or size, not embroidered.									
58071000	-Woven	15								0
58079000	-Other	15								0
5808	Braids in the piece; ornamental trimmings in the piece, without embroidery, other than knitted or crocheted; tassels, pompons and similar articles.									
58081000	-Braids in the piece	15								0
58089000	-Other	15								0
58090000	Woven fabrics of metal thread and woven fabrics of metallised yarn of heading 56.05, of a kind used in apparel, as furnishing fabrics or for similar purposes, not elsewhere specified or included.	15								0
5810	Embroidery in the piece, in strips or in motifs.									
58101000	-Embroidery without visible ground	12					CH			0
58109	-Other embroidery:									
58109100	--Of cotton	10					CH,IN			0
58109200	--Of man-made fibres	10					CH,IN			0
58109900	--Of other textile materials	10					CH,IN			0
58110000	Quilted textile products in the piece, composed of one or more layers of textile materials assembled with padding by stitching or otherwise, other than embroidery of heading 58.10.	15								0
5901	Textile fabrics coated with gum or amylaceous substances, of a kind used for the outer covers of books or the like; tracing cloth; prepared painting canvas; buckram and similar stiffened textile fabrics of a kind used for hat foundations.									
59011000	-Textile fabrics coated with gum or amylaceous substances, of a kind used for the outer covers of books or the like	15								0
590190	-Other									
59019010	---Other: tracing cloth	15								0
59019020	---Other: prepared painting canvas	15								0

HS	Description	Bound rate at date of accession	Interim	Final Bound	Implementation	Present concession established	INR	Concession first incorporated in a GATT Schedule	Earlier INRs	ODCs
59019030	---Other: buckram and similar	15								0
5902	Tyre cord fabric of high tenacity yarn of nylon or other polyamides, polyesters or viscose rayon.									
59021000	-Of nylon or other polyamides	15								0
59022000	-Of polyesters	15								0
59029000	-Other	15								0
5903	Textile fabrics impregnated, coated, covered or laminated with plastics, other than those of heading 59.02.									
59031000	-With poly(vinyl chloride)	10					IN			0
59032000	-With polyurethane	15								0
59039000	-Other	5								0
5904	Linoleum, whether or not cut to shape; floor coverings consisting of a coating or covering applied on a textile backing, whether or not cut to shape.									
59041000	-Linoleum	15								0
59049000	-Other	15								0
5905	Textile wall coverings.									
59050010	---Textile wall coverings of pile fabrics	15								0
59050020	---Textile wall coverings of cotton	15								0
59050030	---Textile wall coverings of wool or fine hair	15								0
59050040	---Textile wall coverings of synthetic fibres	15								0
59050050	---Textile wall coverings of artificial fibres	15								0
59050090	---Textile wall coverings of other fibres	15								0
5906	Rubberised textile fabrics, other than those of heading 59.02.									
59061000	-Adhesive tape of a width not exceeding 20 cm	15								0
59069	-Other:									
59069100	--Knitted or crocheted	15								0
59069900	--Other	15								0
5907	Textile fabrics otherwise impregnated, coated or covered; painted canvas being theatrical scenery, studio back-cloths or the like.									
5907001	---Textile fabrics otherwise impregnated, coated or covered:									

HS	Description	Bound rate at date of accession	Interim	Final Bound	Implementation	Present concession established	INR	Concession first incorporated in a GATT Schedule	Earlier INRs	ODCs
59070011	----Textiles fabrics coated with tar, bitumen	5								0
59070012	----Textile fabrics coated with waxy materials	5								0
59070013	----Soft textile fabrics coated with resins	5								0
59070014	----Textile fabrics coated or impregnated with oil	5								0
59070015	----Textile fabrics silicate-covered to be fire resistant	5								0
59070019	----Other coated or impregnated textile fabrics	5								0
59070020	---Painted canvas for theatrical scenery or the like	5								0
59080000	Textile wicks, woven, plaited or knitted, for lamps, stoves, lighters, candles or the like; incandescent gas mantles and tubular knitted gas mantle fabric therefor, whether or not impregnated.	15								0
5909	Textile hosepiping and similar textile tubing, with or without lining, armour or accessories of other materials.									
59090010	---Textile hosepiping for fire-fighting	15								0
59090090	---Other textile hosepiping	15								0
59100000	Transmission or conveyor belts or belting, of textile material, whether or not impregnated, coated, covered or laminated with plastics, or reinforced with metal or other material.	15								0
5911	Textile products and articles, for technical uses, specified in Note 7 to this Chapter.									
59111000	-Textile fabrics, felt and felt-lined woven fabrics, coated, covered or laminated with rubber, leather or other material, of a kind used for card clothing, and similar fabrics of a kind used for other technical purposes, including narrow fabrics made of velvet impregnated with rubber, for covering weaving spindles (weaving beams)	15								0
59112000	-Bolting cloth, whether or not made up	15								0

HS	Description	Bound rate at date of accession	Interim	Final Bound	Implementation	Present concession established	INR	Concession first incorporated in a GATT Schedule	Earlier INRs	ODCs
59113	-Textile fabrics and felts, endless or fitted with linking devices, of a kind used in paper-making or similar machines (for example, for pulp or asbestos-cement):									
59113100	--Weighing less than 650 g/m2	15								0
59113200	--Weighing 650 g/m2 or more	15								0
59114000	-Straining cloth of a kind used in oil presses or the like, including that of human hair	15								0
59119000	-Other	15								0
6001	Pile fabrics, including "long pile" fabrics and terry fabrics, knitted or crocheted.									
60011000	-"Long pile" fabrics	8					EC			0
60012	-Looped pile fabrics:									
60012100	--Of cotton	15								0
60012200	--Of man-made fibres	15								0
60012900	--Of other textile materials	15								0
60019	-Other:									
60019100	--Of cotton	15								0
60019200	--Of man-made fibres	10								0
60019900	--Of other textile materials	15								0
6002	Knitted or crocheted fabrics of a width not exceeding 30 cm, containing by weight 5 % or more of elastomeric yarn or rubber thread, other than those of heading 60.01.									
60024000	-Containing by weight 5 % or more of elastomeric yarn but not containing rubber thread	15								0
60029000	-Other	12								0
6003	Knitted or crocheted fabrics of a width not exceeding 30 cm, other than those of heading 60.01 or 60.02.									
60031000	-Of wool or fine animal hair	15								0
60032000	-Of cotton	15								0
60033000	-Of synthetic fibres	15								0
60034000	-Of artificial fibres	15								0
60039000	-Other	15								0

HS	Description	Bound rate at date of accession	Interim	Final Bound	Implementation	Present concession established	INR	Concession first incorporated in a GATT Schedule	Earlier INRs	ODCs
6004	Knitted or crocheted fabrics of a width exceeding 30 cm, containing by weight 5 % or more of elastomeric yarn or rubber thread, other than those of heading 60.01.									
60041000	-Containing by weight 5 % or more of elastomeric yarn but not containing rubber thread	15								0
60049000	-Other	15								0
6005	Warp knit fabrics (including those made on galloon knitting machines), other than those of headings 60.01 to 60.04.									
60051000	-Of wool or fine animal hair	15								0
60052	-Of cotton:									
60052100	--Unbleached or bleached	15								0
60052200	--Dyed	15								0
60052300	--Of yarns of different colours	15								0
60052400	--Printed	15								0
60053	-Of synthetic fibres:									
60053100	--Unbleached or bleached	15								0
60053200	--Dyed	15								0
60053300	--Of yarns of different colours	15								0
60053400	--Printed	15								0
60054	-Of artificial fibres:									
60054100	--Unbleached or bleached	15								0
60054200	--Dyed	15								0
60054300	--Of yarns of different colours	15								0
60054400	--Printed	15								0
60059000	-Other	15								0
6006	Other knitted or crocheted fabrics.									
60061000	-Of wool or fine animal hair	15								0
60062	-Of cotton:									
60062100	--Unbleached or bleached	15								0
60062200	--Dyed	15								0
60062300	--Of yarns of different colours	15								0
60062400	--Printed	15								0
60063	-Of synthetic fibres:									
60063100	--Unbleached or bleached	12								0
60063200	--Dyed	12								0
60063300	--Of yarns of different colours	12								0
60063400	--Printed	12								0
60064	-Of artificial fibres:									

HS	Description	Bound rate at date of accession	Interim	Final Bound	Implementation	Present concession established	INR	Concession first incorporated in a GATT Schedule	Earlier INRs	ODCs
60064100	--Unbleached or bleached	12								0
60064200	--Dyed	12								0
60064300	--Of yarns of different colours	12								0
60064400	--Printed	12								0
60069000	-Other	15								0
6101	Men's or boys' overcoats, car-coats, capes, cloaks, anoraks (including ski-jackets), wind-cheaters, wind-jackets and similar articles, knitted or crocheted, other than those of heading 61.03.									
61011000	-Of wool or fine animal hair	12								0
61012000	-Of cotton	12								0
61013000	-Of man-made fibres	10								0
61019000	-Of other textile materials	12								0
6102	Women's or girls' overcoats, car-coats, capes, cloaks, anoraks (including ski-jackets), wind-cheaters, wind- jackets and similar articles, knitted or crocheted, other than those of heading 61.04.									
61021000	-Of wool or fine animal hair	12								0
61022000	-Of cotton	12								0
61023000	-Of man-made fibres	12								0
61029000	-Of other textile materials	12								0
6103	Men's or boys' suits, ensembles, jackets, blazers, trousers, bib and brace overalls, breeches and shorts (other than swimwear), knitted or crocheted.									
61031	-Suits:									
61031100	--Of wool or fine animal hair	12								0
61031200	--Of synthetic fibres	12								0
61031900	--Of other textile materials	10					IN			0
61032	-Ensembles:									
61032100	--Of wool or fine animal hair	12								0
61032200	--Of cotton	10								0
61032300	--Of synthetic fibres	10					CN			0
61032900	--Of other textile materials	10								0
61033	-Jackets and blazers:									
61033100	--Of wool or fine animal hair	8					EC			0
61033200	--Of cotton	12								0
61033300	--Of synthetic fibres	10								0

HS	Description	Bound rate at date of accession	Interim	Final Bound	Implementation	Present concession established	INR	Concession first incorporated in a GATT Schedule	Earlier INRs	ODCs
61033900	--Of other textile materials	12								0
61034	-Trousers, bib and brace overalls, breeches and shorts:									
61034100	--Of wool or fine animal hair	12								0
61034200	--Of cotton	10								0
61034300	--Of synthetic fibres	10								0
61034900	--Of other textile materials	12								0
6104	Women's or girls' suits, ensembles, jackets, blazers, dresses, skirts, divided skirts, trousers, bib and brace overalls, breeches and shorts (other than swimwear), knitted or crocheted.									
61041	-Suits:									
61041100	--Of wool or fine animal hair	12								0
61041200	--Of cotton	12								0
61041300	--Of synthetic fibres	12								0
61041900	--Of other textile materials	12								0
61042	-Ensembles:									
61042100	--Of wool or fine animal hair	12								0
61042200	--Of cotton	10								0
61042300	--Of synthetic fibres	10					CN			0
61042900	--Of other textile materials	10								0
61043	-Jackets and blazers:									
61043100	--Of wool or fine animal hair	12								0
61043200	--Of cotton	12								0
61043300	--Of synthetic fibres	10								0
61043900	--Of other textile materials	12								0
61044	-Dresses:									
61044100	--Of wool or fine animal hair	12								0
61044200	--Of cotton	10					IN			0
61044300	--Of synthetic fibres	12								0
61044400	--Of artificial fibres	12								0
61044900	--Of other textile materials	12								0
61045	-Skirts and divided skirts:									
61045100	--Of wool or fine animal hair	12								0
61045200	--Of cotton	12								0
61045300	--Of synthetic fibres	10								0
61045900	--Of other textile materials	12								0
61046	-Trousers, bib and brace overalls, breeches and shorts:									
61046100	--Of wool or fine animal hair	12								0

HS	Description	Bound rate at date of accession	Interim	Final Bound	Implementation	Present concession established	INR	Concession first incorporated in a GATT Schedule	Earlier INRs	ODCs
61046200	--Of cotton	10								0
61046300	--Of synthetic fibres	10								0
61046900	--Of other textile materials	12								0
6105	Men's or boys' shirts, knitted or crocheted.									
61051000	-Of cotton	10					DO,HN,IN,SV			0
61052000	-Of man-made fibres	12								0
61059000	-Of other textile materials	12								0
6106	Women's or girls' blouses, shirts and shirt-blouses, knitted or crocheted.									
61061000	-Of cotton	10					DO,HN,IN			0
61062000	-Of man-made fibres	12								0
61069000	-Of other textile materials	12								0
6107	Men's or boys' underpants, briefs, nightshirts, pyjamas, bathrobes, dressing gowns and similar articles, knitted or crocheted.									
61071	-Underpants and briefs:									
61071100	--Of cotton	10					DO,HN,SV			0
61071200	--Of man-made fibres	12								0
61071900	--Of other textile materials	12								0
61072	-Nightshirts and pyjamas:									
61072100	--Of cotton	10					DO,HN			0
61072200	--Of man-made fibres	12								0
61072900	--Of other textile materials	12								0
61079	-Other:									
61079100	--Of cotton	12					DO,HN			0
61079200	--Of man-made fibres	12								0
61079900	--Of other textile materials	12								0
6108	Women's or girls' slips, petticoats, briefs, panties, nightdresses, pyjamas, négligés, bathrobes, dressing gowns and similar articles, knitted or crocheted.									
61081	-Slips and petticoats:									
61081100	--Of man-made fibres	12								0
61081900	--Of other textile materials	12								0
61082	-Briefs and panties:									
61082100	--Of cotton	10					DO,HN,SV			0
61082200	--Of man-made fibres	10								0
61082900	--Of other textile materials	12								0
61083	-Nightdresses and pyjamas:									
61083100	--Of cotton	10					DO,HN			0

HS	Description	Bound rate at date of accession	Interim	Final Bound	Implementation	Present concession established	INR	Concession first incorporated in a GATT Schedule	Earlier INRs	ODCs
61083200	--Of man-made fibres	10					CN			0
61083900	--Of other textile materials	10								0
61089	-Other:									
61089100	--Of cotton	12					DO,HN			0
61089200	--Of man-made fibres	8								0
61089900	--Of other textile materials	12								0
6109	T-shirts, singlets and other vests, knitted or crocheted.									
61091000	-Of cotton	10					CN,DO,HN,IN,SV			0
61099000	-Of other textile materials	8					SV			0
6110	Jerseys, pullovers, cardigans, waist-coats and similar articles, knitted or crocheted.									
61101	-Of wool or fine animal hair:									
61101100	--Of wool	8								0
61101200	--Of Kashmir (cashmere) goats	8								0
61101900	--Other	8								0
61102000	-Of cotton	12								0
61103000	-Of man-made fibres	10								0
61109000	-Of other textile materials	12								0
6111	Babies' garments and clothing accessories, knitted or crocheted.									
61111000	-Of wool or fine animal hair	12								0
61112000	-Of cotton	10					DO,HN,IN			0
61113000	-Of synthetic fibres	10								0
61119000	-Of other textile materials	12								0
6112	Track suits, ski suits and swimwear, knitted or crocheted.									
61121	-Track suits:									
61121100	--Of cotton	10					IN			0
61121200	--Of synthetic fibres	10								0
61121900	--Of other textile materials	8								0
61122000	-Ski suits	12								0
61123	-Men's or boys' swimwear:									
61123100	--Of synthetic fibres	12								0
61123900	--Of other textile materials	12								0
61124	-Women's or girls' swimwear:									
61124100	--Of synthetic fibres	12								0
61124900	--Of other textile materials	12								0
61130000	Garments, made up of knitted or crocheted fabrics of heading 59.03, 59.06 or 59.07.	12								0

HS	Description	Bound rate at date of accession	Interim	Final Bound	Implementation	Present concession established	INR	Concession first incorporated in a GATT Schedule	Earlier INRs	ODCs
6114	Other garments, knitted or crocheted.									
61141000	-Of wool or fine animal hair	12					KG			0
61142000	-Of cotton	12					DO,HN			0
61143000	-Of man-made fibres	12								0
61149000	-Of other textile materials	12								0
6115	Panty hose, tights, stockings, socks and other hosiery, including stockings for varicose veins and footwear without applied soles, knitted or crocheted.									
61151	-Panty hose and tights:									
61151100	--Of synthetic fibres, measuring per single yarn less than 67 decitex	8					EC,SV			0
61151200	--Of synthetic fibres, measuring per single yarn 67 decitex or more	12								0
61151900	--Of other textile materials	12								0
61152000	-Women's full-length or knee-length hosiery, measuring per single yarn less than 67 decitex	8								0
61159	-Other:									
61159100	--Of wool or fine animal hair	15								0
61159200	--Of cotton	15					KG			0
61159300	--Of synthetic fibres	15					EC			0
61159900	--Of other textile materials	15								0
6116	Gloves, mittens and mitts, knitted or crocheted.									
61161000	-Impregnated, coated or covered with plastics or rubber	12								0
61169	-Other:									
61169100	--Of wool or fine animal hair	12								0
61169200	--Of cotton	12								0
61169300	--Of synthetic fibres	12								0
61169900	--Of other textile materials	12								0
6117	Other made up clothing accessories, knitted or crocheted; knitted or crocheted parts of garments or of clothing accessories.									
61171000	-Shawls, scarves, mufflers, mantillas, veils and the like	10								0
61172000	-Ties, bow ties and cravats	12								0
61178000	-Other accessories	12								0
61179000	-Parts	12								0

HS	Description	Bound rate at date of accession	Interim	Final Bound	Implementation	Present concession established	INR	Concession first incorporated in a GATT Schedule	Earlier INRs	ODCs
6201	Men's or boys' overcoats, car-coats, capes, cloaks, anoraks (including ski-jackets), wind-cheaters, wind-jackets and similar articles, other than those of heading 62.03.									
62011	-Overcoats, raincoats, car-coats, capes, cloaks and similar articles:									
620111	--Of wool or fine animal hair									
62011110	---Male cloaks, wool, not knitted	10								0
62011190	---Male overcoats, etc., wool, not knitted	10								0
62011200	--Of cotton	12								0
62011300	--Of man-made fibres	12								0
62011900	--Of other textile materials	12								0
62019	-Other:									
62019100	--Of wool or fine animal hair	12								0
62019200	--Of cotton	10								0
62019300	--Of man-made fibres	10								0
62019900	--Of other textile materials	12								0
6202	Women's or girls' overcoats, car-coats, capes, cloaks, anoraks (including ski-jackets), wind-cheaters, wind-jackets and similar articles, other than those of heading 62.04.									
62021	-Overcoats, raincoats, car-coats, capes, cloaks and similar articles:									
62021100	--Of wool or fine animal hair	12								0
62021200	--Of cotton	12								0
620213	--Of man-made fibres									
62021310	---Women's cloaks, of man-made fibres, not knitted	12								0
62021390	---Female overcoats, etc., man-made fibres, not knitted	12								0
620219	--Of other textile materials									
6202191	---Of silk:									
62021911	----Women's cloaks, of silk, not knitted	12								0
62021919	----Other	15								0
62021990	---Other	12								0
62029	-Other:									
62029100	--Of wool or fine animal hair	12								0
62029200	--Of cotton	12								0
62029300	--Of man-made fibres	10								0
62029900	--Of other textile materials	12								0

HS	Description	Bound rate at date of accession	Interim	Final Bound	Implementation	Present concession established	INR	Concession first incorporated in a GATT Schedule	Earlier INRs	ODCs
6203	Men's or boys' suits, ensembles, jackets, blazers, trousers, bib and brace overalls, breeches and shorts (other than swimwear).									
62031	-Suits:									
62031100	--Of wool or fine animal hair	8								0
62031200	--Of synthetic fibres	12								0
62031900	--Of other textile materials (See Endnote 8)	10					IN			0
62032	-Ensembles:									
62032100	--Of wool or fine animal hair	12								0
62032200	--Of cotton	10					IN,TH			0
62032300	--Of synthetic fibres	10					TH			0
62032900	--Of other textile materials	10								0
62033	-Jackets and blazers:									
62033100	--Of wool or fine animal hair	12								0
62033200	--Of cotton	10					IN			0
62033300	--Of synthetic fibres	12								0
62033900	--Of other textile materials	12								0
62034	-Trousers, bib and brace overalls, breeches and shorts:									
62034100	--Of wool or fine animal hair	12								0
62034200	--Of cotton	10					IN,TH			0
62034300	--Of synthetic fibres	10								0
62034900	--Of other textile materials	10								0
6204	Women's or girls' suits, ensembles, jackets, blazers, dresses, skirts, divided skirts, trousers, bib and brace overalls, breeches and shorts (other than swimwear).									
62041	-Suits:									
62041100	--Of wool or fine animal hair	12								0
62041200	--Of cotton	12								0
62041300	--Of synthetic fibres	12								0
62041900	--Of other textile materials	12								0
62042	-Ensembles:									
62042100	--Of wool or fine animal hair	12								0
62042200	--Of cotton	10								0
62042300	--Of synthetic fibres	10								0
62042900	--Of other textile materials	10					IN			0
62043	-Jackets and blazers:									
62043100	--Of wool or fine animal hair	12								0

HS	Description	Bound rate at date of accession	Interim	Final Bound	Implementation	Present concession established	INR	Concession first incorporated in a GATT Schedule	Earlier INRs	ODCs
62043200	--Of cotton	12								0
62043300	--Of synthetic fibres	10								0
62043900	--Of other textile materials	12								0
62044	-Dresses:									
62044100	--Of wool or fine animal hair	8					IN			0
62044200	--Of cotton	10					IN			0
62044300	--Of synthetic fibres	10					IN			0
62044400	--Of artificial fibres	10					IN			0
62044900	--Of other textile materials	10					IN			0
62045	-Skirts and divided skirts:									
62045100	--Of wool or fine animal hair	8								0
62045200	--Of cotton	12								0
62045300	--Of synthetic fibres	12								0
62045900	--Of other textile materials	12								0
62046	-Trousers, bib and brace overalls, breeches and shorts:									
62046100	--Of wool or fine animal hair	12								0
62046200	--Of cotton	10					IN,SV			0
62046300	--Of synthetic fibres	10					IN			0
62046900	--Of other textile materials	12								0
6205	Men's or boys' shirts.									
62051000	-Of wool or fine animal hair	12								0
62052000	-Of cotton (See Endnote 9)	10					DO,HN,IN,SV			0
62053000	-Of man-made fibres	10					IN,TH			0
62059000	-Of other textile materials	10								0
6206	Women's or girls' blouses, shirts and shirt-blouses.									
62061000	-Of silk or silk waste	12								0
62062000	-Of wool or fine animal hair	12								0
62063000	-Of cotton (See Endnote 10)	10					DO,HN,IN			0
62064000	-Of man-made fibres	10								0
62069000	-Of other textile materials	12								0
6207	Men's or boys' singlets and other vests, underpants, briefs, nightshirts, pyjamas, bathrobes, dressing gowns and similar articles.									
62071	-Underpants and briefs:									
62071100	--Of cotton	12					DO,HN			0
62071900	--Of other textile materials	10								0
62072	-Nightshirts and pyjamas:									
62072100	--Of cotton	10					DO,HN			0

HS	Description	Bound rate at date of accession	Interim	Final Bound	Implementation	Present concession established	INR	Concession first incorporated in a GATT Schedule	Earlier INRs	ODCs
62072200	--Of man-made fibres	12								0
62072900	--Of other textile materials	12								0
62079	-Other:									
62079100	--Of cotton	10					DO,HN,IN			0
62079200	--Of man-made fibres	10								0
62079900	--Of other textile materials	12								0
6208	Women's or girls' singlets and other vests, slips, petticoats, briefs, panties, nightdresses, pyjamas, négligés, bathrobes, dressing gowns and similar articles.									
62081	-Slips and petticoats:									
62081100	--Of man-made fibres	10					IN			0
62081900	--Of other textile materials	10					IN			0
62082	-Nightdresses and pyjamas:									
62082100	--Of cotton	10					IN			0
62082200	--Of man-made fibres	10								0
62082900	--Of other textile materials	10								0
62089	-Other:									
62089100	--Of cotton	10					IN,KG			0
62089200	--Of man-made fibres	10								0
62089900	--Of other textile materials	10								0
6209	Babies' garments and clothing accessories.									
62091000	-Of wool or fine animal hair	12								0
62092000	-Of cotton	10					IN			0
62093000	-Of synthetic fibres	10								0
62099000	-Of other textile materials	12								0
6210	Garments, made up of fabrics of heading 56.02, 56.03, 59.03, 59.06 or 59.07.									
621010	-Of fabrics of heading 56.02 or 56.03									
62101010	---Garments and garments suits made up of fabrics of headings No. 5602 or 5603, whether sterilized for operation theaters, of polypropylene, for one time use	8					DO,HN			0
62101090	---Other garments	8					DO,HN			0
62102000	-Other garments, of the type described in subheadings 6201.11 to 6201.19	12								0
62103000	-Other garments, of the type described in subheadings 6202.11 to 6202.19	12								0
62104000	-Other men's or boys' garments	10								0

HS	Description	Bound rate at date of accession	Interim	Final Bound	Implementation	Present concession established	INR	Concession first incorporated in a GATT Schedule	Earlier INRs	ODCs
62105000	-Other women's or girls' garments	12								0
6211	Track suits, ski suits and swimwear; other garments.									
62111	-Swimwear:									
62111100	--Men's or boys'	12								0
62111200	--Women's or girls'	12								0
62112000	-Ski suits	12								0
62113	-Other garments, men's or boys':									
621131	--Of wool or fine animal hair									
62113110	---Thobes "dishdasha"	15								0
62113120	---Training suits of wool	15								0
62113190	---Other men's or boys' garments	12								0
621132	--Of cotton									
62113210	---Thobes "dishdasha"	10								0
62113220	---Training suits of cotton	15								0
62113290	---Other men's or boys' garments	10								0
621133	--Of man-made fibres									
62113310	---Thobes "dishdasha"	10					CN			0
62113320	---Training suits of synthetic fibres	15								0
62113390	---Other men's or boys' garments	10					CN			0
621139	--Of other textile materials									
62113910	---Thobes "dishdasha"	12								0
62113920	---Training suits of other synthetics	15								0
62113990	---Other men's or boys' garments	12								0
62114	-Other garments, women's or girls':									
62114100	--Of wool or fine animal hair	12								0
62114200	--Of cotton	10								0
62114300	--Of man-made fibres	10								0
62114900	--Of other textile materials	12								0
6212	Brassières, girdles, corsets, braces, suspenders, garters and similar articles and parts thereof, whether or not knitted or crocheted.									
62121000	-Brassières	10					DO,HN			0
62122000	-Girdles and panty-girdles	12								0
62123000	-Corselettes	12								0
62129000	-Other	12								0
6213	Handkerchiefs.									
62131000	-Of silk or silk waste	12								0
62132000	-Of cotton	12								0
62139000	-Of other textile materials	12								0

HS	Description	Bound rate at date of accession	Interim	Final Bound	Implementation	Present concession established	INR	Concession first incorporated in a GATT Schedule	Earlier INRs	ODCs
6214	Shawls, scarves, mufflers, mantillas, veils and the like.									
62141000	-Of silk or silk waste	12								0
621420	-Of wool or fine animal hair									
62142010	---Wool shawls	12								0
62142020	---Wool scarves	12								0
62142090	---Other wool mufflers, veils, etc.	12								0
621430	-Of synthetic fibres									
62143010	---Synthetic fiber shawls	10					IN			0
62143020	---Synthetic fiber scarves	10								0
62143030	---Synthetic fiber mufflers	10								0
62143040	---Synthetic fiber veils	10								0
62143090	---Other mantillas and similar of synthetic fibres	10					IN			0
621440	-Of artificial fibres									
62144010	---Artificial fiber shawls	10					IN			0
62144020	---Artificial fiber scarves	10								0
62144030	---Artificial fiber mufflers	10								0
62144040	---Artificial fiber veils	10								0
62144090	---Other mantillas and similar of artificial fibres	10								0
621490	-Of other textile materials									
6214901	---Of cotton:									
62149011	----Cotton shawls	10					IN			0
62149012	----Cotton scarves	10								0
62149013	----Mufflers	10								0
62149014	----Cotton veils	10								0
62149019	----Other cotton mantillas and similar	10								0
62149090	---Shawls, scarves and similar of other textiles	10					IN			0
6215	Ties, bow ties and cravats.									
62151000	-Of silk or silk waste	12								0
62152000	-Of man-made fibres	12								0
62159000	-Of other textile materials	12								0
62160000	Gloves, mittens and mitts.	12								0
6217	Other made up clothing accessories; parts of garments or of clothing accessories, other than those of heading 62.12.									
621710	-Accessories									
62171010	---Stockings accessories, not knitted	12								0
62171020	---Footwear without soles	12								0

HS	Description	Bound rate at date of accession	Interim	Final Bound	Implementation	Present concession established	INR	Concession first incorporated in a GATT Schedule	Earlier INRs	ODCs
6217103	---Belts of all kinds:									
62171031	----Belts with precious stones	12								0
62171039	----Other belts	12								0
62171040	---Shoulder insignia or badges	12								0
62171050	---Badges, labels and initials	12								0
62171060	---Plaited strips (braids) for ornamenting the uniform	12								0
62171070	---Pockets, sleeves, small collars, garment trimmings	12								0
62171090	---Other clothing accessories	12								0
621790	-Parts									
62179010	---Dress shields	12								0
62179020	---Shoulder pads and similar for tailors	12								0
62179090	---Other clothing parts	12								0
6301	Blankets and travelling rugs.									
63011000	-Electric blankets	15								0
63012000	-Blankets (other than electric blankets) and travelling rugs, of wool or of fine animal hair	15								0
63013000	-Blankets (other than electric blankets) and travelling rugs, of cotton	15								0
63014000	-Blankets (other than electric blankets) and travelling rugs, of synthetic fibres	15								0
63019000	-Other blankets and travelling rugs	15								0
6302	Bed linen, table linen, toilet linen and kitchen linen.									
63021000	-Bed linen, knitted or crocheted	15								0
63022	-Other bed linen, printed:									
63022100	--Of cotton	15		12	2008		PK			0
63022200	--Of man-made fibres	15								0
63022900	--Of other textile materials	15								0
63023	-Other bed linen:									
63023100	--Of cotton	15								0
63023200	--Of man-made fibres	15								0
63023900	--Of other textile materials	15								0
63024000	-Table linen, knitted or crocheted	15								0
63025	-Other table linen:									
63025100	--Of cotton	15		13	2010					0
63025200	--Of flax	15								0
63025300	--Of man-made fibres	15								0
63025900	--Of other textile materials	15								0

HS	Description	Bound rate at date of accession	Interim	Final Bound	Implementation	Present concession established	INR	Concession first incorporated in a GATT Schedule	Earlier INRs	ODCs
63026000	-Toilet linen and kitchen linen, of terry towelling or similar terry fabrics, of cotton	5					KG			0
63029	-Other:									
630291	--Of cotton									
63029110	---Pilgrimage towels	15					PK			0
63029120	---Ordinary towels, hand towels and bath towels	15								0
63029130	---Towels joined end to end to be reeled	15								0
63029140	---Kitchen towels for drying and wiping the pots	15								0
63029190	---Other cotton towels	15								0
63029200	--Of flax	15								0
63029300	--Of man-made fibres	15								0
63029900	--Of other textile materials	15								0
6303	Curtains (including drapes) and interior blinds; curtain or bed valances.									
63031	-Knitted or crocheted:									
63031100	--Of cotton	15								0
63031200	--Of synthetic fibres	15								0
63031900	--Of other textile materials	15								0
63039	-Other:									
630391	--Of cotton									
63039110	---Curtains and drapes, cotton, not knitted	15								0
63039120	---Blinds for means of transportation, cotton, not knitted	15								0
63039190	---Other cotton blinds, valalnces, etc., not knitted	15								0
630392	--Of synthetic fibres									
63039210	---Curtains and drapes of synthetic fibres, not knitted	15								0
63039220	---Blinds for transportation, synthetic, not knitted	15								0
63039290	---Other blinds, etc., of synthetic fibres, not knitted	15								0
63039900	--Of other textile materials	15								0
6304	Other furnishing articles, excluding those of heading 94.04.									
63041	-Bedspreads:									
63041100	--Knitted or crocheted	15								0
63041900	--Other	10								0

HS	Description	Bound rate at date of accession	Interim	Final Bound	Implementation	Present concession established	INR	Concession first incorporated in a GATT Schedule	Earlier INRs	ODCs
63049	-Other:									
630491	--Knitted or crocheted									
63049110	---Mosquito nets, knitted	15								0
63049120	---Covers for the seats of vehicles, knitted	15								0
63049190	---Other knitted furnishing	15								0
630492	--Not knitted or crocheted, of cotton									
63049210	---Mosquito nets, not knitted, cotton	15								0
63049220	---Covers for the seats of vehicles, not knitted, cotton	15								0
63049230	---Curtain bands, not knitted, cotton	10					IN			0
63049240	---Pillow cases, not knitted, cotton	10					IN			0
63049290	---Other furnishings, not knitted, cotton	10					IN			0
630493	--Not knitted or crocheted, of synthetic fibres									
63049310	---Mosquito nets, not knitted, synthetic	15								0
63049320	---Covers for vehicle seats, not knitted, synthetic	15								0
63049330	---Curtain bands, not knitted, synthetic	15								0
63049340	---Pillow cases, not knitted, synthetic	15								0
63049390	---Other furnishings, not knitted, synthetic	15								0
630499	--Not knitted or crocheted, of other textile materials									
63049910	---Mosquito nets, not knitted, of other textiles	15								0
63049920	---Covers for vehicle seats, not knitted, other textiles	15								0
63049930	---Curtain bands, not knitted, of other textiles	15								0
63049940	---Pillow cases, not knitted, of other textiles	15								0
63049990	---Other furnishings, not knitted, of other textiles	15								0
6305	Sacks and bags, of a kind used for the packing of goods.									
630510	-Of jute or of other textile bast fibres of heading 53.03									
63051010	---Jute sacks and bags	10					IN			0
63051090	---Other textile bast sacks and bags	10								0
63052000	-Of cotton	15								0
63053	-Of man-made textile materials:									
63053200	--Flexible intermediate bulk containers	15								0

HS	Description	Bound rate at date of accession	Interim	Final Bound	Implementation	Present concession established	INR	Concession first incorporated in a GATT Schedule	Earlier INRs	ODCs
63053300	--Other, of polyethylene or polypropylene strip or the like	15					DO,HN			0
63053900	--Other	15								0
63059000	-Of other textile materials	15								0
6306	Tarpaulins, awnings and sunblinds; tents; sails for boats, sailboards or landcraft; camping goods.									
63061	-Tarpaulins, awnings and sunblinds:									
630611	--Of cotton									
63061110	---Tarpaulins, cotton	15					PK			0
63061120	---Awnings and sunblinds, cotton	15								0
630612	--Of synthetic fibres									
63061210	---Tarpaulins, synthetic fibers	15								0
63061220	---Awnings and sunblinds, synthetic fibres	15								0
630619	--Of other textile materials									
63061910	---Tarpaulins, of other textiles	15								0
63061920	---Awnings and sunblinds, of other textiles	15								0
63062	-Tents:									
63062100	--Of cotton	15					PK			0
63062200	--Of synthetic fibres	15								0
63062900	--Of other textile materials	15					PK			0
63063	-Sails:									
63063100	--Of synthetic fibres	15								0
63063900	--Of other textile materials	15								0
63064	-Pneumatic mattresses:									
63064100	--Of cotton	15								0
63064900	--Of other textile materials	15								0
63069	-Other:									
63069100	--Of cotton	15								0
63069900	--Of other textile materials	15								0
6307	Other made up articles, including dress patterns.									
63071000	-Floor-cloths, dish-cloths, dusters and similar cleaning cloths	15								0
63072000	-Life-jackets and life-belts	15								0
630790	-Other									
63079010	---Dress patterns	15								0
63079020	---Flags, banners, pennants, badges and the like	15								0

HS	Description	Bound rate at date of accession	Interim	Final Bound	Implementation	Present concession established	INR	Concession first incorporated in a GATT Schedule	Earlier INRs	ODCs
63079030	---Laundry sacks, shoe bags and pouches, small bags	15								0
63079040	---Bags for protecting clothes	15								0
63079050	---Car covers, machine covers, suitcase covers, etc.	15								0
63079060	---Bags for filtering the coffee and bags for ice	15								0
63079070	---Decoration knots for contests	15								0
63079080	---Pneumatic pillows other than those used for camping	15								0
63079091	----Covers for tea pots	15								0
63079092	----Pin-cushions	15								0
63079093	----Sanitary towels, except those coated with gum or amylaceous substances (Chapter 5901)	15								0
63079094	----Shoelaces and corsets of fixed ends	15								0
63079095	----Portable cradles	15								0
63079096	----Sheaths and covers of umbrellas and sunshades	15								0
63079097	----Surgeon/medical masks	15								0
63079099	----Other made up articles	12								0
63080000	Sets consisting of woven fabric and yarn, whether or not with accessories, for making up into rugs, tapestries, embroidered table cloths or serviettes, or similar textile articles, put up in packings for retail sale.	15								0
6309	Worn clothing and other worn articles.									
63090020	---Used shamaghs	15								0
63090090	---Other used clothing	15								0
6310	Used or new rags, scrap twine, cordage, rope and cables and worn out articles of twine, cordage, rope or cables, of textile materials.									
63101000	-Sorted	15								0
63109000	-Other	15								0
6401	Waterproof footwear with outer soles and uppers of rubber or of plastics, the uppers of which are neither fixed to the sole nor assembled by stitching, riveting, nailing, screwing, plugging or similar processes.									
64011000	-Footwear incorporating a protective metal toe-cap	15								0

HS	Description	Bound rate at date of accession	Interim	Final Bound	Implementation	Present concession established	INR	Concession first incorporated in a GATT Schedule	Earlier INRs	ODCs
64019	-Other footwear:									
64019100	--Covering the knee	15								0
64019200	--Covering the ankle but not covering the knee	15								0
64019900	--Other	15								0
6402	Other footwear with outer soles and uppers of rubber or plastics.									
64021	-Sports footwear:									
64021200	--Ski-boots, cross-country ski footwear and snowboard boots	15								0
64021900	--Other	10								0
64022000	-Footwear with upper straps or thongs assembled to the sole by means of plugs	10								0
64023000	-Other footwear, incorporating a protective metal toe-cap	10								0
64029	-Other footwear:									
64029100	--Covering the ankle	10								0
64029900	--Other (See Endnote 11)	8					CN			0
6403	Footwear with outer soles of rubber, plastics, leather or composition leather and uppers of leather.									
64031	-Sports footwear:									
64031200	--Ski-boots, cross-country ski footwear and snowboard boots	15								0
64031900	--Other	10								0
64032000	-Footwear with outer soles of leather, and uppers which consist of leather straps across the instep and around the big toe	15								0
64033000	-Footwear made on a base or platform of wood, not having an inner sole or a protective metal toe-cap	15								0
64034000	-Other footwear, incorporating a protective metal toe-cap	15								0
64035	-Other footwear with outer soles of leather:									
640351	--Covering the ankle									
64035110	---Leather footwear covering the ankle, male	15								0
64035120	---Leather footwear covering the ankle, female	15								0

HS	Description	Bound rate at date of accession	Interim	Final Bound	Implementation	Present concession established	INR	Concession first incorporated in a GATT Schedule	Earlier INRs	ODCs
64035130	---Leather footwear covering the ankle, baby	15								0
640359	--Other									
64035910	---Leather footwear not covering the ankle, male	15								0
64035920	---Leather footwear not covering the ankle, female	15								0
64035930	---Leather footwear not covering the ankle, baby	15								0
64039	-Other footwear:									
640391	--Covering the ankle									
64039110	---Male other footwear covering the ankle	10					DO,HN			0
64039120	---Female other footwear covering the ankle	10					DO,HN			0
64039130	---Baby other footwear covering the ankle	10					DO,HN			0
640399	--Other									
64039910	---Male other footwear not covering the ankle	10								0
64039920	---Female other footwear not covering the ankle	10								0
64039930	---Baby other footwear not covering the ankle	10								0
6404	Footwear with outer soles of rubber, plastics, leather or composition leather and uppers of textile materials.									
64041	-Footwear with outer soles of rubber or plastics:									
64041100	--Sports footwear; tennis shoes, basketball shoes, gym shoes, training shoes and the like	10								0
64041900	--Other	10								0
64042000	-Footwear with outer soles of leather or composition leather	15								0
6405	Other footwear.									
64051000	-With uppers of leather or composition leather	15								0
64052000	-With uppers of textile materials	15								0
64059000	-Other	15		13	2010					0

HS	Description	Bound rate at date of accession	Interim	Final Bound	Implementation	Present concession established	INR	Concession first incorporated in a GATT Schedule	Earlier INRs	ODCs
6406	Parts of footwear (including uppers whether or not attached to soles other than outer soles); removable in-soles, heel cushions and similar articles; gaiters, leggings and similar articles, and parts thereof.									
64061000	-Uppers and parts thereof, other than stiffeners	15					DO,HN			0
64062000	-Outer soles and heels, of rubber or plastics	15								0
64069	-Other:									
64069100	--Of wood	15								0
64069900	--Of other materials	15								0
65010000	Hat-forms, hat bodies and hoods of felt, neither blocked to shape nor with made brims; plateaux and manchons (including slit manchons), of felt.	15								0
65020000	Hat-shapes, plaited or made by assembling strips of any material, neither blocked to shape, nor with made brims, nor lined, nor trimmed.	8					EC			0
65030000	Felt hats and other felt headgear, made from the hat bodies, hoods or plateaux of heading 65.01, whether or not lined or trimmed.	10								0
65040000	Hats and other headgear, plaited or made by assembling strips of any material, whether or not lined or trimmed.	8					EC			0
6505	Hats and other headgear, knitted or crocheted, or made up from lace, felt or other textile fabric, in the piece (but not in strips), whether or not lined or trimmed; hair-nets of any material, whether or not lined or trimmed.									
65051000	-Hair-nets	15								0
650590	-Other									
65059010	---Embroidered shamagh	15								0
65059020	---Ghutrahs in the form of shamagh, embroidered	10								0
65059030	---Ordinary ghutrahs	10								0
65059040	---Taqiahs	12								0
65059050	---Agals	12								0
65059060	---Hats	12								0

HS	Description	Bound rate at date of accession	Interim	Final Bound	Implementation	Present concession established	INR	Concession first incorporated in a GATT Schedule	Earlier INRs	ODCs
6505909	---Other:									
65059094	----Berets	12								0
65059095	----Caps used in operations rooms, of propylene, whether sterilised, disposable	15								0
65059096	----Headgear embroidered and non-embroidered	15								0
65059099	----Other knitted headgear	8								0
6506	Other headgear, whether or not lined or trimmed.									
650610	-Safety headgear									
65061010	---Sports safety headgear	15								0
65061020	---Firemen's helmets	15								0
65061030	---Military helmets	15								0
65061040	---Motorcyclists' helmets	15								0
65061050	---Construction workers' helmets	15								0
65061090	---Other safety headgear	15								0
65069	-Other:									
650691	--Of rubber or of plastics									
65069110	---Bathing headgear	15								0
65069190	---Other rubber or plastic headgear	15								0
65069200	--Of furskin	15								0
65069900	--Of other materials	15								0
65070000	Head-bands, linings, covers, hat foundations, hat frames, peaks and chinstraps, for headgear.	15								0
6601	Umbrellas and sun umbrellas (including walking-stick umbrellas, garden umbrellas and similar umbrellas).									
66011000	-Garden or similar umbrellas	15								0
66019	-Other:									
66019100	--Having a telescopic shaft	15								0
66019900	--Other	15								0
6602	Walking-sticks, seat-sticks, whips, riding-crops and the like.									
66020010	---Walking sticks	15								0
66020020	---Whips	15								0
66020090	---Other riding-crops, seat-sticks and the like	15								0
6603	Parts, trimmings and accessories of articles of heading 66.01 or 66.02.									
66031000	-Handles and knobs	15								0

HS	Description	Bound rate at date of accession	Interim	Final Bound	Implementation	Present concession established	INR	Concession first incorporated in a GATT Schedule	Earlier INRs	ODCs
66032000	-Umbrella frames, including frames mounted on shafts (sticks)	15								0
66039000	-Other	15								0
6701	Skins and other parts of birds with their feathers or down, feathers, parts of feathers, down and articles thereof (other than goods of heading 05.05 and worked quills and scapes).									
67010010	---Fans (non-mechanical) of decoration feathers	15								0
67010090	---Other parts of birds like feathers, down, etc.	15								0
6702	Artificial flowers, foliage and fruit and parts thereof; articles made of artificial flowers, foliage or fruit.									
67021000	-Of plastics	10								0
670290	-Of other materials									
67029010	---Artificial flowers, etc., of metal sheets	10								0
67029020	---Artificial flowers, etc., of textiles	10								0
67029090	---Artifical flowers, etc., of other materials	10								0
67030000	Human hair, dressed, thinned, bleached or otherwise worked; wool or other animal hair or other textile materials, prepared for use in making wigs or the like.	15								0
6704	Wigs, false beards, eyebrows and eyelashes, switches and the like, of human or animal hair or of textile materials; articles of human hair not elsewhere specified or included.									
67041	-Of synthetic textile materials:									
67041100	--Complete wigs	15								0
67041900	--Other	15								0
67042000	-Of human hair	15								0
67049000	-Of other materials	15								0
6801	Setts, curbstones and flagstones, of natural stone (except slate).									
68010010	---Curbstones, flagstones of sand stone	15								0
68010020	---Curbstones, flagstones of granite	15								0
68010030	---Curbstones, flagstones of porphyry	15								0
68010040	---Curbstones, flagstones of marble	15								0
68010090	---Curbstones, flagstones of other natural stones	15								0

HS	Description	Bound rate at date of accession	Interim	Final Bound	Implementation	Present concession established	INR	Concession first incorporated in a GATT Schedule	Earlier INRs	ODCs
6802	Worked monumental or building stone (except slate) and articles thereof, other than goods of heading 68.01; mosaic cubes and the like, of natural stone (including slate), whether or not on a backing; artificially coloured granules, chippings and powder, of natural stone (including slate).									
68021000	-Tiles, cubes and similar articles, whether or not rectangular (including square), the largest surface area of which is capable of being enclosed in a square the side of which is less than 7 cm; artificially coloured granules, chippings and powder	15								0
680220	-Other monumental or building stone and articles thereof,									
68022100	--Marble, travertine and alabaster	10					IN			0
68022200	--Other calcareous stone	15								0
68022300	--Granite	10					IN			0
68022900	--Other stone	15								0
68029	-Other:									
680291	--Marble, travertine and alabaster									
68029110	---Stairs, cornices, etc., of marble and other stone	15								0
6802912	---Permanent sanitary ware:									
68029121	----Bathtubs of marble and other stone	15								0
68029122	----Wash basins of marble and other stone	15								0
68029123	----Fountain basins of marble and other stone	15								0
68029129	----Other sanitary fixtures of marble and other stone	15								0
68029130	---Flower vases and the like of marble and other stone	15								0
68029140	---Columns and pedestals of marble and other stone	15								0
68029150	---Cups, boxes and ash trays of marble and other stone	15								0
68029160	---Paper weights and writing aid of marble and other stone	15								0
68029170	---Sheets for furniture surfaces of marble and other stone	15								0

HS	Description	Bound rate at date of accession	Interim	Final Bound	Implementation	Present concession established	INR	Concession first incorporated in a GATT Schedule	Earlier INRs	ODCs
68029190	---Other articles of marble or other stone (See Endnote 12)	12								0
68029200	--Other calcareous stone	15								0
68029300	--Granite	10								0
68029900	--Other stone	15								0
6803	Worked slate and articles of slate or of agglomerated slate.									
68030010	---Tiles and blocks for building and paving of slate	15								0
68030090	---Other slate articles	15								0
6804	Millstones, grindstones, grinding wheels and the like, without frameworks, for grinding, sharpening, polishing, trueing or cutting, hand sharpening or polishing stones, and parts thereof, of natural stone, of agglomerated natural or artificial abrasives, or of ceramics, with or without parts of other materials.									
68041000	-Millstones and grindstones for milling, grinding or pulping	15								0
68042	-Other millstones, grindstones, grinding wheels and the like:									
68042100	--Of agglomerated synthetic or natural diamond	15								0
68042200	--Of other agglomerated abrasives or of ceramics	15								0
68042300	--Of natural stone	15								0
68043000	-Hand sharpening or polishing stones	15								0
6805	Natural or artificial abrasive powder or grain, on a base of textile material, of paper, of paperboard or of other materials, whether or not cut to shape or sewn or otherwise made up.									
68051000	-On a base of woven textile fabric only	15								0
68052000	-On a base of paper or paperboard only	15								0
68053000	-On a base of other materials	15								0

HS	Description	Bound rate at date of accession	Interim	Final Bound	Implementation	Present concession established	INR	Concession first incorporated in a GATT Schedule	Earlier INRs	ODCs
6806	Slag wool, rock wool and similar mineral wools; exfoliated vermiculite, expanded clays, foamed slag and similar expanded mineral materials; mixtures and articles of heat-insulating, sound-insulating or sound-absorbing mineral materials, other than those of heading 68.11 or 68.12 or of Chapter 69.									
68061000	-Slag wool, rock wool and similar mineral wools (including intermixtures thereof), in bulk, sheets or rolls	15								0
68062000	-Exfoliated vermiculite, expanded clays, foamed slag and similar expanded mineral materials (including intermixtures thereof)	15								0
68069000	-Other	15								0
6807	Articles of asphalt or of similar material (for example, petroleum bitumen or coal tar pitch).									
68071000	-In rolls	15								0
680790	-Other									
68079010	---Tiles, setts and paving stones of asphalt	15								0
68079020	---Ceiling and building boards of asphalt	15								0
68079030	---Pipes and fittings thereof of asphalt	15								0
68079040	---Cast or moulded tableware of asphalt	15								0
68079090	---Other articles of asphalt or similar material	15								0
68080000	Panels, boards, tiles, blocks and similar articles of vegetable fibre, of straw or of shavings, chips, particles, sawdust or other waste, of wood, agglomerated with cement, plaster or other mineral binders.	15								0
6809	Articles of plaster or of compositions based on plaster.									
68091	-Boards, sheets, panels, tiles and similar articles, not ornamented:									
68091100	--Faced or reinforced with paper or paperboard only	15		13	2010					0
68091900	--Other	15								0
680990	-Other articles									
68099010	---Ornamented plasterboard	15								0

HS	Description	Bound rate at date of accession	Interim	Final Bound	Implementation	Present concession established	INR	Concession first incorporated in a GATT Schedule	Earlier INRs	ODCs
68099020	---Moulded items or ornamental items of plasterboard	15								0
68099030	---Moulds for industry of plasterboard	15								0
68099090	---Other plasterboard articles	15								0
6810	Articles of cement, of concrete or of artificial stone, whether or not reinforced.									
68101	-Tiles, flagstones, bricks and similar articles:									
68101100	--Building blocks and bricks	15								0
681019	--Other									
68101910	---Roofing tiles of cement or concrete	15								0
6810192	---Other tiles:									
68101921	----Tiles and blocks for road paving	15								0
68101922	----Local tiles for flooring and roofing	15								0
68101923	----Granulated marble tiles	15								0
68101929	----Other tiles of cement or concrete	15								0
68101990	---Other flagstones	15								0
68109	-Other articles:									
68109100	--Prefabricated structural components for building or civil engineering	15								0
681099	--Other									
68109910	---Fixed bathroom equipment of concrete, etc.	15								0
68109990	---Other articles of cement, concrete, etc.	15								0
6811	Articles of asbestos-cement, of cellulose fibre-cement or the like.									
68111000	-Corrugated sheets	15								0
68112000	-Other sheets, panels, tiles and similar articles	15		13	2010					0
681130	-Tubes, pipes and tube or pipe fittings									
68113010	---Ventilating pipes and the likeof asbestos-cement, etc.	15								0
68113020	---Conduits of asbestos-cement and similar	15								0
68113030	---Pipe joints and washers of asbestos-cement and similar	15								0
68113090	---Other tubes and pipes of asbestos-cement and similar	15								0
681190	-Other articles									
68119010	---Tanks of asbestos-cement and similar	15					AU			0

HS	Description	Bound rate at date of accession	Interim	Final Bound	Implementation	Present concession established	INR	Concession first incorporated in a GATT Schedule	Earlier INRs	ODCs
68119020	---Basins of asbestos-cement and similar	15					AU			0
68119030	---Vases of asbestos-cement and similar	15					AU			0
68119090	---Other articles of asbestos-cement and similar	15					AU			0
6812	Fabricated asbestos fibres; mixtures with a basis of asbestos or with a basis of asbestos and magnesium carbonate; articles of such mixtures or of asbestos (for example, thread, woven fabric, clothing, headgear, footwear, gaskets), whether or not reinforced, other than goods of heading 68.11 or 68.13.									
68125000	-Clothing, clothing accessories, footwear and headgear	15								0
68126000	-Paper, millboard and felt	15								0
68127000	-Compressed asbestos fibre jointing, in sheets or rolls	15								0
681290	-Other									
68129010	---Filter blocks and table mats of asbestos fibres	15								0
ex68129010	----For use in civil aircraft	0					US			0
68129020	---Cones of iron covered with asbestos for fires	15								0
ex68129020	----For use in civil aircraft	0					US			0
ex68129090	----For use in civil aircraft	0					US			0
68129090	---Other articles of asbestos fibres	15								0
6813	Friction material and articles thereof (for example, sheets, rolls, strips, segments, discs, washers, pads), not mounted, for brakes, for clutches or the like, with a basis of asbestos, of other mineral substances or of cellulose, whether or not combined with textile or other materials.									
68131000	-Brake linings and pads	15								0
ex68131000	--For use in civil aircraft	0					US			0
68139000	-Other	15								0
ex68139000	--For use in civil aircraft	0					US			0
6814	Worked mica and articles of mica, including agglomerated or reconstituted mica, whether or not on a support of paper, paperboard or other materials.									

HS	Description	Bound rate at date of accession	Interim	Final Bound	Implementation	Present concession established	INR	Concession first incorporated in a GATT Schedule	Earlier INRs	ODCs
68141000	-Plates, sheets and strips of agglomerated or reconstituted mica, whether or not on a support	15								0
681490	-Other									
68149010	---Pipes, channels and the like of mica	15								0
68149090	---Other articles of mica	15								0
6815	Articles of stone or of other mineral substances (including carbon fibres, articles of carbon fibres and articles of peat), not elsewhere specified or included.									
681510	-Non-electrical articles of graphite or other carbon									
68151010	---Filtering pipes and discs of graphite	15								0
68151020	---Shaft bearings of graphite	15								0
68151030	---Worked brick and tiles of graphite	15								0
68151040	---Moulds for the manufacture of small pieces, graphite	15								0
68151090	---Other articles of graphite	15								0
681520	-Articles of peat									
68152010	---Sheets of peat	15								0
68152020	---Cylindrical shapes of peat	15								0
68152030	---Plant pots of peat	15								0
68152090	---Other articles of peat	15								0
68159	-Other articles:									
681591	--Containing magnesite, dolomite or chromite									
68159110	---Brick untreated with fire, made of dolomite	15								0
68159120	---Brick and other shapes made of magnesite	15								0
68159190	---Other articles of magnesite, dolomite or chromite	15								0
681599	--Other									
68159910	---Vats of silica or alum untreated with fire	15								0
68159920	---Touchstone for testing precious metals	15								0
68159930	---Paving blocks and slabs of other minerals	15								0
68159940	---Filtering pipes of agglomerated quartz or flint	15								0

HS	Description	Bound rate at date of accession	Interim	Final Bound	Implementation	Present concession established	INR	Concession first incorporated in a GATT Schedule	Earlier INRs	ODCs
68159950	---Other blocks, slabs or sheets of melted basalt	15								0
68159990	---Other articles of other minerals	15								0
69010000	Bricks, blocks, tiles and other ceramic goods of siliceous fossil meals (for example, kieselguhr, tripolite or diatomite) or of similar siliceous earths.	15								0
6902	Refractory bricks, blocks, tiles and similar refractory ceramic constructional goods, other than those of siliceous fossil meals or similar siliceous earths.									
69021000	-Containing by weight, singly or together, more than 50 % of the elements Mg, Ca or Cr, expressed as MgO, CaO or Cr2O3	15								0
69022000	-Containing by weight more than 50 % of alumina (Al2O3), of silica (SiO2) or of a mixture or compound of these products	15								0
69029000	-Other	15								0
6903	Other refractory ceramic goods (for example, retorts, crucibles, muffles, nozzles, plugs, supports, cupels, tubes, pipes, sheaths and rods), other than those of siliceous fossil meals or of similar siliceous earths.									
69031000	-Containing by weight more than 50 % of graphite or other carbon or of a mixture of these products	15								0
69032000	-Containing by weight more than 50 % of alumina (Al2O3) or of a mixture or compound of alumina and of silica (SiO2)	15								0
69039000	-Other	15								0
6904	Ceramic building bricks, flooring blocks, support or filler tiles and the like.									
69041000	-Building bricks	15								0
69049000	-Other	10								0
6905	Roofing tiles, chimney-pots, cowls, chimney liners, architectural ornaments and other ceramic constructional goods.									
69051000	-Roofing tiles	15								0
690590	-Other									
69059010	---Ceramic chimney cowls	8					EC			0
69059020	---Ceramic architectural ornaments	8					EC			0

HS	Description	Bound rate at date of accession	Interim	Final Bound	Implementation	Present concession established	INR	Concession first incorporated in a GATT Schedule	Earlier INRs	ODCs
69059090	---Other ceramic architectural goods	8					EC			0
69060000	Ceramic pipes, conduits, guttering and pipe fittings.	15								0
6907	Unglazed ceramic flags and paving, hearth or wall tiles; unglazed ceramic mosaic cubes and the like, whether or not on a backing.									
69071000	-Tiles, cubes and similar articles, whether or not rectangular, the largest surface area of which is capable of being enclosed in a square the side of which is less than 7 cm	15								0
690790	-Other									
69079010	---Unglazed ceramic tiles for flooring or walls	15								0
69079090	---Other unglazed ceramic flags and tiles	10								0
6908	Glazed ceramic flags and paving, hearth or wall tiles; glazed ceramic mosaic cubes and the like, whether or not on a backing.									
69081000	-Tiles, cubes and similar articles, whether or not rectangular, the largest surface area of which is capable of being enclosed in a square the side of which is less than 7 cm	15					IN			0
690890	-Other									
69089010	---Glazed ceramic tiles for flooring or walls	15					IN			0
69089090	---Other glazed ceramic flags and tile	10					IN			0
6909	Ceramic wares for laboratory, chemical or other technical uses; ceramic troughs, tubs and similar receptacles of a kind used in agriculture; ceramic pots, jars and similar articles of a kind used for the conveyance or packing of goods.									
69091	-Ceramic wares for laboratory, chemical or other technical uses:									
69091100	--Of porcelain or china	15								0
69091200	--Articles having a hardness equivalent to 9 or more on the Mohs scale	15								0
69091900	--Other	15								0
690990	-Other									
69099010	---Ceramic pots and similar articles for packing	15								0

HS	Description	Bound rate at date of accession	Interim	Final Bound	Implementation	Present concession established	INR	Concession first incorporated in a GATT Schedule	Earlier INRs	ODCs
69099090	---Other ceramic jars, tubs, etc.	15								0
6910	Ceramic sinks, wash basins, wash basin pedestals, baths, bidets, water closet pans, flushing cisterns, urinals and similar sanitary fixtures.									
69101000	-Of porcelain or china	12					IN			0
69109000	-Other	12								0
6911	Tableware, kitchenware, other household articles and toilet articles, of porcelain or china.									
69111000	-Tableware and kitchenware	10					LK			0
69119000	-Other	15								0
69120000	Ceramic tableware, kitchenware, other household articles and toilet articles, other than of porcelain or china.	8								0
6913	Statuettes and other ornamental ceramic articles.									
691310	-Of porcelain or china									
69131010	---Censers of porcelain or china	10								0
69131020	---Paper weights and the like of porcelain or china	10								0
69131030	---Vases of porcelain or china	10								0
69131040	---Ashtrays of porcelain or china	10								0
69131050	---Boxes for jewelleries and the like of porcelain or china	10								0
69131090	---Other ornamental articles of porcelain or china	10								0
691390	-Other									
69139010	---Ceramic vases	15								0
69139090	---Other ornamental ceramic articles (See Endnote 13)	12					PH			0
6914	Other ceramic articles.									
691410	-Of porcelain or china									
69141010	---Door and window accessories of porcelain or china	15								0
69141020	---Sign-plates, numbers, etc., of porcelain or china	15								0
69141090	---Other articles of porcelain or china	15								0
69149	-Other:									
69149010	---Stoves and other heaters made of pottery	15								0
69149020	---Undecorated pots made of ordinary pottery	15								0

HS	Description	Bound rate at date of accession	Interim	Final Bound	Implementation	Present concession established	INR	Concession first incorporated in a GATT Schedule	Earlier INRs	ODCs
69149030	---Jars and containers for general lab or warehouse use	15								0
69149090	---Other ceramic articles not elsewhere classified	15								0
70010000	Cullet and other waste and scrap of glass; glass in the mass.	15								0
7002	Glass in balls (other than microspheres of heading 70.18), rods or tubes, unworked.									
70021000	-Balls	15								0
70022000	-Rods	15								0
70023	-Tubes:									
70023100	--Of fused quartz or other fused silica	15								0
70023200	--Of other glass having a linear coefficient of expansion not exceeding 5 x 10-6 per Kelvin within a temperature range of 0 °C to 300 °C	15								0
70023900	--Other	15								0
7003	Cast glass and rolled glass, in sheets or profiles, whether or not having an absorbent, reflecting or non-reflecting layer, but not otherwise worked.									
70031	-Non-wired sheets:									
70031200	--Coloured throughout the mass (body tinted), opacified, flashed or having an absorbent, reflecting or non-reflecting layer	15								0
70031900	--Other	15								0
70032000	-Wired sheets	15								0
70033000	-Profiles	15								0
7004	Drawn glass and blown glass, in sheets, whether or not having an absorbent, reflecting or non-reflecting layer, but not otherwise worked.									
70042000	-Glass, coloured throughout the mass (body tinted), opacified, flashed or having an absorbent, reflecting or non-reflecting layer	15								0
70049000	-Other glass	15								0
7005	Float glass and surface ground or polished glass, in sheets, whether or not having an absorbent, reflecting or non-reflecting layer, but not otherwise worked.									

HS	Description	Bound rate at date of accession	Interim	Final Bound	Implementation	Present concession established	INR	Concession first incorporated in a GATT Schedule	Earlier INRs	ODCs
70051000	-Non-wired glass, having an absorbent, reflecting or non-reflecting layer	15								0
70052	-Other non-wired glass:									
70052100	--Coloured throughout the mass (body tinted), opacified, flashed or merely surface ground	15								0
70052900	--Other	15		12	2008					0
70053000	-Wired glass	15								0
70060000	Glass of heading 70.03, 70.04 or 70.05, bent, edge-worked, engraved, drilled, enamelled or otherwise worked, but not framed or fitted with other materials.	15								0
7007	Safety glass, consisting of toughened (tempered) or laminated glass.									
70071	-Toughened (tempered) safety glass:									
70071100	--Of size and shape suitable for incorporation in vehicles, aircraft, spacecraft or vessels	15		12	2008					0
70071900	--Other	15								0
70072	-Laminated safety glass:									
70072100	--Of size and shape suitable for incorporation in vehicles, aircraft, spacecraft or vessels	15								0
ex70072100	---For use in civil aircraft	0					US			0
70072900	--Other	15								0
70080000	Multiple-walled insulating units of glass.	15								0
7009	Glass mirrors, whether or not framed, including rear-view mirrors.									
70091000	-Rear-view mirrors for vehicles	12								0
70099	-Other:									
70099100	--Unframed	15								0
70099200	--Framed	15								0
7010	Carboys, bottles, flasks, jars, pots, phials, ampoules and other containers, of glass, of a kind used for the conveyance or packing of goods; preserving jars of glass; stoppers, lids and other closures, of glass.									
70101000	-Ampoules	15								0
70102000	-Stoppers, lids and other closures	15								0
70109000	-Other	15								0

HS	Description	Bound rate at date of accession	Interim	Final Bound	Implementation	Present concession established	INR	Concession first incorporated in a GATT Schedule	Earlier INRs	ODCs
7011	Glass envelopes (including bulbs and tubes), open, and glass parts thereof, without fittings, for electric lamps, cathode-ray tubes or the like.									
70111000	-For electric lighting	15								0
70112000	-For cathode-ray tubes	15								0
70119000	-Other	15								0
70120000	Glass inners for vacuum flasks or for other vacuum vessels.	15								0
7013	Glassware of a kind used for table, kitchen, toilet, office, indoor decoration or similar purposes (other than that of heading 70.10 or 70.18).									
701310	-Of glass-ceramics									
70131010	---Tableware or kitchenware of glass-ceramics	15		12	2008		MX			0
70131030	---Articles for offices of glass-ceramics	15		12	2008		MX			0
7013104	---Articles for toilets:									
70131041	----Decoration perfume bottles of glassy porcelain	15		12	2008					0
70131049	----Other make- up items of glassy porcelain	15		12	2008					0
70131090	---Other articles of glass-ceramics	15		12	2008		MX			0
70132	-Drinking glasses other than of glass ceramics:									
70132100	--Of lead crystal	15		12	2008		MX			0
70132900	--Other	15		12	2008		MX			0
70133	-Glassware of a kind used for table (other than drinking glasses) or kitchen purposes other than of glass-ceramics:									
70133100	--Of lead crystal	15		12	2008		MX			0
70133200	--Of glass having a linear coefficient of expansion not exceeding 5 x 10-6 per Kelvin within a temperature range of 0 °C to 300 °C	15		12	2008		MX			0
70133900	--Other	10					MX			0
70139	-Other glassware:									
701391	--Of lead crystal									
70139110	---Articles for toilets of lead crystal	15		12	2008		MX			0
7013913	---Toilet articles:									
70139131	----Decoration bottles of glass for perfumes	15		12	2008		MX			0
70139139	----Other make-up items of glass	15		12	2008		MX			0

HS	Description	Bound rate at date of accession	Interim	Final Bound	Implementation	Present concession established	INR	Concession first incorporated in a GATT Schedule	Earlier INRs	ODCs
70139190	---Other articles of lead crystal	15		12	2008		MX			0
701399	--Other									
70139910	---Fish aquarium of glass	15		12	2008		MX			0
70139920	---Glass censer	15		12	2008		MX			0
70139990	---Other glass items	15		12	2008		MX			0
7014	Signalling glassware and optical elements of glass (other than those of heading 70.15), not optically worked.									
70140010	---Signalling glassware for transportation equipment	15								0
70140090	---Other signalling glassware and optical elements	15								0
7015	Clock or watch glasses and similar glasses, glasses for non-corrective or corrective spectacles, curved, bent, hollowed or the like, not optically worked; hollow glass spheres and their segments, for the manufacture of such glasses.									
70151000	-Glasses for corrective spectacles	15								0
701590	-Other									
70159010	---Clock and watch glass	15								0
70159020	---Glass for sunglasses and other protecting glass	15								0
70159090	---Other glass for spectacles	15								0
7016	Paving blocks, slabs, bricks, squares, tiles and other articles of pressed or moulded glass, whether or not wired, of a kind used for building or construction purposes; glass cubes and other glass smallwares, whether or not on a backing, for mosaics or similar decorative purposes; leaded lights and the like; multicellular or foam glass in blocks, panels, plates, shells or similar forms.									
70161000	-Glass cubes and other glass smallwares, whether or not on a backing, for mosaics or similar decorative purposes	15								0
70169000	-Other	15								0
7017	Laboratory, hygienic or pharmaceutical glassware, whether or not graduated or calibrated.									
70171000	-Of fused quartz or other fused silica	5		0	2008		US			0

HS	Description	Bound rate at date of accession	Interim	Final Bound	Implementation	Present concession established	INR	Concession first incorporated in a GATT Schedule	Earlier INRs	ODCs
70172000	-Of other glass having a linear coefficient of expansion not exceeding 5 x 10-6 per Kelvin within a temperature range of 0 °C to 300 °C	15								0
70179000	-Other	7								0
7018	Glass beads, imitation pearls, imitation precious or semi-precious stones and similar glass smallwares, and articles thereof other than imitation jewellery; glass eyes other than prosthetic articles; statuettes and other ornaments of lamp-worked glass, other than imitation jewellery; glass microspheres not exceeding 1 mm in diameter.									
701810	-Glass beads, imitation pearls, imitation precious or semi-precious stones and similar glass smallwares									
70181010	---Rosaries of imitation jewellery	15								0
70181090	---Other articles of imitation jewellery	10								0
70182000	-Glass microspheres not exceeding 1 mm in diameter	15					AU			0
70189000	-Other	15								0
7019	Glass fibres (including glass wool) and articles thereof (for example, yarn, woven fabrics).									
70191	-Slivers, rovings, yarn and chopped strands:									
70191100	--Chopped strands, of a length of not more than 50 mm	15								0
70191200	--Rovings	15	13 (2008)	10	2010		IN,NO			0
70191900	--Other	15								0
70193	-Thin sheets (voiles), webs, mats, mattresses, boards and similar nonwoven products:									
70193100	--Mats	15								0
70193200	--Thin sheets (voiles)	15								0
70193900	--Other	15								0
70194000	-Woven fabrics of rovings	15								0
70195	-Other woven fabrics:									
70195100	--Of a width not exceeding 30 cm	15								0
70195200	--Of a width exceeding 30 cm, plain weave, weighing less than 250 g/m², of filaments measuring per single yarn not more than 136 tex	15								0

HS	Description	Bound rate at date of accession	Interim	Final Bound	Implementation	Present concession established	INR	Concession first incorporated in a GATT Schedule	Earlier INRs	ODCs
70195900	--Other	15								0
701990	-Other									
70199010	---Transportation equipment of glass fibres	15								0
70199020	---Water tanks of glass fibres	15								0
70199030	---Furnishings and indoor decoration of glass fibres	15								0
70199040	---Insulation (heat, sound, electricity) of glass fibres	15								0
70199050	---Boxes of electric meters, without electrical fitting	15								0
70199060	---Pipes and tubes	15								0
70199090	---Other articles of glass fibres	15								0
7020	Other articles of glass.									
70200010	---Transportation equipment of glass	15								0
70200020	---Tanks and basins of glass	15								0
70200030	---Letters, numbers and similar of glass	15								0
70200090	---Other articles of glass	15								0
7101	Pearls, natural or cultured, whether or not worked or graded but not strung, mounted or set; pearls, natural or cultured, temporarily strung for convenience of transport.									
71011000	-Natural pearls	15								0
71012	-Cultured pearls:									
71012100	--Unworked	15								0
71012200	--Worked	15								0
7102	Diamonds, whether or not worked, but not mounted or set.									
71021000	-Unsorted	15								0
71022	-Industrial:									
71022100	--Unworked or simply sawn, cleaved or bruted	15								0
71022900	--Other	15								0
71023	-Non-industrial:									
71023100	--Unworked or simply sawn, cleaved or bruted	15								0
71023900	--Other	10					CH,IN			0

HS	Description	Bound rate at date of accession	Interim	Final Bound	Implementation	Present concession established	INR	Concession first incorporated in a GATT Schedule	Earlier INRs	ODCs
7103	Precious stones (other than diamonds) and semi-precious stones, whether or not worked or graded but not strung, mounted or set; ungraded precious stones (other than diamonds) and semi-precious stones, temporarily strung for convenience of transport.									
71031000	-Unworked or simply sawn or roughly shaped	15								0
71039	-Otherwise worked:									
71039100	--Rubies, sapphires and emeralds	12					LK			0
71039900	--Other	15								0
7104	Synthetic or reconstructed precious or semi-precious stones, whether or not worked or graded but not strung, mounted or set; ungraded synthetic or reconstructed precious or semi-precious stones, temporarily strung for convenience of transport.									
71041000	-Piezo-electric quartz	15								0
71042000	-Other, unworked or simply sawn or roughly shaped	15								0
71049000	-Other	15								0
7105	Dust and powder of natural or synthetic precious or semi-precious stones.									
71051000	-Of diamonds	15								0
71059000	-Other	15								0
7106	Silver (including silver plated with gold or platinum), unwrought or in semi-manufactured forms, or in powder form.									
71061000	-Powder	15								0
71069	-Other:									
710691	--Unwrought									
71069110	---Silver ingots	7								0
71069190	---Other unwrought silver	15								0
71069200	--Semi-manufactured	15								0
71070000	Base metals clad with silver, not further worked than semi-manufactured.	15								0
7108	Gold (including gold plated with platinum) unwrought or in semi-manufactured forms, or in powder form.									
71081	-Non-monetary:									
71081100	--Powder	15								0
710812	--Other unwrought forms									

HS	Description	Bound rate at date of accession	Interim	Final Bound	Implementation	Present concession established	INR	Concession first incorporated in a GATT Schedule	Earlier INRs	ODCs
71081210	---Gold ingots	7								0
71081290	---Other unwrought gold	15								0
71081300	--Other semi-manufactured forms	15		13	2008		AU			0
71082000	-Monetary	7								0
71090000	Base metals or silver, clad with gold, not further worked than semi-manufactured.	15								0
7110	Platinum, unwrought or in semi-manufactured forms, or in powder form.									
71101	-Platinum:									
711011	--Unwrought or in powder form									
71101110	---Platinum ingots	7								0
71101190	---Other unwrought platinum	15								0
71101900	--Other	15								0
71102	-Palladium:									
71102100	--Unwrought or in powder form	15								0
71102900	--Other	15								0
71103	-Rhodium:									
71103100	--Unwrought or in powder form	15								0
71103900	--Other	15								0
71104	-Iridium, osmium and ruthenium:									
71104100	--Unwrought or in powder form	15								0
71104900	--Other	15								0
71110000	Base metals, silver or gold, clad with platinum, not further worked than semi-manufactured.	15								0
7112	Waste and scrap of precious metal or of metal clad with precious metal; other waste and scrap containing precious metal or precious metal compounds, of a kind used principally for the recovery of precious metal.									
71123000	-Ash containing precious metal or precious metal compounds	15								0
71129	-Other:									
71129100	--Of gold, including metal clad with gold but excluding sweepings containing other precious metals	15								0
71129200	--Of platinum, including metal clad with platinum but excluding sweepings containing other precious metals	15								0
71129900	--Other	15								0

HS	Description	Bound rate at date of accession	Interim	Final Bound	Implementation	Present concession established	INR	Concession first incorporated in a GATT Schedule	Earlier INRs	ODCs
7113	Articles of jewellery and parts thereof, of precious metal or of metal clad with precious metal.									
71131	-Of precious metal whether or not plated or clad with precious metal:									
71131100	--Of silver, whether or not plated or clad with other precious metal	10					IN			0
711319	--Of other precious metal, whether or not plated or clad with precious metal									
71131910	---Jewellery of gold	15		10	2008		CH,IN			0
71131920	---Jewellery of platinium and the platinum group	15		12	2008		CH,IN			0
71132000	-Of base metal clad with precious metal	15								0
7114	Articles of goldsmiths' or silversmiths' wares and parts thereof, of precious metal or of metal clad with precious metal.									
71141	-Of precious metal whether or not plated or clad with precious metal:									
71141100	--Of silver, whether or not plated or clad with other precious metal	12					PH			0
711419	--Of other precious metal, whether or not plated or clad with precious metal									
71141910	---Goldsmiths' wares of gold	15					CH			0
71141920	---Goldsmiths wares of platinium and the platinium group	15					CH			0
71142000	-Of base metal clad with precious metal	15								0
7115	Other articles of precious metal or of metal clad with precious metal.									
71151000	-Catalysts in the form of wire cloth or grill, of platinum	15								0
71159000	-Other	15								0
7116	Articles of natural or cultured pearls, precious or semi-precious stones (natural, synthetic or reconstructed).									
711610	-Of natural or cultured pearls									
71161010	---Articles of personal ornamentation of pearls	15								0
71161090	---Other articles of pearls	15								0
711620	-Of precious or semi-precious stones (natural, synthetic or reconstructed)									
71162010	---Articles of personal ornamentation of precious stones	15								0

HS	Description	Bound rate at date of accession	Interim	Final Bound	Implementation	Present concession established	INR	Concession first incorporated in a GATT Schedule	Earlier INRs	ODCs
71162020	---Industrial equipment of precious stones	15								0
71162090	---Other articles of precious and semi-precious stones	15								0
7117	Imitation jewellery.									
71171	-Of base metal, whether or not plated with precious metal:									
711711	--Cuff-links and studs									
71171110	---Cuff-links of base metals	15								0
71171190	---Other studs of base metals	10								0
71171900	--Other	10								0
711790	-Other									
71179010	---Imitation jewellery of plastic	10								0
71179020	---Imitation jewellery of glass	10								0
71179030	---Imitation jewellery of wood	10								0
71179090	---Other imitation jewellery	10					IN			0
7118	Coin.									
71181000	-Coin (other than gold coin), not being legal tender	15								0
71189000	-Other	7								0
7201	Pig iron and spiegeleisen in pigs, blocks or other primary forms.									
72011000	-Non-alloy pig iron containing by weight 0.5 % or less of phosphorus	10					IN			0
72012000	-Non-alloy pig iron containing by weight more than 0.5 % of phosphorus	15								0
72015000	-Alloy pig iron; spiegeleisen	10					IN			0
7202	Ferro-alloys.									
72021	-Ferro-manganese:									
72021100	--Containing by weight more than 2 % of carbon	15								0
72021900	--Other	15								0
72022	-Ferro-silicon:									
72022100	--Containing by weight more than 55 % of silicon	15								0
72022900	--Other	15								0
72023000	-Ferro-silico-manganese	12								0
72024	-Ferro-chromium:									
72024100	--Containing by weight more than 4 % of carbon	15								0
72024900	--Other	15								0
72025000	-Ferro-silico-chromium	15								0

HS	Description	Bound rate at date of accession	Interim	Final Bound	Implementation	Present concession established	INR	Concession first incorporated in a GATT Schedule	Earlier INRs	ODCs
72026000	-Ferro-nickel	15								0
72027000	-Ferro-molybdenum	15								0
72028000	-Ferro-tungsten and ferro-silico-tungsten	15								0
72029	-Other:									
72029100	--Ferro-titanium and ferro-silico-titanium	15								0
72029200	--Ferro-vanadium	15								0
72029300	--Ferro-niobium	15								0
72029900	--Other	15								0
7203	Ferrous products obtained by direct reduction of iron ore and other spongy ferrous products, in lumps, pellets or similar forms; iron having a minimum purity by weight of 99.94 %, in lumps, pellets or similar forms.									
72031000	-Ferrous products obtained by direct reduction of iron ore	15								0
72039000	-Other	15								0
7204	Ferrous waste and scrap; remelting scrap ingots of iron or steel.									
72041000	-Waste and scrap of cast iron	15								0
72042	-Waste and scrap of alloy steel:									
72042100	--Of stainless steel	15								0
72042900	--Other	15								0
72043000	-Waste and scrap of tinned iron or steel	15								0
72044	-Other waste and scrap:									
72044100	--Turnings, shavings, chips, milling waste, sawdust, filings, trimmings and stampings, whether or not in bundles	15								0
72044900	--Other	15								0
72045000	-Remelting scrap ingots	15								0
7205	Granules and powders, of pig iron, spiegeleisen, iron or steel.									
72051000	-Granules	15								0
72052	-Powders:									
72052100	--Of alloy steel	15								0
72052900	--Other	15								0
7206	Iron and non-alloy steel in ingots or other primary forms (excluding iron of heading 72.03).									
72061000	-Ingots	12								0
72069000	-Other	15								0
7207	Semi-finished products of iron or non-alloy steel.									

HS	Description	Bound rate at date of accession	Interim	Final Bound	Implementation	Present concession established	INR	Concession first incorporated in a GATT Schedule	Earlier INRs	ODCs
72071	-Containing by weight less than 0.25 % of carbon:									
72071100	--Of rectangular (including square) cross-section, the width measuring less than twice the thickness	10					IN			0
72071200	--Other, of rectangular (other than square) cross-section	12								0
72071900	--Other	12								0
72072000	-Containing by weight 0.25 % or more of carbon	12								0
7208	Flat-rolled products of iron or non-alloy steel, of a width of 600 mm or more, hot-rolled, not clad, plated or coated.									
72081000	-In coils, not further worked than hot-rolled, with patterns in relief	10					IN			0
72082	-Other, in coils, not further worked than hot-rolled, pickled:									
72082500	--Of a thickness of 4.75 mm or more	15								0
72082600	--Of a thickness of 3 mm or more but less than 4.75 mm	15					IN			0
72082700	--Of a thickness of less than 3 mm	15								0
72083	-Other, in coils, not further worked than hot-rolled:									
72083600	--Of a thickness exceeding 10 mm	15								0
72083700	--Of a thickness of 4.75 mm or more but not exceeding 10 mm	15					JP			0
72083800	--Of a thickness of 3 mm or more but less than 4.75 mm	15								0
72083900	--Of a thickness of less than 3 mm	15					JP			0
72084000	-Not in coils, not further worked than hot-rolled, with patterns in relief	12								0
72085	-Other, not in coils, not further worked than hot-rolled:									
72085100	--Of a thickness exceeding 10 mm	15								0
72085200	--Of a thickness of 4.75 mm or more but not exceeding 10 mm	15		13	2008					0
72085300	--Of a thickness of 3 mm or more but less than 4.75 mm	15								0
72085400	--Of a thickness of less than 3 mm	15								0
72089000	-Other	15								0
7209	Flat-rolled products of iron or non-alloy steel, of a width of 600 mm or more, cold-rolled (cold-reduced), not clad, plated or coated.									

HS	Description	Bound rate at date of accession	Interim	Final Bound	Implementation	Present concession established	INR	Concession first incorporated in a GATT Schedule	Earlier INRs	ODCs
72091	-In coils, not further worked than cold-rolled (cold-reduced):									
72091500	--Of a thickness of 3 mm or more	15								0
72091600	--Of a thickness exceeding 1 mm but less than 3 mm	15								0
72091700	--Of a thickness of 0.5 mm or more but not exceeding 1 mm	15								0
72091800	--Of a thickness of less than 0.5 mm	15					IN			0
72092	-Not in coils, not further worked than cold-rolled (cold-reduced):									
72092500	--Of a thickness of 3 mm or more	15								0
72092600	--Of a thickness exceeding 1 mm but less than 3 mm	15								0
72092700	--Of a thickness of 0.5 mm or more but not exceeding 1 mm	15								0
72092800	--Of a thickness of less than 0.5 mm	15								0
72099000	-Other	15								0
7210	Flat-rolled products of iron or non-alloy steel, of a width of 600 mm or more, clad, plated or coated.									
72101	-Plated or coated with tin:									
72101100	--Of a thickness of 0.5 mm or more	15								0
72101200	--Of a thickness of less than 0.5 mm	15		13	2008		AU,JP			0
72102000	-Plated or coated with lead, including terne-plate	15								0
72103000	-Electrolytically plated or coated with zinc	15								0
72104	-Otherwise plated or coated with zinc:									
72104100	--Corrugated	15					IN			0
72104900	--Other	15					AU,JP			0
72105000	-Plated or coated with chromium oxides or with chromium and chromium oxides	12								0
72106	-Plated or coated with aluminium:									
72106100	--Plated or coated with aluminium-zinc alloys	15					AU			0
72106900	--Other	15								0
72107000	-Painted, varnished or coated with plastics	12					AU			0
72109000	-Other	15								0
7211	Flat-rolled products of iron or non-alloy steel, of a width of less than 600 mm, not clad, plated or coated.									
72111	-Not further worked than hot-rolled:									

HS	Description	Bound rate at date of accession	Interim	Final Bound	Implementation	Present concession established	INR	Concession first incorporated in a GATT Schedule	Earlier INRs	ODCs
72111300	--Rolled on four faces or in a closed box pass, of a width exceeding 150 mm and a thickness of not less than 4 mm, not in coils and without patterns in relief	12								0
72111400	--Other, of a thickness of 4.75 mm or more	12								0
72111900	--Other	12								0
72112	-Not further worked than cold-rolled (cold-reduced):									
72112300	--Containing by weight less than 0.25 % of carbon	12								0
72112900	--Other	12								0
72119000	-Other	12								0
7212	Flat-rolled products of iron or non-alloy steel, of a width of less than 600 mm, clad, plated or coated.									
72121000	-Plated or coated with tin	10					IN			0
72122000	-Electrolytically plated or coated with zinc	12								0
72123000	-Otherwise plated or coated with zinc	12								0
72124000	-Painted, varnished or coated with plastics	12								0
72125000	-Otherwise plated or coated	12								0
72126000	-Clad	12								0
7213	Bars and rods, hot-rolled, in irregularly wound coils, of iron or non-alloy steel.									
72131000	-Containing indentations, ribs, grooves or other deformations produced during the rolling process	20								0
72132000	-Other, of free-cutting steel	20								0
72139	-Other:									
72139100	--Of circular cross-section measuring less than 14 mm in diameter	20								0
72139900	--Other	20								0
7214	Other bars and rods of iron or non-alloy steel, not further worked than forged, hot-rolled, hot-drawn or hot-extruded, but including those twisted after rolling.									
72141000	-Forged	20								0
72142000	-Containing indentations, ribs, grooves or other deformations produced during the rolling process or twisted after rolling	15					DO,HN			0
72143000	-Other, of free-cutting steel	20								0

HS	Description	Bound rate at date of accession	Interim	Final Bound	Implementation	Present concession established	INR	Concession first incorporated in a GATT Schedule	Earlier INRs	ODCs
72149	-Other:									
72149100	--Of rectangular (other than square) cross-section	20								0
72149900	--Other	20								0
7215	Other bars and rods of iron or non-alloy steel.									
72151000	-Of free-cutting steel, not further worked than cold-formed or cold-finished	20								0
72155000	-Other, not further worked than cold-formed or cold-finished	20								0
72159000	-Other	20								0
7216	Angles, shapes and sections of iron or non-alloy steel.									
72161000	-U, I or H sections, not further worked than hot-rolled, hot-drawn or extruded, of a height of less than 80 mm	15								0
72162	-L or T sections, not further worked than hot-rolled, hot-drawn or extruded, of a height of less than 80 mm:									
72162100	--L sections	12								0
72162200	--T sections	12								0
72163	-U, I or H sections, not further worked than hot-rolled, hot-drawn or extruded of a height of 80 mm or more:									
72163100	--U sections	15								0
72163200	--I sections	15								0
72163300	--H sections	15								0
72164000	-L or T sections, not further worked than hot-rolled, hot-drawn or extruded, of a height of 80 mm or more	15								0
72165000	-Other angles, shapes and sections, not further worked than hot-rolled, hot-drawn or extruded	12								0
72166	-Angles, shapes and sections, not further worked than cold-formed or cold-finished:									
72166100	--Obtained from flat-rolled products	12								0
72166900	--Other	12								0
72169	-Other:									
72169100	--Cold-formed or cold-finished from flat-rolled products	12								0
72169900	--Other	12								0
7217	Wire of iron or non-alloy steel.									

HS	Description	Bound rate at date of accession	Interim	Final Bound	Implementation	Present concession established	INR	Concession first incorporated in a GATT Schedule	Earlier INRs	ODCs
72171000	-Not plated or coated, whether or not polished	15								0
72172000	-Plated or coated with zinc	15								0
72173000	-Plated or coated with other base metals	15								0
72179000	-Other	15								0
7218	Stainless steel in ingots or other primary forms; semi-finished products of stainless steel.									
72181000	-Ingots and other primary forms	12								0
72189	-Other:									
72189100	--Of rectangular (other than square) cross-section	12								0
72189900	--Other	12								0
7219	Flat-rolled products of stainless steel, of a width of 600 mm or more.									
72191	-Not further worked than hot-rolled, in coils:									
72191100	--Of a thickness exceeding 10 mm	12								0
72191200	--Of a thickness of 4.75 mm or more but not exceeding 10 mm	12								0
72191300	--Of a thickness of 3 mm or more but less than 4.75 mm	12								0
72191400	--Of a thickness of less than 3 mm	12								0
72192	-Not further worked than hot-rolled, not in coils:									
72192100	--Of a thickness exceeding 10 mm	12								0
72192200	--Of a thickness of 4.75 mm or more but not exceeding 10 mm	12								0
72192300	--Of a thickness of 3 mm or more but less than 4.75 mm	12								0
72192400	--Of a thickness of less than 3 mm	12								0
72193	-Not further worked than cold-rolled (cold-reduced):									
72193100	--Of a thickness of 4.75 mm or more	12								0
72193200	--Of a thickness of 3 mm or more but less than 4.75 mm	12								0
72193300	--Of a thickness exceeding 1 mm but less than 3 mm	12								0
72193400	--Of a thickness of 0.5 mm or more but not exceeding 1 mm	12								0
72193500	--Of a thickness of less than 0.5 mm	12								0
72199000	-Other	12								0

HS	Description	Bound rate at date of accession	Interim	Final Bound	Implementation	Present concession established	INR	Concession first incorporated in a GATT Schedule	Earlier INRs	ODCs
7220	Flat-rolled products of stainless steel, of a width of less than 600 mm.									
72201	-Not further worked than hot-rolled:									
72201100	--Of a thickness of 4.75 mm or more	12								0
72201200	--Of a thickness of less than 4.75 mm	12								0
72202000	-Not further worked than cold-rolled (cold-reduced)	12								0
72209000	-Other	12								0
72210000	Bars and rods, hot-rolled, in irregularly wound coils, of stainless steel.	12								0
7222	Other bars and rods of stainless steel; angles, shapes and sections of stainless steel.									
72221	-Bars and rods, not further worked than hot-rolled, hot-drawn or extruded:									
72221100	--Of circular cross-section	12								0
72221900	--Other	12								0
72222000	-Bars and rods, not further worked than cold-formed or cold-finished	10								0
72223000	-Other bars and rods	10								0
72224000	-Angles, shapes and sections	12								0
72230000	Wire of stainless steel.	10								0
7224	Other alloy steel in ingots or other primary forms; semi-finished products of other alloy steel.									
72241000	-Ingots and other primary forms	12								0
72249000	-Other	12								0
7225	Flat-rolled products of other alloy steel, of a width of 600 mm or more.									
72251	-Of silicon-electrical steel:									
72251100	--Grain-oriented	12								0
72251900	--Other	12								0
72252000	-Of high speed steel	10					IN			0
72253000	-Other, not further worked than hot-rolled, in coils	12								0
72254000	-Other, not further worked than hot-rolled, not in coils	12								0
72255000	-Other, not further worked than cold-rolled (cold-reduced)	12								0
72259	-Other:									
72259100	--Electrolytically plated or coated with zinc	12								0
72259200	--Otherwise plated or coated with zinc	12								0

HS	Description	Bound rate at date of accession	Interim	Final Bound	Implementation	Present concession established	INR	Concession first incorporated in a GATT Schedule	Earlier INRs	ODCs
72259900	--Other	12								0
7226	Flat-rolled products of other alloy steel, of a width of less than 600 mm.									
72261	-Of silicon-electrical steel:									
72261100	--Grain-oriented	12								0
72261900	--Other	12								0
72262000	-Of high speed steel	12								0
72269	-Other:									
72269100	--Not further worked than hot-rolled	12								0
72269200	--Not further worked than cold-rolled (cold-reduced)	12								0
72269300	--Electrolytically plated or coated with zinc	12								0
72269400	--Otherwise plated or coated with zinc	12								0
72269900	--Other	12								0
7227	Bars and rods, hot-rolled, in irregularly wound coils, of other alloy steel.									
72271000	-Of high speed steel	12								0
72272000	-Of silico-manganese steel	12								0
72279000	-Other	10								0
7228	Other bars and rods of other alloy steel; angles, shapes and sections, of other alloy steel; hollow drill bars and rods, of alloy or non-alloy steel.									
72281000	-Bars and rods, of high speed steel	12								0
72282000	-Bars and rods, of silico-manganese steel	12								0
72283000	-Other bars and rods, not further worked than hot-rolled, hot-drawn or extruded	12								0
72284000	-Other bars and rods, not further worked than forged	12								0
72285000	-Other bars and rods, not further worked than cold-formed or cold-finished	12								0
72286000	-Other bars and rods	12								0
72287000	-Angles, shapes and sections	12								0
72288000	-Hollow drill bars and rods	12								0
7229	Wire of other alloy steel.									
72291000	-Of high speed steel	12								0
72292000	-Of silico-manganese steel	12								0
72299000	-Other	12								0

HS	Description	Bound rate at date of accession	Interim	Final Bound	Implementation	Present concession established	INR	Concession first incorporated in a GATT Schedule	Earlier INRs	ODCs
7301	Sheet piling of iron or steel, whether or not drilled, punched or made from assembled elements; welded angles, shapes and sections, of iron or steel.									
73011000	-Sheet piling	15								0
73012000	-Angles, shapes and sections	10								0
7302	Railway or tramway track construction material of iron or steel, the following : rails, check-rails and rack rails, switch blades, crossing frogs, point rods and other crossing pieces, sleepers (cross-ties), fish-plates, chairs, chair wedges, sole plates (base plates), rail clips, bedplates, ties and other material specialized for jointing or fixing rails.									
73021000	-Rails	12								0
73023000	-Switch blades, crossing frogs, point rods and other crossing pieces	15								0
73024000	-Fish-plates and sole plates	12								0
73029000	-Other	12								0
73030000	Tubes, pipes and hollow profiles, of cast iron.	15								0
7304	Tubes, pipes and hollow profiles, seamless, of iron (other than cast iron) or steel.									
73041000	-Line pipe of a kind used for oil or gas pipelines	10					MX			0
73042	-Casing, tubing and drill pipe, of a kind used in drilling for oil or gas:									
73042100	--Drill pipe	10								0
73042900	--Other	10					JP,MX			0
73043	-Other, of circular cross-section, of iron or non-alloy steel:									
73043100	--Cold-drawn or cold-rolled (cold-reduced)	8								0
ex73043100	---For use in civil aircraft	0					US			0
73043900	--Other	8								0
ex73043900	---For use in civil aircraft	0					US			0
73044	-Other, of circular cross-section, of stainless steel:									
ex73044100	---For use in civil aircraft	0					US			0
73044100	--Cold-drawn or cold-rolled (cold-reduced)	8								0
73044900	--Other	8								0

HS	Description	Bound rate at date of accession	Interim	Final Bound	Implementation	Present concession established	INR	Concession first incorporated in a GATT Schedule	Earlier INRs	ODCs
ex73044900	---For use in civil aircraft	0					US			0
73045	-Other, of circular cross-section, of other alloy steel:									
ex73045100	---For use in civil aircraft	0					US			0
73045100	--Cold-drawn or cold-rolled (cold-reduced)	8								0
73045900	--Other	8								0
ex73045900	---For use in civil aircraft	0					US			0
ex73049000	--For use in civil aircraft	0					CN,US			0
73049000	-Other	8					CN			0
7305	Other tubes and pipes (for example, welded, riveted or similarly closed), having circular cross-sections, the external diameter of which exceeds 406.4 mm, of iron or steel.									
73051	-Line pipe of a kind used for oil or gas pipelines:									
73051100	--Longitudinally submerged arc welded	15					N			0
ex73051100	--For use in civil aircraft	0								
73051200	--Other, longitudinally welded	15								0
73051900	--Other	15								0
73052000	-Casing of a kind used in drilling for oil or gas	15								0
73053	-Other, welded:									
73053100	--Longitudinally welded	15								0
73053900	--Other	15								0
73059000	-Other	15								0
7306	Other tubes, pipes and hollow profiles (for example, open seam or welded, riveted or similarly closed), of iron or steel.									
73061000	-Line pipe of a kind used for oil or gas pipelines	15								0
73062000	-Casing and tubing of a kind used in drilling for oil or gas	15								0
73063000	-Other, welded, of circular cross-section, of iron or non-alloy steel	15								0
ex73063000	--For use in civil aircraft	0					US			0
ex73064000	--For use in civil aircraft	0					US			0
73064000	-Other, welded, of circular cross-section, of stainless steel	8								0
73065000	-Other, welded, of circular cross-section, of other alloy steel	8								0

HS	Description	Bound rate at date of accession	Interim	Final Bound	Implementation	Present concession established	INR	Concession first incorporated in a GATT Schedule	Earlier INRs	ODCs
ex73065000	--For use in civil aircraft	0					US			0
73066000	-Other, welded, of non-circular cross-section	15								0
ex73066000	--For use in civil aircraft	0					US			0
73069000	-Other	15								0
7307	Tube or pipe fittings (for example, couplings, elbows, sleeves), of iron or steel.									
73071	-Cast fittings:									
73071100	--Of non-malleable cast iron	15								0
73071900	--Other	10								0
73072	-Other, of stainless steel:									
73072100	--Flanges	15								0
73072200	--Threaded elbows, bends and sleeves	12								0
73072300	--Butt welding fittings	15								0
73072900	--Other	15								0
73079	-Other:									
73079100	--Flanges	15								0
73079200	--Threaded elbows, bends and sleeves	12								0
73079300	--Butt welding fittings	15								0
73079900	--Other	12								0
7308	Structures (excluding prefabricated buildings of heading 94.06) and parts of structures (for example, bridges and bridge-sections, lock-gates, towers, lattice masts, roofs, roofing frame-works, doors and windows and their frames and thresholds for doors, shutters, balustrades, pillars and columns), of iron or steel; plates, rods, angles, shapes, sections, tubes and the like, prepared for use in structures, of iron or steel.									
73081000	-Bridges and bridge-sections	12								0
73082000	-Towers and lattice masts	15								0
73083000	-Doors, windows and their frames and thresholds for doors	10					AU,NO			0
73084000	-Equipment for scaffolding, shuttering, propping or pitpropping	12								0
730890	-Other									
73089010	---Boxes fitted in walls for fire fighting	10								0
73089020	---Big shelves to be installed in buildings	10								0

HS	Description	Bound rate at date of accession	Interim	Final Bound	Implementation	Present concession established	INR	Concession first incorporated in a GATT Schedule	Earlier INRs	ODCs
73089030	---Angles ties for fastening decoration tiles in ceilings	15								0
73089040	---Scaffoldings, props, platforms and fittings	10					IN			0
73089050	---Staircases, stationary	10								0
73089060	---Sheds and domes	10								0
73089090	---Other iron or steel structures or parts	10								0
7309	Reservoirs, tanks, vats and similar containers for any material (other than compressed or liquefied gas), of iron or steel, of a capacity exceeding 300 l, whether or not lined or heat-insulated, but not fitted with mechanical or thermal equipment.									
73090010	---Water tanks for household use over 300 litres	5								0
73090090	---Other iron or steel tanks over 300 litres	15								0
7310	Tanks, casks, drums, cans, boxes and similar containers, for any material (other than compressed or liquefied gas), of iron or steel, of a capacity not exceeding 300 l, whether or not lined or heat-insulated, but not fitted with mechanical or thermal equipment									
73101000	-Of a capacity of 50 l or more	15								0
73102	-Of a capacity of less than 50 l:									
731021	--Cans which are to be closed by soldering or crimping									
73102110	---Cans for aerated beverages and fruit juices	15								0
73102120	---Cans for preserving foods	15								0
73102130	---Cans for preserving chemicals and lubricating oils	15								0
73102190	---Other cans under 50 l	15								0
73102900	--Other	15								0
7311	Containers for compressed or liquefied gas, of iron or steel.									
73110010	---Containers for oxygen	15								0
73110020	---Containers for freon	15								0
73110030	---Containers for domestic stoves' gases	15								0
73110090	---Containers for other gases	15								0

HS	Description	Bound rate at date of accession	Interim	Final Bound	Implementation	Present concession established	INR	Concession first incorporated in a GATT Schedule	Earlier INRs	ODCs
7312	Stranded wire, ropes, cables, plaited bands, slings and the like, of iron or steel, not electrically insulated.									
731210	-Stranded wire, ropes and cables									
73121010	---Electric wire and cable, not insulated	15								0
ex73121010	----For use in civil aircraft	0					US			0
ex73121090	----For use in civil aircraft	0					US			0
73121090	---Other stranded wire and cable, steel, not insulated	8								0
731290	-Other									
ex73129010	----For use in civil aircraft	0					US			0
73129010	---Lifting cables	8								0
ex73129090	----For use in civil aircraft	0					US			0
73129090	---Other cables	8								0
73130000	Barbed wire of iron or steel; twisted hoop or single flat wire, barbed or not, and loosely twisted double wire, of a kind used for fencing, of iron or steel.	15								0
7314	Cloth (including endless bands), grill, netting and fencing, of iron or steel wire; expanded metal of iron or steel.									
73141	-Woven cloth:									
73141200	--Endless bands for machinery, of stainless steel	15								0
73141300	--Other endless bands for machinery	15								0
73141400	--Other woven cloth, of stainless steel	15								0
73141900	--Other	15								0
73142000	-Grill, netting and fencing, welded at the intersection, of wire with a maximum cross-sectional dimension of 3 mm or more and having a mesh size of 100 cm^2 or more	15								0
73143	-Other grill, netting and fencing, welded at the intersection:									
73143100	--Plated or coated with zinc	15								0
73143900	--Other	15								0
73144	-Other cloth, grill, netting and fencing:									
73144100	--Plated or coated with zinc	15								0
73144200	--Coated with plastics	15								0
73144900	--Other	15								0
73145000	-Expanded metal	15								0
7315	Chain and parts thereof, of iron or steel.									
73151	-Articulated link chain and parts thereof:									

HS	Description	Bound rate at date of accession	Interim	Final Bound	Implementation	Present concession established	INR	Concession first incorporated in a GATT Schedule	Earlier INRs	ODCs
73151100	--Roller chain	15					KG			0
73151200	--Other chain	12								0
73151900	--Parts	15								0
73152000	-Skid chain	15								0
73158	-Other chain:									
73158100	--Stud-link	15								0
73158200	--Other, welded link	15								0
73158900	--Other	15								0
73159000	-Other parts	15								0
73160000	Anchors, grapnels and parts thereof, of iron or steel.	15								0
7317	Nails, tacks, drawing pins, corrugated nails, staples (other than those of heading 83.05) and similar articles, of iron or steel, whether or not with heads of other material, but excluding such articles with heads of copper.									
73170010	---Steel nails and carpentry nails	15								0
73170020	---Tacks	10								0
73170030	---Drawing pins	10								0
73170040	---Staples	10								0
73170090	---Other nails and staples	10								0
7318	Screws, bolts, nuts, coach screws, screw hooks, rivets, cotters, cotter-pins, washers (including spring washers) and similar articles, of iron or steel.									
73181	-Threaded articles:									
73181100	--Coach screws	15								0
73181200	--Other wood screws	12								0
73181300	--Screw hooks and screw rings	15								0
73181400	--Self-tapping screws	12								0
73181500	--Other screws and bolts, whether or not with their nuts or washers	15		12	2008		IN			0
73181600	--Nuts	15					IN			0
73181900	--Other	10								0
73182	-Non-threaded articles:									
73182100	--Spring washers and other lock washers	15								0
73182200	--Other washers	15								0
73182300	--Rivets	15								0
73182400	--Cotters and cotter-pins	15								0
73182900	--Other	15								0

HS	Description	Bound rate at date of accession	Interim	Final Bound	Implementation	Present concession established	INR	Concession first incorporated in a GATT Schedule	Earlier INRs	ODCs
7319	Sewing needles, knitting needles, bodkins, crochet hooks, embroidery stilettos and similar articles, for use in the hand, of iron or steel; safety pins and other pins of iron or steel, not elsewhere specified or included.									
73191000	-Sewing, darning or embroidery needles	15								0
73192000	-Safety pins	15								0
73193000	-Other pins	15								0
73199000	-Other	15								0
7320	Springs and leaves for springs, of iron or steel.									
73201000	-Leaf-springs and leaves therefor	10								0
73202000	-Helical springs	15								0
73209000	-Other	15								0
7321	Stoves, ranges, grates, cookers (including those with subsidiary boilers for central heating), barbecues, braziers, gas-rings, plate warmers and similar non-electric domestic appliances, and parts thereof, of iron or steel.									
73211	-Cooking appliances and plate warmers:									
732111	--For gas fuel or for both gas and other fuels									
73211110	---Gas cookstoves	15		13	2008					0
73211120	---Gas grills	7								0
73211130	---Gas hearths	5								0
73211190	---Other gas cooking appliances	5								0
732112	--For liquid fuel									
73211210	---Cookstoves of liquid fuel	15								0
73211220	---Grills of liquid fuel	15								0
73211230	---Hearths of liquid fuel	15								0
73211290	---Other liquid fuel cookers	15								0
73211300	--For solid fuel	15								0
73218	-Other appliances:									
732181	--For gas fuel or for both gas and other fuels									
73218110	---Fireplaces with gas fuel	15								0
73218190	---Other appliances with gas fuel	15								0
732182	--For liquid fuel									
73218210	---Heaters with liquid fuel	15								0

HS	Description	Bound rate at date of accession	Interim	Final Bound	Implementation	Present concession established	INR	Concession first incorporated in a GATT Schedule	Earlier INRs	ODCs
73218290	---Other cooking appliances with liquid fuel	15								0
73218300	--For solid fuel	15								0
732190	-Parts									
73219010	---Parts for cookers	15								0
73219020	---Parts for barbecues	15								0
73219030	---Parts for heaters	15								0
73219090	---Other parts for cooking appliances	15								0
7322	Radiators for central heating, not electrically heated, and parts thereof, of iron or steel; air heaters and hot air distributors (including distributors which can also distribute fresh or conditioned air), not electrically heated, incorporating a motor-driven fan or blower, and parts thereof, of iron or steel.									
73221	-Radiators and parts thereof:									
73221100	--Of cast iron	15								0
73221900	--Other	15								0
73229000	-Other	15								0
ex73229000	--For use in civil aircraft	0					US			0
7323	Table, kitchen or other household articles and parts thereof, of iron or steel; iron or steel wool; pot scourers and scouring or polishing pads, gloves and the like, of iron or steel.									
73231000	-Iron or steel wool; pot scourers and scouring or polishing pads, gloves and the like	15					DO,HN			0
73239	-Other:									
73239100	--Of cast iron, not enamelled	15								0
73239200	--Of cast iron, enamelled	15								0
73239300	--Of stainless steel	10					IN			0
73239400	--Of iron (other than cast iron) or steel, enamelled	10					IN			0
73239900	--Other	10								0
7324	Sanitary ware and parts thereof, of iron or steel.									
ex73241000	--For use in civil aircraft	0					US			0
73241000	-Sinks and wash basins, of stainless steel	15								0
73242	-Baths:									

HS	Description	Bound rate at date of accession	Interim	Final Bound	Implementation	Present concession established	INR	Concession first incorporated in a GATT Schedule	Earlier INRs	ODCs
73242100	--Of cast iron, whether or not enamelled	15								0
73242900	--Other	15								0
ex73249000	--For use in civil aircraft	0					US			0
73249000	-Other, including parts	15								0
7325	Other cast articles of iron or steel.									
732510	-Of non-malleable cast iron									
73251010	---Manholes, sink covers and similar articles of cast iron	15								0
73251020	---Fire nozzle plugs; fire alarm pillars of cast iron	10								0
73251030	---Pillar-boxes for mail of cast iron	10								0
73251040	---Rabbit - hutches	10								0
73251090	---Other articles of cast iron	10								0
73259	-Other:									
73259100	--Grinding balls and similar articles for mills	15								0
732599	--Other									
73259910	---Manholes, sink covers and similar items, iron or steel	15								0
73259920	---Fire nozzle plugs; fire alarm pillars of iron or steel	15								0
73259930	---Pillar-boxes for mail of iron or steel	15								0
73259940	---Rabbit - hutches	12								0
73259990	---Other cast articles of iron or steel	10					IN			0
7326	Other articles of iron or steel.									
73261	-Forged or stamped, but not further worked:									
73261100	--Grinding balls and similar articles for mills	15								0
73261900	--Other	10								0
732620	-Articles of iron or steel wire									
73262010	---Rat traps	10								0
ex73262010	----For use in civil aircraft	0					US			0
ex73262020	----For use in civil aircraft	0					US			0
73262020	---Fisheries	10								0
73262030	---Wire ties for stall-feeding	10								0
ex73262030	----For use in civil aircraft	0					US			0
ex73262040	----For use in civil aircraft	0					US			0
73262040	---Waste baskets of iron or steel wire	10								0
ex73262090	----For use in civil aircraft	0					US			0
73262090	---Other articles of iron or steel wire	10								0
732690	-Other									

HS	Description	Bound rate at date of accession	Interim	Final Bound	Implementation	Present concession established	INR	Concession first incorporated in a GATT Schedule	Earlier INRs	ODCs
73269010	---Boot protectors	5								0
73269020	---Climbing irons (spikes)	5								0
73269030	---Non-mechanical air holes	10								0
73269040	---Venetian blinds	10								0
73269050	---Hooping iron	5								0
73269060	---Electric-lines fittings	15								0
73269070	---Fencing pillars	5								0
73269080	---Pegs for tents and stakes for tying domestic animals	5								0
7326909	---Other:									
73269091	----Hoops for gardens' boundaries and trees	5								0
73269092	----Clips for water hoses	5								0
73269093	----Spikes for delineating road lanes	15								0
73269094	----Portable ladders and stairs	5								0
73269095	----Tool boxes	5								0
73269096	----Boxes for jewellery, works of art and cosmetic powders	10								0
73269097	----Electricity (lighting) poles of iron or steel	5								0
73269098	----Rabbit - hutches - hen-coop	5								0
73269099	----Other articles of iron or steel	15					IN			0
7401	Copper mattes; cement copper (precipitated copper).									
74011000	-Copper mattes	15								0
74012000	-Cement copper (precipitated copper)	15								0
74020000	Unrefined copper; copper anodes for electrolytic refining.	15								0
7403	Refined copper and copper alloys, unwrought.									
74031	-Refined copper:									
74031100	--Cathodes and sections of cathodes	10					IN			0
74031200	--Wire-bars	12								0
74031300	--Billets	12								0
74031900	--Other	12								0
74032	-Copper alloys:									
74032100	--Copper-zinc base alloys (brass)	12								0
74032200	--Copper-tin base alloys (bronze)	12								0
74032300	--Copper-nickel base alloys (cupro-nickel) or copper-nickel-zinc base alloys (nickel silver)	12								0

HS	Description	Bound rate at date of accession	Interim	Final Bound	Implementation	Present concession established	INR	Concession first incorporated in a GATT Schedule	Earlier INRs	ODCs
74032900	--Other copper alloys (other than master alloys of heading 74.05)	12								0
74040000	Copper waste and scrap.	12								0
74050000	Master alloys of copper.	12								0
7406	Copper powders and flakes.									
74061000	-Powders of non-lamellar structure	12								0
74062000	-Powders of lamellar structure; flakes	12								0
7407	Copper bars, rods and profiles.									
74071000	-Of refined copper	10					IN			0
74072	-Of copper alloys:									
74072100	--Of copper-zinc base alloys (brass)	10					AU,IN			0
74072200	--Of copper-nickel base alloys (cupro-nickel) or copper-nickel-zinc base alloys (nickel silver)	12								0
74072900	--Other	10					IN			0
7408	Copper wire.									
74081	-Of refined copper:									
74081100	--Of which the maximum cross-sectional dimension exceeds 6 mm	15								0
74081900	--Other	15					AU			0
74082	-Of copper alloys:									
74082100	--Of copper-zinc base alloys (brass)	12								0
74082200	--Of copper-nickel base alloys (cupro-nickel) or copper-nickel-zinc base alloys (nickel silver)	12								0
74082900	--Other	12								0
7409	Copper plates, sheets and strip, of a thickness exceeding 0.15 mm.									
74091	-Of refined copper:									
74091100	--In coils	12								0
74091900	--Other	12								0
74092	-Of copper-zinc base alloys (brass):									
74092100	--In coils	10								0
74092900	--Other	12								0
74093	-Of copper-tin base alloys (bronze):									
74093100	--In coils	12								0
74093900	--Other	12								0
74094000	-Of copper-nickel base alloys (cupro-nickel) or copper- nickel-zinc base alloys (nickel silver)	12								0
74099000	-Of other copper alloys	12								0

HS	Description	Bound rate at date of accession	Interim	Final Bound	Implementation	Present concession established	INR	Concession first incorporated in a GATT Schedule	Earlier INRs	ODCs
7410	Copper foil (whether or not printed or backed with paper, paperboard, plastics or similar backing materials) of a thickness (excluding any backing) not exceeding 0.15 mm.									
74101	-Not backed:									
74101100	--Of refined copper	12								0
74101200	--Of copper alloys	12								0
74102	-Backed:									
74102100	--Of refined copper	12								0
74102200	--Of copper alloys	12								0
7411	Copper tubes and pipes.									
74111000	-Of refined copper	12								0
74112	-Of copper alloys:									
74112100	--Of copper-zinc base alloys (brass)	12								0
74112200	--Of copper-nickel base alloys (cupro-nickel) or copper-nickel-zinc base alloys (nickel silver)	12								0
74112900	--Other	12								0
7412	Copper tube or pipe fittings (for example, couplings, elbows, sleeves).									
74121000	-Of refined copper	12								0
74122000	-Of copper alloys	12								0
74130000	Stranded wire, cables, plaited bands and the like, of copper, not electrically insulated.	15								0
ex74130000	--For use in civil aircraft	0					US			0
7414	Cloth (including endless bands), grill and netting, of copper wire; expanded metal of copper.									
74142000	-Cloth	12								0
74149000	-Other	12								0
7415	Nails, tacks, drawing pins, staples (other than those of heading 83.05) and similar articles, of copper or of iron or steel with heads of copper; screws, bolts, nuts, screw hooks, rivets, cotters, cotter-pins, washers (including spring washers) and similar articles, of copper.									
74151000	-Nails and tacks, drawing pins, staples and similar articles	12								0
74152	-Other articles, not threaded:									
74152100	--Washers (including spring washers)	12								0

HS	Description	Bound rate at date of accession	Interim	Final Bound	Implementation	Present concession established	INR	Concession first incorporated in a GATT Schedule	Earlier INRs	ODCs
74152900	--Other	12								0
74153	-Other threaded articles:									
74153300	--Screws; bolts and nuts	10								0
74153900	--Other	12								0
74160000	Copper springs.	12								0
7417	Cooking or heating apparatus of a kind used for domestic purposes, non-electric, and parts thereof, of copper.									
74170010	---Copper cookers	12								0
74170020	---Copper heaters	12								0
74170090	---Other copper heating appliances	12								0
7418	Table, kitchen or other household articles and parts thereof, of copper; pot scourers and scouring or polishing pads, gloves and the like, of copper; sanitary ware and parts thereof, of copper.									
74181	-Table, kitchen or other household articles and parts thereof; pot scourers and scouring or polishing pads, gloves and the like:									
74181100	--Pot scourers and scouring or polishing pads, gloves and the like	12								0
74181900	--Other	12								0
74182000	-Sanitary ware and parts thereof	10					IN			0
7419	Other articles of copper.									
74191000	-Chain and parts thereof	10								0
74199	-Other:									
741991	--Cast, moulded, stamped or forged, but not further worked									
74199110	---Sheets for radiators	12								0
74199120	---Tanks and similar containers, over 300 l, worked copper	12								0
74199190	---Other	12								0
741999	--Other									
74199910	---Sheets for radiators	12								0
74199920	---Tanks and the like, over 300 l, of other copper	12								0
74199930	---Containers for gas	12								0
74199940	---Electroplating anodes of copper	12								0
74199950	---Articles of copper wire	10					IN			0
74199960	---Non-mechanical ventilators	12								0
74199970	---Venetian blinds	12								0

HS	Description	Bound rate at date of accession	Interim	Final Bound	Implementation	Present concession established	INR	Concession first incorporated in a GATT Schedule	Earlier INRs	ODCs
74199980	---Hose clips	12								0
74199990	---Other	10					IN			0
7501	Nickel mattes, nickel oxide sinters and other intermediate products of nickel metallurgy.									
75011000	-Nickel mattes	12								0
75012000	-Nickel oxide sinters and other intermediate products of nickel metallurgy	12								0
7502	Unwrought nickel.									
75021000	-Nickel, not alloyed	12								0
75022000	-Nickel alloys	12								0
75030000	Nickel waste and scrap.	12								0
75040000	Nickel powders and flakes.	12								0
7505	Nickel bars, rods, profiles and wire.									
75051	-Bars, rods and profiles:									
75051100	--Of nickel, not alloyed	12								0
75051200	--Of nickel alloys	12								0
75052	-Wire:									
75052100	--Of nickel, not alloyed	12								0
75052200	--Of nickel alloys	12								0
7506	Nickel plates, sheets, strip and foil.									
75061000	-Of nickel, not alloyed	12								0
75062000	-Of nickel alloys	12								0
7507	Nickel tubes, pipes and tube or pipe fittings (for example, couplings, elbows, sleeves).									
75071	-Tubes and pipes:									
75071100	--Of nickel, not alloyed	12								0
75071200	--Of nickel alloys	12								0
75072000	-Tube or pipe fittings	12								0
7508	Other articles of nickel.									
75081000	-Cloth, grill and netting, of nickel wire	12								0
750890	-Other									
75089010	---Window frames of nickel, for structures	12								0
75089020	---Tanks and vats of nickel, without mech. or thermal equip.	12								0
75089030	---Nails, tacks, staples, etc., nickel	12								0
75089040	---Springs, nickel	12								0
75089050	---Household and kitchen utensils, nickel	12								0

HS	Description	Bound rate at date of accession	Interim	Final Bound	Implementation	Present concession established	INR	Concession first incorporated in a GATT Schedule	Earlier INRs	ODCs
75089060	---Sanitary ware, nickel	12								0
75089090	---Other articles, nickel	12								0
7601	Unwrought aluminium.									
76011000	-Aluminium, not alloyed	8								0
76012000	-Aluminium alloys	12								0
76020000	Aluminium waste and scrap.	12								0
7603	Aluminium powders and flakes.									
76031000	-Powders of non-lamellar structure	12								0
76032000	-Powders of lamellar structure; flakes	12								0
7604	Aluminium bars, rods and profiles.									
76041000	-Of aluminium, not alloyed	15					DO,HN			0
76042	-Of aluminium alloys:									
76042100	--Hollow profiles	15								0
76042900	--Other	12					DO,HN			0
7605	Aluminium wire.									
76051	-Of aluminium, not alloyed:									
76051100	--Of which the maximum cross-sectional dimension exceeds 7 mm	12								0
76051900	--Other	12								0
76052	-Of aluminium alloys:									
76052100	--Of which the maximum cross-sectional dimension exceeds 7 mm	12								0
76052900	--Other	12								0
7606	Aluminium plates, sheets and strip, of a thickness exceeding 0.2 mm.									
76061	-Rectangular (including square):									
76061100	--Of aluminium, not alloyed	15								0
76061200	--Of aluminium alloys	12					AU			0
76069	-Other:									
76069100	--Of aluminium, not alloyed	12								0
76069200	--Of aluminium alloys	12								0
7607	Aluminium foil (whether or not printed or backed with paper, paperboard, plastics or similar backing materials) of a thickness (excluding any backing) not exceeding 0.2 mm.									
76071	-Not backed:									
760711	--Rolled but not further worked									
76071110	---Aluminium foil, rolled, put up for retail sale	10					SV			0
76071190	---Other aluminium foils, rolled	10					SV			0
760719	--Other									

HS	Description	Bound rate at date of accession	Interim	Final Bound	Implementation	Present concession established	INR	Concession first incorporated in a GATT Schedule	Earlier INRs	ODCs
76071910	---Aluminium foil, rolled, put up for retail sale	12					SV			0
76071990	---Other aluminium foils, rolled	12					SV			0
760720	-Backed									
76072010	---Aluminium foil, rolled, put up for retail sale	12					SV			0
76072090	---Other aluminium foils, rolled	12					SV			0
7608	Aluminium tubes and pipes.									
ex76081000	--For use in civil aircraft	0					US			0
76081000	-Of aluminium, not alloyed	8								0
ex76082000	--For use in civil aircraft	0					US			0
76082000	-Of aluminium alloys	8								0
76090000	Aluminium tube or pipe fittings (for example, couplings, elbows, sleeves).	12								0
7610	Aluminium structures (excluding prefabricated buildings of heading 94.06) and parts of structures (for example, bridges and bridge-sections, towers, lattice masts, roofs, roofing frameworks, doors and windows and their frames and thresholds for doors, balustrades, pillars and columns); aluminium plates, rods, profiles, tubes and the like, prepared for use in structures.									
761010	-Doors, windows and their frames and thresholds for doors									
76101010	---Electrically operated doors for garages, aluminium	12								0
76101090	---Other aluminium doors and windows	12								0
761090	-Other									
76109010	---Bridges and sections thereof, aluminium	12								0
76109020	---Towers and lattice masts, aluminium	12								0
76109030	---Sheds and domes, aluminium	12								0
76109040	---Staircases, stationary, aluminium	12								0
76109050	---Wall partitions for buildings, aluminium	12								0
76109060	---Decoration tiles for ceilings, aluminium	12								0
76109070	---Ties to fasten decoration tile in ceiling, aluminium	12								0
76109090	---Other aluminium structures and parts	12								0

HS	Description	Bound rate at date of accession	Interim	Final Bound	Implementation	Present concession established	INR	Concession first incorporated in a GATT Schedule	Earlier INRs	ODCs
76110000	Aluminium reservoirs, tanks, vats and similar containers, for any material (other than compressed or liquefied gas), of a capacity exceeding 300 litres, whether or not lined or heat-insulated, but not fitted with mechanical or thermal equipment.	12								0
7612	Aluminium casks, drums, cans, boxes and similar containers (including rigid or collapsible tubular containers), for any material (other than compressed or liquefied gas), of a capacity not exceeding 300 l, whether or not lined or heat-insulated, but not fitted with mechanical or thermal equipment.									
76121000	-Collapsible tubular containers	12								0
761290	-Other									
76129010	---Cans for aerating beverages and fruit juices, aluminium	12								0
76129020	---Cans for preserving foods, aluminium	12								0
76129030	---Cans for chemicals and lubrication oils, aluminium	12								0
76129090	---Other aluminium cans, drums and the like	12								0
7613	Aluminium containers for compressed or liquefied gas.									
76130010	---Aluminium containers for gas, capacity 100 litres or less	12								0
76130090	---Other aluminium containers for gas	12								0
7614	Stranded wire, cables, plaited bands and the like, of aluminium, not electrically insulated.									
761410	-With steel core									
76141010	---Aluminium electric wire with steel core, not insulated	12								0
76141090	---Other aluminium wire and cable with steel core	12								0
76149000	-Other	12								0
7615	Table, kitchen or other household articles and parts thereof, of aluminium; pot scourers and scouring or polishing pads, gloves and the like, of aluminium; sanitary ware and parts thereof, of aluminium.									

HS	Description	Bound rate at date of accession	Interim	Final Bound	Implementation	Present concession established	INR	Concession first incorporated in a GATT Schedule	Earlier INRs	ODCs
76151	-Table, kitchen or other household articles and parts thereof; pot scourers and scouring or polishing pads, gloves and the like:									
76151100	--Pot scourers and scouring or polishing pads, gloves and the like	12								0
761519	--Other									
76151910	---Plates and trays of aluminium flakes	15								0
76151990	---Other aluminium household articles	15								0
76152000	-Sanitary ware and parts thereof	12								0
7616	Other articles of aluminium.									
76161000	-Nails, tacks, staples (other than those of heading 83.05), screws, bolts, nuts, screw hooks, rivets, cotters, cotter-pins, washers and similar articles	12					DO,HN			0
76169	-Other:									
76169100	--Cloth, grill, netting and fencing, of aluminium wire	12					DO,HN			0
761699	--Other									
76169910	---Chain and parts thereof, aluminium	12					DO,HN			0
7616992	---Article of aluminium wire:									
76169921	----Extended wire cloth and netting , of alum	12					DO,HN			0
76169922	----Waste baskets, aluminium	12					DO,HN			0
76169929	----Other aluminium wire articles	12					DO,HN			0
76169930	---Non-mechanical ventilation blinds, aluminium	12					DO,HN			0
76169940	---Venetian blinds, aluminium	12					DO,HN			0
76169950	---Fittings for electricity lines, aluminium	12					DO,HN			0
76169960	---Fencing pillars, aluminium	12					DO,HN			0
76169970	---Portable ladders, aluminium	12					DO,HN			0
76169990	---Other aluminium articles	12					DO,HN			0
7801	Unwrought lead.									
78011000	-Refined lead	15								0
78019	-Other:									
78019100	--Containing by weight antimony as the principal other element	15								0
78019900	--Other	15								0
78020000	Lead waste and scrap.	12								0
78030000	Lead bars, rods, profiles and wire.	12								0
7804	Lead plates, sheets, strip and foil; lead powders and flakes.									

HS	Description	Bound rate at date of accession	Interim	Final Bound	Implementation	Present concession established	INR	Concession first incorporated in a GATT Schedule	Earlier INRs	ODCs
78041	-Plates, sheets, strip and foil:									
78041100	--Sheets, strip and foil of a thickness (excluding any backing) not exceeding 0.2 mm	12								0
78041900	--Other	12								0
78042000	-Powders and flakes	12								0
78050000	Lead tubes, pipes and tube or pipe fittings (for example, couplings, elbows, sleeves).	12								0
78060000	Other articles of lead.	12								0
7901	Unwrought zinc.									
79011	-Zinc, not alloyed:									
79011100	--Containing by weight 99.99 % or more of zinc	12					AU			0
79011200	--Containing by weight less than 99.99 % of zinc	12								0
79012000	-Zinc alloys	12								0
79020000	Zinc waste and scrap.	12								0
7903	Zinc dust, powders and flakes.									
79031000	-Zinc dust	12								0
79039000	-Other	12								0
7904	Zinc bars, rods, profiles and wire.									
79040010	---Zinc wire	12								0
79040020	---Zinc bars and rods	12								0
79040090	---Profiles	12								0
7905	Zinc plates, sheets, strip and foil.									
79050010	---Zinc plates for lithography	12								0
79050090	---Other zinc plates	12								0
7906	Zinc tubes, pipes and tube or pipe fittings (for example, couplings, elbows, sleeves).									
79060010	---Zinc tubes and pipes	12								0
79060090	---Zinc tube or pipe fittings	12								0
7907	Other articles of zinc.									
79070010	---Cans, boxes, and similar containers of zinc	10								0
79070020	---Reservoirs and vats of zinc	10								0
79070030	---Zinc tubular containers, for wrapping the products	10								0
79070040	---Gauze of zinc wire and expanded metal plates of zinc	10								0
79070050	---Bolts, tacks, nuts and screws of zinc	10								0

HS	Description	Bound rate at date of accession	Interim	Final Bound	Implementation	Present concession established	INR	Concession first incorporated in a GATT Schedule	Earlier INRs	ODCs
79070060	---Household ware of zinc	10								0
79070070	---Sanitary ware of zinc	10								0
79070080	---Zinc labels for plants and shrubs	10								0
7907009	---Other:									
79070091	----Templates (hollow plates) for making signs, etc., zinc	10								0
79070092	----Electro-plating anodes, zinc	10								0
79070093	----Cathode protection anodes for pipes, zinc	10								0
79070099	----Other articles of zinc	10								0
8001	Unwrought tin.									
80011000	-Tin, not alloyed	12								0
80012000	-Tin alloys	12								0
80020000	Tin waste and scrap.	12								0
8003	Tin bars, rods, profiles and wire.									
80030010	---Hollow bars of tin	12								0
80030090	---Other tin rods, profiles and wire	12								0
80040000	Tin plates, sheets and strip, of a thickness exceeding 0.2 mm.	12								0
80050000	Tin foil (whether or not printed or backed with paper, paperboard, plastics or similar backing materials), of a thickness (excluding any backing) not exceeding 0.2 mm; tin powders and flakes.	12								0
80060000	Tin tubes, pipes and tube or pipe fittings (for example, couplings, elbows, sleeves).	12								0
8007	Other articles of tin.									
80070010	---Tin reservoirs, barrels and similar containers	12								0
80070020	---Tin flexible tubes for packing tooth paste and the like	12								0
80070030	---Tin articles for domestic purposes and tableware	12								0
80070090	---Other tin articles	12								0
8101	Tungsten (wolfram) and articles thereof, including waste and scrap.									
81011000	-Powders	12								0
81019	-Other:									
81019400	--Unwrought tungsten, including bars and rods obtained simply by sintering	12								0

HS	Description	Bound rate at date of accession	Interim	Final Bound	Implementation	Present concession established	INR	Concession first incorporated in a GATT Schedule	Earlier INRs	ODCs
81019500	--Bars and rods, other than those obtained simply by sintering, profiles, plates, sheets, strip and foil	12								0
81019600	--Wire	12								0
81019700	--Waste and scrap	12								0
81019900	--Other	12								0
8102	Molybdenum and articles thereof, including waste and scrap.									
81021000	-Powders	12								0
81029	-Other:									
81029400	--Unwrought molybdenum, including bars and rods obtained simply by sintering	12								0
81029500	--Bars and rods, other than those obtained simply by sintering, profiles, plates, sheets, strip and foil	12								0
81029600	--Wire	12								0
81029700	--Waste and scrap	12								0
81029900	--Other	12								0
8103	Tantalum and articles thereof, including waste and scrap.									
81032000	-Unwrought tantalum, including bars and rods obtained simply by sintering; powders	12								0
81033000	-Waste and scrap	12								0
81039000	-Other	12								0
8104	Magnesium and articles thereof, including waste and scrap.									
81041	-Unwrought magnesium:									
81041100	--Containing at least 99.8 % by weight of magnesium	12								0
81041900	--Other	12								0
81042000	-Waste and scrap	12								0
81043000	-Raspings, turnings and granules, graded according to size; powders	12								0
810490	-Other									
81049010	---Angles, shapes, sheets, plates and the like, magnesium	12					AU			0
81049020	---Wire, rods and bars of magnesium	12					AU			0
81049030	---Pipes and tubes and fillings thereof, of magnesium	12					AU			0
81049090	---Other articles of magnesium	12					AU			0

HS	Description	Bound rate at date of accession	Interim	Final Bound	Implementation	Present concession established	INR	Concession first incorporated in a GATT Schedule	Earlier INRs	ODCs
8105	Cobalt mattes and other intermediate products of cobalt metallurgy; cobalt and articles thereof, including waste and scrap.									
81052000	-Cobalt mattes and other intermediate products of cobalt metallurgy; unwrought cobalt; powders	12								0
81053000	-Waste and scrap	12								0
81059000	-Other	12								0
81060000	Bismuth and articles thereof, including waste and scrap.	12								0
8107	Cadmium and articles thereof, including waste and scrap.									
81072000	-Unwrought cadmium; powders	12								0
81073000	-Waste and scrap	12								0
81079000	-Other	12								0
8108	Titanium and articles thereof, including waste and scrap.									
81082000	-Unwrought titanium; powders	12								0
81083000	-Waste and scrap	12								0
81089000	-Other	8								0
ex81089000	--For use in civil aircraft	0					US			0
8109	Zirconium and articles thereof, including waste and scrap.									
81092000	-Unwrought zirconium; powders	12								0
81093000	-Waste and scrap	12								0
81099000	-Other	12								0
8110	Antimony and articles thereof, including waste and scrap.									
81101000	-Unwrought antimony; powders	12								0
81102000	-Waste and scrap	12								0
81109000	-Other	12								0
81110000	Manganese and articles thereof, including waste and scrap.	12								0
8112	Beryllium, chromium, germanium, vanadium, gallium, hafnium, indium, niobium (columbium), rhenium and thallium, and articles of these metals, including waste and scrap.									
81121	-Beryllium:									
81121200	--Unwrought; powders	12								0
81121300	--Waste and scrap	12								0
81121900	--Other	12								0

HS	Description	Bound rate at date of accession	Interim	Final Bound	Implementation	Present concession established	INR	Concession first incorporated in a GATT Schedule	Earlier INRs	ODCs
81122	-Chromium:									
81122100	--Unwrought; powders	12								0
81122200	--Waste and scrap	12								0
81122900	--Other	12								0
81123000	-Germanium	12								0
81124000	-Vanadium	12								0
81125	-Thallium:									
81125100	--Unwrought; powders	12								0
81125200	--Waste and scrap	12								0
81125900	--Other	12								0
81129	-Other:									
81129200	--Unwrought; waste and scrap; powders	12								0
81129900	--Other	12								0
81130000	Cermets and articles thereof, including waste and scrap.	12								0
8201	Hand tools, the following : spades, shovels, mattocks, picks, hoes, forks and rakes; axes, bill hooks and similar hewing tools; secateurs and pruners of any kind; scythes, sickles, hay knives, hedge shears, timber wedges and other tools of a kind used in agriculture, horticulture or forestry.									
82011000	-Spades and shovels	15								0
82012000	-Forks	15								0
82013000	-Mattocks, picks, hoes and rakes	15								0
82014000	-Axes, bill hooks and similar hewing tools	15					DO,HN			0
82015000	-Secateurs and similar one-handed pruners and shears (including poultry shears)	15								0
82016000	-Hedge shears, two-handed pruning shears and similar two-handed shears	15								0
82019000	-Other hand tools of a kind used in agriculture, horticulture or forestry	10								0
8202	Hand saws; blades for saws of all kinds (including slitting, slotting or toothless saw blades).									
82021000	-Hand saws	15								0
82022000	-Band saw blades	15								0
82023	-Circular saw blades (including slitting or slotting saw blades):									
82023100	--With working part of steel	15								0

HS	Description	Bound rate at date of accession	Interim	Final Bound	Implementation	Present concession established	INR	Concession first incorporated in a GATT Schedule	Earlier INRs	ODCs
82023900	--Other, including parts	15								0
82024000	-Chain saw blades	15								0
82029	-Other saw blades:									
82029100	--Straight saw blades, for working metal	15								0
82029900	--Other	15								0
8203	Files, rasps, pliers (including cutting pliers), pincers, tweezers, metal cutting shears, pipe-cutters, bolt croppers, perforating punches and similar hand tools.									
82031000	-Files, rasps and similar tools	15					DO,HN			0
82032000	-Pliers (including cutting pliers), pincers, tweezers and similar tools	5								0
82033000	-Metal cutting shears and similar tools	15								0
82034000	-Pipe-cutters, bolt croppers, perforating punches and similar tools	15								0
8204	Hand-operated spanners and wrenches (including torque meter wrenches but not including tap wrenches); interchangeable spanner sockets, with or without handles.									
82041	-Hand-operated spanners and wrenches:									
82041100	--Non-adjustable	10								0
82041200	--Adjustable	15								0
82042000	-Interchangeable spanner sockets, with or without handles	15								0
8205	Hand tools (including glaziers' diamonds), not elsewhere specified or included; blow lamps; vices, clamps and the like, other than accessories for and parts of, machine tools; anvils; portable forges; hand or pedal-operated grinding wheels with frameworks.									
82051000	-Drilling, threading or tapping tools	15					KG			0
82052000	-Hammers and sledge hammers	15								0
82053000	-Planes, chisels, gouges and similar cutting tools for working wood	15								0
82054000	-Screwdrivers	15								0
82055	-Other hand tools (including glaziers' diamonds):									
82055100	--Household tools	15								0
820559	--Other									
82055910	---Rivet guns by cartridges	5								0

HS	Description	Bound rate at date of accession	Interim	Final Bound	Implementation	Present concession established	INR	Concession first incorporated in a GATT Schedule	Earlier INRs	ODCs
82055920	---Hand greasers	5								0
82055990	---Other hand tools	5								0
82056000	-Blow lamps	15								0
82057000	-Vices, clamps and the like	10								0
82058000	-Anvils; portable forges; hand or pedal-operated grinding wheels with frameworks	15								0
820590	-Sets of articles of two or more of the foregoing subheadings									
82059010	---Hand tools, not for household use, in sets	15								0
82059020	---Household hand tools in sets	15								0
82060000	Tools of two or more of the headings 82.02 to 82.05, put up in sets for retail sale.	15								0
8207	Interchangeable tools for hand tools, whether or not power-operated, or for machine-tools (for example, for pressing, stamping, punching, tapping, threading, drilling, boring, broaching, milling, turning or screw driving), including dies for drawing or extruding metal, and rock drilling or earth boring tools.									
82071	-Rock drilling or earth boring tools:									
82071300	--With working part of cermets	15								0
82071900	--Other, including parts	12								0
82072000	-Dies for drawing or extruding metal	15								0
82073000	-Tools for pressing, stamping or punching	15								0
82074000	-Tools for tapping or threading	15								0
82075000	-Tools for drilling, other than for rock drilling	15								0
82076000	-Tools for boring or broaching	15								0
82077000	-Tools for milling	15								0
82078000	-Tools for turning	15								0
82079000	-Other interchangeable tools	12								0
8208	Knives and cutting blades, for machines or for mechanical appliances.									
82081000	-For metal working	15								0
82082000	-For wood working	15								0
82083000	-For kitchen appliances or for machines used by the food industry	7								0

HS	Description	Bound rate at date of accession	Interim	Final Bound	Implementation	Present concession established	INR	Concession first incorporated in a GATT Schedule	Earlier INRs	ODCs
82084000	-For agricultural, horticultural or forestry machines	15								0
82089000	-Other	15								0
82090000	Plates, sticks, tips and the like for tools, unmounted, of cermets.	15								0
82100000	Hand-operated mechanical appliances, weighing 10 kg or less, used in the preparation, conditioning or serving of food or drink.	15								0
8211	Knives with cutting blades, serrated or not (including pruning knives), other than knives of heading 82.08, and blades therefor.									
82111000	-Sets of assorted articles	15								0
82119	-Other:									
821191	--Table knives having fixed blades									
82119110	---Table knives with fixed blades and valuable handles	15								0
82119190	---Table knives with fixed blades and other handles	15								0
82119200	--Other knives having fixed blades	15								0
821193	--Knives having other than fixed blades									
82119310	---Pruning knives	15								0
82119390	---Other knives without fixed blades	15								0
82119400	--Blades	15								0
82119500	--Handles of base metal	15								0
8212	Razors and razor blades (including razor blade blanks in strips).									
821210	-Razors									
82121010	---Safety shaving machines, metallic	15								0
82121020	---Safety shavers of plastics with their blades	15								0
82121090	---Other razors	10								0
82122000	-Safety razor blades, including razor blade blanks in strips	10								0
82129000	-Other parts	15								0
82130000	Scissors, tailors' shears and similar shears, and blades therefor.	15								0

HS	Description	Bound rate at date of accession	Interim	Final Bound	Implementation	Present concession established	INR	Concession first incorporated in a GATT Schedule	Earlier INRs	ODCs
8214	Other articles of cutlery (for example, hair clippers, butchers' or kitchen cleavers, choppers and mincing knives, paper knives); manicure or pedicure sets and instruments (including nail files).									
821410	-Paper knives, letter openers, erasing knives, pencil sharpeners and blades therefor									
82141010	---Pencil sharpeners and blades thereof	15								0
82141090	---Other paper knives, letter openers and the like	15								0
82142000	-Manicure or pedicure sets and instruments (including nail files)	15								0
821490	-Other									
82149010	---Butchers' or kitchen cleavers	15								0
82149090	---Other articles of cutlery	15								0
8215	Spoons, forks, ladles, skimmers, cake-servers, fish-knives, butter-knives, sugar tongs and similar kitchen or tableware.									
82151000	-Sets of assorted articles containing at least one article plated with precious metal	15								0
82152000	-Other sets of assorted articles	10								0
82159	-Other:									
82159100	--Plated with precious metal	15								0
82159900	--Other	10								0
8301	Padlocks and locks (key, combination or electrically operated), of base metal; clasps and frames with clasps, incorporating locks, of base metal; keys for any of the foregoing articles, of base metal.									
83011000	-Padlocks	15					DO,HN			0
83012000	-Locks of a kind used for motor vehicles	15					DO,HN			0
83013000	-Locks of a kind used for furniture	15					DO,HN			0
830140	-Other locks									
83014010	---Key or combination operated locks	7					DO,HN			0
83014020	---Electrically operated locks	7					DO,HN			0
83014030	---Locks for handbags or trunks	7					DO,HN			0
83014040	---Locks for bikes	7					DO,HN			0
83014090	---Other locks	10					DO,HN			0

HS	Description	Bound rate at date of accession	Interim	Final Bound	Implementation	Present concession established	INR	Concession first incorporated in a GATT Schedule	Earlier INRs	ODCs
83015000	-Clasps and frames with clasps, incorporating locks	15					DO,HN			0
83016000	-Parts	15					DO,HN			0
83017000	-Keys presented separately	15					DO,HN			0
8302	Base metal mountings, fittings and similar articles suitable for furniture, doors, staircases, windows, blinds, coachwork, saddlery, trunks, chests, caskets or the like; base metal hat-racks, hat-pegs, brackets and similar fixtures; castors with mountings of base metal; automatic door closers of base metal.									
83021000	-Hinges	10					DO,HN			0
ex83021000	--For use in civil aircraft	0					DO,HN,US			0
83022000	-Castors	15					DO,HN			0
ex83022000	--For use in civil aircraft	0					DO,HN,US			0
83023000	-Other mountings, fittings and similar articles suitable for motor vehicles	15					DO,HN			0
83024	-Other mountings, fittings and similar articles:									
83024100	--Suitable for buildings	10					DO,HN			0
83024200	--Other, suitable for furniture	10					DO,HN			0
ex83024200	---For use in civil aircraft	0					DO,HN,US			0
830249	--Other									
83024910	---Door handles	15					DO,HN			0
ex83024910	----For use in civil aircraft	0					DO,HN,US			0
83024990	---Other mountings and fittings	15					DO,HN			0
ex83024990	----For use in civil aircraft	0					DO,HN,US			0
83025000	-Hat-racks, hat-pegs, brackets and similar fixtures	15								0
83026000	-Automatic door closers	15								0
ex83026000	--For use in civil aircraft	0					US			0
83030000	Armoured or reinforced safes, strong-boxes and doors and safe deposit lockers for strong-rooms, cash or deed boxes and the like, of base metal.	15								0
8304	Filing cabinets, card-index cabinets, paper trays, paper rests, pen trays, office-stamp stands and similar office or desk equipment, of base metal, other than office furniture of heading 94.03.									
83040010	---Filing cabinets, paper trays and the like, base metal	15								0

HS	Description	Bound rate at date of accession	Interim	Final Bound	Implementation	Present concession established	INR	Concession first incorporated in a GATT Schedule	Earlier INRs	ODCs
8304002	---Desk equipment (such as book-ends, paperweights, ink-stands and ink-pot, etc.) :									
83040021	----Iron office or desk equipment	15								0
83040029	----Office or desk equipment of other base metals	15								0
83040030	---Paper holders for typing machines	15								0
83040040	---Shelves of the kind to be put on office desks	15								0
83040090	---Other office or desk equipment	15								0
8305	Fittings for loose-leaf binders or files, letter clips, letter corners, paper clips, indexing tags and similar office articles, of base metal; staples in strips (for example, for offices, upholstery, packaging), of base metal.									
83051000	-Fittings for loose-leaf binders or files	15								0
83052000	-Staples in strips	15								0
83059000	-Other, including parts	15								0
8306	Bells, gongs and the like, non-electric, of base metal; statuettes and other ornaments, of base metal; photograph, picture or similar frames, of base metal; mirrors of base metal.									
83061000	-Bells, gongs and the like	15								0
83062	-Statuettes and other ornaments:									
83062100	--Plated with precious metal	15								0
83062900	--Other	12								0
83063000	-Photograph, picture or similar frames; mirrors	15								0
8307	Flexible tubing of base metal, with or without fittings.									
ex83071000	--For use in civil aircraft	0					US			0
83071000	-Of iron or steel	15								0
ex83079000	--For use in civil aircraft	0					US			0
83079000	-Of other base metal	15								0
8308	Clasps, frames with clasps, buckles, buckle-clasps, hooks, eyes, eyelets and the like, of base metal, of a kind used for clothing, footwear, awnings, handbags, travel goods or other made up articles; tubular or bifurcated rivets, of base metal; beads and spangles, of base metal.									

HS	Description	Bound rate at date of accession	Interim	Final Bound	Implementation	Present concession established	INR	Concession first incorporated in a GATT Schedule	Earlier INRs	ODCs
83081000	-Hooks, eyes and eyelets	15								0
83082000	-Tubular or bifurcated rivets	15								0
830890	-Other, including parts									
83089010	---Clasps, buckle-clasps and the like of base metal	12								0
83089020	---Beads and spangles (tartar)	15								0
83089090	---Other buckles, parts and the like of base metal	15								0
8309	Stoppers, caps and lids (including crown corks, screw caps and pouring stoppers), capsules for bottles, threaded bungs, bung covers, seals and other packing accessories, of base metal.									
83091000	-Crown corks	15								0
830990	-Other									
83099010	---Metal stoppers lined with cork, with toothed edges	15								0
83099020	---Stoppers, screw covers and the like for bottles	15								0
83099030	---Threaded bung covers	10								0
83099040	---Pouring stoppers, measuring stoppers and the like	15								0
83099050	---Seals of all kinds	15								0
83099060	---Ties for sealing bags and similar containers	15								0
83099070	---Can covers and bottoms	12					DO,HN			0
83099090	---Other stoppers and lids	15								0
8310	Sign-plates, name-plates, address-plates and similar plates, numbers, letters and other symbols, of base metal, excluding those of heading 94.05.									
83100010	---Name-plates for districts, roads, streets and the like	15								0
83100020	---Sign-plates for general agencies and traffic	15								0
83100030	---Signs for houses, stores, factories, etc.	15								0
83100040	---Signs for commercials (advertisements)	15								0
83100050	---Address-plates for doors, mail boxes and the like	15								0

HS	Description	Bound rate at date of accession	Interim	Final Bound	Implementation	Present concession established	INR	Concession first incorporated in a GATT Schedule	Earlier INRs	ODCs
83100060	---Plates and similar signs for machinery, equipment, etc.	15								0
83100070	---Separate numbers, letters for name-plates and the like	15								0
83100090	---Other sign and name-plates	15								0
8311	Wire, rods, tubes, plates, electrodes and similar products, of base metal or of metal carbides, coated or cored with flux material, of a kind used for soldering, brazing, welding or deposition of metal or of metal carbides; wire and rods, of agglomerated base metal powder, used for metal spraying.									
83111000	-Coated electrodes of base metal, for electric arc-welding	15								0
83112000	-Cored wire of base metal, for electric arc-welding	15								0
83113000	-Coated rods and cored wire, of base metal, for soldering, brazing or welding by flame	15								0
83119000	-Other, including parts	15								0
8401	Nuclear reactors; fuel elements (cartridges), non-irradiated, for nuclear reactors; machinery and apparatus for isotopic separation.									
84011000	-Nuclear reactors	15								0
84012000	-Machinery and apparatus for isotopic separation, and parts thereof	15								0
84013000	-Fuel elements (cartridges), non-irradiated	15								0
84014000	-Parts of nuclear reactors	15								0
8402	Steam or other vapour generating boilers (other than central heating hot water boilers capable also of producing low pressure steam); super-heated water boilers.									
84021	-Steam or other vapour generating boilers:									
84021100	--Watertube boilers with a steam production exceeding 45 tonnes per hour	15								0
84021200	--Watertube boilers with a steam production not exceeding 45 tonnes per hour	15								0

HS	Description	Bound rate at date of accession	Interim	Final Bound	Implementation	Present concession established	INR	Concession first incorporated in a GATT Schedule	Earlier INRs	ODCs
84021900	--Other vapour generating boilers, including hybrid boilers	15								0
84022000	-Super-heated water boilers	15								0
84029000	-Parts	7								0
8403	Central heating boilers other than those of heading 84.02.									
84031000	-Boilers	15								0
84039000	-Parts	15								0
8404	Auxiliary plant for use with boilers of heading 84.02 or 84.03 (for example, economisers, super-heaters, soot removers, gas recoverers); condensers for steam or other vapour power units.									
84041000	-Auxiliary plant for use with boilers of heading 84.02 or 84.03	15								0
84042000	-Condensers for steam or other vapour power units	15								0
84049000	-Parts	15								0
8405	Producer gas or water gas generators, with or without their purifiers; acetylene gas generators and similar water process gas generators, with or without their purifiers.									
84051000	-Producer gas or water gas generators, with or without their purifiers; acetylene gas generators and similar water process gas generators, with or without their purifiers	15								0
84059000	-Parts	15								0
8406	Steam turbines and other vapour turbines.									
84061000	-Turbines for marine propulsion	15								0
84068	-Other turbines:									
84068100	--Of an output exceeding 40 MW	15								0
84068200	--Of an output not exceeding 40 MW	15								0
84069000	-Parts	7								0
8407	Spark-ignition reciprocating or rotary internal combustion piston engines.									
ex84071000	--For use in civil aircraft	0					US			0
84071000	-Aircraft engines	15								0
84072	-Marine propulsion engines:									
84072100	--Outboard motors	15								0
84072900	--Other	15								0

HS	Description	Bound rate at date of accession	Interim	Final Bound	Implementation	Present concession established	INR	Concession first incorporated in a GATT Schedule	Earlier INRs	ODCs
84073	-Reciprocating piston engines of a kind used for the propulsion of vehicles of Chapter 87:									
84073100	--Of a cylinder capacity not exceeding 50 cc	15								0
84073200	--Of a cylinder capacity exceeding 50 cc but not exceeding 250 cc	15								0
84073300	--Of a cylinder capacity exceeding 250 cc but not exceeding 1,000 cc	15								0
840734	--Of a cylinder capacity exceeding 1,000 cc									
84073410	---Motor vehicle piston engines 1001-1500 cc, spark/rotary	5								0
84073420	---Motor vehicle piston engines 1501-3000 cc, spark/rotary	5								0
84073430	---Motor vehicle piston engines over 3000 cc, spark/rotary	5								0
84079000	-Other engines	15								0
8408	Compression-ignition internal combustion piston engines (diesel or semi-diesel engines).									
84081000	-Marine propulsion engines	15								0
84082000	-Engines of a kind used for the propulsion of vehicles of Chapter 87	7								0
ex84089000	--For use in civil aircraft	0					US			0
84089000	-Other engines	10								0
8409	Parts suitable for use solely or principally with the engines of heading 84.07 or 84.08.									
84091000	-For aircraft engines	15								0
ex84091000	--For use in civil aircraft	0					US			0
84099	-Other:									
840991	--Suitable for use solely or principally with spark-ignition internal combustion piston engines									
84099110	---Pistons and piston rings for spark-ignition engines	7					AU			0
84099120	---Cylinders and their parts for spark-ignition engines	7					AU			0
84099130	---Fuel feeding valves and pipes for spark-ignition engine	7					AU			0
84099140	---Exhaust relief valves, pipes for spark-ignition engines	7					AU			0

HS	Description	Bound rate at date of accession	Interim	Final Bound	Implementation	Present concession established	INR	Concession first incorporated in a GATT Schedule	Earlier INRs	ODCs
84099150	---Carburetors and nozzles for spark-ignition engines	7					AU			0
84099190	---Other parts for spark-ignition engines	7					AU			0
84099900	--Other	5								0
8410	Hydraulic turbines, water wheels, and regulators therefor.									
84101	-Hydraulic turbines and water wheels:									
84101100	--Of a power not exceeding 1,000 kW	15								0
84101200	--Of a power exceeding 1,000 kW but not exceeding 10,000 kW	15								0
84101300	--Of a power exceeding 10,000 kW	10								0
84109000	-Parts, including regulators	15								0
8411	Turbo-jets, turbo-propellers and other gas turbines.									
84111	-Turbo-jets:									
84111100	--Of a thrust not exceeding 25 kN	15								0
ex84111100	---For use in civil aircraft	0					US			0
84111200	--Of a thrust exceeding 25 kN	15								0
ex84111200	---For use in civil aircraft	0					US			0
84112	-Turbo-propellers:									
84112100	--Of a power not exceeding 1,100 kW	15								0
ex84112100	---For use in civil aircraft	0					US			0
ex84112200	---For use in civil aircraft	0					US			0
84112200	--Of a power exceeding 1,100 kW	15								0
84118	-Other gas turbines:									
84118100	--Of a power not exceeding 5,000 kW	15								0
ex84118100	---For use in civil aircraft	0					US			0
84118200	--Of a power exceeding 5,000 kW	15								0
ex84118200	---For use in civil aircraft	0					US			0
84119	-Parts:									
84119100	--Of turbo-jets or turbo-propellers	15					CH			0
ex84119100	---For use in civil aircraft	0					CH,US			0
84119900	--Other	10					CH			0
ex84119900	---For use in civil aircraft	0					CH,US			0
8412	Other engines and motors.									
84121000	-Reaction engines other than turbo-jets	15								0
ex84121000	--For use in civil aircraft	0					US			0
84122	-Hydraulic power engines and motors:									
84122100	--Linear acting (cylinders)	15								0
ex84122100	---For use in civil aircraft	0					US			0
84122900	--Other	15								0

HS	Description	Bound rate at date of accession	Interim	Final Bound	Implementation	Present concession established	INR	Concession first incorporated in a GATT Schedule	Earlier INRs	ODCs
ex84122900	---For use in civil aircraft	0					US			0
84123	-Pneumatic power engines and motors:									
84123100	--Linear acting (cylinders)	15								0
ex84123100	---For use in civil aircraft	0					US			0
ex84123900	---For use in civil aircraft	0					US			0
84123900	--Other	15								0
84128000	-Other	15								0
ex84128000	--For use in civil aircraft	0					US			0
ex84129000	--For use in civil aircraft	0					CA,US			0
84129000	-Parts	15					CA			0
8413	Pumps for liquids, whether or not fitted with a measuring device; liquid elevators.									
84131	-Pumps fitted or designed to be fitted with a measuring device:									
84131100	--Pumps for dispensing fuel or lubricants, of the type used in filling-stations or in garages	7								0
841319	--Other									
84131910	---Fire pumps	15								0
ex84131910	----For use in civil aircraft	0					US			0
84131990	---Other liquid pumps with a measuring device	15								0
ex84131990	----For use in civil aircraft	0					US			0
84132000	-Hand pumps, other than those of subheading 8413.11 or 8413.19	15								0
ex84132000	--For use in civil aircraft	0					US			0
84133000	-Fuel, lubricating or cooling medium pumps for internal combustion piston engines	15								0
ex84133000	--For use in civil aircraft	0					US			0
84134000	-Concrete pumps	15								0
ex84135000	--For use in civil aircraft	0					US			0
84135000	-Other reciprocating positive displacement pumps	15								0
ex84136000	--For use in civil aircraft	0					US			0
84136000	-Other rotary positive displacement pumps	15								0
84137000	-Other centrifugal pumps	15					KG			0
ex84137000	--For use in civil aircraft	0					KG,US			0
84138	-Other pumps; liquid elevators:									
841381	--Pumps									

HS	Description	Bound rate at date of accession	Interim	Final Bound	Implementation	Present concession established	INR	Concession first incorporated in a GATT Schedule	Earlier INRs	ODCs
84138110	---Other liquid pumps for agricultural use	15					AU			0
ex84138110	----For use in civil aircraft	0					AU,US			0
ex84138120	----For use in civil aircraft	0					AU,US			0
84138120	---Other liquid pumps for domestic use	10					AU			0
ex84138190	----For use in civil aircraft	0					AU,US			0
84138190	---Other liquid pumps	10					AU			0
84138200	--Liquid elevators	15								0
84139	-Parts:									
ex84139100	---For use in civil aircraft	0					CH,US			0
84139100	--Of pumps	15					CH			0
84139200	--Of liquid elevators	15								0
8414	Air or vacuum pumps, air or other gas compressors and fans; ventilating or recycling hoods incorporating a fan, whether or not fitted with filters.									
ex84141000	--For use in civil aircraft	0					US			0
84141000	-Vacuum pumps	15								0
84142000	-Hand- or foot-operated air pumps	15								0
ex84142000	--For use in civil aircraft	0					US			0
84143000	-Compressors of a kind used in refrigerating equipment	10					IN			0
ex84143000	--For use in civil aircraft	0					IN,US			0
84144000	-Air compressors mounted on a wheeled chassis for towing	10								0
84145	-Fans:									
84145100	--Table, floor, wall, window, ceiling or roof fans, with a self-contained electric motor of an output not exceeding 125 W	10								0
ex84145100	---For use in civil aircraft	0					US			0
ex84145900	---For use in civil aircraft	0					US			0
84145900	--Other	15								0
84146000	-Hoods having a maximum horizontal side not exceeding 120 cm	15								0
ex84148000	--For use in civil aircraft	0					CH,US			0
84148000	-Other	15					CH			0
84149000	-Parts	15					CH			0
ex84149000	--For use in civil aircraft	0					CH,US			0
8415	Air conditioning machines, comprising a motor-driven fan and elements for changing the temperature and humidity, including those machines in which the humidity cannot be separately regulated.									

HS	Description	Bound rate at date of accession	Interim	Final Bound	Implementation	Present concession established	INR	Concession first incorporated in a GATT Schedule	Earlier INRs	ODCs
841510	-Window or wall types, self-contained or "split-system"									
84151020	---Air conditioners (freon), self-contained wall units	15					JP			0
84151090	---Other self-contained wall air conditioners	10					TH			0
84152000	-Of a kind used for persons, in motor vehicles	15								0
84158	-Other:									
841581	--Incorporating a refrigerating unit and a valve for reversal of the cooling/heat cycle (reversible heat pumps)									
8415812	---Air conditioning machines (freon):									
84158121	----Central freon air conditioner, refrig and reverse valve	15					JP			0
ex84158121	-----For use in civil aircraft	0					US			0
84158129	----Other freon air conditioners, refrig and reverse valve	15								0
ex84158129	-----For use in civil aircraft	0					US			0
ex84158190	----For use in civil aircraft	0					US			0
84158190	---Other air conditioners, refrigeration and reverse valve	15					JP			0
841582	--Other, incorporating a refrigerating unit									
8415822	---Air conditioning machines (freon):									
ex84158221	-----For use in civil aircraft	0					US			0
84158221	----Other freon central air conditioner with refrigeration	15								0
84158229	----Other freon air conditioners with refrigeration units	15								0
ex84158229	-----For use in civil aircraft	0					US			0
ex84158290	----For use in civil aircraft	0					TH,US			0
84158290	---Other air conditioners with refrigeration units	10					JP,TH			0
841583	--Not incorporating a refrigerating unit									
8415832	---Central freon air conditioners without refrigeration									
ex84158321	-----For use in civil aircraft	0					US			0
84158321	----Central freon air conditioners without refrigeration	15					JP			0
84158329	----Other freon air conditioners without refrigeration unit	15								0
ex84158329	-----For use in civil aircraft	0					US			0
ex84158390	----For use in civil aircraft	0					US			0

HS	Description	Bound rate at date of accession	Interim	Final Bound	Implementation	Present concession established	INR	Concession first incorporated in a GATT Schedule	Earlier INRs	ODCs
84158390	---Other air conditioners without refrigeration unit	15								0
84159000	-Parts	10					JP			0
ex84159000	--For use in civil aircraft	0					US			0
8416	Furnace burners for liquid fuel, for pulverised solid fuel or for gas; mechanical stokers, including their mechanical grates, mechanical ash dischargers and similar appliances.									
84161000	-Furnace burners for liquid fuel	15								0
84162000	-Other furnace burners, including combination burners	15								0
84163000	-Mechanical stokers, including their mechanical grates, mechanical ash dischargers and similar appliances	15								0
84169000	-Parts	7								0
8417	Industrial or laboratory furnaces and ovens, including incinerators, non-electric.									
84171000	-Furnaces and ovens for the roasting, melting or other heat-treatment of ores, pyrites or of metals	15								0
84172000	-Bakery ovens, including biscuit ovens	15								0
841780	-Other									
84178010	---Wood charring kiln	15								0
84178020	---Rotating furnaces for cement and mixing furnaces	15								0
84178030	---Furnaces for the manufacture of ceramics and enamelling	15								0
84178040	---Glass manufacturing furnaces	15								0
84178090	---Other industrial or laboratory furnaces	15								0
84179000	-Parts	5								0
8418	Refrigerators, freezers and other refrigerating or freezing equipment, electric or other; heat pumps other than air conditioning machines of heading 84.15.									
ex84181000	--For use in civil aircraft	0					US			0
84181000	-Combined refrigerator-freezers, fitted with separate external doors	15		10	2008					0
84182	-Refrigerators, household type:									
84182100	--Compression-type	15		10	2008					0
84182200	--Absorption-type, electrical	15								0

HS	Description	Bound rate at date of accession	Interim	Final Bound	Implementation	Present concession established	INR	Concession first incorporated in a GATT Schedule	Earlier INRs	ODCs
84182900	--Other	15								0
84183000	-Freezers of the chest type, not exceeding 800 litres capacity	15								0
ex84183000	--For use in civil aircraft	0					US			0
84184000	-Freezers of the upright type, not exceeding 900 litres capacity	15								0
ex84184000	--For use in civil aircraft	0					US			0
84185000	-Other refrigerating or freezing chests, cabinets, display counters, show-cases and similar refrigerating or freezing furniture	15		10	2008					0
84186	-Other refrigerating or freezing equipment; heat pumps:									
ex84186100	---For use in civil aircraft	0					US			0
84186100	--Compression type units whose condensers are heat exchangers	15								0
841869	--Other									
84186910	---Potable water coolers	15								0
ex84186910	----For use in civil aircraft	0					US			0
84186920	---Ice-cream making machines	15								0
ex84186920	----For use in civil aircraft	0					US			0
84186930	---Beverage cooling machines	15								0
ex84186930	----For use in civil aircraft	0					US			0
84186940	---Refrigerating or freezing rooms over 900 l	15								0
ex84186940	----For use in civil aircraft	0					US			0
84186950	---Ice-cubes making machines	15								0
84186990	---Other refrigeration equipment; heat pumps	15								0
ex84186990	----For use in civil aircraft	0					US			0
84189	-Parts:									
84189100	--Furniture designed to receive refrigerating or freezing equipment	15								0
841899	--Other									
84189910	---Compression-type refrigerating units	7								0
84189990	---Other parts for refrigeration equipment	15								0

HS	Description	Bound rate at date of accession	Interim	Final Bound	Implementation	Present concession established	INR	Concession first incorporated in a GATT Schedule	Earlier INRs	ODCs
8419	Machinery, plant or laboratory equipment, whether or not electrically heated (excluding furnaces, ovens and other equipment of heading 85.14), for the treatment of materials by a process involving a change of temperature such as heating, cooking, roasting, distilling, rectifying, sterilising, pasteurising, steaming, drying, evaporating, vaporising, condensing or cooling, other than machinery or plant of a kind used for domestic purposes; instantaneous or storage water heaters, non-electric.									
84191	-Instantaneous or storage water heaters, non-electric:									
84191100	--Instantaneous gas water heaters	15								0
841919	--Other									
84191910	---Water heaters by solar energy	15								0
84191990	---Other water heaters	15								0
84192000	-Medical, surgical or laboratory sterilisers	5								0
84193	-Dryers:									
84193100	--For agricultural products	15								0
84193200	--For wood, paper pulp, paper or paperboard	15								0
84193900	--Other	15								0
84194000	-Distilling or rectifying plant	15								0
84195000	-Heat exchange units	15								0
ex84195000	--For use in civil aircraft	0					US			0
84196000	-Machinery for liquefying air or other gases	15								0
84198	-Other machinery, plant and equipment:									
ex84198100	---For use in civil aircraft	0								0
84198100	--For making hot drinks or for cooking or heating food	15								0
84198900	--Other	5		0	2008		CH,US			0
84199000	-Parts	5		0	2008		US			0
ex84199000	--For use in civil aircraft	0					US			0
8420	Calendering or other rolling machines, other than for metals or glass, and cylinders therefor.									
84201000	-Calendering or other rolling machines	15								0
84209	-Parts:									

HS	Description	Bound rate at date of accession	Interim	Final Bound	Implementation	Present concession established	INR	Concession first incorporated in a GATT Schedule	Earlier INRs	ODCs
84209100	--Cylinders	15								0
84209900	--Other	15								0
8421	Centrifuges, including centrifugal dryers; filtering or purifying machinery and apparatus, for liquids or gases.									
84211	-Centrifuges, including centrifugal dryers:									
84211100	--Cream separators	15								0
84211200	--Clothes-dryers	15								0
84211900	--Other	5		0	2008		US			0
ex84211900	---For use in civil aircraft	0					US			0
84212	-Filtering or purifying machinery and apparatus for liquids:									
842121	--For filtering or purifying water									
84212110	---Water filtering apparatus for household use	15								0
ex84212110	----For use in civil aircraft	0					US			0
84212190	---Other water filtering machinery	15								0
ex84212190	----For use in civil aircraft	0					US			0
84212200	--For filtering or purifying beverages other than water	15								0
84212300	--Oil or petrol-filters for internal combustion engines	15								0
ex84212300	---For use in civil aircraft	0					US			0
842129	--Other									
84212910	---Blood filtering machines	15								0
ex84212910	----For use in civil aircraft	0					US			0
84212990	---Other filtering or purifying machinery for liquids	15								0
ex84212990	----For use in civil aircraft	0					US			0
84213	-Filtering or purifying machinery and apparatus for gases:									
84213100	--Intake air filters for internal combustion engines	15								0
ex84213100	---For use in civil aircraft	0					US			0
ex84213900	---For use in civil aircraft	0					CH,US			0
84213900	--Other	10					CH			0
84219	-Parts:									
84219100	--Of centrifuges, including centrifugal dryers	5		0	2008		US			0
84219900	--Other	5								0

HS	Description	Bound rate at date of accession	Interim	Final Bound	Implementation	Present concession established	INR	Concession first incorporated in a GATT Schedule	Earlier INRs	ODCs
8422	Dish washing machines; machinery for cleaning or drying bottles or other containers; machinery for filling, closing, sealing or labelling bottles, cans, boxes, bags or other containers; machinery for capsuling bottles, jars, tubes and similar containers; other packing or wrapping machinery (including heat-shrink wrapping machinery); machinery for aerating beverages.									
84221	-Dish washing machines:									
84221100	--Of the household type	15								0
84221900	--Other	15								0
84222000	-Machinery for cleaning or drying bottles or other containers	5								0
842230	-Machinery for filling, closing, sealing, or labelling bottles, cans, boxes, bags or other containers; machinery for capsuling bottles, jars, tubes and similar containers; machinery for aerating beverages									
84223010	---Machinery for filling, closing, etc., containers	5								0
84223020	---Machinery for the manufacture of carbonated beverages	5								0
84224000	-Other packing or wrapping machinery (including heat-shrink wrapping machinery)	15								0
84229000	-Parts	5								0
8423	Weighing machinery (excluding balances of a sensitivity of 5 cg or better), including weight operated counting or checking machines; weighing machine weights of all kinds.									
84231000	-Personal weighing machines, including baby scales; household scales	15								0
84232000	-Scales for continuous weighing of goods on conveyors	15								0
84233000	-Constant weight scales and scales for discharging a predetermined weight of material into a bag or container, including hopper scales	15								0
84238	-Other weighing machinery:									

HS	Description	Bound rate at date of accession	Interim	Final Bound	Implementation	Present concession established	INR	Concession first incorporated in a GATT Schedule	Earlier INRs	ODCs
84238100	--Having a maximum weighing capacity not exceeding 30 kg	15								0
84238200	--Having a maximum weighing capacity exceeding 30 kg but not exceeding 5 000 kg	15								0
84238900	--Other	15								0
84239000	-Weighing machine weights of all kinds; parts of weighing machinery	15								0
8424	Mechanical appliances (whether or not hand-operated) for projecting, dispersing or spraying liquids or powders; fire extinguishers, whether or not charged; spray guns and similar appliances; steam or sand blasting machines and similar jet projecting machines.									
ex84241000	--For use in civil aircraft	0					US			0
84241000	-Fire extinguishers, whether or not charged	15								0
842420	-Spray guns and similar appliances									
84242010	---Spray guns for building materials	15								0
84242090	---Other spraying appliances	15								0
84243000	-Steam or sand blasting machines and similar jet projecting machines	15								0
84248	-Other appliances:									
842481	--Agricultural or horticultural									
84248110	---Complete irrigation systems of all kinds	15								0
84248120	---Insecticide spraying appliances	5								0
84248130	---Water sprinkling appliances for irrigating	5								0
84248190	---Other agricultural spraying appliances	5								0
84248900	--Other	5		0	2008		US			0
842490	-Parts									
84249010	---Sprayer head parts for mechanical or jet projecting appliances	5		0	2008		US			0
84249020	---Parts of irrigation systems of subheading 84248110	12		0	2008		US			0
84249090	---Other parts for mechanical or jet projecting appliances, nec	5		0	2008		US			0
8425	Pulley tackle and hoists other than skip hoists; winches and capstans; jacks.									

HS	Description	Bound rate at date of accession	Interim	Final Bound	Implementation	Present concession established	INR	Concession first incorporated in a GATT Schedule	Earlier INRs	ODCs
84251	-Pulley tackle and hoists other than skip hoists or hoists of a kind used for raising vehicles:									
ex84251100	---For use in civil aircraft	0					KG,US			0
84251100	--Powered by electric motor	8					KG			0
84251900	--Other	8								0
ex84251900	---For use in civil aircraft	0					US			0
84252000	-Pit-head winding gear; winches specially designed for use underground	8								0
84253	-Other winches; capstans:									
84253100	--Powered by electric motor	8								0
ex84253100	---For use in civil aircraft	0					US			0
84253900	--Other	8								0
ex84253900	---For use in civil aircraft	0					US			0
84254	-Jacks; hoists of a kind used for raising vehicles:									
84254100	--Built-in jacking systems of a type used in garages	8					US			0
84254200	--Other jacks and hoists, hydraulic	8								0
ex84254200	---For use in civil aircraft	0					US			0
84254900	--Other	8								0
ex84254900	---For use in civil aircraft	0					US			0
8426	Ships' derricks; cranes, including cable cranes; mobile lifting frames, straddle carriers and works trucks fitted with a crane.									
84261	-Overhead travelling cranes, transporter cranes, gantry cranes, bridge cranes, mobile lifting frames and straddle carriers:									
84261100	--Overhead travelling cranes on fixed support	8					US			0
84261200	--Mobile lifting frames on tyres and straddle carriers	8					US			0
84261900	--Other	8					US			0
84262000	-Tower cranes	10								0
84263000	-Portal or pedestal jib cranes	8					US			0
84264	-Other machinery, self-propelled:									
84264100	--On tyres	6					US			0
84264900	--Other	6					US			0
84269	-Other machinery:									
84269100	--Designed for mounting on road vehicles	8					US			0

HS	Description	Bound rate at date of accession	Interim	Final Bound	Implementation	Present concession established	INR	Concession first incorporated in a GATT Schedule	Earlier INRs	ODCs
ex84269900	---For use in civil aircraft	0					US			0
84269900	--Other	8								0
8427	Fork-lift trucks; other works trucks fitted with lifting or handling equipment.									
84271000	-Self-propelled trucks powered by an electric motor	5								0
84272000	-Other self-propelled trucks	15								0
84279000	-Other trucks	5								0
8428	Other lifting, handling, loading or unloading machinery (for example, lifts, escalators, conveyors, teleferics).									
ex84281000	--For use in civil aircraft	0					US			0
84281000	-Lifts and skip hoists	8								0
ex84282000	--For use in civil aircraft	0					US			0
84282000	-Pneumatic elevators and conveyors	8								0
84283	-Other continuous-action elevators and conveyors, for goods or materials:									
84283100	--Specially designed for underground use	8								0
84283200	--Other, bucket type	8								0
84283300	--Other, belt type	8								0
ex84283300	---For use in civil aircraft	0					US			0
84283900	--Other	8								0
ex84283900	---For use in civil aircraft	0					US			0
84284000	-Escalators and moving walkways	8								0
84285000	-Mine wagon pushers, locomotive or wagon traversers, wagon tippers and similar railway wagon handling equipment	8								0
84286000	-Teleferics, chair-lifts, ski-draglines; traction mechanisms for funiculars	8								0
ex84289000	--For use in civil aircraft	0					US			0
84289000	-Other machinery	8								0
8429	Self-propelled bulldozers, angledozers, graders, levellers, scrapers, mechanical shovels, excavators, shovel loaders, tamping machines and road rollers.									
84291	-Bulldozers and angledozers:									
84291100	--Track laying	6					JP,US			0
84291900	--Other	6					US			0
84292000	-Graders and levellers	6					US			0
84293000	-Scrapers	8					US			0
84294000	-Tamping machines and road rollers	6					US			0

HS	Description	Bound rate at date of accession	Interim	Final Bound	Implementation	Present concession established	INR	Concession first incorporated in a GATT Schedule	Earlier INRs	ODCs
84295	-Mechanical shovels, excavators and shovel loaders:									
84295100	--Front-end shovel loaders	6					US			0
84295200	--Machinery with a 360° revolving superstructure	8					JP,US			0
84295900	--Other	10					US			0
8430	Other moving, grading, levelling, scraping, excavating, tamping, compacting, extracting or boring machinery, for earth, minerals or ores; pile-drivers and pile-extractors; snow-ploughs and snow-blowers.									
84301000	-Pile-drivers and pile-extractors	8					US			0
84302000	-Snow-ploughs and snow-blowers	8								0
84303	-Coal or rock cutters and tunnelling machinery:									
84303100	--Self-propelled	8								0
84303900	--Other	6					US			0
84304	-Other boring or sinking machinery:									
84304100	--Self-propelled	6					EC,US			0
84304900	--Other	6					EC,US			0
84305000	-Other machinery, self-propelled	6					US			0
84306	-Other machinery, not self-propelled:									
84306100	--Tamping or compacting machinery	8					US			0
84306900	--Other	6					US			0
8431	Parts suitable for use solely or principally with the machinery of headings 84.25 to 84.30.									
84311000	-Of machinery of heading 84.25	6					US			0
84312000	-Of machinery of heading 84.27	5								0
84313	-Of machinery of heading 84.28:									
84313100	--Of lifts, skip hoists or escalators	10					US			0
84313900	--Other	6					US			0
84314	-Of machinery of heading 84.26, 84.29 or 84.30:									
84314100	--Buckets, shovels, grabs and grips	8					US			0
84314200	--Bulldozer or angledozer blades	8					US			0
843143	--Parts for boring or sinking machinery of subheading 8430.41 or 8430.49									
84314310	---Well boring drills	6					EC,US			0
84314390	---Other parts for boring machinery	6					EC,US			0
84314900	--Other	6					US			0

HS	Description	Bound rate at date of accession	Interim	Final Bound	Implementation	Present concession established	INR	Concession first incorporated in a GATT Schedule	Earlier INRs	ODCs
8432	Agricultural, horticultural or forestry machinery for soil preparation or cultivation; lawn or sports-ground rollers.									
84321000	-Ploughs	8					US			0
84322	-Harrows, scarifiers, cultivators, weeders and hoes:									
84322100	--Disc harrows	8					US			0
84322900	--Other	8								0
84323000	-Seeders, planters and transplanters	8					US			0
84324000	-Manure spreaders and fertiliser distributors	8								0
84328000	-Other machinery	8					US			0
84329000	-Parts	8					US			0
8433	Harvesting or threshing machinery, including straw or fodder balers; grass or hay mowers; machines for cleaning, sorting or grading eggs, fruit or other agricultural produce, other than machinery of heading 84.37.									
84331	-Mowers for lawns, parks or sports-grounds:									
84331100	--Powered, with the cutting device rotating in a horizontal plane	8					US			0
84331900	--Other	8					US			0
84332000	-Other mowers, including cutter bars for tractor mounting	8					US			0
84333000	-Other haymaking machinery	8					US			0
84334000	-Straw or fodder balers, including pick-up balers	8					US			0
84335	-Other harvesting machinery; threshing machinery:									
84335100	--Combine harvester-threshers	8					US			0
84335200	--Other threshing machinery	8								0
84335300	--Root or tuber harvesting machines	8								0
84335900	--Other	8								0
84336000	-Machines for cleaning, sorting or grading eggs, fruit or other agricultural produce	8					US			0
84339000	-Parts	8					US			0
8434	Milking machines and dairy machinery.									
84341000	-Milking machines	8								0
84342000	-Dairy machinery	8					US			0

HS	Description	Bound rate at date of accession	Interim	Final Bound	Implementation	Present concession established	INR	Concession first incorporated in a GATT Schedule	Earlier INRs	ODCs
84349000	-Parts	8					US			0
8435	Presses, crushers and similar machinery used in the manufacture of wine, cider, fruit juices or similar beverages.									
84351000	-Machinery	15								0
84359000	-Parts	15								0
8436	Other agricultural, horticultural, forestry, poultry-keeping or bee-keeping machinery, including germination plant fitted with mechanical or thermal equipment; poultry incubators and brooders.									
84361000	-Machinery for preparing animal feeding stuffs	15								0
84362	-Poultry-keeping machinery; poultry incubators and brooders:									
84362100	--Poultry incubators and brooders	15								0
84362900	--Other	5								0
843680	-Other machinery									
84368010	---Machinery for incubating micro-organisms in laboratories	15								0
84368090	---Other	15								0
84369	-Parts:									
84369100	--Of poultry-keeping machinery or poultry incubators and brooders	15								0
84369900	--Other	15								0
8437	Machines for cleaning, sorting or grading seed, grain or dried leguminous vegetables; machinery used in the milling industry or for the working of cereals or dried leguminous vegetables, other than farm-type machinery.									
84371000	-Machines for cleaning, sorting or grading seed, grain or dried leguminous vegetables	15								0
84378000	-Other machinery	15								0
84379000	-Parts	15								0

HS	Description	Bound rate at date of accession	Interim	Final Bound	Implementation	Present concession established	INR	Concession first incorporated in a GATT Schedule	Earlier INRs	ODCs
8438	Machinery, not specified or included elsewhere in this Chapter, for the industrial preparation or manufacture of food or drink, other than machinery for the extraction or preparation of animal or fixed vegetable fats or oils.									
84381000	-Bakery machinery and machinery for the manufacture of macaroni, spaghetti or similar products	15								0
84382000	-Machinery for the manufacture of confectionery, cocoa or chocolate	15								0
84383000	-Machinery for sugar manufacture	15								0
84384000	-Brewery machinery	15								0
84385000	-Machinery for the preparation of meat or poultry	15								0
84386000	-Machinery for the preparation of fruits, nuts or vegetables	15								0
84388000	-Other machinery	15								0
84389000	-Parts	15								0
8439	Machinery for making pulp of fibrous cellulosic material or for making or finishing paper or paperboard.									
84391000	-Machinery for making pulp of fibrous cellulosic material	15								0
84392000	-Machinery for making paper or paperboard	15								0
84393000	-Machinery for finishing paper or paperboard	15								0
84399	-Parts:									
84399100	--Of machinery for making pulp of fibrous cellulosic material	15								0
84399900	--Other	15								0
8440	Book-binding machinery, including book-sewing machines.									
84401000	-Machinery	15								0
84409000	-Parts	15								0
8441	Other machinery for making up paper pulp, paper or paperboard, including cutting machines of all kinds.									
84411000	-Cutting machines	15								0
84412000	-Machines for making bags, sacks or envelopes	15								0

HS	Description	Bound rate at date of accession	Interim	Final Bound	Implementation	Present concession established	INR	Concession first incorporated in a GATT Schedule	Earlier INRs	ODCs
84413000	-Machines for making cartons, boxes, cases, tubes, drums or similar containers, other than by moulding	15								0
84414000	-Machines for moulding articles in paper pulp, paper or paperboard	5								0
84418000	-Other machinery	5								0
84419000	-Parts	5								0
8442	Machinery, apparatus and equipment (other than the machine-tools of headings 84.56 to 84.65), for type-founding or type-setting, for preparing or making printing blocks, plates, cylinders or other printing components; printing type, blocks, plates, cylinders and other printing components; blocks, plates, cylinders and lithographic stones, prepared for printing purposes (for example, planed, grained or polished).									
84421000	-Phototype-setting and composing machines	15								0
84422000	-Machinery, apparatus and equipment for type-setting or composing by other processes, with or without founding device	15								0
84423000	-Other machinery, apparatus and equipment	15								0
84424000	-Parts of the foregoing machinery, apparatus or equipment	15								0
84425000	-Printing type, blocks, plates, cylinders and other printing components; blocks, plates, cylinders and lithographic stones, prepared for printing purposes (for example, planed, grained or polished)	15								0
8443	Printing machinery used for printing by means of the printing type, blocks, plates, cylinders and other printing components of heading 84.42; ink-jet printing machines, other than those of heading 84.71; machines for uses ancillary to printing.									
84431	-Offset printing machinery:									
84431100	--Reel fed	15								0

HS	Description	Bound rate at date of accession	Interim	Final Bound	Implementation	Present concession established	INR	Concession first incorporated in a GATT Schedule	Earlier INRs	ODCs
84431200	--Sheet fed, office type (sheet size not exceeding 22 x 36 cm)	15								0
84431900	--Other	15								0
84432	-Letterpress printing machinery, excluding flexographic printing:									
84432100	--Reel fed	15								0
84432900	--Other	15								0
84433000	-Flexographic printing machinery	5								0
84434000	-Gravure printing machinery	15								0
84435	-Other printing machinery:									
84435100	--Ink-jet printing machines	15								0
84435900	--Other	5								0
84436000	-Machines for uses ancillary to printing	15								0
84439000	-Parts	5								0
84440000	Machines for extruding, drawing, texturing or cutting man-made textile materials.	15								0
8445	Machines for preparing textile fibres; spinning, doubling or twisting machines and other machinery for producing textile yarns; textile reeling or winding (including weft-winding) machines and machines for preparing textile yarns for use on the machines of heading 84.46 or 84.47.									
84451	-Machines for preparing textile fibres:									
84451100	--Carding machines	15								0
84451200	--Combing machines	15								0
84451300	--Drawing or roving machines	15								0
84451900	--Other	5								0
84452000	-Textile spinning machines	15								0
84453000	-Textile doubling or twisting machines	15								0
84454000	-Textile winding (including weft-winding) or reeling machines	15								0
84459000	-Other	15								0
8446	Weaving machines (looms).									
84461000	-For weaving fabrics of a width not exceeding 30 cm	15								0
84462	-For weaving fabrics of a width exceeding 30 cm, shuttle type:									
84462100	--Power looms	15								0
84462900	--Other	15								0

HS	Description	Bound rate at date of accession	Interim	Final Bound	Implementation	Present concession established	INR	Concession first incorporated in a GATT Schedule	Earlier INRs	ODCs
84463000	-For weaving fabrics of a width exceeding 30 cm, shuttleless type	15								0
8447	Knitting machines, stitch-bonding machines and machines for making gimped yarn, tulle, lace, embroidery, trimmings, braid or net and machines for tufting.									
84471	-Circular knitting machines:									
84471100	--With cylinder diameter not exceeding 165 mm	15								0
84471200	--With cylinder diameter exceeding 165 mm	15								0
84472000	-Flat knitting machines; stitch-bonding machines	15								0
84479000	-Other	5								0
8448	Auxiliary machinery for use with machines of heading 84.44, 84.45, 84.46 or 84.47 (for example, dobbies, Jacquards, automatic stop motions, shuttle changing mechanisms); parts and accessories suitable for use solely or principally with the machines of this heading or of heading 84.44, 84.45, 84.46 or 84.47 (for example, spindles and spindle flyers, card clothing, combs, extruding nipples, shuttles, healds and heald-frames, hosiery needles).									
84481	-Auxiliary machinery for machines of heading 84.44, 84.45, 84.46 or 84.47:									
84481100	--Dobbies and Jacquards; card reducing, copying, punching or assembling machines for use therewith	15								0
84481900	--Other	15								0
84482000	-Parts and accessories of machines of heading 84.44 or of their auxiliary machinery	15								0
84483	-Parts and accessories of machines of heading 84.45 or of their auxiliary machinery:									
84483100	--Card clothing	15								0
84483200	--Of machines for preparing textile fibres, other than card clothing	15								0
84483300	--Spindles, spindle flyers, spinning rings and ring travellers	15								0

HS	Description	Bound rate at date of accession	Interim	Final Bound	Implementation	Present concession established	INR	Concession first incorporated in a GATT Schedule	Earlier INRs	ODCs
84483900	--Other	15								0
84484	-Parts and accessories of weaving machines (looms) or of their auxiliary machinery:									
84484100	--Shuttles	15								0
84484200	--Reeds for looms, healds and heald-frames	15								0
84484900	--Other	15								0
84485	-Parts and accessories of machines of heading 84.47 or of their auxiliary machinery:									
84485100	--Sinkers, needles and other articles used in forming stitches	15								0
84485900	--Other	15								0
84490000	Machinery for the manufacture or finishing of felt or nonwovens in the piece or in shapes, including machinery for making felt hats; blocks for making hats.	15								0
8450	Household or laundry-type washing machines, including machines which both wash and dry.									
84501	-Machines, each of a dry linen capacity not exceeding 10 kg:									
84501100	--Fully-automatic machines	5								0
84501200	--Other machines, with built-in centrifugal drier	5					TH			0
84501900	--Other	15								0
84502000	-Machines, each of a dry linen capacity exceeding 10 kg	15								0
84509000	-Parts	15								0
8451	Machinery (other than machines of heading 84.50) for washing, cleaning, wringing, drying, ironing, pressing (including fusing presses), bleaching, dyeing, dressing, finishing, coating or impregnating textile yarns, fabrics or made up textile articles and machines for applying the paste to the base fabric or other support used in the manufacture of floor coverings such as linoleum; machines for reeling, unreeling, folding, cutting or pinking textile fabrics.									
84511000	-Dry-cleaning machines	15								0

HS	Description	Bound rate at date of accession	Interim	Final Bound	Implementation	Present concession established	INR	Concession first incorporated in a GATT Schedule	Earlier INRs	ODCs
84512	-Drying machines:									
84512100	--Each of a dry linen capacity not exceeding 10 kg	5								0
84512900	--Other	15								0
84513000	-Ironing machines and presses (including fusing presses)	15								0
84514000	-Washing, bleaching or dyeing machines	15								0
84515000	-Machines for reeling, unreeling, folding, cutting or pinking textile fabrics	15								0
84518000	-Other machinery	5								0
84519000	-Parts	5								0
8452	Sewing machines, other than book-sewing machines of heading 84.40; furniture, bases and covers specially designed for sewing machines; sewing machine needles.									
84521000	-Sewing machines of the household type	15								0
84522	-Other sewing machines:									
84522100	--Automatic units	15								0
84522900	--Other	15								0
84523000	-Sewing machine needles	15								0
84524000	-Furniture, bases and covers for sewing machines and parts thereof	15								0
84529000	-Other parts of sewing machines	15								0
8453	Machinery for preparing, tanning or working hides, skins or leather or for making or repairing footwear or other articles of hides, skins or leather, other than sewing machines.									
84531000	-Machinery for preparing, tanning or working hides, skins or leather	15								0
84532000	-Machinery for making or repairing footwear	15								0
84538000	-Other machinery	15								0
84539000	-Parts	15								0
8454	Converters, ladles, ingot moulds and casting machines, of a kind used in metallurgy or in metal foundries.									
84541000	-Converters	10								0
84542000	-Ingot moulds and ladles	15								0
84543000	-Casting machines	15								0

HS	Description	Bound rate at date of accession	Interim	Final Bound	Implementation	Present concession established	INR	Concession first incorporated in a GATT Schedule	Earlier INRs	ODCs
84549000	-Parts	15								0
8455	Metal-rolling mills and rolls therefor.									
84551000	-Tube mills	15								0
84552	-Other rolling mills:									
84552100	--Hot or combination hot and cold	15								0
84552200	--Cold	15								0
84553000	-Rolls for rolling mills	15								0
84559000	-Other parts	15								0
8456	Machine-tools for working any material by removal of material, by laser or other light or photon beam, ultrasonic, electro-discharge, electro-chemical, electron beam, ionic-beam or plasma arc processes.									
84561000	-Operated by laser or other light or photon beam processes	5		0	2008		US			0
84562000	-Operated by ultrasonic processes	15								0
84563000	-Operated by electro-discharge processes	15								0
84569	-Other:									
84569100	--For dry-etching patterns on semiconductor materials	5		0	2008		US			0
84569900	--Other	5		0	2008		US			0
8457	Machining centres, unit construction machines (single station) and multi-station transfer machines, for working metal.									
84571000	-Machining centres	15								0
84572000	-Unit construction machines (single station)	15								0
84573000	-Multi-station transfer machines	15								0
8458	Lathes (including turning centres) for removing metal.									
84581	-Horizontal lathes:									
84581100	--Numerically controlled	15								0
84581900	--Other	15								0
84589	-Other lathes:									
84589100	--Numerically controlled	15								0
84589900	--Other	15								0

HS	Description	Bound rate at date of accession	Interim	Final Bound	Implementation	Present concession established	INR	Concession first incorporated in a GATT Schedule	Earlier INRs	ODCs
8459	Machine-tools (including way-type unit head machines) for drilling, boring, milling, threading or tapping by removing metal, other than lathes (including turning centres) of heading 84.58.									
84591000	-Way-type unit head machines	15								0
84592	-Other drilling machines:									
84592100	--Numerically controlled	5								0
84592900	--Other	15								0
84593	-Other boring-milling machines:									
84593100	--Numerically controlled	15								0
84593900	--Other	10								0
84594000	-Other boring machines	15								0
84595	-Milling machines, knee-type:									
84595100	--Numerically controlled	15								0
84595900	--Other	15								0
84596	-Other milling machines:									
84596100	--Numerically controlled	15								0
84596900	--Other	15								0
84597000	-Other threading or tapping machines	15								0
8460	Machine-tools for deburring, sharpening, grinding, honing, lapping, polishing or otherwise finishing metal or cermets by means of grinding stones, abrasives or polishing products, other than gear cutting, gear grinding or gear finishing machines of heading 84.61.									
84601	-Flat-surface grinding machines, in which the positioning in any one axis can be set up to an accuracy of at least 0.01 mm:									
84601100	--Numerically controlled	15								0
84601900	--Other	10								0
84602	-Other grinding machines, in which the positioning in any one axis can be set up to an accuracy of at least 0.01 mm:									
84602100	--Numerically controlled	15								0
84602900	--Other	15								0
84603	-Sharpening (tool or cutter grinding) machines:									
84603100	--Numerically controlled	15								0
84603900	--Other	15								0

HS	Description	Bound rate at date of accession	Interim	Final Bound	Implementation	Present concession established	INR	Concession first incorporated in a GATT Schedule	Earlier INRs	ODCs
84604000	-Honing or lapping machines	15								0
84609000	-Other	15								0
8461	Machine-tools for planing, shaping, slotting, broaching, gear cutting, gear grinding or gear finishing, sawing, cutting-off and other machine-tools working by removing metal or cermets, not elsewhere specified or included.									
84612000	-Shaping or slotting machines	10								0
84613000	-Broaching machines	15								0
84614000	-Gear cutting, gear grinding or gear finishing machines	15								0
84615000	-Sawing or cutting-off machines	15								0
84619000	-Other	10								0
8462	Machine-tools (including presses) for working metal by forging, hammering or die-stamping; machine-tools (including presses) for working metal by bending, folding, straightening, flattening, shearing, punching or notching; presses for working metal or metal carbides, not specified above.									
84621000	-Forging or die-stamping machines (including presses) and hammers	5								0
84622	-Bending, folding, straightening or flattening machines (including presses):									
84622100	--Numerically controlled	15								0
84622900	--Other	15								0
84623	-Shearing machines (including presses), other than combined punching and shearing machines:									
84623100	--Numerically controlled	15								0
84623900	--Other	15								0
84624	-Punching or notching machines (including presses), including combined punching and shearing machines:									
84624100	--Numerically controlled	15								0
84624900	--Other	15								0
84629	-Other:									
84629100	--Hydraulic presses	15								0
84629900	--Other	15								0
8463	Other machine-tools for working metal or cermets, without removing material.									

HS	Description	Bound rate at date of accession	Interim	Final Bound	Implementation	Present concession established	INR	Concession first incorporated in a GATT Schedule	Earlier INRs	ODCs
84631000	-Draw-benches for bars, tubes, profiles, wire or the like	15								0
84632000	-Thread rolling machines	15								0
84633000	-Machines for working wire	15								0
84639000	-Other	15								0
8464	Machine-tools for working stone, ceramics, concrete, asbestos-cement or like mineral materials or for cold working glass.									
84641000	-Sawing machines	5		0	2008		US			0
84642000	-Grinding or polishing machines	5		0	2008		US			0
84649000	-Other	5		0	2008		US			0
8465	Machine-tools (including machines for nailing, stapling, glueing or otherwise assembling) for working wood, cork, bone, hard rubber, hard plastics or similar hard materials.									
84651000	-Machines which can carry out different types of machining operations without tool change between such operations	15								0
84659	-Other:									
84659100	--Sawing machines	15								0
84659200	--Planing, milling or moulding (by cutting) machines	15								0
84659300	--Grinding, sanding or polishing machines	15								0
84659400	--Bending or assembling machines	15								0
84659500	--Drilling or morticing machines	15								0
84659600	--Splitting, slicing or paring machines	15								0
84659900	--Other	15								0
8466	Parts and accessories suitable for use solely or principally with the machines of headings 84.56 to 84.65, including work or tool holders, self-opening dieheads, dividing heads and other special attachments for machine-tools; tool holders for any type of tool for working in the hand.									
84661000	-Tool holders and self-opening dieheads	15					KG			0
84662000	-Work holders	15					KG			0
84663000	-Dividing heads and other special attachments for machine-tools	15								0
84669	-Other:									
84669100	--For machines of heading 84.64	5		0	2008		US			0

HS	Description	Bound rate at date of accession	Interim	Final Bound	Implementation	Present concession established	INR	Concession first incorporated in a GATT Schedule	Earlier INRs	ODCs
84669200	--For machines of heading 84.65	15								0
84669300	--For machines of headings 84.56 to 84.61	5		0	2008		US			0
84669400	--For machines of heading 84.62 or 84.63	7								0
8467	Tools for working in the hand, pneumatic, hydraulic or with self-contained electric or non-electric motor.									
84671	-Pneumatic:									
84671100	--Rotary type (including combined rotary-percussion)	15								0
846719	--Other									
84671910	---Drilling, lathing and threading tools, hand, pneumatic	15								0
84671920	---Screw drivers and bolt equipment, hand, pneumatic	15								0
84671930	---Surface grinders, polishers, etc., hand, pneumatic	15								0
84671940	---Saws and cutters, hand, pneumatic	15								0
84671950	---Rust scaling hammers and the like, hand, pneumatic	15								0
84671960	---Jaw riveting machines, hand, pneumatic	15								0
84671970	---Plate-shearing machines, hand, pneumatic	15								0
84671980	---Construction tamping, paving machines, hand, pneumatic	15								0
84671990	---Other hand, pneumatic tools	15								0
84672	-With self-contained electric motor:									
84672100	--Drills of all kinds	5								0
84672200	--Saws	15								0
84672900	--Other	15								0
84678	-Other tools:									
84678100	--Chain saws	15								0
84678900	--Other	15								0
84679	-Parts:									
84679100	--Of chain saws	15								0
84679200	--Of pneumatic tools	15								0
84679900	--Other	15								0

HS	Description	Bound rate at date of accession	Interim	Final Bound	Implementation	Present concession established	INR	Concession first incorporated in a GATT Schedule	Earlier INRs	ODCs
8468	Machinery and apparatus for soldering, brazing or welding, whether or not capable of cutting, other than those of heading 85.15; gas-operated surface tempering machines and appliances.									
84681000	-Hand-held blow pipes	15								0
84682000	-Other gas-operated machinery and apparatus	15								0
84688000	-Other machinery and apparatus	15								0
84689000	-Parts	15								0
8469	Typewriters other than printers of heading 84.71; word-processing machines.									
84691	-Automatic typewriters and word-processing machines:									
84691100	--Word-processing machines	5		0	2008		US			0
84691200	--Automatic typewriters	15								0
84692000	-Other typewriters, electric	15								0
84693000	-Other typewriters, non-electric	15								0
8470	Calculating machines and pocket-size data recording, reproducing and displaying machines with calculating functions; accounting machines, postage-franking machines, ticket-issuing machines and similar machines, incorporating a calculating device; cash registers.									
84701000	-Electronic calculators capable of operation without an external source of electric power and pocket-size data recording, reproducing and displaying machines with calculating functions	5		0	2008		US			0
84702	-Other digital automatic data processing machines:									
84702100	--Incorporating a printing device	5		0	2008		US			0
84702900	--Other	5		0	2008		US			0
84703000	-Other calculating machines	5		0	2008		US			0
84704000	-Accounting machines	5		0	2008		US			0
84705000	-Cash registers	5		0	2008		US			0
847090	-Other									
84709010	---Stamp franking machines	5		0	2008		US			0
84709020	---Ticket-issuing machines	5		0	2008		US			0
84709090	---Other postage and similar machines	5		0	2008		US			0

HS	Description	Bound rate at date of accession	Interim	Final Bound	Implementation	Present concession established	INR	Concession first incorporated in a GATT Schedule	Earlier INRs	ODCs
8471	Automatic data processing machines and units thereof; magnetic or optical readers, machines for transcribing data onto data media in coded form and machines for processing such data, not elsewhere specified or included.									
84711000	-Analogue or hybrid automatic data processing machines	5		0	2008		US			0
ex84711000	--For use in civil aircraft	0					US			0
84713000	-Portable digital automatic data processing machines, weighing not more than 10 kg, consisting of at least a central processing unit, a keyboard and a display	5		0	2008		US			0
ex84713000	--For use in civil aircraft	0					US			0
84714	-Other automatic data processing machines:									
84714100	--Comprising in the same housing at least a central processing unit and an input and output unit, whether or not combined	5		0	2008		US			0
ex84714100	---For use in civil aircraft	0					US			0
84714900	--Other, presented in the form of systems	5		0	2008		US			0
ex84714900	---For use in civil aircraft	0					US			0
84715000	-Digital processing units other than those of sub-heading 8471.41 or 8471.49, whether or not containing in the same housing one or two of the following types of unit: storage units, input units, output units	5		0	2008		US			0
ex84715000	--For use in civil aircraft	0					US			0
84716000	-Input or output units, whether or not containing storage units in the same housing	5		0	2008		US			0
ex84716000	--For use in civil aircraft	0					US			0
84717000	-Storage units	5		0	2008		US			0
ex84717000	--For use in civil aircraft	0					US			0
84718000	-Other units of automatic data processing machines	5		0	2008		US			0
84719000	-Other	5		0	2008		US			0

HS	Description	Bound rate at date of accession	Interim	Final Bound	Implementation	Present concession established	INR	Concession first incorporated in a GATT Schedule	Earlier INRs	ODCs
8472	Other office machines (for example, hectograph or stencil duplicating machines, addressing machines, automatic banknote dispensers, coin-sorting machines, coin-counting or wrapping machines, pencil-sharpening machines, perforating or stapling machines).									
84721000	-Duplicating machines	15								0
84722000	-Addressing machines and address plate embossing machines	15								0
84723000	-Machines for sorting or folding mail or for inserting mail in envelopes or bands, machines for opening, closing or sealing mail and machines for affixing or cancelling postage stamps	15								0
847290	-Other									
84729010	---Other ticket-issuing machines not elsewhere	5		0	2008		US			0
84729020	---Coin-sorting, counting and wrapping machines	5		0	2008		US			0
84729030	---Pencil sharpening machines	5		0	2008		US			0
84729040	---Paper-perforating machines	5		0	2008		US			0
84729050	---Small machines for stapling the papers	5		0	2008		US			0
84729060	---Small machines for shredding	5		0	2008		US			0
84729070	---Cash registers without calculating devices	15								0
84729090	---Other office machines	5		0	2008		US			0
8473	Parts and accessories (other than covers, carrying cases and the like) suitable for use solely or principally with machines of headings 84.69 to 84.72.									
84731000	-Parts and accessories of the machines of heading 84.69	15					US			0

HS	Description	Bound rate at date of accession	Interim	Final Bound	Implementation	Present concession established	INR	Concession first incorporated in a GATT Schedule	Earlier INRs	ODCs
ex84731000	--Printed Circuit Assemblies for products falling within this agreement, including such assemblies for external connections such as cards that conform to the PCMCIA standard. Such printed circuit assemblies consist of one or more printed circuits of heading 8534 with one or more active elements assembled thereon, with or without passive elements "Active elements" means diodes, transistors, and similar semiconductor devices, whether or not photosensitive, of heading 8541, and integrated circuits and micro assemblies of heading 8542.	15		0	2008		US			0
84732	-Parts and accessories of the machines of heading 84.70:									
84732100	--Of the electronic calculating machines of subheading 8470.10, 8470.21 or 8470.29	5		0	2008		US			0
84732900	--Other	5		0	2008		US			0
84733000	-Parts and accessories of the machines of heading 84.71	5		0	2008		US			0
84734000	-Parts and accessories of the machines of heading 84.72	5								0
ex84734000	--Printed Circuit Assemblies for products falling within this agreement, including such assemblies for external connections such as cards that conform to the PCMCIA standard. Such printed circuit assemblies consist of one or more printed circuits of heading 8534 with one or more active elements assembled thereon, with or without passive elements "Active elements" means diodes, transistors, and similar semiconductor devices, whether or not photosensitive, of heading 8541, and integrated circuits and micro assemblies of heading 8542.	5		0	2008					0
84735000	-Parts and accessories equally suitable for use with machines of two or more of the headings 84.69 to 84.72	5		0	2008		US			0

HS	Description	Bound rate at date of accession	Interim	Final Bound	Implementation	Present concession established	INR	Concession first incorporated in a GATT Schedule	Earlier INRs	ODCs
8474	Machinery for sorting, screening, separating, washing, crushing, grinding, mixing or kneading earth, stone, ores or other mineral substances, in solid (including powder or paste) form; machinery for agglomerating, shaping or moulding solid mineral fuels, ceramic paste, unhardened cements, plastering materials or other mineral products in powder or paste form; machines for forming foundry moulds of sand.									
84741000	-Sorting, screening, separating or washing machines	8								0
84742000	-Crushing or grinding machines	8								0
84743	-Mixing or kneading machines:									
84743100	--Concrete or mortar mixers	8								0
84743200	--Machines for mixing mineral substances with bitumen	8								0
84743900	--Other	8								0
84748000	-Other machinery	8								0
84749000	-Parts	5								0
8475	Machines for assembling electric or electronic lamps, tubes or valves or flashbulbs, in glass envelopes; machines for manufacturing or hot working glass or glassware.									
84751000	-Machines for assembling electric or electronic lamps, tubes or valves or flashbulbs, in glass envelopes	15								0
84752	-Machines for manufacturing or hot working glass or glassware:									
84752100	--Machines for making optical fibres and preforms thereof	15								0
84752900	--Other	15								0
84759000	-Parts	15								0
8476	Automatic goods-vending machines (for example, postage stamp, cigarette, food or beverage machines), including money-changing machines.									
84762	-Automatic beverage-vending machines:									
84762100	--Incorporating heating or refrigerating devices	15								0
84762900	--Other	15								0
84768	-Other machines:									

HS	Description	Bound rate at date of accession	Interim	Final Bound	Implementation	Present concession established	INR	Concession first incorporated in a GATT Schedule	Earlier INRs	ODCs
84768100	--Incorporating heating or refrigerating devices	15								0
84768900	--Other	15								0
84769000	-Parts	15								0
8477	Machinery for working rubber or plastics or for the manufacture of products from these materials, not specified or included elsewhere in this Chapter.									
84771000	-Injection-moulding machines	5		0	2008		CA,US			0
84772000	-Extruders	15								0
84773000	-Blow moulding machines	15								0
84774000	-Vacuum moulding machines and other thermoforming machines	15								0
84775	-Other machinery for moulding or otherwise forming:									
84775100	--For moulding or retreading pneumatic tyres or for moulding or otherwise forming inner tubes	15								0
84775900	--Other	15								0
84778000	-Other machinery	5								0
84779000	-Parts	5		0	2008		US			0
8478	Machinery for preparing or making up tobacco, not specified or included elsewhere in this Chapter.									
84781000	-Machinery	15								0
84789000	-Parts	15								0
8479	Machines and mechanical appliances having individual functions, not specified or included elsewhere in this Chapter.									
847910	-Machinery for public works, building or the like									
84791010	---Levelling machinery used for constructing roads	8					US			0
84791020	---Machinery for bedding gravel or asphalt on roads	8					US			0
84791030	---Appliances for marking traffic signs on roads	8					US			0
84791090	---Other machinery for public roads or works	8					US			0
84792000	-Machinery for the extraction or preparation of animal or fixed vegetable fats or oils	15								0

HS	Description	Bound rate at date of accession	Interim	Final Bound	Implementation	Present concession established	INR	Concession first incorporated in a GATT Schedule	Earlier INRs	ODCs
84793000	-Presses for the manufacture of particle board or fibre building board of wood or other ligneous materials and other machinery for treating wood or cork	15								0
84794000	-Rope or cable-making machines	15								0
84795000	-Industrial robots, not elsewhere specified or included	5		0	2008		US			0
84796000	-Evaporative air coolers	15								0
84798	-Other machines and mechanical appliances:									
84798100	--For treating metal, including electric wire coil-winders	5								0
84798200	--Mixing, kneading, crushing, grinding, screening, sifting, homogenising, emulsifying or stirring machines	15								0
847989	--Other									
84798910	---Machines and equipment for making soaps	5		0	2008					0
84798920	---Basketware and wickerwork machines	5		0	2008		US			0
ex84798920	----For use in civil aircraft	0					US			0
84798930	---Machines and equipment for making brushes	5		0	2008		US			0
ex84798930	----For use in civil aircraft	0					US			0
84798940	---Air-moistening and air-drying equipment	5		0	2008		US			0
ex84798940	----For use in civil aircraft	0					US			0
84798950	---Automatic grease pumping equipment for machinery	5		0	2008		US			0
ex84798950	----For use in civil aircraft	0					US			0
84798960	---Match dipping machines	5		0	2008		US			0
ex84798960	----For use in civil aircraft	0					US			0
84798970	---Electrode welding machines	5		0	2008		US			0
ex84798970	----For use in civil aircraft	0					US			0
84798980	---Machines for tightening screws, nuts, bolts, etc.	5		0	2008		US			0
ex84798980	----For use in civil aircraft	0					US			0
8479899	---Other:									
84798991	----Machines for maintaining the pipe lines	5		0	2008		US			0
ex84798991	-----For use in civil aircraft	0					US			0
84798992	----Machines for stuffing and upholstering mattresses	5		0	2008		US			0
ex84798992	-----For use in civil aircraft	0					US			0

HS	Description	Bound rate at date of accession	Interim	Final Bound	Implementation	Present concession established	INR	Concession first incorporated in a GATT Schedule	Earlier INRs	ODCs
84798993	----Machines for fixing grinding materials on supports	5		0	2008		US			0
ex84798993	-----For use in civil aircraft	0					US			0
84798994	----Diving bells and suits, of metals	5		0	2008		US			0
ex84798994	-----For use in civil aircraft	0					US			0
84798999	----Other machinery having only individual function	5		0	2008		US			0
ex84798999	-----For use in civil aircraft	0					US			0
84799000	-Parts	5		0	2008		US			0
ex84799000	--For use in civil aircraft	0					US			0
8480	Moulding boxes for metal foundry; mould bases; moulding patterns; moulds for metal (other than ingot moulds), metal carbides, glass, mineral materials, rubber or plastics.									
84801000	-Moulding boxes for metal foundry	15								0
84802000	-Mould bases	15								0
848030	-Moulding patterns									
84803010	---Molding patterns of wood or iron	15								0
84803090	---Molding patterns of other materials	15								0
84804	-Moulds for metal or metal carbides:									
84804100	--Injection or compression types	15								0
84804900	--Other	15								0
84805000	-Moulds for glass	15								0
84806000	-Moulds for mineral materials	15								0
84807	-Moulds for rubber or plastics:									
84807100	--Injection or compression types	5		0	2008		US			0
84807900	--Other	15		13	2010					0
8481	Taps, cocks, valves and similar appliances for pipes, boiler shells, tanks, vats or the like, including pressure-reducing valves and thermostatically controlled valves.									
84811000	-Pressure-reducing valves	10								0
84812000	-Valves for oleohydraulic or pneumatic transmissions	10								0
84813000	-Check (nonreturn) valves	10								0
84814000	-Safety or relief valves	10								0
848180	-Other appliances									
84818010	---Valves of tubes for wheels	5								0
84818020	---Valves for draining the radiator	5					IN			0
84818030	---Valves for gas cylinders	5								0

HS	Description	Bound rate at date of accession	Interim	Final Bound	Implementation	Present concession established	INR	Concession first incorporated in a GATT Schedule	Earlier INRs	ODCs
84818040	---Float operated valves	5								0
84818050	---Fire-extinguishing nozzles and valves	5								0
84818060	---Nozzles and valves for cultivation and irrigation hoses	5								0
84818070	---Valves for draining the water from bathrooms and sinks	5								0
84818080	---Caps for spraying cans filled with insecticides, etc.	5								0
84818090	---Other valves, cocks, etc.	5					IN			0
84819000	-Parts	5								0
8482	Ball or roller bearings.									
84821000	-Ball bearings	15								0
84822000	-Tapered roller bearings, including cone and tapered roller assemblies	15		12	2008					0
84823000	-Spherical roller bearings	15								0
84824000	-Needle roller bearings	15								0
84825000	-Other cylindrical roller bearings	15								0
84828000	-Other, including combined ball/roller bearings	15								0
84829	-Parts:									
84829100	--Balls, needles and rollers	15								0
84829900	--Other	15								0
8483	Transmission shafts (including cam shafts and crank shafts) and cranks; bearing housings and plain shaft bearings; gears and gearing; ball or roller screws; gear boxes and other speed changers, including torque converters; flywheels and pulleys, including pulley blocks; clutches and shaft couplings (including universal joints).									
ex84831000	--For use in civil aircraft	0					US			0
84831000	-Transmission shafts (including cam shafts and crank shafts) and cranks	15		12	2008					0
84832000	-Bearing housings, incorporating ball or roller bearings	15								0
84833000	-Bearing housings, not incorporating ball or roller bearings; plain shaft bearings	15								0
ex84833000	--For use in civil aircraft	0					US			0
ex84834000	--For use in civil aircraft	0					US			0

HS	Description	Bound rate at date of accession	Interim	Final Bound	Implementation	Present concession established	INR	Concession first incorporated in a GATT Schedule	Earlier INRs	ODCs
84834000	-Gears and gearing, other than toothed wheels, chain sprockets and other transmission elements presented separately; ball or roller screws; gear boxes and other speed changers, including torque converters	10								0
84835000	-Flywheels and pulleys, including pulley blocks	15								0
ex84835000	--For use in civil aircraft	0					US			0
ex84836000	--For use in civil aircraft	0					US			0
84836000	-Clutches and shaft couplings (including universal joints)	15		12	2008					0
84839000	-Toothed wheels, chain sprockets and other transmission elements presented separately; parts	15								0
ex84839000	--For use in civil aircraft	0					US			0
8484	Gaskets and similar joints of metal sheeting combined with other material or of two or more layers of metal; sets or assortments of gaskets and similar joints, dissimilar in composition, put up in pouches, envelopes or similar packings; mechanical seals.									
ex84841000	--For use in civil aircraft	0					US			0
84841000	-Gaskets and similar joints of metal sheeting combined with other material or of two or more layers of metal	15								0
84842000	-Mechanical seals	15								0
ex84849000	--For use in civil aircraft	0					US			0
84849000	-Other	15		12	2008					0
8485	Machinery parts, not containing electrical connectors, insulators, coils, contacts or other electrical features, not specified or included elsewhere in this Chapter.									
84851000	-Ships' or boats' propellers and blades therefor	15								0
84859000	-Other	5								0
8501	Electric motors and generators (excluding generating sets).									
85011000	-Motors of an output not exceeding 37.5 W	5								0
ex85012000	--For use in civil aircraft	0					US			0

HS	Description	Bound rate at date of accession	Interim	Final Bound	Implementation	Present concession established	INR	Concession first incorporated in a GATT Schedule	Earlier INRs	ODCs
85012000	-Universal AC/DC motors of an output exceeding 37.5 W	15								0
85013	-Other DC motors; DC generators:									
ex85013100	---For use in civil aircraft	0					US			0
85013100	--Of an output not exceeding 750 W	15								0
85013200	--Of an output exceeding 750 W but not exceeding 75 kW	15					KG			0
ex85013200	---For use in civil aircraft	0					KG,US			0
85013300	--Of an output exceeding 75 kW but not exceeding 375 kW	15					KG			0
ex85013300	---For use in civil aircraft	0					KG,US			0
85013400	--Of an output exceeding 375 kW	15					KG			0
ex85013400	---For use in civil aircraft	0					KG,US			0
85014000	-Other AC motors, single-phase	10					IN,KG			0
ex85014000	--For use in civil aircraft	0					IN,KG,US			0
85015	-Other AC motors, multi-phase:									
85015100	--Of an output not exceeding 750 W	15					KG			0
ex85015100	---For use in civil aircraft	0					KG,US			0
ex85015200	---For use in civil aircraft	0					KG,US			0
85015200	--Of an output exceeding 750 W but not exceeding 75 kW	15					KG			0
ex85015300	---For use in civil aircraft	0					KG,US			0
85015300	--Of an output exceeding 75 kW	15					KG			0
85016	-AC generators (alternators):									
ex85016100	---For use in civil aircraft	0					US			0
85016100	--Of an output not exceeding 75 kVA	15								0
ex85016200	---For use in civil aircraft	0					US			0
85016200	--Of an output exceeding 75 kVA but not exceeding 375 kVA	15								0
85016300	--Of an output exceeding 375 kVA but not exceeding 750 kVA	15								0
ex85016300	---For use in civil aircraft	0					US			0
85016400	--Of an output exceeding 750 kVA	5								0
8502	Electric generating sets and rotary converters.									
85021	-Generating sets with compression-ignition internal combustion piston engines (diesel or semi-diesel engines):									
ex85021100	---For use in civil aircraft	0					US			0
85021100	--Of an output not exceeding 75 kVA	15								0
ex85021200	---For use in civil aircraft	0					US			0

HS	Description	Bound rate at date of accession	Interim	Final Bound	Implementation	Present concession established	INR	Concession first incorporated in a GATT Schedule	Earlier INRs	ODCs
85021200	--Of an output exceeding 75 kVA but not exceeding 375 kVA	15								0
ex85021300	---For use in civil aircraft	0					US			0
85021300	--Of an output exceeding 375 kVA	15								0
85022000	-Generating sets with spark-ignition internal combustion piston engines	15								0
ex85022000	--For use in civil aircraft	0					US			0
85023	-Other generating sets:									
ex85023100	---For use in civil aircraft	0					US			0
85023100	--Wind-powered	15								0
85023900	--Other	15					KG			0
ex85023900	---For use in civil aircraft	0					KG,US			0
ex85024000	--For use in civil aircraft	0					US			0
85024000	-Electric rotary converters	15								0
85030000	Parts suitable for use solely or principally with the machines of heading 85.01 or 85.02.	5					AU,CH			0
8504	Electrical transformers, static converters (for example, rectifiers) and inductors.									
ex85041000	--For use in civil aircraft	0					US			0
85041000	-Ballasts for discharge lamps or tubes	10								0
85042	-Liquid dielectric transformers:									
85042100	--Having a power handling capacity not exceeding 650 kVA	15					AU			0
85042200	--Having a power handling capacity exceeding 650 kVA but not exceeding 10,000 kVA	15								0
85042300	--Having a power handling capacity exceeding 10,000 kVA	15								0
85043	-Other transformers:									
85043100	--Having a power handling capacity not exceeding 1 kVA	15								0
ex85043100	---For use in civil aircraft	0					US			0
ex85043200	---For use in civil aircraft	0					US			0
85043200	--Having a power handling capacity exceeding 1 kVA but not exceeding 16 kVA	15								0
85043300	--Having a power handling capacity exceeding 16 kVA but not exceeding 500 kVA	15								0
ex85043300	---For use in civil aircraft	0					US			0

HS	Description	Bound rate at date of accession	Interim	Final Bound	Implementation	Present concession established	INR	Concession first incorporated in a GATT Schedule	Earlier INRs	ODCs
85043400	--Having a power handling capacity exceeding 500 kVA	15								0
85044000	-Static converters	5		0	2008		KG,US			0
ex85044000	--For use in civil aircraft	0					KG,US			0
85045000	-Other inductors	5		0	2008		US			0
ex85045000	--For use in civil aircraft	0					US			0
85049000	-Parts	5					US			0
ex85049000	--Printed Circuit Assemblies for products falling within this agreement, including such assemblies for external connections such as cards that conform to the PCMCIA standard. Such printed circuit assemblies consist of one or more printed circuits of heading 8534 with one or more active elements assembled thereon, with or without passive elements "Active elements" means diodes, transistors, and similar semiconductor devices, whether or not photosensitive, of heading 8541, and integrated circuits and micro assemblies of heading 8542.	5		0	2008		US			0
8505	Electro-magnets; permanent magnets and articles intended to become permanent magnets after magnetisation; electro-magnetic or permanent magnet chucks, clamps and similar holding devices; electro-magnetic couplings, clutches and brakes; electro-magnetic lifting heads.									
85051	-Permanent magnets and articles intended to become permanent magnets after magnetisation:									
85051100	--Of metal	15								0
85051900	--Other	15								0
85052000	-Electro-magnetic couplings, clutches and brakes	15								0
85053000	-Electro-magnetic lifting heads	15								0
85059000	-Other, including parts	15								0
8506	Primary cells and primary batteries.									
850610	-Manganese dioxide									
85061010	---Dry batteries, 1.5 volt and over, portable	10								0
85061090	---Other manganese dioxide batteries	10								0
850630	-Mercuric oxide									

HS	Description	Bound rate at date of accession	Interim	Final Bound	Implementation	Present concession established	INR	Concession first incorporated in a GATT Schedule	Earlier INRs	ODCs
85063010	---Mercuric oxide dry batteries, 1.5 volt and over, portable	15								0
85063090	---Other mercuric oxide batteries	15								0
850640	-Silver oxide									
85064010	---Silver oxide dry batteries, 1.5 volt and over, portable	15								0
85064090	---Other	15								0
850650	-Lithium									
85065010	---Lithium dry batteries, 1.5 volt and over, portable	15								0
85065090	---Other lithium dry batteries	15								0
850660	-Air-zinc									
85066010	---Air zinc dry batteries, 1.5 volt and over, portable	15								0
85066090	---Other air zinc batteries	15								0
850680	-Other primary cells and primary batteries									
85068010	---Dry batteries, 1.5 volt and over, portable	5								0
85068090	---Other electric cells and batteries	15								0
85069000	-Parts	15								0
8507	Electric accumulators, including separators therefor, whether or not rectangular (including square).									
ex85071000	--For use in civil aircraft	0					US			0
85071000	-Lead-acid, of a kind used for starting piston engines	15								0
ex85072000	--For use in civil aircraft	0					US			0
85072000	-Other lead-acid accumulators	15								0
ex85073000	--For use in civil aircraft	0					US			0
85073000	-Nickel-cadmium	15								0
85074000	-Nickel-iron	15								0
ex85074000	--For use in civil aircraft	0					US			0
85078000	-Other accumulators	15								0
ex85078000	--For use in civil aircraft	0					US			0
ex85079000	--For use in civil aircraft	0					US			0
85079000	-Parts	15								0
8509	Electro-mechanical domestic appliances, with self-contained electric motor.									
85091000	-Vacuum cleaners, including dry and wet vacuum cleaners	5								0

HS	Description	Bound rate at date of accession	Interim	Final Bound	Implementation	Present concession established	INR	Concession first incorporated in a GATT Schedule	Earlier INRs	ODCs
85092000	-Floor polishers	15								0
85093000	-Kitchen waste disposers	15								0
85094000	-Food grinders and mixers; fruit or vegetable juice extractors	10								0
850980	-Other appliances									
85098010	---Potato peeling and cutting machines	15					AU			0
85098020	---Different machines for cutting meats, cheese, etc.	15					AU			0
85098030	---Machines for grinding or polishing table knives	15					AU			0
85098040	---Electric tooth brushes	15					AU			0
85098090	---Other domestic appliances with electric motor	15					AU			0
85099000	-Parts	5								0
8510	Shavers, hair clippers and hair-removing appliances, with self-contained electric motor.									
85101000	-Shavers	15								0
85102000	-Hair clippers	15								0
85103000	-Hair-removing appliances	15								0
85109000	-Parts	15								0
8511	Electrical ignition or starting equipment of a kind used for spark-ignition or compression-ignition internal combustion engines (for example, ignition magnetos, magneto-dynamos, ignition coils, sparking plugs and glow plugs, starter motors); generators (for example, dynamos, alternators) and cut-outs of a kind used in conjunction with such engines.									
ex85111000	--For use in civil aircraft	0					MX,US			0
85111000	-Sparking plugs	15		12	2008		MX			0
ex85112000	--For use in civil aircraft	0					US			0
85112000	-Ignition magnetos; magneto-dynamos; magnetic flywheels	15								0
85113000	-Distributors; ignition coils	15								0
ex85113000	--For use in civil aircraft	0					US			0
85114000	-Starter motors and dual purpose starter-generators	15								0
ex85114000	--For use in civil aircraft	0					US			0
85115000	-Other generators	15								0
ex85115000	--For use in civil aircraft	0					US			0

HS	Description	Bound rate at date of accession	Interim	Final Bound	Implementation	Present concession established	INR	Concession first incorporated in a GATT Schedule	Earlier INRs	ODCs
85118000	-Other equipment	15								0
ex85118000	--For use in civil aircraft	0					US			0
85119000	-Parts	5								0
8512	Electrical lighting or signalling equipment (excluding articles of heading 85.39), windscreen wipers, defrosters and demisters, of a kind used for cycles or motor vehicles.									
85121000	-Lighting or visual signalling equipment of a kind used on bicycles	15								0
85122000	-Other lighting or visual signalling equipment	5								0
85123000	-Sound signalling equipment	5								0
85124000	-Windscreen wipers, defrosters and demisters	15								0
85129000	-Parts	5								0
8513	Portable electric lamps designed to function by their own source of energy (for example, dry batteries, accumulators, magnetos), other than lighting equipment of heading 85.12.									
85131000	-Lamps	10								0
85139000	-Parts	15								0
8514	Industrial or laboratory electric furnaces and ovens (including those functioning by induction or dielectric loss); other industrial or laboratory equipment for the heat treatment of materials by induction or dielectric loss.									
85141000	-Resistance heated furnaces and ovens	5		0	2008		US			0
85142000	-Furnaces and ovens functioning by induction or dielectric loss	5		0	2008		US			0
85143000	-Other furnaces and ovens	5		0	2008		US			0
85144000	-Other equipment for the heat treatment of materials by induction or dielectric loss	15								0
85149000	-Parts	5		0	2008		US			0

HS	Description	Bound rate at date of accession	Interim	Final Bound	Implementation	Present concession established	INR	Concession first incorporated in a GATT Schedule	Earlier INRs	ODCs
8515	Electric (including electrically heated gas), laser or other light or photon beam, ultrasonic, electron beam, magnetic pulse or plasma arc soldering, brazing or welding machines and apparatus, whether or not capable of cutting; electric machines and apparatus for hot spraying of metals or cermets.									
85151	-Brazing or soldering machines and apparatus:									
85151100	--Soldering irons and guns	15								0
85151900	--Other	5								0
85152	-Machines and apparatus for resistance welding of metal:									
85152100	--Fully or partly automatic	15								0
85152900	--Other	15								0
85153	-Machines and apparatus for arc (including plasma arc) welding of metals:									
85153100	--Fully or partly automatic	5								0
85153900	--Other	5								0
85158000	-Other machines and apparatus	15								0
85159000	-Parts	15								0
8516	Electric instantaneous or storage water heaters and immersion heaters; electric space heating apparatus and soil heating apparatus; electro-thermic hair-dressing apparatus (for example, hair dryers, hair curlers, curling tong heaters) and hand dryers; electric smoothing irons; other electro-thermic appliances of a kind used for domestic purposes; electric heating resistors, other than those of heading 85.45.									
85161000	-Electric instantaneous or storage water heaters and immersion heaters	15								0
85162	-Electric space heating apparatus and electric soil heating apparatus:									
85162100	--Storage heating radiators	15								0
851629	--Other									
85162910	---Electric household heating apparatus	15								0
85162990	---Other electric space and soil heating apparatus	15								0

HS	Description	Bound rate at date of accession	Interim	Final Bound	Implementation	Present concession established	INR	Concession first incorporated in a GATT Schedule	Earlier INRs	ODCs
85163	-Electro-thermic hair-dressing or hand-drying apparatus:									
85163100	--Hair dryers	15								0
85163200	--Other hair-dressing apparatus	15								0
85163300	--Hand-drying apparatus	15								0
85164000	-Electric smoothing irons	15								0
85165000	-Microwave ovens	10								0
85166000	-Other ovens; cookers, cooking plates, boiling rings; grillers and roasters	7								0
85167	-Other electro-thermic appliances:									
85167100	--Coffee or tea makers	15								0
85167200	--Toasters	15								0
851679	--Other									
85167910	---Coffee roasters or popcorn makers	15								0
85167920	---Electric incense burners	15								0
85167990	---Other electro-thermic appliances	15								0
85168000	-Electric heating resistors	15								0
ex85168000	--For use in civil aircraft	0					US			0
85169000	-Parts	5								0
8517	Electrical apparatus for line telephony or line telegraphy, including line telephone sets with cordless handsets and telecommunication apparatus for carrier-current line systems or for digital line systems; videophones.									
85171	-Telephone sets; videophones:									
85171100	--Line telephone sets with cordless handsets	5		0	2008		US			0
851719	--Other									
85171910	---Wire telephone sets with hand sets	5		0	2008		US			0
85171990	---Other telephone sets	5		0	2008		US			0
85172	-Facsimile machines and teleprinters:									
85172100	--Facsimile machines	5		0	2008		US			0
851722	--Teleprinters									
85172210	---Telex machines	5		0	2008		US			0
85172290	---Other teleprinters and facsimile	5		0	2008		US			0
85173000	-Telephonic or telegraphic switching apparatus	5		0	2008		US			0
85175000	-Other apparatus, for carrier-current line systems or for digital line systems	5		0	2008		US			0
85178000	-Other apparatus	5		0	2008		US			0
851790	-Parts									

HS	Description	Bound rate at date of accession	Interim	Final Bound	Implementation	Present concession established	INR	Concession first incorporated in a GATT Schedule	Earlier INRs	ODCs
85179010	---Parts for use with headings 85.17 and 85.25 to 85.28	5		0	2008		CA,US			0
85179090	---Other parts for line telephony or telegraphy	5		0	2008		CA,US			0
8518	Microphones and stands therefor; loudspeakers, whether or not mounted in their enclosures; headphones and earphones, whether or not combined with a microphone, and sets consisting of a microphone and one or more loudspeakers; audio-frequency electric amplifiers; electric sound amplifier sets.									
85181000	-Microphones and stands therefor	5		0	2008		US			0
ex85181000	--For use in civil aircraft	0					US			0
85182	-Loudspeakers, whether or not mounted in their enclosures:									
ex85182100	---For use in civil aircraft	0					US			0
85182100	--Single loudspeakers, mounted in their enclosures	15		13	2010					0
85182200	--Multiple loudspeakers, mounted in the same enclosure	15								0
ex85182200	---For use in civil aircraft	0					US			0
85182900	--Other	5		0	2008		US			0
ex85182900	---For use in civil aircraft	0					US			0
85183000	-Headphones and earphones, whether or not combined with a microphone, and sets consisting of a microphone and one or more loudspeakers	5		0	2008		US			0
ex85183000	--For use in civil aircraft	0					US			0
ex85184000	--For use in civil aircraft	0					US			0
85184000	-Audio-frequency electric amplifiers	15					US			0
ex85184000	--Electric amplifiers when used as repeaters in line telephony products falling within this agreement, and parts thereof	15		0	2008		US			0
ex85185000	--For use in civil aircraft	0					US			0
85185000	-Electric sound amplifier sets	15								0
85189000	-Parts	15					US			0

HS	Description	Bound rate at date of accession	Interim	Final Bound	Implementation	Present concession established	INR	Concession first incorporated in a GATT Schedule	Earlier INRs	ODCs
ex85189000	--Electric amplifiers when used as repeaters in line telephony products falling within this agreement, and parts thereof; Printed Circuit Assemblies for products falling within this agreement, including such assemblies for external connections such as cards that conform to the PCMCIA standard. Such printed circuit assemblies consist of one or more printed circuits of heading 8534 with one or more active elements assembled thereon, with or without passive elements "Active elements" means diodes, transistors, and similar semiconductor devices, whether or not photosensitive, of heading 8541, and integrated circuits and micro assemblies of heading 8542.	15		0	2008		US			0
8519	Turntables (record-decks), record-players, cassette-players and other sound reproducing apparatus, not incorporating a sound recording device.									
85191000	-Coin- or disc-operated record-players	15								0
85192	-Other record-players:									
85192100	--Without loudspeaker	10								0
85192900	--Other	15								0
85193	-Turntables (record-decks):									
85193100	--With automatic record changing mechanism	15								0
85193900	--Other	15								0
85194000	-Transcribing machines	15								0
85199	-Other sound reproducing apparatus:									
85199200	--Pocket-size cassette-players	10								0
85199300	--Other, cassette-type	15								0
85199900	--Other	15		13	2010					0
8520	Magnetic tape recorders and other sound recording apparatus, whether or not incorporating a sound reproducing device.									
85201000	-Dictating machines not capable of operating without an external source of power	15								0
85202000	-Telephone answering machines	5		0	2008		US			0

HS	Description	Bound rate at date of accession	Interim	Final Bound	Implementation	Present concession established	INR	Concession first incorporated in a GATT Schedule	Earlier INRs	ODCs
85203	-Other magnetic tape recorders incorporating sound reproducing apparatus:									
85203200	--Digital audio type	15								0
85203300	--Other, cassette-type	15		13	2010					0
85203900	--Other	15								0
ex85209000	--For use in civil aircraft	0					US			0
85209000	-Other	15					JP			0
8521	Video recording or reproducing apparatus, whether or not incorporating a video tuner.									
85211000	-Magnetic tape-type	10					JP			0
ex85211000	--For use in civil aircraft	0					US			0
85219000	-Other	10								0
8522	Parts and accessories suitable for use solely or principally with the apparatus of headings 85.19 to 85.21.									
85221000	-Pick-up cartridges	15								0
85229000	-Other	15		13	2010		US			0
ex85229000	--For use in civil aircraft	0					US			0
ex85229000	--Printed Circuit Assemblies for products falling within this agreement, including such assemblies for external connections such as cards that conform to the PCMCIA standard. Such printed circuit assemblies consist of one or more printed circuits of heading 8534 with one or more active elements assembled thereon, with or without passive elements "Active elements" means diodes, transistors, and similar semiconductor devices, whether or not photosensitive, of heading 8541, and integrated circuits and micro assemblies of heading 8542.	15		0	2008		US			0
8523	Prepared unrecorded media for sound recording or similar recording of other phenomena, other than products of Chapter 37.									
85231	-Magnetic tapes:									
852311	--Of a width not exceeding 4 mm									
85231110	---Recorder magnetic tape not over 4 mm wide	12		0	2008		US			0

350

HS	Description	Bound rate at date of accession	Interim	Final Bound	Implementation	Present concession established	INR	Concession first incorporated in a GATT Schedule	Earlier INRs	ODCs
85231120	---Videotape magnetic tape not over 4 mm wide	12		0	2008		US			0
85231130	---Computer magnetic tape not over 4 mm wide	5		0	2008		US			0
85231190	---Other magnetic tape not over 4 mm wide	5		0	2008		US			0
852312	--Of a width exceeding 4 mm but not exceeding 6.5 mm									
85231210	---Recorder magnetic tape over 4 but not over 6.5 mm wide	12		0	2008		US			0
85231220	---Videotape magnetic tape over 4 but not over 6.5 mm wide	12		0	2008		US			0
85231230	---Computer magnetic tape over 4 but not over 6.5 mm wide	5		0	2008		US			0
85231290	---Other magnetic tape over 4 but not over 6.5 mm wide	5		0	2008		US			0
852313	--Of a width exceeding 6.5 mm									
85231310	---Recorder magnetic tape over 6.5 mm wide	12		0	2008		US			0
85231320	---Videotape magnetic tape over 6.5 mm wide	12		0	2008		US			0
85231330	---Computer magnetic tape over 6.5 mm wide	5		0	2008		US			0
85231390	---Other magnetic tape over 6.5 mm wide	5		0	2008		US			0
852320	-Magnetic discs									
85232010	---Computer magnetic discs	5		0	2008		US			0
85232090	---Other magnetic discs	5		0	2008		US			0
85233000	-Cards incorporating a magnetic stripe	15								0
852390	-Other									
85239010	---Other unrecorded media for recorders	5		0	2008		US			0
85239020	---Other unrecorded media for videotape apparatus	5		0	2008		US			0
85239030	---Other unrecorded media for computers	12		0	2008		US			0
85239090	---Other unrecorded media for sound recording	5		0	2008		US			0
8524	Records, tapes and other recorded media for sound or other similarly recorded phenomena, including matrices and masters for the production of records, but excluding products of Chapter 37.									
85241000	-Gramophone records	8					EC			0

HS	Description	Bound rate at date of accession	Interim	Final Bound	Implementation	Present concession established	INR	Concession first incorporated in a GATT Schedule	Earlier INRs	ODCs
85243	-Discs for laser reading systems:									
85243100	--For reproducing phenomena other than sound or image	5		0	2008		EC,US			0
85243200	--For reproducing sound only	8					EC			0
85243900	--Other	5		0	2008		EC,US			0
85244000	-Magnetic tapes for reproducing phenomena other than sound or image	5		0	2008		IN,US			0
85245	-Other magnetic tapes:									
852451	--Of a width not exceeding 4 mm									
85245110	---Recorded magnetic tapes not over 4 mm wide for recorder	8								0
85245120	---Recorded magnetic tapes not over 4mm wide for videotape	8					EC			0
85245130	---Recorded magnetic tapes not over 4 mm wide for computer	8					EC			0
85245190	---Recorded magnetic tapes not over 4 mm wide for other	8								0
852452	--Of a width exceeding 4 mm but not exceeding 6.5 mm									
85245210	---Recorded magnetic tapes over 4 to 6.5 mm wide, recorder	8								0
85245220	---Recorded magnetic tapes over 4 to 6.5mm wide, videotape	8								0
85245230	---Recorded magnetic tapes over 4 to 6.5 mm wide, computer	5								0
85245290	---Recorded magnetic tape over 4 to 6.5 mm wide, other	5								0
852453	--Of a width exceeding 6.5 mm									
85245310	---Recorded magnetic tapes over 6.5 mm wide for recorders	8								0
85245320	---Recorded magnetic tapes over 6.5 mm wide for videotape	8								0
85245330	---Recorded magnetic tapes over 6.5 mm wide for computers	5								0
85245390	---Recorded magnetic tapes over 6.5 mm wide for other uses	5								0
85246000	-Cards incorporating a magnetic stripe	8								0
85249	-Other:									
85249100	--For reproducing phenomena other than sound or image	5		0	2008		IN,US			0
852499	--Other									
85249910	---Other recorded media for recorders	5		0	2008		EC,US			0

HS	Description	Bound rate at date of accession	Interim	Final Bound	Implementation	Present concession established	INR	Concession first incorporated in a GATT Schedule	Earlier INRs	ODCs
85249920	---Other recorded media for videotape apparatus	5		0	2008		EC,US			0
85249930	---Other recorded media for computers	5		0	2008		US			0
85249990	---Other recorded media for other uses	5		0	2008		US			0
8525	Transmission apparatus for radio-telephony, radio-telegraphy, radio-broadcasting or television, whether or not incorporating reception apparatus or sound recording or reproducing apparatus; television cameras; still image video cameras and other video camera recorders; digital cameras.									
852510	-Transmission apparatus									
85251010	---Transmission apparatus for language interpretation	5		0	2008		US			0
ex85251010	----For use in civil aircraft	0					US			0
85251020	---Automatic hazard signalling apparatus in ships, etc.	5		0	2008		US			0
ex85251020	----For use in civil aircraft	0					US			0
85251030	---Wireless microphone with small cable or metal antenna	5		0	2008		US			0
ex85251030	----For use in civil aircraft	0					US			0
85251090	---Other transmission apparatus for radio or tv	5		0	2008		US			0
ex85251090	----For use in civil aircraft	0					US			0
852520	-Transmission apparatus incorporating reception apparatus									
8525201	---Portable transmission apparatus, usually electric cell operated, of walky talky type, or the like:									
85252011	----Transmission apparatus for military purposes	5		0	2008		US			0
ex85252011	-----For use in civil aircraft	0					US			0
85252019	----Other	5		0	2008		US			0
ex85252019	-----For use in civil aircraft	0					US			0
85252020	---Facsimile apparatus for transmitting documents	5		0	2008		US			0
ex85252020	----For use in civil aircraft	0					US			0
85252030	---Transmission sets for remote signals	5		0	2008		US			0
ex85252030	----For use in civil aircraft	0					US			0
85252040	---Immobile radio sets for telephone and telegraph	5		0	2008		US			0
ex85252040	----For use in civil aircraft	0					US			0

HS	Description	Bound rate at date of accession	Interim	Final Bound	Implementation	Present concession established	INR	Concession first incorporated in a GATT Schedule	Earlier INRs	ODCs
85252050	---Broadcast transmission and receiving sets (radio)	5		0	2008		US			0
ex85252050	----For use in civil aircraft	0					US			0
85252060	---Television transmission and receiving sets	5		0	2008		US			0
ex85252060	----For use in civil aircraft	0					US			0
85252070	---Transmission and receiving sets for mobile telephone	5		0	2008		US			0
ex85252070	----For use in civil aircraft	0					US			0
85252090	---Other transmission apparatus with reception apparatus	5		0	2008		US			0
ex85252090	----For use in civil aircraft	0					US			0
85253000	-Television cameras	15		0	2008		US			0
85254000	-Still image video cameras and other video camera recorders; digital cameras	5		0	2008		JP,US			0
8526	Radar apparatus, radio navigational aid apparatus and radio remote control apparatus.									
85261000	-Radar apparatus	7								0
ex85261000	--For use in civil aircraft	0					US			0
85269	-Other:									
85269100	--Radio navigational aid apparatus	7								0
ex85269100	---For use in civil aircraft	0					US			0
85269200	--Radio remote control apparatus	7								0
ex85269200	---For use in civil aircraft	0					US			0
8527	Reception apparatus for radio-telephony, radio-telegraphy or radio-broadcasting, whether or not combined, in the same housing, with sound recording or reproducing apparatus or a clock.									
85271	-Radio-broadcast receivers capable of operating without an external source of power, including apparatus capable of receiving also radio-telephony or radio-telegraphy:									
85271200	--Pocket-size radio cassette-players	15		13	2010					0
85271300	--Other apparatus combined with sound recording or reproducing apparatus	10								0
85271900	--Other	15								0

HS	Description	Bound rate at date of accession	Interim	Final Bound	Implementation	Present concession established	INR	Concession first incorporated in a GATT Schedule	Earlier INRs	ODCs
85272	-Radio-broadcast receivers not capable of operating without an external source of power, of a kind used in motor vehicles, including apparatus capable of receiving also radio-telephony or radio-telegraphy:									
85272100	--Combined with sound recording or reproducing apparatus	10								0
85272900	--Other	15								0
85273	-Other radio-broadcast receivers, including apparatus capable of receiving also radio-telephony or radio-telegraphy:									
85273100	--Combined with sound recording or reproducing apparatus	10								0
85273200	--Not combined with sound recording or reproducing apparatus but combined with a clock	15								0
85273900	--Other	15								0
852790	-Other apparatus									
85279010	---Automatic paging sets (pagers)	5		0	2008		US			0
ex85279010	----For use in civil aircraft	0					US			0
85279090	---Other	5		0	2008		US			0
ex85279090	----For use in civil aircraft	0					US			0
8528	Reception apparatus for television, whether or not incorporating radio-broadcast receivers or sound or video recording or reproducing apparatus; video monitors and video projectors.									
85281	-Reception apparatus for television, whether or not incorporating radio-broadcast receivers or sound or video recording or reproducing apparatus:									
852812	--Colour									
85281210	---Color tv sets for household use	10					CN,TH			0
8528129	---Other:									
85281291	----Receivers	10					CN,TH,US			0
ex85281291	-----Set top boxes which have a communication function: a microprocessor-based device incorporating a modem for gaining access to the Internet, and having a function of interactive information exchange	10		0	2008		CN,TH,US			0

HS	Description	Bound rate at date of accession	Interim	Final Bound	Implementation	Present concession established	INR	Concession first incorporated in a GATT Schedule	Earlier INRs	ODCs
85281299	----Other	10					CN,TH,US			0
ex85281299	-----Set top boxes which have a communication function: a microprocessor-based device incorporating a modem for gaining access to the Internet, and having a function of interactive information exchange	10		0	2008		CN,TH,US			0
852813	--Black and white or other monochrome									
85281310	---Black and white tv sets for household use	15								0
85281390	---Other black and white tv sets	15								0
85282	-Video monitors:									
85282100	--Colour	15								0
85282200	--Black and white or other monochrome	15								0
85283000	-Video projectors	15								0
8529	Parts suitable for use solely or principally with the apparatus of headings 85.25 to 85.28.									
85291000	-Aerials and aerial reflectors of all kinds; parts suitable for use therewith	5		0	2008		US			0
ex85291000	--For use in civil aircraft	0					US			0
85299000	-Other	5		0	2008		US			0
ex85299000	--For use in civil aircraft	0					US			0
8530	Electrical signalling, safety or traffic control equipment for railways, tramways, roads, inland waterways, parking facilities, port installations or airfields (other than those of heading 86.08).									
85301000	-Equipment for railways or tramways	15								0
85308000	-Other equipment	15								0
85309000	-Parts	5								0
8531	Electric sound or visual signalling apparatus (for example, bells, sirens, indicator panels, burglar or fire alarms), other than those of heading 85.12 or 85.30.									
85311000	-Burglar or fire alarms and similar apparatus	15								0
ex85311000	--For use in civil aircraft	0					US			0
85312000	-Indicator panels incorporating liquid crystal devices (LCD) or light emitting diodes (LED)	5		0	2008		US			0

HS	Description	Bound rate at date of accession	Interim	Final Bound	Implementation	Present concession established	INR	Concession first incorporated in a GATT Schedule	Earlier INRs	ODCs
ex85312000	--For use in civil aircraft	0					US			0
853180	-Other apparatus									
85318010	---Electric bells for doors	15								0
ex85318010	----For use in civil aircraft	0					US			0
ex85318090	----For use in civil aircraft	0					US			0
85318090	---Other electric sound or visual signalling apparatus	15					US			0
ex85318090	----Paging alert devices, and parts thereof; Flat panel display devices (including LCD, Electro Luminescence, Plasma, Vacuum-Fluorescence and other technologies) for products falling within this agreement, and parts thereof.	15		0	2008		US			0
85319000	-Parts	5		0	2008		US			0
8532	Electrical capacitors, fixed, variable or adjustable (pre-set).									
85321000	-Fixed capacitors designed for use in 50/60 Hz circuits and having a reactive power handling capacity of not less than 0.5 kvar (power capacitors)	5		0	2008		US			0
85322	-Other fixed capacitors:									
85322100	--Tantalum	5		0	2008		US			0
85322200	--Aluminium electrolytic	5		0	2008		US			0
85322300	--Ceramic dielectric, single layer	5		0	2008		US			0
85322400	--Ceramic dielectric, multilayer	5		0	2008		US			0
85322500	--Dielectric of paper or plastics	5		0	2008		US			0
85322900	--Other	5		0	2008		US			0
85323000	-Variable or adjustable (pre-set) capacitors	5		0	2008		US			0
85329000	-Parts	5		0	2008		US			0
8533	Electrical resistors (including rheostats and potentiometers), other than heating resistors.									
85331000	-Fixed carbon resistors, composition or film types	5		0	2008		US			0
85332	-Other fixed resistors:									
85332100	--For a power handling capacity not exceeding 20 W	5		0	2008		US			0
85332900	--Other	5		0	2008		US			0
85333	-Wirewound variable resistors, including rheostats and potentiometers:									
85333100	--For a power handling capacity not exceeding 20 W	5		0	2008		US			0

HS	Description	Bound rate at date of accession	Interim	Final Bound	Implementation	Present concession established	INR	Concession first incorporated in a GATT Schedule	Earlier INRs	ODCs
85333900	--Other	5		0	2008		US			0
85334000	-Other variable resistors, including rheostats and potentiometers	5		0	2008		US			0
85339000	-Parts	5		0	2008		US			0
85340000	Printed circuits.	5		0	2008		US			0
8535	Electrical apparatus for switching or protecting electrical circuits, or for making connections to or in electrical circuits (for example, switches, fuses, lightning arresters, voltage limiters, surge suppressors, plugs, junction boxes), for a voltage exceeding 1,000 volts.									
85351000	-Fuses	5								0
85352	-Automatic circuit breakers:									
85352100	--For a voltage of less than 72.5 kV	15								0
85352900	--Other	15								0
85353000	-Isolating switches and make-and-break switches	15					CH			0
85354000	-Lightning arresters, voltage limiters and surge suppressors	15								0
85359000	-Other	5					CH			0
8536	Electrical apparatus for switching or protecting electrical circuits, or for making connections to or in electrical circuits (for example, switches, relays, fuses, surge suppressors, plugs, sockets, lamp-holders, junction boxes), for a voltage not exceeding 1,000 volts.									
85361000	-Fuses	5								0
85362000	-Automatic circuit breakers	15								0
85363000	-Other apparatus for protecting electrical circuits	5								0
85364	-Relays:									
85364100	--For a voltage not exceeding 60 V	15								0
85364900	--Other	15								0
85365000	-Other switches	5		0	2008		US			0
85366	-Lamp-holders, plugs and sockets:									
85366100	--Lamp-holders	15								0
85366900	--Other	5		0	2008		US			0
85369000	-Other apparatus	5		0	2008		KG,US			0

HS	Description	Bound rate at date of accession	Interim	Final Bound	Implementation	Present concession established	INR	Concession first incorporated in a GATT Schedule	Earlier INRs	ODCs
8537	Boards, panels, consoles, desks, cabinets and other bases, equipped with two or more apparatus of heading 85.35 or 85.36, for electric control or the distribution of electricity, including those incorporating instruments or apparatus of Chapter 90, and numerical control apparatus, other than switching apparatus of heading 85.17.									
85371000	-For a voltage not exceeding 1,000 V	15								0
85372000	-For a voltage exceeding 1,000 V	15		10	2010					0
8538	Parts suitable for use solely or principally with the apparatus of heading 85.35, 85.36 or 85.37.									
85381000	-Boards, panels, consoles, desks, cabinets and other bases for the goods of heading 85.37, not equipped with their apparatus	15								0
85389000	-Other	10					AU,CH,NO,US			0
ex85389000	--Printed Circuit Assemblies for products falling within this agreement, including such assemblies for external connections such as cards that conform to the PCMCIA standard. Such printed circuit assemblies consist of one or more printed circuits of heading 8534 with one or more active elements assembled thereon, with or without passive elements "Active elements" means diodes, transistors, and similar semiconductor devices, whether or not photosensitive, of heading 8541, and integrated circuits and micro assemblies of heading 8542.	10		0	2008		AU,CH,NO,US			0
8539	Electric filament or discharge lamps, including sealed beam lamp units and ultra-violet or infra-red lamps; arc-lamps.									
85391000	-Sealed beam lamp units	15								0
ex85391000	--For use in civil aircraft	0					US			0
85392	-Other filament lamps, excluding ultra-violet or infra-red lamps:									
85392100	--Tungsten halogen	15								0
85392200	--Other, of a power not exceeding 200 W and for a voltage exceeding 100 V	15					KG			0

HS	Description	Bound rate at date of accession	Interim	Final Bound	Implementation	Present concession established	INR	Concession first incorporated in a GATT Schedule	Earlier INRs	ODCs
85392900	--Other	15					KG			0
85393	-Discharge lamps, other than ultra-violet lamps:									
85393100	--Fluorescent, hot cathode	5								0
85393200	--Mercury or sodium vapour lamps; metal halide lamps	15								0
85393900	--Other	5								0
85394	-Ultra-violet or infra-red lamps; arc-lamps:									
85394100	--Arc-lamps	15								0
85394900	--Other	15								0
85399000	-Parts	15								0
8540	Thermionic, cold cathode or photo-cathode valves and tubes (for example, vacuum or vapour or gas filled valves and tubes, mercury arc rectifying valves and tubes, cathode-ray tubes, television camera tubes).									
85401	-Cathode-ray television picture tubes, including video monitor cathode-ray tubes:									
85401100	--Colour	10								0
85401200	--Black and white or other monochrome	15								0
85402000	-Television camera tubes; image converters and intensifiers; other photo-cathode tubes	15								0
85404000	-Data/graphic display tubes, colour, with a phosphor dot screen pitch smaller than 0.4 mm	15								0
85405000	-Data/graphic display tubes, black and white or other monochrome	15								0
85406000	-Other cathode-ray tubes	15								0
85407	-Microwave tubes (for example, magnetrons, klystrons, travelling wave tubes, carcinotrons), excluding grid-controlled tubes:									
85407100	--Magnetrons	15								0
85407200	--Klystrons	15								0
85407900	--Other	15								0
85408	-Other valves and tubes:									
85408100	--Receiver or amplifier valves and tubes	15								0
85408900	--Other	15								0
85409	-Parts:									

HS	Description	Bound rate at date of accession	Interim	Final Bound	Implementation	Present concession established	INR	Concession first incorporated in a GATT Schedule	Earlier INRs	ODCs
85409100	--Of cathode-ray tubes	15								0
85409900	--Other	15								0
8541	Diodes, transistors and similar semiconductor devices; photosensitive semiconductor devices, including photovoltaic cells whether or not assembled in modules or made up into panels; light emitting diodes; mounted piezo-electric crystals.									
85411000	-Diodes, other than photosensitive or light emitting diodes	5		0	2008		US			0
85412	-Transistors, other than photosensitive transistors:									
85412100	--With a dissipation rate of less than 1 W	5		0	2008		US			0
85412900	--Other	5		0	2008		US			0
85413000	-Thyristors, diacs and triacs, other than photosensitive devices	5		0	2008		US			0
85414000	-Photosensitive semiconductor devices, including photovoltaic cells whether or not assembled in modules or made up into panels; light emitting diodes	5		0	2008		US			0
85415000	-Other semiconductor devices	5		0	2008		US			0
85416000	-Mounted piezo-electric crystals	5		0	2008		US			0
85419000	-Parts	5		0	2008		US			0
8542	Electronic integrated circuits and microassemblies.									
85421000	-Cards incorporating an electronic integrated circuit ("smart" cards)	5		0	2008		US			0
85422	-Monolithic integrated circuits:									
85422100	--Digital	5		0	2008		KG,US			0
85422900	--Other	5		0	2008		US			0
85426000	-Hybrid integrated circuits	5		0	2008		US			0
85427000	-Electronic microassemblies	5		0	2008		US			0
85429000	-Parts	5		0	2008		US			0
8543	Electrical machines and apparatus, having individual functions, not specified or included elsewhere in this Chapter.									
85431	-Particle accelerators:									
85431100	--Ion implanters for doping semiconductor materials	5		0	2008		US			0
85431900	--Other	15								0

HS	Description	Bound rate at date of accession	Interim	Final Bound	Implementation	Present concession established	INR	Concession first incorporated in a GATT Schedule	Earlier INRs	ODCs
85432000	-Signal generators	15								0
85433000	-Machines and apparatus for electroplating, electrolysis or electrophoresis	5		0	2008		US			0
85434000	-Electric fence energisers	15		0	2008		US			0
85438	-Other machines and apparatus:									
85438100	--Proximity cards and tags	5		0	2008		US			0
854389	--Other									
85438910	---Sound fusion equipment, used in the sound recording	5		0	2008		US			0
ex85438910	----For use in civil aircraft	0					US			0
85438920	---Mine and metal elements detectors	5		0	2008		US			0
ex85438920	----For use in civil aircraft	0					US			0
85438930	---Electric detonators	5		0	2008		US			0
ex85438930	----For use in civil aircraft	0					US			0
85438940	---Electric shock insecticide sets	5		0	2008		US			0
ex85438940	----For use in civil aircraft	0					US			0
85438990	---Other electric machinery with only individual function	5								0
ex85438990	----For use in civil aircraft	0					US			0
ex85438990	----Electrical machines with translation or dictionary functions; Flat panel display devices (including LCD, Electro Luminescence, Plasma, Vacuum-Fluorescence and other technologies) for products falling within this agreement, and parts thereof.	5		0	2008		US			0
85439000	-Parts	5		0	2008		US			0
ex85439000	--For use in civil aircraft	0					US			0
8544	Insulated (including enamelled or anodised) wire, cable (including co-axial cable) and other insulated electric conductors, whether or not fitted with connectors; optical fibre cables, made up of individually sheathed fibres, whether or not assembled with electric conductors or fitted with connectors.									
85441	-Winding wire:									
85441100	--Of copper	15								0
85441900	--Other	15								0
854420	-Co-axial cable and other co-axial electric conductors									

HS	Description	Bound rate at date of accession	Interim	Final Bound	Implementation	Present concession established	INR	Concession first incorporated in a GATT Schedule	Earlier INRs	ODCs
85442010	---Co-axial cable over 10 mm wide and over 300 volts	15					IN			0
85442020	---Co-axial cable with 10 or more pairs	15					IN			0
85442030	---Co-axial cable with less than 10 pairs	15					IN			0
85442090	---Other co-axial cable	15					IN			0
85443000	-Ignition wiring sets and other wiring sets of a kind used in vehicles, aircraft or ships	15								0
ex85443000	--For use in civil aircraft	0					US			0
85444	-Other electric conductors, for a voltage not exceeding 80 V:									
85444100	--Fitted with connectors	12		0	2008		US			0
85444900	--Other	12		0	2008		US			0
85445	-Other electric conductors, for a voltage exceeding 80 V but not exceeding 1,000 V:									
854451	--Fitted with connectors									
85445110	---Other conductors with connectors over 10 mm and 300 v	20		0	2008		US			0
85445120	---Other conductors with connectors not exceeding 10 mm in c.s.	12		0	2008		US			0
85445130	---Other conductors with connectors and 10 or more pairs	12		0	2008		US			0
85445140	---Other conductors with connectors and less than 10 pairs	12		0	2008		US			0
85445190	---Other conductors with connectors 81 to 1000 v	12		0	2008		US			0
854459	--Other									
85445910	---Other conductors without connectors over 10 mm and 300 v	15								0
85445920	---Other conductors without connectors and c.s. < 10 mm	15								0
85445930	---Other conductors without connectors and with 10 or more pairs	15								0
85445940	---Other conductors without connectors and < 10 pairs	15								0
85445990	---Other conductors without connectors 81 to 1000 v	15								0
854460	-Other electric conductors, for a voltage exceeding 1,000 V									
85446010	---Other conductors over 10 mm wide and over 1000 v	15								0

HS	Description	Bound rate at date of accession	Interim	Final Bound	Implementation	Present concession established	INR	Concession first incorporated in a GATT Schedule	Earlier INRs	ODCs
85446020	---Other conductors without connectors and c.s. < 10 mm	15								0
85446030	---Other conductors without connectors and with 10 or more pairs	15								0
85446090	---Other conductors over 1000 v and under 11 mm wide	15								0
85447000	-Optical fibre cables	12		0	2008		US			0
8545	Carbon electrodes, carbon brushes, lamp carbons, battery carbons and other articles of graphite or other carbon, with or without metal, of a kind used for electrical purposes.									
85451	-Electrodes:									
85451100	--Of a kind used for furnaces	5								0
85451900	--Other	15								0
85452000	-Brushes	15								0
85459000	-Other	15								0
8546	Electrical insulators of any material.									
85461000	-Of glass	15								0
85462000	-Of ceramics	10					IN			0
85469000	-Other	10					IN			0
8547	Insulating fittings for electrical machines, appliances or equipment, being fittings wholly of insulating material apart from any minor components of metal (for example, threaded sockets) incorporated during moulding solely for purposes of assembly, other than insulators of heading 85.46; electrical conduit tubing and joints therefor, of base metal lined with insulating material.									
85471000	-Insulating fittings of ceramics	15								0
85472000	-Insulating fittings of plastics	15								0
85479000	-Other	7					IN			0
8548	Waste and scrap of primary cells, primary batteries and electric accumulators; spent primary cells, spent primary batteries and spent electric accumulators; electrical parts of machinery or apparatus, not specified or included elsewhere in this Chapter.									

HS	Description	Bound rate at date of accession	Interim	Final Bound	Implementation	Present concession established	INR	Concession first incorporated in a GATT Schedule	Earlier INRs	ODCs
85481000	-Waste and scrap of primary cells, primary batteries and electric accumulators; spent primary cells, spent primary batteries and spent electric accumulators	15								0
85489000	-Other	7								0
8601	Rail locomotives powered from an external source of electricity or by electric accumulators.									
86011000	-Powered from an external source of electricity	15								0
86012000	-Powered by electric accumulators	15								0
8602	Other rail locomotives; locomotive tenders.									
86021000	-Diesel-electric locomotives	5								0
86029000	-Other	15								0
8603	Self-propelled railway or tramway coaches, vans and trucks, other than those of heading 86.04.									
86031000	-Powered from an external source of electricity	15								0
86039000	-Other	15								0
86040000	Railway or tramway maintenance or service vehicles, whether or not self-propelled (for example, workshops, cranes, ballast tampers, trackliners, testing coaches and track inspection vehicles).	15								0
86050000	Railway or tramway passenger coaches, not self-propelled; luggage vans, post office coaches and other special purpose railway or tramway coaches, not self-propelled (excluding those of heading 86.04).	15								0
8606	Railway or tramway goods vans and wagons, not self-propelled.									
86061000	-Tank wagons and the like	15								0
86062000	-Insulated or refrigerated vans and wagons, other than those of subheading 8606.10	15								0
86063000	-Self-discharging vans and wagons, other than those of subheading 8606.10 or 8606.20	15								0
86069	-Other:									
86069100	--Covered and closed	15								0

HS	Description	Bound rate at date of accession	Interim	Final Bound	Implementation	Present concession established	INR	Concession first incorporated in a GATT Schedule	Earlier INRs	ODCs
86069200	--Open, with non-removable sides of a height exceeding 60 cm	15								0
86069900	--Other	15								0
8607	Parts of railway or tramway locomotives or rolling-stock.									
86071	-Bogies, bissel-bogies, axles and wheels, and parts thereof:									
86071100	--Driving bogies and bissel-bogies	15								0
86071200	--Other bogies and bissel-bogies	15								0
86071900	--Other, including parts	15								0
86072	-Brakes and parts thereof:									
86072100	--Air brakes and parts thereof	15								0
86072900	--Other	15								0
86073000	-Hooks and other coupling devices, buffers, and parts thereof	15								0
86079	-Other:									
86079100	--Of locomotives	15								0
86079900	--Other	15								0
86080000	Railway or tramway track fixtures and fittings; mechanical (including electro-mechanical) signalling, safety or traffic control equipment for railways, tramways, roads, inland waterways, parking facilities, port installations or airfields; parts of the foregoing.	15								0
86090000	Containers (including containers for the transport of fluids) specially designed and equipped for carriage by one or more modes of transport.	10								0
8701	Tractors (other than tractors of heading 87.09).									
87011000	-Pedestrian controlled tractors	15								0
87012000	-Road tractors for semi-trailers	15								0
87013000	-Track-laying tractors	8					US			0
87019000	-Other	8					US			0
8702	Motor vehicles for the transport of ten or more persons, including the driver.									
87021000	-With compression-ignition internal combustion piston engine (diesel or semi-diesel)	7								0
87029000	-Other	7								0

HS	Description	Bound rate at date of accession	Interim	Final Bound	Implementation	Present concession established	INR	Concession first incorporated in a GATT Schedule	Earlier INRs	ODCs
8703	Motor cars and other motor vehicles principally designed for the transport of persons (other than those of heading 87.02), including station wagons and racing cars.									
87031000	-Vehicles specially designed for travelling on snow; golf cars and similar vehicles	5								0
87032	-Other vehicles, with spark-ignition internal combustion reciprocating piston engine:									
870321	--Of a cylinder capacity not exceeding 1,000 cc									
8703211	---Saloon cars:									
87032111	----Private cars, current, spark-ignition, not over 1000 cc	7								0
87032112	----Private cars, 1-year, spark-ignition, not over 1000 cc	7								0
8703213	---Four-wheeled motor vehicles:									
87032131	----Jeeps, current, spark ignition, not over 1000 cc	7								0
87032132	----Jeeps, 1 year old, spark ignition, not over 1000 cc	7								0
87032150	---Emergency vehicles, spark ignition, not over 1000 cc	7								0
87032160	---Motor homes, spark ignition, not over 1000 cc	7								0
87032170	---Light cars, 3-wheels, spark ignition, not over 1000cc	7								0
87032180	---Vehicles for crippled, spark ignition, not over 1000 cc	7								0
87032190	---Other vehicles, spark ignition, not over 1000 cc	7								0
870322	--Of a cylinder capacity exceeding 1,000 cc but not exceeding 1,500 cc									
8703221	---Saloon cars:									
87032211	----Private cars, current, spark ignition, 1001 to 1500 cc	7								0
87032212	----Private cars, 1 year, spark ignition, 1001 to 1500 cc	7								0
8703223	---Four-wheeled motor vehicles:									
87032231	----Jeeps, current, spark ignition, 1001 to 1500 cc	7								0

HS	Description	Bound rate at date of accession	Interim	Final Bound	Implementation	Present concession established	INR	Concession first incorporated in a GATT Schedule	Earlier INRs	ODCs
87032232	----Jeeps, 1 year old, spark ignition, 1001 to 1500 cc	7								0
87032250	---Emergency vehicles, spark ignition, 1001 to 1500 cc	7								0
87032260	---Motor homes, spark ignition, 1001 to 1500 cc	7								0
87032270	---Light cars, 3-wheels, spark ignition, 1001 to 1500 cc	7								0
87032280	---Vehicles for crippled, spark ignition, 1001 to 1500 cc	7								0
87032290	---Other vehicles, spark ignition, 1001 to 1500 cc	7								0
870323	--Of a cylinder capacity exceeding 1,500 cc but not exceeding 3,000 cc									
8703231	---Saloon cars:									
87032311	----Private cars, current, spark ignition, 1501 to 3000 cc	7					AU			0
87032312	----Private cars, 1 year, spark ignition, 1501 to 3000 cc	7								0
8703233	---Four-wheeled motor vehicles:									
87032331	----Jeeps, current, spark ignition, 1501 to 3000 cc	7					JP			0
87032332	----Jeeps, 1 year old, spark ignition, 1501 to 3000 cc	7					JP			0
87032350	---Emergency vehicles, spark ignition, 1501 to 3000 cc	7					JP			0
87032360	---Motor homes, spark ignition, 1501 to 3000 cc	7					JP			0
87032370	---Light cars, 3-wheels, spark ignition, 1501 to 3000 cc	7					JP			0
87032380	---Vehicles for crippled, spark ignition, 1501 to 3000 cc	7					JP			0
87032390	---Other vehicles, spark ignition, 1501 to 3000 cc	7					AU,JP			0
870324	--Of a cylinder capacity exceeding 3,000 cc									
8703241	---Motor cars:									
87032411	----Private cars, current, spark ignition, over 3000 cc	7					AU,JP			0
87032412	----Private cars, 1 year old, spark ignition, over 3000 cc	7					JP			0
8703243	---Four-wheeled motor vehicles:									
87032431	----Jeeps, current year, spark ignition, over 3000 cc	7					JP			0

HS	Description	Bound rate at date of accession	Interim	Final Bound	Implementation	Present concession established	INR	Concession first incorporated in a GATT Schedule	Earlier INRs	ODCs
87032432	----Jeeps, 1 year old, spark ignition, over 3000 cc	7					JP			0
87032450	---Emergency vehicles, spark ignition, over 3000 cc	7					JP			0
87032460	---Motor homes, spark ignition, over 3000 cc	7					JP			0
87032470	---Vehicles for crippled, spark ignition, over 3000 cc	7					JP			0
87032490	---Other vehicles, spark ignition, over 3000 cc	7					AU,JP			0
87033	-Other vehicles, with compression-ignition internal combustion piston engine (diesel or semi-diesel):									
87033100	--Of a cylinder capacity not exceeding 1,500 cc	15								0
87033200	--Of a cylinder capacity exceeding 1,500 cc but not exceeding 2,500 cc	7								0
87033300	--Of a cylinder capacity exceeding 2,500 cc	7								0
87039000	-Other	7								0
8704	Motor vehicles for the transport of goods.									
87041000	-Dumpers designed for off-highway use	6					US			0
87042	-Other, with compression-ignition internal combustion piston engine (diesel or semi-diesel):									
870421	--g.v.w. not exceeding 5 tonnes									
87042110	---Pickups, compression ignition, 5 tonnes and less	7								0
8704212	---Light transport trucks (dyna trucks, half-lorry and the like), whether or not fitted with tipping body:									
87042121	----Light truck, chassis-cabs, compression, 5 tonnes and less	15								0
87042122	----Light truck, body chassis, compression, 5 tonnes or less	15								0
8704213	---Tankers:									
87042131	----Tanker chassis-cabs, compression ignition, 5 tonnes and less	15								0
87042132	----Tankers, body chassis, compression, 5 tonnes and less	15								0
8704214	---Refuse collectors whether or not fitted with loading, compressing, damping, etc., devices:									

HS	Description	Bound rate at date of accession	Interim	Final Bound	Implementation	Present concession established	INR	Concession first incorporated in a GATT Schedule	Earlier INRs	ODCs
87042141	----Garbage vehicles chassis-cabs, compression, 5 tonnes and less	15								0
87042142	----Garbage body chassis, compression ignition, 5 tonnes and less	15								0
87042150	---Other vehicle chassis-cabs, compression, 5 tonnes or less	15								0
87042160	---Refrigerator vehicles, compression, 5 tonnes or less	15								0
87042190	---Other transport vehicles, compression, 5 tonnes or less	15								0
870422	--g.v.w. exceeding 5 tonnes but not exceeding 20 tonnes									
8704221	---Heavy-duty lorries:									
87042211	----Lorry chassis-cabs, compression ignition, 5+ to 20 tonnes	15								0
87042212	----Lorry body chassis, compression ignition, 5+ to 20 tonnes	15								0
8704222	---Vehicles fitted with tipping body:									
87042221	----Tipper chassis-cabs, compression ignition, 5+ to 20 tonnes	15								0
87042222	----Tipper body chassis, compression ignition, 5+ to 20 tonnes	15								0
8704223	---Tankers:									
87042231	----Tanker chassis-cabs, compression ignition, 5+ to 20 tonnes	15								0
87042232	----Tanker body chassis, compression ignition, 5+ to 20 tonnes	15								0
8704224	---Refuse collectors whether or not fitted with loading, compressing, damping, etc., devices:									
87042241	----Garbage vehicle chassis-cabs, compression, 5+ to 20 tonnes	15								0
87042242	----Garbage body chassis, compression ignition, 5+ to 20 tonnes	15								0
87042250	---Shuttle cars, compression ignition, 5+ to 20 tonnes	15								0
87042260	---Hoist vehicles, compression ignition, 5+ to 20 tonnes	15								0
87042270	---Concrete, gas vehicles, compression, 5+ to 20 tonnes	15								0
87042280	---Other vehicle chassis-cabs, compression, 5+ to 20 tonnes	15								0
8704229	---Other:									

HS	Description	Bound rate at date of accession	Interim	Final Bound	Implementation	Present concession established	INR	Concession first incorporated in a GATT Schedule	Earlier INRs	ODCs
87042291	----Refrigerator vehicles, compression ignition, 5+ to 20 tonnes	15								0
87042299	----Other transport vehicles, compression, 5+ to 20 tonnes	15								0
870423	--g.v.w. exceeding 20 tonnes									
8704231	---Ordinary lorries:									
87042311	----Lorry chassis-cabs, compression ignition, over 20 tonnes	15								0
87042312	----Lorry body chassis, compression ignition, over 20 tonnes	15								0
8704232	---Vehicles fitted with tipping body:									
87042321	----Tipper chassis-cabs, compression ignition, over 20 tonnes	15								0
87042322	----Tipper body chassis, compression ignition, over 20 tonnes	15								0
8704233	---Tankers:									
87042331	----Tanker chassis-cabs, compression ignition, over 20 tonnes	15								0
87042332	----Tanker body chassis, compression ignition, over 20 tonnes	15								0
8704234	---Refuse collectors whether or not fitted with loading, compressing, damping, etc., devices:									
87042341	----Garbage vehicle chassis-cabs, compression, over 20 tonnes	15								0
87042342	----Garbage body chassis, compression ignition, over 20 tonnes	15								0
87042350	---Hoist vehicles, compression ignition, over 20 tonnes	7								0
87042360	---Cement vehicles, compression ignition, over 20 tonnes	7								0
87042370	---Chemical vehicles, compression ignition, over 20 tonnes	7								0
87042380	---Other vehicle chassis-cabs, compression, over 20 tonnes	15								0
8704239	---Other:									
87042391	----Refrigerator vehicles, compression ignition, over 20 tonnes	15								0
87042399	----Other transport vehicles, compression, over 20 tonnes	7								0
87043	-Other, with spark-ignition internal combustion piston engine:									
870431	--g.v.w. not exceeding 5 tonnes									

HS	Description	Bound rate at date of accession	Interim	Final Bound	Implementation	Present concession established	INR	Concession first incorporated in a GATT Schedule	Earlier INRs	ODCs
87043110	---Pickups, one cab, spark ignition, 5 tonnes or less	5								0
87043120	---Pickups, two cabs, spark ignition, 5 tonnes or less	5								0
8704313	---Light transport trucks (dyna trucks, half-lorry and the like), fitted with ordinary body:									
87043131	----Light truck chassis-cabs, normal box, spark, 5 tonnes or less	10								0
87043132	----Light truck body chassis, normal box, spark, 5 tonnes or less	10								0
8704314	---Light transport trucks (dyna trucks, half-lorry and the like), fitted with tipping body:									
87043141	----Light truck chassis-cabs, trip box, spark, 5 tonnes or less	10								0
87043142	----Light truck body chassis, trip box, spark, 5 tonnes or less	10								0
8704315	---Tankers:									
87043151	----Chassis fitted with cabs	10								0
87043152	----Tanker body chassis, spark ignition, 5 tonnes or less	10								0
8704316	---Refuse collectors whether or not fitted with loading, compressing, damping, etc., devices:									
87043161	----Garbage vehicle chassis-cabs, spark, 5 tonnes or less	10								0
87043162	----Garbage vehicle body chassis, spark, 5 tonnes or less	10								0
87043170	---Other vehicle chassis-cabs, spark, 5 tonnes or less	10								0
87043180	---Refrigerator vehicles, spark ignition, 5 tonnes or less	10								0
87043190	---Other transport vehicles, spark ignition, 5 tonnes or less	10								0
870432	--g.v.w. exceeding 5 tonnes									
8704321	---Heavy-duty lorries, trucks with tipping body, and tankers:									
87043211	----Lorry, etc., chassis-cabs, spark ignition, over 5 tonnes	15								0
87043212	----Lorry, etc., body chassis, spark ignition, over 5 tonnes	15								0

HS	Description	Bound rate at date of accession	Interim	Final Bound	Implementation	Present concession established	INR	Concession first incorporated in a GATT Schedule	Earlier INRs	ODCs
8704322	---Refuse collectors whether or not fitted with loading, compressing, damping, etc., devices:									
87043221	----Garbage vehicle chassis-cabs, spark ignition, over 5 tonnes	15								0
87043222	----Garbage vehicle body chassis, spark ignition, over 5 tonnes	15								0
87043290	---Other transport vehicles, spark ignition, over 5 tonnes	7								0
87049000	-Other	7								0
8705	Special purpose motor vehicles, other than those principally designed for the transport of persons or goods (for example, breakdown lorries, crane lorries, fire fighting vehicles, concrete-mixer lorries, road sweeper lorries, spraying lorries, mobile workshops, mobile radiological units).									
87051000	-Crane lorries	7								0
87052000	-Mobile drilling derricks	15								0
87053000	-Fire fighting vehicles	7								0
87054000	-Concrete-mixer lorries	15								0
870590	-Other									
87059010	---Towing and repair trucks, mobile workshops	15								0
87059020	---Trucks fitted with ladders or elevator platforms	15								0
87059030	---Vehicles equipped for cleaning streets and the like	15								0
87059040	---Spraying vehicles for all uses	15								0
87059050	---Stacking vehicles	15								0
87059060	---Vehicles equipped with power generators	15								0
87059070	---Vehicles for radiography	15								0
87059080	---Vehicles for surgical and medical purposes	15								0
8705909	---Other:									
87059091	----Searchlight trucks with light projectors	15								0
87059092	----Broadcasting vehicles, telegraph vehicles and the like	15								0
87059093	----Bakery vehicles with complete equipment	15								0

HS	Description	Bound rate at date of accession	Interim	Final Bound	Implementation	Present concession established	INR	Concession first incorporated in a GATT Schedule	Earlier INRs	ODCs
87059094	----Vehicles equipped with tanks and water pumps	15								0
87059099	----Other special purpose motor vehicles	15								0
87060000	Chassis fitted with engines, for the motor vehicles of headings 87.01 to 87.05.	7								0
8707	Bodies (including cabs), for the motor vehicles of headings 87.01 to 87.05.									
87071000	-For the vehicles of heading 87.03	15								0
870790	-Other									
87079010	---Bodies of tractors falling under heading 87.01	7								0
87079020	---Bodies of vehicles falling under heading 87.02	15								0
8707903	---Bodies (including cabs), for the motor vehicles of heading 87.04:									
87079031	----Bodies for pickups	5								0
87079032	----Bodies for light transportation trucks	15								0
87079033	----Bodies for garbage collection vehicles	15								0
87079034	----Bodies for lorries	15								0
87079035	----Boxes for tippers	15								0
87079036	----Refrigerators for foodstuffs transportation vehicles	15								0
87079039	----Other bodies for transport motor vehicles	15								0
87079090	---Other bodies for motor vehicles	15								0
8708	Parts and accessories of the motor vehicles of headings 87.01 to 87.05.									
87081000	-Bumpers and parts thereof	7								0
87082	-Other parts and accessories of bodies (including cabs):									
87082100	--Safety seat belts	15								0
870829	--Other									
87082910	---Luggage carriers or nets	7								0
87082990	---Other body parts	7					AU			0
87083	-Brakes and servo-brakes and parts thereof:									
87083100	--Mounted brake linings	15					AU			0
87083900	--Other	15					AU			0
87084000	-Gear boxes	7								0

HS	Description	Bound rate at date of accession	Interim	Final Bound	Implementation	Present concession established	INR	Concession first incorporated in a GATT Schedule	Earlier INRs	ODCs
87085000	-Drive-axles with differential, whether or not provided with other transmission components	7								0
87086000	-Non-driving axles and parts thereof	15								0
87087000	-Road wheels and parts and accessories thereof	7					AU			0
87088000	-Suspension shock-absorbers	7					AU			0
87089	-Other parts and accessories:									
87089100	--Radiators	15					KG			0
87089200	--Silencers and exhaust pipes	15								0
87089300	--Clutches and parts thereof	7					AU			0
87089400	--Steering wheels, steering columns and steering boxes	15								0
87089900	--Other	7					AU,CA,IN			0
8709	Works trucks, self-propelled, not fitted with lifting or handling equipment, of the type used in factories, warehouses, dock areas or airports for short distance transport of goods; tractors of the type used on railway station platforms; parts of the foregoing vehicles.									
87091	-Vehicles:									
87091100	--Electrical	7								0
87091900	--Other	15								0
87099000	-Parts	15								0
87100000	Tanks and other armoured fighting vehicles, motorised, whether or not fitted with weapons, and parts of such vehicles.	7								0
8711	Motorcycles (including mopeds) and cycles fitted with an auxiliary motor, with or without side-cars; side-cars.									
87111000	-With reciprocating internal combustion piston engine of a cylinder capacity not exceeding 50 cc	15								0
87112000	-With reciprocating internal combustion piston engine of a cylinder capacity exceeding 50 cc but not exceeding 250 cc	15								0
87113000	-With reciprocating internal combustion piston engine of a cylinder capacity exceeding 250 cc but not exceeding 500 cc	15								0

HS	Description	Bound rate at date of accession	Interim	Final Bound	Implementation	Present concession established	INR	Concession first incorporated in a GATT Schedule	Earlier INRs	ODCs
87114000	-With reciprocating internal combustion piston engine of a cylinder capacity exceeding 500 cc but not exceeding 800 cc	15								0
87115000	-With reciprocating internal combustion piston engine of a cylinder capacity exceeding 800 cc	7								0
87119000	-Other	15								0
8712	Bicycles and other cycles (including delivery tricycles), not motorised.									
87120010	---Bicycles for children	10								0
87120020	---Invalid cycles (carriages)	10								0
87120090	---Other bicycles and similar	10								0
8713	Carriages for disabled persons, whether or not motorised or otherwise mechanically propelled.									
87131000	-Not mechanically propelled	5								0
87139000	-Other	5								0
8714	Parts and accessories of vehicles of headings 87.11 to 87.13.									
87141	-Of motorcycles (including mopeds):									
87141100	--Saddles	15								0
87141900	--Other	10								0
87142000	-Of carriages for disabled persons	5								0
87149	-Other:									
87149100	--Frames and forks, and parts thereof	15								0
87149200	--Wheel rims and spokes	15								0
87149300	--Hubs, other than coaster braking hubs and hub brakes, and free-wheel sprocket-wheels	15								0
87149400	--Brakes, including coaster braking hubs and hub brakes, and parts thereof	15								0
87149500	--Saddles	15								0
87149600	--Pedals and crank-gear, and parts thereof	15								0
87149900	--Other	7								0
8715	Baby carriages and parts thereof.									
87150010	---Baby carriages	10								0
87150090	---Parts of baby carriages	10								0
8716	Trailers and semi-trailers; other vehicles, not mechanically propelled; parts thereof.									

HS	Description	Bound rate at date of accession	Interim	Final Bound	Implementation	Present concession established	INR	Concession first incorporated in a GATT Schedule	Earlier INRs	ODCs
87161000	-Trailers and semi-trailers of the caravan type, for housing or camping	7								0
87162000	-Self-loading or self-unloading trailers and semi-trailers for agricultural purposes	15								0
87163	-Other trailers and semi-trailers for the transport of goods:									
87163100	--Tanker trailers and tanker semi-trailers	15								0
871639	--Other									
87163910	---Trailers for public works, not mechanical	7								0
87163920	---Refrigerator trailers for transport, not mechanical	7								0
87163930	---Special trailers for furniture, not mechanical	7								0
87163940	---Trailers for animals, not mechanical	7								0
87163950	---Trailers for vehicles. not mechanical	7								0
87163960	---Small trailers for bikes	7								0
87163970	---Trailers with low platforms for heavy equipment	7								0
87163990	---Other trailers for transport of goods, not mechanical	7								0
871640	-Other trailers and semi-trailers									
87164010	---Trailers for the transport of people, not mechanical	7								0
87164020	---Exhibition trailers	7								0
87164030	---Trailers prepared in the form of libraries	7								0
87164090	---Other trailers, not elsewhere	7								0
871680	-Other vehicles									
8716801	---Vehicles pulled by hands:									
87168011	----Carriages for cleaning and building	10								0
87168012	----Carriages containing a barrel for drainage	10								0
87168013	----Carriages for cleaning and trash, small, hand-driven	10								0
87168014	----Carriages for carrying and hauling carpets	7								0
87168015	----Carriages of metal wires for shopping in stores	7								0
87168016	----Carriages for transportation of medical tools	7								0

HS	Description	Bound rate at date of accession	Interim	Final Bound	Implementation	Present concession established	INR	Concession first incorporated in a GATT Schedule	Earlier INRs	ODCs
87168017	----Carriages prepared for carrying and selling food	7								0
87168018	----Small carriages for selling cold drinks	7								0
87168019	----Other carriages, non-mechanical	7								0
87168090	---Other vehicles non-mechanical, not elsewhere	7								0
871690	-Parts									
87169010	---Parts of motor vehicles specified in (ex) s.h 8716	10								0
87169090	---Other parts	7								0
8801	Balloons and dirigibles; gliders, hang gliders and other non-powered aircraft.									
ex88011000	--For use in civil aircraft	0					US			0
88011000	-Gliders and hang gliders	7								0
88019000	-Other	7								0
ex88019000	--For use in civil aircraft	0					US			0
8802	Other aircraft (for example, helicopters, aeroplanes); spacecraft (including satellites) and suborbital and spacecraft launch vehicles.									
88021	-Helicopters:									
88021100	--Of an unladen weight not exceeding 2,000 kg	7								0
ex88021100	---For use in civil aircraft	0					US			0
ex88021200	---For use in civil aircraft	0					CA,US			0
88021200	--Of an unladen weight exceeding 2,000 kg	7					CA			0
ex88022000	--For use in civil aircraft	0					US			0
88022000	-Aeroplanes and other aircraft, of an unladen weight not exceeding 2,000 kg	7								0
88023000	-Aeroplanes and other aircraft, of an unladen weight exceeding 2,000 kg but not exceeding 15,000 kg	7					CA			0
ex88023000	--For use in civil aircraft	0					CA,US			0
88024000	-Aeroplanes and other aircraft, of an unladen weight exceeding 15,000 kg	7								0
ex88024000	--For use in civil aircraft	0					US			0
88026000	-Spacecraft (including satellites) and suborbital and spacecraft launch vehicles	7								0
8803	Parts of goods of heading 88.01 or 88.02.									
88031000	-Propellers and rotors and parts thereof	7								0

HS	Description	Bound rate at date of accession	Interim	Final Bound	Implementation	Present concession established	INR	Concession first incorporated in a GATT Schedule	Earlier INRs	ODCs
ex88031000	--For use in civil aircraft	0					US			0
88032000	-Under-carriages and parts thereof	7								0
ex88032000	--For use in civil aircraft	0					US			0
ex88033000	--For use in civil aircraft	0					US			0
88033000	-Other parts of aeroplanes or helicopters	7								0
88039000	-Other	7								0
ex88039000	--For use in civil aircraft	0					US			0
88040000	Parachutes (including dirigible parachutes and paragliders) and rotochutes; parts thereof and accessories thereto.	7								0
8805	Aircraft launching gear; deck-arrestor or similar gear; ground flying trainers; parts of the foregoing articles.									
88051000	-Aircraft launching gear and parts thereof; deck-arrestor or similar gear and parts thereof	7								0
88052	-Ground flying trainers and parts thereof:									
88052100	--Air combat simulators and parts thereof	7					CA			0
88052900	--Other	0					CA			0
8901	Cruise ships, excursion boats, ferry-boats, cargo ships, barges and similar vessels for the transport of persons or goods.									
89011000	-Cruise ships, excursion boats and similar vessels principally designed for the transport of persons; ferry-boats of all kinds	15								0
89012000	-Tankers	15								0
89013000	-Refrigerated vessels, other than those of subheading 8901.20	15								0
89019000	-Other vessels for the transport of goods and other vessels for the transport of both persons and goods	7								0
89020000	Fishing vessels; factory ships and other vessels for processing or preserving fishery products.	15								0
8903	Yachts and other vessels for pleasure or sports; rowing boats and canoes.									
89031000	-Inflatable	15								0
89039	-Other:									

HS	Description	Bound rate at date of accession	Interim	Final Bound	Implementation	Present concession established	INR	Concession first incorporated in a GATT Schedule	Earlier INRs	ODCs
89039100	--Sailboats, with or without auxiliary motor	15								0
89039200	--Motorboats, other than outboard motorboats	7								0
890399	--Other									
89039910	---Fiber-glass boats with mobile outward engines	15								0
89039920	---Fiber-glass boats without engines	15								0
89039990	---Other touring boats	15								0
89040000	Tugs and pusher craft.	10					CN			0
8905	Light-vessels, fire-floats, dredgers, floating cranes and other vessels the navigability of which is subsidiary to their main function; floating docks; floating or submersible drilling or production platforms.									
89051000	-Dredgers	15								0
89052000	-Floating or submersible drilling or production platforms	15								0
890590	-Other									
89059010	---Fire-floats	7								0
89059020	---Light-vessels	15								0
89059090	---Other floating docks and the like	15								0
8906	Other vessels, including warships and lifeboats other than rowing boats.									
89061000	-Warships	7								0
890690	-Other									
89069010	---Boats and warships of all kinds including lifeboats	7								0
89069090	---Other	7								0
8907	Other floating structures (for example, rafts, tanks, coffer-dams, landing-stages, buoys and beacons).									
89071000	-Inflatable rafts	15								0
89079000	-Other	15								0
89080000	Vessels and other floating structures for breaking up.	15								0

HS	Description	Bound rate at date of accession	Interim	Final Bound	Implementation	Present concession established	INR	Concession first incorporated in a GATT Schedule	Earlier INRs	ODCs
9001	Optical fibres and optical fibre bundles; optical fibre cables other than those of heading 85.44; sheets and plates of polarising material; lenses (including contact lenses), prisms, mirrors and other optical elements, of any material, unmounted, other than such elements of glass not optically worked.									
90011000	-Optical fibres, optical fibre bundles and cables	15					IN			0
90012000	-Sheets and plates of polarising material	15								0
90013000	-Contact lenses	5								0
90014000	-Spectacle lenses of glass	10								0
90015000	-Spectacle lenses of other materials	15					AU			0
90019000	-Other	15								0
ex90019000	--For use in civil aircraft	0					US			0
9002	Lenses, prisms, mirrors and other optical elements, of any material, mounted, being parts of or fittings for instruments or apparatus, other than such elements of glass not optically worked.									
90021	-Objective lenses:									
90021100	--For cameras, projectors or photographic enlargers or reducers	15								0
90021900	--Other	15								0
90022000	-Filters	5								0
90029000	-Other	15								0
ex90029000	--For use in civil aircraft	0					US			0
9003	Frames and mountings for spectacles, goggles or the like, and parts thereof.									
90031	-Frames and mountings:									
90031100	--Of plastics	15								0
90031900	--Of other materials	15								0
90039000	-Parts	15								0
9004	Spectacles, goggles and the like, corrective, protective or other.									
90041000	-Sunglasses	15								0
900490	-Other									
90049010	---Spectacles (eyeglasses), corrective	15								0
90049020	---Protective goggles	15								0
90049090	---Other corrective or protective spectacles or goggles	15								0

HS	Description	Bound rate at date of accession	Interim	Final Bound	Implementation	Present concession established	INR	Concession first incorporated in a GATT Schedule	Earlier INRs	ODCs
9005	Binoculars, monoculars, other optical telescopes, and mountings therefor; other astronomical instruments and mountings therefor, but not including instruments for radio-astronomy.									
90051000	-Binoculars	15								0
90058000	-Other instruments	15								0
90059000	-Parts and accessories (including mountings)	15								0
9006	Photographic (other than cinematographic) cameras; photographic flashlight apparatus and flashbulbs other than discharge lamps of heading 85.39.									
90061000	-Cameras of a kind used for preparing printing plates or cylinders	15								0
90062000	-Cameras of a kind used for recording documents on microfilm, microfiche or other microforms	15								0
90063000	-Cameras specially designed for underwater use, for aerial survey or for medical or surgical examination of internal organs; comparison cameras for forensic or criminological purposes	15								0
90064000	-Instant print cameras	15								0
90065	-Other cameras:									
90065100	--With a through-the-lens viewfinder (single lens reflex (SLR)), for roll film of a width not exceeding 35 mm	15								0
90065200	--Other, for roll film of a width less than 35 mm	15								0
90065300	--Other, for roll film of a width of 35 mm	10								0
90065900	--Other	15								0
90066	-Photographic flashlight apparatus and flashbulbs:									
90066100	--Discharge lamp ("electronic") flashlight apparatus	15								0
90066200	--Flashbulbs, flashcubes and the like	15								0
90066900	--Other	15								0
90069	-Parts and accessories:									
90069100	--For cameras	5								0
90069900	--Other	15								0

HS	Description	Bound rate at date of accession	Interim	Final Bound	Implementation	Present concession established	INR	Concession first incorporated in a GATT Schedule	Earlier INRs	ODCs
9007	Cinematographic cameras and projectors, whether or not incorporating sound recording or reproducing apparatus.									
90071	-Cameras:									
90071100	--For film of less than 16 mm width or for double-8 mm film	15								0
90071900	--Other	15								0
90072000	-Projectors	15								0
90079	-Parts and accessories:									
90079100	--For cameras	15								0
90079200	--For projectors	15								0
9008	Image projectors, other than cinematographic; photographic (other than cinematographic) enlargers and reducers.									
90081000	-Slide projectors	15								0
90082000	-Microfilm, microfiche or other microform readers, whether or not capable of producing copies	15								0
90083000	-Other image projectors	15								0
90084000	-Photographic (other than cinematographic) enlargers and reducers	15								0
90089000	-Parts and accessories	15								0
9009	Photocopying apparatus incorporating an optical system or of the contact type and thermo-copying apparatus.									
90091	-Electrostatic photocopying apparatus:									
90091100	--Operating by reproducing the original image directly onto the copy (direct process)	5		0	2008		US			0
90091200	--Operating by reproducing the original image via an intermediate onto the copy (indirect process)	10								0
90092	-Other photocopying apparatus:									
90092100	--Incorporating an optical system	5		0	2008		US			0
90092200	--Of the contact type	15								0
90093000	-Thermo-copying apparatus	15								0
90099	-Parts and accessories:									
90099100	--Automatic document feeders (See Endnote 14)	5		0	2008		US			0
90099200	--Paper feeders (See Endnote 14)	5		0	2008		US			0

HS	Description	Bound rate at date of accession	Interim	Final Bound	Implementation	Present concession established	INR	Concession first incorporated in a GATT Schedule	Earlier INRs	ODCs
90099300	--Sorters (See Endnote 14)	5		0	2008		US			0
90099900	--Other (See Endnote 14)	5		0	2008		US			0
9010	Apparatus and equipment for photographic (including cinematographic) laboratories (including apparatus for the projection or drawing of circuit patterns on sensitised semiconductor materials), not specified or included elsewhere in this Chapter; negatoscopes; projection screens.									
90101000	-Apparatus and equipment for automatically developing photographic (including cinematographic) film or paper in rolls or for automatically exposing developed film to rolls of photographic paper	5								0
90104	-Apparatus for the projection or drawing of circuit patterns on sensitised semiconductor materials:									
90104100	--Direct write-on-wafer apparatus	5		0	2008		US			0
90104200	--Step and repeat aligners	5		0	2008		US			0
90104900	--Other	5		0	2008		US			0
90105000	-Other apparatus and equipment for photographic (including cinematographic) laboratories; negatoscopes	10								0
90106000	-Projection screens	15								0
90109000	-Parts and accessories	5		0	2008		US			0
9011	Compound optical microscopes, including those for photomicrography, cinephotomicrography or microprojection.									
90111000	-Stereoscopic microscopes	5		0	2008		US			0
90112000	-Other microscopes, for photomicrography, cinephoto-micrography or microprojection	5		0	2008		US			0
90118000	-Other microscopes	15								0
90119000	-Parts and accessories	5		0	2008		US			0
9012	Microscopes other than optical microscopes; diffraction apparatus.									
90121000	-Microscopes other than optical microscopes; diffraction apparatus	5		0	2008		US			0
90129000	-Parts and accessories	5		0	2008		US			0

HS	Description	Bound rate at date of accession	Interim	Final Bound	Implementation	Present concession established	INR	Concession first incorporated in a GATT Schedule	Earlier INRs	ODCs
9013	Liquid crystal devices not constituting articles provided for more specifically in other headings; lasers, other than laser diodes; other optical appliances and instruments, not specified or included elsewhere in this Chapter.									
90131000	-Telescopic sights for fitting to arms; periscopes; telescopes designed to form parts of machines, appliances, instruments or apparatus of this Chapter or Section XVI	15								0
90132000	-Lasers, other than laser diodes	15								0
901380	-Other devices, appliances and instruments									
90138010	---Magnifying lenses (pocket, desk, etc.)	15								0
90138020	---Magic eyes for doors, ovens and the like	15								0
90138090	---Other optical appliances and instruments	15					US			0
ex90138090	----Flat panel display devices (including LCD, Electro Luminescence, Plasma, Vacuum-Fluorescence and other technologies) for products falling within this agreement, and parts thereof.	15		0	2008		US			0
90139000	-Parts and accessories	5					US			0
ex90139000	Flat panel display devices (including LCD, Electro Luminescence, Plasma, Vacuum-Fluorescence and other technologies) for products falling within this agreement, and parts thereof; Printed Circuit Assemblies for products falling within this agreement, including such assemblies for external connections such as cards that conform to the PCMCIA standard. Such printed circuit assemblies consist of one or more printed circuits of heading 8534 with one or more active elements assembled thereon, with or without passive elements "Active elements" means diodes, transistors, and similar semiconductor devices, whether or not photosensitive, of heading 8541, and integrated circuits and micro assemblies of heading 8542.	5		0	2008		US			0

HS	Description	Bound rate at date of accession	Interim	Final Bound	Implementation	Present concession established	INR	Concession first incorporated in a GATT Schedule	Earlier INRs	ODCs
9014	Direction finding compasses; other navigational instruments and appliances.									
90141000	-Direction finding compasses	15								0
ex90141000	--For use in civil aircraft	0					US			0
90142000	-Instruments and appliances for aeronautical or space navigation (other than compasses)	15								0
ex90142000	--For use in civil aircraft	0					US			0
90148000	-Other instruments and appliances	8								0
ex90149000	--For use in civil aircraft	0					US			0
90149000	-Parts and accessories	8								0
9015	Surveying (including photogrammetrical surveying), hydrographic, oceanographic, hydrological, meteorological or geophysical instruments and appliances, excluding compasses; rangefinders.									
90151000	-Rangefinders	15								0
90152000	-Theodolites and tachymeters (tacheometers)	15								0
90153000	-Levels	15								0
90154000	-Photogrammetrical surveying instruments and appliances	15								0
90158000	-Other instruments and appliances	5								0
90159000	-Parts and accessories	15								0
90160000	Balances of a sensitivity of 5 cg or better, with or without weights.	15								0
9017	Drawing, marking-out or mathematical calculating instruments (for example, drafting machines, pantographs, protractors, drawing sets, slide rules, disc calculators); instruments for measuring length, for use in the hand (for example, measuring rods and tapes, micrometers, callipers), not specified or included elsewhere in this Chapter.									
90171000	-Drafting tables and machines, whether or not automatic	15					DO,HN,US			0
ex90171000	--Plotters whether input or output units of HS heading No 8471 or drawing or drafting machines of HS heading No 9017.	15		0	2008		DO,HN,US			0

HS	Description	Bound rate at date of accession	Interim	Final Bound	Implementation	Present concession established	INR	Concession first incorporated in a GATT Schedule	Earlier INRs	ODCs
90172000	-Other drawing, marking-out or mathematical calculating instruments	5		0	2008		DO,HN,US			0
90173000	-Micrometers, callipers and gauges	5					DO,HN			0
901780	-Other instruments									
90178010	---School rulers and the like	15					DO,HN			0
90178020	---Longitudinal meters, foldable, etc.	15					DO,HN			0
90178090	---Other measuring, drawing and similar instruments	15					DO,HN			0
90179000	-Parts and accessories	5		0	2008		DO,HN,US			0
9018	Instruments and appliances used in medical, surgical, dental or veterinary sciences, including scintigraphic apparatus, other electro-medical apparatus and sight-testing instruments.									
90181	-Electro-diagnostic apparatus (including apparatus for functional exploratory examination or for checking physiological parameters):									
90181100	--Electro-cardiographs	5								0
90181200	--Ultrasonic scanning apparatus	5					NO			0
90181300	--Magnetic resonance imaging apparatus	5								0
90181400	--Scintigraphic apparatus	5								0
901819	--Other									
90181910	---Diagnostic ultrasonic apparatus	5								0
90181920	---Apparatus for measuring the blood pressure	5								0
90181990	---Other electro-diagnostic apparatus	5								0
90182000	-Ultra-violet or infra-red ray apparatus	5								0
90183	-Syringes, needles, catheters, cannulae and the like:									
901831	--Syringes, with or without needles									
90183110	---Syringes for plastering	5								0
90183120	---Syringes for eyes, ears and larynx	5								0
90183130	---Uterus syringes- gynecology	5								0
90183140	---Subcutaneous disposable syringes	5								0
90183190	---Other syringes	5								0
90183200	--Tubular metal needles and needles for sutures	5								0
901839	--Other									
90183910	---Trocar and cannula	5								0
90183920	---Scalpels, dissectors, probes and the like	5								0

HS	Description	Bound rate at date of accession	Interim	Final Bound	Implementation	Present concession established	INR	Concession first incorporated in a GATT Schedule	Earlier INRs	ODCs
90183930	---Intravenous catheter	5								0
90183990	---Other syringes, needles and the like	5								0
90184	-Other instruments and appliances, used in dental sciences:									
90184100	--Dental drill engines, whether or not combined on a single base with other dental equipment	5								0
901849	--Other									
90184910	---Spittons with fountains	5								0
90184920	---Teeth filling tools	5								0
90184930	---Dentists' chairs	5								0
90184990	---Other dental equipment	5								0
901850	-Other ophthalmic instruments and appliances									
90185010	---Diagnosing appliances (ophthalmoscope, etc.)	5								0
90185020	---Eye examination instruments and equipment	5								0
90185090	---Other ophthalmic instruments	5								0
901890	-Other instruments and appliances									
90189010	---Appliances for ear medicine	5								0
90189020	---Equipment and appliances for anaesthesia	5								0
90189030	---Appliances for nose and throat medicine	5								0
90189040	---Artificial kidney appliances	5								0
90189050	---Needles, of gold, silver or steel, for puncturing	5								0
90189060	---Endoscopes	5								0
90189070	---Veterinary instruments and equipment	5								0
90189090	---Other medical equipment	5								0
9019	Mechano-therapy appliances; massage apparatus; psychological aptitude-testing apparatus; ozone therapy, oxygen therapy, aerosol therapy, artificial respiration or other therapeutic respiration apparatus.									
90191000	-Mechano-therapy appliances; massage apparatus; psychological aptitude-testing apparatus	5								0
90192000	-Ozone therapy, oxygen therapy, aerosol therapy, artificial respiration or other therapeutic respiration apparatus	5								0

HS	Description	Bound rate at date of accession	Interim	Final Bound	Implementation	Present concession established	INR	Concession first incorporated in a GATT Schedule	Earlier INRs	ODCs
90200000	Other breathing appliances and gas masks, excluding protective masks having neither mechanical parts nor replaceable filters.	15								0
ex90200000	-For use in civil aircraft	0					US			0
9021	Orthopaedic appliances, including crutches, surgical belts and trusses; splints and other fracture appliances; artificial parts of the body; hearing aids and other appliances which are worn or carried, or implanted in the body, to compensate for a defect or disability.									
902110	-Orthopaedic or fracture appliances									
90211010	---Orthopaedic foot appliances (talipes appliances, leg braces, with or without spring support for the foot, surgical boots, etc.)	5								0
90211020	---Appliances for jaw bones	5								0
90211030	---Finger orthopaedic appliances	5								0
90211040	---Head and spine orthopaedic appliances	5								0
90211050	---Appliances for correcting scoliosis and curvature of the spine, surgical corsets and belts (excluding those of heading 62.12)	5								0
90211060	---Crutches, other than walking sticks of heading 66.02	5								0
90211070	---Orthopaedic appliances for animals	5								0
90211090	---Other	5								0
90212	-Artificial teeth and dental fittings:									
90212100	--Artificial teeth	5								0
90212900	--Other	5								0
90213	-Other artificial parts of the body:									
90213100	--Artificial joints	5								0
902139	--Other									
90213910	---Artificial ocular fittings (artificial eyes, intra-ocular lenses)	5								0
90213920	---Arms, forearms, hands, legs, feet, noses and heart vales	5								0
90213990	---Other	5								0
90214000	-Hearing aids, excluding parts and accessories	5								0

HS	Description	Bound rate at date of accession	Interim	Final Bound	Implementation	Present concession established	INR	Concession first incorporated in a GATT Schedule	Earlier INRs	ODCs
90215000	-Pacemakers for stimulating heart muscles, excluding parts and accessories	5								0
902190	-Other									
90219010	---Talking appliances for persons who cannot talk	5								0
90219020	---Electronic appliances for the blind	5								0
90219090	---Other orthopaedic appliances	5								0
9022	Apparatus based on the use of X-rays or of alpha, beta or gamma radiations, whether or not for medical, surgical, dental or veterinary uses, including radiography or radiotherapy apparatus, X-ray tubes and other X-ray generators, high tension generators, control panels and desks, screens, examination or treatment tables, chairs and the like.									
90221	-Apparatus based on the use of X-rays, whether or not for medical, surgical, dental or veterinary uses, including radiography or radiotherapy apparatus:									
90221200	--Computed tomography apparatus	5								0
90221300	--Other, for dental uses	5								0
90221400	--Other, for medical, surgical or veterinary uses	5								0
902219	--For other uses									
90221910	---X-ray equipment for luggage and suitcases	5								0
90221990	---Other x-ray and detection equipment	5								0
90222	-Apparatus based on the use of alpha, beta or gamma radiations, whether or not for medical, surgical, dental or veterinary uses, including radiography or radiotherapy apparatus:									
90222100	--For medical, surgical, dental or veterinary uses	5								0
90222900	--For other uses	7								0
90223000	-X-ray tubes	7								0
90229000	-Other, including parts and accessories	5								0
90230000	Instruments, apparatus and models, designed for demonstrational purposes (for example, in education or exhibitions), unsuitable for other uses.	8								0

HS	Description	Bound rate at date of accession	Interim	Final Bound	Implementation	Present concession established	INR	Concession first incorporated in a GATT Schedule	Earlier INRs	ODCs
9024	Machines and appliances for testing the hardness, strength, compressibility, elasticity or other mechanical properties of materials (for example, metals, wood, textiles, paper, plastics).									
90241000	-Machines and appliances for testing metals	15								0
90248000	-Other machines and appliances	10								0
90249000	-Parts and accessories	5								0
9025	Hydrometers and similar floating instruments, thermometers, pyrometers, barometers, hygrometers and psychrometers, recording or not, and any combination of these instruments.									
90251	-Thermometers and pyrometers, not combined with other instruments:									
ex90251100	---For use in civil aircraft	0					US			0
90251100	--Liquid-filled, for direct reading	5								0
ex90251900	---For use in civil aircraft	0					US			0
90251900	--Other	15								0
902580	-Other instruments									
90258010	---Hydrometers	15								0
ex90258010	----For use in civil aircraft	0					US			0
ex90258020	----For use in civil aircraft	0					US			0
90258020	---Hygrometers	15								0
ex90258090	----For use in civil aircraft	0					US			0
90258090	---Other floating instruments	15								0
90259000	-Parts and accessories	15								0
ex90259000	--For use in civil aircraft	0					US			0
9026	Instruments and apparatus for measuring or checking the flow, level, pressure or other variables of liquids or gases (for example, flow meters, level gauges, manometers, heat meters), excluding instruments and apparatus of heading 90.14, 90.15, 90.28 ou 90.32.									
90261000	-For measuring or checking the flow or level of liquids	5		0	2008		US			0
ex90261000	--For use in civil aircraft	0					US			0
90262000	-For measuring or checking pressure	5		0	2008		US			0
ex90262000	--For use in civil aircraft	0					US			0
90268000	-Other instruments or apparatus	5		0	2008		US			0

HS	Description	Bound rate at date of accession	Interim	Final Bound	Implementation	Present concession established	INR	Concession first incorporated in a GATT Schedule	Earlier INRs	ODCs
ex90268000	--For use in civil aircraft	0					US			0
90269000	-Parts and accessories	5		0	2008		US			0
ex90269000	--For use in civil aircraft	0					US			0
9027	Instruments and apparatus for physical or chemical analysis (for example, polarimeters, refractometers, spectrometers, gas or smoke analysis apparatus); instruments and apparatus for measuring or checking viscosity, porosity, expansion, surface tension or the like; instruments and apparatus for measuring or checking quantities of heat, sound or light (including exposure meters); microtomes.									
90271000	-Gas or smoke analysis apparatus	15								0
90272000	-Chromatographs and electrophoresis instruments	5		0	2008		US			0
90273000	-Spectrometers, spectrophotometers and spectrographs using optical radiations (UV, visible, IR)	5		0	2008		US			0
90274000	-Exposure meters	15								0
90275000	-Other instruments and apparatus using optical radiations (UV, visible, IR)	5		0	2008		US			0
902780	-Other instruments and apparatus									
90278010	---Blood test tools and devices	5		0	2008		CH,US			0
90278090	---Other instruments for chemical analysis and the like	5		0	2008		CH,US			0
90279000	-Microtomes; parts and accessories	5		0	2008		US			0
9028	Gas, liquid or electricity supply or production meters, including calibrating meters therefor.									
90281000	-Gas meters	5								0
902820	-Liquid meters									
90282010	---Water meters	15								0
90282090	---Other liquid meters	15								0
90283000	-Electricity meters	15								0
90289000	-Parts and accessories	5								0
9029	Revolution counters, production counters, taximeters, mileometers, pedometers and the like; speed indicators and tachometers, other than those of heading 90.14 or 90.15; stroboscopes.									

HS	Description	Bound rate at date of accession	Interim	Final Bound	Implementation	Present concession established	INR	Concession first incorporated in a GATT Schedule	Earlier INRs	ODCs
902910	-Revolution counters, production counters, taximeters, mileometers, pedometers and the like									
90291010	---Production counters	15								0
ex90291010	----For use in civil aircraft	0					US			0
ex90291020	----For use in civil aircraft	0					US			0
90291020	---Taximeters	15								0
ex90291090	----For use in civil aircraft	0					US			0
90291090	---Other revolution counters, pedometers and the like	15								0
ex90292000	--For use in civil aircraft	0					US			0
90292000	-Speed indicators and tachometers; stroboscopes	15								0
90299000	-Parts and accessories	15								0
ex90299000	--For use in civil aircraft	0					US			0
9030	Oscilloscopes, spectrum analysers and other instruments and apparatus for measuring or checking electrical quantities, excluding meters of heading 90.28; instruments and apparatus for measuring or detecting alpha, beta, gamma, X-ray, cosmic or other ionising radiations.									
90301000	-Instruments and apparatus for measuring or detecting ionising radiations	8								0
ex90301000	--For use in civil aircraft	0					US			0
ex90302000	--For use in civil aircraft	0					US			0
90302000	-Cathode-ray oscilloscopes and cathode-ray oscillographs	8								0
90303	-Other instruments and apparatus, for measuring or checking voltage, current, resistance or power, without a recording device:									
ex90303100	---For use in civil aircraft	0					US			0
90303100	--Multimeters	8								0
ex90303900	---For use in civil aircraft	0					US			0
90303900	--Other	8								0
90304000	-Other instruments and apparatus, specially designed for telecommunications (for example, cross-talk meters, gain measuring instruments, distortion factor meters, psophometers)	5		0	2008		US			0

HS	Description	Bound rate at date of accession	Interim	Final Bound	Implementation	Present concession established	INR	Concession first incorporated in a GATT Schedule	Earlier INRs	ODCs
ex90304000	--For use in civil aircraft	0					US			0
90308	-Other instruments and apparatus:									
90308200	--For measuring or checking semiconductor wafers or devices	5		0	2008		US			0
90308300	--Other, with a recording device	8								0
ex90308300	---For use in civil aircraft	0					US			0
90308900	--Other	8								0
ex90308900	---For use in civil aircraft	0					US			0
90309000	-Parts and accessories	5		0	2008		US			0
ex90309000	--For use in civil aircraft	0					US			0
9031	Measuring or checking instruments, appliances and machines, not specified or included elsewhere in this Chapter; profile projectors.									
90311000	-Machines for balancing mechanical parts	15								0
90312000	-Test benches	15								0
90313000	-Profile projectors	15								0
90314	-Other optical instruments and appliances:									
90314100	--For inspecting semiconductor wafers or devices or for inspecting photomasks or reticles used in manufacturing semiconductor devices	5		0	2008		US			0
90314900	--Other	5		0	2008		US			0
903180	-Other instruments, appliances and machines									
ex90318010	----For use in civil aircraft	0					US			0
90318010	---Instruments for inspecting and adjusting engines	5								0
ex90318090	----For use in civil aircraft	0					US			0
90318090	---Other instruments for checking or measuring	5								0
90319000	-Parts and accessories	5		0	2008		US			0
ex90319000	--For use in civil aircraft	0					US			0
9032	Automatic regulating or controlling instruments and apparatus.									
90321000	-Thermostats	8								0
ex90321000	--For use in civil aircraft	0					US			0
ex90322000	--For use in civil aircraft	0					US			0
90322000	-Manostats	8								0
90328	-Other instruments and apparatus:									
90328100	--Hydraulic or pneumatic	8								0

HS	Description	Bound rate at date of accession	Interim	Final Bound	Implementation	Present concession established	INR	Concession first incorporated in a GATT Schedule	Earlier INRs	ODCs
ex90328100	---For use in civil aircraft	0					US			0
ex90328900	---For use in civil aircraft	0					CA,US			0
90328900	--Other	8					CA			0
ex90329000	--For use in civil aircraft	0					US			0
90329000	-Parts and accessories	8								0
90330000	Parts and accessories (not specified or included elsewhere in this Chapter) for machines, appliances, instruments or apparatus of Chapter 90.	5								0
9101	Wrist-watches, pocket-watches and other watches, including stop-watches, with case of precious metal or of metal clad with precious metal.									
91011	-Wrist-watches, electrically operated, whether or not incorporating a stop-watch facility:									
91011100	--With mechanical display only	12					CH			0
91011200	--With opto-electronic display only	15					CH			0
91011900	--Other	15					CH			0
91012	-Other wrist-watches, whether or not incorporating a stop-watch facility:									
91012100	--With automatic winding	12					CH			0
91012900	--Other	12					CH			0
91019	-Other:									
91019100	--Electrically operated	15					CH			0
91019900	--Other	15					CH			0
9102	Wrist-watches, pocket-watches and other watches, including stop-watches, other than those of heading 91.01.									
91021	-Wrist-watches, electrically operated, whether or not incorporating a stop-watch facility:									
91021100	--With mechanical display only	12					CH,JP			0
91021200	--With opto-electronic display only	15					CH,JP			0
91021900	--Other	15					CH			0
91022	-Other wrist-watches, whether or not incorporating a stop-watch facility:									
91022100	--With automatic winding	12					CH,JP			0
91022900	--Other	12					CH			0
91029	-Other:									
91029100	--Electrically operated	15					CH			0
91029900	--Other	15					CH			0

HS	Description	Bound rate at date of accession	Interim	Final Bound	Implementation	Present concession established	INR	Concession first incorporated in a GATT Schedule	Earlier INRs	ODCs
9103	Clocks with watch movements, excluding clocks of heading 91.04.									
91031000	-Electrically operated	15					CH			0
91039000	-Other	15					CH			0
ex91040000	-For use in civil aircraft	0					CH,US			0
91040000	Instrument panel clocks and clocks of a similar type for vehicles, aircraft, spacecraft or vessels.	15					CH			0
9105	Other clocks.									
91051	-Alarm clocks:									
91051100	--Electrically operated	10					CH			0
91051900	--Other	15					CH			0
91052	-Wall clocks:									
91052100	--Electrically operated	10					CH			0
91052900	--Other	15					CH			0
91059	-Other:									
91059100	--Electrically operated	15					CH			0
91059900	--Other	15					CH			0
9106	Time of day recording apparatus and apparatus for measuring, recording or otherwise indicating intervals of time, with clock or watch movement or with synchronous motor (for example, time-registers, time-recorders).									
91061000	-Time-registers; time-recorders	15					CH			0
91062000	-Parking meters	15					CH			0
91069000	-Other	15					CH			0
91070000	Time switches with clock or watch movement or with synchronous motor.	15					CH			0
9108	Watch movements, complete and assembled.									
91081	-Electrically operated:									
91081100	--With mechanical display only or with a device to which a mechanical display can be incorporated	15					CH			0
91081200	--With opto-electronic display only	15					CH			0
91081900	--Other	15					CH			0
91082000	-With automatic winding	15					CH			0
91089000	-Other	15					CH			0
9109	Clock movements, complete and assembled.									
91091	-Electrically operated:									
91091100	--Of alarm clocks	15					CH			0

HS	Description	Bound rate at date of accession	Interim	Final Bound	Implementation	Present concession established	INR	Concession first incorporated in a GATT Schedule	Earlier INRs	ODCs
ex91091900	---For use in civil aircraft	0					CH,US			0
91091900	--Other	15					CH			0
ex91099000	--For use in civil aircraft	0					CH,US			0
91099000	-Other	15					CH			0
9110	Complete watch or clock movements, unassembled or partly assembled (movement sets); incomplete watch or clock movements, assembled; rough watch or clock movements.									
91101	-Of watches:									
91101100	--Complete movements, unassembled or partly assembled (movement sets)	15					CH			0
91101200	--Incomplete movements, assembled	15					CH			0
91101900	--Rough movements	15					CH			0
91109000	-Other	15					CH			0
9111	Watch cases and parts thereof.									
91111000	-Cases of precious metal or of metal clad with precious metal	15					CH			0
91112000	-Cases of base metal, whether or not gold- or silver-plated	15					CH			0
91118000	-Other cases	15					CH			0
91119000	-Parts	15					CH			0
9112	Clock cases and cases of a similar type for other goods of this Chapter, and parts thereof.									
91122000	-Cases	15					CH			0
91129000	-Parts	15					CH			0
9113	Watch straps, watch bands and watch bracelets, and parts thereof.									
91131000	-Of precious metal or of metal clad with precious metal	15					CH			0
91132000	-Of base metal, whether or not gold- or silver-plated	15					CH			0
911390	-Other									
91139010	---Watch bands of artificial plastic materials	15					CH			0
91139020	---Watch bands of natural leather or composition leather	15					CH			0
91139030	---Watch bands of woven fabrics	15					CH			0
91139040	---Watch bands with pearls, precious, semi-precious stones	15					CH			0
91139090	---Other watch bands and the like	15					CH			0
9114	Other clock or watch parts.									

HS	Description	Bound rate at date of accession	Interim	Final Bound	Implementation	Present concession established	INR	Concession first incorporated in a GATT Schedule	Earlier INRs	ODCs
91141000	-Springs, including hair-springs	15					CH			0
91142000	-Jewels	15					CH			0
91143000	-Dials	15					CH			0
91144000	-Plates and bridges	15					CH			0
91149000	-Other	15					CH			0
9201	Pianos, including automatic pianos; harpsichords and other keyboard stringed instruments.									
92011000	-Upright pianos	15								0
92012000	-Grand pianos	15								0
92019000	-Other	15								0
9202	Other string musical instruments (for example, guitars, violins, harps).									
92021000	-Played with a bow	15								0
920290	-Other									
92029010	---Lutes	15								0
92029090	---Other string musical instruments	15								0
92030000	Keyboard pipe organs; harmoniums and similar keyboard instruments with free metal reeds.	15								0
9204	Accordions and similar instruments; mouth organs.									
92041000	-Accordions and similar instruments	15								0
92042000	-Mouth organs	15								0
9205	Other wind musical instruments (for example, clarinets, trumpets, bagpipes).									
92051000	-Brass-wind instruments	15								0
92059000	-Other	15								0
9206	Percussion musical instruments (for example, drums, xylophones, cymbals, castanets, maracas).									
92060010	---Drums	15								0
92060020	---Cymbals	15								0
92060030	---Triangles (and rods)	15								0
92060040	---Xylophones	15								0
92060090	---Other percussion instruments	15								0
9207	Musical instruments, the sound of which is produced, or must be amplified, electrically (for example, organs, guitars, accordions).									
92071000	-Keyboard instruments, other than accordions	15								0
92079000	-Other	15								0

HS	Description	Bound rate at date of accession	Interim	Final Bound	Implementation	Present concession established	INR	Concession first incorporated in a GATT Schedule	Earlier INRs	ODCs
9208	Musical boxes, fairground organs, mechanical street organs, mechanical singing birds, musical saws and other musical instruments not falling within any other heading of this Chapter; decoy calls of all kinds; whistles, call horns and other mouth-blown sound signalling instruments.									
92081000	-Musical boxes	15								0
920890	-Other									
92089010	---Fairground organs	15								0
92089020	---Musical saws	15								0
92089030	---Decoy calls and effects	15								0
92089040	---Mouth-blown whistles for leadership and the like	15								0
92089090	---Other musical instruments not elsewhere specified	15								0
9209	Parts (for example, mechanisms for musical boxes) and accessories (for example, cards, discs and rolls for mechanical instruments) of musical instruments; metronomes, tuning forks and pitch pipes of all kinds.									
92091000	-Metronomes, tuning forks and pitch pipes	15								0
92092000	-Mechanisms for musical boxes	15								0
92093000	-Musical instrument strings	15								0
92099	-Other:									
92099100	--Parts and accessories for pianos	15								0
92099200	--Parts and accessories for the musical instruments of heading 92.02	15								0
92099300	--Parts and accessories for the musical instruments of heading 92.03	15								0
92099400	--Parts and accessories for the musical instruments of heading 92.07	15								0
92099900	--Other	15								0
9301	Military weapons, other than revolvers, pistols and the arms of heading 93.07.									
93011	-Artillery weapons (for example, guns, howitzers and mortars):									
93011100	--Self-propelled	7								0
93011900	--Other	7								0

HS	Description	Bound rate at date of accession	Interim	Final Bound	Implementation	Present concession established	INR	Concession first incorporated in a GATT Schedule	Earlier INRs	ODCs
93012000	-Rocket launchers; flame-throwers; grenade launchers; torpedo tubes and similar projectors	7								0
93019000	-Other	7								0
93020000	Revolvers and pistols, other than those of heading 93.03 or 93.04.	7								0
9303	Other firearms and similar devices which operate by the firing of an explosive charge (for example, sporting shotguns and rifles, muzzle-loading firearms, Very pistols and other devices designed to project only signal flares, pistols and revolvers for firing blank ammunition, captive-bolt humane killers, line-throwing guns).									
93031000	-Muzzle-loading firearms	15								0
93032000	-Other sporting, hunting or target-shooting shotguns, including combination shotgun-rifles	15								0
93033000	-Other sporting, hunting or target-shooting rifles	15								0
93039000	-Other	15								0
9304	Other arms (for example, spring, air or gas guns and pistols, truncheons), excluding those of heading 93.07.									
93040010	---Fishguns (underwater)	15								0
93040090	---Other arms	15								0
9305	Parts and accessories of articles of headings 93.01 to 93.04.									
93051000	-Of revolvers or pistols	7								0
93052	-Of shotguns or rifles of heading 93.03:									
93052100	--Shotgun barrels	15								0
93052900	--Other	15								0
93059	-Other:									
93059100	--Of military weapons of heading 93.01	7								0
93059900	--Other	15								0
9306	Bombs, grenades, torpedoes, mines, missiles and similar munitions of war and parts thereof; cartridges and other ammunition and projectiles and parts thereof, including shot and cartridge wads.									

HS	Description	Bound rate at date of accession	Interim	Final Bound	Implementation	Present concession established	INR	Concession first incorporated in a GATT Schedule	Earlier INRs	ODCs
93061000	-Cartridges for riveting or similar tools or for captive-bolt humane killers and parts thereof	15								0
93062	-Shotgun cartridges and parts thereof; air gun pellets:									
930621	--Cartridges									
93062110	---Cartridges for hunting and sports shooting	15		13	2008					0
93062190	---Other cartridges	7								0
930629	--Other									
93062910	---Parts and accessories of cartridges	15								0
93062990	---Other of cartridges	7								0
930630	-Other cartridges and parts thereof									
93063010	---Other cartridges, parts and accessories, hunting/sports	15								0
93063090	---Other cartridges, parts, accessories for other purposes	7								0
93069000	-Other	7								0
9307	Swords, cutlasses, bayonets, lances and similar arms and parts thereof and scabbards and sheaths therefor.									
93070010	---Military swords, bayonets and the like	7								0
93070090	---Swords, bayonets and the like for non-military	15								0
9401	Seats (other than those of heading 94.02), whether or not convertible into beds, and parts thereof.									
94011000	-Seats of a kind used for aircraft	15								0
ex94011000	--For use in civil aircraft	0					US			0
94012000	-Seats of a kind used for motor vehicles	15								0
94013000	-Swivel seats with variable height adjustment	15								0
94014000	-Seats other than garden seats or camping equipment, convertible into beds	15								0
94015000	-Seats of cane, osier, bamboo or similar materials	15					PH			0
94016	-Other seats, with wooden frames:									
94016100	--Upholstered	15					PY			0
94016900	--Other	15					PY			0
94017	-Other seats, with metal frames:									
940171	--Upholstered									

HS	Description	Bound rate at date of accession	Interim	Final Bound	Implementation	Present concession established	INR	Concession first incorporated in a GATT Schedule	Earlier INRs	ODCs
94017110	---Baby seats with metal frames, upholstered	15								0
94017120	---Walker seats with metal frames, upholstered	15								0
94017190	---Other seats with metal frames, upholstered	15								0
940179	--Other									
94017910	---Baby seats with metal frames, not upholstered	15								0
94017920	---Other walker seats with metal frames, not upholstered	15								0
94017990	---Other seats with metal frames not upholstered	15								0
940180	-Other seats									
9401801	---Other seats, with plastic frames:									
94018011	----Baby seats with plastic frames	15								0
94018012	----Other walker seats with plastic frames, not upholstered	15								0
94018019	----Other seats with plastic frames	15								0
94018020	---Seats of stones, mixture of asbestos or ceramics	15								0
94018090	---Other seats not elsewhere included (See Endnote 15)	15								0
94019000	-Parts	15								0
9402	Medical, surgical, dental or veterinary furniture (for example, operating tables, examination tables, hospital beds with mechanical fittings, dentists' chairs); barbers' chairs and similar chairs, having rotating as well as both reclining and elevating movements; parts of the foregoing articles.									
940210	-Dentists', barbers' or similar chairs and parts thereof									
94021010	---Dentists' chairs and parts thereof	5								0
94021020	---Barbers' chairs and parts thereof	5								0
94021090	---Other chairs similar to dentist or barber	5								0
940290	-Other									
94029010	---Medical and surgical furniture and parts	5								0
94029090	---Other	5								0
9403	Other furniture and parts thereof.									

HS	Description	Bound rate at date of accession	Interim	Final Bound	Implementation	Present concession established	INR	Concession first incorporated in a GATT Schedule	Earlier INRs	ODCs
940310	-Metal furniture of a kind used in offices									
94031010	---Office desks, metal	15					DO,HN			0
94031020	---Tables with wheels, metal	15					DO,HN			0
94031030	---Cabinets, electrical, for keeping files, metal	15					DO,HN			0
94031090	---Other metal office furniture	15					DO,HN			0
940320	-Other metal furniture									
94032010	---Wardrobes, metal	15								0
ex94032010	----For use in civil aircraft	0					US			0
94032020	---Clothes stands for placing on the floor, metal	15								0
ex94032020	----For use in civil aircraft	0					US			0
ex94032030	----For use in civil aircraft	0					US			0
94032030	---Lab benches fitted with nozzles or water taps, metal	15								0
ex94032040	----For use in civil aircraft	0					US			0
94032040	---Draught screens used as metal furniture	15								0
94032090	---Other metal furniture	15								0
ex94032090	----For use in civil aircraft	0					US			0
940330	-Wooden furniture of a kind used in offices									
94033010	---Office desks, wood	15					EC			0
94033020	---Tables with wheels, wood	15					EC			0
94033030	---Cabinets, electrical, for keeping files, wood	15					EC			0
94033090	---Other wood office furniture	15					EC			0
940340	-Wooden furniture of a kind used in the kitchen									
94034010	---Wooden cupboards for pots and tableware	15								0
94034020	---Wooden dining room sets, complete	8					EC			0
94034090	---Other wood kitchen furniture	8					EC			0
940350	-Wooden furniture of a kind used in the bedroom									
94035010	---Wooden bedroom sets, complete (See Endnote 16)	15								0
94035020	---Wardrobes, wood	15								0
94035090	---Other wooden bedroom furniture (See Endnote 16)	15								0
940360	-Other wooden furniture									

HS	Description	Bound rate at date of accession	Interim	Final Bound	Implementation	Present concession established	INR	Concession first incorporated in a GATT Schedule	Earlier INRs	ODCs
94036010	---Lab benches fitted with nozzles and water taps, wood	10								0
94036020	---Clothes stands for placing on the floor, wood	15								0
94036030	---Wall cabinets (first aid kits), wood	15								0
94036040	---Cabinets used as supports for wash basins, wood	15								0
94036090	---Other wooden furniture	15								0
ex94037000	--For use in civil aircraft	0					US			0
94037000	-Furniture of plastics	15								0
940380	-Furniture of other materials, including cane, osier, bamboo or similar materials									
94038010	---Furniture of stones, of asbestos mixture or ceramics (See Endnote 17)	10								0
94038090	---Furniture of other materials not specified elsewhere (See Endnote 18)	15								0
94039000	-Parts	15								0
9404	Mattress supports; articles of bedding and similar furnishing (for example, mattresses, quilts, eiderdowns, cushions, pouffes and pillows) fitted with springs or stuffed or internally fitted with any material or of cellular rubber or plastics, whether or not covered.									
94041000	-Mattress supports	15								0
94042	-Mattresses:									
940421	--Of cellular rubber or plastics, whether or not covered									
94042110	---Spring mattresses of cellular rubber or plastics	15								0
94042120	---Spring mattresses of cellular rubber or plastic, 100 x 200 cm	15								0
94042190	---Other mattresses of cellular rubber or plastics	15								0
940429	--Of other materials									
94042910	---Spring mattresses of other materials	15								0
94042920	---Spring mattresses of other materials, 100 x 200 cm	15								0
94042990	---Other mattresses of other materials	15								0
94043000	-Sleeping bags	15								0
940490	-Other									
94049010	---Quilts	10								0
94049020	---Pillows	10								0

HS	Description	Bound rate at date of accession	Interim	Final Bound	Implementation	Present concession established	INR	Concession first incorporated in a GATT Schedule	Earlier INRs	ODCs
94049030	---Cushions and puff seats	10								0
94049040	---Sets of quilts, bedspreads and counterpanes	15								0
94049090	---Other articles of bedding	10								0
9405	Lamps and lighting fittings including searchlights and spotlights and parts thereof, not elsewhere specified or included; illuminated signs, illuminated name-plates and the like, having a permanently fixed light source, and parts thereof not elsewhere specified or included.									
94051000	-Chandeliers and other electric ceiling or wall lighting fittings, excluding those of a kind used for lighting public open spaces or thoroughfares	10								0
ex94051000	--For use in civil aircraft	0					US			0
94052000	-Electric table, desk, bedside or floor-standing lamps	10								0
94053000	-Lighting sets of a kind used for Christmas trees	10								0
940540	-Other electric lamps and lighting fittings									
94054010	---Lamps for external lighting	15								0
94054020	---Special lamps	7								0
94054090	---Other electric lamps and lighting fixtures	10								0
94055000	-Non-electrical lamps and lighting fittings	15								0
94056000	-Illuminated signs, illuminated name-plates and the like	15								0
ex94056000	--For use in civil aircraft	0					US			0
94059	-Parts:									
94059100	--Of glass	15								0
ex94059200	---For use in civil aircraft	0					US			0
94059200	--Of plastics	15								0
ex94059900	---For use in civil aircraft	0					US			0
94059900	--Other	15								0
9406	Prefabricated buildings.									
9406001	---Of plastics:									
94060011	----Greenhouses for cultivation purposes, plastic	7								0
94060012	----Barns and cages for animal production, plastic	5								0

HS	Description	Bound rate at date of accession	Interim	Final Bound	Implementation	Present concession established	INR	Concession first incorporated in a GATT Schedule	Earlier INRs	ODCs
94060013	----Warehouses, plastic	7								0
94060014	----Buildings for residence or school, plastic	5								0
94060019	----Other plastic prefabricated buildings	5								0
9406002	---Of wood:									
94060021	----Greenhouses for cultivation purposes, wood	5								0
94060022	----Barns and cages for animal production, wood	5								0
94060023	----Warehouses, wood	5								0
94060024	----Buildings for residence or school, wood	5								0
94060029	----Other wooden prefabricated buildings	5								0
9406003	---Of iron:									
94060031	----Greenhouses for cultivation purposes, iron	15								0
94060032	----Barns and cages for animal production, iron	5								0
94060033	----Warehouses, iron	15								0
94060034	----Buildings for residence or school, iron	15								0
94060039	----Other iron prefabricated buildings	5								0
9406004	---Of aluminium:									
94060041	----Greenhouses for cultivation purposes, aluminium	15								0
94060042	----Barns and cages for animal production, aluminium	7								0
94060043	----Warehouses, aluminium	7								0
94060044	----Buildings for residence or school, aluminium	7								0
94060049	----Other aluminium prefabricated buildings	7								0
9406005	---Of fibreglass:									
94060051	----Greenhouses for cultivation purposes, fibreglass	15								0
94060052	----Barns and cages for animal production, fibreglass	15								0
94060053	----Warehouses, fibreglass	15								0
94060054	----Buildings for residence or school, fibreglass	5								0
94060059	----Other fibreglass prefabricated buildings	5								0

HS	Description	Bound rate at date of accession	Interim	Final Bound	Implementation	Present concession established	INR	Concession first incorporated in a GATT Schedule	Earlier INRs	ODCs
94060090	---Prefabricated buildings of other materials	5								0
9501	Wheeled toys designed to be ridden by children (for example, tricycles, scooters, pedal cars); dolls' carriages.									
95010010	---Children's tricycles	10								0
95010020	---Children's pedal cars	10								0
95010090	---Other children's wheeled toys	10								0
9502	Dolls representing only human beings.									
95021000	-Dolls, whether or not dressed	15								0
95029	-Parts and accessories:									
95029100	--Garments and accessories therefor, footwear and headgear	15								0
95029900	--Other	15								0
9503	Other toys; reduced-size ("scale") models and similar recreational models, working or not; puzzles of all kinds.									
95031000	-Electric trains, including tracks, signals and other accessories therefor	15								0
95032000	-Reduced-size ("scale") model assembly kits, whether or not working models, excluding those of subheading 9503.10	15								0
95033000	-Other construction sets and constructional toys	15								0
95034	-Toys representing animals or non-human creatures:									
95034100	--Stuffed	10								0
95034900	--Other	15								0
95035000	-Toy musical instruments and apparatus	15								0
95036000	-Puzzles	15								0
95037000	-Other toys, put up in sets or outfits	15								0
95038000	-Other toys and models, incorporating a motor	15								0
95039000	-Other	10								0
9504	Articles for funfair, table or parlour games, including pintables, billiards, special tables for casino games and automatic bowling alley equipment.									
95041000	-Video games of a kind used with a television receiver	10								0
950420	-Articles and accessories for billiards									
95042010	---Billiards	15								0

HS	Description	Bound rate at date of accession	Interim	Final Bound	Implementation	Present concession established	INR	Concession first incorporated in a GATT Schedule	Earlier INRs	ODCs
95042020	---Billiards' chalk	15								0
95042090	---Billiards' chalk	10								0
95043000	-Other games, operated by coins, banknotes (paper currency), discs or other similar articles, other than bowling alley equipment	15								0
95044000	-Playing cards	15								0
95049000	-Other	10								0
9505	Festive, carnival or other entertainment articles, including conjuring tricks and novelty jokes.									
95051000	-Articles for Christmas festivities	15								0
95059000	-Other	15								0
9506	Articles and equipment for general physical exercise, gymnastics, athletics, other sports (including table-tennis) or outdoor games, not specified or included elsewhere in this Chapter; swimming pools and paddling pools.									
95061	-Snow-skis and other snow-ski equipment:									
95061100	--Skis	15								0
95061200	--Ski-fastenings (ski-bindings)	15								0
95061900	--Other	5								0
95062	-Water-skis, surf-boards, sailboards and other water-sport equipment:									
95062100	--Sailboards	15								0
95062900	--Other	5								0
95063	-Golf clubs and other golf equipment:									
95063100	--Clubs, complete	15								0
95063200	--Balls	15								0
95063900	--Other	15								0
95064000	-Articles and equipment for table-tennis	15								0
95065	-Tennis, badminton or similar rackets, whether or not strung:									
95065100	--Lawn-tennis rackets, whether or not strung	15								0
95065900	--Other	15								0
95066	-Balls, other than golf balls and table-tennis balls:									
95066100	--Lawn-tennis balls	10					PH			0
95066200	--Inflatable	10								0
95066900	--Other	15								0

HS	Description	Bound rate at date of accession	Interim	Final Bound	Implementation	Present concession established	INR	Concession first incorporated in a GATT Schedule	Earlier INRs	ODCs
95067000	-Ice skates and roller skates, including skating boots with skates attached	15								0
95069	-Other:									
95069100	--Articles and equipment for general physical exercise, gymnastics or athletics	5								0
95069900	--Other	5								0
9507	Fishing rods, fish-hooks and other line fishing tackle; fish landing nets, butterfly nets and similar nets; decoy "birds" (other than those of heading 92.08 or 97.05) and similar hunting or shooting requisites.									
95071000	-Fishing rods	15								0
95072000	-Fish-hooks, whether or not snelled	15								0
95073000	-Fishing reels	15								0
95079000	-Other	15								0
9508	Roundabouts, swings, shooting galleries and other fairground amusements; travelling circuses and travelling menageries; travelling theatres.									
95081000	-Travelling circuses and travelling menageries	15								0
950890	-Other									
95089010	---Roundabouts, swings	15								0
95089090	---Other	15								0
9601	Worked ivory, bone, tortoise-shell, horn, antlers, coral, mother-of-pearl and other animal carving material, and articles of these materials (including articles obtained by moulding).									
96011000	-Worked ivory and articles of ivory	15								0
96019000	-Other	10								0
9602	Worked vegetable or mineral carving material and articles of these materials; moulded or carved articles of wax, of stearin, of natural gums or natural resins or of modelling pastes, and other moulded or carved articles, not elsewhere specified or included; worked, unhardened gelatin (except gelatin of heading 35.03) and articles of unhardened gelatin.									
96020010	---Artificial honeycombs for beehives	15								0

HS	Description	Bound rate at date of accession	Interim	Final Bound	Implementation	Present concession established	INR	Concession first incorporated in a GATT Schedule	Earlier INRs	ODCs
96020020	---Pearls of wax	15								0
96020030	---Articles made of wax-based and unhardened gelatin	15								0
96020040	---Articles of paraffin like vessels for hydrofluoric acid	15								0
96020050	---Articles for stearin	15								0
96020090	---Other worked vegetable or mineral carving articles	15								0
9603	Brooms, brushes (including brushes constituting parts of machines, appliances or vehicles), hand-operated mechanical floor sweepers, not motorised, mops and feather dusters; prepared knots and tufts for broom or brush making; paint pads and rollers; squeegees (other than roller squeegees).									
96031000	-Brooms and brushes, consisting of twigs or other vegetable materials bound together, with or without handles	15		12	2008		MX			0
96032	-Tooth brushes, shaving brushes, hair brushes, nail brushes, eyelash brushes and other toilet brushes for use on the person, including such brushes constituting parts of appliances:									
96032100	--Tooth brushes, including dental-plate brushes	15								0
960329	--Other									
96032910	---Shaving brushes	15					CH,DO,HN			0
96032920	---Hair brushes	15					CH,DO,HN			0
96032990	---Other brushes for use on people	15					CH,DO,HN			0
96033000	-Artists' brushes, writing brushes and similar brushes for the application of cosmetics	15								0
96034000	-Paint, distemper, varnish or similar brushes (other than brushes of subheading 9603.30); paint pads and rollers	15								0
96035000	-Other brushes constituting parts of machines, appliances or vehicles	15								0
960390	-Other									
96039010	---Brushes of rubber or plastic for house-keeping	15								0
96039020	---Brushes for cleaning clothes or shoes	15								0

HS	Description	Bound rate at date of accession	Interim	Final Bound	Implementation	Present concession established	INR	Concession first incorporated in a GATT Schedule	Earlier INRs	ODCs
96039030	---Sweeping brushes for cleaning the roads, floors, etc.	15								0
96039040	---Manual brushes of metal wires	15								0
96039090	---Other brushes and the like	15								0
96040000	Hand sieves and hand riddles.	15								0
96050000	Travel sets for personal toilet, sewing or shoe or clothes cleaning.	15								0
9606	Buttons, press-fasteners, snap-fasteners and press-studs, button moulds and other parts of these articles; button blanks.									
96061000	-Press-fasteners, snap-fasteners and press-studs and parts therefor	15								0
96062	-Buttons:									
96062100	--Of plastics, not covered with textile material	15								0
96062200	--Of base metal, not covered with textile material	15								0
96062900	--Other	15								0
96063000	-Button moulds and other parts of buttons; button blanks	15								0
9607	Slide fasteners and parts thereof.									
96071	-Slide fasteners:									
96071100	--Fitted with chain scoops of base metal	15								0
96071900	--Other	10								0
96072000	-Parts	15								0
9608	Ball point pens; felt tipped and other porous-tipped pens and markers; fountain pens, stylograph pens and other pens; duplicating stylos; propelling or sliding pencils; pen-holders, pencil-holders and similar holders; parts (including caps and clips) of the foregoing articles, other than those of heading 96.09.									
96081000	-Ball point pens	15					CH,JP			0
96082000	-Felt tipped and other porous-tipped pens and markers	15					JP			0
96083	-Fountain pens, stylograph pens and other pens:									
96083100	--Indian ink drawing pens	15								0
96083900	--Other	15								0
96084000	-Propelling or sliding pencils	15								0

HS	Description	Bound rate at date of accession	Interim	Final Bound	Implementation	Present concession established	INR	Concession first incorporated in a GATT Schedule	Earlier INRs	ODCs
96085000	-Sets of articles from two or more of the foregoing subheadings	15								0
96086000	-Refills for ball point pens, comprising the ball point and ink-reservoir	15								0
96089	-Other:									
96089100	--Pen nibs and nib points	15								0
96089900	--Other	15					CH			0
9609	Pencils (other than pencils of heading 96.08), crayons, pencil leads, pastels, drawing charcoals, writing or drawing chalks and tailors' chalks.									
96091000	-Pencils and crayons, with leads encased in a rigid sheath	15								0
96092000	-Pencil leads, black or coloured	15								0
960990	-Other									
96099010	---Slate pencils	15								0
96099020	---Drawing charcoals	15								0
96099030	---Crayons	15								0
96099040	---Writing and drawing chalk	15								0
96099050	---Tailors' chalk	15								0
96099090	---Other pencils, chalk, crayon and the like	15								0
9610	Slates and boards, with writing or drawing surfaces, whether or not framed.									
96100010	---Slate boards for writing or drawing	15								0
96100090	---Other slates and boards	15								0
96110000	Date, sealing or numbering stamps, and the like (including devices for printing or embossing labels), designed for operating in the hand; hand-operated composing sticks and hand printing sets incorporating such composing sticks.	15								0
9612	Typewriter or similar ribbons, inked or otherwise prepared for giving impressions, whether or not on spools or in cartridges; ink-pads, whether or not inked, with or without boxes.									
96121000	-Ribbons	15								0
96122000	-Ink-pads	15								0

HS	Description	Bound rate at date of accession	Interim	Final Bound	Implementation	Present concession established	INR	Concession first incorporated in a GATT Schedule	Earlier INRs	ODCs
9613	Cigarette lighters and other lighters, whether or not mechanical or electrical, and parts thereof other than flints and wicks.									
96131000	-Pocket lighters, gas fuelled, non-refillable	15								0
96132000	-Pocket lighters, gas fuelled, refillable	15								0
96138000	-Other lighters	15								0
96139000	-Parts	15								0
9614	Smoking pipes (including pipe bowls) and cigar or cigarette holders, and parts thereof.									
96142000	-Pipes and pipe bowls	15								0
96149000	-Other	15								0
9615	Combs, hair-slides and the like; hairpins, curling pins, curling grips, hair-curlers and the like, other than those of heading 85.16, and parts thereof.									
96151	-Combs, hair-slides and the like:									
96151100	--Of hard rubber or plastics	10								0
96151900	--Other	15								0
96159000	-Other	15								0
9616	Scent sprays and similar toilet sprays, and mounts and heads therefor; powder-puffs and pads for the application of cosmetics or toilet preparations.									
96161000	-Scent sprays and similar toilet sprays, and mounts and heads therefor	15								0
96162000	-Powder-puffs and pads for the application of cosmetics or toilet preparations	15								0
9617	Vacuum flasks and other vacuum vessels, complete with cases; parts thereof other than glass inners.									
96170010	---Thermos bottles used for tea or coffee	10					IN,JP			0
96170090	---Other vacuum flasks and vessels	10					IN,JP			0
96180000	Tailors' dummies and other lay figures; automata and other animated displays used for shop window dressing.	15								0

HS	Description	Bound rate at date of accession	Interim	Final Bound	Implementation	Present concession established	INR	Concession first incorporated in a GATT Schedule	Earlier INRs	ODCs
9701	Paintings, drawings and pastels, executed entirely by hand, other than drawings of heading 49.06 and other than hand-painted or hand-decorated manufactured articles; collages and similar decorative plaques.									
97011000	-Paintings, drawings and pastels	15								0
97019000	-Other	15								0
97020000	Original engravings, prints and lithographs.	15								0
97030000	Original sculptures and statuary, in any material.	15								0
97040000	Postage or revenue stamps, stamp-postmarks, first-day covers, postal stationery (stamped paper), and the like, used or unused, other than those of heading 49.07.	15								0
97050000	Collections and collectors' pieces of zoological, botanical, mineralogical, anatomical, historical, archaeological, palaeontological, ethnographic or numismatic interest.	15								0
970600	Antiques of an age exceeding 100 years									
97060010	---Antique furniture and parts over 100 years old	15								0
97060020	---Antique carpets of all kinds over 100 years old	15								0
97060030	---Antique works of painting and caligraphy over 100 years old	15								0
97060090	---Other antiques over 100 years old	15								0
	Endnote 1--Milkfish and tilapia are included in HS 030379.									
	Endnote 2--Powders, whether or not compressed, are included in HS 33049190.									
	Endnote 3--Creams and balms are included in HS 33049910, 33049920, 33049930, 33049940, and 33049990.									
	Endnote 4--Basketwork, wickerwork and other articles, made directly to shape from plaiting materials or made up from goods of heading 4601, of vegetable materials are included in HS 46021010.									

HS	Description	Bound rate at date of accession	Interim	Final Bound	Implementation	Present concession established	INR	Concession first incorporated in a GATT Schedule	Earlier INRs	ODCs
	Endnote 5--Handbags, wallets, purses and similar articles, of vegetable plaiting materials are included in HS 46021020.									
	Endnote 6--Polyester shirtings are included in HS 54075200.									
	Endnote 7--Twine, cordage, rope & cables, of abaca (Manila hemp or Musa textilis) or other hard (leaf) fibers are included in HS 56079010 and 56079020.									
	Endnote 8--Suits of cotton are included in HS 62031900.									
	Endnote 9--Handloom and millmade are included in HS 62052000.									
	Endnote 10--Blouses are included in HS 62063000.									
	Endnote 11--B867 slippers of rubbers are included in HS 64029900.									
	Endnote 12--Marble, travertine and alabaster, other than tiles, cubes and similar articles and other than monumental or building stones and articles thereof are included in HS 68029190.									
	Endnote 13--Statuettes & other ornamental ceramic articles, other than porcelain or china are included in HS 69139090.									
	Endnote 14--Parts and accessories of photocopying apparatus incorporating an optical system or of the contact type and the thermo-copying apparatus are included in HS 90099100, 90099200, 90099300, and 90099900.									
	Endnote 15--Other seats, of other materials, of wood, of metal are included in HS 94018090.									
	Endnote 16--Beds, of wood, are included in HS 94035010 and 94035090.									
	Endnote 17--Furniture of marble is included in HS 94038010.									

HS	Description	Bound rate at date of accession	Interim	Final Bound	Implementation	Present concession established	INR	Concession first incorporated in a GATT Schedule	Earlier INRs	ODCs
	Endnote 18--Furniture, of other materials, including cane, osier bamboo or similar materials, nes, of rattan are included in HS 94038090.									

Schedule CLVIII - Kingdom of Saudi Arabia

PART II - PREFERENTIAL TARIFF

NIL

Schedule CLVIII - Kingdom of Saudi Arabia

PART III - NON-TARIFF CONCESSIONS

Tariff item number	Description of products	Concessions
02013000	Boneless meat of fresh bovine animals	None of these products are subject to quantitative restrictions (QRs).
02071200	Frozen whole chicken	None of these products are subject to quantitative restrictions (QRs).
02071410	Cuts and offal frozen, poultry minced meat	None of these products are subject to quantitative restrictions (QRs).
02071490	Cuts and offal frozen, other	None of these products are subject to quantitative restrictions (QRs).
03062100	Rock lobster and other sea crawfish	None of these products are subject to quantitative restrictions (QRs).
03062200	Lobsters	None of these products are subject to quantitative restrictions (QRs).
03062300	Shrimp and prawns	None of these products are subject to quantitative restrictions (QRs).
03071000	Oysters	None of these products are subject to quantitative restrictions (QRs).
03072100	Scallops, live, fresh or chilled	None of these products are subject to quantitative restrictions (QRs).
03074100	Cuttle fish, live, fresh or chilled	None of these products are subject to quantitative restrictions (QRs).
03074900	Other cuttle fish	None of these products are subject to quantitative restrictions (QRs).
03075100	Octopus, live, fresh or chilled	None of these products are subject to quantitative restrictions (QRs).
03076000	Snails, other than sea snails	None of these products are subject to quantitative restrictions (QRs).
03079100	Other molluscs, live, fresh or chilled	None of these products are subject to quantitative restrictions (QRs).
04090000	Natural honey	None of these products are subject to quantitative restrictions (QRs).
06031000	Fresh cut flowers	None of these products are subject to quantitative restrictions (QRs).
06039000	Other cut flowers	None of these products are subject to quantitative restrictions (QRs).
07032000	Garlic, fresh	None of these products are subject to quantitative restrictions (QRs).
07132000	Chickpeas, dried	None of these products are subject to quantitative restrictions (QRs).
08030000	Bananas, including plantains	None of these products are subject to quantitative restrictions (QRs).
08044000	Avocados	None of these products are subject to quantitative restrictions (QRs).
08045010	Guavas	None of these products are subject to quantitative restrictions (QRs).
08045020	Mangoes	None of these products are subject to quantitative restrictions (QRs).
08055010	Fresh lemons	None of these products are subject to quantitative restrictions (QRs).
08059000	Other citrus fruits (citrus latifolia)	None of these products are subject to quantitative restrictions (QRs).
08111000	Strawberries, frozen	None of these products are subject to quantitative restrictions (QRs).
09011100	Unroasted coffee, not decaffeinated	None of these products are subject to quantitative restrictions (QRs).
09011200	Unroasted coffee, decaffeinated	None of these products are subject to quantitative restrictions (QRs).
09012100	Coffee, roasted and not decaffeinated	None of these products are subject to quantitative restrictions (QRs).
09012200	Coffee, roasted and decaffeinated	None of these products are subject to quantitative restrictions (QRs).
09019000	Other coffee	None of these products are subject to quantitative restrictions (QRs).

Tariff item number	Description of products	Concessions
12074000	Sesame seeds	None of these products are subject to quantitative restrictions (QRs).
16041400	Tuna, processed	None of these products are subject to quantitative restrictions (QRs).
17011110	Cane sugar for industrial refining and filtering	None of these products are subject to quantitative restrictions (QRs).
17011190	Other cane sugar	None of these products are subject to quantitative restrictions (QRs).
17011210	Beet sugar for industrial refining and filtering	None of these products are subject to quantitative restrictions (QRs).
17011290	Other beet sugar	None of these products are subject to quantitative restrictions (QRs).
17029010	Maltose, whether or nor chemically pure	None of these products are subject to quantitative restrictions (QRs).
17029020	Sucrose, chemically impure	None of these products are subject to quantitative restrictions (QRs).
17029030	Invert sugar, whether or not chemically pure	None of these products are subject to quantitative restrictions (QRs).
17029040	Fructose, chemically impure	None of these products are subject to quantitative restrictions (QRs).
17029050	Sugar liquids	None of these products are subject to quantitative restrictions (QRs).
17029060	Caramel	None of these products are subject to quantitative restrictions (QRs).
17029070	Artificial honey	None of these products are subject to quantitative restrictions (QRs).
17029090	Other sugar	None of these products are subject to quantitative restrictions (QRs).
17049090	Other sugar confectionery	None of these products are subject to quantitative restrictions (QRs).
20091100	Frozen orange juice	None of these products are subject to quantitative restrictions (QRs).
21011100	Extracts, essences and concentrates	None of these products are subject to quantitative restrictions (QRs).
21013010	Roasted chicory and other roasted coffee substitutes	None of these products are subject to quantitative restrictions (QRs).
21013020	Chicory extracts, concentrates and essences	None of these products are subject to quantitative restrictions (QRs).
21031000	Soya sauce	The import of soya sauce is allowed with 3-MCPD at a maximum level of 0.1 mg/kg.
24011000	Unmanufactured tobacco; tobacco refuse; not stemmed/stripped	None of these products are subject to quantitative restrictions (QRs).
24012000	Unmanufactured tobacco; tobacco refuse; partly or wholly stemmed/stripped	None of these products are subject to quantitative restrictions (QRs).
24013010	Tobacco waste suitable for use as tobacco	None of these products are subject to quantitative restrictions (QRs).
24013090	Other tobacco waste	None of these products are subject to quantitative restrictions (QRs).
24021000	Cigars, cheroots and cigarillos, of tobacco	None of these products are subject to quantitative restrictions (QRs).
24022000	Cigarettes containing tobacco	None of these products are subject to quantitative restrictions (QRs).
24031010	Chopped or pressed tobacco for smoking	None of these products are subject to quantitative restrictions (QRs).
24031020	Chopped or pressed tobacco for pipes	None of these products are subject to quantitative restrictions (QRs).
24031030	Chopped or pressed tunbak for retail sale	None of these products are subject to quantitative restrictions (QRs).
24031090	Other smoking tobacco	None of these products are subject to quantitative restrictions (QRs).
24039100	Homogenized or reconstituted tobacco	None of these products are subject to quantitative restrictions (QRs).
25232100	White Portland cement	None of these products are subject to quantitative restrictions (QRs).
25232910	Other Portland cement	None of these products are subject to quantitative restrictions (QRs).
25232920	Sulphate resistant cement	None of these products are subject to quantitative restrictions (QRs).
37012000	Instant print packs, flat	None of these products are subject to quantitative restrictions (QRs).
70052900	Other non-wired float glass	None of these products are subject to quantitative restrictions (QRs).
70071100	Tempered safety glass for transportation	None of these products are subject to quantitative restrictions (QRs).
70109000	Carboys, bottles, flasks, jars, pots, phials, and other containers, of glass, of a kind used for the conveyance or packing of goods; preserving jars of glass	None of these products are subject to quantitative restrictions (QRs).
70131010	Tableware or kitchenware of glass-ceramics	None of these products are subject to quantitative restrictions (QRs).
70131020	Perfume bottles for toilet of glass-ceramics	None of these products are subject to quantitative restrictions (QRs).
70131041	Decoration perfume bottles of glassy porcelain	None of these products are subject to quantitative restrictions (QRs).

Tariff item number	Description of products	Concessions
70131049	Other make- up items of glassy porcelain	None of these products are subject to quantitative restrictions (QRs).
70131090	Other articles of glass-ceramics	None of these products are subject to quantitative restrictions (QRs).
70132100	Drinking glasses of lead crystal	None of these products are subject to quantitative restrictions (QRs).
70132900	Other drinking glasses, not of glass	None of these products are subject to quantitative restrictions (QRs).
70133100	Table glassware of lead crystal	None of these products are subject to quantitative restrictions (QRs).
70133200	Table glassware with linear coefficient of expansion not exceeding 5 x 10-6 per Kelvin within a temperature range of 0 °C to 300 °C	None of these products are subject to quantitative restrictions (QRs).
70133900	Other table glassware	None of these products are subject to quantitative restrictions (QRs).
70139110	Articles for toilets of lead crystal	None of these products are subject to quantitative restrictions (QRs).
70139131	Decoration bottles of glass for perfumes, of lead crystal	None of these products are subject to quantitative restrictions (QRs).
70139139	Other make-up items of glass, of lead crystal	None of these products are subject to quantitative restrictions (QRs).
70139190	Other articles of lead crystal	None of these products are subject to quantitative restrictions (QRs).
70139910	Fish aquarium of glass	None of these products are subject to quantitative restrictions (QRs).
70139920	Glass censer	None of these products are subject to quantitative restrictions (QRs).
70139990	Other glass items	None of these products are subject to quantitative restrictions (QRs).
73041000	Line pipe used for oil or gas	None of these products are subject to quantitative restrictions (QRs).
73042900	Other tubes and pipes and hollow	None of these products are subject to quantitative restrictions (QRs).
85111000	Sparking plugs	None of these products are subject to quantitative restrictions (QRs).
96031000	Brooms and brushes, consisting of twigs	None of these products are subject to quantitative restrictions (QRs).
various	Coconut products	There is no import ban on coconut products and the import of fresh and processed coconut products and by-products is allowed in accordance with WTO-consistent measures and procedures.
various	Fresh/frozen/canned marine and dairy products	There is no import ban on cholera-free countries as certified by the WHO.

Schedule CLVIII - Kingdom of Saudi Arabia

PART IV - AGRICULTURAL PRODUCTS: COMMITMENTS LIMITING SUBSIDIZATION

(Article 3 of the Agreement on Agriculture)

SECTION I - Domestic Support: Total AMS Commitments

Million Saudi Riyals

BASE TOTAL AMS	Annual and final bound commitment levels 2006-2015										Relevant Support
2001-2003	2006	2007	2008	2009	2010	2011	2012	2013	2014	2015	Tables and document
3,711.97	3,662.60	3,613.23	3,563.86	3,514.49	3,465.12	3,415.76	3,366.39	3,317.02	3,267.65	3,218.28	WT/ACC/SPEC/SAU/1/Rev.10

Schedule CLVIII - Kingdom of Saudi Arabia

PART IV - AGRICULTURAL PRODUCTS: COMMITMENTS LIMITING SUBSIDIZATION

SECTION II - Export Subsidies: Budgetary Outlay and Quantity Reduction Commitment

Description of products and tariff item no.	Base outlay level	Calendar/other year applied	Annual and final outlay commitment levels	Base quantity	Calendar/other year applied	Annual and final quantity commitment levels	Relevant Supporting Tables and document reference

WT/ACC/SPEC/SAU/1/Rev.10

Schedule CLVIII - Kingdom of Saudi Arabia

PART IV - AGRICULTURAL PRODUCTS: COMMITMENTS LIMITING SUBSIDIZATION

SECTION III - Commitments Limiting the Scope of Export Subsidies

Description of products	Nature of Commitments

NIL

Kingdom of Saudi Arabia--Attachment B

With respect to any product described in or for Attachment B to the Annex to the Ministerial Declaration on Trade in Information Technology Products (WT/MIN(96)/16), to the extent not specifically provided for in this Schedule, the customs duties on such product, as well any other duties and charges of any kind (within the meaning of Article II:1(b) of the General Agreement on Tariffs and Trade 1994), shall be bound and eliminated, as set forth in paragraph 2(a) of the Annex to the Declaration, wherever the product is classified.

Description	HS
Quartz reactor tubes and holders designed for insertion into diffusion and oxidation furnaces for production of semiconductor wafers	70171000
Chemical vapor deposition apparatus for semiconductor production	84198900
Parts of chemical vapor deposition apparatus for semiconductor production	84199000
Apparatus for stripping or cleaning semiconductor wafers	84569100
Lasercutters for cutting contacting tracks in semiconductor production by laser beam	84569900
Machines for sawing monocrystal semiconductor boules into slices, or wafers into chips	84641000
Parts for machines for sawing monocrystal semiconductor boules into slices, or wafers into chips	84669100
Parts of dicing machines for scribing or scoring semiconductor wafers	84669100
Parts of lasercutters for cutting contacting tracks in semiconductor production by laser beam	84669300
Parts of apparatus for stripping or cleaning semiconductor wafers	84669300
Encapsulation equipment for assembly of semiconductors	84771000
Parts of encapsulation equipment	84779000
Automated machines for transport, handling and storage of semiconductor wafers, wafer cassettes, wafer boxes and other material for semiconductor devices	84795000
Apparatus for physical deposition by sputtering on semiconductor wafers	84798999
Apparatus for wet etching, developing, stripping or cleaning semiconductor wafers and flat panel displays	84798999
Die attach apparatus, tape automated bonders, and wire bonders for assembly of semiconductors	84798999
Encapsulation equipment for assembly of semiconductors	84798999
Machines for bending, folding and straightening semiconductor leads	84798999
Physical deposition apparatus for semiconductor production	84798999

Description	HS
Spinners for coating photographic emulsions on semiconductor wafers	84798999
Part of apparatus for physical deposition by sputtering on semiconductor wafers	84799000
Parts for die attach apparatus, tape automated bonders, and wire bonders for assembly of semiconductors	84799000
Parts for spinners for coating photographic emulsions on semiconductor wafers	84799000
Parts of apparatus for wet etching, developing, stripping or cleaning semiconductor wafers and flat panel displays	84799000
Parts of automated machines for transport, handling and storage of semiconductor wafers, wafer cassettes, wafer boxes and other material for semiconductor devices	84799000
Parts of encapsulation equipment for assembly of semiconductors	84799000
Parts of machines for bending, folding and straightening semiconductor leads	84799000
Parts of physical deposition apparatus for semiconductor production	84799000
Apparatus for rapid heating of semiconductor wafers	85143000
Parts of apparatus for rapid heating of wafers	85149000
Wafer probers	85369000
Apparatus for wet etching, developing, stripping or cleaning semiconductor wafers and flat panel displays	85433000
Parts of apparatus for wet etching, developing, stripping or cleaning semiconductor wafers and flat panel displays	85439000
Optical stereoscopic microscopes fitted with equipment specifically designed for the handling and transport of semiconductor wafers or reticles	90111000
Photomicrographic microscopes fitted with equipment specifically designed for the handling and transport of semiconductor wafers or reticles	90112000
Parts and accessories of optical stereoscopic microscopes fitted with equipment specifically designed for the handling and transport of semiconductor wafers or reticles	90119000
Parts and accessories of photomicrographic microscopes fitted with equipment specifically designed for the handling and transport of semiconductor wafers or reticles	90119000

Description	HS
Electron beam microscopes fitted with equipment specifically designed for the handling and transport of semiconductor wafers or reticles	90121000
Parts and accessories of electron beam microscopes fitted with equipment specifically designed for the handling and transport of semiconductor wafers or reticles	90129000
Pattern generating apparatus of a kind used for producing masks or reticles from photoresist coated substrates	90172000
Parts and accessories for pattern generating apparatus of a kind used for producing masks or reticles from photoresist coated substrates	90179000
Parts of such pattern generating apparatus	90179000
Computers: automatic data processing machines capable of 1) storing the processing program or programs and at least the data immediately necessary for the execution of the program; 2) being freely programmed in accordance with the requirements of the user; 3) performing arithmetical computations specified by the user; and 4) executing, without human intervention, a processing program which requires them to modify their execution, by logical decision during the processing run. The agreement covers such automatic data processing machines whether or not they are able to receive and process with the assistance of central processing unit telephony signals, television signals, or other analogue or digitally processed audio or video signals. Machines performing a specific function other than data processing, or incorporating or working in conjunction with an automatic data processing machine, and not otherwise specified under Attachment A or B, are not covered by this agreement.	84711000,84713000,84714900,84715000
Electric amplifiers when used as repeaters in line telephony products falling within this agreement, and parts thereof	85184000,85189000
Flat panel display devices (including LCD, Electro Luminescence, Plasma, Vacuum-Fluorescence and other technologies) for products falling within this agreement, and parts thereof.	84714900,84715000,84716000,84733000,85312000,85318090,85319000,85438990,85439000,90138090,90139000
Network equipment: Local Area Network (LAN) and Wide Area Network (WAN) apparatus, including those products dedicated for use solely or principally to permit the interconnection of automatic data processing machines and units thereof for a network that is used primarily for the sharing of resources such as central processor units, data storage devices and input or output units - including adapters, hubs, in-line repeaters, converters, concentrators, bridges and routers, and printed circuit assemblies for physical incorporation into automatic data processing machines and units thereof.	84714900,84718000

Description	HS
Monitors : display units of automatic data processing machines with a cathode ray tube with a dot screen pitch smaller than 0,4 mm not capable of receiving and processing television signals or other analogue or digitally processed audio or video signals without assistance of a central processing unit of a computer as defined in this agreement. The agreement does not, therefore, cover televisions, including high definition televisions.	84714900,84716000
Optical disc storage units, for automatic data processing machines (including CD drives and DVD-drives), whether or not having the capability of writing/recording as well as reading, whether or not in their own housings.	84714900,84717000
Paging alert devices, and parts thereof .	85252011,85252019,85252020,85252030,85252040,85252050,85252060,85252070,85252090,85279010,85279090,85291000,85299000,85318090,85319000
Plotters whether input or output units of HS heading No 8471 or drawing or drafting machines of HS heading No 9017.	84714900,84716000,90171000,90172000
Printed Circuit Assemblies for products falling within this agreement, including such assemblies for external connections such as cards that conform to the PCMCIA standard. Such printed circuit assemblies consist of one or more printed circuits of heading 8534 with one or more active elements assembled thereon, with or without passive elements "Active elements" means diodes, transistors, and similar semiconductor devices, whether or not photosensitive, of heading 8541, and integrated circuits and micro assemblies of heading 8542.	84715000,84731000,84732100,84732900,84733000,84734000,84735000,85044000,85049000,85175000,85179010,85179090,85189000,85202000,85229000,85299000,85319000,85389000,85439000,90099100,90099200,90099300,90099900,90139000,90179000,90269000,90279000,90309000,90319000
Projection type flat panel display units used with automatic data processing machines which can display digital information generated by the central processing unit.	84714900,84716000
Proprietary format storage devices including media therefor for automatic data processing machines, with or without removable media and whether magnetic, optical or other technology, including Bernoulli Box, Syquest, or Zipdrive cartridge storage units.	84714900,84717000,85232010,85239030,85243100,85243900,85249100,85249930
Multimedia upgrade kits for automatic data processing machines, and units thereof, put up for retail sale, consisting of, at least, speakers and/or microphones as well as a printed circuit assembly that enables the ADP machines and units thereof to process audio signals (sound cards).	84733000,85175000
Set top boxes which have a communication function: a microprocessor-based device incorporating a modem for gaining access to the Internet, and having a function of interactive information exchange	85175000,85251090,85281291,85281299

Kingdom of Saudi Arabia--Staging Matrix

The respective reductions, as noted in the columns, shall be the month/day of the Kingdom of Saudi Arabia's accession in the year indicated.

HS	Base rate	2006	2007	2008
38180000	5	5	5	0
70171000	5	5	5	0
84198900	5	5	5	0
84199000	5	5	5	0
84211900	5	5	5	0
84219100	5	5	5	0
84248900	5	5	5	0
84249090	5	5	5	0
84561000	5	5	5	0
84569100	5	5	5	0
84569900	5	5	5	0
84641000	5	5	5	0
84642000	5	5	5	0
84649000	5	5	5	0
84669100	5	5	5	0
84669300	5	5	5	0
84691100	5	5	5	0
84701000	5	5	5	0
84702100	5	5	5	0
84702900	5	5	5	0
84703000	5	5	5	0
84704000	5	5	5	0
84705000	5	5	5	0
84709010	5	5	5	0
84709020	5	5	5	0
84709090	5	5	5	0
84711000	5	5	5	0
84713000	5	5	5	0
84714100	5	5	5	0
84714900	5	5	5	0
84715000	5	5	5	0
84716000	5	5	5	0
84717000	5	5	5	0

HS	Base rate	2006	2007	2008
84718000	5	5	5	0
84719000	5	5	5	0
84729090	5	5	5	0
ex84731000	15	15	15	0
84732100	5	5	5	0
84732900	5	5	5	0
84733000	5	5	5	0
ex84734000	5	5	5	0
84735000	5	5	5	0
84771000	5	5	5	0
84779000	5	5	5	0
84795000	5	5	5	0
84798999	5	5	5	0
84799000	5	5	5	0
84807100	5	5	5	0
85044000	5	5	5	0
85045000	5	5	5	0
ex85049000	5	5	5	0
85141000	5	5	5	0
85142000	5	5	5	0
85143000	5	5	5	0
85149000	5	5	5	0
85171100	5	5	5	0
85171910	5	5	5	0
85171990	5	5	5	0
85172100	5	5	5	0
85172210	5	5	5	0
85172290	5	5	5	0
85173000	5	5	5	0
85175000	5	5	5	0
85178000	5	5	5	0
85179010	5	5	5	0
85179090	5	5	5	0
85181000	5	5	5	0
85182900	5	5	5	0
85183000	5	5	5	0

HS	Base rate	2006	2007	2008
ex85184000	15	15	15	0
ex85189000	15	15	15	0
85202000	5	5	5	0
ex85229000	15	15	15	0
85231110	12	12	12	0
85231120	12	12	12	0
85231130	5	5	5	0
85231190	5	5	5	0
85231210	12	12	12	0
85231220	12	12	12	0
85231230	5	5	5	0
85231290	5	5	5	0
85231310	12	12	12	0
85231320	12	12	12	0
85231330	5	5	5	0
85231390	5	5	5	0
85232010	5	5	5	0
85232090	5	5	5	0
85239010	5	5	5	0
85239020	5	5	5	0
85239030	12	12	12	0
85239090	5	5	5	0
85243100	5	5	5	0
85243900	5	5	5	0
85244000	5	5	5	0
85249100	5	5	5	0
85249930	5	5	5	0
85251010	5	5	5	0
85251020	5	5	5	0
85251030	5	5	5	0
85251090	5	5	5	0
85252011	5	5	5	0
85252019	5	5	5	0
85252020	5	5	5	0
85252030	5	5	5	0
85252040	5	5	5	0

HS	Base rate	2006	2007	2008
85252050	5	5	5	0
85252060	5	5	5	0
85252070	5	5	5	0
85252090	5	5	5	0
85254000	5	5	5	0
85279010	5	5	5	0
85279090	5	5	5	0
ex85281291	10	10	10	0
ex85281299	10	10	10	0
85291000	5	5	5	0
85299000	5	5	5	0
85312000	5	5	5	0
ex85318090	15	15	15	0
85319000	5	5	5	0
85321000	5	5	5	0
85322100	5	5	5	0
85322200	5	5	5	0
85322300	5	5	5	0
85322400	5	5	5	0
85322500	5	5	5	0
85322900	5	5	5	0
85323000	5	5	5	0
85329000	5	5	5	0
85331000	5	5	5	0
85332100	5	5	5	0
85332900	5	5	5	0
85333100	5	5	5	0
85333900	5	5	5	0
85334000	5	5	5	0
85339000	5	5	5	0
85340000	5	5	5	0
85365000	5	5	5	0
85366900	5	5	5	0
85369000	5	5	5	0
ex85389000	10	10	10	0
85411000	5	5	5	0

HS	Base rate	2006	2007	2008
85412100	5	5	5	0
85412900	5	5	5	0
85413000	5	5	5	0
85414000	5	5	5	0
85415000	5	5	5	0
85416000	5	5	5	0
85419000	5	5	5	0
85421000	5	5	5	0
85422100	5	5	5	0
85422900	5	5	5	0
85426000	5	5	5	0
85427000	5	5	5	0
85429000	5	5	5	0
85431100	5	5	5	0
85433000	5	5	5	0
85438100	5	5	5	0
ex85438990	5	5	5	0
85439000	5	5	5	0
85444100	12	12	12	0
85444900	12	12	12	0
85445190	12	12	12	0
85447000	12	12	12	0
90091100	5	5	5	0
90092100	5	5	5	0
90099100	5	5	5	0
90099200	5	5	5	0
90099300	5	5	5	0
90099900	5	5	5	0
90104100	5	5	5	0
90104200	5	5	5	0
90104900	5	5	5	0
90109000	5	5	5	0
90111000	5	5	5	0
90112000	5	5	5	0
90119000	5	5	5	0
90121000	5	5	5	0

HS	Base rate	2006	2007	2008
90129000	5	5	5	0
ex90138090	15	15	15	0
ex90139000	5	5	5	0
ex90171000	15	15	15	0
90172000	5	5	5	0
90179000	5	5	5	0
90261000	5	5	5	0
90262000	5	5	5	0
90268000	5	5	5	0
90269000	5	5	5	0
90272000	5	5	5	0
90273000	5	5	5	0
90275000	5	5	5	0
90278010	5	5	5	0
90278090	5	5	5	0
90279000	5	5	5	0
90304000	5	5	5	0
90308200	5	5	5	0
90309000	5	5	5	0
90314100	5	5	5	0
90314900	5	5	5	0
90319000	5	5	5	0

Kingdom of Saudi Arabia

Schedule of Specific
Commitments in Services
List of Article II MFN Exemptions

Authentic only in the English language.

Modes of supply: (1) Cross-border supply; (2) Consumption abroad; (3) Commercial presence; (4) Presence of natural persons.

Sector or Sub-sector	Limitation on market access	Limitations on national treatment	Additional commitments
I. HORIZONTAL COMMITMENTS			
All Sectors and Sub-Sectors of Services included in this Offer	(3) (i) Commercial presence for all services listed in this Schedule, other than business services (as listed below)[1] subject to incorporation under the Companies Act either as joint-stock companies or as limited liability companies. (ii) Commercial presence for business services (as listed below)[1] subject to formation of a company, and registration of such a company under the Professional Companies Law.	(3) (i) Foreign service suppliers require approval from the Saudi Arabian General Investment Authority for establishing commercial presence in Saudi Arabia according to the Foreign Investment Law of April 2000 and Article 5:3 of the Regulation of the Foreign Investment Act. (ii) Non Saudi nationals may acquire the right to own real estate in Saudi Arabia by succession. Foreign establishments authorized to carry on their activities in the Kingdom under the Foreign Investment Law may own real estate in accordance with the present laws and regulations governing foreign ownership of real estate. (iii) Non Saudi business entities and foreign natural persons are subject to income tax while Saudi entities and Saudi individuals are subject to Zakat. Future changes in Saudi tax code will not be less favourable to foreign service providers than the existing code. (iv) Foreign service entities and foreign natural persons shall have access to subsidies available in the country. However some subsidies on	All modes of supply: In all respects other than Zakat, taxation measures will be applied in conformity with Articles II and XVII and all other relevant provisions of the GATS.

[1] Professional Services (1A), as in document W/120.

Modes of supply: (1) Cross-border supply; (2) Consumption abroad; (3) Commercial presence; (4) Presence of natural persons.

Sector or Sub-sector	Limitation on market access	Limitations on national treatment	Additional commitments
		certain services will be available to Saudis only.	
	(4) Unbound, except for measures concerning the entry and temporary stay of natural persons in the following categories: (i) <u>Business Visitors</u> A natural person who stays in Saudi Arabia, without acquiring remuneration from within Saudi Arabia and without engaging in making direct sales to the general public or supplying services, for the purposes of participating in business meetings, business contacts including negotiations for the sale of services and/or other similar activities including those to prepare for establishing a commercial presence in Saudi Arabia. Entry and stay shall be for a period of no more than 180 days, including multiple entries.	(4) Unbound, except as in the column for limitation on market access	

Modes of supply: (1) Cross-border supply; (2) Consumption abroad; (3) Commercial presence; (4) Presence of natural persons.

Sector or Sub-sector	Limitation on market access	Limitations on national treatment	Additional commitments
	(ii) Intra-corporate transferees (ICT) Intra-corporate transferees of managers, executives and specialists (as defined below), who have work experience for a period of at least three years in the same field prior to the date of application for entry into the Kingdom, to an affiliate in Saudi Arabia of a juridical person. Entry and stay of such managers, executives and specialists shall be subject to the following conditions: - Their number shall be limited to 25% of the total workforce of each service supplier. However, a minimum of three persons will be allowed. Alternatively to the above, the service supplier may have the following option, the number of managers, executives and specialists of each service supplier shall be limited to 15%; and the number of other foreign employees (i.e. other than managers, executives, or specialists) of each service supplier shall be limited to 10%, or vice versa. However, a minimum of two ICT will be allowed as compliant with the 15% threshold. - Their entry and stay shall be for a period of two years, renewable for similar periods. - Certain positions in a company may be reserved for Saudi nationals in all categories. These positions are recruitment		

Modes of supply: (1) Cross-border supply; (2) Consumption abroad; (3) Commercial presence; (4) Presence of natural persons.

Sector or Sub-sector	Limitation on market access	Limitations on national treatment	Additional commitments
	and personnel, receptionists, cashiers, civil security guards, and transaction (government relations) follow up. Definitions: Managers: Persons within an organization, who primarily direct the organization or a department or sub-division of the organization, supervise and control the work of other supervisory, professional or managerial employees, have the authority to hire or fire or recommend hiring, firing or other personnel action (such as promotion or leave authorisation) and exercise discretionary authority over day-to-day operation, does not include first-line supervisor unless the employees supervised are professional, nor does include employees who primarily perform tasks necessary for the provision of the service. Executives: Persons within an organization, who primarily direct the management of the organization, establish the goals and policies of the organization, exercise wide latitude in decision-making and receive only general supervision or direction from higher-level executives, the board of directors or stockholders of the business. Executives would not directly perform tasks related to the actual provision of service or services of the organization. Specialists: Persons within an organization who possess knowledge at an advanced level of expertise and who possess proprietary knowledge of the		

Modes of supply: (1) Cross-border supply; (2) Consumption abroad; (3) Commercial presence; (4) Presence of natural persons.

Sector or Sub-sector	Limitation on market access	Limitations on national treatment	Additional commitments
	organizations services, research, equipment, techniques or management. (iii) <u>Contractual service suppliers</u> Employees of contractual service suppliers, i.e. employees of juridical persons with no commercial presence in Saudi Arabia, who have obtained a service contract in Saudi Arabia requiring the presence of their employees in order to fulfil the contract. Entry and stay of such persons shall be for a period of no more than 180 days which would be renewable. Entry of such persons shall be allowed only for the following sub-sectors on business services: - Legal services (Part of CPC 861) - Architectural services (CPC 8671) - Urban planning and landscape architectural services (CPC 8674) - Engineering services (CPC 8672) - Integrated engineering services (CPC 8673) - Related scientific and technical consulting (CPC 8675) - Technical testing & analysis services (CPC 8676) - Translation services (CPC 87905) - Environmental services (all-sub sectors)		

Modes of supply: (1) Cross-border supply; (2) Consumption abroad; (3) Commercial presence; (4) Presence of natural persons.

Sector or Sub-sector	Limitation on market access	Limitations on national treatment	Additional commitments
	(CPC 94010 + 94020 + 9403 + 9404 + 9405 + 9406 + 9409) - Services incidental to mining (CPC 883 + 5115) - Management consulting services (CPC 8650) - Services related to management consulting (CPC 8660) - Maintenance and repair of equipment (not including maritime vessels, aircraft or other transport equipment) (CPC 633 + 8861-8866) - Accounting, auditing & bookkeeping (CPC 8621 + 8622) - Medical & dental services (CPC 9312) - Inter-disciplinary Research and Development Services (CPC 85300) - Computer & related services (CPC 841-845 + 849) - Construction and related engineering services (CPC 511-518) - Travel Agency and Tour Operator services, excluding for Umra and Hajj (CPC 7471) - Restaurant Services, including catering services (except bars, nightclubs, etc.) (CPC 6421 + 6422 + 6423)		

Modes of supply: (1) Cross-border supply; (2) Consumption abroad; (3) Commercial presence; (4) Presence of natural persons.

Sector or Sub-sector	Limitation on market access	Limitations on national treatment	Additional commitments
	(iv) <u>Independent Professionals</u> Independent Professionals (i.e. natural persons) as part of a service contract with juridical person in Saudi Arabia for rendering professional services in which he/she possesses the necessary academic credentials and professional qualifications with three years experience in the same field. Their entry and stay shall be for a period of 180 days, which may be renewable. Entry of such persons shall be allowed only for the following: - Computer & related services (CPC 841-845 + 849) - Construction & related engineering services (CPC 512, 513, 516 + 517) - Accounting, auditing and bookkeeping services (CPC 8621 + 8622) - Taxation services (CPC 87905) - Architectural services (CPC 8671) - Pilot & Crews - Legal services (part of CPC 861) - Medical & dental services (CPC 9312) - Interdisciplinary Research and Development Services (CPC 85300) - Management consulting services (CPC 8650) - Building – cleaning services		

Modes of supply: (1) Cross-border supply; (2) Consumption abroad; (3) Commercial presence; (4) Presence of natural persons.

Sector or Sub-sector	Limitation on market access	Limitations on national treatment	Additional commitments
	(CPC 874) For other education services (only Thai cooking and Thai language (as part of CPC 9290)), entry and stay shall be for a period of 90 days, which would be renewable for similar period. (v) <u>Installers and maintainers</u> Qualified specialists supplying installation or maintenance services. The supply of that service has to occur on a contractual basis between the builder of the machinery or equipment and the owner of that machinery or equipment, both of them being juridical persons. Temporary entry is granted for a period of stay of no more than 90 days which would be renewable.		

Modes of supply: (1) Cross-border supply; (2) Consumption abroad; (3) Commercial presence; (4) Presence of natural persons.

Sector or Sub-sector	Limitation on market access	Limitations on national treatment	Additional commitments
II. SPECIFIC SECTOR COMMITMENTS			
1. BUSINESS SERVICES			
A. Professional Services			
a. Legal Services Consultancy on the law of jurisdiction where the services supplier is qualified as a lawyer and on international law (Part of CPC 861)	(1) None (2) None (3) Foreign equity limited to 75% (4) Unbound, except as indicated in the horizontal section	(1) None (2) None (3) Non-Saudi lawyers cannot appear in courts to plead cases (4) Unbound, except as indicated in the horizontal section	
b. Accounting, auditing and bookkeeping services (CPC 8621 and 8622) c. Taxation services (CPC 8630) d. Architectural services (CPC 8671) e. Engineering services (CPC 8672) f. Integrated engineering services (CPC 8673) g. Urban planning and landscape architectural services (CPC 8674) h. Medical and dental services (CPC 9312) i. Veterinary services (CPC 93201)	(1) None (2) None (3) Foreign equity limited to 75% (4) Unbound, except as indicated in the horizontal section	(1) None (2) None (3) None (4) Unbound, except as indicated in the horizontal section	

Modes of supply: (1) Cross-border supply; (2) Consumption abroad; (3) Commercial presence; (4) Presence of natural persons.

Sector or Sub-sector	Limitation on market access	Limitations on national treatment	Additional commitments
B. Computer and Related Services a.-e. (CPC 841-45 and 849)	(1) None (2) None (3) None (4) Unbound, except as indicated in the horizontal section	(1) None (2) None (3) None (4) Unbound, except as indicated in the horizontal section	
C. Research and Development Services a.-c. (CPC 851, 852, 853)	(1) None (2) None (3) None (4) Unbound, except as indicated in the horizontal section	(1) None (2) None (3) None (4) Unbound, except as indicated in the horizontal section	
E. Rental/Leasing Services without Operators			
a. Relating to ships (CPC 83103) b. Relating to aircraft (CPC 83104) c. Relating to other transport equipment (CPC 83101+83102+83105) d. Relating to other machinery and equipment (CPC 83106-83109) e. Leasing or rental services concerning household goods (CPC 832)	(1) None (2) None (3) None (4) Unbound, except as indicated in the horizontal section	(1) None (2) None (3) None (4) Unbound, except as indicated in the horizontal section	
F. Other Business Services			
a. Advertising services (CPC 8711) b. Market research services (CPC 86401) c. Management consulting services (CPC 8650) d. Services related to management consulting (CPC 8660) e. Technical testing and analysis services (CPC 8676) f. Services incidental to agriculture, hunting and forestry (CPC 881) h. Services incidental to mining (CPC 883+5115) i. Services incidental to manufacturing (CPC 884 (except 88442)+885) j. Services incidental to energy	(1) None (2) None (3) None (4) Unbound, except as indicated in the horizontal section	(1) None (2) None (3) None (4) Unbound, except as indicated in the horizontal section	

Modes of supply: (1) Cross-border supply; (2) Consumption abroad; (3) Commercial presence; (4) Presence of natural persons.

Sector or Sub-sector	Limitation on market access	Limitations on national treatment	Additional commitments
distribution (CPC 887) m. Related to scientific and technical consulting services (CPC 8675) n. Maintenance and repair of equipment (not including maritime vessels, aircraft or other transport equipment) (CPC 633+8861-8866) p. Photographic services (CPC 8750) q. Packaging services (CPC 8760) r. Printing and publishing services (CPC 88442) s. Convention services (CPC 87909)* t. Other (e.g. public relations services) - Translation services (CPC 87905) - Speciality design services (CPC 87907)			
2. COMMUNICATION SERVICES			
B. Courier services (CPC 7512)	(1) None (2) None (3) None (4) Unbound, except as indicated in the horizontal section	(1) None (2) None (3) None (4) Unbound, except as indicated in the horizontal section	- Foreign express delivery operators will have a treatment no less favourable than that accorded to the Postal Office for its activities in express delivery. - When Consultancy related to the provision of postal services (CPC 7511**) are privatized, they will also be opened for foreign service suppliers.

Modes of supply: (1) Cross-border supply; (2) Consumption abroad; (3) Commercial presence; (4) Presence of natural persons.

Sector or Sub-sector	Limitation on market access	Limitations on national treatment	Additional commitments
C. Telecommunication services			
General conditions for this sub-sector: The commitments taken by the Kingdom of Saudi Arabia are based on the scheduling principles provided by the following documents: Notes for scheduling Basic Telecom Services Commitments (S/GBT/W/2/Rev.1) and Market Access Limitations on Spectrum Availability (S/GBT/W/3). This commitment is subject to the following general conditions: - The Kingdom of Saudi Arabia undertakes commitments as contained in the basic telecommunications reference paper, included in Annex. - Any telecom service supplied in Saudi Arabia on a commercial presence basis (Mode 3) must be supplied by a company registered in Saudi Arabia, the foreign equity of which shall be limited to the percentage levels mentioned below. - This schedule on basic telecommunication does not include any broadcasting services[2]. - Cross-border supply is subject to commercial agreement with a legal entity/entities licensed or authorized by CITC in the Kingdom of Saudi Arabia.			
1. Basic telecommunication services - Public Fixed – facilities-based a. Voice telephone services f. Facsimile services i. Voice mail	(1) None as of the end of 2006 (2) None (3) None, except services offered as public telecommunications services must be provided by a joint stock company. Foreign equity is limited to 49% upon accession, to go to 51% by the end of 2007 and 60% by the end of 2008 (4) Unbound, except as indicated in the horizontal section	(1) None (2) None (3) None (4) Unbound, except as indicated in the horizontal section	
Public Fixed – non-facilities-based Private fixed – facilities-based or non-facilities based a. Voice telephone services f. Facsimile services i. Voice mail	(1) None as of the end of 2006 (2) None (3) None, except foreign equity shall be limited to 49% upon accession, to go to 51% by the end of 2006, and to 70% after 3 years from accession (4) Unbound, except as indicated in the horizontal section	(1) None (2) None (3) None (4) Unbound, except as indicated in the horizontal section	

[2] A broadcasting service is defined as a radio communication service in which the transmissions are intended for direct reception by the general public, including sound transmissions, or television transmissions. However, carrying a signal between broadcasting stations and transmitters is part of telecommunications services.

Modes of supply: (1) Cross-border supply; (2) Consumption abroad; (3) Commercial presence; (4) Presence of natural persons.

Sector or Sub-sector	Limitation on market access	Limitations on national treatment	Additional commitments
2. Public or Private – facilities-based or non-facilities-based b. Packet-switched data transmission services c. Circuit-switched data transmission services d. Telex services e. Telegraph services g. Private leased circuit services - Value-added services h. Electronic mail j. On-line information and data base retrieval k. Electronic data interchange (EDI) l. Enhanced/value-added facsimile services, including store and forward, store and retrieve m. Code and protocol conversion n. On-line information and/or data processing (incl. transaction processing) o. Paging p. Internet services	(1) None (2) None (3) None, except foreign equity shall be limited to 49% upon accession, to go to 51% by the end of 2006, and to 70% after 3 years from accession (4) Unbound, except as indicated in the horizontal section	(1) None (2) None (3) None (4) Unbound, except as indicated in the horizontal section	

Modes of supply: (1) Cross-border supply; (2) Consumption abroad; (3) Commercial presence; (4) Presence of natural persons.

Sector or Sub-sector	Limitation on market access	Limitations on national treatment	Additional commitments
3. Others Mobile telephone services A.1. Public Mobile – facilities-based a. Voice f. Facsimile i. Voice mail	(1) None (2) None (3) None, except that mobile voice services offered as a facilities-based public telecommunications service must be provided by a joint stock company. Foreign equity shall be limited to 49% upon accession, to go to 51% by the end of 2005 and 60% by the end 2008. (4) Unbound, except as indicated in the horizontal section	(1) None (2) None (3) None (4) Unbound, except as indicated in the horizontal section	
A.2. Private Mobile (facilities-based or non-facilities based) and Public Mobile non-facilities-based a. Voice f. Facsimile i. Voice mail Satellite services[3]: - VSAT - GMPCS - Sale of satellite capacity to legal entities licensed or authorized by CITC to use such capacity in the Kingdom of Saudi Arabia.	(1) None (2) None (3) None, except: - Foreign equity shall be limited to 49% upon accession, to go to 51% by end of 2005, and to 70% after 3 years from accession. - The number of licenses for VSAT services may be limited to 5 until 1 January 2006. After that date, there will be no limit on the number of licenses. (4) Unbound, except as indicated in the horizontal section	(1) None (2) None (3) None (4) Unbound, except as indicated in the horizontal section	
D. Audiovisual Services 1. References below to "home video entertainment" include, but are not limited to, video tapes and digitally encoded video. 2. Nothing in this commitment shall require Saudi Arabia to provide a means of exhibition or transmission of audiovisual services not offered by the Saudi Government to the public generally.			
a. Motion picture and home video entertainment distribution services (CPC 96113) to other industries for public entertainment, television broadcasting, or sale or rental to others[4]	(1) None (2) None (3) Unbound (4) Unbound, except as indicated in the horizontal section	(1) None (2) None (3) Unbound (4) Unbound, except as indicated in the horizontal section	

[3] The GMPCS and VSAT Satellite Operators shall be required until 1 January 2006 to pass traffic via STC network through transit and gateway exchanges, especially in the case of overseas communication from Saudi Arabia.

[4] For purposes of clarity, this commitment relates only to the distribution, i.e., licensing of motion pictures of videotapes, and does not cover their television broadcast.

Modes of supply: (1) Cross-border supply; (2) Consumption abroad; (3) Commercial presence; (4) Presence of natural persons.

Sector or Sub-sector	Limitation on market access	Limitations on national treatment	Additional commitments
b. Radio and television production and distribution services (licensing of radio and television programs whether live, on tape, on other recording medium or on digitally encoded video for subsequent broadcast, whether by terrestrial broadcasting, by satellite television, by cable, or by other similar medium, including DTH and DBS. These programs, and channels of programming, may be for entertainment, for promotion or plays that are normally produced in television studios. Also included are products such as sports coverage, weather forecasting, interviews, etc.)	(1) Unbound (2) None (3) Unbound (4) Unbound, except as indicated in the horizontal section	(1) Unbound (2) None (3) Unbound (4) Unbound, except as indicated in the horizontal section	
3. CONSTRUCTION AND RELATED ENGINEERING SERVICES			
A. General construction work for buildings (CPC 512) B. General construction work for civil engineering (CPC 513) C. Installation and assembly work (CPC 516+514) D. Building completion and finishing work (CPC 517) E. Other (CPC 511, 515, 518)	(1) Unbound* except for consultancy and advisory related services (2) None (3) None (4) Unbound, except as indicated in the horizontal section	(1) Unbound* except for consultancy and advisory related services (2) None (3) None (4) Unbound, except as indicated in the horizontal section	

Modes of supply: (1) Cross-border supply; (2) Consumption abroad; (3) Commercial presence; (4) Presence of natural persons.

Sector or Sub-sector	Limitation on market access	Limitations on national treatment	Additional commitments
4. DISTRIBUTION SERVICES			
B. Wholesale trade services (CPC 622, 6111, 6113, 6121) C. Retailing services (CPC 631, 632, 6111, 6113, 6121 and 613) For purposes of this schedule wholesale and retail trade in country includes engaging private national individuals on a contract basis to sell products and services at retail for which compensation is received both for the sales effort and for sales support services that result in additional sales by other contracted distributors.	(1) None (2) None (3) None, except: - Foreign equity limited to 51% upon accession and to 75% after 3 years from the date of accession. - Minimum foreign investment of Saudi Riyals 20 million by each service supplier. - Minimum size of outlets may be prescribed. - Minimum of 15% Saudi employees to be trained each year. (4) Unbound, except as indicated in the horizontal section	(1) None (2) None (3) None (4) Unbound, except as indicated in the horizontal section	
D. Franchising (CPC 8929)	(1) Unbound (2) None (3) None, except: - Foreign equity limited to 51% upon accession and to 75% after 3 years from the date of accession. - Foreigner should be authorized in his own country to practice franchising or be a partner in an authorized company for a period no less than five years without interruption. (4) Unbound, except as indicated in the horizontal section	(1) Unbound (2) None (3) None (4) Unbound, except as indicated in the horizontal section	

Modes of supply: (1) Cross-border supply; (2) Consumption abroad; (3) Commercial presence; (4) Presence of natural persons.

Sector or Sub-sector	Limitation on market access	Limitations on national treatment	Additional commitments
5. EDUCATIONAL SERVICES			
A. Primary education services (CPC 921) B. Secondary education services (CPC 922) C. Higher education services (CPC 923) D. Adult education (CPC 924) E. Other (technical + Thai cooking and Thai language) (CPC 929)	(1) None (2) None (3) None (4) Unbound, except as indicated in the horizontal section	(1) None (2) None (3) None (4) Unbound, except as indicated in the horizontal section	
6. ENVIRONMENTAL SERVICES			
A. Sewage services (CPC 94010) B. Refuse disposal services (CPC 94020) C. Sanitation and similar services (CPC 9403) D. Other - Cleaning services for exhaust gases (CPC 9404) - Nature and landscape protection services (CPC 9406) - Noise abatement services (CPC 9405) - Other environmental services (CPC 9409) (including environmental impact assessment)	(1) None (2) None (3) None (4) Unbound, except as indicated in the horizontal section	(1) None (2) None (3) None (4) Unbound, except as indicated in the horizontal section	

Modes of supply: (1) Cross-border supply; (2) Consumption abroad; (3) Commercial presence; (4) Presence of natural persons.

Sector or Sub-sector	Limitation on market access	Limitations on national treatment	Additional commitments
7. FINANCIAL SERVICES			
A. Insurance and Insurance-Related Services (Market access allowed only for cooperative insurance services)			
Foreign insurance service providers operating through a Saudi Arabian agent are allowed to operate, including the ability to continue existing business operations without disruption, as well as to offer new products and servicing new clients, for a period of 3 years from the date of the Royal Decree No. 3120/MB dated 4/3/1426H (13 April 2005), and in accordance with that Decree.			
a. Protection and savings insurance[5] b. Non-life insurance (General insurance and health insurance) c. Reinsurance and retrocession d. Insurance Intermediation (Brokerage and Agency) e. Services auxiliary to insurance (consultancy, actuarial, risk assessment and claims settlement services)	(1) Unbound, except none for: (b) Insurance of risks relating to marine shipping and commercial aviation and space launching and freight (including satellites), with such insurance to cover any or all of the following: - the goods being transported, the vehicle transporting the goods and any liability arising there from. - Insurance of risks relating to goods in international transit. (c) Reinsurance and retrocession. (d) Brokerage and Agency. (e) Services auxiliary to insurance consultancy, actuarial, risk assessment and claims settlement services. (2) None (3) For (a), (b), and (c) Commercial presence is permissible in the form of a locally incorporated cooperative insurance joint-stock company, or as an established direct branch of an international insurance company operating in Saudi Arabia as a cooperative insurance provider[6]. Non-Saudi participation in the joint-stock company in Saudi Arabia is permitted up to 60% from the date of	(1) Unbound, except none for: (b) Insurance of risks relating to marine shipping and commercial aviation and space launching and freight (including satellites), with such insurance to cover any or all of the following: - the goods being transported, the vehicle transporting the goods and any liability arising there from. - Insurance of risks relating to goods in international transit. (c) Reinsurance and retrocession. (d) Brokerage and Agency. (e) Services auxiliary to insurance consultancy, actuarial, risk assessment and claims settlement services. (2) None (3) None	

[5] As defined in Article 3, Part 3:1-3 of the Cooperative Insurance Companies Control Law Implementing Regulations, published 25 April 2004, including protection against longevity.
[6] For clarity's sake, branches of foreign insurance companies operating as cooperative insurance providers are not required to operate as joint-stock companies in Saudi Arabia.

Modes of supply: (1) Cross-border supply; (2) Consumption abroad; (3) Commercial presence; (4) Presence of natural persons.

Sector or Sub-sector	Limitation on market access	Limitations on national treatment	Additional commitments

	accession.
	
	For (d) Commercial presence is permissible in the form of a locally incorporated joint-stock company or a limited liability company. Non-Saudi participation is permitted up to 60% from the date of accession.
	
	For (e) Commercial presence for claims services and risk assessment is permissible in the form of a locally incorporated joint-stock company or a limited liability company. Non-Saudi participation is permitted up to 60% from the date of accession. For actuarial and consultancy commercial presence is permitted as a natural person or a juristic entity.
	
	(4) Unbound, except as indicated in the horizontal section
		(4) Unbound, except as indicated in the horizontal section	

B. Banking and other financial services (excluding insurance)			
a. Acceptance of deposits and other repayable funds from the public b. Lending of all types, including consumer credit, mortgage credit, factoring and financing of commercial transaction c. Financial leasing d. All payment and money transmission services, including credit, charge and debit cards, travellers cheques and bankers drafts e. Guarantees and commitments f. Trading for own account or for account of customers, whether on an exchange, in an over-the-counter market or otherwise, the following: - money market instruments (including cheques, bills,	(1) Unbound, except for 'l.', 'k.' and, under 'i.', only for cash or portfolio management, all forms of collective investment, custodial, depository and trust services to be provided by institutions to institutional clients, including collective investment schemes, upon accession. (2) None, except unbound for pension fund management under 'i.' and all domestic settlement and clearing services provided exclusively by SAMA under 'j.'. This also limits national treatment. (3) None, except: - Commercial presence of banks is permissible in the form of a locally incorporated joint-stock	(1) Unbound, except as indicated in the M.A. column (2) None (3) None	When pension schemes supplementary to the public pension scheme are provided by Saudi Financial institutions, it will also be open for foreign service suppliers for mode (2) and (3) only.

Modes of supply: (1) Cross-border supply; (2) Consumption abroad; (3) Commercial presence; (4) Presence of natural persons.

Sector or Sub-sector	Limitation on market access	Limitations on national treatment	Additional commitments
certificates of deposits); - foreign exchange; - derivative products including, but not limited to, futures and options; - exchange rate and interest rate instruments, including products such as swaps, forward rate agreements; - transferable securities; - other negotiable instruments and financial assets, including bullion. g. participation in issues of all kinds of securities, including underwriting and placement as agent (whether publicly or privately) and provision of services related to such issues h. Money broking i. Asset management, such as cash or portfolio management, all forms of collective investment management, pension fund management, custodial, depository and trust services j. Settlement and clearing services for financial assets, including securities, derivative products, and other negotiable instruments k. Advisory and other auxiliary financial services on all the activities listed in sub paragraphs 'a.' through 'l.', including credit reference and analysis, investment and portfolio research and advice, advice on acquisitions and on corporate restructuring and strategy l. Provision and transfer of financial information, and financial data processing and related software.	company or as a branch of an international bank. - Non-Saudi participation in a joint-venture in Saudi Arabia is permitted up to 60% from the date of accession. - These financial services are to be provided by commercial banks except that asset management 'i.' and advisory services 'k.' may be provided by non-commercial banking financial institutions under the capital market law. - Unbound for pension fund management under 'i.'. This also limits national treatment. - Unbound for all domestic settlement and clearing services provided exclusively by SAMA under 'j.'. This also limits national treatment. (4) Unbound, except as indicated in the horizontal section	(4) Unbound, except as indicated in the horizontal section	

Modes of supply: (1) Cross-border supply; (2) Consumption abroad; (3) Commercial presence; (4) Presence of natural persons.

Sector or Sub-sector	Limitation on market access	Limitations on national treatment	Additional commitments
8. HEALTH RELATED AND OTHER SERVICES			
A. Hospital services (CPC 9311)	(1) Unbound* (2) None (3) None, except subject to formation of a company between a foreign hospital company and a licensed Saudi medical professional (4) Unbound, except as indicated in the horizontal section	(1) Unbound* (2) None (3) None (4) Unbound, except as indicated in the horizontal section	
B. Other human health services (CPC 9319, except 93191)	(1) Unbound* (2) None (3) None, except subject to formation of a company between a foreign health company and a licensed Saudi medical professional (4) Unbound, except as indicated in the horizontal section	(1) Unbound* (2) None (3) None (4) Unbound, except as indicated in the horizontal section	

Modes of supply: (1) Cross-border supply; (2) Consumption abroad; (3) Commercial presence; (4) Presence of natural persons.

Sector or Sub-sector	Limitation on market access	Limitations on national treatment	Additional commitments
9. TOURISM AND TRAVEL RELATED SERVICES			
A. Hotels and restaurants (including catering) (CPC 64110, 64120, 642 & 643) (Except bars, nightclubs, etc.)	(1) None (2) None (3) None (4) Unbound, except as indicated in the horizontal section	(1) None (2) None (3) None (4) Unbound, except as indicated in the horizontal section	
B. Travel agencies and tour operators services (CPC 7471) (excluding for Umra and Hajj)	(1) None (2) None (3) None, except economic needs test applied to travel agencies only, based on the ratio of total population to the number of travel agencies (4) Unbound, except as indicated in the horizontal section	(1) None (2) None (3) None (4) Unbound, except as indicated in the horizontal section	
C. Tourist guides services (CPC 74720) (excluding for Umra and Hajj)	(1) None (2) None (3) None (4) Unbound, except as indicated in the horizontal section	(1) None (2) None (3) None (4) Unbound, except as indicated in the horizontal section	
10. RECREATIONAL CULTURAL AND SPORTING SERVICES			
B. News agency services (CPC 962) D. Recreational services (CPC 96491) (Only parks and public gardens services)	(1) None (2) None (3) None (4) Unbound, except as indicated in the horizontal section	(1) None (2) None (3) None (4) Unbound, except as indicated in the horizontal section	
11. TRANSPORT SERVICES			
A. Maritime Transport Services a. Passenger transportation (CPC 7211) b. Freight transportation (CPC 7212) c. Rental of vessels with crew (CPC 72130) d. Maintenance and repair of vessels	(1) None (2) None (3) None (4) Unbound, except as indicated in the horizontal section	(1) None (2) None (3) None (4) Unbound, except as indicated in the horizontal section	The following services at the port are made available to international maritime transport suppliers on reasonable and non-discriminatory terms and conditions: - port and waterway operation services (excluding cargo handling) - pilotage and perthing services; - navigation aid services; - vessel salvage and re-floating services; - all other supporting services for water transport.

Modes of supply: (1) Cross-border supply; (2) Consumption abroad; (3) Commercial presence; (4) Presence of natural persons.

Sector or Sub-sector	Limitation on market access	Limitations on national treatment	Additional commitments
C. Air Transport Services d. Maintenance and repair of aircraft e. Supporting services for air transport (CPC 746) - Computer reservation system	(1) None (2) None (3) None (4) Unbound, except as indicated in the horizontal section	(1) None (2) None (3) None (4) Unbound, except as indicated in the horizontal section	
E. Rail Transport Services a. Passenger transportation (CPC 7111) b. Freight transportation (CPC 7112) c. Pushing and towing services (CPC 7130) d. Maintenance and repair of rail transport equipment (CPC 8868) e. Supporting services for rail transport services (CPC 743)	(1) None (2) None (3) Foreign investment in the form of Build, Operate and Transfer (BOT) arrangement (4) Unbound, except as indicated in the horizontal section	(1) None (2) None (3) None (4) Unbound, except as indicated in the horizontal section	
G. Pipeline transport a. Transportation of fuels (CPC 7131) b. Transportation of other goods (CPC 7139)	(1) None (2) None (3) None (4) Unbound, except as indicated in the horizontal section	(1) None (2) None (3) None (4) Unbound, except as indicated in the horizontal section	
H. Services auxiliary to all modes of transport (limited to maritime, rail, and air transport services in accordance with the Annex on Air Transport Services) a. Cargo handling services (CPC 741) b. Storage and warehouse services (CPC 742) c. Freight transport agency services (CPC 748)	(1) None (2) None (3) None (4) Unbound, except as indicated in the horizontal section	(1) None (2) None (3) None (4) Unbound, except as indicated in the horizontal section	The services related to CPC 749 are currently provided by the public sector. As far as market access to services included in CPC 749 become open under the Saudi legislation to private entities, national treatment will be granted.

REFERENCE PAPER

Scope

The following are definitions and principles on the regulatory framework for the basic telecommunications services.

Definitions

Users mean service consumers and service suppliers.

Essential facilities mean facilities of a public telecommunications transport network or service that

(a) are exclusively or predominantly provided by a single or limited number of suppliers; and

(b) cannot feasibly be economically or technically substituted in order to provide a service.

A major supplier is a supplier which has the ability to materially affect the terms of participation (having regard to price and supply) in the relevant market for basic telecommunications services as a result of:

(a) control over essential facilities; or

(b) use of its position in the market.

1. Competitive safeguards

1.1 Prevention of anti-competitive practices in telecommunications

Appropriate measures shall be maintained for the purpose of preventing suppliers who, alone or together, are a major supplier from engaging in or continuing anti-competitive practices.

1.2 Safeguards

The anti-competitive practices referred to above shall include in particular:

(a) engaging in anti-competitive cross-subsidization;

(b) using information obtained from competitors with anti-competitive results; and

(c) not making available to other services suppliers on a timely basis technical information about essential facilities and commercially relevant information which are necessary for them to provide services.

2. Interconnection

2.1 This section applies to linking with suppliers providing public telecommunications transport networks or services in order to allow the users of one supplier to communicate with users of another supplier and to access services provided by another supplier, where specific commitments are undertaken.

2.2 Interconnection to be ensured

Interconnection with a major supplier will be ensured at any technically feasible point in the network. Such interconnection is provided:

(a) Under non-discriminatory terms, conditions (including technical standards and specifications) and rates and of a quality no less favourable than that provided for its own like services or for like services of non-affiliated service suppliers or for its subsidiaries or other affiliates;
(b) In a timely fashion, on terms, conditions (including technical standards and specifications) and cost-oriented rates that are transparent, reasonable, having regard to economic feasibility, and sufficiently unbundled so that the supplier need not pay for network components or facilities that it does not require for the service to be provided; and
(c) Upon request, at points in addition to the network termination points offered to the majority of users, subject to charges that reflect the cost of construction of necessary additional facilities.

2.3 Public availability of the procedures for interconnection negotiations

The procedures applicable for interconnection to a major supplier will be made publicly available.

2.4 Transparency of interconnection arrangements

It is ensured that a major supplier will make publicly available either its interconnection agreements or a reference interconnection offer.

2.5 Interconnection: dispute settlement

A service supplier requesting interconnection with a major supplier will have recourse, either:

(a) At any time; or
(b) After a reasonable period of time which has been made publicly known to an independent domestic body, which may be a regulatory body as referred to in paragraph 5 below, to resolve disputes regarding appropriate terms, conditions and rates for interconnection within a reasonable period of time, to the extent that these have not been established previously.

3. Universal service

Any Member has the right to define the kind of universal service obligation it wishes to maintain. Such obligations will not be regarded as anti-competitive *per se*, provided they are administered in a transparent, non-discriminatory and competitively neutral manner and are not more burdensome than necessary for the kind of universal service defined by the Member.

4. Public availability of licensing criteria

Where a licence is required, the following will be made publicly available:

(a) all the licensing criteria and the period of time normally required to reach a decision concerning an application for a licence; and
(b) the terms and conditions of individual licences.

The reasons for the denial of a licence will be made known to the applicant upon request.

5. Independent regulators

The regulatory body is separate from, and not accountable to, any supplier of basic telecommunications services. The decisions of and the procedures used by regulators shall be impartial with respect to all market participants.

6. Allocation and use of scarce resources

Any procedures for the allocation and use of scarce resources, including frequencies, numbers and rights of way, will be carried out in an objective, timely, transparent and non-discriminatory manner. The current state of allocated frequency bands will be made publicly available, but detailed identification of frequencies allocated for specific government uses is not required.

List of Article II (MFN) Exemptions

Sector or sub-sector	Description of measure indicating its inconsistency with Article II	Countries to which the measure applies	Intended duration	Conditions creating the need for the exemption
Road Transport Services	Reciprocal preferential treatment for cross-border services	Egypt, Jordan	Indefinite	Existing bilateral agreements
Maritime Shipping and Road Transport Services	Preference for use of national shipping lines and road transport vehicles in bilateral trade	Egypt, Tunisia	Indefinite	Existing bilateral agreements
Road Transport Services	Reciprocal preferential treatment	Lebanon, Syria, Turkey	Indefinite	Existing bilateral agreements

Le Royaume d'Arabie saoudite

Liste d'engagements spécifiques concernant les services
Liste d'exemptions des obligations énoncées à l'article II (NPF)

Seul le texte anglais fait foi.

Modes de fourniture: 1) Fourniture transfrontières 2) Consommation à l'étranger 3) Présence commerciale 4) Présence de personnes physiques

Secteur ou sous-secteur	Limitations concernant l'accès aux marchés	Limitations concernant le traitement national	Engagements additionnels
I. ENGAGEMENTS HORIZONTAUX			
Ensemble des secteurs et sous-secteurs des services inclus dans la présente offre	3) i) Présence commerciale pour tous les services énumérés dans la présente liste, autres que les services fournis aux entreprises (énumérés ci-dessous)[1] sous réserve de la constitution en société conformément à la Loi sur les sociétés, soit comme société par actions soit comme société à responsabilité limitée. ii) Présence commerciale pour les services fournis aux entreprises (énumérés ci-dessous)[1] sous réserve de l'établissement d'une société et de son enregistrement en vertu de la Loi sur les sociétés professionnelles.	3) i) Les fournisseurs de services étrangers doivent obtenir l'approbation de la Direction générale de l'investissement pour établir une présence commerciale en Arabie saoudite conformément à la Loi d'avril 2000 sur l'investissement étranger et à l'article 5:3 du Règlement relatif à la Loi sur l'investissement étranger. ii) Les ressortissants non saoudiens peuvent acquérir des biens immobiliers en Arabie saoudite par héritage. Les établissements étrangers autorisés à exercer leurs activités dans le Royaume en vertu de la Loi sur l'investissement étranger peuvent posséder des biens immobiliers conformément aux lois et règlements régissant la participation étrangère dans des actifs immobiliers. iii) Les entités commerciales non saoudiennes sont assujetties à un impôt sur le revenu tandis que les entités saoudiennes sont assujetties au Zakat. Les modifications qui seront apportées à l'avenir au code fiscal saoudien ne seront pas moins favorables aux fournisseurs de services étrangers qu'elles ne le sont en vertu du code actuel.	Tous les modes de fournitures: les mesures de fiscalité seront à tous égards, sauf pour le Zakat, appliquées conformément aux articles II et XVII et à toutes les autres dispositions pertinentes de l'AGCS.

[1] Services professionnels (1A), voir document W/120.

Modes de fourniture: 1) Fourniture transfrontières 2) Consommation à l'étranger 3) Présence commerciale 4) Présence de personnes physiques

Secteur ou sous-secteur	Limitations concernant l'accès aux marchés	Limitations concernant le traitement national	Engagements additionnels
		iv) Les fournisseurs de services étrangers et les personnes physiques étrangères auront accès aux subventions disponibles dans le pays. Toutefois, seuls les Saoudiens pourront bénéficier de subventions sur certains services.	
	4) Non consolidé, sauf en ce qui concerne les mesures applicables à l'entrée et au séjour temporaire des personnes physiques appartenant aux catégories suivantes: i) <u>Personnes en voyage d'affaires</u>: Personnes physiques qui séjournent en Arabie saoudite sans recevoir de rémunération en Arabie saoudite ni effectuer de ventes directes au grand public ni fournir de services, en vue de participer à des réunions d'affaires, de nouer des contacts d'affaires, y compris de participer à des négociations pour la vente de services et/ou à d'autres activités similaires, y compris pour préparer l'établissement d'une présence commerciale en Arabie saoudite. L'entrée et le séjour sont limités à une période n'excédant pas 180 jours, y compris les entrées multiples. ii) <u>Personnes transférées à l'intérieur d'une société</u> Personnel d'encadrement, dirigeants et spécialistes (au sens indiqué plus loin) qui, à la date de leur demande d'entrée dans le Royaume, sont employés depuis trois ans au moins dans le même domaine par une personne morale et sont transférés vers une entreprise qui lui est apparentée en Arabie saoudite. L'entrée et le séjour de ces membres du personnel d'encadrement, dirigeants et spécialistes sont subordonnés aux conditions suivantes:	4) Non consolidé, sauf comme indiqué sous "limitations concernant l'accès aux marchés"	

Modes de fourniture: 1) Fourniture transfrontières 2) Consommation à l'étranger 3) Présence commerciale 4) Présence de personnes physiques

Secteur ou sous-secteur	Limitations concernant l'accès aux marchés	Limitations concernant le traitement national	Engagements additionnels
	- Leur nombre ne peut excéder 25 pour cent de l'effectif total de chaque fournisseur de services. Toutefois, un minimum de trois personnes sera autorisé. Il est également possible pour le fournisseur de services de choisir l'option suivante: le nombre de ces membres du personnel d'encadrement, dirigeants et spécialistes ne dépassera pas 15 pour cent; et le nombre des autres employés étrangers (c'est-à-dire autres que les membres du personnel d'encadrement, dirigeants et spécialistes) sera limité à 10 pour cent, ou vice-versa. Toutefois, le transfert d'un minimum de deux personnes sera considéré comme étant conforme au seuil de 15 pour cent. - Leur entrée et leur séjour seront autorisés pour une période de deux ans, renouvelable pour des durées similaires. - Certains postes dans une entreprise peuvent être réservés aux ressortissants saoudiens de toutes catégories. Ces postes sont ceux ayant trait au recrutement et au personnel, les postes de réceptionniste, caissier, garde de la sécurité civile et les postes ayant trait au suivi des transactions (relations avec le gouvernement).		

Modes de fourniture: 1) Fourniture transfrontières 2) Consommation à l'étranger 3) Présence commerciale 4) Présence de personnes physiques

Secteur ou sous-secteur	Limitations concernant l'accès aux marchés	Limitations concernant le traitement national	Engagements additionnels
	Définitions: Personnel d'encadrement: personnes qui, dans une organisation, ont essentiellement pour tâche de diriger celle-ci, ou un de ses départements ou services, supervisent et contrôlent le travail d'autres superviseurs, professionnels ou cadres, sont habilitées à recruter et à licencier ou à recommander le recrutement et le licenciement de personnel, ou à prendre d'autres décisions (par exemple en ce qui concerne les promotions ou l'autorisation de congés), et ont un pouvoir discrétionnaire pour les activités courantes. Cette catégorie ne comprend ni les superviseurs de premier rang – sauf si les employés qu'ils supervisent sont des professionnels – ni les employés qui exécutent essentiellement des tâches nécessaires à la fourniture du service considéré. Dirigeants: personnes qui, dans une organisation, ont essentiellement pour tâche de gérer celle-ci, fixent ses objectifs et déterminent ses politiques, disposent d'un large pouvoir de décision et auxquelles les cadres de rang supérieur, le conseil d'administration ou les actionnaires de l'entreprise n'adressent que des indications ou directives de caractère général. Ils n'exécutent pas directement des tâches liées à la fourniture effective du service ou des services de l'organisation. Spécialistes: personnes qui, dans une organisation, ont de très grandes compétences et des connaissances très poussées, entretenues par une pratique suivie des services, des activités de recherche, du matériel, des techniques ou de la gestion de l'organisation.		

Modes de fourniture: 1) Fourniture transfrontières 2) Consommation à l'étranger 3) Présence commerciale 4) Présence de personnes physiques

Secteur ou sous-secteur	Limitations concernant l'accès aux marchés	Limitations concernant le traitement national	Engagements additionnels
	iii) <u>Fournisseurs de services contractuels</u> Employés de fournisseurs de services contractuels, c'est-à-dire employés de personnes morales sans présence commerciale en Arabie saoudite, qui ont obtenu un contrat de services en Arabie saoudite dont l'exécution exige la présence de leurs employés dans le pays. L'entrée et le séjour de ces personnes seront autorisés pour une période n'excédant pas 180 jours renouvelable. L'entrée de ces personnes sera autorisée uniquement pour les sous-secteurs ci-après des services fournis aux entreprises: - services juridiques (partie de CPC 861) - services d'architecture (CPC 8671) - services d'aménagement urbain et d'architecture paysagère (CPC 8674) - services d'ingénierie (CPC 8672) - services intégrés d'ingénierie (CPC 8673) - services connexes de consultations scientifiques et techniques (CPC 8675) - services d'essais et d'analyses techniques (CPC 8676) - services de traduction (CPC 87905) - services liés à l'environnement (tous les sous-secteurs) (CPC 94010 + 94020 + 9403 + 9404 + 9405 + 9406 + 9409)		

Modes de fourniture: 1) Fourniture transfrontières 2) Consommation à l'étranger 3) Présence commerciale 4) Présence de personnes physiques

Secteur ou sous-secteur	Limitations concernant l'accès aux marchés	Limitations concernant le traitement national	Engagements additionnels
	- services annexes aux industries extractives (CPC 883 + 5115) - services de conseil en gestion (CPC 8650) - services connexes aux services de consultations en matière de gestion (CPC 8660) - services d'entretien et de réparation de matériel (à l'exclusion des véhicules maritimes, aériens ou d'autres matériels de transport) (CPC 633 + 8861 à 8866) - services comptables, d'audit et de tenue de livres (CPC 8621 + 8622) - services médicaux et dentaires (CPC 9312) - services fournis à la recherche et au développement expérimental interdisciplinaires (CPC 85300) - services informatiques et services connexes (CPC 841 à 845 + 849) - services de construction et d'ingénierie connexes (CPC 511 à 518) - services d'agences de voyages et d'organisateurs touristiques, à l'exclusion des services pour l'Umra et le Hadj (CPC 7471) - services de restauration, y compris les services de traiteur (à l'exception des bars, boîtes de nuit, etc.) (CPC 6421 + 6422 + 6423)		

Modes de fourniture: 1) Fourniture transfrontières 2) Consommation à l'étranger 3) Présence commerciale 4) Présence de personnes physiques

Secteur ou sous-secteur	Limitations concernant l'accès aux marchés	Limitations concernant le traitement national	Engagements additionnels
	iv) Professionnels indépendants Professionnels indépendants (c'est-à-dire personnes physiques) engagés au titre d'un contrat de services par une personne morale établie en Arabie saoudite afin de rendre des services professionnels pour lesquels ils possèdent les diplômes universitaires et les qualifications professionnelles nécessaires ainsi que trois ans d'expérience dans le domaine concerné. L'entrée et le séjour de ces personnes seront autorisés pour une période de 180 jours, qui pourra être renouvelée. L'entrée de ces personnes sera autorisée uniquement pour les services suivants: - services informatiques et services connexes (CPC 841 à 845 + 849) - services de construction et services d'ingénierie connexes (CPC 512, 513 et 516 + 517) - services comptables, d'audit et de tenue de livres (CPC 8621 + 8622) - services de conseil fiscal (CPC 87905) - services d'architecture (CPC 8671) - pilotes et équipage services juridiques (partie de CPC 861)		

Modes de fourniture: 1) Fourniture transfrontières 2) Consommation à l'étranger 3) Présence commerciale 4) Présence de personnes physiques

Secteur ou sous-secteur	Limitations concernant l'accès aux marchés	Limitations concernant le traitement national	Engagements additionnels
	- services médicaux et dentaires CPC 9312) - services fournis à la recherche et au développement expérimental interdisciplinaires (CPC 85300) - services de conseil en gestion (CPC 8650) - services de nettoyage de bâtiments (CPC 874) Pour les autres services d'enseignement (uniquement l'enseignement de la cuisine thaïlandaise et de la langue thaïe (en tant que partie de CPC 9290)), l'entrée et le séjour seront autorisés pour une période de 90 jours, qui pourra être renouvelée pour une durée similaire. v) <u>Installateurs et agents d'entretien</u> Spécialistes qualifiés qui fournissent des services d'installation ou d'entretien. Ces services doivent être fournis sous contrat entre le constructeur des machines ou matériels et leur propriétaire, l'un comme l'autre étant des personnes morales. L'entrée temporaire est accordée pour une période ne dépassant pas 90 jours, qui peut être renouvelée.		

Modes de fourniture: 1) Fourniture transfrontières 2) Consommation à l'étranger 3) Présence commerciale 4) Présence de personnes physiques

Secteur ou sous-secteur	Limitations concernant l'accès aux marchés	Limitations concernant le traitement national	Engagements additionnels
II. ENGAGEMENTS SECTORIELS			
1. SERVICES FOURNIS AUX ENTREPRISES			
A. Services professionnels			
a. Services juridiques Services de conseil juridique dans le droit de la juridiction pour lequel le fournisseur de services a qualité de juriste et en droit international (partie de CPC 861)	1) Néant 2) Néant 3) Participation du capital étranger limitée à 75 pour cent 4) Non consolidé, sauf comme indiqué sous "Engagements horizontaux"	) Néant 2) Néant 3) Les juristes qui ne sont pas des ressortissants saoudiens ne peuvent pas plaider une affaire devant les tribunaux 4) Non consolidé, sauf comme indiqué sous "Engagements horizontaux"	
b. Services comptables, d'audit et de tenue de livres (CPC 8621 et 8622) c. Services de conseil fiscal (CPC 8630) d. Services d'architecture (CPC 8671) e. Services d'ingénierie (CPC 8672) f. Services intégrés d'ingénierie (CPC 8673) g. Services d'aménagement urbain et d'architecture paysagère (CPC 8674) h. Services médicaux et dentaires (CPC 9312) i. Services vétérinaires (CPC 93201)	1) Néant 2) Néant 3) Participation du capital étranger limitée à 75 pour cent 4) Non consolidé, sauf comme indiqué sous "Engagements horizontaux"	1) Néant 2) Néant 3) Néant 4) Non consolidé, sauf comme indiqué sous "Engagements horizontaux"	

Modes de fourniture: 1) Fourniture transfrontières 2) Consommation à l'étranger 3) Présence commerciale 4) Présence de personnes physiques

Secteur ou sous-secteur	Limitations concernant l'accès aux marchés	Limitations concernant le traitement national	Engagements additionnels
B. Services informatiques et services connexes			
a-e. (CPC 841 à 845 et 849)	1) Néant 2) Néant 3) Néant 4) Non consolidé, sauf comme indiqué sous "Engagements horizontaux"	1) Néant 2) Néant 3) Néant 4) Non consolidé, sauf comme indiqué sous "Engagements horizontaux"	
C. Services de recherche-développement			
a-c. (CPC 851, 852 et 853)	1) Néant 2) Néant 3) Néant 4) Non consolidé, sauf comme indiqué sous "Engagements horizontaux"	1) Néant 2) Néant 3) Néant 4) Non consolidé, sauf comme indiqué sous "Engagements horizontaux"	
E. Services de crédit-bail ou de location sans opérateurs			
a. De bateaux (CPC 83103) b. D'aéronefs (CPC 83104) c. D'autres matériels de transport (CPC 83101 + 83102 + 83105) d. D'autres machines et matériel (CPC 83106 à 83109) e. Services de location simple ou en crédit-bail d'articles domestiques (CPC 832)	1) Néant 2) Néant 3) Néant 4) Non consolidé, sauf comme indiqué sous "Engagements horizontaux"	1) Néant 2) Néant 3) Néant 4) Non consolidé, sauf comme indiqué sous "Engagements horizontaux"	

Modes de fourniture: 1) Fourniture transfrontières 2) Consommation à l'étranger 3) Présence commerciale 4) Présence de personnes physiques

Secteur ou sous-secteur	Limitations concernant l'accès aux marchés	Limitations concernant le traitement national	Engagements additionnels
F. Autres services fournis aux entreprises			
a. Services de publicité (CPC 8711) b. Services d'études de marchés (CPC 86401) c. Services de conseil en gestion (CPC 8650) d. Services connexes aux services de consultations en matière de gestion (CPC 8660) e. Services d'essais et d'analyses techniques (CPC 8676) f. Services annexes à l'agriculture, à la chasse, à la sylviculture et à la pêche (CPC 881) h. Services annexes aux industries extractives (CPC 883 + 5115) i. Services annexes aux industries manufacturières (CPC 884 (à l'exception de 88442) + 885) j. Services annexes à la distribution d'énergie (CPC 887) m. Services connexes de consultations scientifiques et techniques (CPC 8675)	1) Néant 2) Néant 3) Néant 4) Non consolidé, sauf comme indiqué sous "Engagements horizontaux"	1) Néant 2) Néant 3) Néant 4) Non consolidé, sauf comme indiqué sous "Engagements horizontaux"	

Modes de fourniture: 1) Fourniture transfrontières 2) Consommation à l'étranger 3) Présence commerciale 4) Présence de personnes physiques

Secteur ou sous-secteur	Limitations concernant l'accès aux marchés	Limitations concernant le traitement national	Engagements additionnels
n. Services d'entretien et de réparation de matériel (à l'exclusion des véhicules maritimes, aériens ou d'autres matériels de transport) (CPC 633 + 8861 à 8866) p. Services photographiques (CPC 8750) q. Services de conditionnement (CPC 8760) r. Services d'impression et de publication (CPC 88442) s. Services de congrès (CPC 87909)* t. Autres services (par exemple services de relations publiques) - Services de traduction (CPC 87905) - Services de conception spécialisés (CPC 87907)			

Modes de fourniture: 1) Fourniture transfrontières 2) Consommation à l'étranger 3) Présence commerciale 4) Présence de personnes physiques

Secteur ou sous-secteur	Limitations concernant l'accès aux marchés	Limitations concernant le traitement national	Engagements additionnels
2. SERVICES DE COMMUNICATION			
B. Services de courrier (CPC 7512)	1) Néant 2) Néant 3) Néant 4) Non consolidé, sauf comme indiqué sous "Engagements horizontaux	1) Néant 2) Néant 3) Néant 4) Non consolidé, sauf comme indiqué sous "Engagements horizontaux"	- Les exploitants de services de livraison exprès bénéficieront d'un traitement non moins favorable que celui qui est accordé à la poste pour ses activités de livraison exprès. - Lorsque les services de consultation relatifs à la fourniture de services postaux (CPC 7511**) seront privatisés, ils seront aussi ouverts aux fournisseurs de services étrangers
C. Services de télécommunication			

Conditions générales pour ce sous-secteur: Les engagements contractés par le Royaume d'Arabie saoudite sont conformes aux principes énoncés aux fins de l'établissement des listes dans les documents ci-après: "Notes sur l'établissement des listes d'engagements pour les télécommunications de base" (S/GBT/W/2/Rev.1) et "Limitations concernant l'accès aux marchés qui ont trait à la disponibilité du spectre" (S/GBT/W/3).

Ces engagements sont subordonnés aux conditions générales ci-après:

- Le Royaume d'Arabie saoudite contracte des engagements conformément au document de référence sur les télécommunications de base figurant en annexe.
- Tout service de télécommunication fourni en Arabie saoudite sur la base d'une présence commerciale (mode 3) doit être fourni par une entreprise enregistrée en Arabie saoudite, dans laquelle la participation étrangère ne dépassera pas les pourcentages mentionnés ci-après.
- La présente liste relative aux télécommunications de base n'inclut aucun service de diffusion.[2]
- La fourniture transfrontières est subordonnée à un accord commercial avec une/des entité(s) juridique(s) ayant obtenu une licence ou un agrément de la CITC dans le Royaume d'Arabie saoudite

[2] Les services de diffusion sont définis comme étant des services de radiocommunication dans lesquels les transmissions sont conçues pour être reçues directement par le grand public, y compris les transmissions sonores ou les transmissions télévisuelles. Toutefois, le transport d'un signal entre les stations de diffusion et les émetteurs fait partie des services de télécommunication.

Modes de fourniture: 1) Fourniture transfrontières 2) Consommation à l'étranger 3) Présence commerciale 4) Présence de personnes physiques

Secteur ou sous-secteur	Limitations concernant l'accès aux marchés	Limitations concernant le traitement national	Engagements additionnels
1. Services de télécommunication de base - Services publics, fixes – fournis par la mise à disposition d'installations a. Services de téléphone f. Services de télécopie i. Services d'audio-messagerie téléphonique	1) Néant à compter de fin 2006 2) Néant 3) Néant, sauf que les services offerts en tant que services de télécommunication publics doivent être fournis par une société par actions. La participation étrangère au capital est limitée à 49 pour cent au moment de l'accession; elle pourra être de 51 pour cent d'ici à la fin de 2007 et de 60 pour cent d'ici à la fin de 2008 4) Non consolidé, sauf comme indiqué sous "Engagements horizontaux"	1) Néant 2) Néant 3) Néant 4) Non consolidé, sauf comme indiqué sous "Engagements horizontaux	
Publics, fixes – sans mise à disposition d'installations et privés, fixes – avec ou sans mise à disposition d'installations a. Services de téléphone f. Services de télécopie i. Services d'audio-messagerie téléphonique	1) Néant à compter de fin 2006 2) Néant 3) Néant, sauf que la participation étrangère au capital sera limitée à 49 pour cent au moment de l'accession, puis à 51 pour cent d'ici à la fin de 2006 et à 70 pour cent trois ans après l'accession 4) Non consolidé, sauf comme indiqué sous "Engagements horizontaux"	1) Néant 2) Néant 3) Néant 4) Non consolidé, sauf comme indiqué sous "Engagements horizontaux"	
2. Publics ou privés – avec ou sans mise à disposition d'installations b. Services de transmission de données avec commutation par paquets c. Services de transmission de données avec commutation de circuits	1) Néant 2) Néant 3) Néant, sauf que la participation étrangère au capital sera limitée à 49 pour cent au moment de l'accession, puis à 51 pour cent d'ici à la fin de 2006 et à 70 pour cent trois ans après l'accession 4) Non consolidé, sauf comme indiqué sous "Engagements horizontaux"	1) Néant 2) Néant 3) Néant 4) Non consolidé, sauf comme indiqué sous "Engagements horizontaux"	

Modes de fourniture: 1) Fourniture transfrontières 2) Consommation à l'étranger 3) Présence commerciale 4) Présence de personnes physiques

Secteur ou sous-secteur	Limitations concernant l'accès aux marchés	Limitations concernant le traitement national	Engagements additionnels
d. Services de télex e. Services de télégraphe g. Services de circuits privés loués - Services à valeur ajoutée h. Courrier électronique j. Services directs de recherche d'informations permanente et de serveurs de bases de données k. Échange électronique de données l. Services à valeur ajoutée/améliorés de télécopie, y compris enregistrement et retransmission et enregistrement et recherche m. Services de conversion de codes et de protocoles n. Services de traitement direct de l'information et/ou de données (y compris traitement transactionnel) o. Services de recherche de personnes p. Services de fournisseurs d'accès à Internet			

Modes de fourniture: 1) Fourniture transfrontières 2) Consommation à l'étranger 3) Présence commerciale 4) Présence de personnes physiques

Secteur ou sous-secteur	Limitations concernant l'accès aux marchés	Limitations concernant le traitement national	Engagements additionnels
3. Autres Services de radiotéléphonie mobile A.1. Services de radiotéléphonie mobile publics – avec mise à disposition d'installations a. Services de téléphone f. Services de télécopie i. Services d'audio-messagerie téléphonique	1) Néant 2) Néant 3) Néant, sauf que les services de téléphone mobile offerts en tant que service de télécommunication public avec mise à disposition d'installations doivent être fournis par une société par actions. La participation étrangère au capital sera limitée à 49 pour cent au moment de l'accession, elle pourra être de 51 pour cent d'ici à la fin de 2005 et de 60 pour cent d'ici à la fin de 2008. 4) Non consolidé, sauf comme indiqué sous "Engagements horizontaux"	1) Néant 2) Néant 3) Néant 4) Non consolidé, sauf comme indiqué sous "Engagements horizontaux	
A.2. Services de radiotéléphonie mobile privés (avec ou sans mise à disposition d'installations) et services de radiotéléphonie mobile publics sans mise à disposition d'installations a. Services de téléphone f. Services de télécopie i. Services d'audio-messagerie téléphonique	1) Néant 2) Néant 3) Néant, sauf: - La participation étrangère au capital sera limitée à 49 pour cent au moment de l'accession, elle pourra être de 51 pour cent d'ici à la fin de 2005, puis de 70 pour cent trois ans après l'accession. - Le nombre de licences pour les services VSAT sera limité à cinq jusqu'au 1er janvier 2006. Après cette date, il n'y aura aucune limitation du nombre des licences.	1) Néant 2) Néant 3) Néant	

Modes de fourniture: 1) Fourniture transfrontières 2) Consommation à l'étranger 3) Présence commerciale 4) Présence de personnes physiques

Secteur ou sous-secteur	Limitations concernant l'accès aux marchés	Limitations concernant le traitement national	Engagements additionnels
Services par satellite[3]: - VSAT - GMPCS - Vente de capacité satellite à des entités juridiques ayant obtenu une licence ou un agrément de la CITC pour utiliser cette capacité dans le Royaume d'Arabie saoudite	4) Non consolidé, sauf comme indiqué sous "Engagements horizontaux"	4) Non consolidé, sauf comme indiqué sous "Engagements horizontaux"	
D. Services audiovisuels 1. Les "produits récréatifs vidéo grand public" mentionnés ci-après comprennent sans s'y limiter les cassettes vidéo et les vidéodisques numériques. 2. Rien dans le présent engagement n'oblige l'Arabie saoudite à fournir un moyen de présentation ou de transmission des services audiovisuels qui n'est pas offert par le gouvernement saoudien au public d'une manière générale.			
a. Services de distribution de films cinématographiques et de produits vidéo récréatifs grand public (CPC 96113) à d'autres établissements à des fins récréatives, pour diffusion télévisuelle ou pour la vente ou la location à des tiers.[4]	1) Néant 2) Néant 3) Non consolidé 4) Non consolidé, sauf comme indiqué sous "Engagements horizontaux"	1) Néant 2) Néant 3) Non consolidé 4) Non consolidé, sauf comme indiqué sous "Engagements horizontaux"	

[3] Les exploitants de systèmes par satellite GMPCS et VSAT seront tenus jusqu'au 1er janvier 2006 d'acheminer le trafic sur le réseau de la STC par l'intermédiaire de centres de transit et de centres tête de ligne, en particulier dans le cas des communications de l'Arabie saoudite vers l'étranger.

[4] Dans un souci de clarté, cet engagement a uniquement trait à la distribution de films cinématographiques ou de bandes vidéo, c'est-à-dire à l'octroi de licences y relatives, et ne porte pas sur leur diffusion télévisuelle.

Modes de fourniture: 1) Fourniture transfrontières 2) Consommation à l'étranger 3) Présence commerciale 4) Présence de personnes physiques

Secteur ou sous-secteur	Limitations concernant l'accès aux marchés	Limitations concernant le traitement national	Engagements additionnels
b. Services de production et de distribution radiophoniques et télévisuels (octroi de licences pour des émission de radio et de télévision, qu'il s'agisse d'émissions en direct, enregistrées sur bande, sur un autre support d'enregistrement ou sur vidéodisque numérique pour une émission ultérieure, qu'il s'agisse d'une radiodiffusion terrestre, par télévision satellite, par câble ou par tout autre moyen similaire, y compris la DTH et la DBS. Ces programmes, et chaînes de programmation, peuvent être produits à des fins récréatives, publicitaires ou inclure des pièces habituellement réalisées dans les studios de télévision. Ces services comprennent également la production d'émissions sur l'actualité sportive et les prévisions météorologiques ainsi que la réalisation d'interviews, etc.).	1) Non consolidé 2) Néant 3) Non consolidé 4) Non consolidé, sauf comme indiqué sous "Engagements horizontaux"	1) Non consolidé 2) Néant 3) Non consolidé 4) Non consolidé, sauf comme indiqué sous "Engagements horizontaux"	

Modes de fourniture: 1) Fourniture transfrontières 2) Consommation à l'étranger 3) Présence commerciale 4) Présence de personnes physiques

Secteur ou sous-secteur	Limitations concernant l'accès aux marchés	Limitations concernant le traitement national	Engagements additionnels
3. SERVICES DE CONSTRUCTION ET SERVICES D'INGÉNIERIE CONNEXES			
A. Travaux de construction de bâtiments (CPC 512) B. Travaux de construction d'ouvrages de génie civil (CPC 513) C. Travaux de pose d'installations et d'assemblage (CPC 516 + 514) D. Travaux d'achèvement et de finition des bâtiments (CPC 517) E. Autres (CPC 511, 515 et 518)	1) Non consolidé* sauf pour les services de consultation et de conseil connexes 2) Néant 3) Néant 4) Non consolidé, sauf comme indiqué sous "Engagements horizontaux"	1) Non consolidé* sauf pour les services de consultation et de conseil connexes 2) Néant 3) Néant 4) Non consolidé, sauf comme indiqué sous "Engagements horizontaux"	
4. SERVICES DE DISTRIBUTION			
B. Services de commerce de gros (CPC 622, 6111, 6113, 6121) C. Services de commerce de détail (CPC 631, 632, 6111, 6113, 6121 et 613)	1) Néant 2) Néant 3) Néant, sauf: - Participation étrangère au capital limitée à 51 pour cent au moment de l'accession puis à 75 pour cent trois ans après la date d'accession.	1) Néant 2) Néant 3) Néant	

Modes de fourniture: 1) Fourniture transfrontières 2) Consommation à l'étranger 3) Présence commerciale 4) Présence de personnes physiques

Secteur ou sous-secteur	Limitations concernant l'accès aux marchés	Limitations concernant le traitement national	Engagements additionnels
Aux fins de la présente liste, le commerce de gros et de détail dans le pays inclut l'embauche de personnes physiques ressortissantes du pays sur une base contractuelle pour vendre des produits et des services au détail moyennant une rémunération qui sera perçue à la fois pour l'effort de vente et pour les services de soutien à la vente qui se traduisent par des ventes supplémentaires par d'autres distributeurs sous contrat.	- L'investissement étranger minimum est de 20 millions de riyals saoudiens pour chaque fournisseur de services. - La taille minimum des points de vente pourra être fixée. - 15 pour cent des employés saoudiens au minimum devront être formés chaque année. 4) Non consolidé, sauf comme indiqué sous "Engagements horizontaux"	4) Non consolidé, sauf comme indiqué sous "Engagements horizontaux"	
D. Franchisage (CPC 8929)	1) Non consolidé 2) Néant 3) Néant, sauf: - Participation étrangère au capital limitée à 51 pour cent au moment de l'accession puis à 75 pour cent trois ans après la date d'accession. - Un étranger doit être autorisé dans son propre pays à pratiquer le franchisage ou être associé dans une société agréée depuis au moins cinq ans sans interruption. 4) Non consolidé, sauf comme indiqué sous "Engagements horizontaux"	1) Non consolidé 2) Néant 3) Néant 4) Non consolidé, sauf comme indiqué sous "Engagements horizontaux"	

Modes de fourniture: 1) Fourniture transfrontières 2) Consommation à l'étranger 3) Présence commerciale 4) Présence de personnes physiques

Secteur ou sous-secteur	Limitations concernant l'accès aux marchés	Limitations concernant le traitement national	Engagements additionnels
5. SERVICES D'ÉDUCATION			
A. Services d'enseignement primaire (CPC 921) B. Services d'enseignement secondaire (CPC 922) C. Services d'enseignement supérieur (CPC 923) D. Services d'enseignement pour adultes (CPC 924) E. Autres (enseignement technique + cuisine thaïlandaise et langue thaïe) (CPC 929)	1) Néant 2) Néant 3) Néant 4) Non consolidé, sauf comme indiqué sous "Engagements horizontaux"	1) Néant 2) Néant 3) Néant 4) Non consolidé, sauf comme indiqué sous "Engagements horizontaux"	
6. SERVICES ENVIRONNEMENTAUX			
A. Services d'assainissement (CPC 94010) B. Services d'enlèvement des ordures (CPC 94020) C. Services de voierie et services analogues (CPC 9403)	1) Néant 2) Néant 3) Néant 4) Non consolidé, sauf comme indiqué sous "Engagements horizontaux"	1) Néant 2) Néant 3) Néant 4) Non consolidé, sauf comme indiqué sous "Engagements horizontaux"	

Modes de fourniture: 1) Fourniture transfrontières 2) Consommation à l'étranger 3) Présence commerciale 4) Présence de personnes physiques

Secteur ou sous-secteur	Limitations concernant l'accès aux marchés	Limitations concernant le traitement national	Engagements additionnels
D. Autres - Services de purification des gaz brûlés (CPC 9404) - Services de protection de la nature et des paysages (CPC 9406) - Services de lutte contre le bruit (CPC 9405) - Autres services de protection de l'environnement (CPC 9409) (y compris évaluation des retombées sur l'environnement)			

Modes de fourniture: 1) Fourniture transfrontières 2) Consommation à l'étranger 3) Présence commerciale 4) Présence de personnes physiques

Secteur ou sous-secteur	Limitations concernant l'accès aux marchés	Limitations concernant le traitement national	Engagements additionnels
7. SERVICES FINANCIERS			
A. Services d'assurance et relatifs à l'assurance (L'accès aux marchés est permis uniquement aux services d'assurance fournis selon un système coopératif)			
Les fournisseurs étrangers de services d'assurance exerçant leurs activités par l'intermédiaire d'un agent saoudien sont autorisés à exercer ces activités, y compris à poursuivre les opérations commerciales existantes sans interruption, ainsi qu'à offrir de nouveaux produits et services à de nouveaux clients, pendant une période de trois ans à compter de la date d'adoption du Décret royal n° 3120/MB daté du 4/3/1426H (13 avril 2005) et conformément à ce décret.			
a. Services d'assurance – Protection et épargne[5] b. Services d'assurance autre que sur la vie (assurance générale et assurance maladie) c. Réassurance et rétrocession d. Intermédiation en assurance (y compris services de courtage et d'agence) e. Services auxiliaires de l'assurance (services de consultation, actuariels, d'évaluation du risque et de liquidation des sinistres)	1) Non consolidé, sauf néant pour: b) Assurance contre les risques en rapport avec le transport maritime, le transport aérien commercial, le lancement d'engins spatiaux et le transport effectué par ces engins (y compris les satellites), cette assurance couvrant la totalité ou une partie des éléments ci-après: - marchandises transportées, véhicules transportant les marchandises et toute responsabilité en découlant. - assurance contre les risques en rapport avec les marchandises en transit international c) Réassurance et rétrocession d) Courtage et agence e) Services auxiliaires de l'assurance, services de consultation, actuariels, d'évaluation du risque et de liquidation des sinistres	1) Non consolidé, sauf néant pour: b) Assurance contre les risques en rapport avec le transport maritime, le transport aérien commercial, le lancement d'engins spatiaux et le transport effectué par ces engins (y compris les satellites), cette assurance couvrant la totalité ou une partie des éléments ci-après: - marchandises transportées, véhicules transportant les marchandises et toute responsabilité en découlant. - assurance contre les risques en rapport avec les marchandises en transit international c) Réassurance et rétrocession d) Courtage et agence e) Services auxiliaires de l'assurance, services de consultation, actuariels, d'évaluation du risque et de liquidation des sinistres.	

[5] Tels qu'ils sont définis à l'article 3, partie 3:1 à 3, du règlement d'application de la Loi sur le contrôle des sociétés coopératives d'assurance, publié le 25 avril 2004, y compris l'assurance-vieillesse.

Modes de fourniture: 1) Fourniture transfrontières 2) Consommation à l'étranger 3) Présence commerciale 4) Présence de personnes physiques

Secteur ou sous-secteur	Limitations concernant l'accès aux marchés	Limitations concernant le traitement national	Engagements additionnels
	2) Néant 3) Pour a), b) et c), la présence commerciale est autorisée sous la forme d'une société par actions d'assurance coopérative constituée localement, ou sous la forme d'une succursale directe, établie dans le pays, d'une compagnie d'assurance internationale exerçant en Arabie saoudite en tant que fournisseur de services d'assurance coopérative.[6] La participation étrangère aux sociétés par actions en Arabie saoudite est autorisée dans la limite de 60 pour cent du capital à compter de la date d'accession. Pour d), la présence commerciale est autorisée sous la forme d'une société par actions constituée localement ou d'une société à responsabilité limitée. La participation étrangère est autorisée dans la limite de 60 pour cent du capital à compter de la date d'accession. Pour e), la présence commerciale pour les services de liquidation des sinistres et d'évaluation du risque est autorisée sous la forme d'une société par actions constituée localement ou d'une société à responsabilité limitée. La participation étrangère est autorisée dans la limite de 60 pour cent du capital à compter de la date d'accession. Pour les services actuariels et les services de consultation, la présence commerciale est autorisée pour les personnes physiques ou les entités juridiques. 4) Non consolidé, sauf comme indiqué sous "Engagements horizontaux"	2) Néant 3) Néant 4) Non consolidé, sauf comme indiqué sous "Engagements horizontaux"	

[6] Dans un souci de clarté, les succursales des compagnies d'assurance étrangères exerçant en tant que fournisseurs de services d'assurance coopérative ne sont pas tenues d'exercer leurs activités en tant que sociétés par actions en Arabie saoudite.

Modes de fourniture: 1) Fourniture transfrontières 2) Consommation à l'étranger 3) Présence commerciale 4) Présence de personnes physiques

Secteur ou sous-secteur	Limitations concernant l'accès aux marchés	Limitations concernant le traitement national	Engagements additionnels
B. Services bancaires et autres services financiers (à l'exclusion de l'assurance)			
a. Acceptation de dépôts et d'autres fonds remboursables du public; b. Prêts de tout type, y compris crédit à la consommation, crédit hypothécaire, affacturage et financement de transactions commerciales; c. Crédit-bail; d. Tous services de règlement et de transferts monétaires, y compris cartes de crédit, de paiement et similaires, chèques de voyage et traites; e. Garanties et engagements; f. Opérations pour compte propre ou pour compte de clients, que ce soit dans une bourse, sur un marché hors cote ou autre, sur: - instruments du marché monétaire (y compris chèques, effets, certificats de dépôt); - devises; - produits dérivés, y compris, mais pas uniquement, instruments à terme et options;	1) Non consolidé, sauf pour "l", "k" et, sous "i", uniquement pour la gestion de trésorerie ou de portefeuille, toutes formes de gestion d'investissement collectif, services de garde, services de dépositaire et services fiduciaires doivent être fournis par des institutions pour les clients institutionnels, y compris les régimes d'investissement collectif, au moment de l'accession. 2) Néant, sauf non consolidé pour la gestion de fonds de pension sous "i". Sous "j", tous les services de règlement et de compensation sont fournis exclusivement par la SAMA. Cela limite également le traitement national. 3) Néant, sauf: - La présence commerciale des banques est autorisée sous la forme d'une société par actions constituée localement ou d'une succursale d'une banque internationale. - La participation étrangère au capital d'une coentreprise en Arabie saoudite est autorisée dans la limite de 60 pour cent à compter de la date d'accession. - Ces services financiers doivent être fournis par des banques commerciales à l'exception de la gestion des actifs, sous "i", et des services de conseil, sous "k", qui peuvent être fournis par des établissements financiers bancaires non commerciaux conformément à la législation sur le marché des capitaux	1) Non consolidé, sauf comme indiqué dans la colonne sur l'accès aux marchés 2) Néant 3) Néant	Lorsque les services de régime de pension complémentaire du régime public de pension sont fournis par des institutions financières saoudiennes, ils seront aussi ouverts à des fournisseurs de services étrangers pour les modes 2 et 3 uniquement.

Modes de fourniture: 1) Fourniture transfrontières 2) Consommation à l'étranger 3) Présence commerciale 4) Présence de personnes physiques

Secteur ou sous-secteur	Limitations concernant l'accès aux marchés	Limitations concernant le traitement national	Engagements additionnels
- instruments du marché des changes et du marché monétaire, y compris swaps, accords de taux à terme; - valeurs mobilières négociables; - autres instruments et actifs financiers négociables, y compris métal. g. Participation à des émissions de tout type de valeurs mobilières, y compris garantie et placement en qualité d'agent (dans le public ou à titre privé) et prestation de services relatifs à ces émissions; h. Courtage monétaire; i. Gestion d'actifs, par exemple gestion de trésorerie ou de portefeuille, toutes formes de gestion d'investissement collectif, gestion de fonds de pension, services de garde, services de dépositaire et services fiduciaires;	- Non consolidé pour la gestion des fonds de pension sous "i". Cela limite aussi le traitement national - Non consolidé pour tous les services de règlement et de compensation nationaux, sous "j", fournis exclusivement par la SAMA. Cela limite également le traitement national. 4) Non consolidé, sauf comme indiqué sous "Engagements horizontaux"	4) Non consolidé, sauf comme indiqué sous "Engagements horizontaux"	

Modes de fourniture: 1) Fourniture transfrontières 2) Consommation à l'étranger 3) Présence commerciale 4) Présence de personnes physiques

Secteur ou sous-secteur	Limitations concernant l'accès aux marchés	Limitations concernant le traitement national	Engagements additionnels
j. Services de règlement et de compensation afférents à des actifs financiers, y compris valeurs mobilières, produits dérivés et autres instruments négociables; k. Services de conseil et autres services financiers auxiliaires afférents à toutes les activités reprises aux alinéas a) à l), y compris cote de crédit et analyse financière, recherche et conseil en investissements et en placements et conseil en matière d'acquisitions, de restructurations et de stratégies d'entreprises. l. Fourniture et transfert d'informations financières, et traitement de données financières et logiciels y relatifs.			
8. SERVICES DE SANTÉ ET AUTRES			
A. Services hospitaliers (CPC 9311)	1) Non consolidé* 2) Néant 3) Néant, sauf sous réserve de la constitution d'une entreprise entre une entreprise hospitalière étrangère et un professionnel de la médecine agréé en Arabie saoudite 4) Non consolidé, sauf comme indiqué sous "Engagements horizontaux"	1) Non consolidé* 2) Néant 3) Néant 4) Non consolidé, sauf comme indiqué sous "Engagements horizontaux"	

Modes de fourniture: 1) Fourniture transfrontières 2) Consommation à l'étranger 3) Présence commerciale 4) Présence de personnes physiques

Secteur ou sous-secteur	Limitations concernant l'accès aux marchés	Limitations concernant le traitement national	Engagements additionnels
B. Autres services de santé humaine (CPC 9319, sauf 93191)	1) Non consolidé* 2) Néant 3) Néant, sauf sous réserve de la constitution d'une entreprise entre une entreprise hospitalière étrangère et un professionnel de la médecine agréé en Arabie saoudite 4) Non consolidé, sauf comme indiqué sous "Engagements horizontaux"	1) Non consolidé* 2) Néant 3) Néant 4) Non consolidé, sauf comme indiqué sous "Engagements horizontaux"	
9. SERVICES RELATIFS AU TOURISME ET AUX VOYAGES			
A. Services d'hôtellerie et de restauration (y compris les services de traiteur) (CPC 64110, 64120, 642 et 643) (à l'exception des bars, boîtes de nuit, etc.)	1) Néant 2) Néant 3) Néant 4) Non consolidé, sauf comme indiqué sous "Engagements horizontaux"	1) Néant 2) Néant 3) Néant 4) Non consolidé, sauf comme indiqué sous "Engagements horizontaux"	
B. Services d'agences de voyages et d'organisateurs touristiques (CPC 7471) (sauf pour l'Umra et le Hadj)	1) Néant 2) Néant 3) Néant, sauf examen des besoins économiques, appliqué aux agences de voyages uniquement sur la base du rapport entre la population totale et le nombre d'agences de voyages 4) Non consolidé, sauf comme indiqué sous "Engagements horizontaux"	1) Néant 2) Néant 3) Néant 4) Non consolidé, sauf comme indiqué sous "Engagements horizontaux"	
C. Services de guides touristiques (CPC 74720) (sauf pour l'Umra et le Hadj)	1) Néant 2) Néant 3) Néant 4) Non consolidé, sauf comme indiqué sous "Engagements horizontaux"	1) Néant 2) Néant 3) Néant 4) Non consolidé, sauf comme indiqué sous "Engagements horizontaux"	

Modes de fourniture: 1) Fourniture transfrontières 2) Consommation à l'étranger 3) Présence commerciale 4) Présence de personnes physiques

Secteur ou sous-secteur	Limitations concernant l'accès aux marchés	Limitations concernant le traitement national	Engagements additionnels
10. SERVICES RÉCRÉATIFS, CULTURELS ET SPORTIFS			
B. Services d'agence de presse (CPC 962) D. Services récréatifs (CPC 96491) (Uniquement les services des parcs et jardins publics)	1) Néant 2) Néant 3) Néant 4) Non consolidé, sauf comme indiqué sous "Engagements horizontaux"	1) Néant 2) Néant 3) Néant 4) Non consolidé, sauf comme indiqué sous "Engagements horizontaux"	
11. SERVICES DE TRANSPORT			
A. Services de transport maritime a. Transport de voyageurs (CPC 7211) b. Transport de marchandises (CPC 7212) c. Location de navires avec équipage (CPC 72130) d. Maintenance et réparation des navires	1) Néant 2) Néant 3) Néant 4) Non consolidé, sauf comme indiqué sous "Engagements horizontaux"	1) Néant 2) Néant 3) Néant 4) Non consolidé, sauf comme indiqué sous "Engagements horizontaux"	Les services portuaires ci-après seront mis à la disposition des fournisseurs de transports maritimes internationaux à des conditions raisonnables et non discriminatoires: - services d'exploitation des ports et voies navigables (à l'exclusion de la manutention des cargaisons); - services de pilotage et d'accostage; - services d'aide à la navigation; - services de sauvetage et de renflouement; - tous les autres services annexes des transports par eau.

Modes de fourniture: 1) Fourniture transfrontières 2) Consommation à l'étranger 3) Présence commerciale 4) Présence de personnes physiques

Secteur ou sous-secteur	Limitations concernant l'accès aux marchés	Limitations concernant le traitement national	Engagements additionnels
C. Services de transport aérien d. Maintenance et réparation des aéronefs e. Services annexes des transports aériens (CPC 746) - Systèmes informatisés de réservation	1) Néant 2) Néant 3) Néant 4) Non consolidé, sauf comme indiqué sous "Engagements horizontaux"	1) Néant 2) Néant 3) Néant 4) Non consolidé, sauf comme indiqué sous "Engagements horizontaux"	
E. Services de transport ferroviaire a. Transport de voyageurs (CPC 7111) b. Transport de marchandises (CPC 7112) c. Services de poussage et de remorquage (CPC 7130) d. Maintenance et réparation de matériel de transport ferroviaire (CPC 8868) e. Services annexes des transports ferroviaires (CPC 743)	1) Néant 2) Néant 3) Investissement étranger dans le cadre d'arrangements dits de construction-exploitation-transfert (CET) 4) Non consolidé, sauf comme indiqué sous "Engagements horizontaux"	1) Néant 2) Néant 3) Néant 4) Non consolidé, sauf comme indiqué sous "Engagements horizontaux"	
G. Services de transport par conduites a. Transport de combustibles (CPC 7131) b. Transport d'autres marchandises (CPC 7139)	1) Néant 2) Néant 3) Néant 4) Non consolidé, sauf comme indiqué sous "Engagements horizontaux"	1) Néant 2) Néant 3) Néant 4) Non consolidé, sauf comme indiqué sous "Engagements horizontaux"	

Modes de fourniture: 1) Fourniture transfrontières 2) Consommation à l'étranger 3) Présence commerciale 4) Présence de personnes physiques

Secteur ou sous-secteur	Limitations concernant l'accès aux marchés	Limitations concernant le traitement national	Engagements additionnels
H. Services annexes et auxiliaires de tous les modes de transport (limités aux services de transport maritime, ferroviaire et aérien conformément à l'Annexe sur les services de transport aérien) a. Services de manutention (CPC 741) b. Services d'entreposage (CPC 742) c. Services d'agences de transport de marchandises (CPC 748)	1) Néant 2) Néant 3) Néant 4) Non consolidé, sauf comme indiqué sous "Engagements horizontaux"	1) Néant 2) Néant 3) Néant 4) Non consolidé, sauf comme indiqué sous "Engagements horizontaux"	Les services relevant de la catégorie CPC 749 sont actuellement fournis par le secteur public. Dans la mesure où l'accès aux marchés pour les services inclus dans la catégorie CPC 749 sera ouvert aux entités privées au titre de la législation saoudienne, le traitement national sera accordé.

DOCUMENT DE RÉFÉRENCE

Objet

Le présent document contient des définitions et des principes concernant le cadre réglementaire pour les services de télécommunications de base.

Définitions

Le terme utilisateurs désigne les consommateurs et les fournisseurs de services.

L'expression installations essentielles désigne les installations d'un réseau ou service public de transport des télécommunications:

a) qui sont fournies exclusivement ou essentiellement par un seul fournisseur ou un nombre limité de fournisseurs; et

b) qu'il n'est pas possible de remplacer d'un point de vue économique ou technique pour fournir un service.

Un fournisseur principal est un fournisseur qui a la capacité d'influer de manière importante sur les modalités de la participation (en ce qui concerne le prix et l'offre) sur un marché donné de services de télécommunication de base par suite:

a) du contrôle qu'il exerce sur des installations essentielles; ou

b) de l'utilisation de sa position sur le marché.

1. Sauvegardes en matière de concurrence

1.1 Prévention des pratiques anticoncurrentielles dans les télécommunications

Des mesures appropriées seront appliquées en vue d'empêcher des fournisseurs qui, seuls ou ensemble, sont un fournisseur principal, d'adopter ou de maintenir des pratiques anticoncurrentielles.

1.2 Sauvegardes

Les pratiques anticoncurrentielles mentionnées ci-dessus consistent en particulier:

a) à pratiquer un subventionnement croisé anticoncurrentiel;

b) à utiliser des renseignements obtenus auprès de concurrents d'une manière qui donne des résultats anticoncurrentiels; et

c) à ne pas mettre à la disposition des autres fournisseurs de services en temps opportun les renseignements techniques sur les installations essentielles et les renseignements commercialement pertinents qui leur sont nécessaires pour fournir des services.

2. Interconnexion

2.1 La présente section traite des liaisons avec les fournisseurs de réseaux ou services publics de transport des télécommunications permettant aux utilisateurs relevant d'un fournisseur de communiquer avec les utilisateurs relevant d'un autre fournisseur et d'avoir accès à des services fournis par un autre fournisseur, dans les cas où des engagements spécifiques sont souscrits.

2.2 Interconnexion à assurer

L'interconnexion avec un fournisseur principal sera assurée à tout point du réseau où cela sera techniquement possible. Cette interconnexion est assurée:

a) suivant des modalités, à des conditions (y compris les normes et spécifications techniques) et à des tarifs non discriminatoires et sa qualité est non moins favorable que celle qui est prévue pour les services similaires dudit fournisseur ou pour les services similaires des fournisseurs de services non affiliés ou pour des filiales ou autres sociétés affiliées;

b) en temps opportun, suivant des modalités, à des conditions (y compris les normes et spécifications techniques) et moyennant des taxes fondées sur les coûts qui soient transparentes, raisonnables, compte tenu de la faisabilité économique, et suffisamment détaillées pour que le fournisseur n'ait pas à payer pour des éléments ou installations du réseau dont il n'a pas besoin pour le service à fournir; et

c) sur demande, à des points en plus des points de terminaison du réseau accessibles à la majorité des utilisateurs, moyennant des tarifs qui reflètent le coût de la construction des installations additionnelles nécessaires.

2.3 Accès du public aux procédures concernant les négociations en matière d'interconnexion

Le public aura accès aux procédures applicables pour une interconnexion avec un fournisseur principal.

2.4 Transparence des arrangements en matière d'interconnexion

Il est fait en sorte qu'un fournisseur principal mette à la disposition du public soit ses accords d'interconnexion soit une offre d'interconnexion de référence.

2.5 Interconnexion: règlement des différends

Un fournisseur de services demandant l'interconnexion avec un fournisseur principal aura recours, soit:

a) à tout moment, soit

b) après un délai raisonnable qui aura été rendu public,

à un organe interne indépendant, qui peut être l'organe réglementaire mentionné au paragraphe 5 ci-après pour régler les différends concernant les modalités, conditions et taxes d'interconnexion pertinentes dans un délai raisonnable, dans la mesure où celles-ci n'ont pas été établies au préalable.

3. Service universel

Tout Membre a le droit de définir le type d'obligation en matière de service universel qu'il souhaite maintenir. Ces obligations ne seront pas considérées comme étant anticoncurrentielles en soi, à condition qu'elles soient administrées de manière transparente, non discriminatoire et neutre du point de vue de la concurrence et qu'elles ne soient pas plus rigoureuses qu'il n'est nécessaire pour le type de service universel défini par le Membre.

4. Accès du public aux critères en matière de licences

Lorsqu'une licence sera nécessaire, le public aura accès aux informations suivantes:

a) tous les critères en matière de licences et le délai normalement requis pour qu'une décision soit prise au sujet d'une demande de licence; et

b) les modalités et conditions des licences individuelles.

Les raisons du refus d'une licence seront communiquées au requérant sur demande.

5. Indépendance des organes réglementaires

L'organe réglementaire est distinct de tout fournisseur de services de télécommunications de base et ne relève pas d'un tel fournisseur. Les décisions des organes réglementaires et les procédures qu'ils utilisent seront impartiales à l'égard de tous les participants sur le marché.

6. Répartition et utilisation des ressources limitées

Toutes les procédures concernant l'attribution et l'utilisation des ressources limitées, y compris les fréquences, les numéros et les servitudes, seront mises en œuvre de manière objective, opportune, transparente et non discriminatoire. Les renseignements sur la situation courante des bandes de fréquences attribuées seront mis à la disposition du public, mais il n'est pas obligatoire d'indiquer de manière détaillée les fréquences attribuées pour des utilisations spécifiques relevant de l'État.

Liste d'exemptions de l'article II (NPF)

Secteur ou sous-secteur	Description de la mesure, y compris les raisons pour lesquelles elle est incompatible avec l'article II	Pays auxquels la mesure s'applique	Durée projetée	Conditions qui rendent l'exemption nécessaire
Services de transport routier	Traitement préférentiel réciproque pour les services transfrontières	Égypte, Jordanie	Indéterminée	Accords bilatéraux existants
Services de transport maritime et de transport routier	Préférence pour l'utilisation des compagnies maritimes et des véhicules de transport routier nationaux dans les échanges bilatéraux	Égypte, Tunisie	Indéterminée	Accords bilatéraux existants
Services de transport routier	Traitement préférentiel réciproque	Liban, Syrie, Turquie	Indéterminée	Accords bilatéraux existants

El Reino de Arabia Saudita

Lista de compromisos específicos en materia de servicios
Lista de exenciones de las obligaciones del artículo II (NMF)

Será auténtica sólo en idioma inglés.

Modos de suministro: 1) Suministro transfronterizo 2) Consumo en el extranjero 3) Presencia comercial 4) Presencia de personas físicas

Sector o subsector	Limitaciones al acceso a los mercados	Limitaciones al trato nacional	Compromisos adicionales
I. COMPROMISOS HORIZONTALES.			
Todos los sectores y subsectores incluidos en la presente oferta	3) i) La presencia comercial respecto de todos los servicios consignados en la presente Lista, excepto los servicios prestados a las empresas (enumerados *infra*)[1], está supeditada a que la empresa se constituya con arreglo a la Ley de Sociedades, bien como sociedad anónima, bien como sociedad de responsabilidad limitada. ii) La presencia comercial respecto de los servicios prestados a las empresas (enumerados *infra*)[1] está supeditada a la constitución de una empresa y su registro con arreglo a la Ley de Empresas de Servicios Profesionales.	3) i) Los proveedores de servicios extranjeros deben obtener la autorización de la Dirección General de Inversiones de Arabia Saudita para poder establecer una presencia comercial en el país de conformidad con la Ley de Inversiones Extranjeras y del párrafo 3 del artículo 5 del Reglamento de la Ley de Inversiones Extranjeras. ii) Las personas que no sean nacionales de Arabia Saudita pueden adquirir por sucesión el derecho a ser propietarios de bienes inmuebles en Arabia Saudita. Los establecimientos extranjeros autorizados para desarrollar sus actividades en el Reino en virtud de la Ley de Inversiones Extranjeras pueden ser propietarios de bienes inmuebles de conformidad con las leyes y reglamentos vigentes relativos a la propiedad extranjera de bienes inmuebles. iii) Las entidades comerciales y personas físicas que no sean árabes sauditas están sujetas al impuesto sobre la renta, mientras que las entidades y particulares árabes sauditas están sujetos al Zakat. Los cambios que en el futuro se introduzcan en el código fiscal árabe saudita no serán menos favorables para los proveedores de servicios extranjeros que el código existente.	Todos los modos de suministro: en todos los aspectos, salvo en lo que concierne al Zakat, las medidas fiscales se aplicarán de conformidad con los artículos II y XVII y demás disposiciones pertinentes del AGCS.

[1] Servicios profesionales (1A), según el documento W/120.

Modos de suministro: 1) Suministro transfronterizo 2) Consumo en el extranjero 3) Presencia comercial 4) Presencia de personas físicas

Sector o subsector	Limitaciones al acceso a los mercados	Limitaciones al trato nacional	Compromisos adicionales
	4) Sin consolidar, excepto en lo que se refiere a las medidas que afecten a la entrada y estancia temporal de personas físicas de las siguientes categorías: i) <u>Personas en visita de negocios</u> Personas físicas que permanecen en Arabia Saudita sin recibir remuneración alguna en el país y sin dedicarse a la venta directa o el suministro de servicios al público, con el fin de participar en reuniones de trabajo, entablar contactos comerciales, incluidas las negociaciones para la venta de servicios y/u otras actividades similares, como los preparativos para el establecimiento de una presencia comercial en Arabia Saudita. Se permiten la entrada y estancia por un período no superior a 180 días, incluidas entradas múltiples. ii) <u>Personas trasladadas dentro de la misma empresa</u> Gerentes, ejecutivos y especialistas (definidos *infra*) trasladados dentro de la misma empresa que cuenten con una experiencia laboral mínima de tres años en el mismo campo antes de la fecha de solicitud de entrada en el Reino para trabajar en una empresa afiliada establecida en Arabia Saudita de una persona jurídica. Su entrada y estancia estarán sujetas a las siguientes condiciones:	iv) Las entidades extranjeras de servicios y las personas físicas extranjeras tendrán acceso a las subvenciones disponibles en el país. No obstante, algunas subvenciones para determinados servicios sólo estarán a disposición de los árabes sauditas. 4) Sin consolidar, excepto lo indicado en la columna relativa al acceso a los mercados	

Modos de suministro: 1) Suministro transfronterizo 2) Consumo en el extranjero 3) Presencia comercial 4) Presencia de personas físicas

Sector o subsector	Limitaciones al acceso a los mercados	Limitaciones al trato nacional	Compromisos adicionales
	- Su número estará limitado al 25% del total de empleados de cada proveedor de servicios. No obstante, se autorizará un mínimo de tres personas. Como alternativa a lo anterior, el proveedor de servicios podrá disponer de la opción siguiente: el número de gerentes, ejecutivos y especialistas de cada proveedor de servicios se limitará al 15%, y el número del resto de los empleados extranjeros (es decir, los que no sean gerentes, ejecutivos o especialistas) de cada proveedor de servicios se limitará al 10%, o viceversa. No obstante, se permitirá un mínimo de dos personas trasladadas dentro de la misma empresa respetando el umbral del 15%. - Se permitirá su entrada y estancia por un período de dos años, renovable por períodos similares. - Podrán reservarse a los nacionales árabes sauditas ciertos puestos de todas las categorías dentro de una empresa. Estos puestos son los de contratación y personal, recepcionistas, cajeros, guardias de seguridad civil y encargados del seguimiento de las transacciones (relaciones con el Gobierno).		

Modos de suministro: 1) Suministro transfronterizo 2) Consumo en el extranjero 3) Presencia comercial 4) Presencia de personas físicas

Sector o subsector	Limitaciones al acceso a los mercados	Limitaciones al trato nacional	Compromisos adicionales
	Definiciones: Gerentes: Personas que en una organización se encargan fundamentalmente de la dirección de ésta o de alguno de sus departamentos o subdivisiones, supervisan y controlan el trabajo de otros empleados de supervisión, profesionales o de gestión, tienen la facultad de contratar o despedir o de recomendar que se contrate o se despida y de tomar otras disposiciones en materia de personal (tales como autorizar ascensos o permisos), y ejercen una autoridad discrecional sobre las actividades cotidianas. No están incluidos los supervisores directos, a menos que los empleados supervisados sean profesionales, ni los empleados que principalmente realizan tareas necesarias para el suministro del servicio. Ejecutivos: Personas que en una organización se encargan fundamentalmente de la gestión de ésta, fijan sus metas y su política, ejercen amplia latitud en la toma de decisiones, y sólo están sujetas a la supervisión o dirección general de ejecutivos de rango superior, el consejo de administración o los accionistas de la empresa. Los ejecutivos no realizan directamente tareas relacionadas con el suministro efectivo de un servicio o de servicios de la organización. Especialistas: Personas que en una organización poseen conocimientos especializados avanzados y conocimientos de dominio privado de los servicios, la investigación, el equipo, las técnicas o la gestión de la organización.		

Modos de suministro: 1) Suministro transfronterizo 2) Consumo en el extranjero 3) Presencia comercial 4) Presencia de personas físicas

Sector o subsector	Limitaciones al acceso a los mercados	Limitaciones al trato nacional	Compromisos adicionales
	iii) Proveedores de servicios por contrato Empleados de proveedores de servicios por contrato, es decir, los empleados de una persona jurídica sin presencia comercial en Arabia Saudita que ha obtenido en el país un contrato cuyo cumplimiento requiere la presencia de sus empleados. Se permitirá la entrada y estancia de esas personas por un período no superior a 180 días que sería renovable. Sólo se permitirá la entrada de esas personas respecto de los siguientes subsectores de servicios prestados a las empresas: - Servicios jurídicos (Parte de CPC 861) - Servicios de arquitectura (CPC 8671) - Servicios de planificación urbana y de arquitectura paisajista (CPC 8674) - Servicios de ingeniería (CPC 8672) - Servicios integrados de ingeniería (CPC 8673) - Servicios de consultores en ciencia y tecnología relacionados con la ingeniería (CPC 8675) - Servicios de ensayos y análisis técnicos (CPC 8676) - Servicios de traducción (CPC 87905) - Servicios relacionados con el medio ambiente (todos los subsectores) (CPC 94010 + 94020 + 9403 + 9404 + 9405 + 9406 + 9409)		

Modos de suministro: 1) Suministro transfronterizo 2) Consumo en el extranjero 3) Presencia comercial 4) Presencia de personas físicas

Sector o subsector	Limitaciones al acceso a los mercados	Limitaciones al trato nacional	Compromisos adicionales
	- Servicios relacionados con la minería (CPC 883 + 5115) - Servicios de consultores en administración (CPC 8650) - Servicios relacionados con los de los consultores en administración (CPC 8660) - Servicios de mantenimiento y reparación de equipo (con exclusión de las embarcaciones, las aeronaves y demás equipo de transporte) (CPC 633 + 8861-8866) - Servicios de contabilidad, auditoría y teneduría de libros (CPC 8621 + 8622) - Servicios médicos y dentales (CPC 9312) - Servicios interdisciplinarios de investigación y desarrollo (CPC 85300) - Servicios de informática y servicios conexos (CPC 841-845 + 849) - Servicios de construcción y servicios de ingeniería conexos (CPC 511-518) - Servicios de agencias de viajes y organización de viajes en grupo, con exclusión de los relacionados con el Umra y el Hajj. (CPC 7471) - Servicios de restaurante, incluidos los servicios de suministro de comidas al exterior por contrato (excepto bares, clubes nocturnos, etc.) (CPC 6421 + 6422 + 6423)		

Modos de suministro: 1) Suministro transfronterizo 2) Consumo en el extranjero 3) Presencia comercial 4) Presencia de personas físicas

Sector o subsector	Limitaciones al acceso a los mercados	Limitaciones al trato nacional	Compromisos adicionales
	iv) Profesionales independientes Profesionales independientes (es decir, personas físicas) en el marco de un contrato de servicios con una persona jurídica en Arabia Saudita destinado a la prestación de servicios profesionales para los que el/la profesional posea la titulación académica y las calificaciones profesionales necesarias, así como tres años de experiencia en el mismo campo. Se permitirá su entrada y estancia por un período 180 días que podría ser renovable. Sólo se permitirá la entrada de esas personas para los siguientes subsectores: - Servicios de informática y servicios conexos (CPC 841-845 + 849) - Servicios de construcción y servicios de ingeniería conexos (CPC 512, 513, 516 + 517) - Servicios de contabilidad, auditoría y teneduría de libros (CPC 8621 + 8622) - Servicios de asesoramiento tributario (CPC 87905) - Servicios de arquitectura (CPC 8671) - Pilotos y tripulantes - Servicios jurídicos (parte de CPC 861) - Servicios médicos y dentales (CPC 9312) - Servicios interdisciplinarios de investigación y desarrollo (CPC 85300)		

Modos de suministro: 1) Suministro transfronterizo 2) Consumo en el extranjero 3) Presencia comercial 4) Presencia de personas físicas

Sector o subsector	Limitaciones al acceso a los mercados	Limitaciones al trato nacional	Compromisos adicionales
	- Servicios de consultores en administración (CPC 8650) - Servicios de limpieza de edificios (CPC 874) Para otros servicios de enseñanza (únicamente los relacionados con la cocina tailandesa y el idioma tailandés, como parte de CPC 9290), se permitirá la entrada y la estancia por un período de 90 días que sería renovable por un período similar. v) Personal de instalación y mantenimiento Especialistas calificados que presten servicios de instalación o mantenimiento. El suministro de ese servicio ha de realizarse por contrato entre el constructor de la maquinaria o equipo y el propietario de esa maquinaria o equipo, siendo ambos personas jurídicas. Se permite la entrada temporal por un período de estancia no superior a 90 días que sería renovable.		

Modos de suministro: 1) Suministro transfronterizo 2) Consumo en el extranjero 3) Presencia comercial 4) Presencia de personas físicas

Sector o subsector	Limitaciones al acceso a los mercados	Limitaciones al trato nacional	Compromisos adicionales
II. COMPROMISOS RELATIVOS A SECTORES ESPECÍFICOS			
1. SERVICIOS PRESTADOS A LAS EMPRESAS			
A. Servicios profesionales			
a. Servicios jurídicos Servicios de consultoría relativos al derecho de la jurisdicción para la que el proveedor de servicios tiene un título de abogado, y relativos al derecho internacional (Parte de CPC 861)	1) Ninguna 2) Ninguna 3) La participación extranjera en el capital social está limitada al 75%. 4) Sin consolidar, excepto lo indicado en los compromisos horizontales.	1) Ninguna 2) Ninguna 3) Los abogados que no sean árabes sauditas no pueden actuar ante los tribunales. 4) Sin consolidar, excepto lo indicado en los compromisos horizontales.	
b. Servicios de contabilidad, auditoría y teneduría de libros (CPC 8621 y 8622) c. Servicios de asesoramiento tributario (CPC 8630) d. Servicios de arquitectura (CPC 8671) e. Servicios de ingeniería (CPC 8672) f. Servicios integrados de ingeniería (CPC 8673) g. Servicios de planificación urbana y de arquitectura paisajista (CPC 8674) h. Servicios médicos y dentales (CPC 9312) i. Servicios de veterinaria (CPC 93201)	1) Ninguna 2) Ninguna 3) La participación extranjera en el capital social está limitada al 75%. 4) Sin consolidar, excepto lo indicado en los compromisos horizontales.	1) Ninguna 2) Ninguna 3) Ninguna 4) Sin consolidar, excepto lo indicado en los compromisos horizontales.	
B. Servicios de informática y servicios conexos			
a.-e. (CPC 841-45 y 849)	1) Ninguna 2) Ninguna 3) Ninguna 4) Sin consolidar, excepto lo indicado en los compromisos horizontales.	1) Ninguna 2) Ninguna 3) Ninguna 4) Sin consolidar, excepto lo indicado en los compromisos horizontales.	

Modos de suministro: 1) Suministro transfronterizo 2) Consumo en el extranjero 3) Presencia comercial 4) Presencia de personas físicas

Sector o subsector	Limitaciones al acceso a los mercados	Limitaciones al trato nacional	Compromisos adicionales
C. Servicios de investigación y desarrollo			
a.-c. (CPC 851, 852, 853)	1) Ninguna 2) Ninguna 3) Ninguna 4) Sin consolidar, excepto lo indicado en los compromisos horizontales.	1) Ninguna 2) Ninguna 3) Ninguna 4) Sin consolidar, excepto lo indicado en los compromisos horizontales.	
E. Servicios de arrendamiento o alquiler sin operarios			
a. De buques (CPC 83103) b. De aeronaves (CPC 83104) c. De otros medios de transporte (CPC 83101+83102+83105) d. De otro tipo de maquinaria y equipo (CPC 83106-83109) e. Servicios de arrendamiento o alquiler de enseres domésticos (CPC 832)	1) Ninguna 2) Ninguna 3) Ninguna 4) Sin consolidar, excepto lo indicado en los compromisos horizontales.	1) Ninguna 2) Ninguna 3) Ninguna 4) Sin consolidar, excepto lo indicado en los compromisos horizontales.	
F. Otros servicios prestados a las empresas			
a. Servicios de publicidad (CPC 8711) b. Servicios de investigación de mercados y servicios similares (CPC 86401) c. Servicios de consultores en administración (CPC 8650) d. Servicios relacionados con los de los consultores en administración (CPC 8660) e. Servicios de ensayos y análisis técnicos (CPC 8676) f. Servicios relacionados con la agricultura, la caza y la silvicultura (CPC 881)	1) Ninguna 2) Ninguna 3) Ninguna 4) Sin consolidar, excepto lo indicado en los compromisos horizontales.	1) Ninguna 2) Ninguna 3) Ninguna 4) Sin consolidar, excepto lo indicado en los compromisos horizontales.	

Modos de suministro: 1) Suministro transfronterizo 2) Consumo en el extranjero 3) Presencia comercial 4) Presencia de personas físicas

Sector o subsector	Limitaciones al acceso a los mercados	Limitaciones al trato nacional	Compromisos adicionales
h. Servicios relacionados con la minería (CPC 883+5115) i. Servicios relacionados con las manufacturas (CPC 884 (excepto 88442)+885) j. Servicios relacionados con la distribución de energía (CPC 887) m. Servicios de consultores en ciencia y tecnología relacionados con la ingeniería (CPC 8675) n. Servicios de mantenimiento y reparación de equipo (con exclusión de las embarcaciones, las aeronaves y demás equipo de transporte) (CPC 633+8861-8866) p. Servicios fotográficos (CPC 8750) q. Servicios de empaque (CPC 8760) r. Servicios de imprenta y publicación (CPC 88442) s. Servicios prestados con ocasión de asambleas o convenciones (CPC 87909)* t. Otros (por ejemplo, servicios de relaciones públicas) - Servicios de traducción (CPC 87905) - Servicios especializados de diseño (CPC 87907)			

Modos de suministro: 1) Suministro transfronterizo 2) Consumo en el extranjero 3) Presencia comercial 4) Presencia de personas físicas

Sector o subsector	Limitaciones al acceso a los mercados	Limitaciones al trato nacional	Compromisos adicionales
2. SERVICIOS DE COMUNICACIONES			
B. Servicios de mensajeros (CPC 7512)	1) Ninguna 2) Ninguna 3) Ninguna 4) Sin consolidar, excepto lo indicado en los compromisos horizontales.	1) Ninguna 2) Ninguna 3) Ninguna 4) Sin consolidar, excepto lo indicado en los compromisos horizontales.	- Los operadores extranjeros de servicios de entrega urgente tendrán un trato no menos favorable que el otorgado a la Administración Postal por sus actividades de entrega urgente. - Cuando se privaticen los servicios de consultores relacionados con los servicios postales (CPC 7511**), también se abrirán estos servicios a los proveedores de servicios extranjeros.

C. Servicios de telecomunicaciones

Condiciones generales de este subsector: Los compromisos asumidos por el Reino de Arabia Saudita se basan en los principios de consignación en listas contenidos en los siguientes documentos: "Notas a efectos de la consignación en listas de los compromisos sobre servicios de telecomunicaciones básicas" (S/GBT/W/2/Rev.1) y "Limitaciones del acceso a los mercados relativas a la disponibilidad de espectro" (S/GBT/W/3).

Este compromiso está sujeto a las siguientes condiciones generales:

- El Reino de Arabia Saudita se compromete a observar lo que se indica en el documento de referencia sobre servicios de telecomunicaciones básicas, que figura en anexo.
- Todo servicio de telecomunicaciones suministrado en Arabia Saudita sobre la base de una presencia comercial (modo 3) debe ser suministrado por una empresa registrada en Arabia Saudita, en la que la participación extranjera en el capital social esté limitada a los porcentajes que figuran *supra*.
- Esta lista relativa a las telecomunicaciones básicas no incluye los servicios de transmisión de programas.[2]
- El suministro transfronterizo está sujeto a acuerdos comerciales con una o más personas jurídicas titulares de la licencia correspondiente o autorizadas por la Comisión de Comunicaciones y Tecnología de la Información (CCTI) del Reino de Arabia Saudita.

[2] Se entiende por servicio de transmisión de programas un servicio de comunicación por radio en que el objeto de las transmisiones es la recepción directa por el gran público, y que incluye las transmisiones de sonido o las de televisión. No obstante, la transmisión de señales entre estaciones de transmisión y transmisores forma parte de los servicios de telecomunicaciones.

Modos de suministro: 1) Suministro transfronterizo 2) Consumo en el extranjero 3) Presencia comercial 4) Presencia de personas físicas

Sector o subsector	Limitaciones al acceso a los mercados	Limitaciones al trato nacional	Compromisos adicionales
1. Servicios de telecomunicaciones básicas - Red pública fija - basada en la utilización de instalaciones a. Servicios telefónicos de voz f. Servicios de facsímil i. Correo vocal	1) Ninguna desde finales de 2006 2) Ninguna 3) Ninguna, salvo que los servicios públicos ofrecidos como servicios de telecomunicaciones deben ser suministrados por una sociedad anónima. La participación extranjera en el capital social está limitada al 49% en el momento de la adhesión, y llegará al 51% al final de 2007 y al 60% al final de 2008. 4) Sin consolidar, excepto lo indicado en los compromisos horizontales.	1) Ninguna 2) Ninguna 3) Ninguna 4) Sin consolidar, excepto lo indicado en los compromisos horizontales.	
Red pública fija - no basada en la utilización de instalaciones Red privada fija - basada o no en la utilización de instalaciones a. Servicios telefónicos de voz f. Servicios de facsímil i. Correo vocal	1) Ninguna desde el final de 2006 2) Ninguna 3) Ninguna, salvo que la participación extranjera en el capital social estará limitada al 49% en el momento de la adhesión, llegará al 51% al final de 2006 y al 70% tres años después. 4) Sin consolidar, excepto lo indicado en los compromisos horizontales.	1) Ninguna 2) Ninguna 3) Ninguna 4) Sin consolidar, excepto lo indicado en los compromisos horizontales.	
2. Red pública o privada - basada o no en la utilización de instalaciones b. Servicios de transmisión de datos con conmutación de paquetes c. Servicios de transmisión de datos con conmutación de circuitos d. Servicios de télex e. Servicios de telégrafo g. Servicios de circuitos privados arrendados - Servicios de valor añadido h. Correo electrónico	1) Ninguna 2) Ninguna 3) Ninguna, salvo que la participación extranjera en el capital social estará limitada al 49% en el momento de la adhesión, llegará al 51% al final de 2006 y al 70% tres años después. 4) Sin consolidar, excepto lo indicado en los compromisos horizontales.	1) Ninguna 2) Ninguna 3) Ninguna 4) Sin consolidar, excepto lo indicado en los compromisos horizontales.	

Modos de suministro: 1) Suministro transfronterizo 2) Consumo en el extranjero 3) Presencia comercial 4) Presencia de personas físicas

Sector o subsector	Limitaciones al acceso a los mercados	Limitaciones al trato nacional	Compromisos adicionales
j) Extracción de información en línea y de bases de datos k) Servicios de intercambio electrónico de datos (IED) l) servicios de facsímil mejorados/de valor añadido, incluidos los de almacenamiento y retransmisión y los de almacenamiento y recuperación m. Conversión de códigos y protocolos n. Procesamiento de datos y/o información en línea (con inclusión del procesamiento de transacciones) o. Radiobúsqueda p. Servicios de Internet			
3. Los demás Servicios de telefonía móvil A.1. Servicio de telefonía móvil público - basado en la utilización de instalaciones a) Servicios de voz f) Facsímil i) Correo vocal	1) Ninguna 2) Ninguna 3) Ninguna, salvo que los servicios de telefonía móvil de voz ofrecidos como servicios públicos de telecomunicaciones basados en la utilización de instalaciones deben ser suministrados por una sociedad anónima. La participación extranjera en el capital social estará limitada al 49% en el momento de la adhesión, y llegará al 51% al final de 2005 y al 60% al final de 2008. 4) Sin consolidar, excepto lo indicado en los compromisos horizontales.	1) Ninguna 2) Ninguna 3) Ninguna 4) Sin consolidar, excepto lo indicado en los compromisos horizontales.	

Modos de suministro: 1) Suministro transfronterizo 2) Consumo en el extranjero 3) Presencia comercial 4) Presencia de personas físicas

Sector o subsector	Limitaciones al acceso a los mercados	Limitaciones al trato nacional	Compromisos adicionales
A.2. Telefonía móvil privada (incluso no basada en la utilización de instalaciones) y telefonía móvil pública no basada en la utilización de instalaciones a. Servicios de voz f. Facsímil i. Correo vocal Servicios por satélite[3]: - VSAT - GMPCS - Venta de capacidad de satélite a personas jurídicas titulares de la licencia correspondiente o autorizadas por la Comisión de Comunicaciones y Tecnología de la Información (CCTI) para utilizar esa capacidad en el Reino de Arabia Saudita.	1) Ninguna 2) Ninguna 3) Ninguna, con las excepciones siguientes: - la participación extranjera en el capital social estará limitada al 49% en el momento de la adhesión, llegará al 51% al final de 2005 y al 70% tres años después - el número de licencias de servicios de VSAT podrá estar limitado a cinco hasta el 1º de enero de 2006. A partir de esa fecha, no habrá límites al número de licencias. 4) Sin consolidar, excepto lo indicado en los compromisos horizontales.	1) Ninguna 2) Ninguna 3) Ninguna 4) Sin consolidar, excepto lo indicado en los compromisos horizontales.	

[3] Los operadores de comunicaciones por satélite tipo GMPCS y VSAT deberán cursar el tráfico por la red STC a través de las centrales de tránsito y portales hasta el 1º de enero de 2006, especialmente en el caso de comunicaciones con el exterior desde Arabia Saudita.

Modos de suministro: 1) Suministro transfronterizo 2) Consumo en el extranjero 3) Presencia comercial 4) Presencia de personas físicas

Sector o subsector	Limitaciones al acceso a los mercados	Limitaciones al trato nacional	Compromisos adicionales
D. Servicios audiovisuales 1. Las referencias que se hacen *infra* a "cintas de vídeo para uso doméstico con fines de esparcimiento" incluyen las cintas de vídeo y los videodiscos digitales, pero no se limitan a ellos. 2. Nada de lo establecido en este compromiso obligará a Arabia Saudita a suministrar medios de exhibición o transmisión de servicios audiovisuales no ofrecidos por el Gobierno árabe saudita al público en general.			
a) Servicios de distribución de películas cinematográficas y cintas de vídeo para uso doméstico con fines de esparcimiento (CPC 96113) a otros sectores de actividad para espectáculos públicos, transmisión por televisión, o venta o alquiler a terceros[4]	1) Ninguna 2) Ninguna 3) Sin consolidar 4) Sin consolidar, excepto lo indicado en los compromisos horizontales.	1) Ninguna 2) Ninguna 3) Sin consolidar 4) Sin consolidar, excepto lo indicado en los compromisos horizontales.	
b. Servicios de distribución y producción de radio y televisión (concesión de licencias de programas de radio y televisión, ya sean en directo, en cinta, en otro soporte de grabación o en videodiscos digitales para su posterior transmisión, por vía terrestre, por televisión por satélite, por cable o por otro medio similares, incluidos DTH y DBS. Estos programas y canales de programación podrán utilizarse para esparcimiento, para promoción o para piezas que suelen producirse en estudios de televisión. Se incluyen asimismo productos como la transmisión de encuentros deportivos, el pronóstico del tiempo, entrevistas, etc.)	1) Sin consolidar 2) Ninguna 3) Sin consolidar 4) Sin consolidar, excepto lo indicado en los compromisos horizontales.	1) Sin consolidar 2) Ninguna 3) Sin consolidar 4) Sin consolidar, excepto lo indicado en los compromisos horizontales.	

[4] A efectos de claridad, este compromiso guarda relación con la distribución únicamente, es decir, la concesión de licencias de películas cinematográficas o de vídeo y no afecta a su transmisión por televisión.

Modos de suministro: 1) Suministro transfronterizo 2) Consumo en el extranjero 3) Presencia comercial 4) Presencia de personas físicas

Sector o subsector	Limitaciones al acceso a los mercados	Limitaciones al trato nacional	Compromisos adicionales
3. SERVICIOS DE CONSTRUCCIÓN Y SERVICIOS DE INGENIERÍA CONEXOS			
A. Trabajos generales de construcción para la edificación (CPC 512) B. Trabajos generales de construcción para ingeniería civil (CPC 513) C. Armado de construcciones prefabricadas y trabajos de instalación (CPC 516+514) D. Trabajos de terminación de edificios (CPC 517) E. Los demás (CPC 511, 515, 518)	1) Sin consolidar*, excepto los servicios de consultores y servicios de asesoramiento conexos. 2) Ninguna 3) Ninguna 4) Sin consolidar, excepto lo indicado en los compromisos horizontales.	1) Sin consolidar*, excepto los servicios de consultores y servicios de asesoramiento conexos. 2) Ninguna 3) Ninguna 4) Sin consolidar, excepto lo indicado en los compromisos horizontales.	
4. SERVICIOS DE DISTRIBUCIÓN			
B. Servicios comerciales al por mayor (CPC 622, 6111, 6113, 6121) C. Servicios comerciales al por menor (CPC 631, 632, 6111, 6113, 6121 y 613) A efectos de esta lista, el comercio al por mayor y al por menor en el país comprende la contratación de particulares que sean ciudadanos del país para la venta de productos y servicios al por menor con una remuneración por la actividad de venta y por los servicios de apoyo a las ventas que dan lugar a nuevas ventas de otros distribuidores por contrato.	1) Ninguna 2) Ninguna 3) Ninguna, con las excepciones siguientes: - la participación extranjera en el capital social estará limitada al 51% en el momento de la adhesión, y al 75% tres años después. - la inversión extranjera mínima será de 20 millones de riyals árabes sauditas por cada proveedor de servicios. - podrá exigirse un tamaño mínimo de los puntos de venta. - cada año un mínimo del 15% de empleados árabes sauditas deberá recibir formación. 4) Sin consolidar, excepto lo indicado en los compromisos horizontales.	1) Ninguna 2) Ninguna 3) Ninguna 4) Sin consolidar, excepto lo indicado en los compromisos horizontales.	

Modos de suministro: 1) Suministro transfronterizo 2) Consumo en el extranjero 3) Presencia comercial 4) Presencia de personas físicas

Sector o subsector	Limitaciones al acceso a los mercados	Limitaciones al trato nacional	Compromisos adicionales
D. Servicios de franquicia (CPC 8929)	1) Sin consolidar 2) Ninguna 3) Ninguna, con las excepciones siguientes: - la participación extranjera en el capital social estará limitada al 51% en el momento de la adhesión, y al 75 % tres años después. - los extranjeros deberán estar autorizados en su propio país para prestar servicios de franquicia o actuar como socios de una empresa autorizada por un período mínimo de cinco años sin interrupción. 4) Sin consolidar, excepto lo indicado en los compromisos horizontales.	1) Sin consolidar 2) Ninguna 3) Ninguna 4) Sin consolidar, excepto lo indicado en los compromisos horizontales.	
5. SERVICIOS DE ENSEÑANZA			
A. Servicios de enseñanza primaria (CPC 921) B. Servicios de enseñanza secundaria (CPC 922) C. Servicios de enseñanza superior (CPC 923) D. Servicios de enseñanza de adultos (CPC 924) E. Los demás enseñanza técnica más cocina tailandesa e idioma tailandés) (CPC 929)	1) Ninguna 2) Ninguna 3) Ninguna 4) Sin consolidar, excepto lo indicado en los compromisos horizontales.	1) Ninguna 2) Ninguna 3) Ninguna 4) Sin consolidar, excepto lo indicado en los compromisos horizontales.	

Modos de suministro: 1) Suministro transfronterizo 2) Consumo en el extranjero 3) Presencia comercial 4) Presencia de personas físicas

Sector o subsector	Limitaciones al acceso a los mercados	Limitaciones al trato nacional	Compromisos adicionales
6. SERVICIOS RELACIONADOS CON EL MEDIO AMBIENTE			
A. Servicios de alcantarillado (CPC 94010) B. Servicios de eliminación de desperdicios (CPC 94020) C. Servicios de saneamiento y servicios similares (CPC 9403) D. Los demás - Servicios de limpieza de gases de escape (CPC 9404) - Servicios de protección de la naturaleza y el paisaje (CPC 9406) - Servicios de lucha contra el ruido (CPC 9405) - Otros servicios relacionados con el medio ambiente (CPC 9409) (incluida la evaluación del impacto ambiental)	1) Ninguna 2) Ninguna 3) Ninguna 4) Sin consolidar, excepto lo indicado en los compromisos horizontales.	1) Ninguna 2) Ninguna 3) Ninguna 4) Sin consolidar, excepto lo indicado en los compromisos horizontales.	

Modos de suministro: 1) Suministro transfronterizo 2) Consumo en el extranjero 3) Presencia comercial 4) Presencia de personas físicas

Sector o subsector	Limitaciones al acceso a los mercados	Limitaciones al trato nacional	Compromisos adicionales
7. SERVICIOS FINANCIEROS			
A. Servicios de seguros y relacionados con los seguros (Sólo se permite el acceso a los mercados a los servicios de seguros cooperativos)			
Los proveedores de servicios de seguros extranjeros que actúan por intermedio de un agente árabe saudita están autorizados a operar y a continuar sin interrupción las actividades comerciales existentes, así como a ofrecer nuevos productos y prestar servicios a nuevos clientes, por un período de tres años a partir de la fecha del Real Decreto Nº 3120/MB de fecha 4/3/1426H (13 de abril de 2005), y de conformidad con ese Decreto.			
a. Seguro de ahorro y protección[5] b. Servicios de seguros distintos de los seguros de vida (Seguro general y seguro de salud) c. Servicios de reaseguro y retrocesión d. Actividades de intermediación de seguros (servicios de corredores y agencias de seguros) e. Servicios auxiliares de los seguros (servicios de consultores en seguros, servicios actuariales, servicios de evaluación de riesgos y servicios de indemnización de siniestros)	1) Sin consolidar, pero ninguna en los siguientes casos: b) Seguro contra los riesgos relativos al transporte marítimo y la aviación comercial y lanzamiento y transporte espacial (incluidos satélites), en que el seguro cubra cualquiera o la totalidad de los elementos siguientes: - las mercancías transportadas, el vehículo que las transporta y la responsabilidad civil que pueda derivarse de los mismos - seguro contra riesgos relativos a mercancías en tránsito internacional c) Servicios de reaseguro y retrocesión d) Servicios de corretaje y agencias de seguros. e) Servicios auxiliares de los seguros (servicios de consultores en seguros, servicios actuariales, servicios de evaluación de riesgos y servicios de indemnización de siniestros)	1) Sin consolidar, pero ninguna en los siguientes casos: b) Seguro contra los riesgos relacionados con el transporte marítimo y la aviación comercial y lanzamiento y transporte espacial (incluidos satélites), en que el seguro cubra cualquiera o la totalidad de los elementos siguientes: - las mercancías transportadas, el vehículo que las transporta y la responsabilidad civil que pueda derivarse de los mismos - seguro contra riesgos relativos a mercancías en tránsito internacional c) Servicios de reaseguro y retrocesión d) Servicios de corretaje y agencias de seguros. e) Servicios auxiliares de los servicios de consultores en seguros, servicios actuariales, servicios de evaluación de riesgos y servicios de indemnización de siniestros)	

[5] En virtud de la definición que figura en el artículo 3, parte 3:1-3 del Reglamento de aplicación de la Ley de fiscalización de las empresas de seguros cooperativos, publicado el 25 de abril de 2004, incluida la protección respecto de la longevidad.

Modos de suministro: 1) Suministro transfronterizo 2) Consumo en el extranjero 3) Presencia comercial 4) Presencia de personas físicas

Sector o subsector	Limitaciones al acceso a los mercados	Limitaciones al trato nacional	Compromisos adicionales
	2) Ninguna 3) En los casos a), b) y c), se admite la presencia comercial en forma de sociedad anónima de seguros cooperativos, constituida en el país, o de sucursal directa establecida de una empresa internacional de seguros que opere en Arabia Saudita como proveedor de servicios de seguros cooperativos.[6] A partir de la fecha de la adhesión se admitirá hasta el 60% de participación no árabe saudita en la sociedad anónima de Arabia Saudita. En el caso d) se admite la presencia comercial en forma de sociedad anónima o de responsabilidad limitada constituida en el país. A partir de la fecha de la adhesión se admitirá hasta el 60% de participación no árabe saudita. En el caso e) se admite la presencia comercial para los servicios de indemnización de siniestros y evaluación de riesgos en forma de sociedad anónima o de responsabilidad limitada constituida en el país. A partir de la fecha de la adhesión se admitirá hasta el 60% de participación no árabe saudita. Para los servicios actuariales y de consultores de seguros, se admite la presencia comercial de una persona física o una persona jurídica. 4) Sin consolidar, excepto lo indicado en los compromisos horizontales.	2) Ninguna 3) Ninguna 4) Sin consolidar, excepto lo indicado en los compromisos horizontales.	

[6] A efectos de claridad, las sucursales de empresas extranjeras de seguros que actúan como proveedores de seguros mutuos no están obligadas a funcionar como sociedades anónimas en Arabia Saudita.

Modos de suministro: 1) Suministro transfronterizo 2) Consumo en el extranjero 3) Presencia comercial 4) Presencia de personas físicas

Sector o subsector	Limitaciones al acceso a los mercados	Limitaciones al trato nacional	Compromisos adicionales
B. Servicios bancarios y demás servicios financieros (excluidos los seguros)			
a. Aceptación de depósitos y otros fondos reembolsables del público b. Préstamos de todo tipo, incluidos los créditos personales, los créditos hipotecarios, el *factoring* y la financiación de transacciones comerciales. c. Servicios de arrendamiento financieros d. Todos los servicios de pago y transferencia monetaria, con inclusión de tarjetas de crédito, de pago y similares, cheques de viajeros y giros bancarios e. Garantías y compromisos f. Intercambio comercial por cuenta propia o de clientes, ya sea en una bolsa, en un mercado extrabursátil o de otro modo, de lo siguiente: - instrumentos del mercado monetario (incluidos cheques, letras y certificados de depósito); - divisas; - productos derivados, incluidos, aunque no exclusivamente, futuros y opciones; - instrumentos de los mercados cambiario y monetario, por ejemplo, *swaps*, y acuerdos a plazo sobre tipos de interés; - valores transferibles;	1) Sin consolidar, salvo para l), k) y, en i), únicamente para la administración de fondos en efectivo o de carteras de valores, gestión de inversiones colectivas en todas sus formas, servicios de depósito y custodia y servicios fiduciarios que se presten por instituciones a clientes institucionales, incluidos los sistemas de inversión colectiva, en el momento de la adhesión. 2) Ninguna, salvo: sin consolidar la administración de fondos de pensiones en i) y todos los servicios de pago y compensación nacionales prestados exclusivamente por el Instituto Monetario de Arabia Saudita mencionados en j). Esto también limita el trato nacional. 3) Ninguna, excepto: - Se admite la presencia comercial en forma de sociedad anónima, constituida en el país, o de sucursal establecida y directa de un banco internacional. - A partir de la fecha de la adhesión se admitirá hasta el 60% de participación no árabe saudita en empresas mixtas de Arabia Saudita. - Estos servicios financieros han de ser prestados por bancos comerciales, salvo que la administración de activos que se menciona en i) y los servicios de asesoramiento que se mencionan en k) los podrán proporcionar instituciones financieras que no sean bancos comerciales con arreglo a la Ley del Mercado de Capitales. - Sin consolidar para la administración de fondos de pensiones mencionados en i). Esto también limita el trato nacional.	1) Sin consolidar, excepto lo indicado en los columna de acceso a los mercados 2) Ninguna 3) Ninguna	Cuando las instituciones financieras ofrezcan planes de pensiones complementarios del plan de pensiones público, también se abrirán a los proveedores de servicios extranjeros, únicamente para el modo 2 y 3.

Modos de suministro: 1) Suministro transfronterizo 2) Consumo en el extranjero 3) Presencia comercial 4) Presencia de personas físicas

Sector o subsector	Limitaciones al acceso a los mercados	Limitaciones al trato nacional	Compromisos adicionales
- otros instrumentos y activos financieros negociables, metal inclusive; g. Participación en emisiones de toda clase de valores, con inclusión de la suscripción y colocación como agentes (pública o privadamente) y el suministro de servicios relacionados con esas emisiones. h. Corretaje de cambios i. Administración de activos; por ejemplo, administración de fondos en efectivo o de carteras de valores, administración de fondos de pensiones, servicios de depósito y custodia y servicios fiduciarios j. Servicios de pago y compensación respecto de activos financieros, con inclusión de valores, productos derivados y otros instrumentos negociables k. Servicios de asesoramiento y otros servicios financieros auxiliares respecto de cualesquiera de las actividades enumeradas en los apartados a) a l), con inclusión de informes y análisis de crédito, estudios y asesoramiento sobre inversiones y carteras de valores, y asesoramiento sobre adquisiciones y sobre reestructuración y estrategia de las empresas	- Sin consolidar para todos los servicios de pago y compensación nacionales prestados exclusivamente por el Instituto Monetario de Arabia Saudita mencionados en j). Esto también limita el trato nacional. 4) Sin consolidar, excepto lo indicado en los compromisos horizontales.	4) Sin consolidar, excepto lo indicado en los compromisos horizontales.	

Modos de suministro: 1) Suministro transfronterizo 2) Consumo en el extranjero 3) Presencia comercial 4) Presencia de personas físicas

Sector o subsector	Limitaciones al acceso a los mercados	Limitaciones al trato nacional	Compromisos adicionales
l. Suministro y transferencia de información financiera, y procesamiento de datos financieros y soporte lógico con ellos relacionado.			
8. SERVICIOS DE SALUD Y DE OTRO TIPO			
A. Servicios de hospital (CPC 9311)	1) Sin consolidar* 2) Ninguna 3) Ninguna, pero con sujeción a la constitución de una sociedad entre una empresa extranjera de servicios de hospital y un profesional médico árabe saudita titular de una licencia. 4) Sin consolidar, excepto lo indicado en los compromisos horizontales.	1) Sin consolidar* 2) Ninguna 3) Ninguna 4) Sin consolidar, excepto lo indicado en los compromisos horizontales.	
B. Otros servicios de salud humana (CPC 9319, excepto 93191)	1) Sin consolidar* 2) Ninguna 3) Ninguna, pero con sujeción a la constitución de una sociedad entre una empresa extranjera de servicios de salud y un profesional médico árabe saudita titular de una licencia. 4) Sin consolidar, excepto lo indicado en los compromisos horizontales.	1) Sin consolidar* 2) Ninguna 3) Ninguna 4) Sin consolidar, excepto lo indicado en los compromisos horizontales.	
9. SERVICIOS DE TURISMO Y SERVICIOS RELACIONADOS CON LOS VIAJES			
A. Hoteles y restaurantes (incluidos los servicios de suministro de comidas al exterior por contrato) (CPC 64110, 64120, 642 y 643) (Excepto bares, clubes nocturnos, etc.)	1) Ninguna 2) Ninguna 3) Ninguna 4) Sin consolidar, excepto lo indicado en los compromisos horizontales.	1) Ninguna 2) Ninguna 3) Ninguna 4) Sin consolidar, excepto lo indicado en los compromisos horizontales.	
B. Servicios de agencias de viajes y organización de viajes en grupo (CPC 7471) (Con exclusión de los relacionados con el Umra y el Hajj)	1) Ninguna 2) Ninguna 3) Ninguna, excepto que se aplica una prueba de necesidades económicas a las agencias de viajes únicamente, sobre la base de la relación entre el número de agencias y la población total. 4) Sin consolidar, excepto lo indicado en los compromisos horizontales.	1) Ninguna 2) Ninguna 3) Ninguna 4) Sin consolidar, excepto lo indicado en los compromisos horizontales.	

Modos de suministro: 1) Suministro transfronterizo 2) Consumo en el extranjero 3) Presencia comercial 4) Presencia de personas físicas

Sector o subsector	Limitaciones al acceso a los mercados	Limitaciones al trato nacional	Compromisos adicionales
C. Servicios de guías de turismo (CPC 74720) (Con exclusión de los relacionados con el Umra y el Hajj)	1) Ninguna 2) Ninguna 3) Ninguna 4) Sin consolidar, excepto lo indicado en los compromisos horizontales.	1) Ninguna 2) Ninguna 3) Ninguna 4) Sin consolidar, excepto lo indicado en los compromisos horizontales.	
10. SERVICIOS DE ESPARCIMIENTO, CULTURALES Y DEPORTIVOS			
B. Servicios de agencias de noticias (CPC 962) D. Servicios de esparcimiento (CPC 96491) (Únicamente los servicios de parques y jardines públicos)	1) Ninguna 2) Ninguna 3) Ninguna 4) Sin consolidar, excepto lo indicado en los compromisos horizontales.	1) Ninguna 2) Ninguna 3) Ninguna 4) Sin consolidar, excepto lo indicado en los compromisos horizontales.	
11. SERVICIOS DE TRANSPORTE			
A. Servicios de transporte marítimo a. Transporte de pasajeros (CPC 7211) b. Transporte de carga (CPC 7212) c. Alquiler de embarcaciones con tripulación (CPC 72130) d. Mantenimiento y reparación de embarcaciones	1) Ninguna 2) Ninguna 3) Ninguna 4) Sin consolidar, excepto lo indicado en los compromisos horizontales.	1) Ninguna 2) Ninguna 3) Ninguna 4) Sin consolidar, excepto lo indicado en los compromisos horizontales.	Los siguientes servicios portuarios se ponen a disposición de los proveedores de servicios de transporte marítimo internacional en condiciones razonables y no discriminatorias: - servicios de explotación de puertos y vías de navegación (con exclusión de carga y descarga); - servicios de pilotaje y atracamiento; - servicios de ayuda a la navegación; - servicios de salvamento y reflotamiento de embarcaciones; - los demás servicios complementarios para el transporte por vías de navegación.

Modos de suministro: 1) Suministro transfronterizo 2) Consumo en el extranjero 3) Presencia comercial 4) Presencia de personas físicas

Sector o subsector	Limitaciones al acceso a los mercados	Limitaciones al trato nacional	Compromisos adicionales
C. Servicios de transporte aéreo d. Mantenimiento y reparación de aeronaves e. Servicios complementarios para el transporte por vía aérea (CPC 746) - Sistemas de reserva informatizados	1) Ninguna 2) Ninguna 3) Ninguna 4) Sin consolidar, excepto lo indicado en los compromisos horizontales.	1) Ninguna 2) Ninguna 3) Ninguna 4) Sin consolidar, excepto lo indicado en los compromisos horizontales.	
E. Servicios de transporte por ferrocarril a. Transporte de pasajeros (CPC 7111) b. Transporte de carga (CPC 7112) c. Servicios de tracción y remolque (CPC 7130) d. Mantenimiento y reparación de equipo de transporte por ferrocarril (CPC 8868) e. Servicios complementarios para los servicios de transporte por ferrocarril (CPC 743)	1) Ninguna 2) Ninguna 3) La inversión extranjera se realizará mediante acuerdos de construcción -operación-transferencia 4) Sin consolidar, excepto lo indicado en los compromisos horizontales.	1) Ninguna 2) Ninguna 3) Ninguna 4) Sin consolidar, excepto lo indicado en los compromisos horizontales.	
G. Servicios de transporte por tuberías a) Transporte de combustibles (CPC 7131) b. Transporte de otros elementos (CPC 7139)	1) Ninguna 2) Ninguna 3) Ninguna 4) Sin consolidar, excepto lo indicado en los compromisos horizontales.	1) Ninguna 2) Ninguna 3) Ninguna 4) Sin consolidar, excepto lo indicado en los compromisos horizontales.	

Modos de suministro: 1) Suministro transfronterizo 2) Consumo en el extranjero 3) Presencia comercial 4) Presencia de personas físicas

Sector o subsector	Limitaciones al acceso a los mercados	Limitaciones al trato nacional	Compromisos adicionales
H. Servicios auxiliares en relación con todos los medios de transporte (limitados al transporte marítimo, por ferrocarril y aéreo de conformidad con el Anexo sobre Servicios de Transporte Aéreo) a. Servicios de carga y descarga (CPC 741) b. Servicios de almacenamiento (CPC 742) c. Servicios de agencias de transporte de carga (CPC 748)	1) Ninguna 2) Ninguna 3) Ninguna 4) Sin consolidar, excepto lo indicado en los compromisos horizontales.	1) Ninguna 2) Ninguna 3) Ninguna 4) Sin consolidar, excepto lo indicado en los compromisos horizontales.	En la actualidad, el sector público presta los servicios relacionados con el grupo 749 de la CPC. Se otorgará el trato nacional a medida que, de conformidad con la legislación árabe saudita, se vaya abriendo a la entidades privadas el acceso al mercado de los servicios incluidos en dicho grupo.

DOCUMENTO DE REFERENCIA

Alcance

A continuación figuran definiciones y principios relativos al marco reglamentario de los servicios de telecomunicaciones básicas.

Definiciones

Por usuarios se entiende los consumidores de servicios y los proveedores de servicios.

Por instalaciones esenciales se entiende toda instalación de una red o servicio públicos de transporte de telecomunicaciones que:

a) sea suministrada exclusivamente o de manera predominante por un solo proveedor o por un número limitado de proveedores; y

b) cuya sustitución con miras al suministro de un servicio no sea factible en lo económico o en lo técnico.

Un proveedor importante es un proveedor que tenga la capacidad de afectar de manera importante las condiciones de participación (desde el punto de vista de los precios y del suministro) en un mercado dado de servicios de telecomunicaciones básicas como resultado de:

a) el control de las instalaciones esenciales; o

b) la utilización de su posición en el mercado.

1. Salvaguardias de la competencia

1.1 Prevención de las prácticas anticompetitivas en la esfera de las telecomunicaciones

Se mantendrán medidas adecuadas con el fin de impedir que aquellos proveedores que, individual o conjuntamente, sean un proveedor importante empleen o sigan empleando prácticas anticompetitivas.

1.2 Salvaguardias

Las prácticas anticompetitivas a las que se hace referencia *supra* incluirán, en particular, las siguientes:

a) realizar actividades anticompetitivas de subvención cruzada;

b) utilizar información obtenida de competidores con resultados anticompetitivos; y

c) no poner oportunamente a disposición de los demás proveedores de servicios la información técnica sobre las instalaciones esenciales y la información comercialmente pertinente que éstos necesiten para suministrar servicios.

2. Interconexión

2.1 Esta sección se refiere al enlace con los proveedores que suministran redes o servicios públicos de transporte de telecomunicaciones, con objeto de que los usuarios de un proveedor puedan comunicarse con los usuarios de otro proveedor y tener acceso a los servicios suministrados por otro proveedor, respecto de los que se contraigan compromisos específicos.

2.2 Interconexión que se ha de asegurar

La interconexión con un proveedor importante quedará asegurada en cualquier punto técnicamente viable de la red. Esta interconexión se facilitará:

a) en términos y condiciones (incluidas las normas y especificaciones técnicas) y con tarifas que no sean discriminatorios, y será de una calidad no menos favorable que la facilitada para sus propios servicios similares o para servicios similares de proveedores de servicios no afiliados o para sus filiales u otras sociedades afiliadas;
b) en una forma oportuna, en términos y condiciones (incluidas las normas y especificaciones técnicas) y con tarifas basadas en el costo que sean transparentes y razonables, tengan en cuenta la viabilidad económica, y estén suficientemente desagregados para que el proveedor no deba pagar por componentes o instalaciones de la red que no necesite para el suministro del servicio; y
c) previa solicitud, en puntos adicionales a los puntos de terminación de la red ofrecidos a la mayoría de los usuarios, a un precio que refleje el costo de construcción de las instalaciones adicionales necesarias.

2.3 Disponibilidad pública de los procedimientos de negociación de interconexiones

Se pondrán a disposición del público los procedimientos aplicables a la interconexión con un proveedor importante.

2.4 Transparencia de los acuerdos de interconexión

Se garantiza que todo proveedor importante pondrá a disposición del público sus acuerdos de interconexión o una oferta de interconexión de referencia.

2.5 Interconexión: solución de diferencias

Todo proveedor de servicios que solicite la interconexión con un proveedor importante podrá presentar recurso:

a) en cualquier momento, o
b) después de un plazo razonable que se haya dado a conocer públicamente

ante un órgano nacional independiente, que podrá ser el órgano de reglamentación al que se hace referencia en el párrafo 5 *infra*, para resolver dentro de un plazo razonable las diferencias con respecto a los términos, condiciones y tarifas apropiados de interconexión, siempre que éstos no hayan sido establecidos previamente.

3. Servicio universal

Todo Miembro tiene derecho a definir el tipo de obligación de servicio universal que desee mantener. No se considerará que las obligaciones de esa naturaleza son anticompetitivas *per se*, a condición de que sean administradas de manera transparente y no discriminatoria y con neutralidad en la competencia y no sean más gravosas de lo necesario para el tipo de servicio universal definido por el Miembro.

4. Disponibilidad pública de los criterios de concesión de licencias

Cuando se exija una licencia, se pondrán a disposición del público:

a) todos los criterios de concesión de licencias y los plazos normalmente requeridos para tomar una decisión relativa a una solicitud de licencia y
b) los términos y condiciones de las licencias individuales.

A solicitud del interesado le serán comunicadas las razones de la denegación de la licencia.

5. Independencia de la entidad de reglamentación

El órgano de reglamentación será independiente de todo proveedor de servicios de telecomunicaciones básicas, y no responderá ante él. Las decisiones del órgano de reglamentación y los procedimientos aplicados serán imparciales con respecto a todos los participantes en el mercado.

6. Asignación y utilización de recursos escasos

Todo procedimiento para la asignación y utilización de recursos escasos, como las frecuencias, los números y los derechos de paso, se llevará a la práctica de manera objetiva, oportuna, transparente y no discriminatoria. Se pondrá a disposición del público el estado actual de las bandas de frecuencia asignadas, pero no es preciso identificar detalladamente las frecuencias asignadas a usos oficiales específicos.

Lista final de exenciones del artículo II (NMF)

Sector o subsector	Descripción de la medida con indicación de su incompatibilidad con el artículo II	Países a los que se aplica la medida	Duración prevista	Condiciones que motivan la necesidad de la exención
Servicios de transporte por carretera	Trato preferencial recíproco para los servicios transfronterizos	Egipto, Jordania	Indefinida	Acuerdos bilaterales en vigor
Servicios de transporte marítimo y por carretera	Preferencia en el uso de las líneas de transporte marítimo y de los vehículos de transporte por carretera en el comercio bilateral	Egipto, Túnez	Indefinida	Acuerdos bilaterales en vigor
Servicios de transporte por carretera	Trato preferencial recíproco	Líbano, Siria, Turquía	Indefinida	Acuerdos bilaterales en vigor

For the Kingdom of Saudi Arabia   Pour le Royaume d'Arabie saoudite   Por el Reino de Arabia Saudita

I hereby certify that the foregoing text is a true copy of the Protocol on the Accession of the Kingdom of Saudi Arabia, done at Geneva on 11 November 2005, the original of which is deposited with the Director-General of the World Trade Organization.

Je certifie que le texte qui précède est la copie conforme du Protocole d'Accession du Royaume d'Arabie saoudite, établi à Genève le 11 novembre 2005, dont le texte original est déposé auprès du Directeur Général de l'Organisation Mondiale du Commerce.

Certifico que el texto que antecede es copia conforme del Protocolo de Adhesión del Reino de Arabia Saudita, hecho en Ginebra el 11 de noviembre de 2005 de cuyo texto original es depositario el Director General de la Organización Mundial del Comercio.

Pascal Lamy

Director-General

Directeur général

Director General